ROUTLEDGE HANDBOOK OF MEDITERRANEAN POLITICS

The Mediterranean space, defined by a major sea, a large number of littoral countries and to some extent their hinterlands, is at the same time an interface between Europe, Africa and Asia. This brings complex challenges in terms of achieving peace and stability. Recently it has received intense international attention through the internal destructiveness and spill-over from conflicts, primarily those waged in Libya, Syria and, more remotely, Iraq.

This *Handbook* provides an overview of the political processes that shape the Mediterranean region in the contemporary context. It explores the issues of crucial importance to Mediterranean dynamics through a series of analytical sections that guide the reader towards a comprehensive understanding of the main regional interactions and trends.

The *Handbook* explores:

- the complex historical formation of the contemporary Mediterranean
- geopolitical perspectives
- issues around peace and conflict
- the political economy of the region
- the role of non-state actors and social movements
- societal and cultural trends.

The wide range of contributions from many of the leading academic experts on the region offers not only insights into the debates and processes that structure each theme, but also key pointers for a more general understanding of how distinct political, economic, social and cultural dynamics interact across the region. It will therefore be a key resource for policy-makers and students and scholars of Mediterranean politics and international relations.

Richard Gillespie is Professor of Politics at the University of Liverpool and was the founding editor of the journal *Mediterranean Politics*.

Frédéric Volpi is Senior Lecturer in International Politics at the School of International Relations at the University of Saint Andrews.

ROUTLEDGE HANDBOOK OF MEDITERRANEAN POLITICS

Edited by Richard Gillespie and Frédéric Volpi

Routledge
Taylor & Francis Group
LONDON AND NEW YORK

First published 2018 by Routledge

2 Park Square, Milton Park, Abingdon, Oxfordshire OX14 4RN
52 Vanderbilt Avenue, New York, NY 10017

Routledge is an imprint of the Taylor & Francis Group, an informa business

First issued in paperback 2019

British Library Cataloguing-in-Publication Data
A catalogue record for this book is available from the British Library

Library of Congress Cataloging-in-Publication Data
Names: Gillespie, Richard, 1952- editor. | Volpi, Frédéric, editor.
Title: Routledge handbook of Mediterranean politics/edited by Richard Gillespie and Frédéric Volpi.
Other titles: Handbook of Mediterranean politics
Description: Abingdon, Oxon; New York, NY: Routledge, 2018. | Includes bibliographical references and index.
Identifiers: LCCN 2017008253 | ISBN 9781138903982 (hbk) | ISBN 9781315696577 (ebk)
Subjects: LCSH: Mediterranean Region–Politics and government–21st century. | Mediterranean Region–Foreign relations–21st century. | Geopolitics–Mediterranean Region. | Political culture–Mediterranean Region. | Mediterranean Region–Emigration and immigration–Government policy. | Social movements–Political aspects–Mediterranean Region.
Classification: LCC DE100.R68 2018 | DDC 909/.09822083–dc23LC record available at https://lccn.loc.gov/2017008253

ISBN: 978-1-138-90398-2 (hbk)
ISBN: 978-0-367-87257-1 (pbk)

Typeset in Bembo
by Sunrise Setting Ltd., Brixham, UK

CONTENTS

Notes on contributors *ix*

1 Introduction: the growing international relevance of Mediterranean politics 1
Richard Gillespie and Frédéric Volpi

PART I
Historical constructions **11**

2 The historical construction of the Mediterranean 13
Dominic Fenech and Michelle Pace

3 Historical/geopolitical turning points in the modern Mediterranean: Cold War, post-Cold War and Arab Spring 24
Francesco Cavatorta

4 Regionalism and the Mediterranean: long history, odd partners 37
Federica Bicchi

5 Securing the Mediterranean, inventing the 'Middle East' 50
Pinar Bilgin

6 From imperialism to failed liberal peace: how Europe contributed to MENA's failing states system and how MENA blowback threatens Europe 60
Raymond Hinnebusch

7 A new era in Euro-Mediterranean relations 72
Richard Youngs

PART II
Geopolitical perspectives **83**

8 EU member states' representation and positioning and the north–south divide in Euro-Mediterranean affairs 85
Tobias Schumacher

9 The north–south divide: southern perceptions of the Mediterranean 97
Yahia H. Zoubir

10 US outlook on the Mediterranean 110
Katerina Dalacoura

11 Israeli regional perspectives and the Mediterranean 120
Daniela Huber

12 Turkish regional perspectives and the Mediterranean 132
Bill Park

PART III
Peace and conflict **143**

13 The Mediterranean observes the world, the world observes the Mediterranean: conflict and peace in the Mediterranean 145
Stephan Stetter

14 Military and politics in the Mediterranean 157
Aurel Croissant and Tanja Eschenauer

15 Stalled conflicts in the Mediterranean 171
Neophytos Loizides

16 Insurgencies, terrorism and political violence in the Mediterranean region 182
Krista E. Wiegand

17 Do regional organizations contribute to security? Perspectives on Euro-Mediterranean cooperation 194
Niklas Bremberg

18 Regime resilience and the Arab uprisings in the southern Mediterranean: four emerging approaches for explaining authoritarian persistence 207
Matt Buehler and Amnah Ibraheem

PART IV
Political economy 219

19 Beyond state and market: development strategies in the Arab world 221
Amr Adly

20 The political economy of energy in the Mediterranean 232
Gonzalo Escribano

21 Globalization and the Mediterranean 244
Patrick Holden

22 Minding development gaps in EU Mediterranean policies: a variegated neoliberalization thesis? 255
Karim Knio

23 Climate change, environmental degradation and renewable energy 268
Michael Mason

24 Politics and tourism in the Mediterranean region 279
Raoul Bianchi and Tom Selwyn

PART V
Non-state actors and social movements 293

25 Debates on civil society in the Mediterranean 295
Benoit Challand

26 Transnational advocacy networks and human rights activism 309
Laura Feliu

27 Islamist movements in the Mediterranean: modernist Islam, Islamism and Salafism 320
Roel Meijer

28 Women's movements within Euro-Mediterranean politics: the need to go beyond 'the Arab woman' 331
Ali Bilgic

29 Youth activism and protest around the Mediterranean 342
Emma C. Murphy

PART VI
Societal and cultural trends 357

30 New media, activism, and the transformative Arab political landscape 359
Sahar Khamis

31 Digital communications and social networks: co-evolution of digital activism and repression during the Arab Uprisings 371
Ben Wagner

32 Mediterranean migrants and refugees: historical and political continuities and discontinuities 382
Sarah Wolff and Leila Hadj-Abdou

33 Intercultural dialogue across the Mediterranean troubled waters: challenges to the Anna Lindh Foundation 394
Stefania Panebianco

Index *408*

CONTRIBUTORS

Amr Adly is a non-resident scholar at Carnegie – Middle East. He worked as a postdoctoral fellow at the Center on Democracy, Development, and the Rule of Law at Stanford University, and as a senior researcher at the Egyptian Initiative for Personal Rights, heading the unit for social and economic rights. He has a PhD in political economy from the European University Institute, Florence. Adly is the author of *State Reform and Development in the Middle East: Turkey and Egypt in the Post-Liberalization Era* (Routledge, 2012). He has also written several other academic publications that have appeared in *Business and Politics*, *Turkish Studies*, and *Middle Eastern Studies*, amongst others.

Raoul Bianchi is a Reader in International Tourism and Development at the University of East London. He is the co-author of the book *Tourism and Citizenship* (Routledge, 2014) and has published widely on the sociology, politics and international political economy of tourism. He has carried out extensive fieldwork on the politics and development of tourism and cultural heritage in the Canary Islands as well as having been the co-director of a major European research project on urban cultural heritage in the Mediterranean.

Federica Bicchi is Associate Professor in the Department of International Relations at the London School of Economics and Political Science. She holds a PhD in political science from the European University Institute. Her research interests include EU foreign policy towards its southern neighbourhood, a topic on which she has published articles and books, including *European Foreign Policy Making towards the Mediterranean* (Palgrave, 2007), *The Struggle for Influence in the Middle East* (co-edited with Benoit Challand and Steven Heydeman, Palgrave, 2015) and *The Union for the Mediterranean: Continuity or Change in Euro-Mediterranean Relations?* (co-edited with Richard Gillespie, Palgrave, 2012).

Ali Bilgic is Lecturer at Loughborough University, Department of Politics, History and International Relations. He holds a PhD from Aberystwyth University in the UK. His research interests include feminist postcolonial approaches, critical security studies with a focus on feminist approaches to security, contemporary social movements, Middle East and North African politics, migration and Turkey's foreign policy. He is the author of *Turkey, Power and the West: Gendered International Relations and Foreign Policy* (I. B. Tauris, 2016) and *Rethinking Security in the Age of Migration: Trust and Emancipation in Europe* (Routledge, 2013).

Pinar Bilgin is a Professor of International Relations at Bilkent University. She specializes in critical approaches to the study of security and international relations. She is the author of *Regional Security in the Middle East: A Critical Perspective* (Routledge, 2005), *The International in Security, Security in the International* (2016) and co-editor of *Routledge Handbook of International Political Sociology* (with Xavier Guillaume, Routledge, 2017), *Asia in International Relations: Unthinking Imperial Power Relations* (co-edited with L. H. M. Ling, Routledge, 2017).

Niklas Bremberg is Research Fellow at the Swedish Institute of International Affairs. He holds a PhD in political science from the University of Stockholm and has been visiting researcher at the University of Toronto, the University of Liverpool and Universitat Autònoma de Barcelona. His research focuses on regional security practices, security communities and EU foreign and security policy, especially towards North Africa. His publications include the research monograph *Diplomacy and Security Community-Building: EU Crisis Management in the Western Mediterranean* (Routledge, 2016) and articles in *Journal of Common Market Studies, Cooperation and Conflict, European Security*, and *Mediterranean Politics*.

Matt Buehler is an Assistant Professor at the University of Tennessee, where he researches politics of the Middle East and North Africa. He is also a Global Security Fellow at the Howard H. Baker Jr Center for Public Policy. He has held research fellowships at Georgetown's Center for International and Regional Studies and also Harvard University's Middle East Initiative. Dr Buehler is working on a book manuscript entitled, *Why Alliances Fail: Opposition Coalitions between Islamists and Leftists in North Africa*. His research has appeared in peer-reviewed journals, including *Political Research Quarterly, Mediterranean Politics, British Journal of Middle Eastern Studies, Middle East Law and Governance* and *Terrorism and Political Violence*.

Francesco Cavatorta is Associate Professor in the Department of Political Science at Université Laval, Quebec, Canada. His research focuses on processes of democratization and authoritarian resilience in the Arab world, Islamist parties and movements and civil society activism. He has authored or co-authored over 50 peer-reviewed journal articles. He authored the monograph *The International Dimension of the Failed Algerian Transition* (Manchester University Press, 2009) and co-authored the book *Civil Society and Democratisation in the Arab World* (Routledge, 2010). His most recent book is the edited volume *Salafism after the Arab Awakening* (Hurst/Oxford University Press, 2017, co-edited with Fabio Merone).

Benoit Challand is Associate Professor in Sociology at the New School for Social Research in New York. He holds a PhD in social and political science from the European University Institute in Florence (2005) and has taught, among others, at the University of Fribourg and at NYU (Kevorkian Center for Near East Studies, New York). He has published on civil society promotion, popular mobilization, and Islamic charities in the Arab world, with a focus on Palestine and Tunisia.

Aurel Croissant is a Professor of Comparative Politics at Heidelberg University. His research focuses mainly on the comparative study of democratization, authoritarianism, civil–military relations and Asian politics. He is co-editor of the journal *Democratization* and coordinates a multi-year research project on military reactions to anti-incumbent mass protests in authoritarian regimes. He has recently co-edited *Armies and Insurgencies in the Arab Spring* (University of Pennsylvania Press, 2016) and *Reforming Civil–Military Relations in New Democracies* (Springer, 2017). Currently, he is writing a book manuscript on civil–military relations and democratization in the third wave.

Katerina Dalacoura is Associate Professor in International Relations at the London School of Economics and Political Science. In 2015/16, she was British Academy Mid-Career Fellow. Her main areas of expertise are in: human rights, democracy and democracy promotion in the Middle East; political Islam; and culture and religion in international relations. Her work has recently focused particularly on Turkey. She is author of *Islam, Liberalism and Human Rights: Implications for International Relations* (I. B. Tauris, 2007), *Islamist Terrorism and Democracy in the Middle East* (Cambridge University Press, 2011) and of a number of chapters and articles in peer-reviewed journals.

Tanja Eschenauer is a Research Fellow and PhD student at Heidelberg University. She works on the project 'Dictator's Endgame: Theory and empirical analysis of military behavior in authoritarian regime crises, 1946–2014'. Her research interests include political–military relations in autocracies, military coups and (quantitative) measurement of military influence. Her regional focus is the Middle East and Maghreb. Between 2009 and 2014, she worked at the Heidelberg Institute for International Conflict Research (HIIK) and monitored conflicts in Iraq, Iran and Afghanistan.

Gonzalo Escribano is the Director of the Energy Programme at the Elcano Royal Institute (Madrid), and Professor of Economics at the Spanish Open University (UNED). He holds a degree and a PhD in economics from the Universidad Complutense, and his research agenda focuses on the international political economy of energy. Among his most recent publications are *Energy Security for the EU in the 21st Century* (Routledge, 2012) and several articles in journals like *Energy Policy, Renewable and Sustainable Energy Reviews, European Journal of Political Economy, Global Policy, Turkish Studies* and *Mediterranean Politics*. He can be followed at his Twitter account @g_escribano.

Laura Feliu is a Senior Lecturer in International Relations at the Faculty of Political Science and Sociology of the Universitat Autònoma de Barcelona, Spain. She has extensively worked and published on international human rights promotion, international relations of the MENA region, and Spanish foreign policy. She leads the research project 'Popular revolts from the Mediterranean to Central Asia', financed by the Spanish Ministry of Economy and Competitiveness. Her latest publication is 'The Western Saharan Members of the Moroccan Parliament: Diplomacy and Perceptions of Identity' (with A. Parejo), in Ojeda-García, Fernández-Molina and Veguilla (eds), *Global, Regional and Local Dimensions of Western Sahara's Protracted Decolonization* (Palgrave, 2016).

Dominic Fenech is a Professor of Modern and Contemporary History, Head of the History Department and Dean of the Faculty of Arts at the University of Malta. His main teaching, research interests and publications are in the areas of modern and contemporary Mediterranean history, and Maltese constitutional history and politics. He is a regular contributor in *Western European Politics*, the *European Journal of Political Research* and *The Annual Register of World Events*.

Richard Gillespie holds the established Chair of Politics at the University of Liverpool where he is co-director of the Europe and the World Centre. Founding editor of *Mediterranean Politics*, he was editor or co-editor of this (yearbook and eventual) journal from 1994 to 2014. His contributions to Mediterranean studies have focused mainly on European region-building initiatives, the evolution of Euro-Mediterranean relations and the influential role of Spain in the region. Publications include *Spain and the Mediterranean* (Macmillan, 2000), *The Union for the Mediterranean* (with Federica Bicchi, Routledge, 2012) and articles in journals such as the *Journal of Common Market Studies, International Politics* and *Geopolitics*.

Leila Hadj-Abdou is an Adjunct Lecturer at the Department of Political Sciences of the University of Vienna, and a project coordinator in the field of asylum and immigration in an educational centre. She specializes in international migration and asylum governance, immigrant integration and immigration policies, and the populist right. Before moving to Vienna Leila was working as a Research Fellow at the University of Sheffield (UK), and the Centre for Transatlantic Relations in Washington DC. Leila holds a PhD in social and political sciences from the European University Institute (2013).

Raymond Hinnebusch is Professor of International Relations and Middle East Politics at the University of St Andrews. His major works include *Egyptian Politics under Sadat* (Cambridge University Press, 1985); *The International Politics of the Middle East* (2nd edition, Manchester University Press, 2015); and *Syria: Revolution from Above* (Routledge, 2001). He co-edited *The Foreign Policies of Middle East States* (2nd edition, Lynne Rienner, 2014); *Turkey–Syria Relations: Between Enmity and Amity* (Ashgate, 2013); *Sovereignty after Empire: Comparing the Middle East and Central Asia* (Edinburgh University Press, 2011); *The Iraq War: Causes and Consequences* (Lynne Rienner, 2006); and *Syria: From Reform to Revolt* (Syracuse University Press, 2014).

Patrick Holden is an Associate Professor in International Relations, at Plymouth University. He previously studied at University College Dublin and the University of Limerick. He is a former Marie Curie Visiting Fellow at the Centre for International Studies, Cambridge. His research interests focus on the politics of international development, and his doctoral thesis focused on Euro-Mediterranean relations. While researching for his doctorate, he worked at the Euro-Mediterranean Human Rights Network. He is the Programme Leader of the MA in International Relations: Global Security and Development at Plymouth.

Daniela Huber is Research Fellow at LUISS University in Rome and Senior Researcher at the Istituto Affari Internazionali (IAI) in the Mediterranean and Middle East programme. Her current research project, supported by the Gerda Henkel Foundation and pursued at LUISS University, focuses on the role construction of key powers in the Middle East in the case of the Israeli–Palestinian conflict. She also co-coordinates a Horizon 2020 project on Mediterranean relations at the IAI. She holds a PhD from the Hebrew University of Jerusalem and an MA in international relations from the Free University of Berlin.

Amnah Ibraheem is a doctoral student in political science at the University of Tennessee. Her research focuses on local perceptions and responses to governmental policies in the Middle East and North Africa. She also serves as a Graduate Research Assistant at the Howard H. Baker Jr Center for Public Policy, facilitating a variety of ongoing research projects, under the supervision of the Center's Global Security Fellows.

Sahar Khamis is an Associate Professor in the Department of Communication at the University of Maryland. She is an expert on Arab and Muslim media, and the former Head of the Mass Communication Department in Qatar University. She is the co-author of the books *Islam Dot Com: Contemporary Islamic Discourses in Cyberspace* (Palgrave Macmillan, 2009) and *Egyptian Revolution 2.0: Political Blogging, Civic Engagement and Citizen Journalism* (Palgrave Macmillan, 2013). Dr Khamis is a media commentator, a public speaker, a human rights commissioner in Montgomery County, Maryland, and a radio host presenting a monthly programme on 'US Arab Radio'.

Karim Knio (PhD University of Birmingham) is Senior Lecturer in Politics at the International Institute of Social Studies of Erasmus University Rotterdam. His research focuses on the political economy of governance with a focus on regionalism and trade. He also has interests in EU democracy promotion programmes, the politics of crisis management and Lebanese politics. He is the author of *The European Union's Mediterranean Policy: Model or Muddle? A New Institutionalist Perspective* (Palgrave Macmillan, 2013); *The South China Sea and Asian Regionalism: A Critical Realist Perspective* (with Thanhdam Truong, Springer, 2016). He is also the associate editor of *European Political Science Review* (*EPSR*).

Neophytos Loizides is Professor in International Conflict Analysis at the University of Kent and the author of more than thirty academic articles and chapters on conflict regulation in deeply divided societies and the eastern Mediterranean in particular. His most recent monographs include *The Politics of Majority Nationalism: Framing Peace, Stalemates, and Crises* (Stanford University Press, 2015) and *Designing Peace: Cyprus and Institutional Innovations in Divided Societies* (University of Pennsylvania Press, 2016).

Michael Mason is an Associate Professor in the Department of Geography and Environment at the London School of Economics and Political Science. His research interests include environmental politics and governance in the eastern Mediterranean region and accountability/transparency in global environmental policy-making. Alongside articles in a wide range of scholarly journals, he is the author/editor of four books, most recently *Transparency in Global Environmental Governance* (co-edited with Aarti Gupta, MIT Press, 2014).

Roel Meijer is Lecturer in Middle East History at the Department of Religious Studies at the Radboud University, Nijmegen and the International Institute of Social History (IISH) in Amsterdam. He has edited seven volumes, including *Global Salafism: Islam's New Religious Movement* (Hurst/Columbia UP, 2009, translated into Chinese) and focuses on social movements and the political situation in Egypt, Saudi Arabia, Iraq and Bahrain. His latest interest is in concepts of citizenship in the Middle East. A new anthology, edited with Nils Butenschøn, *The Crisis of Citizenship in the Arab World*, will be published by Brill in 2017.

Emma C. Murphy is Professor of Political Economy in the School of Government and International Affairs, Durham University. Her research includes diverse aspects of the MENA region's political economy including economic and political liberalization, information and communications technologies, food security and most recently youth and youth policy. She has a particular interest in Tunisia, Israel and Palestine.

Michelle Pace is Professor with special responsibilities in EU–MENA Politics at Roskilde University in Denmark and Honorary Professor in Politics and International Studies at the University of Birmingham in the UK. She is principal investigator on a Ministry of Foreign Affairs (Denmark) funded project entitled 'Change in Exile: Re-invigorating principles of reform and social stability amongst young Syrian refugees in Denmark and Lebanon' as well as a Carlsberg Foundation funded project on 'The Struggle of State Building in Palestine: Exploring "State-less"-Society Relations in the West Bank'. She has published widely on Mediterranean politics and society.

Stefania Panebianco has a PhD in international relations and is Associate Professor of Political Science, University of Catania. She teaches Mediterranean politics, institutions of global trade, security and migration and is holder of the Jean Monnet Chair EUMedEA (EU Mediterranean Border Crises and European External Action). Her main research interests are the Mediterranean migration crisis, EU foreign policies, EU relations with the Middle East and North Africa. Her most recent books include *Sulle onde del Mediterraneo: cambiamenti globali e risposte alla crisi migratoria* (EGEA, 2016), *L'Unione Europea 'potenza divisa' nel Mediterraneo* (EGEA, 2012), *Winds of Democratic Change in the Mediterranean? Actors, Processes and Outcomes* (edited with Rosa Rossi, Rubbettino, Soveria-Mannelli, 2012).

Bill Park is a Senior Lecturer in the Defence Studies Department, King's College London. He serves as a council member for the British Institute at Ankara (BIAA), is an editorial board member for the journal *Mediterranean Politics*, sits on the international advisory panel for the journal *Turkish Studies*, and is an advisor to the Centre for Turkish Studies (CEFTUS). He is also a Visiting Scholar at TOBB-ET University in Ankara.

Tobias Schumacher holds the Chair in European Neighbourhood Policy at the College of Europe, Natolin Campus (Warsaw, Poland). He is also a Senior Research Associate at the Centre for International Studies (CEI-IUL) at the Lisbon University Institute, and he was a John F. Kennedy Memorial Fellow at the Minda de Gunzburg Center for European Studies at Harvard University during the first half of 2016. He has recently co-edited *The European Neighbourhood Policy: Continuity and Change in EU Foreign Policy* (Palgrave, 2016) and he is the lead editor of the *Routledge Handbook on the European Neighbourhood Policy*.

Tom Selwyn is Professorial Research Associate at the School of Oriental and African Studies (SOAS) at the University of London where he holds a Leverhulme Emeritus Professorial Fellowship. He is widely published in the field of anthropology of travel, tourism, and pilgrimage with a regional interest in the Mediterranean, in particular Palestine/Israel. He has directed/co-directed four major projects for the European Commission on the topic of Mediterranean and Balkan cultural heritage, with a special focus on Sarajevo and Bethlehem/Jerusalem. He was awarded the Royal Anthropological Institute's Lucy Mair medal in 2009.

Stephan Stetter is Professor of World Politics and Conflict Studies at the University of the Bundeswehr Munich and Dean of the Faculty of Social Sciences and Public Affairs. He is editor of the leading German-language political science journal, the *Zeitschrift für Internationale Beziehungen*. His research foci are historical-sociological theories of globalization, social evolution theories, Middle East politics and society as well as EU foreign affairs.

Frédéric Volpi is Senior Lecturer in International Politics in the School of International Relations at the University of Saint Andrews. He specializes on Middle East politics, with a focus on contentious politics, democratization and Islamism. He is the author of *Revolution and Authoritarianism in North Africa* (Oxford University Press/Hurst, 2017) and *Political Islam Observed* (Oxford University Press/Hurst, 2010). His articles have appeared in the *Journal of Democracy*, *Democratization*, *Third World Quarterly*, *International Studies Review*, etc. He is also the editor of the journal *Mediterranean Politics*.

Ben Wagner is the Director of the Centre of Internet and Human Rights (CIHR). His research focuses on communicative ruptures, digital rights and the Internet in foreign policy. Ben holds a PhD in political and social sciences from European University Institute in Florence. He was previously a post doctoral research fellow at University of Pennsylvania and a Visiting Fellow at Human Rights Watch, Humboldt University and the European Council on Foreign Relations. His research has been published in *Politics*, *Telecommunications Policy*, *JITP* and the *International Journal of Communications*.

Krista E. Wiegand (PhD Duke University) is Associate Professor of Political Science at the University of Tennessee-Knoxville and Director of the Conflict Processes-Global Security Research Program at the Howard H. Baker Jr Center for Public Policy. Dr Wiegand specializes in international conflict management and political violence, specifically dispute resolution, territorial and maritime disputes, and Islamist political group violence. Her work has been published in her first book, *Bombs and Ballots: Governance by Islamic Terrorist and Guerrilla Groups* (Routledge, 2010), journal articles, and edited books about radical Islam, extremism, religious violence, and terrorism and insurgency in the Middle East.

Sarah Wolff is Lecturer in Public Policy at Queen Mary, University of London. She is an expert on EU–Mediterranean cooperation on justice and home affairs, migration and border management policies. Her monograph *The Mediterranean Dimension of the European Union's Internal Security* (Palgrave, 2012) builds upon fieldwork in Europe, Morocco, Egypt and Jordan. In 2014/15 she was awarded a Fulbright Schuman fellowship and a Leverhulme Research Grant to research EU engagement with Islamist actors. She holds a PhD in international relations (LSE, 2009), an MSc in European politics and governance (LSE, 2004) and a BA in public administration (Sciences Po Grenoble, 1999).

Richard Youngs is Senior Associate at the Carnegie Endowment for International Peace and Professor of International Relations at Warwick University, UK. He is author of eleven books, including most recently *The Puzzle of Non-Western Democracy* (Carnegie, 2015) and *Europe in the New Middle East* (Oxford University Press, 2014). He was previously director of FRIDE, Madrid and senior analyst at the Foreign and Commonwealth Office.

Yahia H. Zoubir is Professor of International Relations and Director of Research in geopolitics at KEDGE Business School. He has published extensively on international political, foreign policy, governance and security issues. His recent works include *North African Politics: Continuity and Change* (co-edited with Gregory White, Routledge, 2015); *Building a New Silk Road: China and the Middle East in the 21st Century* (co-edited with Sun Degang, World Affairs Press, 2014); 'Algeria after the Arab Spring', *Foreign Affairs* (2016), 'China's Economic Diplomacy towards the Arab Countries', *Journal of Contemporary China* (2015) and 'China's Response to the Revolts in the Arab World: A Case of Pragmatic Diplomacy', *Mediterranean Politics* (2014).

1

INTRODUCTION

The growing international relevance of Mediterranean politics

Richard Gillespie and Frédéric Volpi

Since 2010 the map of the Mediterranean has returned to international news coverage as a result of the Arab uprisings and their aftermath, initially providing a series of epic events involving direct regime–opposition power struggles yet since then mostly featuring the frustration of those movements that have aimed to bring change and the ouster of authoritarian rulers. This Mediterranean space, defined by a major sea, a large number of littoral countries and even to some extent their hinterlands, is at the same time an interface between Europe, Africa and Asia, posing complex challenges in terms of achieving peace and stability. Only recently re-established as a focus of compelling international interest, for decades it had been regarded as something of a backwater of global and international politics, with the great exception of the enduring conflict in the Middle East. As occurred periodically in earlier phases of history, it has become a focus of international attention once more through the internal destructiveness and spill-over from conflicts, primarily those waged in Libya, Syria and (more remotely) Iraq. Syria has been the cause of the largest, most desperate migration of asylum-seekers to reach European shores since the creation of the European Union, and indeed since long beforehand, while refuge from its conflict has also been provided by several eastern Mediterranean countries, notwithstanding their weaker economic status. Although conflicts often have a tendency to place prime emphasis on the actions of states and international organizations, the refugee crisis has brought the people of the area more into the picture, through the most appalling human tragedy.

Thus the recent succession of events within this space has generated both a number of specific flashpoints as well as more unremitting human dramas. Amplified by the revolution in digital information technologies, both phenomena have contributed to rising international public interest and awareness, while further south from the shores of the Mediterranean Sea an equally daunting set of growing security challenges remain far less visible in the Sahel and in sub-Saharan Africa, but also cast doubt on the durability of the old order. Adding to the sense of a pan-Mediterranean dimension has been the divisive north–south dimension of the Eurozone crisis, giving rise to the somewhat simplistic notion of problematic southern member states within the EU. As in the 1980s, when some observers in the western world conceptualized this space as 'Mediterranean Europe' and not merely as 'southern Europe' (Pridham, 1984; Payne, 1986; Judt, 1989), the northern shores of the Mediterranean are attracting wider interest among social scientists.

Yet even at this time of uncommonly high interest in the countries around the Mediterranean and in the Sea itself, now the scene of human tragedy as it frequently devours the bodies of those desperate to migrate to safer or richer countries, it is still not the entire Mediterranean as region that tends to draw attention, so much as the flashpoints, together with the networks, communication channels, transit routes and economic exchanges that connect the space with the outside world. Its own regional integration, at least at the economic level, remains critically weak, accounting for only 1 per cent of its trade (EU Neighbourhood Info Centre, 2016). None the less, connectivity at the human level has grown, owing to local initiatives, to some extent, while also being promoted by external agency, with the Euro-Mediterranean Partnership, for all its shortcomings, giving rise to a plethora of links below state level (Youngs, Chapter 7, this volume). Transnational networks have also been boosted hugely by the impact of new communications technologies and, in parts of the region, by the decline of territorial sovereignty (Huber, Chapter 11, this volume).

Research on Mediterranean politics has tended to reflect the fragmentation of the space and the tendency of the parts to sometimes eclipse the whole. The monumental works on the Mediterranean writ large have been historical works, from Fernand Braudel (1972) to Peregrine Horden and Nicholas Purcell (2000).[1] To interpret present day events, it requires the combined and sometimes concerted endeavours of academic journals, collaborative research projects, think tanks and advocacy networks to bring coalitions of researchers, analysts and commentators together, ideally with practitioners, to make sense of the wider complex picture at a time of such great flux and movement, posing far greater challenges than existed during the Cold War when state structures and institutions were relatively stable and maps seemed permanent and authoritative enough to become familiar.

The task of making sense of developments across the Mediterranean space is impeded by its complexity and by fragmentation. While a number of quite ambitious efforts have been made to promote or build academic networks,[2] of late there has been a sense that the structures and dynamics have been evolving faster than our ability to interpret them, and that in some respects fragmentation has increased (Jones, 2014). Yet complexity does not invariably push in the direction of fragmentation: for example, as shown by Murphy (Chapter 29, this volume), global tendencies have also done much to unify the experience of youth across the Mediterranean, thus showing the continued and indeed enhanced relevance of this shared space 'in terms of the exclusionary political, economic and social experiences which are propelling them into new formats for political action', both in southern Europe and North Africa. Such a depiction is entirely compatible with tracing specific trajectories of youth movement activism distinguishable in southern Europe and in eastern as well as southern Mediterranean countries.

Definition of the 'area' of study of Mediterranean politics is a messy and inconclusive business and we have not attempted here to impose a particular geographical framework on our contributors, preferring to regard this issue as an, often implicit, ongoing debate among scholars. In any case, an excellent discussion of the validity and shortcomings of a vast range of different historical notions of the Mediterranean is already available in the impressive work of Horden and Purcell, *The Corrupting Sea* (2000: 9–49). The relevant scope of analysis for Mediterranean political issues is by no means uniform, but rather tends to shift over time and differs from one policy domain to another, regardless of state frontiers, while also extending into hinterlands or even more globally. Thus the scholar of Mediterranean politics stands to benefit from a wider familiarity with the discipline or sub-disciplines of international relations and international political economy and will do well to extend their purview to the literatures pertaining to 'adjacent' area-focused studies, on European, Middle Eastern and North African politics. Equally, for the purposes of this collection, they will benefit from dipping into the specialized thematic literatures, such as those on civil society, regime transition, etc.

The literature specifically on Mediterranean politics has grown impressively since the 1990s, with interest rekindled by developments such as the (short-lived) promise of an end to the Israeli–Palestinian conflict and the launch of the Barcelona process, as well as the accession of southern European countries into the EU, with specific foreign policy priorities in the Mediterranean (Stavridis *et al.*, 1999; Gillespie, 2000). Judging by the special issues of *Mediterranean Politics* published over the last 20 years, the main focuses of research have been the experience of Euro-Mediterranean regional initiatives and the politics of change or continuity in the Arab world. While many collections of this journal have contained contributions from scholars from diverse Mediterranean countries, language remains a barrier to inclusive debates. Multilingual journals such as *Afkar/Ideas*, published by the European Institute for the Mediterranean (IEMed) in Barcelona and occasional contemporary issues of the more historically focused *Cahiers de la Méditerranée* published by the Centre de la Méditerranée Moderne et Contemporaine (CMMC) at the University of Nice have been welcome initiatives, but difficult to sustain in an era of austerity. Thus, although it is fair to depict some degree of regionalization of the Mediterranean research agenda, one must always be aware that not all debates taking place in this area and not all research is reflected in publications that have a largely global distribution.

Global themes in Mediterranean politics

In the contemporary context, perhaps the most symbolic, if not the most instrumentally effective, embodiment of a regional Mediterranean synergy remains the Euro-Mediterranean Partnership officially launched by the EU in 1995, in Barcelona. Underpinning this 'Barcelona process' of regional collaboration is an ideal of political, socio-economic, and cultural rapprochement in the region (Adler *et al.*, 2006). This vision of, and for, the Mediterranean reflects both a regionalization of crucial global political, cultural and economic transformations of the last few decades and longer processes that are grounded in the Mediterranean context. The promotion of a liberal democratic peace in the region illustrated both the post-Cold War rebirth of a global discourse on democracy and much older views of a politically unified Mediterranean world. The institutionalization of trade agreements across the Mediterranean, and between EU and non-EU European states, also reflected the global dominance of a neoliberal economic order and long-standing mercantilist networks between the countries of the region. Culturally, the self-image of the EU as a normative civilian power, facilitated once again in this historical context the promotion of rights and values which were deemed to have universal appeal, even though here, as in the other EMP policies, elite views tended to frame the debate in a very specific light.

Politically, the globalized narrative about democratization that grew in strength in the 1970s and 1980s in the policy-making and scholarly spheres has shaped many approaches to, and expectations of, the Mediterranean region. In his classic article 'Transitions to Democracy' (1970), Rustow stressed the importance of an agreement between elites on the relevance of a democratic system as a means to resolve apparently unsurmountable political tensions. Rustow, also a specialist on Turkish politics, emphasized the importance of a process of habituation for the population at large to adopt such an elite consensus about democracy. Successful transitions from authoritarianism in southern European countries in the 1970s (Greece, Portugal, Spain) began to entrench this transitologist view that presented liberal democracy as a natural outcome of the process of modernization. The landmark four volumes of O'Donnell, Schmitter and Whitehead *Transitions from Authoritarian Rule* (1986) complexified the debate about trajectories of authoritarianism and democratization, but the outlook remained generally positive right into the 1990s. The collapse of the communist bloc in eastern Europe at the end of the 1980s and the wave of 'velvet revolutions' producing democratic systems in eastern and south-eastern Europe confirmed these expectations. Even on the southern shores of the Mediterranean, some former 'Arab-socialist' regimes appeared to be following the same trend, at least initially, as with the Algerian democratic experiment (Volpi, 2003). The relevance of standard democratization models and mechanisms to the Middle East remained, however, a moot point throughout the 1990s. Culturalist views of democratization articulated notably by Huntington's article 'The Clash of Civilizations?' (1993), hinted that a mainly Arab and Muslim Middle East could not produce a working liberal democracy. Just as the Barcelona process began to articulate a democratic agenda for the Mediterranean region, scholars and policy makers alike began to think about the possibility of a Middle Eastern exceptionalism (Salamé, 1994). Progressively, the optimism of the 1990s turned into pessimism in the 2000s, and scholars focused increasingly on explaining the resilience of authoritarianism rather than the progression of democratization (Levitsky and Way, 2002; Diamond, 2002; Heydemann, 2007). By the end of the 2000s, a seemingly increasingly unbridgeable political gap had appeared between a democratic northern shore and an autocratic southern shore, as democratization discourses and democracy promotion policies were upstaged by the securitization narratives and policies of the 'war on terror' (Schlumberger, 2007). Whilst the 2011 Arab uprisings reintroduced the possibility of democratic changes in polities on the southern shores of the Mediterranean, the post-uprising situations showed the fragility of these political developments (Gunning and Baron, 2014; Volpi, 2017). If the early 2010s have illustrated that the Middle East was not that exceptional, the making of a democratic Mediterranean region has also proved to be more elusive than some had hoped at the end of the Cold War. All the chapters of this *Handbook*, directly or indirectly addressing the issue of democracy, point to the multiplicity of factors – be they rooted in policies from the north or from the south – that interact and underpin this difficult construction of a domestic and regional political consensus.

The cultural pendant to a democratic political agenda for the Mediterranean is a liberal conception of rights, enshrined in policies designed to promote human rights across the region (and beyond). This normative ambition of the Barcelona process may be linked to older schemes of a civilizing mission that had rhetorically justified some of the actions of the European empires on the southern shores of the Mediterranean. Even Tocqueville (1988 [1837]) was at first quite enthusiastic about the impact that France could have in Algeria. In practice, French (and British, and Italian) colonial policies commonly proved to be far less uplifting for the local population, and Spain's protectorate in Morocco was hardly benevolent (Balfour, 2002: part II). Colonial policies were often taken up by indigenous authoritarian actors, sometimes with eventual consequences for the metropolis, as in the Spanish civil war or the military challenge to de Gaulle during the Algerian war. The colonial period initiated a new period of multiculturalism and cosmopolitanism in the south; while the post-colonial period was characterized by the same process in the north. In the Middle East and North Africa, earlier forms of multiculturalism were reshaped to accommodate the secularizing dynamics initiated by European powers – a process that outlived colonialism itself (Meijer, 2014; Ruedy, 1996). This difficult process of mutual accommodation, particularly visible in relation to the place of Islam in society, contributed to the evolution of Islamism over the ensuing decades, first in the countries on the southern shores of the Mediterranean, and then in the European countries themselves (Esposito and Burgat, 2003). The cultural transformations initiated by colonial powers in the nineteenth century laid the foundation for the social reconfigurations of the end of the twentieth century, when the implications of migration from the south began to impact states and societies on both shores of the Mediterranean (Brand, 2006). Whilst the discourse of 'rights' has undeniably established itself across the region over the years, its significance has tended to vary with its political uses

(Slyomovics, 2005). Despite the normative promotion of its 'acquis communautaire' in the region, European Union policies de facto prioritized the implementation of security and economic agreements as the basis of a regional 'community' of sorts (Kausch and Youngs, 2009).

The socio-economic dimension of community building in the Mediterranean has always been central to the formation of a Mediterranean nexus, be it in classical times, in the period studied by Braudel, or in the contemporary context. In the modern period, colonial policies shaped an extractive relationship in which colonies on the southern shores provided countries on the northern shores with cheap raw material (and then manpower); and Europe sent some manufactured goods in return. This imbalanced relationship continued in the post-colonial period, even as oil-rich countries in the south tried to use their newfound wealth to develop their economies. In practice, reliance on oil and gas entrenched a dependence on natural resources and hindered the domestic economy, not least due to an ill-thought-through spate of state dirigisme (Luciani, 1990). The post-WWII period was marked by an ever-greater economic union on the northern shores of the Mediterranean through the creation and expansion of what evolved into the European Union. The post-colonial period did not produce a similar integration of the economies of the countries of the Middle East and North Africa. Despite the pan-Arabist and Arab-socialist rhetoric, political division between the different authoritarian regimes of the region remained strong and hindered cross-national collaboration. North–south relations structured by the neo liberal economic agenda of the EU thus kept structuring regional wealth exchanges and constrained the developmental options of the MENA countries (Henry and Springborg, 2010). Despite the narrative of the EU as a 'normative power', the emphasis on technical bilateral collaboration as a developmental solution in the new 2008 EU initiative, the Union for the Mediterranean, illustrated this diminished ambition for regional political and socio-economic collaboration (Bicchi and Gillespie, 2012). As with the process of European integration within the EU, the building of stronger Mediterranean ties followed the ups and downs of the economy; expanding and deepening in periods of growth, weakening and contracting in periods of recession. In recent years the specifically Mediterranean aspect of this downturn has been particularly important, as southern European countries (Italy, Spain, Portugal, Cyprus, and worse of all Greece) have gone through severe economic crises. The Arab uprisings, despite their potent political message, did not give rise to a sizeable economic turnover in MENA countries still dominated by crony capitalism (Malik and Awadallah, 2013). For their part, emerging Mediterranean economic powers, such as Turkey or Israel, proved to be too tied up in their own political problems to provide a dependable economic impetus in the region.

A handbook for the Mediterranean

The *Routledge Handbook of Mediterranean Politics* is part of a 'handbook' suite of volumes possessing a shared publishing rationale. Its appearance is particularly significant for the domain of Mediterranean politics, which has not hitherto seen such an ambitious single collection attempted on such a scale by academics.[3] This *Handbook* attempts to bring together the perspectives of most of the leading contemporary academic experts who have researched the Mediterranean, either as a unit of some kind or through more partial focuses. They have been asked in some cases to revisit their earlier work on a topic, to provide an overview of the evolution of their subject or to focus on quite recent developments. Diverse notions of the Mediterranean lie behind their contributions. Just to encapsulate this in sweeping geographical terms, some of these authors take the north–south axis as key while others see a need to focus equally on the specificities of the eastern and/or western Mediterranean, deemed relevant to elucidate the dimensionality of their own subject area. While we believe that the volume achieves what it set out to in terms of mapping the contours and dimensions as well as key themes of Mediterranean politics, it would be unrealistic to claim that even a handbook of this size addresses everything one ideally needs to know about the political realities of the Mediterranean Basin. While we set out to be as comprehensive as we could, we are only too aware of the time it takes for solidly researched analysis to follow in the aftermath of actual developments on the ground and for theoretical reflections to ensue; and of the fact that, while certain topics (such as the travails of efforts aimed at regime change in the Arab countries) have attracted huge interest, others remain under-researched or in very early stages of social science investigation.

Even so, we hope that the studies offered here map onto key areas of study in universities and will thus be much used by students looking either for authoritative work on a particular theme or insights into the overall context of the Mediterranean, its evolution and major linkages with other parts of the world. Equally, for subjects that we have not been able to address in depth on this occasion, we trust that what is offered here will inspire further research by this and the next generation of scholars.

The *Handbook* is articulated around six key parts: historical constructions, geopolitical perspectives, peace and conflict, political economy, non-state actors and social movements, and societal and cultural trends. The first part investigates the recent political constructions of the Mediterranean as an integrated and institutionalized space in an historical perspective. Several contributors examine how different influential ideas and policies have shaped this space, with external actors playing key roles in the historical construction of both 'Mediterranean' and 'Middle East' over the last hundred years. The eventual failures of western powers to achieve many of their main political objectives should not be allowed to obscure the profound impact of external policies, arguably debilitating local regimes in the long run and thus having a destabilizing effect in an area already deemed unstable. In recent decades, European policy, with its emphasis on soft power and the export of its own political and economic experience (much of it somewhat mythicized) set out to offer a distinctive strategic approach, yet it is shown here to have been markedly inconsistent, in the long run shifting from a liberal to a realist emphasis while continuing to eschew the use of hard power. In parallel to these outside–inside dynamics between external and internal actors, there remain the complex structures of the space itself, certainly traversed by a north–south divide but also featuring regional dynamics, seen by several contributors as emerging more assertively recently at the level of civil society, which – despite an accentuation of repression or chaos in many parts of the Arab Mediterranean – are looking to their own collective experiences as bases for challenging the status quo.

The second part complements the first by recognizing that, once a general framing of Mediterranean dynamics has been proposed, one still needs to be very aware of the specificities shaping the attitudes and roles of different states. There are major limits to how far one can generalize about the Arab Mediterranean, for instance. The discussion presented here certainly points to much commonality in the way that Arab states and societies have perceived north–south issues and Euro-Mediterranean initiatives, though not always producing uniform political responses, nor so far prompting effective inter-Arab cooperation. In contrast, Europe is often depicted in much Euro-Mediterranean analysis as a single actor, yet is shown here to be marked by important north–south divergence within Europe and by distinctive northern, southern and eastern outlooks, which have been a factor in the EU's overall ineffectiveness. Even the USA, often presented as having the great advantage over the EU of being a single state actor, is shown to be lacking a unified outlook on the Mediterranean, apart from a shared tendency *not* to visualize the space integrally. Within the area, yet facing other important areas as well insofar as their external relations are concerned, both Israel and Turkey are shown to have been somewhat 'odd fits' (to use a term deployed by Park, Chapter 12, this volume) within the

Barcelona process and Mediterranean regional context and to have identified more crucial priorities, particularly as events around the Mediterranean have evolved in the twenty-first century. The political dynamics set in motion by powerful state actors to address the dilemmas that affected them most are shown to have multiple consequences for the regional system.

The third part investigates the mobilization, organization and utilization of coercion and violence in the making and unmaking of models for political collaboration across the region. Despite blatant contemporary examples of military dictatorships and ongoing conflicts in the Arab world, the Mediterranean region as a whole generally has followed global patterns of democratization since decolonization at least to the extent that most countries have slowly and eventually pushed military actors away from the centre of power. Over time the playing out of power struggles between military and civilian elites has been one factor impacting political evolution. Also affecting it has been the political instrumentalization of ethno-religious and economic conflicts, which has provided many opportunities for violent organizations – whether nationalist movements or religious groups – to undermine the possibility of domestic and international collaboration and power sharing. The extreme crystallization of such conflicts in specific locations can not only durably hinder the formation of more stable and democratic political orders, but also can produce additional difficulties for the emergence of productive regional collaborations. Bilateral collaborations and EU initiatives are shown to be useful at the margins to resolve some of these predicaments, but they appear to have a limited impact on some of the more serious conflicts, especially when local actors frame these disagreements as existential identity threats. The 2011 Arab uprisings have shown both the possibilities for substantive political reform in the region brought about by different state and non-state actors, as well as the limits on change that can be imposed by resilient authoritarian actors.

Part IV addresses the economic calculus and dynamics that enabled and/or hindered different models of regional cooperation, as well as underpinning competition between Mediterranean actors. The north–south economic inequalities that constitute a continuing source of tension between regional actors have fed on the repeated failures of southern states to put in place dependable strategies of development. Even the sizeable natural resources and energy assets of many countries of the southern shores of the Mediterranean have not been put to their best use by incumbent elites owing to political calculations, both at the national and regional level. The slow but increasing integration of Mediterranean countries into a globalized economy is shown not to be in and of itself a factor favouring socio-economic improvement, nor is it necessarily detrimental to these developing economies. It is suggested that the limited understanding of the multifarious impacts and consequences of neoliberal policies, by both economic and political actors at the domestic and regional levels, itself contributes to the unpredictable developmental dynamics of the region.

Part V investigates in more depth the role of non-state actors in the formation of transnational Mediterranean networks, some of which directly or indirectly sustain a distinct regional identity and practice while also having locally specific features. The contributors indicate how social actors and movements insert themselves in larger institutional dynamics and attempt to influence the policy agendas managed by state actors, but they are also increasingly involved in the construction of horizontal transnational networks in order to overcome their disadvantages *vis-à-vis* the holders of political and economic power. The Arab uprisings, and to some extent the anti-austerity campaigns waged by youthful alternative left movements in southern Europe, have been key transnational points of reference for debates about the nature of civil society, for strategic and tactical lessons available to social movement activists, and for policy makers and diplomats whose remit has a Euro-Mediterranean dimension. Particularly significant at this juncture has been the transient or more sustained opening of political systems to the participation of Islamist parties in certain southern Mediterranean countries, along with incipient engagement between Islamist and more secular advocacy networks in the course of protest actions, dialogue and political activity.

The final, sixth part continues to examine issues at the sub-state and transnational levels but focuses less on actors and movements than on cultural and social interactions, both virtual and physical, that shape the perceptions and practices of communities across the Mediterranean space. The development of global communication networks and the appeal of new social media promised to liberate and empower citizens and even to facilitate the growth of shared identity in the area, yet much of the evidence presented points to successful defences of the fundamentals of pre-existing institutions and established identity stereotypes by making use of the very same technological innovations. While new media have undoubtedly facilitated social mobilization and increased the rapidity and scope of 'contagion' effects, at times the same media that help generate global public interest in developments at the same time distort their public imagery and thus make it harder for well-conceived policy responses or actions taken in support of movements for change. Following the Arab uprisings and the emergence of a refugee crisis which heightened global public attention, many observers still fail to grasp the political complexities and cultural diversity of the Mediterranean space and thus continue to entertain simplistic notions of, for example, 'the Arab people'. As the case of the Anna Lindh Foundation illustrates, even those Europeans who oppose the tendency of policy makers to view dramatic news-feeding events through a narrow security prism may also be investing their hopes in somewhat elitist initiatives somewhat detached from social realities and blind to certain cultural identities.

Mediterranean politics are so complex and varied that the current *Handbook* can only claim to provide a useful entry point for an informed exploration of the multiple actors and processes that shape the contemporary Mediterranean world. The interconnections between the different aspects of politics highlighted in the different sections of the volume are in our view key to appreciating the dynamics of change in the region. The contributions contained in this work offer not only insights into the debates and processes that structure each theme, but also key pointers for a more general understanding of how distinct political, economic, social and cultural dynamics interact across the region. The only broad 'lesson' that can be learnt from this work is that there is no single linear story to tell about the Mediterranean. Yet, there are practical and conceptual synergies that can be identified in these multifaceted regional processes. Notably, national and supranational processes that aimed at forging more cohesive political identities have repeatedly created not only a higher degree of social, economic and cultural integration, but also multiple resistances and alternative solidarities; with the use of repression or structural violence inducing in return specific types of grassroots rejection. Centrifugal forces in the creation of a contemporary Mediterranean region are shown here to include amongst other things the imposition of exclusive political identities and ideologies, as well as segregated models of socio-economic development. By contrast, centripetal forces are shown to be made of more diffuse mechanisms – often unintended consequences of larger political, economic or cultural dynamics – which are only loosely tied to institutional processes. The interplay between centrifugal and centripetal forces will continue to shape the destinies of Mediterranean peoples in the years ahead.

Notes

1 For its scope, mention should also be made of the work of David Abulafia and others, cited in Fenech and Pace (Chapter 2, this volume), including his concluding chapter, 'A Globalized Mediterranean: 1900–2000', in Abulafia (2003).

2 Jones (2014: 2) mentions the British–Spanish 'Encuentro' project supported by the British Council in 2006 (on which see Gillespie and Martín, 2006) and a more recent event convened by the Centre de la Méditerranée Moderne et Contemporaine in Nice and Sciences-Po in Menton in 2013. Academics

specializing in security studies have been given new opportunities to collaborate since 1996 owing to the existence of EuroMeSCo (the Euro-Mediterranean Study Commission), an EU-funded network of research centres on politics and security in the Mediterranean. At present it comprises 107 institutes, coming from 32 countries. Besides networks, recent years have seen the creation of modest Euro-Mediterranean universities in Slovenia and Morocco, funded by the Union for the Mediterranean.

3 Precedents include the two *Mediterranean Politics* yearbooks edited by Richard Gillespie (1994, 1996), before the journal of the same name was launched in 1996, and the *IEMed Yearbook* published by the European Institute for the Mediterranean and CIDOB in Barcelona since 2003, the latter with a larger number of relatively short contributions, mostly though not exclusively by academics.

References

Abulafia, David (2003). 'A Globalized Mediterranean: 1900–2000'. In Abulafia, D. (ed.), *The Mediterranean in History*. London: Thames & Hudson.

Adler, Emanuel, Federica Bicchi, Beverly Crawford and Raffaella Del Sarto (eds) (2006). *The Convergence of Civilizations: Constructing a Mediterranean Region*. Toronto: University of Toronto Press.

Balfour, Sebastian (2002). *Deadly Embrace: Morocco and the Road to the Spanish Civil War*. Oxford: Oxford University Press.

Bicchi, Federica and Richard Gillespie (eds) (2012). *The Union for the Mediterranean*. London: Routledge.

Brand, Laurie A. (2006). *Citizens Abroad: Emigration and the State in the Middle East and North Africa*. Cambridge: Cambridge University Press.

Braudel, Fernand (1972). *The Mediterranean and the Mediterranean World in the Age of Philip II* (*La Méditerrannée et le Monde Méditeranéen à l'époque de Philippe II*, 1st edn 1949), 2 vols. London and New York: HarperCollins.

Diamond, Larry J. (2002). 'Thinking about Hybrid Regimes', *Journal of Democracy* 13(2): 21–35.

Esposito, John L. and François Burgat (eds) (2003). *Modernizing Islam: Religion in the Public Sphere in the Middle East and Europe*. New Brunswick: Rutgers University Press.

EU Neighbourhood Info Centre (2016). *EuroMed News* (Brussels), 1 April, electronic newsletter, available online at www.euneighbours.eu.

Gillespie, Richard (1994, 1996). *Mediterranean Politics*, 2 vols. London: Pinter.

Gillespie, Richard (2000). *Spain and the Mediterranean: Developing a European Policy towards the South*. Basingstoke: Macmillan.

Gillespie, Richard and Iván Martín (eds) (2006). *Researching the Mediterranean*. Barcelona: British Council, CIDOB Foundation and Institut Europeu de la Mediterrània. Spanish edn, *Investigando el Mediterráneo* (same publishers, 2006).

Gunning, Jeroen and Ilan Zvi Baron (2014). *Why Occupy a Square? People, Protests and Movements in the Egyptian Revolution*. New York: Oxford University Press.

Henry, Clement Moore and Robert Springborg (2010). *Globalization and the Politics of Development in the Middle East*, 2nd edn. Cambridge: Cambridge University Press.

Heydemann, Steven (2007). 'Upgrading Authoritarianism in the Arab World', Analysis Paper 13, Washington DC: Saban Center for Middle East Policy.

Horden, Peregrine and Nicholas Purcell (2000). *The Corrupting Sea: A Study of Mediterranean History*. Oxford: Blackwell.

Huntington, Samuel P. (1993). 'The Clash of Civilizations?', *Foreign Affairs* 72(3): 22–49.

Jones, Anthony (2014). 'Research Agendas for the Mediterranean Region: Opportunities and Challenges', *Cahiers de la Méditerranée*, 89: 1–6.

Judt, Tony (ed.) (1989). *Resistance and Revolution in Mediterranean Europe*. London: Routledge.

Kausch, Kristina and Richard Youngs (2009). 'The End of the "Euro-Mediterranean vision"', *International Affairs* 85(5): 963–75.

Levitsky, Steven and Lucan A. Way (2002). 'The Rise of Competitive Authoritarianism', *Journal of Democracy* 13(2): 51–65.

Luciani, Giacomo (ed.) (1990). *The Arab State*. Berkeley: University of California Press.

Malik, Adeel and Bassem Awadallah (2013). 'The Economics of the Arab Spring', *World Development* 45: 296–313.

Meijer, Roel (ed.) (2014). *Cosmopolitanism, Identity and Authenticity in the Middle East*. New York: Routledge.

O'Donnell, Guillermo, Philippe Schmitter and Laurence Whitehead (eds) (1986). *Transitions from Authoritarian Rule: Prospects for Democracy*, 4 vols. Baltimore: Johns Hopkins University Press.

Payne, Stanley G. (1986). 'The Concept of "Southern Europe" and Political Development', *Mediterranean Historical Review* 1(1): 100–16.
Pridham, Geoffrey (ed.) (1984). *The New Mediterranean Democracies*. London: Frank Cass.
Ruedy, John (ed.) (1996). *Islamism and Secularism in North Africa*. New York: Palgrave.
Rustow, Dankwart A. (1970). 'Transitions to Democracy: Toward a Dynamic Model', *Comparative Politics* 2(3): 337–63.
Salamé, Ghassan (1994). *Democracy without Democrats? The Renewal of Politics in the Muslim World*. London: I. B. Tauris.
Schlumberger, Oliver (ed.) (2007). *Debating Arab Authoritarianism: Dynamics and Durability in Nondemocratic Regimes*. Stanford: Stanford University Press.
Slyomovics, Susan (2005). *The Performance of Human Rights in Morocco*. Philadelphia: University of Pennsylvania Press.
Stavridis, Stelios, Theodore Couloumbis, Thanos Veremis and Neville Waites (1999). *The Foreign Policies of the European Union's Member States and Applicant Countries in the 1990s*. Basingstoke: Macmillan.
Tocqueville, Alexis de (1988 [1837]). *De la Colonie en Algérie*. Brussels: Éditions Complexe.
Volpi, Frédéric (2003). *Islam and Democracy: The Failure of Dialogue in Algeria*. London: Pluto Press.
Volpi, Frédéric (2017). *Revolution and Authoritarianism in North Africa*. New York: Oxford University Press.

PART I

Historical constructions

2

THE HISTORICAL CONSTRUCTION OF THE MEDITERRANEAN

Dominic Fenech and Michelle Pace

When we think about a 'region' we mostly have in mind a rather homogeneous area with distinct characteristics that contrast it with surrounding areas. Movement within such an imagined geographical area is usually depicted through certain regular patterns of relations and interactions between the countries making up that area. A distinction is clear between macro (large-scale geographical spaces of continental proportions) and micro (very small structures) regions. Uniform regions are identified through common region-wide characteristics while focal regions are those in which the characteristics are most strongly discernible at or near the centre of the region and least strongly at the boundaries. The Mediterranean can be conceptualized as either a 'region' with sub-regions (encompassing southern Europe, North Africa or the Maghreb and the Levant or the Mashrek) or as an interface or bridge between coherent regions (for example, between Europe and the Middle East and North Africa, MENA). In the case of the former, the Mediterranean is said to embody at least parts of Turkey, southern European Union member states – Italy, Spain, France, Malta, Cyprus, Greece, Portugal to an extent and Algeria, Libya, Mauritania, Morocco, and Tunisia as well as Egypt, Israel, the Occupied Palestinian Territories, Jordan, Lebanon and Syria (Pace, 2006). These classifications are highly debatable. What is important for us for the purpose of this handbook is that the Mediterranean has been central to the development of humanity since known history began, and while it ceased to be a primary junction of global convergence after the late Middle Ages, it remained a focal point of international affairs, whether as subject or as object. A measure of such continuity is the extent to which terms coined in our times could easily have been applied to the region centuries ago. Here began, and persisted, the north–south divide, as did Europe's imperialism. Here too was played out more than one east–west contest. From imperial collapse to postcolonial transitions and legacies and now post-postcolonial ones, to concerns over Islamist militancy, to mass movement of people, so many world developments and phenomena featured, if not originated, here and in many cases they remain rampant today. The Mediterranean is more than just a list of problems, but depth of civilization, the olive and the vine, and holidays in the sun are only one side of a very crowded coin.

No discussion of the historical construction of the Mediterranean can get underway without a tentative few words about locating its 'regionality' and without acknowledging the interminability of the debate about what exactly one has in mind when invoking the 'Mediterranean'. As Iver B. Neumann puts it, one way of reading the Mediterranean is through symbolic geography, that is the lens through which the Mediterranean can be perceived as a land mass, that has an inside that is material (a territory) and an outside that is represented (a map) (Neumann in Pace, 2006: preface). But what is important here is that the Mediterranean is a represented entity. By understanding who is making these representations of the Mediterranean, in what context, for which purpose, etc., we can then appreciate that power is at play. Therefore, symbolic geography helps us focus on our object of study, namely the Mediterranean, by shedding light on the preconditions and, crucially, the effects of operating with one set of geographical delineations in mind rather than another. Hence, the way in which the Mediterranean has been, continues to be, and will be, defined – in terms of territory, functions, institutions, etc. – makes it a social fact that exists. Those representations that win the day dominate the discourse of the Mediterranean (Neumann in Pace, 2006: preface).

Thus, the Mediterranean has often been represented as a distinct 'Other' in historical narratives, symbolic geography and anthropological discourses and especially in relation to the larger context of Europe. The cultural construction of the Mediterranean as 'inside outsider' within Europe has been debated through theories of modernization, colonial culture and power relations as well as critical race and ethnic studies. This chapter charts a historical trajectory of the Mediterranean by highlighting defining moments of its social construction at specific periods in the past up to the present day. Each defining moment in the history of the Mediterranean is synthesized with the dominant narrative of the 'region' at the time and the theoretical and political dilemmas that shaped and continue to shape such discursive practices.

The attributes that one may give to the historical Mediterranean, if one so wishes, are endless. It is a connector of continents, a precocious superhighway, a murderous frontier, a layered ecosystem, a cultural soup, a romantic ideal, a theoretical convention, a deconstructionist's laboratory, a historian's arsenal – and the deeper one delves the more the horizons broaden, instead of narrowing. There is so much to it that it has inversely been criticized for being too sprawling, lacking in focus and therefore meaning, if not being, with one eminent skeptic proposing that 'Mediterraneanism' provided 'excuses for everything, from epistemology to eating' (Herzfeld, 2005). Even historians, who have been the vanguard of scholars of the Mediterranean, are challenged by the unevenness of its status and homogeneity in different periods of its history, which is perhaps why they prefer to concentrate on certain periods rather than on others. The homogeneity that the Mediterranean enjoyed under the Roman Empire gave it a completeness that is unmatched by any other epoch of history, so there is no difficulty there, but what about when that homogeneity was lost? The question of when that completeness ceased produced one of the most important historiographical debates of the twentieth century, when Henri Pirenne (1937) proposed that the coherence of the Mediterranean was broken by the Islamic conquests of the eighth century and not, as commonly held, by the fall of Rome in 476 CE. Not that political unity is a prerequisite for regionality of course, for if that were the case one should be hard put to treat, for example, Europe's history as a regional one. However one interprets it, the fracture between the Christian Mediterranean and the Muslim one, with their respective European and Afro-Asian hinterlands, was anything but a mark of decline for the region as a whole. For one thing, as has been pointed out, the flipside of the formal contest between the two was a degree of cultural synthesis (Said, 2001). And the institutional state of confrontation in early modern history was certainly no problem for the patriarchal Fernand Braudel (1949) when opting to write about the 'Mediterranean *world*' of a time when the mightiest political players of the day were located here in the Mediterranean. On the contrary, the choice of the sixteenth century, as it were the last fling of the Mediterranean as the centre of the world before decline set in, could not have been more calculated. Meanwhile, given how the Mediterranean moved in and out of the limelight over the centuries, it is not perhaps surprising that historians have been reluctant to write long-range Mediterranean historical narratives, although John Julius Norwich (2007) and David Abulafia (2011) took up the challenge in recent years.

One lasting effect of the Braudelian historical tradition has been the acknowledgement that the physical geographic characteristics of the Mediterranean provide the inescapable parameters for human agency. Abulafia, who sees trade as the paramount human activity and a prime agent of Mediterranean coherence, thinks that Braudel takes his point too far (Abulafia, 2011: xxvi–xxvii) and to make his own point subtitled his landmark history 'A *Human* History of the Mediterranean'. Still, he implicitly concedes the importance of geography, notably when proposing mass tourism as one of the defining features of the contemporary Mediterranean (2011: 631–8), inasmuch as mass tourism has been driven primarily by climate, much more even than the civilizational heritage that earlier had attracted the elite visitors on the Grand Tour. Opening up the Mediterranean to the world (and in turn impelling the growth of several Mediterranean economies), mass tourism indeed commodified the Mediterranean, as did important byproducts such as regional tastes in food (Abulafia, 2003: 306–12), not without feeding somewhat the tendency to typecast the Mediterranean with such constructions as 'Mediterranean cuisine' or 'Mediterranean diet'. Climate – the geographical element most responsible for tourism, produce, consumption and lifestyle – is probably the most enduring of those features where the Mediterranean is cast as a global model. Who has not heard of the Mediterranean climate – in California, or indeed nowadays in any part of the planet that is capable of producing New World wine, making it Mediterranean by definition – a 'Mediterraneanoid' ecosystem (Broodbank, 2013: 61)? Such labels make out the Mediterranean as something of a prototype, if not a nickname.

The tendency to stretch the definition of the Mediterranean is not unusual among the scholars who study it. As mentioned already, the countries that are conjured up in our minds when thinking about the Mediterranean often depend on where one is located. For example, if one is located in northern Europe the Mediterranean can stretch as far as Greece, Italy, France, Malta and Cyprus, perhaps Portugal. We want to make the point that such interpretations of the Mediterranean, and the endless debates about whether to stick strictly to the coastal states surrounding the Mediterranean Sea or whether to include certain hinterlands, may lead observers to imagine a fractured space. Our point is that breaking down the region into sub-regions serves certain (political, economic) purposes. But the Mediterranean is much more than the sum of its parts. To understand and appreciate the history of the Mediterranean, what matters are relations among its inhabitants and those of other regions, in other words, networks of exchanges – be these material, cultural or human, over time and continuing up to this day. The evolution of the interactions of this inexhaustive, expansive and ever-changing space have been thoroughly documented over time in major works including those of Fernand Braudel, Peregrine Horden and Nicholas Purcell, and David Abulafia, amongst others.

Braudel sees the Mediterranean in the light of a hub with geography as key to its regional credentials, as noted, whence, however, human agency takes over to create the Greater Mediterranean, 'a wide zone, extending well beyond the shores of the sea in all directions . . . an electric or magnetic field' (1949: 168), practically reaching as far as human networks can extend. Horden and Purcell, in their stout defence of the Mediterranean as an area worth investigating as a region, while not claiming that its history is a global history in itself, see it nonetheless as 'a peculiar and important segment', which in any eventual framing of a maritime-centred global history must stand out on account of 'how different it is from the rest of the show' (2006: 740). In this definition of its distinctiveness the Mediterranean is more leader than prototype or hub.

Our own view is that the Mediterranean, besides being richly deserving of treatment as a region, albeit a constructed one – on account of its deep-rooted history and civilization, its sheer complexity, its uninterrupted prominence in world affairs and its ongoing newsworthiness – continues to represent, if no more the centre as such, a microcosm or scale-model of world affairs. In terms of Arjun Appadurai's (1996) notions of mediascapes, ethnoscapes, technoscapes, financescapes and ideoscapes, no other region in the world conjures up as many daily images, debates and movements – be these of people, goods, money or political ideas – as the Mediterranean. As shall be suggested, there is far too much going on in today's Mediterranean that is one with world events not to make it distinctive. The fluidity of the Mediterranean is indeed endless.

The very origin of its name speaks volumes about the global importance attributed to it since antiquity. It remains etymologically uncertain whether the name 'Mediterranean' was originally coined to mean 'the sea in the middle of the Earth' or simply and prosaically, 'water enclosed by land'. Whichever is correct does not matter, since the land surrounding the sea belongs to three converging continents, and three continents that between them comprised the entire known world. Until Vasco da Gama and Christopher Columbus opened up the oceans, the Mediterranean was an exclusive node of convergence for global trade and encounters of civilizations. It was also at the centre of international relations, housing the main protagonists of world affairs, from the Ottoman Turks, to the Spanish Habsburgs, the papacy, France and the great Italian trading empires.

This concentration of major international players in such a confined space gave the Mediterranean a distinct cosmopolitanism. In particular – though one must not look for symmetry in the shifting sands of alignments of medieval and early modern times – the Mediterranean for almost a millennium had been the main point of contact for one of the most ambiguous relationships in cultural history, that between Christians and Muslims. That historical relationship has been debated interminably, and will no doubt continue to be so and with increasing intensity as long as the world remains preoccupied with fundamentalist militancy. Historians of the Mediterranean from Braudel to Horden and Purcell to Abulafia are careful to point out the Sea's inherent 'connectivities', especially insofar as the imperative of profitable international trade may have been stronger than religious fanaticism. At the same time, aggressive imperialist warfare and widespread private or state-sanctioned terrorism (notably corsairing, an early form of hijacking), sometimes licensed and waged under the guise of holy war, were equally a fact of life. And even on the commercial plane, cross-border fraternizing was hamstrung by monopolistic and extortionate state practices, which was partly what drove the Iberian states to turn their back on the Mediterranean and explore oceanic trade routes to eastern Asia in preference to the overland ones trodden since antiquity (Crowley, 2013, 2015).

As it happened the success of these oceanic exploits would contribute significantly, though by no means solely, to the sidelining of the Mediterranean as the epicentre of world economics and politics. There followed a commercial revolution and the flourishing of a modern 'capitalist world economy' that would soon give emergent northern European states a decisive edge over the old Mediterranean centres of power. This north–south divide – to use the first of many anachronistic terms – appeared here in the Euro-Mediterranean area, in the course of the sixteenth and seventeenth centuries. The context was the turmoil of the Reformation and Counterreformation, which witnessed a successful political rebellion of the rising north against the old suffocating powers of the south (Wallerstein, 1979: 1–36). This new intra-Christian north–south contest-cum-divide crisscrossed the other long-established one played on an east–west axis, the last peaking before the fizzling out of the 900-year-old contest for territory and hegemony that had seen the Christian–Muslim frontier moving back and forth across the Mediterranean. Played out like a Cold War between virtual superpowers, the Ottomans and the Habsburgs, and underpinned by opposing ideological world-views, the contest led to all out physical clashes in the sixteenth century Mediterranean twice – in Malta and in Lepanto. Both were won by Christians but neither amounted to a meaningful or conclusive victory for any side (Fenech, 1993). (The Ottomans won lesser clashes at Prevesa and Djerba.)

The ascendancy of the Christian west over the Islamic east would occur later, on a north–south axis. It would consist of the slow contraction of the Ottoman Empire, starting from the late seventeenth century and dragging all the way down to the First World War, its territory a contested ground between the big powers of Europe. As the old Mediterranean centres of power, not just the Ottomans, atrophied and as the region slid into underdevelopment, the mostly northern European powers turned their avid eyes onto it, competing for succession, access, patronage, influence, privileges, and ultimately territory in the form of the systematic colonization of all the Arab shoreline of the region. No stranger to imperialism in its millennial history, the Mediterranean featured amply and conspicuously in imperialism's modern version, that of European domination over non-Europeans, because this is just where non-Europe began.

The nineteenth century Mediterranean acted as the arena for another east–west contest, one whose top protagonists were respectively the world's biggest maritime and land empires. Like some prequel to the twentieth century Cold War, a global Atlantic player from the west secured naval predominance over the waters and developed a strategy of containment against the mammoth state of the east. To stem Russian encroachment on its Balkan and Central Asian neighbourhoods, Britain shored up the ailing Ottoman Empire and Central Asian states such as Persia and Afghanistan, in what were termed the 'Near Eastern Question' and the 'Great Game' (Fenech, 1993).

As the world grew broader and more and more of it entered the scope of Eurocentric history, the Mediterranean, while no longer 'the sea in the middle of the Earth' held on to its role of microcosm of world affairs. With Europe still paramount in the world, and in control of large swathes of its Mediterranean semi-periphery, there was no shortage of developments of world import occurring there. Big Power brinkmanship in Bosnia, Morocco, Albania and Serbia during the early years of the twentieth century set the stage for the First World War, until the Powers, having bickered over the Balkan lands for a couple of centuries, tripped and stumbled over events in that most tragic of cities, Sarajevo. Just as the war left in its wake great changes in the European map, so also it brought about messy changes in the Middle East that gave birth to the most intractable of conflicts in our time, one that in turn spawned endless toxic byproducts. The Balfour Declaration would eventually mark the birth of one nation (Israel) and the tragedy ('nakba') of another (Segev, 2000). For the rest the interwar years saw the consolidation of European imperialism in the Mediterranean, even as the principles of self-determination and democracy were proclaimed, however prematurely, as the hallmark of future peace and prosperity in Europe.

After the Second World War, the Mediterranean experienced at first hand, and earlier than most other parts of the world, the two great phenomena that defined world affairs for the rest of the twentieth century, namely the Cold War and the end of European empires. It was right here in the Mediterranean that these east–west and north–south axes intersected. In October 1944, four months before Yalta, Churchill and Stalin in Moscow were already dividing the Balkans into spheres of influence (Resis, 1978; Carlton, 1983). Three years later, in 1947, it was with reference to the northeastern shores of the Mediterranean, specifically Greece and Turkey, that Harry Truman proclaimed his doctrine, committing the United States to lead the defence of the west against international communism, while pronouncing that a state of Cold War had come to exist in the world. Soon the Mediterranean was roped into the grand strategy of the western alliance, the North Atlantic Treaty Organization (NATO), through the early membership of countries as improbably North Atlantic as Italy (1949), Greece and Turkey (1952). The Mediterranean Sea became NATO's 'southern flank', the front where the western alliance felt particularly vulnerable and hence resolved to secure. Through the eastern Mediterranean the alliance linked on to other alliance sets in Asia – the Baghdad Pact and the South East Asia Treaty Organization (SEATO) – to extend the chain of Soviet containment all the way to the Far East (Fenech, 2000). In the confined and volatile space of the Mediterranean Sea the superpowers maintained dedicated fleets – the Sixth Fleet and the Fifth Eskadra – and played risky games, showing the flag or like waterborne 'Top Guns' shadowing and upstaging each other in their warships (Rosenthal and Duchêne, 1982).

In parallel with all the above, the non-European Mediterranean joined the rest of the world to experience the wide-ranging phenomenon of decolonization. Here occurred some of the most spectacular and discrediting episodes of European imperialism, notably in Egypt following the hapless Suez War, Algeria in one of the bloodiest wars of independence on record, and most of all Palestine, where it left behind the almightiest of messes in the Middle East. The legacy of colonialism reverberates still, notably where it left behind divided communities – Palestine, Lebanon, Cyprus – while residual issues like Ceuta and Melilla's future remain unresolved.

Featuring so centrally in these two world-changing phenomena of Cold War and decolonization, it is not surprising that the Mediterranean threw up two world-class leaders – Yugoslavia's Tito and Egypt's Nasser – who in a resolute attempt to resist superpower neo-imperialism helped put together the World Nonaligned Movement.

Amazingly, during these years it was difficult to get anyone to recognize the Mediterranean as a single interconnected unit. To be sure the superpowers clearly treated the sea as one geostrategic area, but while each saw it as directly relevant to their own strategic and defence interests neither of them took kindly to discussing, much less addressing, its problems. The most telling instance was the respective allies' hostility to a proposal by Malta to include the Mediterranean in the scope of the Conference on Security and Co-operation in Europe (CSCE), when it met in Helsinki in 1975; and if the final document ended up including a so-called 'Mediterranean Chapter', it was only thanks to the use of the veto by the proposer (Holsti, 1982; Badalassi 2012).

More benignly, the European Community (EC), being less hyperopic and more concerned about the problems and opportunities in its immediate neighbourhood, did take an early and sustained interest in the Mediterranean as a whole. During 1972, building on a string of treaties with Mediterranean states from the previous decade, the EC went on to develop a system of association agreements and preferential tariffs, giving it the grand name of Global Mediterranean Policy or GMP. Shortly after, the 1973 Yom Kippur War and the world oil crisis that followed in its wake led to a French initiative, known as the Euro-Arab Dialogue, that was launched in Copenhagen during the European Council meeting. For the Europeans this was a forum where they could discuss economic affairs with third Mediterranean partners, whereas for the Arab side the Dialogue represented a talking shop where they could discuss political affairs with their European former masters (Jawad, 1992). These were eventful years in the Mediterranean. Among other things during the period 1973 to 1975 Polisaro 'insurgents' rose against Spanish colonial forces in Western Sahara and thereafter remained engaged in a war with Morocco (from 1975 until 1991) when Spain relinquished its control. It was also in this period, in 1974, that Cyprus's brief existence as a bi-communal state came to a tragic end, first when a coup instigated by Greece's military junta installed a nationalist regime committed to a union with Greece (*enosis*) and next when Turkey responded by invading northern Cyprus, thereby effectively partitioning the island.

In 1982, the Commission launched a development plan for the southern neighbours, who were encouraged to diversify their agricultural produce. With the end of the Cold War, a second period of EC activism *vis-à-vis* the Mediterranean began. Talks of a Renovated Mediterranean Policy (RMP) already started in 1989, with the EC emphasizing the need to 'balance' relations with the east and the south. Adopting the policy in 1990, the EC increased funds for the Mediterranean and promoted multilateral networks and decentralized cooperation, and moved towards a public-private partnership. However, the RMP neither addressed trade, nor did it give new political momentum to Euro-Mediterranean relations (Foundation for European Progressive Studies, 2009).

Such, however, were the limits of regional recognition, and it is fair to say that even the coastal states themselves paid no more than lip service to the Mediterranean idea, when they did at all. Notable exceptions were Malta, which was busy constructing a whole new Mediterranean-grounded foreign policy (Fenech, 1997), and Yugoslavia, which especially after the 1967 Israeli–Arab war was alarmed by the Soviet naval buildup in the Mediterranean (Rubenstein, 1972). During the Cold War years many were those who questioned the currency of Mediterranean regionality (Fenech, 1991), and it is only relatively recently that the larger world started to accept the concept (Pace, 2006). Until 30 or 40 years ago you could hold the contemporary books about the Mediterranean in your embrace – mostly a crop of publications from the 1970s and 1980s dealing with either Cold War rivalry or EC relations (Fenech, 1991). Nowadays that has changed. Even excluding cookery books – which spring at you from the screen whenever you type Mediterranean on Amazon – books on the Mediterranean are appearing with regular frequency. Periodicals emerged earlier, but it was in the late 1980s and the 1990s that they started picking up. The development of Mediterranean political problems in the post-Cold War years motivated journals like *Mediterranean Politics* (1994) and *Mediterranean Quarterly* (1997). A number of universities spawned institutes and centres for Mediterranean Studies (see e.g. Gillespie and Martin, 2009). So what happened?

What happened was a rush of sudden limelight, thrown by gathering turmoil, always a good motivator for academics and writers. For example, the region's newsworthiness as a result of Mussolini's antics in the interwar years had caused a flurry of publications on the Mediterranean, among which Elizabeth Monroe's *The Mediterranean in Politics* (1938) and Piero Silva's sweeping *Il Mediterraneo dall'Unità di Roma all'Impero Italiano* (1939), to name just two (Fenech, 1991). Back to our times, the curious thing about contemporary authors' newfound inspiration to write about the Mediterranean – excluding those who write in the dedicated periodicals on contemporary affairs just mentioned – is that they don't often write about the problems that brought the region to their attention. As if they remember that the Mediterranean had always been there and beckoning, they write about its archaeology, its classical legacy, its anthropology, its history. Scholars like Horden and Purcell, John Julius Norwich, David Abulafia, Cyprian Broodbank, Averil Cameron, Arthur Eckstein, Faruk Tabak, Robert Holland, Roger Crowley, Noel Malcolm and others rediscover the Mediterranean as a place about which so much *is left to be said*. A thread of subconscious, sometimes self-conscious, revisionism informed by our own times runs through some of these narratives, especially with respect to cross-cultural relations and in particular those between Christians and Muslims, whether referring to *Convivencia* in Muslim Iberia, multiculturalism in Norman Sicily or cross-language trading on the high sea.

Still, Mediterranean awareness was not among the very first byproducts of the post-Cold War years, even if the Cold War had served to conceal a lot of unsavoury realities there. On the contrary, the moment the Iron Curtain was lifted it was eastern Europe that claimed the undivided attention of the west, as a race against time began to quickly galvanize the region before the Russians could change their mind. In addition, having some years before admitted Greece, Spain and Portugal, the renamed European Union was simultaneously preoccupied with its own transformation – its 'deepening' – and for a time appeared, if anything, to be closing ranks on the Mediterranean.

But while everyone seemed to be looking the other way, tidings began to arrive that all was not well in the south. In 1992 a thriving and triumphant Europe woke up with a start to the full force of southern underdevelopment when, a stone's throw away, an abortive experiment in democratic transition showed the majority of the Algerian population to have turned Muslim fundamentalist, revealing the true extent of state failure. Sensing a multiple threat to its prosperity and security, coming also on top of a discernible wave of Arab clandestine migration, Europe took notice. European leaders in unison, accustomed to ascribing Europe's post-war stability and success to the integration project, now devised an integrative approach to the southern problem through the launch, in 1995, of the very hopeful Euro-Mediterranean Partnership (EMP). The initiative should have been a model for north–south relations worldwide had it produced lasting results, but in practice it has had to be kick-started more than once since (Gillespie, 2006). What was actually witnessed by the creation of the EMP is a successfully deployed regime of EU governance of the Mediterranean, a space for 'subject peoples' that ensured a certain control over it (Escobar, 2011). In the late Edward Said (1977)'s terminology, this Mediterranean space as a geopolitical space represents a political will to spatial power as implicit in expressions such as north (Europe) and south (the Mediterranean). This pattern of practices – the GMP, RMP, European Neighborhood Policy (ENP), Union for the Mediterranean (UfM) – 'formulates the Mediterranean as a discursive formation, giving rise to an efficient apparatus that systematically relates forms of knowledge [the Mediterranean] and techniques of power [the EU's]' (adapted from Escobar's (1995: 10) work on development in Pace, 2006).

For all its domination of world politics of nearly half a century, the east–west intra-European divide had turned out to be surprisingly easy to resolve by comparison to the north–south chasm that its termination exposed, most notably in the Mediterranean, a chasm that before long returned the region to the centre of the incipient global contest that succeeded the Cold War. For contemporaneously the Mediterranean became the laboratory for experimenting in new post-Cold War international 'order', by the world's biggest military alliance, as NATO expanded its scope exponentially once the purpose for which it had been created disappeared (Fenech, 1997). Unsatiated by its eastward expansion, its consultants warned that it must next go 'out-of-area or out of business' (Schwarz, 1994). What better place to start than the Mediterranean? The secession wars in Yugoslavia created its first occasion for military action outside its own borders. Next, taking a leaf out of Samuel Huntington's (1993) belligerent grand theory of clashing civilizations, NATO counsels identified Islamic fundamentalism as the post-Communist enemy to look out for. They singled out the MENA as a specific 'arc of crisis' to be closely watched (Asmus et al., 1993, Asmus et al., 1996). An outreach strategy called 'NATO's Mediterranean Dialogue' found, in addition to Jordan and Israel in the Middle East, willing partners in all the North African states except Libya, the regimes there being suitably challenged by any Islamic opposition for their own reasons of survival (Musu, 2006).

Mostly carryovers from the movements that drew legitimacy from their role in the independence struggle, these regimes had eminently failed to deliver the dividends of independence. Inertia and stagnation were mistaken for stability, until a Tunisian spark in December 2010 set North Africa alight. Here was another Mediterranean first. Dictatorial postcolonial regimes and stagnant or failed states abounded in the world. But here was a movement that was endemically Mediterranean and epoch-making. The Arab 'Spring' (or uprisings) may have been rashly named as such, but where it did make history was in drawing a stiff line under the so-called postcolonial era. Here at least that era came to an end, as people said 'enough' to the postcolonial posturing with which their ruling classes had prolonged their autocracy. With this historical event, the so-called Arab exceptionalism came to an end in that it is now no longer possible to argue that the people of the 'south' are not ripe for democracy. MENA citizens packed main city squares across the region calling for more governmental accountability and called for their political, social, economic and civil rights. The protests across the Arab world were not ignited by external actors' democracy promotion efforts but instead by a loose coalition of individual dissidents who organized themselves on the basis of interpersonal trust. The protests were targeted at both internal ossified power structures as well as external meddling in the region, highlighting in particular the unfair distribution of their countries' wealth. And in spite of the huge momentum that these uprisings created, the EU and the US, amongst other external actors, show very little redirection by way of their treatment of the Mediterranean other in their external policies (Pace and Cavatorta, 2012).

The Arab uprisings are the latest illustration of the scale of problems, events, movements, phenomena, currents that occur in the Mediterranean, sometimes originating from it and radiating outwards, sometimes mirroring what goes on in the wider world. And we have not even started to touch on some other big questions of our time, such as the implications of the changing global balance between old and new economic powers; or how the international financial crisis of recent years and the wakeup calls it sounded have been felt, typically more in Mediterranean Europe than the rest of the continent; or how the Mediterranean has found itself at the centre – as highway, frontier and graveyard – of the transcontinental migration flow between Africa, Asia and Europe. For sure, these flows show that the Mediterranean continues to be an evolving space – one that is always on the move. However, as Youngs (2015) argues, with over 20 years of the EMP, what we are faced with today when we, amongst others, see Syria and Libya in tatters, at the same time as Egypt experiences huge political turmoil, is deeper conflict, violence, instability, one humanitarian tragedy after another and political reforms still struggling to take root across the Mediterranean (with some exceptions to an extent in the case of Tunisia). The EU's defensive response has been to build more borders and fences and for its members to shift gears and public funds to defence policies.

To propose the Mediterranean as a scale model of world affairs may sound like an exceptionalist claim, but it is hard to think of another region of comparable size that matches the international resonance and intensity of its eventfulness, for better or worse. In case that might sound like Cicero speaking *pro domo sua*, coming from natives of the area, we conclude with a quote from John Gallagher (2015), reviewing a recent book on sixteenth century Mediterranean history:

> It remains a zone of contact and conflict, a region that both defies and defines our ideas of Europe, Asia, Africa and the world in between . . . it continues to resist our indifference: the Mediterranean remains, as it was for the Romans, 'our sea'.

Bibliography

Abulafia, D. (ed.) (2003). *The Mediterranean in History*. Thames & Hudson.

Abulafia, D. (2011). *The Great Sea: A Human History of the Mediterranean*. Allen Lane.

Appadurai, A. (1996). *Modernity at Large: Cultural Dimensions of Globalization*. University of Minnesota Press.

Asmus, R. D., Kugler, R. L. and Larrabee, F. S. (1993). Building a New NATO, *Foreign Affairs*, 72, 4, 28–40.

Asmus, R. D., Larrabee, F. S. and Lesser, I. O. (1996). Mediterranean Security: New Challenges, New Tasks, *NATO Review*, 44, 3, 25–31.

Badalassi, N. (2012). Sea and Détente in Helsinki: The Mediterranean Stake of the CSCE, 1972–1975, in Calandri, E., Varsori, A. and Caviglia, D. (eds), *Détente in Cold War Europe: Politics and Diplomacy in the Mediterranean and the Middle East*. Tauris, pp. 61–74.

Broodbank C. (2013). *The Making of the Middle Sea: A History of the Mediterranean from the Beginning to the Emergence of the Classical World.* Oxford University Press.

Braudel, F. (1949). *The Mediterranean and the Mediterranean World in the Age of Philip II*, 2 vols. Originally appeared in 1949; revised several times; reprint edition 1995. University of California Press.

Cameron, A. (1993). *The Mediterranean World in Late Antiquity, AD 395–600.* Routledge.

Carlton, D. (1983). Great Power Spheres of Influence in the Balkans, 1944 and After, in Carlton, D. and Schaerf, C. (eds), *South-Eastern Europe after Tito: A Powder Keg for the 1980s.* Macmillan.

Crowley, R. (2006). *1453: The Holy War for Constantinople and the Clash of Islam and the West.* Hachette Books.

Crowley, R. (2009). *Empires of the Sea: The Siege of Malta, the Battle of Lepanto, and the Contest for the Center of the World.* Random House Trade Paperbacks.

Crowley, R. (2013). *City of Fortune: How Venice Ruled the Seas.* Random House Trade Paperbacks.

Crowley, R. (2015). *Conquerors: How Portugal Seized the Indian Ocean and Forged the First Global Empire.* Faber and Faber.

Eckstein, A. M. (2006). *Mediterranean Anarchy, Interstate War and the Rise of Rome.* University of California Press.

Escobar, A. (1995 and 2011). *Encountering Development: The Making and Unmaking of the Third World.* Princeton University Press.

Fenech, D. (1991). Mediterranean Regionality, in Fiorini, S. and Mallia-Milanes, V. (eds), *Malta: A Case Study in International Cross Currents.* Malta University Publications, pp. 267–77.

Fenech, D. (1993). East–West to North–South in the Mediterranean, *Geojournal*, 31, 2, 129–40.

Fenech, D. (1997). The Relevance of European Security Structures for the Mediterranean (and Vice-Versa), in Gillespie, R. (ed.), *The Euro-Mediterranean Partnership: Political and Economic Perspectives.* Frank Cass, pp. 149–76.

Fenech, D. (1997). Malta's External Security, *Geojournal*, 41, 2, 153–63.

Fenech, D. (2000). The Mediterranean Region during the Cold War and After, in Hattendorf, J. B. (ed.) *Naval Policy and Strategy in the Mediterranean: Past, Present, and Future.* Frank Cass, pp. 226–40.

Foundation for European Progressive Studies (2009). The Euro-Mediterranean Dialogue: Prospects for an Area of Prosperity and Security. Available online at: www.feps-europe.eu/assets/b87820bf-4b3f-4fc4-a5c8-3787c88fec55/feps_ie_euromed.pdf

Gallagher, J. (2015). Agents of Empire by Noel Malcolm: A Dazzling History of the 16th-Century Mediterranean, *The Guardian*, 10 June.

Gillespie, R. (ed.) (1997). *The Euro-Mediterranean Partnership: Political and Economic Perspectives.* Frank Cass Publishers.

Gillespie, R. (2006). Onward but not Upward: The Barcelona Conference of 2005, *Mediterranean Politics*, 11, 2, 271–8.

Gillespie, R. and Martin, I. (eds) (2009). *Researching the Mediterranean* (second edition). CIDOB.

Gold, P. (2000). *Europe or Africa? A Contemporary Study of the Spanish North African Enclaves of Ceuta and Melilla.* Liverpool University Press.

Harris, W. V. (ed.) (2005). *Rethinking the Mediterranean.* Oxford University Press.

Holland, R. (2013). *Blue Water Empire: The British in the Mediterranean since 1800.* Penguin Books.

Herzfeld, M. (2005). Practical Mediterraneanism: Excuses for Everything, from Epistemology to Eating, in Harris, W. V. (ed.), *Rethinking the Mediterranean.* Oxford University Press, pp. 45–63.

Holsti, K. J. (1982). Bargaining Theory and Diplomatic Reality, the CSCE Negotiations, *Review of International Studies*, 8, 159–70.

Horden, P. and Purcell, N. (2000). *The Corrupting Sea: A Study of Mediterranean History.* Wiley-Blackwell.

Horden, P. and Purcell, N. (2006). The Mediterranean and the New Thalassology, *The American Historical Review*, 111, 3, 722–40.

Huntington, S. (1993). The Clash of Civilizations?, *Foreign Affairs*, 72, 3, 22–49.

Huntington, S. (1996). *The Clash of Civilizations and the Remaking of World Order.* Simon & Schuster.

Jawad, H. (1992). *Euro-Arab Relations: A Study in Collective Diplomacy.* Garnet Publishing.

Khader, B. (2013). The European Union and the Arab World: From the Rome Treaty to the Arab Spring. IEMed/EuroMeSCo. Working Paper, No. 17, pp. 1–46.

Malcolm, N. (2015). *Agents of Empire: Knights, Corsairs, Jesuits and Spies in the Sixteenth-Century Mediterranean World.* Oxford University Press.

Martín, I. and Gillespie, R. (eds) (2009). *Researching the Mediterranean*, (second edition). CIDOB Barcelona.

Monroe, E. (1938). *The Mediterranean in Politics.* Oxford University Press.

Musu, C. (2006). NATO's Mediterranean Dialogue: More than Just an Empty Shell?, *Mediterranean Politics*, 11, 3, 419–24.

Norwich, J. J. (2007). *The Middle Sea: A History of the Mediterranean*. Vintage.

Pace, M. (2006). *The Politics of Regional Identity: Meddling with the Mediterranean*. Routledge. New International Relations series.

Pace, M. and Cavatorta, F. (2012). The Arab Uprisings in Theoretical Perspective: An Introduction, *Mediterranean Politics*, 17, 2, 125–38.

Pirenne, H. (1937). *Mohammed and Charlemagne*. George Allen & Unwin.

Resis, A. (1978). The Churchill Stalin Secret 'Percentages' Agreement on the Balkans, Moscow, October 1944, *The American Historical Review*, 83, 2, 368–87.

Rosenthal, G. G. and Duchêne, F. (1982). *The Mediterranean Basin: Its Political Economy and Changing International Relations*. Butterworth-Heinemann.

Rubenstein, A. Z. (1972). The Evolution of Yugoslavia's Mediterranean Policy, *International Journal*, 27, 4, 528–45.

Said, E. W. (1977). *Orientalism*. Penguin.

Said, E. W. (2001). The Clash of Ignorance, *The Nation*, 273, 12, 11–13.

Schwarz, B. C. (1994). NATO at the Crossroads: Reexamining America's Role in Europe, RAND January 1994, available online at https://www.rand.org/content/dam/rand/pubs/issue_papers/2006/IP133.pdf

Segev, T. (2000). *One Palestine, Complete: Jews and Arabs under the British Mandate*. Translated by Haim Watzman. Abacus.

Silva, P. (1939). *Il Mediterraneo dall'unità di Roma all'Impero Italiano*. Istituto per gli Studi di Politicia Internazionale.

Tabak, F. (2008). *The Waning of the Mediterranean, 1550–1870*. Johns Hopkins University Press.

Wallerstein, I. (1979). *The Capitalist World Economy*. Cambridge University Press.

Youngs, R. (2015). 20 Years of the Euro-Mediterranean Partnership. Virtual Special Issue of *Mediterranean Politics*. 18 May. Available online at: http://carnegieeurope.eu/publications/?fa=60337

3

HISTORICAL/GEOPOLITICAL TURNING POINTS IN THE MODERN MEDITERRANEAN

Cold War, post-Cold War and Arab Spring[1]

Francesco Cavatorta

The modern Mediterranean has always been considered an important region from the broad perspective of international relations. It has a prominent geo-strategic position, it contains vast hydrocarbon resources and it is a hotbed of domestic and international political violence. By the mid-1990s these traits convinced many scholars that the Mediterranean was a 'fracture line' where the most problematic issues plaguing international politics seem to concentrate and divide the west from the rest with a modern, democratic, economically developed and peaceful northern bank facing a pre-modern, authoritarian, underdeveloped and war prone southern one. This chapter partly rejects the notion that the Mediterranean represents such a clear fracture line. In fact, the historical vantage point allows us to look at the Mediterranean as an area where political, economic and cultural dynamics go beyond pre-defined boundaries based on essentialised notions such as north–south, development/underdevelopment, democracy/authoritarianism or Islam/Christianity. This is relevant to underscore in contemporary international politics because there is a tendency in the region to play a political 'blame game' whereby all the difficult issues come either from imperialist Europe or, conversely, from the 'barbarians at the gates' in North Africa and the Middle East. Thus, while there are clear differences between the southern bank and the northern one in the Mediterranean, there are also shared dynamics. It follows that the modern Mediterranean cannot be understood in its complexity through simplistic lenses.

This chapter focuses on the ways in which countries in the region interact with the international system and how major historical turning points impacted the Mediterranean. In turn, it should also be underscored that events occurring in the region have also had a considerable influence on global politics. The chapter focuses specifically on the post-colonial period of the countries on the southern bank of the Mediterranean, up to the Arab uprisings of 2011. There is little doubt that the legacy of colonial rule as well as the influence of post-World War II international politics contributed to shape the history of the region and the relations between its constituent parts. Post-colonial and Cold War politics prevented the realisation of pan-Arab dynamics, with the region becoming a crucial locus in the global struggle between the Soviet Union and the United States. Cold War politics inserted itself in an already unstable post-colonial environment and contributed to increase the divisions among Arab states, leading them to take divergent paths of economic, social and political development. For a brief interlude after the end of the Cold War, it seemed that a genuine Mediterranean dimension could be generated whereby the wealthier countries on the northern bank could become the locomotive for the creation of a shared area of democracy and prosperity. However, the reality played out differently. The war on terror and the 2008 economic crisis unleashed powerful destabilising dynamics across the Mediterranean with popular movements challenging regimes (Arab world) and governments (southern Europe) to make fundamental changes in the way they governed. Finally, the Arab Spring further destabilised the region with security becoming even more of an obsession for all countries in the region and further distancing European powers from the pursuit of normative objectives.

The post-colonial Mediterranean: the influence of the Cold War

During the Cold War, the Middle East and North Africa (MENA) was a central arena for the confrontation between the United States and the Soviet Union and countries in the region were effectively forced to side with one or other superpower. After World War II, countries in southern Europe became pillars of the US-led western camp with Turkey and Greece freezing their disputes in the context of the NATO alliance. Spain and Portugal also chose the western camp, as did France and Italy, although the French operated outside of NATO structures. On the southern bank, Cold War dynamics influenced and overlapped with post-colonial dynamics, rendering politics in the region complex to navigate. From an 'ideological' perspective, one would have expected the newly independent countries to become close allies with the Soviet Union. The rhetoric of anti-imperialism at the time belonged to the Soviet camp and the former colonial powers in the region all belonged to the western camp. This should have favoured Soviet penetration of the southern bank of the Mediterranean, therefore allowing the USSR to share control of the region with the United States. In reality, the complexity of national post-colonial politics generated profound divisions among the countries of the south. Thus, broadly speaking, post-colonial conservative monarchies such as Morocco fell within the sphere of influence of the United States, while the radical republics of Egypt, Libya and Algeria gravitated towards the Soviet Union, although all maintained a certain distance from Moscow.

This notion of distance is quite significant because it suggested that genuinely anti-imperialist attitudes applied to both the US-led camp and the Soviet one. These newly independent countries were not about to cede their recently acquired sovereignty to another foreign entity and opted for a businesslike relationship. Post-independence dynamics in Morocco favoured the monarchy over nationalist parties and this meant that pro-French attitudes sat at the top of the political system, making the country a vital ally for the western camp in the Mediterranean. The newly independent countries of Tunisia and Mauritania followed the same pattern as Morocco despite their republican institutions.

The problematic nature of post-colonial politics had both an internal and external dimension with feedback loops in place whereby domestic and international developments were closely intertwined and influenced each other. For instance the traumatic war of independence between Algeria and France meant that the Algerian post-colonial leadership preferred to distance itself rhetorically and ideologically from its former French masters. Thus, it embraced a socialist model of economic development and became a beacon of third-world anti-imperialism. Despite a degree of ideological proximity and cordial relations Algeria's third worldism (Malley, 1996) was not subservient to Soviet interests. Algeria therefore, with the Soviet Union, pursued a reasonably aggressive and autonomous foreign policy in the neighbourhood, particularly when it perceived that 'imperialist' rivals like Morocco were attempting to vie for regional supremacy. It was therefore no great surprise that Morocco and Algeria fought a war over territory soon after Algerian independence. At the other end of the spectrum, Morocco, Tunisia and Mauritania had a much less traumatic experience of separation from France and the respective post-colonial leadership chose to accommodate its colonial legacy and gravitate towards France. This had inevitable international repercussions because it also meant that the foreign policy choices they made largely coincided with the ones the west made. This could be seen, for instance, in the far more moderate stance that both Morocco and Tunisia took with respect to the issue of Israel. Both post-colonial dynamics and Cold War ones structured the foreign policy choices of Mediterranean countries. While on the northern bank this meant the freezing of conflicts and disputes because the parties belonged to the same camp, on the southern bank regional disputes broke out in all-out wars at times. In addition, regional rivalries deepened throughout the Cold War period because they found both domestic and international justifications with the Morocco–Algeria dispute over Western Sahara and the Egypt–Libya armed conflict of 1977 being the most prominent examples.

Thus, military and political conflicts between Arab states in addition to larger geo-strategic rivalries between the Soviet and American blocs rendered the Mediterranean a very 'hot' area during the Cold War. It should, however, be noted that relations between the two superpowers and their allies in the Mediterranean were not unidirectional or unchangeable. For once, many of the Arab countries sought to keep their powerful patrons at arm's length and, at times, attempted to play one superpower off against the other, in order to maximise benefits. There was the realisation on the part of Arab leaders that they could try to secure their domestic power by 'playing' both sides while projecting internally an image of autonomy from international constraints through, for instance, the non-aligned movement. For example, Egypt left the Soviet sphere in the 1970s to become a linchpin of the US strategy in the region. This occurred at the height of the Cold War when shifting from one bloc to another was particularly difficult. In the same vein, superpowers sought to keep Mediterranean allies onside through the provision of material resources and interfered in domestic politics when it seemed that local dynamics might undermine a country's place in one's camp. It is for this reason that, for instance, military coups were tolerated – when not actually encouraged – in countries like Greece and Turkey when it seemed that local political actors were pushing for distancing their respective countries from the NATO alliance. These shared dynamics in countries of both banks therefore indicate that the idea of clear-cut fracture line should be problematised.

Scholars like Karsh (1997) insisted that the end of the Cold War did not actually alter regional dynamics. Karsh's argument is largely misguided, but he is correct about the case of Israel. For Israeli policy-makers the end of the Cold War did not change much in strategic terms because the enmity and hostility of the vast majority of Arab states did not subside with the fall of the Soviet Union. In short, the politics of the Cold War had a significant influence on the region and the end of the rivalry between the US and the Soviet Union had a profound effect on both regional relations and on the internal politics of individual countries. The following section will deal with the most significant post-Cold War consequences.

The Mediterranean in a unipolar world

The most dramatic change was the emergence of the United States as the sole superpower, leading some to hail this new era of 'unipolarity' because the hegemonic superpower was a benign one (Krauthammer, 1990). In this privileged position, the US, and its western allies, wished to remake the world according to their strategic interests – access to oil resources and expansion of markets first among them – and to promote their constitutive values of liberalism, democracy and economic openness. By the time the Cold War ended, the northern bank of the

Mediterranean had been almost fully integrated into the economic, political and military system that the United States had led during the struggle against the Soviet Union. For its part, the southern bank had undergone a much more difficult Cold War period and by the early 1990s was mired in economic and political difficulties and facing considerable challenges. This is where the idea of a fracture line is more convincing, but it was presented as a natural 'cultural' outcome rather than the product, for instance, of decades-long western support for authoritarianism and specific political choices such as the refusal of the European Union to let Morocco accede while admitting Spain, Portugal and Greece. In this respect the Mediterranean as a fracture line dividing the basin between economically successful, democratic and liberal countries and underdeveloped, poorer and authoritarian ones was ultimately the product of a series of political choices. In any case, the fracture line began to be perceived as a serious problem to be addressed in the aftermath of the Cold War, as authoritarianism, economic underdevelopment, localised conflicts and the rise of Islamism became a menace to regional stability. As a result of both unipolarity and the emergence of new threats to the stability of the new world order, the west began to invest considerable resources to promote the power of universal ideas and values, namely democracy, human rights and the market economy. This had significant repercussions because there was suddenly the sentiment that realist concerns could be better defended through ethical policies. Concern for human rights abuses, international law and democratic accountability on the part of the US, France and the UK were not priorities during the Cold War and they insulated their allies from criticism. In order to avoid any risk of 'losing' precious allies in the war against communism, ethical concerns about supporting authoritarian regimes were usually set aside and realpolitik imperatives prevailed. The end of the Cold War offered the opportunity to attenuate realist imperatives and reintroduce an ethical dimension in foreign policy. The promotion of democracy became a central tenet of this new policy. At the same time, countries that had been under Soviet influence, like Algeria, felt both internal and external pressures to fall in line with the dominant discourse on democracy and market economics. On foreign policy matters, this meant that they had to abandon their anti-imperialist positions. Thus, the promotion of neo-liberal economic reforms and democratic values became the mainstay of post-Cold War international politics for the United States and its European partners. Indeed, there was a conflation between US strategic interests – unquestioned leadership in global affairs and international peace (Jervis, 2002) – and its ethical position – liberal democracy as a universal good that all should enjoy. The significance of these geo-strategic changes in the Mediterranean crystallised during the Gulf crisis of 1990–91 following Iraq's invasion of Kuwait when the United States, without any challenge from the Soviet Union, decided to put together an international coalition under UN mandate to oust Iraqi troops from Kuwait. The US president George H. Bush argued that in the new post-Cold War world order international legality should prevail and he set about making an example of Iraq. All Mediterranean countries rallied around the United States' decision. Among the countries siding with the US, there were both its traditional Arab allies – with the exception of Jordan and Yemen – and a number of rivals such as Syria and, indirectly, Iran. This testifies to the considerable changes that the end of the rivalry between superpowers brought about in the Mediterranean.

In addition to changes in foreign policy, Arab countries began to undertake proto-democratic reforms to project an image of renewal which the US and European countries could be satisfied with. Thus, in Egypt and Jordan for example, a number of liberalising political and economic reforms were introduced. Tunisia and Morocco also witnessed liberalising initiatives in the late 1980s and 1990s respectively as did Algeria and, to a lesser extent, some of the Gulf countries, in an effort to inject renewed legitimacy into their respective political systems and ailing economies. Finally, it is worth noting that the post-Cold War environment facilitated the

Arab–Israeli peace process. While it might be argued that the seeds for peace had been sown before the collapse of the Soviet Union, it is in the aftermath of the 1991 Gulf war and through US pressure on both allies and rivals in the region that Israel, Jordan, the Palestinians and Syria sat down to work out a comprehensive peace deal. In conclusion, the 1991 Gulf war, the pro-democracy initiatives that the west promoted and the pressure on both Arabs and Israelis to come up with a peace deal demonstrated that the world had changed. Following the US line was a requirement for traditional allies as well as former rivals.

While the US was the superpower, its European partners contributed to solidifying the US's grip on global affairs. In the Mediterranean in particular, the United States, the European Union and individual member states pursued very similar policies centred on democracy promotion, trade liberalisation and strategic primacy. After the Cold War, the process of European integration accelerated and closer coordination in external relations led the European Union to take a significant role in supporting US unipolarity. Central to this process of increased integration was the idea that the EU would become an ethical actor in international politics, attempting to promote universal norms and human rights. The EU would engage all actors on the global scene without resorting to threats, but rather through positive inducements and the power of example, pointing specifically to the way in which economic integration was the instrument for achieving both domestic development and international peace. It is through this self-perception of what it is, and what it does on the international stage, that the EU is referred to as 'normative power Europe' (Manners, 2002). Given the ideals that the pursuit of external relations was built upon, the Mediterranean became a privileged area for the EU's external activism. It was during the early 1990s that the reading of the Mediterranean basin as a fracture line appeared, leading the EU and its constituent parts to believe that such a fracture could be 'healed' through the policies of democracy promotion and trade liberalisation, as well as the military partnerships the United States was advocating and implementing on a greater global scale. This EU policy of 'constructive engagement' did not differ much from how the United States, under George H. Bush and, at least initially, Bill Clinton, sought to reshape international relations. In fact there seemed to be both a coincidence of interests and ideals between the US and the European Union on how to integrate the southern bank of the Mediterranean into the global economy and international security structures. The clearest example of this post-Cold War strategy on the part of the European Union was the effort made to engage Turkey and 'absorb' it in the European space albeit without guaranteeing full accession.

The end of unipolarity

The moment of unipolarity did not last for very long and the Mediterranean has since been a source of instability, leading to considerable security problems across both banks of the sea and further afield. By the mid-1990s, it had become clear that the United States was unable to consolidate its role as the sole benign superpower. While no other country was and would be capable of challenging the US militarily, the assumption that all actors in the global system would accept a new world order with the US at its helm was mistaken. Although military challengers were unlikely to emerge for a long time, two broad reasons explain how unipolarity was unlikely to go unchallenged politically. Firstly, the conflation of US material interests and ethical values proved problematic. While many countries were happy to accept US economic, military, political and cultural dominance because they were able to also reconcile material and ethical interests within US hegemony, others were much more sceptical and pointed to significant inconsistencies in US behaviour. This was particularly true in the Mediterranean where the tension between the norms and interests the US and its European partners pursued was at its strongest, particularly after it became clear that the promotion of democracy on the southern bank of the Mediterranean might have adverse consequences for the pursuit of material interests. Secondly, a number of regional and international actors became more assertive over time on the international stage. Following the realist tenet that imbalances in the international system would be corrected with the rise of emerging powers, new challengers did indeed defy US hegemony, and the Mediterranean has become once more an area of fierce competition.

Democracy promotion in the Mediterranean

The policies of democracy and human rights promotion together with trade liberalisation and market reforms encapsulate both the hopes and contradictions of the moment of unipolarity. The logic behind these policies was that democracies solve their disputes peacefully, contribute to international stability, cooperate more closely on economic matters and, ultimately, produce better living conditions for citizens. The same logic applied to the adoption of genuine market reforms and progressive integration into the global trade system. The changes promoted on the southern bank would have therefore positive repercussions for all actors involved. The US and the European Union would achieve both material and ethical objectives – international stability, the promotion of the 'good life' and economic growth. The Arab countries would achieve better governance, economic success and responsive state institutions. Finally, the wider regional environment would become more peaceful with solutions found to long-standing conflicts, including the Arab–Israeli one. Unfortunately, very little of this occurred and the unipolar moment collapsed under the weight of its contradictions. First and foremost, the promotion of democracy did not deliver the stability the US and the EU sought. In fact, it quickly became clear that the outcome of genuinely democratic elections would be 'counterproductive' if those who were elected did not wish to conform to external requirements, values and interests. Contributing to opening up political systems in Arab countries placed the United States and the European Union in a very awkward position because political *ouvertures* coincided with the success of parties and movements holding anti-western policy positions. These views were expressed through the instruments and mechanics of democracy and open political debate, making them very difficult to dismiss. From the early 1990s the rise of Islamism, in all of its guises, became a considerable preoccupation for the United States, the European Union, and local governments, as the 'green peril' (Miller, 1993) came to be identified as the most significant challenge to western civilisation (Huntington, 1993). While it should be noted that Islamism is a very broad and divided family, the electoral weight of Islamist parties, whether actual or potential, represented a powerful obstacle to the continuation of pro-democracy policies. Mistrust of Islamism was the product of the belief that Islamists in power would pursue an aggressive anti-western foreign policy in a region where there are vast oil and gas resources, where Israel, the most important US ally in the region, stands alone, and where the proliferation of weapons is a genuine concern (Kepel, 2004). In addition, Islamism represented a potent threat to Arab regimes, which had, for the most part and to different degrees, thrown in their lot with the remaining superpower.

Thus, the idea that pro-democracy and pro-human rights policies could coincide with the defence and promotion of material interests began to lose its momentum rapidly. The outcome of free and fair Algerian elections in 1991, the subsequent military coup to prevent the Islamists from gaining power and the ensuing civil war became a powerful 'lesson' on the divergence that might exist between ethical and self-interested positions for the western community of states (Cavatorta, 2009). The events in Algeria produced two mutually reinforcing outcomes. Arab rulers saw the opportunity to roll back on liberal reforms or, more precisely, to implement façade reforms that would ultimately strengthen their grip on power (Heydemann, 2007). At the same time, the US drew back from genuine democracy promotion across the Arab world, reassuring allies that processes of liberalisation and reform would only continue at a pace dictated by Arab rulers. For its part the European Union launched over time a number of pan-Mediterranean initiatives including the Euro-Mediterranean Partnership and the Neighbourhood Policy, with the objective of creating a shared area of democracy and prosperity. Repairing the 'fracture' between the two banks of the Mediterranean through increased trade, the promotion of good governance and greater cultural exchanges was, and still is, a laudable objective, but policy implementation proved complicated and the initiatives ultimately failed under the weight of their internal contradictions. According to some critics (Cavatorta et al., 2008) these initiatives were effectively designed to place democracy and democratisation on the back burner, privileging instead economic links even if they meant strengthening authoritarian rulers in place. Despite the implementation of three different policy frameworks, the adoption of Association Agreements with a number of Arab states and a significant increase in bilateral relations on economic, security and political matters, the overarching objective of the EU, namely the promotion of democracy as the path to international peace and stability, failed.

In addition to the failure of democracy promotion and the decision to favour short-term authoritarian stability, the end of the unipolar moment had negative consequences for the Arab–Israeli peace process. Thus, the gamble the United States took under Bush senior in seeking to resolve the issue of Palestine did not pay off. The peace process launched in Madrid following the first Gulf war against Iraq proved to be a reasonable success in the medium run, and Bill Clinton, who became president in 1992, was able to build on it to get the Israelis and the Palestinians to sign a comprehensive peace deal, the Oslo Accords, in 1993. The early 1990s were years of great hope for peace across the region. But, when the peace process encountered its first obstacles, it seemed to many in the Arab world that the US was not an honest broker. As the situation progressively worsened, the disappointment of ordinary Arabs with US policies in Palestine grew, with accusations of hypocrisy being laid at the US door. The unravelling of the peace process further undermined the image of the United States for two specific reasons. It became apparent that, in its effort to maintain the peace process, the US was prepared to pressure only the weaker side, namely the Palestinians, directly, as well as through its special relationships with Jordan and Egypt. Also, US talk about a new world order underpinned by international legality and justice was exposed as cynicism. Through the Euro-Mediterranean Partnership, the European Union had included Israel in its framework for the creation of a shared peaceful area of prosperity and democracy, gambling that through progressive economic integration and enhanced dialogue both Israelis and Arabs would see the benefits of cooperation. In turn this would have had positive repercussions on the peace process. This did not occur and the 'peace process' stalled. Overall, the EU, instead of providing an alternative to the hegemony of the US in the region, simply strengthened it (Youngs, 2004).

The impact of September 11

The fallout for the Mediterranean of the terrorist attacks against the United States in 2001 accelerated and consolidated the dynamics in place since the early 1990s. In fact the attacks simply entrenched US assumptions and policies in the region and hardened the European ones. Despite a change in rhetoric, the war on terror did not modify existing trends, even if, for a brief moment, George W. Bush seemed to give thought to overhauling US policy framework towards the Arab world and the Middle East more generally (Durac and Cavatorta, 2009). The reality is that the requirements of the war on terror led the US to pursue the same policies adopted in the past. Fighting the war on terror required the support of authoritarian regimes in the region. In the name of the war on terror the United States cooperated even more closely with the security services of countries that had used such services extensively to repress domestic dissent and European countries did the same. Rather than healing the supposed regional fracture, the war on terror instead exposed the connivance between ruling elites on both sides of the Mediterranean (Pace, 2009). On the one side, local autocrats began a new wave of repression that affected all sorts of dissenters, be they peaceful or violent, secular or Islamist. On the other, European and US leaders sold out the very principles of democracy and respect for human rights by contracting out abuses and sanctioning anti-democratic policies. Ultimately, the supposed fracture line did not impede the close relations between western and Arab leaders. Furthermore, while conducting the war on terror with the help of autocratic leaders, the US was finalising plans for the invasion of Iraq, which began in March 2003. The war has left a legacy of instability affecting regional politics ever since, radicalising sectors of the population on both banks of the Mediterranean and undermining the prospects of peaceful change of power. In short, the conflict between realist imperatives and the 'normative' commitment to democracy saw the 'securitisers' win out. The accusation of hypocrisy reverberated across the region once again, leaving the US in the same dilemma as before, except that it was now embroiled in an unwinnable war in Iraq, which provided many young Muslim radicals the opportunity to fight for a new pan-Arab cause, with considerable negative consequences on regional peace and domestic stability on both banks of the Mediterranean. While powerful European states such as France and Germany stayed out of the war in Iraq, European powers as whole did not much deviate from the requirements of the war on terror, particularly when terrorist attacks occurred in Spain and the UK.

In all of this, there is also another dimension worth discussing because it would reveal its importance during the Arab uprisings of 2010–11. During the 1990s and the 2000s, the United States and the European Union promoted policies of economic liberalisation that found an audience in Mediterranean countries on both banks, seeking a 'map' to revitalise their ailing economies. Neo-liberal policies were therefore adopted throughout the region, including southern Europe. The post-Cold War era had provided the opportunity for reshaping local economies in order to integrate them into the neo-liberal economic system. While countries such as Morocco and Tunisia had already gone through a number of market-oriented economic reforms before the collapse of the Soviet Union, dramatic economic change followed the launch of the 'Washington Consensus' and a greater push for European economic integration. Many countries in the region, including Turkey and Israel, adopted the neo-liberal economic model. The US, through its leadership in international financial institutions and through its extensive contacts with ruling regimes in the Middle East and North Africa, pushed for a series of economic reforms based on an end to price subsidies, privatisation, strict fiscal policies, and free trade, as the agreements with Morocco and Jordan indicate (White, 2005). Reforming stagnant economies was certainly necessary and these reforms led indeed to economic growth over time and contributed to the insertion of the Mediterranean in global trade patterns, but failed to ensure wealth redistribution. In fact labour markets suffered with the rise in unemployment, poorer working conditions, increasing informal employment and poor job prospects for graduates. In addition reforms were hijacked by authoritarian ruling elites and increased income distribution gaps and corrupt practices of resource allocation (Dillman, 2001). Countries in southern Europe experienced a similar trend with the push towards greater market integration within the EU. Although authoritarian political structures made the situation more explosive in Arab countries, rising unemployment, poor prospects for young people and welfare restrictions characterised the politics of southern Europe throughout the late 1990s and the 2000s. Ultimately, the politics of protests on both banks of the Mediterranean exploded in 2010 following the financial crisis of 2008.

The uprisings in the Mediterranean

A combination of socioeconomic and political factors therefore explains the reasons behind the protests, which took place, in different forms and to different degrees, across the Mediterranean, including Israel, Spain, Greece and Turkey. This is relevant because it undermines the assumption of a permanent north–south fracture when in fact all countries of the region were affected. As mentioned earlier, from the 1990s onwards, the adoption of neo-liberal economic reforms across the region began the process of erosion of social contracts, insofar as the state withdrew from a number of activities, most specifically welfare provisions. On the southern bank, measures to liberalise foreign trade, the lifting of import restrictions, changing tariff protection and removing barriers against exports were all enforced while state intervention in the economy was scaled back. Government subsidies were reduced, as was employment in the state sector (Sika, 2012). As a result, the reforms prompted widespread unease and led to the Arab Spring. At the same time, an economic downward spiral struck the countries of southern Europe after the 2008 financial crisis. While the signs of crisis were present before this date (the launch of the euro being particularly problematic), the financial crisis demonstrated that the power of the unrestricted market to deliver economic benefits for all was a sham. Increasing unemployment, reduction of safety nets, and the seeming inability to influence the political process despite the existence of democratic institutions added to the frustration of considerable sectors of the population. While protests in Europe and Israel were not uprisings, they suggest that economic frustration was a shared sentiment in the Mediterranean.

However, neo-liberal reforms had a much greater effect on less developed economies because authoritarian political structures remained largely unchanged. This meant that there were few venues for citizens to express their grievances. While their counterparts in Europe, Israel and Turkey could gather, protest and eventually vote as well as channel their dissent through meaningful civil society activism, dissatisfied citizens in the Arab world had no real option but to defy the authoritarian regime. Corruption at the highest and lowest levels of the bureaucracy and in the private sector with the predominance of *wasta* (nepotist patronage) weighed on ordinary citizens. Thus, by the 2000s a pernicious combination of economic de-development and arbitrary political rule alienated many from the regimes in power. The uprisings were a testimony to the failed economic policies of recent decades and it was no coincidence that it was in Tunisia, the model of neo-liberal economic governance according to international financial institutions, that the uprisings began. Demographic patterns contributed to the explosion of protests as younger people were much more affected by unemployment and lack of prospects (Achcar, 2013).

The Arab uprisings have had tremendous repercussion on the Mediterranean and while it is too early to offer a final verdict, it can be safely argued that in the short term they have generated instability, violence and renewed authoritarianism (the exception being Tunisia). From an international perspective, the uprisings for a time re-focused attention away from the war on terror and towards the possibility of rebuilding the Mediterranean order on inclusive and democratic political bases. The US seemed to realise that it had backed the wrong horse for too long, as the picture of widespread political protest drawing on basic human rights, dignity and governmental accountability emerged from the streets of Arab capitals. Former friendly dictators were ditched and calls for the establishment of democracy began. In addition, and crucially, Obama opted to intervene militarily, through NATO, to support the anti-Gaddafi rebellion in Libya. The European Union also re-evaluated its pan-Mediterranean initiatives, admitting that in the past it did not pay sufficient attention to the democratic will of the people (Teti, 2012). Promoting democracy through cooperation with the institutions of authoritarian governments had not worked, and the EU and its members, despite some initial dithering, eventually supported the uprisings, with France and the UK also contributing militarily to the fall of the Gaddafi regime.

For a brief moment it appeared that the Mediterranean could finally be on its way to the construction of what the EU hoped to be an area of peace, economic prosperity and democratic accountability. This, however, did not occur and old 'habits' returned to dominate the politics of the region. The initial enthusiasm for the democratic wave faded rapidly as Islamist electoral victories in Tunisia in 2011 and Egypt in 2012 brought back fears of anti-western policies. The inability and unwillingness of domestic actors to settle their differences through consensual politics brought chaos in Libya. The ability of the Algerian, Mauritanian and Moroccan elites to consolidate their grip on power despite mass protests and therefore to remain stable made international actors weary of promoting changes that might backfire. The regional chaos further afield with the civil wars in Yemen and Syria empowered violent Islamist groups, heightening the quest for security and stability. Finally, the collapse of Iraqi authority on its territory and the rise of the so called Islamic State decisively shifted the momentum from support for change to the quest for stability at almost any price. At the same time, the rise of populism in southern Europe reinforced this quest for stability with governments unwilling to support policies that might make them look weak and unprepared in the face of mounting regional challenges.

New global powers and the Middle East

It is in this context that new global powers have made their presence felt in the Mediterranean, although it should be underscored that their influence is more limited. China and Russia were not interested or strong enough for quite some time to challenge the US and the EU in the Mediterranean, but more recently they have come to play a somewhat greater role, particularly when it comes to the expansion of their commercial links, with Russia also interested in developing greater security cooperation and attempting to divide the European Union. While both acquiesced in the attack on Libya in 2011, Russia and China drew the line when it came to Syria, with their position having significant consequences for the wider Mediterranean.

Aside from having a historical involvement in the region, Russia appears to be more determined to become involved in the regional politics and reassert its status as a global power. Building on its renewed economic development, Russia has sought to provide some sort of counterbalance to the US and the EU, while offering its considerable resources in the fight against Islamism, which Russia considers a domestic threat (Malashenko, 2013). This is evident in the Russian intervention in Syria where international and domestic concerns are both central in Russia's thinking about the role of the Mediterranean. The region represented a strategic and therefore important locus of confrontation during the Cold War, but in its aftermath such significance has, if anything, become stronger. Major wars have taken place in the Mediterranean and it is the only region where US military expansion has known few bounds since the early 1990s. In many ways the southern bank of the Mediterranean has become a '*chasse gardée*' of western powers with Russia being rather firmly shut out of major decisions concerning the region. Russia has, however, been in a position to object to its marginalisation and it has acquired the strength – both diplomatic and military – to challenge the US and its allies, in part because of the 2003 US blunder in Iraq and western wavering about the Arab uprisings, and it has taken a stand over Syria. Russian interventionism is not only the product of global concerns about counterbalancing the United States, but is also driven by significant worries about the rise of violent Islamism. It is on this issue that the international and the domestic dimensions are linked according to the Russians. While Russia is interested in preventing western dominance of the global system, this becomes a concern only when the effects of misguided western policies have a deleterious impact on Russia's internal security. Thus, it is the blunder in Iraq in 2003 and its consequences, the unwavering support for Israel and anti-Iranian stance of the United States that are seen in Russia as the drivers for the rise of extremist Islamism. This perceived anti-imperialist struggle then takes on a transnational character that undermines Russia's internal security, as Muslim communities within the country can radicalise through this transnational discourse and employ violence to subvert the Russian domestic order (Allison, 2013) equating western imperialism with the Russian one. The Russian strategy in Syria has been coherent from the beginning of the crisis, and this coherence has played well in the rest of the region with a number of governments willing to build better relations with Russia, allowing it to have a greater degree of regional influence (Katz, 2013). However, it would be erroneous to argue that Russia's Mediterranean policy simply focuses on the Arab world to counter the effects of what it sees as western-fuelled violent religious extremism. In this respect, Russia has attempted to gain traction as a viable political and economic partner for countries in southern Europe, employing the economic crisis and the dissatisfaction in Greece in particular to divide the EU countries over the issue of sanctions against Russia following its takeover of Crimea and Moscow's role in the crisis in Ukraine (Williams, 2015). While this strategy yet has to produce tangible results, it is indicative of the role that Russia intends to play globally and regionally.

China for its part has thus far stayed away from political and security issues, preferring to focus on building economic linkages, but there are political undertones to China's engagement, particularly because it contributes to consolidate the authoritarianism of Arab countries (Sun and Zoubir, 2014). While China is not as invested as Russia in the survival of the Syrian regime, it has also drawn a line in the sand when it comes to western attempts at managing regional affairs unilaterally and through the use of force. This is because China too sees western policies in the region as somewhat self-defeating insofar as they increase tensions and instability with consequences that go beyond the Arab world. China too has domestic concerns about the rise of Islamist violent extremism and while violent groups are sufficiently far not to be considered an immediate threat, there are transnational links that China worries about when it comes to keep its own Muslim population under political control. From a security perspective though, China prefers to remain aloof from the disputes that characterise the region and argues that all issues should be solved regionally without outside intervention and interference. The main priorities for China in the region remain those of increasing its access to the natural resources and expanding the markets for its products, suggesting that these economic imperatives drive Chinese security policy. Accessing resources is certainly a priority given the needs of the Chinese economy, but finding new markets has also been prioritised. As Neill (2014: 206-7) argues: 'the value of China's exports to the Middle East grew from $6.47 billion in 1999 to $121 bn in 2012, and large-scale infrastructure and other construction projects have become a major feature of the Chinese economic activity in the region'. Thus, Chinese leaders are reluctant to be perceived as a regional alternative challenging the United States and prefer a 'strictly business' approach. This is particularly welcome in the region, although security matters for all Arab countries remain important and cannot be dealt with adequately without US diplomatic, economic and military commitments.

Conclusion

The Mediterranean region is a concentrate of problematic issues, and the countries in the area have more in common than traditionally has been perceived. While it is true that there exists a divide between the Arab world, southern Europe, Israel and Turkey, there are also points of convergence and shared challenges. Despite periodic attempts at constructing an area of prosperity and good governance, these have foundered amidst the primacy of narrow national interests, fears and recriminations. The challenges the region faces are unlikely to be dealt with in the short term and this does not bode well for those who aspire to construct a progressive regional order where integration could take place according to the shared values that do exist even though they might not always have the strength to emerge.

Note

1 This chapter draws in part from the chapters 'The Arab Awakening' and 'The Middle East and the Wider World' in Vincent Durac and Francesco Cavatorta, *Politics and Governance of the Middle East*, Palgrave, 2015.

References

Achcar, Gilbert. 2013. *The People Want*. London: Saqi Books.

Allison, Roy. 2013. 'Russia and Syria: explaining alignment with a regime in crisis', *International Affairs* 89(4): 795–823.

Cavatorta, Francesco. 2009. *The International Dimension of the Failed Algerian Transition*. Manchester: Manchester University Press.

Cavatorta, Francesco, R. Chari, S. Kritzinger and A. Gomez. 2008. 'EU external policy-making: "realistically" dealing with authoritarianism? The case of Morocco', *European Foreign Affairs Review* 13(3): 357–76.

Dillman, Bradford. 2001. 'Facing the Market in North Africa', *Middle East Journal* 55(2): 198–215.

Durac, Vincent and Francesco Cavatorta. 2009. 'Strengthening Authoritarian Rule through Democracy Promotion? Examining the paradox of the US and EU security strategies: the case of Tunisia', *British Journal of Middle Eastern Studies* 36(1): 3–19.

Heydemann, Steven. 2007. 'Upgrading Authoritarianism in the Arab World', The Brookings Institution, Analysis Paper, 13: 1–37. Available at http://www.brookings.edu/,/media/Files/rc/papers/2007/10arabworld/10arabworld.pdf

Huntington, Samuel. 1993. 'The Clash of Civilizations?', *Foreign Affairs* 72(3): 22–49.

Jervis, Robert. 2002. 'Theories of War in an Era of Leading-Power Peace', *American Political Science Review* 96(1): 1–14.

Karsh, Efraim. 1997. 'Cold War, Post-Cold War: does it make a difference for the Middle East?', *Review of International Studies* 23(2): 271–91.

Katz, Mark. 2013. 'Russia and the Conflict in Syria: four myths', *Middle East Policy* 20(2): 38–46.

Kepel, Gilles. 2004. *Fitna: Guerre au coeur de l'Islam*. Paris: Gallimard.

Krauthammer, Charles. 1990. 'The Unipolar Moment', *Foreign Affairs* 70(1): 23–33.

Malashenko, Alexey. 2013. 'Russia and the Arab Spring', *Carnegie Moscow Center*. Available at: http://carnegieendowment.org/files/russia_arab_spring2013.pdf

Malley Robert. 1996. *The Call from Algeria: Third worldism, revolution and the turn to Islam*. Oakland: California University Press.

Manners, Ian. 2002. 'Normative Power Europe: a contradiction in terms?', *Journal of Common Market Studies* 40(2): 235–58.

Miller, Judith. 1993. 'The Challenge of Radical Islam', *Foreign Affairs* 72(2): 47–56.

Neill, Alexander. 2014. 'China and the Middle East', *Adelphi Series* 54 (447–8): 205–24.

Pace, Michelle. 2009. 'Paradoxes and Contradictions in EU Democracy Promotion in the Mediterranean: the limits on EU normative power', *Democratization* 16(1): 39–58.

Sika, Nadine. 2012. 'Youth Political Engagement in Egypt: from abstention to revolution', *British Journal of Middle Eastern Studies* 39(2): 181–99.

Sun, Degang and Yahia Zoubir. 2014. 'China's Response to the Uprisings in the Arab World: a case of pragmatic diplomacy', *Mediterranean Politics* 19(1): 2–20.

Teti, Andrea. 2012. 'The EU's First Response to the "Arab Spring": a critical discourse analysis of the partnership for democracy and shared prosperity', *Mediterranean Politics* 17(3): 265–82.

White, Gregory. 2005. 'Free Trade as a Strategic Instrument in the War on Terror? The 2004 US–Moroccan free trade agreement', *Middle East Journal* 59(4): 597–616.

Williams, Carol. 2015. 'Russia and Greece Consider Collaborating to Circumvent Sanctions', *Los Angeles Times*, June 21. Available at: www.latimes.com/world/europe/la-fg-greece-russia-europe-20150621-story.html

Youngs, Richard. 2004. 'Normative Dynamics and Strategic Interests in the EU's External Identity', *Journal of Common Market Studies* 42(2): 415–35.

4

REGIONALISM AND THE MEDITERRANEAN

Long history, odd partners

Federica Bicchi

Introduction

The Mediterranean sits uneasily across the literature on regionalism. While it could be disqualified from the start on the basis that it is not a piece of land, it is also sufficiently charged with a historical pedigree to have been at times considered as a region in and of itself. It is thus difficult to dismiss beforehand expressions such as 'cradle of civilizations' and Fernand Braudel's 'Mediterranean world', which testify to the Mediterranean being more than a stretch of water. However, as we are going to see, processes of regionalism and regionalisation have been ambiguous when it comes to the Mediterranean and when they have been clearly identifiable, they have been tinged with hegemony and imperialism, as one shore arguably imposed (or attempted to impose) its views on the other. As it has been put, 'the idea of a *Mediterranean region* is far from being self-evident' (Del Sarto, 2006, p. 13, emphasis in the original). The Mediterranean is thus better defined as a regional complex, in which broad practices interact, spread, clash and merge, the overall picture at times being cooperation, but often also conflict.

In order to embark on an analysis of regionalism in the Mediterranean case, it is vital to have a clear understanding of the terms. The literature on the topic has enjoyed a revival, based on the idea that, rather than geographical facts, regions are social constructions or, to put it differently, conceptual and discursive tools (Van Langenhove, 2013). Therefore, although geographical contiguity is generally considered essential, 'institutional facts' (Searle, 1995) have come to matter more when analysing the range of intentional activities in an area (Fawn, 2009, p. 13). The focus, especially in political science and international relations, is thus on networks of various types and boundaries as the product of human labour, which can span rivers and seas too. Within this understanding of 'regions', the new wave of studies about 'regionalism' has centred on the top-down analysis of usually state-led formal institution-building processes and has addressed the regional institutions and organisations that have been set up among at least three states (Börzel and Risse, 2016, p. 7). The scholarly interest has been driven by the wave of publications that have considered the future of global governance to rest on regional building blocks or that have looked at regions as reactions to globalisation.

'Regionalisation', on the contrary, is generally defined as bottom-up social, economic and political exchanges involving market and society actors among contiguous states and societies. Early studies, especially in European integration, highlighted the relevance of this type of transactions, including for the development of regional institutions and thus regionalism (Deutsch, 1957; Haas, 1964). This is a research line that remains useful, if somehow less glamorous, in the case of the Mediterranean. Region-building, for its part, tends to be used as a synonym of regionalism, but with less of an emphasis on formal institutions and more of a focus on other political processes (e.g. Adler and Crawford, 2006; Del Sarto, 2006; Neumann, 1994).

Without too much conceptual stretching, therefore, we can look at regionalism as involving the 'politics of regionalisation', meaning the attempt to harness regionalisation and 'relocate the governance of particular issues beyond the scope of national governance and politics' (Hameiri, 2013, p. 314). This brief conceptual clarification should thus help in sifting through the literature on the Mediterranean, by providing a distinction between e.g. Panebianco's (2010) analysis of 'volatile regionalism' in the area and Tovias' (1999) description of regionalisation in the Mediterranean, while appreciating the meaning of the work on the 'construction of the Mediterranean region' (Adler et al., 2006).

There are conceptual problems that are left unsolved, however, when looking at the Mediterranean through the lenses of regionalism and regionalisation, due to the bias in the literature towards processes moving towards 'more' regional structures and interaction, in a one-way street system. This is problematic because, as we are going to see, the Mediterranean has often been notable for *not* being a site of regionalism and regionalisation, especially not like European integration. Most regionalist efforts, in fact, have centred on attempting to manage and limit unwanted forms of regionalisation, with mixed results. One way to avoid the bias would be to look at the Mediterranean as having its own 'regional order', depicting the specific mix of regionalism and regionalisation, which is understood to vary from one place to the other (Acharya, 2004). But this expression too carries the implication that 'the order is orderly', again something that the Mediterranean cannot vouch for, being almost by definition a crossroads of different influences. Going beyond the literature on regions, therefore, we will need also to rely on security studies and focus on security regions (Del Sarto, 2006) or, in my view even more to the point, on the concept of regional security 'complexes', in terms of patterns of amity and enmity confined within a given geographical area. Regional security complexes identify the interdependence of shared interests but also of rivalry, which can create a regional security complex because of its 'inward-looking character' (Buzan, 1991). The focus on regional security complexes thus depicts the Mediterranean *a contrario*, as a place from which it is impossible to neatly disentangle other regions, such as Europe, the Middle East and North Africa.

Therefore, this chapter will argue that, despite having 'a history and a destiny of its own' (Braudel, 1972[1949], p. 20, preface to the first edition), the Mediterranean has been more of a regional security complex than a region, as regionalism and regionalisation have rarely found a stable balance that could be described as a regional order.

The chapter will first look at how the Mediterranean has fared across history in the debate of scholars of international history, before moving on to more contemporary times and zooming in on the post-Cold War period, as analysed in international relations. In the last section, I will focus on current developments and the pattern of fragmentation in which cooperation and conflict intertwine.

The pattern across history

Given the breadth of the Mediterranean's history (and the limited size of this chapter), I will highlight only the macro-picture that emerges when surveying the Mediterranean across the ages, by pointing to the rare moments of political and economic regional order. These need to be understood, however, against a background in which historians, ethnographers and anthropologists have clashed over how to represent the history of the area – witness the lively debates around 'Mediterraneanism' (Harris, 2004; Horden and Purcell, 2000; Shavit, 1988), 'Mediterraneanisation' (e.g. Morris, 2003) and the existence/relevance of a Mediterranean culture overlapping with the cultivation of the vine or of the olive tree (e.g. Purcell, 2003). The focus here is just on histories *of* the Mediterranean (and whether there is such a thing as a Mediterranean region), as opposed to histories *in* the Mediterranean, in which the Mediterranean just provides a scenery and not an entity in its own right (Horden and Purcell, 2006).

The most famous account of the Mediterranean in history is surely by Fernand Braudel, who in 1949 provided a monumental overview of what, in his view, is to be considered a region, unified by the structural and largely immutable force of geography. According to Braudel, the shared Mediterranean environment was the main feature of this area, while its social history and the 'history of events', triggered by 'individual men', just skimmed the surface of history, as 'crests of foam that the tides of history carry on their strong backs' (Braudel, 1972[1949], p. 21). It is not surprising, therefore, that Braudel's vision of the Mediterranean as a region of continuity rather than change has long since become associated with his idea of history as the 'long durée'. Reinterpreted in the light of the analytical concepts introduced above, Braudel's account depicts a Mediterranean region based on bottom-up regionalisation, whereas regionalism and region-building have been transient forces that have neither contributed to nor hindered the fundamental homogeneity of the place. In more recent times, a very similar position considering the Mediterranean as a region and 'a discriminable whole' has been expressed by Horden and Purcell (2000, p. 2), but on a different basis than geography. Their emphasis is still on regionalisation, but more in the form of networks and 'connectivity' between micro-environments (microecologies, in their language) around the Mediterranean. The distinguishing and unifying factor thus is 'the unique concentration of factors that are not themselves peculiar to the region' (Horden and Purcell, 2006, p. 735). The two scholars make very clear, however, that they do not believe that this unity has been carried into the third millennium, as modernisation has diverted the attention of coastal nations and led to the disintegration of the Mediterranean region (ibid, p. 3).

This vision, depicting unity as central to the Mediterranean's history, has not gone unchallenged. Starting from the opposite perspective but in an equally sweeping account, Abulafia has centred Mediterranean history on the key role of the Mediterranean *sea* (as opposed to a history of the lands around it, à la Braudel), as well as on the fundamental role of the people, and particularly men, who crossed it (Abulafia, 2011a). Unsurprisingly, he suggests that '[r]ather than searching for unity, we should note diversity' in the Mediterranean (Abulafia, 2011b, p. 221), because the unity of Mediterranean history 'lies, paradoxically, in its swirling changeability' (Abulafia, 2011b, p. 211 and 228). His history is thus an account of periods of integration, inevitably followed by violent disintegration, 'through warfare or plague', reflecting a variety of processes at stake. Recast in the terms introduced earlier, Abulafia's history is thus an account of regionalism and especially of its defeats, as the diversity of the area and its changeability defied homogenisation.

Looking at specific aspects of this complex matter, the attention is drawn to the issue of political domination. The political dimension of the Mediterranean across millennia shows just one success, which occurred during Roman times. This was the first and only instance of a single polity for the whole of the Mediterranean. For roughly 500 years,[1] Rome governed all the lands around the Mediterranean (and most of northern Europe as well), imposing a common set of legal and political principles, as well as affecting economic and social relations. While this could be depicted as a 'European' form of governance, it was first and foremost a Mediterranean one: 'from about 27 BC to AD 235, the political axis and cultural base of the empire were to be found in the Mediterranean' (Garnsey and Saller, 2014[1987], p. 22) and the pendulum did not swing away from the Mediterranean until the second half of the third century.[2]

After Roman times, Mediterranean-centred political unity was never recovered and there was no longer a political regional order, but rather several attempts to establish it in and across the Mediterranean, generally entangled with religious elements that pitted Christianity against Islam. A sweeping attempt was made by the political forces emerging from the rise of Islam in the Arabian peninsula during the seventh and eighth centuries, which brought together territories from Spain to south-east Turkey (and beyond). Their advance was stopped at Tours, where the Franks defeated the Islamic empire in 732. Despite crusaders' attempts, spurred by the Pope and expansionist forces in Europe, the east and the south of the Mediterranean became absorbed by their own trajectory at times but not always characterised by political unity (Hourani, 1991, p. 38). It was the evolution of the Ottoman Empire that brought a common political framework over large parts of the Mediterranean, even though at times just a symbolic one. But its expansion towards the north was stopped at Lepanto in 1571. For centuries, the northern European parts of the Mediterranean and the south-eastern parts looked at the world from different political perspectives, while still embedded in a net of cultural, social and economic contacts. This regional complex and its endless possibilities of cross-fertilisation are probably best captured by the map, shown in Figure 4.1, drawn in Sicily around the mid-twelfth century by a Muslim cartographer working at the court of the Normans, its inverted poles upsetting more Eurocentric traditions.

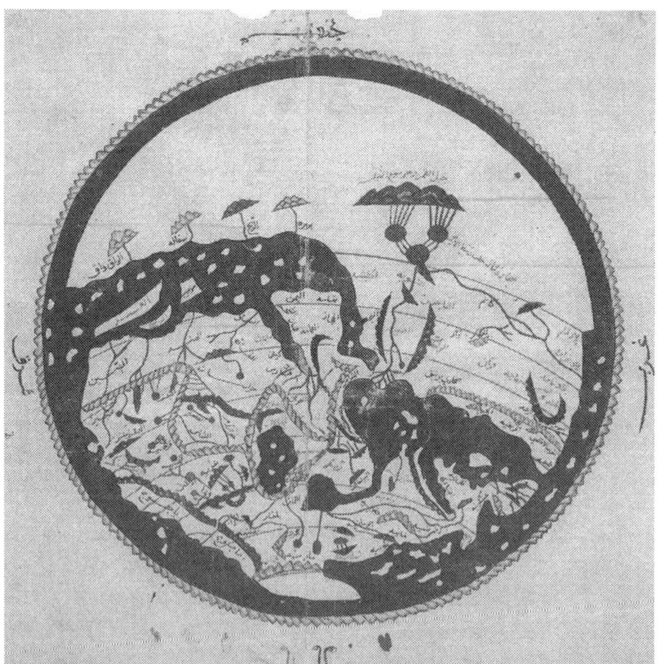

Figure 4.1 Map of the world, by al-Idrisi, Bodleian Library, University of Oxford, MS. Pococke 375, ff. 3b–4a

As the Ottoman Empire's political unity began to crumble, European colonial powers started to infiltrate its vast domains, a process that characterised large parts of the nineteenth century. It came to the fore with the end of World War I with the collapse of the Ottoman Empire. New political dynamics, in the form of direct or indirect colonisation, once again brought together actors in the Mediterranean in a new form of (partial) regional order. In various guises, France, Italy, Spain and the UK colonised the southern and eastern parts of the Mediterranean, imposing political links that connected them to the northern shore of the Mediterranean and established similar patterns of political control, economic exploitation and social links. It was this regional order that unravelled at various points after World War II.

The political processes in the Mediterranean that have achieved or have attempted to achieve a political regional order have thus often had to settle for a regional security complex, in which the pattern of friendships and rivalries kept this 'region' together more than shared regional political institutions. Moreover, political forces with regionalist aspirations have been historically intertwined with imperial aspirations. From the perspective of politics, regionalism in the Mediterranean has relied on force, be it in the case of the Romans, the Arabs, the Crusaders, the Ottomans or the colonial powers. Despite the often peaceful periods that characterised empires across the Mediterranean, wars and conflicts characterised all the beginnings and ends of imperial aspirations.

Does European integration promote regionalism in the Mediterranean?

In contemporary times, the novelty is represented, in political terms, by the process of European integration (a mix of regionalism and regionalisation), which has pooled together an increasing number of countries on the northern shore of the Mediterranean since the creation of the EEC in 1957. While at times considered to echo medieval overlapping orders (e.g. Zielonka, 2013), this political process raises the issue of how this post-World War II new region, under construction with all the institutional and interactive trimmings, relates to the Mediterranean. As we are going to see, Europeans' engagement with regionalism in their southern neighbourhood has come and gone. With a broad generalisation, we can distinguish five stages in the EC/EU relations with its southern partners (cf. Bicchi, 2007), only two of which witnessed a genuine attempt to share political dynamics with non-EC/EU countries around the Mediterranean.

At first, there was little interest and few ties were established. Between 1957 and 1972, the EEC 'lacked a policy framework to organize and structure' Euro-Mediterranean relations (Ginsberg, 1989, p. 119–20) and the non-members on the southern border ranked low on the agenda. The EEC seemingly tackled problems as they arose, without an agreed overall conception (Shlaim, 1976, p. 80), and while it signed several agreements with its neighbours, they were uncoordinated and the result was a 'patchwork' of agreements (Gomez, 1998, p. 134). Each problem was examined individually and was given a different solution – no regionalist approach indeed.

This changed in the 1970s, which marked the first period of regionalism during which the Europeans 'invented' the Mediterranean, used this label to identify their southern neighbours as a relatively homogeneous, Mediterranean, group and aimed to capitalise on the move. Greece, Portugal and Spain, as well as countries on the southern and eastern shores were thus placed in the Mediterranean group, with the goal to emphasise similarities over differences. The instruments for regionalism were the Global Mediterranean Policy (GMP), launched in 1972, and the Euro-Arab Dialogue, which began in 1974. The GMP is particularly relevant, for our concern. It consisted of a series of copy-cat economic and technical agreements, which were meant to create free trade areas for industrial goods between the EEC and each Mediterranean country, thus harmonising different economic regimes. This was an important innovation (Tovias, 1977; Tsoukalis, 1977). The underlying rationale was to create economies of scale for Mediterranean countries, tying them to the European market and encouraging development. Still, the project was stifled by the fact that the EEC called for exceptions in areas (such as agriculture, textiles and phosphate products) where Mediterranean countries were highly competitive. As a consequence, with few exceptions, Mediterranean exports to the EEC – and thus regionalisation – did not increase significantly (Shlaim and Yannopoulos, 1976). No Mediterranean region was (re)born.

Interest for the Mediterranean flagged in the 1980s, a period that marked the construction of a rift in the area. This was a decade of contradictions in Euro-Mediterranean relations. On one hand, regionalism in Europe soared. The EC enlarged to include Greece in 1981, as well as Spain and Portugal in 1986, thus shifting the EC's internal balance towards the south for the first time since its creation. The institutional framework kept growing and the EC entered a long season of institutional reform, starting from the Single European Act in 1984. It was clear by the end of the 1980s that the EC was experiencing one of its most positive periods. On the other hand, these internal developments did not translate into new initiatives towards the Mediterranean. On the contrary, a rift in Euro-Mediterranean relations opened. The southern enlargement absorbed most of member states' attention in terms of southern neighbours, thus concentrating regionalism on the European project. Moreover, enlargement increased the EC self-sufficiency in several sectors, thus delivering a blow also to regionalisation. During the 1980s, the Mediterranean non-members experienced a net loss of relevance vis-à-vis their northern neighbours and the few compensatory measures drafted by the EC did little to change the overall picture (Pierros et al., 1999, p. 105). The burden of adjusting to Europe-centred regionalism was, in fact, left to Mediterranean non-member countries (Grilli, 1993, p. 203), prompting Morocco's and Turkey's applications to the EC in 1987 as a gesture to stress the exclusiveness of the European club. In fact, this period is a micro-case in terms of de-regionalisation and de-regionalism, if these terms were ever to be explored with reference to the Mediterranean.

The end of the Cold War paved the way to the main regionalist attempt of the EU, namely the launching of the Euro-Mediterranean Partnership (EMP) in 1995. The EMP was on a different scale than all previous EC/EU initiatives. It introduced three main novelties in terms of regionalism: 1) a multilayered institutional structure to dialogue, which aimed at institutionalising the regional discussion; 2) a broader number of topics on the agenda, which gave substance to the dialogue and aimed to produce regionalisation; and 3) a new approach to economic questions and development, geared at (re)launching an area of free trade and shared prosperity. The EMP thus put in place a structure with the potential to transform geographical closeness into actual collaboration and partnership, thus 'constructing' a Euro-Mediterranean region and putting flesh on the bones of the Mediterranean project suggested in the 1970s (Adler et al., 2006). It was at the height of this cooperative period in 1999 that Turkey received candidate status, thus significantly enhancing its chances of acquiring EU membership and 'becoming a European country'.

The scholarly debate the EMP engendered has been huge. The process leading to the launch of the initiative was scrutinised (Barbé, 1996; Bicchi, 2007; Bistolfi, 1995; Pierros et al., 1999), and the initiative's different aspects described and assessed (Edwards and Philippart, 1997; Gillespie, 1997; Joffé, 1999; Jünemann, 2004; Khader, 1997; Kienle, 1998; Pace, 2004; Philippart, 2003; Tovias and Ugur, 2004). The academic journal *Mediterranean Politics* became the main venue for this debate.

Much of the analytical attention was directed at addressing a key point, precisely in relation to regionalism. Was the EU aiming to build a comprehensive macro Euro-Mediterranean region, including neighbouring areas and avoiding to establish a 'fortress Europe'? Or was the EU building itself as a region, with the regionalist developments in the Mediterranean just as window-dressing for the continuation of the European project against the backdrop of its Mediterranean periphery? Could the EU go beyond the hegemonic drive that had guided previous attempts at regionalism in the area?

Several positions have developed on this issue. The literature on external governance (e.g. Lavenex, 2008, 2014) has maintained that regionalism in Europe has contributed to regionalism in and regionalisation of Euro-Mediterranean relations. It has shown that Europe's regulatory borders have progressively expanded beyond the EU so that it becomes impossible to analyse the neighbouring countries without taking into account the EU. The progressive extension of the *acquis communautaire*, also through the negotiation of specific agreements or through the use of specific EU instruments, would thus suggest a region building – or even a regionalist – approach on the part of the EU in its relations with Mediterranean neighbours, which in turn have fostered regionalisation. This has been in tune with the literature on regionalism, which has argued that the EU has a long tradition of promoting regionalism. Several studies have convincingly contended this (e.g. Grugel, 2004), and this remains a blossoming research field based on recent developments in theories of new regionalism and comparative regionalism (Börzel, 2012; Jetschke and Lenz, 2013).

From a constructivist foreign policy perspective, the EMP was considered to aim at the creation of a regional order encompassing the whole of the EU and its southern Mediterranean countries in a 'Euro-Mediterranean region'. This line of thought has argued that despite the lack of a membership perspective, the EU has aimed to tie the southern Mediterranean neighbours into a 'regional security partnership' (Attinà, 2006) if not yet into a 'pluralistic security community' based on reasonable expectations of peaceful change (rather than conflict) (Adler et al., 2006). The proposed new identities would not supplant the pre-existing national identities, but rather pool them into a larger collective, regional 'we' (ibid.).

These were not the only arguments in town, however. Another line of thought has stressed the narratives of 'otherness', and the role Russia and the Mediterranean have had in strengthening the 'we-feeling' of Europeans, as opposed to the Russian or Arab 'other'. Security, societal and economic challenges have been seen here not just as opportunities to promote European norms, but also as problems around which discourses coalesce and attitudes are defined *against* external actors (Neumann, 1995; Pace, 2006). While often this perspective has been informed by post-structuralism, this has also been the leitmotiv in traditional approaches to the neighbourhood, which tend to reflect realist tenets and highlight security issues (e.g. Aliboni, 1999). Moreover, due to the evident asymmetry between the parties, the Mediterranean policy of the European countries has been sometimes portrayed as a form of hegemony, enabling the Europeans to pursue their economic and political goals within their periphery (Del Sarto, 2016; Holden, 2009; Philippart, 2003).

Be this as it may, the EMP's ambitious plans were unable to create whatever region, and regionalism was toned down in the fifth stage of Euro-Mediterranean relations, with the launch of the European Neighbourhood Policy (ENP) in 2004 and then of the Union for the Mediterranean (UfM) in 2008 (Bicchi and Lavenex, 2015; Bicchi, Noutcheva and Voltolini, in press). The ENP was conceived as a way to smoothen relations with non-candidate countries in the wake of the east's enlargement in 2004, exactly to avoid the replication of the south's enlargement effect on the Mediterranean. Behind an egalitarian veneer, which promised all neighbours the same chances and opportunities, the ENP, however, marked a clear shift towards bilateralism. While Kelley (2006), stressed the continuity with the EU enlargement policy others highlighted the fundamental differences with previous practices, as Del Sarto and Schumacher (2005) did in relation to the EMP. The UfM's goal was to breathe new life into the more than decade-long regionalist initiative in the Mediterranean, but it represented a further downscaling of the EU's ambitions in the region (Bicchi and Gillespie, 2011), as it actually crystallised an approach à-la-carte that emptied the project of political momentum (Barbé and Herranz-Surrallés, 2013) while maintaining power asymmetries (Cardwell, 2011).

The scholarly debate about region building in the neighbourhood cooled down following the adoption of the ENP in 2004 and the de facto abrogation of regionalism as an EU objective in its southern neighbourhood. Developments such as the Arab Spring only contributed to the further fragmentation of the neighbourhood, as they unleashed processes sparking from similar contingent aspects but capitalising on different structural conditions and leading to different directions. With old and new conflicts tearing the Middle East apart, any narrative about regionalism and a regional neighbourhood ground to a halt, both in academic and policy-making circles.

Regionalisation in current times

While the top-down interest in dealing with the entire Mediterranean area has faded, does this reflect lack of regionalisation and of bottom-up processes keeping the area together? A picture of Euro-Mediterranean relations taken in 2016 shows strong contrasts. A static analysis shows a deep economic and security chasm across the Mediterranean, but this feeds into a dynamic set of flows in relation to trade and people that aim to cross it.

On the one hand, the northern and southern shores of the Mediterranean are very far in terms of economy and security. A comparison of GDP per capita shows that only Israel compares favourably with the average GDP of the EU member states (see Figure 4.2). While the growth rate of Arab economies is impressive (less so after 2013), compared to European rates, its impact is significantly lowered by the high population growth rate, which detracts from economic growth. Demographic trends are changing, as lower birth rates spread across the Arab countries. But it will take a long time even in the best of conditions to close the gap between the two shores.

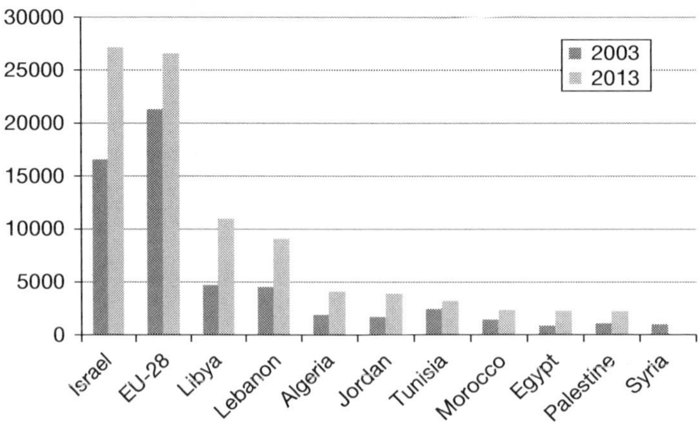

Figure 4.2 GDP per inhabitant, 2003 and 2013, in €

Source: Eurostat 2015.

From a security perspective, it is telling that Europeans' perceptions of the southern Mediterranean rim depict a situation of unprecedented security challenges. The best visual summary is probably provided by the French foreign travel advice, issued in August 2016 (Figure 4.3), which shows the Middle East and North Africa as largely 'no go' areas (red, in the map), while Europe is entirely 'normal' (green, on the French scale, not shown). The French assessment also portrays the southern Mediterranean countries as the most dangerous set of neighbours in comparison to the situation in other regions, with only parts of Morocco in which travellers should act 'normally'.

Therefore, looked at separately and in comparison, the northern and the southern shore of the Mediterranean seem to belong to two different worlds, in terms of wealth and personal safety, and the Mediterranean itself can be seen as Europe's 'Rio Grande' or 'a frontier region of Europe', albeit one in which 'the divisive function of the sea is often overstressed when compared to the common patterns and mutual interests across the Basin' (King, 1998, pp. 109–10).

On the other hand, this apparent chasm has not fed into complete separation. On the contrary, it has led to trade and – in particular – population movements. In trade terms, European countries trade marginally with their southern neighbours, whereas southern neighbours' trade with Europe is crucial, especially for North Africa. In 2013, 'the EU-28 accounted for a majority of the total trade (imports plus exports) in goods for Tunisia, Algeria and Morocco', three countries that import more than 60 per cent of goods from the EU (Eurostat, 2015, p. 72). Trade with the EU is also important for Egypt and Israel (both trading around 30 per cent of imports and of exports with the EU), whereas Jordan and Lebanon are more integrated in the Middle East economic bloc.

The hottest dossier of all remains migration. Also, because of the differential between the two shores in terms of wealth and personal safety, people have been crossing the Mediterranean in unprecedented numbers in 2015 (more than 1 million people, according to the International Organization for Migration[3]). In 2016, numbers have decreased to roughly one-third, but the issue remains very high on the political agenda as an 'unwanted' form of regionalisation.

The political instruments put at use to manage disparities and migration flows bring us back to regionalism (and its absence). Rather than trying to create regional institutions or to

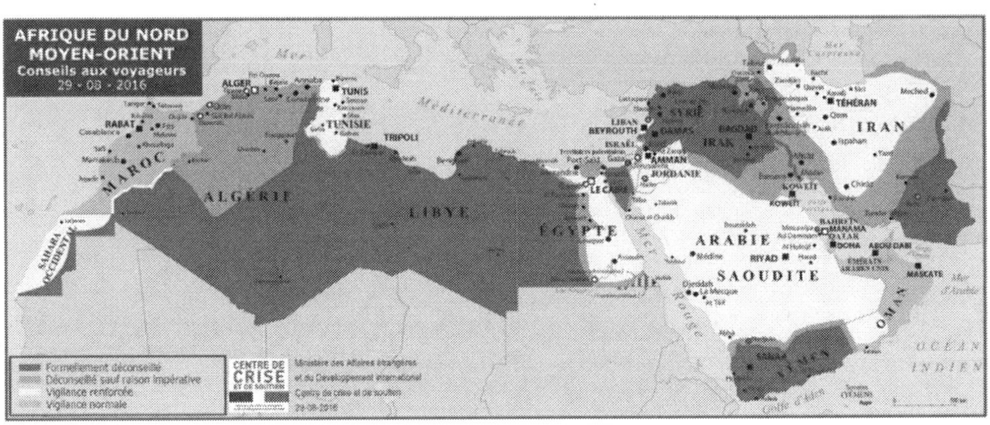

Figure 4.3 Foreign travel advice, Middle East and North Africa

Source: Quai d'Orsay, website.

extend forms of control to the whole area, European countries have largely relied on bilateral deals between the EU and single southern Mediterranean countries in the form of re-admission agreements. While the phenomenon has a regional, Mediterranean dimension, the response is predominantly bilateral, between the European region and its southern neighbours.

Conclusions

This chapter has provided an overview of the insights that emerge from bringing together the Mediterranean with the study of regionalism. It aimed to show that the Mediterranean has lost the characteristics of a single political system that it had during Roman times, never to acquire political unity again, despite several regionalist attempts, tainted to varying degrees by hegemonic aspirations, and against a backdrop of cultural cross-fertilisation. In political terms, the Mediterranean has tended throughout history to resemble a regional security complex more than a regional order, or a crystallised equilibrium between regionalism and regionalisation. The recent attempts by the EU to promote regionalism through the EMP attracted much scholarly attention, but the ambiguities of the project, as well as its over-ambitious agenda, have clashed with the tensions that have arisen throughout global governance institutions, especially in the post-2004 context of EU eastern enlargement and post-2011 fragmentation of the Arab world. The more recent picture of the Mediterranean shows a deep chasm in terms of welfare and personal safety, which, however, does not stop (in fact, feeds into) bottom-up regional trends.

We are still to trace and fully conceptualise the path leading to the decline in regionalism in the Mediterranean (rather: *of* the Mediterranean as a whole, as the debate among historians would suggest), as well as developments in new and recurring trends in regionalisation. However, with regionalism in (and of) Europe also under attack, it is clear that top-down political processes aiming at the creation of political institutions for the whole of the Mediterranean are unlikely to make a return soon, in the absence of committed political leadership.

Notes

1 Dates are difficult to indicate with precision here, given the turbulence of the times, but this period stretches from approximately the end of the Punic wars against Carthage (149 BCE) to the sack of Rome (410 CE).
2 See the addendum to the chapter on 'A Mediterranean Empire' in Garnsey and Saller (2014[1987]) for a three page review of the literature on the topic.
3 See https://missingmigrants.iom.int/mediterranean-update-7-april-2017

References

Abulafia, D. (2011a). *The Great Sea: A Human History of the Mediterranean*. Oxford: Oxford University Press.

Abulafia, D. (2011b). Mediterranean History as Global History. *History and Theory*, 50(2), 220–8.

Acharya, A. (2004). How Ideas Spread: Whose Norms Matter? Norm Localization and Institutional Change in Asian Regionalism. *International Organization*, 58(2), 239–75.

Adler, E. and Crawford, B. (2006). Normative Power: The European Practice of Region Building and the Case of the Euro-Mediterranean Partnership (EMP). In E. Adler, F. Bicchi, B. Crawford and R. Del Sarto (Eds), *The Convergence of Civilizations: Constructing the Mediterranean Region*. Toronto: University of Toronto Press.

Adler, E., Bicchi, F., Crawford, B. and Del Sarto, R. (2006). *The Convergence of Civilizations: Constructing a Mediterranean Region*. Toronto: University of Toronto Press.

Aliboni, R. (1999). European Union Perceptions and Policies towards the Mediterranean. In S. J. Blank (Ed.), *Mediterranean Security into the Coming Millennium*. Strategic Studies Institute.

Attinà, F. (2006). The Building of Regional Security Partnership and the Security–Culture Divide in the Mediterranean Region. In E. Adler, F. Bicchi, B. Crawford and R. Del Sarto (Eds), *The Convergence of Civilizations: Constructing a Mediterranean Region*. Toronto: University of Toronto Press.

Barbé, E. (1996). The Barcelona Conference: Launching Pad of a Process. *Mediterranean Politics*, 1(1), 25–42.

Barbé, E. and Herranz-Surrallés, A. (2013). *The Challenge of Differentiation in Euro-Mediterranean Relations: Flexible Regional Cooperation or Fragmentation?* Abingdon: Routledge.

Bicchi, F. (2007). *European Foreign Policy Making toward the Mediterranean*. New York/Basingstoke: Palgrave Macmillan.

Bicchi, F. and Gillespie, R. (2011). The Union for the Mediterranean or the Changing Euro-Mediterranean Relations. Special issue. *Mediterranean Politics*, 16(1), 1–219.

Bicchi, F. and Lavenex, S. (2015). The European Neighbourhood: Between European Integration and International Relations. In K. E. Jørgensen, A. Kalland Aarstad, E. Drieskens, K. V. Laatikainen, and B. Tonra (Eds), *The SAGE Handbook of European Foreign Policy*. London: SAGE.

Bicchi, F. Noutcheva, G. and Voltolini, B. (In press). The European Neighbourhood Policy between Bilateralism and Region-Building. In T. Schumacher (Ed.), *The Routledge Handbook on the European Neighbourhood Policy*, Routledge.

Bistolfi, R. (1995). *Euro-Méditerranée: une région à construire*. Paris: Publisud.

Börzel, T. A. (2012). Comparative Regionalism: European Integration and Beyond. *Handbook of International Relations*. London: SAGE, pp. 503–30.

Börzel, T. A. and Risse, T. (2016). Introduction. In T. A. Börzel and T. Risse (Eds), *The Oxford Handbook of Comparative Regionalism*. Oxford: Oxford University Press.

Braudel, F. (1972[1949]). *The Mediterranean and the Mediterranean World in the Age of Philip II*. London: Fontana/Collins.

Buzan, B. (1991). *People, States, and Fear* (2nd edn). Hemel Hempstead (UK)/Boulder: Harvester Wheatsheaf/Lynne Rienner.

Cardwell, Paul J. (2011). EuroMed, European Neighbourhood Policy and the Union for the Mediterranean: Overlapping Policy Frames in the EU's Governance of the Mediterranean. *Journal of Common Market Studies*, 49(2), 219–41.

Del Sarto, R. A. (2006). *Contested State Identities and Regional Security in the Euro-Mediterranean Area*. New York/Basingstoke: Palgrave Macmillan.

Del Sarto, R. A. (2016). Normative Empire Europe: The European Union, its Borderlands, and the 'Arab Spring'. *Journal of Common Market Studies*, 54(2), 215–32, doi:10.1111/jcms.12282

Del Sarto, R. A. and Schumacher, T. (2005). From EMP to ENP: What's at Stake with the European Neighbourhood Policy towards the Southern Mediterranean? *European Foreign Affairs Review*, 10(1), 17–38.

Deutsch, K. W. (1957). *Political Community and the North Atlantic Area*. Princeton: Princeton University Press.

Edwards, G. and Philippart, E. (1997). The Euro-Mediterranean Partnership: Fragmentation and Reconstruction. *European Foreign Affairs Review*, 2(4), 465–89.

Eurostat (2015). *Euro-Mediterranean Statistics*. Brussels: Eurostat.

Fawn, R. (2009). 'Regions' and their Study: Wherefrom, What For and Whereto? *Review of International Studies*, 35(S1), 5–34, doi:10.1017/S0260210509008419

Garnsey, P. and Saller, R. P. (2014[1987]). *The Roman Empire: Economy, Society and Culture*. Berkeley: University of California Press.

Gillespie, R. (Ed.) (1997). *The Euro-Mediterranean Partnership: Political and Economic Perspectives*. London/Portland (OR): Frank Cass.

Ginsberg, R. H. (1989). *Foreign Policy Actions of the European Community: The Politics of Scale*. Boulder/London: Lynne Rienner Publishers/Adamantine Press.

Gomez, R. (1998). The EU's Mediterranean Policy: Common Foreign Policy by the Back Door? In J. Peterson and H. Sjursen (Eds), *A Common Foreign Policy for Europe? Competing Visions of the CFSP*. London/New York: Routledge.

Grilli, E. R. (1993). *The European Community and the Developing Countries*. Cambridge: Cambridge University Press.

Grugel, J. B. (2004). New Regionalism and Modes of Governance: Comparing US and EU Strategies in Latin America. *European Journal of International Relations*, 10(4), 603–26.

Haas, E. B. (1964). *Beyond the Nation-State: Functionalism and International Organization*. Stanford (CA): Stanford University Press.

Hameiri, S. (2013). Theorising Regions through Changes in Statehood: Rethinking the Theory and Method of Comparative Regionalism. *Review of International Studies*, 39(2), 313–35, doi:10.1017/S026021051100074X

Harris, W. V. (Ed.) (2004). *Rethinking the Mediterranean*. Oxford: Oxford University Press.

Holden, P. (2009). *In Search of Structural Power: EU Aid Policy as a Global Political Instrument*: Farnham: Ashgate Publishing.

Horden, P. and Purcell, N. (2000). *The Corrupting Sea: A Study of Mediterranean History*. Oxford (UK)/Malden (MA): Blackwell.

Horden, P. and Purcell, N. (2006). The Mediterranean and 'the New Thalassology'. *The American Historical Review*, 111(3), 722–40, doi:10.1086/ahr.111.3.722

Hourani, A. (1991). *A History of the Arab Peoples*. London: Faber and Faber.

Jetschke, A. and Lenz, T. (2013). Does Regionalism Diffuse? A New Research Agenda for the Study of Regional Organizations. *Journal of European Public Policy*, 20(4), 626–37.

Joffé, G. (1999). The Euro-Mediterranean Partnership Initiative: Problems and Prospects. In G. Joffé (Ed.), *Perspectives on Development: The Euro-Mediterranean Partnership*. London/Portland (OR): Frank Cass, pp. 247–66.

Jünemann, A. (Ed.) (2004). *Euro-Mediterranean Relations after September 11: International, Regional and Domestic Dynamics*. London/Portland (OR): Frank Cass.

Kelley, J. (2006). New Wine in Old Wineskins: Promoting Political Reforms through the New European Neighbourhood Policy. *Journal of Common Market Studies*, 44(1), 29–55, doi:10.1111/j.1468-5965.2006.00613.x

Khader, B. (1997). *Le Partenariat Euro-Méditerranéen après la conférence de Barcelone*. Paris: L'Harmattan.

Kienle, E. (1998). Destabilization through Partnership? Euro-Mediterranean Relations after the Barcelona Declaration. *Mediterranean Politics*, 3(2), 1–20.

King, R. (1998). The Mediterranean: Europe's Rio Grande. In M. Anderson and E. Bort (Eds), *The Frontiers of Europe*. London/Washington: Pinter.

Lavenex, S. (2008). A Governance Perspective on the European Neighbourhood Policy: Integration Beyond Conditionality? *Journal of European Public Policy*, 15(6), 938–55.

Lavenex, S. (2014). The Power of Functionalist Extension: How EU Rules Travel. *Journal of European Public Policy*, 21(6), 885–903.

Morris, I. (2003). Mediterraneanization. *Mediterranean Historical Review*, 18(2), 30–55, doi:10.1080/0951896032000230471

Neumann, I. B. (1994). A Region-Building Approach to Northern Europe. *Review of International Studies*, 20(1), 53–74.

Neumann, I. B. (1995). *Russia and the Idea of Europe: A Study in Identity and International Relations*. London: Routledge.

Pace, M. (2004). The Euro-Mediterranean Partnership and the Common Mediterranean Strategy? European Union Policy from a Discursive Perspective. *Geopolitics*, 9(2), 292–309.

Pace, M. (2006). *The Politics of Regional Identity: Meddling with the Mediterranean*. London/New York: Routledge.

Panebianco, A. (2010). Volatile Regionalism in the Mediterranean Area. *L'Europe en Formation*, 356(2), 153–67.

Philippart, E. (2003). The Euro-Mediterranean Partnership: A Critical Evaluation of an Ambitious Scheme. *European Foreign Affairs Review*, 8, 201–20.

Pierros, F., Meunier, J. and Abrams, S. (1999). *Bridges and Barriers: The European Union's Mediterranean Policy, 1961–1998*. Aldershot: Ashgate.

Purcell, N. (2003). The Boundless Sea of Unlikeness? On Defining the Mediterranean. *Mediterranean Historical Review*, 18(2), 9–29, doi:10.1080/0951896032000230462

Searle, J. R. (1995). *The Construction of Social Reality*. London: Allen Lane.

Shavit, Y. (1988). The Mediterranean World and 'Mediterraneanism': The Origins, Meaning, and Application of a Geo-Cultural Notion in Israel. *Mediterranean Historical Review*, 3(2), 96–117, doi:10.1080/09518968808569552

Shlaim, A. (1976). The Community and the Mediterranean Basin. In K. J. Twitchett (Ed.), *Europe and the World: The External Relations of the Common Market*. London: Europa Publications.

Shlaim, A. and Yannopoulos, G. N. (Eds) (1976). *The EEC and the Mediterranean Countries*. Cambridge: Cambridge University Press.

Tovias, A. (1977). *Tariff Preferences in Mediterranean Diplomacy*. London: Macmillan.

Tovias, A. (1999). Regionalisation and the Mediterranean. In G. Joffé (Ed.), *Perspectives on Development: The Euro-Mediterranean Partnership*. London/Portland (OR): Frank Cass, pp. 75–88.

Tovias, A. and Ugur, M. (2004). Can the EU Anchor Policy Reform in Third Countries? An Analysis of the Euro-Med Partnership. *European Union Politics*, 5(4), 395–418.

Tsoukalis, L. (1977). The EEC and the Mediterranean: Is 'Global' Policy a Misnomer? *International Affairs*, 53(3), 422–38.

Van Langenhove, L. (2013). What is a Region? Towards a Statehood Theory of Regions. *Contemporary Politics*, 19(4), 474–90.

Zielonka, J. (2013). The International System in Europe: Westphalian Anarchy or Medieval Chaos? *Journal of European Integration*, 35(1), 1–18.

5

SECURING THE MEDITERRANEAN, INVENTING THE 'MIDDLE EAST'

Pinar Bilgin

As a spatial conception, the Mediterranean has a centuries-long history. Mediterranean littoral peoples and societies were referred to as 'Mediterranean' in ancient Greece. Indeed, some findings suggest that the very first references to the 'West' as a political construct were to the lands surrounding the Mediterranean Sea, whereas the lands to the east and south of the Sea were referred to as the 'East' (Hentsch, 1992). Later, with the 'Arab' invasion of the territories to the south of the Mediterranean and later under Ottoman rule, the south of the Mediterranean got dropped out of the 'West' and was pushed into the 'East'. While both Egyptian and Lebanese intellectuals remained in touch with the Mediterranean identity of their respective countries, it took the agency of the European Union during the 1990s to construct the 'Euro-Mediterranean' as a subject of security in counter-distinction to the 'Middle East' (see Moulakis, 2005).

The 'Middle East', in turn, is relatively new. It was invented at the beginning of the twentieth century as part of debates on securing the waterway to India for the purpose of furthering Britain's imperial interests. Throughout the Cold War, the United States' interests in this part of the world focused on securing the 'Middle East'. Notwithstanding the protests of some local actors who framed their insecurities in terms of another spatial construct, the 'Arab World' (as with Egypt, for instance), over the years many other local actors' discourses have come to be aligned with the US discourse and practices designed to secure the 'Middle East' (as with Saudi Arabia, Iran [until the revolution], Israel and Turkey) (Bilgin, 2005).

This chapter traces the entry onto the world stage of the 'Euro-Mediterranean' as a subject of security in counter-distinction to the 'Middle East' in the 1990s. Where the latter prioritised insecurities as experienced by the United States and its local allies, the former was designed to address insecurities identified by the European Union. What is more, the former constituted a short-lived attempt to re-cast the 'Euro-Mediterranean' as a region and a security community (Adler et al., 2006).

Before we proceed, a caveat is in order. The significance of tracing the emergence and evolution of spatial constructs such as the 'Euro-Mediterranean' and the 'Middle East' is not about the so-called 'artificiality' of 'regions', for all regions are 'artificial' (Lewis and Wigen, 1997). Rather, my aim here is to highlight insecurities that shape the construction of regions, and practices that have been shaped in line with these spatial constructs. Studying the 'Mediterranean', 'Arab World' or the 'Middle East' is no innocent task since 'our' spatial constructs are shaped as part of the attempt to respond to 'our' insecurities 'in here' while insecuring 'others' 'out there'.

Accordingly, defining regions and studying regional security in X or Y 'region' is a political act worthy of critical scrutiny (Bilgin, 2004).

Britain seeks to secure the route to India: inventing the 'Middle East'

The Levant (al Mashreq or 'the land where the sun rises' in Arabic) had been central to the imaginary of those belonging to the three Abrahamic religions. Crusades were organised to secure the Christian 'holy lands'. Muslim holy sites were captured and re-captured by Arabic and Ottoman forces throughout the ages. Jews fleeing persecution in Europe in the early twentieth century sought a home in Jerusalem and its surrounds. Those with more secular agendas also had their eyes on the Levant until the end of World War II – be it Italian city states or the Ottoman and British Empires.

The invention of the 'Middle East' hinted at a shift in policy focus from the Levant to the broader Arabian peninsula, thus signalling an adjustment in British imperial insecurity practices vis-à-vis this part of the world and (eventually) beyond. There is no consensus on the exact moment of 'origin' for the Middle East as a spatial construct (Koppes, 1976). There is more of a consensus on who it was that used the term 'Middle East' for the first time. That honour belongs to a military officer; either Captain Alfred Thayer Mahan, US naval officer and public intellectual, author of several key works on naval strategy, or British General Sir Thomas Edward Gordon. In an article published in *The National Review* in 1902, Mahan suggested that Britain should take up the responsibility of securing an area that he labelled as the 'Middle East' by virtue of its strategic position on the route to the 'Far East' for the purpose of furthering its colonial interests in India and helping out with checking the Russian power in Asia (Mahan, 1902). Two years before that, writing for *The Nineteenth Century*, General Gordon had elaborated on the security of Britain's interests in India in an article entitled 'The Problem of the Middle East' (Koppes, 1976). Whether it was General Gordon or Captain Mahan, what is important for our purposes here is that the 'Middle East' was invented when thinking about securing British imperial interests in the early twentieth century.

Throughout the twentieth century, the 'Middle East' remained an object of security for external powers: initially Britain, later the United States and their local allies. Still, while the term itself became popular in the usage of British and US policy practitioners, for many decades there remained widespread confusion as to where the 'Middle East' began and ended. So much so that a well-respected scholar of the region asked 'Where is the Middle East?' (Davison, 1959). Another scholar pushed further: 'Is there a Middle East?' (Keddie, 1973). In later decades, it became customary for those discussing the affairs of this part of the world to delimit what they meant by the 'Middle East'.

That said, not all those who have addressed the question 'Is there a Middle East?' have considered it to be a purely academic question that can be pushed aside by coming up with a clear definition delineating one's research focus. For, such ostensibly depoliticised discussions on delineating 'regions', however useful they may be in identifying the 'cartographic slipperiness' (Lewis and Wigen, 1997: 71) of the Middle East, have, at the same time, distracted us from focusing on the political dynamics behind such slipperiness: the changing insecurities and shifting practices of actors – local and global. Put differently, the question 'Is there a Middle East?' cannot be answered in seminar rooms, in apparent isolation from policy debates on how to secure this part of the world. Insofar as policy-makers have constructed a 'Middle East' via their discourses of security, our task, as students of world politics, becomes one of understanding the relationship between the invention of regions and the security practices of relevant actors.

Over the years, some critics have pointed to the British colonial and US imperial interests behind lumping together this part of the world in the mind's eye and labelling it as the

'Middle East'. As will be seen later, the proponents of the 'Arab World' as a subject of security have pointed to this eventuality. Still, over the years, a significant number of local actors adopted the Middle East discourse in discussing their insecurities. Notable among them are Israel, Turkey and Saudi Arabia (and also Iran until the revolution). This, in turn, suggests a gradual aligning of some local and global actors' insecurities. Yet, some others resisted, as with the proponents of the 'Arab World' as a subject of security.

Resisting the security agenda of external actors, insisting on the 'Arab World'

The 'Arab World' is a spatial construct that inscribes the 'Arabness' of this part of the world. Inscribing the 'Arabness' of this part of the world comes across as uncontested insofar as many people in this area self-identify as 'Arab'. However, 'Arabness' is only one of the identities of people living in this part of the world. In the years that immediately followed decolonisation, it was far from being obvious that the leaders of the newly independent states would locate themselves in the 'Arab World'. Where early designations distinguished between the 'Maghreb' (the 'West') and the 'Mashreq', the 'Arab World' as a subject of security lumped together all the Arab states in the region, glossing over the ethnic, religious and socio-economic differences. As such, 'Arab World' was (re)constructed following decolonisation as a subject of security in counter-distinction to the 'Middle East'.

The emergence of the 'Arab World' as a subject of security in counter-distinction to the 'Middle East' can be traced in the foreign policy discourses of Egyptian policy-makers (Nasser, 1955). From the mid-1950s until the late 1960s, Egyptian President Gamal Abdel Nasser was the most prominent voice behind constructing the 'Arab World' as a subject of security. That said, in the early twentieth century, Egyptian identity was characterized by fluidity. During the 1920s and 1930s many Egyptian intellectuals also favoured a Mediterranean identity which they viewed as 'neither completely European or Western nor completely divorced from the Arab–Islamic world' (Salem, 1997: 38). It was only in the second half of the 1950s, when a choice was made under President Nasser to firmly locate Egypt in the 'Arab World', that Egypt's 'Arabness' came to be emphasized and the Mediterranean de-emphasized.

Indeed, global actors' insecurities shaping the 'Middle East' were questioned by none better than President Nasser when he asked, in response to US Secretary of State John Foster Dulles' invitation to join the Northern Tier scheme, designed to help contain the Soviet Union: 'How can I go to my people and tell them I am disregarding a killer with a pistol sixty miles from me at the Suez Canal to worry about someone who is holding a knife 5000 miles away?' (quoted in Brands, 1991: 277). In this question, President Nasser highlighted US and allied insecurities that shaped the Northern Tier scheme, but pointed to the fact that these insecurities did not head the Egyptian agenda. For Egypt was preoccupied with other insecurities including the Israeli treatment of Palestinian peoples that took highly militarised forms.

Still, Nasser's concerns began to take an institutionalised form only after global actors insisted on organising local actors under the umbrella of the Middle East Defence Treaty or Organisation, designed as an anti-Soviet grouping of local actors. Turkey played an active role in its formation, enlisting the participation of the Shah's Iran and the newly independent Kingdom of Iraq. The so-called Baghdad Pact was established in 1955. As Turkey's leaders pushed for Egyptian and other Arab participation, President Nasser made the case for the need to organise under the Arab League, thereby underscoring the different insecurities shaping these two spatial conceptions, the 'Middle East' versus the 'Arab World'. Where the former reflected insecurities as experienced by the US and its local allies, the latter reflected the concerns of

Egypt and its allies. Where the former focused on containing Soviet expansionism, the latter prioritised decolonisation, achieving full sovereignty and addressing the Palestinian predicament (Bilgin, 2012).

It is significant to highlight here that insecurities tied up with developing statehood were prioritised by all local actors. Yet, they differed in their responses. Turkey, Saudi Arabia and Iran framed their insecurities within the Cold War framework, identifying their enemies as 'communists' and seeking security through close alignment with the United States. They found themselves a place in the Middle Eastern fold. Egypt, on the other hand, framed its insecurities outside the Cold War framework. President Nasser was one of the leaders of the non-aligned movement that met in Bandung in 1955. When President Nasser articulated the insecurities that shaped the 'Arab World' as a subject of security, he was also resisting US pressure to join the Middle Eastern fold. Indeed, 'neither East nor West' was the guiding principle of this movement long before Iranian Ayatollah Ruhollah Khomeini turned it into a foreign policy slogan for revolutionary Iran in 1979 (Adib-Moghaddam, 2005).

President Nasser's death in 1970 marked the beginning of the decline of the 'Arab World' as a subject of security. During the early 1970s, even as it fought yet another Arab–Israeli war, Egypt no longer seemed committed to addressing Egyptian insecurities within an Arab versus non-Arab framework. That said, scholarly articulations of the 'Arab World' as a subject of security persisted through the 1980s. The most powerful of these articulations came from two Egyptian scholars, Ali Eddin Hillal Dessouki and Jamil Matar, who registered their opposition to the 'Middle East' as a subject of security when they wrote that

> (1) the term Middle East does not refer to a geographical area but rather it represents a political term in its creation and usage; (2) the term is not derived from the nature of the area or its political, cultural, civilizational and demographic characteristics; . . . (3) the term tears up the Arab homeland as a distinct unit since it has always included non-Arab states.
>
> *(Dessouki and Matar quoted in Abdel Aal, 1986: 197–8)*

As such, Dessouki and Matar identified the insecurities that shaped the construction of the 'Middle East' as a subject of security from the perspective of the US and its allies, and reclaimed the agency of local actors by offering the 'Arab regional system' as an alternative. Needless to say, this spatial construct was shaped by a state-centric conception of security and rested on the Arab/non-Arab divide, assuming insecurities to be stemming from outside the 'Arab World' thereby overlooking those that originated from within or across the inside/outside divide (Bilgin, 2012). That said, by way of critiquing the 'Middle East' as a spatial construct and as a term, Dessouki and Matar laid bare the relationship between insecurities and spatial constructs in a way that had not been done before in the literature on regional security (Bilgin, 2005).

By the end of the 1980s, the 'Arab World' no longer seemed to be considered as a subject of security by any state-level actor. Indeed, in the immediate aftermath of the Iraq war of 1990–91, the 'Arab World' seemed to be in free fall. That one Arab country (Iraq) invaded another Arab country (Kuwait) and threatened another (Saudi Arabia) was the first decisive development of this period. That Saudi Arabia asked for US help for securing the Muslim holy sites was a second. That many Arab countries joined the US-led alliance in the war against Iraq was a third decisive development that fuelled commentary regarding 'the shattered consensus' in the 'Arab World' (Said Ali, 1996; also see Karawan, 1994). Accordingly, to EU policy-makers' eyes, the circumstances seemed suitable for offering an alternative spatial construct – more aligned with EU insecurities.

The European Community/Union joins the fray: constructing the Mediterranean

The 'Euro-Mediterranean' as a subject of security has taken shape, from the 1970s onwards, through the European Community's (EC) attempts to formulate its own approach to securing this part of the world as distinct from the other global actor with interests in this part of the world, the United States. The European Community's attempt to distance itself from US-led policies toward the 'Middle East' evolved in a context where the differences between US and EC insecurities vis-à-vis this part of the world became apparent to EC leaders. The most immediate context was the 1973 OPEC oil embargo and the 1973 Arab–Israeli war and the sensibilities both events generated among the Arab and/or Muslim diaspora in EC member states. During this period, a re-thinking on the part of some EC/EU leaders led to the emergence of a more equivocal attitude toward the Arab–Israeli conflict, culminating in the establishment of the Euro-Arab dialogue in 1973 (Jawad, 1992).

The relationship between EU and the geographically close Mediterranean states was institutionalised with the so-called Euro-Mediterranean Partnership (EMP) scheme, also known as the Barcelona Process, after the Barcelona Declaration of 1995. The tripartite set-up of the Barcelona Declaration covering 'politics and security', 'economics and finance' and 'social, cultural and human affairs' revealed a prime EU concern to prevent southern problems from becoming northern problems. As such, the EMP constructed the Euro-Mediterranean as a subject of security for the European Union.

While the EMP was constructed as a partnership between the EU and the 'Mediterranean', the set-up was riddled with a tension from the very beginning. The Mediterranean was viewed by some EU actors as entering this partnership as the 'other' of the European Union. Accordingly, Mediterranean littoral EU members were written out of the 'Mediterranean' and into 'Europe', while overlapping 'European' and 'Mediterranean' identities were de-emphasised. To be fair, several enthusiastic attempts were made to construct the Mediterranean as a shared (civilisational) space (Adler et al., 2006). However, this tension was never resolved in favour of a more inclusive spatial construct (Demmelhuber, 2006; Holm, 2004; Malmvig, 2005). Put differently, the 'Euro-Mediterranean', by way of delineating 'Europe' and the 'Mediterranean' as distinct regions and/or civilisations, has served to pull further apart 'Europe' and the 'Mediterranean' while seeking to bring them closer.

Another tension within the EU's approach to the Mediterranean became apparent through the years: was the EU pursuing common security with the Mediterranean or security against the Mediterranean? The common security understanding behind the CSCE (Conference on Security and Cooperation in Europe) model was underlined by the attempts to construct the aforementioned inclusive Mediterranean 'we', that could, in turn, be the foundation of 'a Euro-Mediterranean security community' (Calleja, 1992). By then, security through non-military means (even though it was not explicitly identified as a 'security policy') had become a trademark of aspects of policy-making by the EU as a so-called 'normative power' (Manners, 2002; Adler and Crawford, 2006; compare with Bicchi, 2006), which gave it a different stance in world politics. However, by the mid-2000s, with the transition to the European Neighbourhood Policy (ENP), the EU no longer seemed to be pursuing common security (Joenniemi, 2008). The country-to-country cooperation that became the trademark of the Union for the Mediterranean (UfM) finally resolved this tension (Bicchi, 2011). By the mid-2000s, the EU was increasingly viewed as seeking to secure itself against the Mediterranean (Bilgin et al., 2011).

The point here is that, if the CSCE model did not work in the context of the Mediterranean, and the attempt to construct the 'Euro-Mediterranean' as a subject of security was not successful, this had to do not only with a southern lack of willingness over democratisation (as frequently argued) but also with EU ambivalence in its relations with the south, and indecisiveness regarding the best way to approach insecurities in this part of the world (Holm, 2004; Malmvig, 2004). There are two related points.

First, during the Cold War, the CSCE insisted on human mobility and the right to leave one's country as 'human rights'. The Euro-Mediterranean Partnership, on the other hand, denied that very right. People-to-people diplomacy and cultural exchanges were designed to keep southern peoples in the south. Whereas the CSCE sought to work with people in an attempt to influence governmental behaviour, the Euro-Mediterranean Partnership sought to work with governments to influence people's migratory behaviour. There is no mistaking the differences in the philosophical outlook of the two efforts.

Second, the CSCE rested on the assumption that peoples could work together only if the obstacles created by the governments could be overcome. A similar pattern did not emerge in north–south interactions in the Mediterranean in that in EU actors' interactions with their southern counterparts, the very identity and value system of the 'south' was often identified as a source of insecurity. It is not only the southern governments (as was the case with the eastern bloc during the Cold War) but also the southern peoples (or their 'Muslimhood') that were viewed as contributing to the tension between the two shores of the Mediterranean. In the CSCE framework, when 'western' citizens looked to their 'eastern' counterparts, they saw potential partners. Now, the northerners when they looked to the south, saw people who were impossible to co-exist with and therefore had to be kept where they were. When southerners looked to the north, in turn, they saw former colonial actors who spoke about the virtues of 'European values' while failing to uphold them when the referent of security happened to be located in the south of the Mediterranean, and not the north (Bilgin, 2016a).

The point here is that the 'Euro-Mediterranean' was constructed by the European Union as a subject of security to address its own insecurities in counter-distinction to the 'Middle East' which was viewed as prioritising the insecurities of the US and its local allies. What was not clear was how these insecurities were going to be addressed: 'with' the Mediterranean or against it? Through pursuing common security or not? Over the years, the tension built into the EMP was resolved when, in the mid-2000s, EU policy-makers dropped the CSCE model of common security. The EMP's replacement, the ENP, was launched in a political context characterised by the shortcomings of the former, a heightened sense of insecurity in the EU in relation to immigration within the context of the 'global war on terror', and the global ambitions of the Union (Bilgin et al., 2011).

Writing more than a decade ago, I concluded that, while the EU's policies toward securing the 'Euro-Mediterranean' prioritised the security interests of the EU and had very few backers in the 'Middle East', it did not have many enemies either; and that this might eventually turn out to be its greatest strength, especially if the EU policy of actively engaging with civil societal actors on its side were to bear fruit in the long run (Bilgin, 2005). This is no longer the case. Indeed not even the European Union seems to be interested in the 'Euro-Mediterranean' as a subject of security. While it is the European Neighbourhood Policy that is often blamed for this eventuality, arguably it is the European Union's externalisation of its security practices (Wolff, 2006) and state-to-state cooperation across the Mediterranean, which involved close collaboration with some of the most authoritarian regimes of the region, that brought the demise of the Mediterranean perspective. Owing to this latter kind of cooperation, northern partners are viewed as having made use of the weaknesses of their southern partners to the detriment of individual citizens on both sides (as well as citizens of third countries who are in transit to the north) (Bilgin et al., 2011).

Needless to say, it is not only EU actors whose practices deserve scrutiny. During the 2000s, with unfolding security cooperation between some EU member states and their Mediterranean counterparts, some authoritarian regimes assumed the role of enforcers of EU anti-terrorism policies vis-à-vis their own citizens and immigrants in transit to the EU. Some authoritarian Mediterranean leaders (not all of whom survived the Arab Spring) also made use of the context of the 'global war on terror' to pursue their own security agendas at the expense of their citizens' security (Bilgin, 2016b).

Finally, NATO also came to assume an evolving role in the Mediterranean following the Cold War. NATO had a 'southern flank' approach to this part of the world throughout the Cold War, focusing mostly on the threat of Soviet expansionism. Since the fall of the Berlin Wall but especially since the dissolution of the Soviet Union, NATO has come to be interested in a wider variety of military and non-military threats emanating from parts of the world that, in an earlier era, would have been considered as 'out of area'. As a collective defence organisation, NATO is designed to address threats directed against its members. Re-definition of NATO as a security community in the post-Cold War era also meant seeking to address insecurities that are not directly threatening the security of members but generating insecurities for security in Europe, as defined by NATO. NATO-led interventions in Kosovo and Libya were undertaken within this evolving context (on NATO as a security community see Williams and Neumann, 2000). That the Libya intervention was endorsed by the Arab League crystallises not only the evolving role of NATO in the Mediterranean but also the decline of the 'Arab World' as a spatial construct shaping (and being shaped by) the insecurities of self-identified Arab actors. In contrast, the African Union resisted giving its stamp of approval to the NATO-led intervention, underscoring the different insecurities of its members as shaped around concerns with external interventionism (Grovogui, 2011).

Thus, by the mid-2000s the 'Euro-Mediterranean', as a spatial construct and a potential security community, was in decline. At the high-time of the Euro-Mediterranean Partnership, the European Union contributed significantly to the strengthening of civil society in the south of the Mediterranean, reviving civil societal activism and empowering a variety of civil-minded actors (Aubarell et al., 2006; Bayoumi, 2007; Kandil, 2011). Yet, by the end of the 2000s, the significance of European Union good deeds had diminished through its allying with repressive regimes of the south as part of the north's externalisation policies (Bilgin et al., 2011).

Arguably, while EU practices have not been successful in constructing the 'Euro-Mediterranean' as a subject of security, they may have, albeit unintentionally, contributed to the persistence of the 'Arab World' among non-state actors, but in a different way. As noted above, the EU has significantly contributed to civil society activism across the Arab World. However, during the 2000s the EU increasingly cooperated with authoritarian regimes through its externalisation practices while at the same time allowing state-to-state north–south cooperation, utilising the failures of southern partners in the process. Still, as the European Union lost its appeal as a champion of civil society activism, Arab civil societal actors have increasingly turned to each other for solidarity and collaboration. Since the decline of the Euro-Mediterranean Partnership, civil societal activism is reported to have further increased in the Arab world, with actors focusing on political reform, democracy, freedom and human rights (Kandil, 2011: 43).

Conclusion

Now that the EU's rival spatial construct, the 'Euro-Mediterranean' has declined and the 'Arab World' has no state-level backers, does this mean that the 'Middle East' as a subject of security remains unrivalled? Given the upheavals that have characterised this part of the world since the

US-led war on Iraq in 2003, no analyst that pays attention to politics below the state level can comfortably reach this conclusion. While state-to-state level interactions point to the 'Middle East' as the subject of security for most Arab states, and many EU members as well as Turkey and Israel align themselves closely with the United States, non-state actors are increasingly voicing their opposition to the practices adopted by their own regimes as warranted by their superpower ally's 'war against terrorism'. Writing in 2005, one author pointed to the decline of US 'soft power' in the 'Middle East' (Aysha, 2005) insofar as regional regimes were increasingly facing protests from their own citizens regarding their cooperation with the United States. Put differently, since 2003, if not before, the 'Middle East' as a subject of security has been in decline as viewed through the prism of non-state actors in this part of the world (Fattah and Fierke, 2009).

Furthermore, the Arab uprisings have been a serious source of inter-state tension for the 'Middle East' as a spatial construct (Korany, 2011). Until the uprisings, Egypt was a linchpin of policies designed to secure the 'Middle East', and received a significant amount of US aid. In the aftermath of the removal of Muslim Brotherhood from power, Saudi Arabia stepped in to support the new regime in Egypt, thereby sustaining its stability-focused security policies in the Middle East. Yet, throughout the Arab uprisings, Saudi policy-makers were critical of their US allies for failing to take the lead in maintaining 'regional stability'. In particular, they were worried that the 'United States is more concerned about being on the right side of history, instead of standing by its friends and working to advance stability in the region' (Boucek, 2011). In other words, since the Arab uprisings, Saudi leadership has been critical of their US counterparts for not fulfilling the precepts of their own regional security perspective: states, regimes and their stability come first, peoples can wait. The rift between the two major actors, the United States and Saudi Arabia, and what they decide to do about this rift, is likely to shape insecurities in the 'Middle East' in the foreseeable future.

To conclude, considering the insecurities that shape the construction of regions, and practices that were shaped in line with these spatial constructs, is no mere academic task. Highlighting the insecurities shaping the 'Middle East' or the 'Euro-Mediterranean' is not to pose 'artificial' versus 'natural' regions. For all spatial constructs (we call them regions) are 'artificial'. As discussed earlier, the 'Arab World' is no more 'natural' as a subject of security than the 'Euro-Mediterranean'. It is only through becoming aware of the insecurities shaping particular spatial constructs that one can identify different insecurities, our own culpability in the re-inscription of our differences and construction of insecurities, and recognise the potential for adopting common security approaches. Contra popular representations of the 'Middle East' as an 'artificial' region, its failures are rooted in the top-down ordering of the insecurities of superpowers and their regional allies while marginalising insecurities voiced by non-state actors.

References

Abdel Aal, A. M. S. A. 1986. The Superpowers and Regional Security in the Middle East. In: Ayoob, M. (ed.) *Regional Security in the Third World: Case Studies from Southeast Asia and the Middle East*. London: Croom Helm.

Adib-Moghaddam, A. 2005. Islamic Utopian Romanticism and the Foreign Policy Culture of Iran. *Critique: Critical Middle Eastern Studies*, 14, 265–92.

Adler, E. and Crawford, B. 2006. Normative Power: The European Practice of Region Building and the Case of the Euro-Mediterranean Partnership. In: Adler, E., Bicchi, F., Crawford, B. and Del Sarto, R. (eds), *The Convergence of Civilizations: Constructing a Mediterranean Region*. Toronto: University of Toronto Press.

Adler, E., Bicchi, F., Crawford, B. and Del Sarto, R. (eds) 2006. *The Convergence of Civilizations: Constructing a Mediterranean Region*. Toronto: University of Toronto Press.

Aubarell, G., Olivan, H. and Rovira, M. 2006. *The Barcelona Process Ten Years On. An Assessment from the Point of View of Civil Society*. IEMed: CIDOB.

Aysha, E. E.-D. 2005. September 11 and the Middle East Failure of US 'Soft Power': Globalisation contra Americanisation in the 'New' US Century. *International Relations*, 19, 193–210.

Bayoumi, S. 2007. Egyptian Views of the EU: Pragmatic, Paternalistic and Partnership Concerns. *European Foreign Affairs Review*, 12, 331–47.

Bicchi, F. 2006. 'Our Size Fits All': Normative Power Europe and the Mediterranean. *Journal of European Public Policy*, 13, 286–303.

Bicchi, F. 2011. The Union for the Mediterranean, or the Changing Context of Euro-Mediterranean Relations. *Mediterranean Politics*, 16, 3–19.

Bilgin, P. 2004. Whose Middle East? Geopolitical Inventions and Practices of Security. *International Relations*, 18, 17–33.

Bilgin, P. 2005. *Regional Security in the Middle East: A Critical Perspective*. London: Routledge Curzon.

Bilgin, P. 2012. Security in the Arab World and Turkey: Differently Different. In: Tickner, A. and Blaney, D. (eds), *Thinking International Relations Differently*. London: Routledge.

Bilgin, P. 2016a. How Not to Think about the Mediterranean Refugee Crisis. Center for Contemporary Middle East Studies, SDU, News Analysis [Available online at http://www.sdu.dk/-/media/files/om_sdu/centre/c_mellemoest/videncenter/artikler/2016/bilgin+article+(feb+16).pdf?la=en].

Bilgin, P. 2016b. Temporalizing Security: Securing the Citizen, Insecuring the Immigrant in the Mediterranean. In: Agathangelou, A. M. and Killian, K. D. (eds), *Time, Temporality and Violence in International Relations: (De)Fatalizing the Present, Forging Radical Alternatives*. London: Routledge.

Bilgin, P., Lecha, E. S. and Bilgic, A. 2011. *European Security Practices vis-à-vis the Mediterranean: Implications in Value Terms*. Copenhagen: Danish Institute for International Studies.

Boucek, C. 2011. US–Saudi Relations in the Shadow of the Arab Spring. Online article. [Available online at http://carnegieendowment.org/2011/06/21/u.s.-saudi-relations-in-shadow-of-arab-spring/1il Accessed 20 May 2014].

Brands, H. W. 1991. *Inside the Cold War: Loy Henderson and the Rise of the American Empire, 1918–1961*. New York: Oxford University Press.

Calleja, J. 1992. Security and Cooperation in the Mediterranean. *International Journal on World Peace*, 9, 17–29.

Davison, R. H. 1959. Where is the Middle East? *Foreign Affairs*, 38, 665–75.

Demmelhuber, T. 2006. The Euro-Mediterranean Space as an Imagined (Geo-)Political, Economic and Cultural Entity. ZEI Discussion Paper C 159. [Available online at https://www.zei.uni-bonn.de/dateien/discussion-paper/dp_c159demmelhuber.pdf].

Fattah, K. and Fierke, K. M. 2009. A Clash of Emotions: The Politics of Humiliation and Political Violence in the Middle East. *European Journal of International Relations*, 15, 67–93.

Grovogui, S. N. 2011. Looking beyond Spring for the Season: An African Perspective on the World Order after the Arab Revolt. *Globalizations*, 8, 567–72.

Hentsch, T. 1992. *Imagining the Middle East*. Montréal and New York: Black Rose Books.

Holm, U. 2004. The EU's Security Policy towards the Mediterranean: An (Im)possible Combination of Export of European Political Values and Anti-Terror Measures? DIIS Working Paper 2004/13 [Available online at https://www.files.ethz.ch/isn/18446/EU_Security_Policy_Mediterranean.pdf].

Jawad, H. 1992. *The Euro-Arab Dialogue: A Study in Collective Diplomacy*. Reading: Ithaca Press.

Joenniemi, P. 2008. Re-negotiating Europe's Identity: The European Neighbourhood Policy as a Form of Differentiation. *Journal of Borderlands Studies*, 23, 83–94.

Kandil, A. 2011. An Attempt to Evaluate the Development of Arab Civil Society. In: Korany, B. (ed.) *The Changing Middle East: A New Look at Regional Dynamics*. Cairo: The American University in Cairo Press.

Karawan, I. 1994. Arab Dilemmas in the 1990s: Breaking Taboos and Searching for Signposts. *The Middle East Journal*, 48, 433–54.

Keddie, N. R. 1973. Is there a Middle East? *International Journal of Middle East Studies*, 4, 255–71.

Koppes, C. R. 1976. Captain Mahan, General Gordon, and the Origins of the Term 'Middle East'. *Middle Eastern Studies*, 12, 95–8.

Korany, B. 2011. Looking at the Middle East Differently: An Alternative Conceptual Lens. In: Korany, B. (ed.) *The Changing Middle East: A New Look at Regional Dynamics*. Cairo: The American University in Cairo Press.

Lewis, M. W. and Wigen, K. 1997. *The Myth of Continents: A Critique of Metageography*. Berkeley: University of California Press.

Mahan, A. T. 1902. The Persian Gulf and International Relations. *The National Review*, September, 38–9.

Malmvig, H. 2004. Cooperation or Democratisation? The EU's Conflicting Mediterranean Security Discourses. Danish Institute for International Studies (DIIS) Working Paper 2004/8 [Available online at http://pure.diis.dk/ws/files/55832/WP_2004_8_Final.pdf].

Malmvig, H. 2005. Security through Intercultural Dialogue? Implications of the Securitization of Euro-Mediterranean Dialogue between Cultures. *Mediterranean Politics*, 10, 349–64.

Manners, I. 2002. Normative Power Europe: A Contradiction in Terms? *Journal of Common Market Studies*, 40, 235–58.

Moulakis, A. 2005. The Mediterranean Region: Reality, Delusion or Euro-Mediterranean Project? *Mediterranean Quarterly*, 16, 11–38.

Nasser, G. A. 1955. The Egyptian Revolution. *Foreign Affairs*, 32, 199–211.

Said Ali, A. M. 1996. The Shattered Consensus? Arab Perceptions of Security. *International Spectator*, 31, 23–52.

Salem, P. 1997. Arab Political Currents, Arab–European Relations and Mediterraneanism. In: Guazzone, L. (ed.) *The Middle East in Global Change: The Politics and Economics of Interdependence versus Fragmentation*. London: Macmillan.

Williams, M. C. and Neumann, I. B. 2000. From Alliance to Security Community: NATO, Russia, and the Power of Identity. *Millennium Journal of International Studies*, 29, 357–87.

Wolff, S. 2006. The Externalization of Justice and Home Affairs to the Southern Neighbours: The EU's Dilemmas in the Fight against Terrorism. EuroMesCo 2006 Annual Conference. Istanbul.

6

FROM IMPERIALISM TO FAILED LIBERAL PEACE

How Europe contributed to MENA's failing states system and how MENA blowback threatens Europe

Raymond Hinnebusch

The Middle East and North Africa (MENA) area was profoundly reshaped under European imperialism, especially by the "peace to end all peace" (Fromkin 1989) imposed after WWI. The Euro-Mediterranean Partnership was designed to deal with the long-term consequence: a dysfunctional regional states system whose instabilities were always liable to spill across to the north of the Mediterranean. The partnership would establish a liberal peace on Europe's Mediterranean borders via the export of economic and political reform, via soft rather than hard power, through the spread of norms by example, quite different from the failed US attempt at military hegemony, epitomized by the 2003 invasion of Iraq.

Conceptual framing: liberalism vs. structuralism, soft vs. hard power

The EU relation to MENA allows testing of rival IR paradigms' understanding of core–periphery relations. In the liberal paradigm, EU–MENA relations can be interpreted as an attempt to use soft power to export a liberal peace through norm diffusion mechanisms such as linkage and leverage (Levitsky and Way 2005) and norm cascading (Finnamore and Sikkink 1998) that produces a benign win–win situation for both. The opposite structuralist paradigm, including neo-Gramscianism (Cox 1996) and world systems theory (Arrighi and Silver 2001), sees norm export as an instrument of the global hegemon's attempt to establish the dominance over the periphery of the world capitalist core's finance capital. The equivalent of soft power in this paradigm, ideological hegemony, is merely the ideational superstructure of hard power, rooted in economic dominance, and backed up by military intervention where needed. It is moreover, part of what Clark (2001) depicted as an attempt to reverse the power diffusion from the spread of sovereignty to the periphery under de-colonialization so that, rather than a win–win outcome, various forms of resistance in the periphery may lead to "imperial overstretch" (Burbach and Tarbell 2004; Marshall 2016) in which the core incurs high costs, including "blowback" on itself of the turbulence in the periphery that it precipitates (Johnson 2004). Moreover, contradictions between the use of hard and soft power, and in the norms exported, for example between neo-liberalism and democracy, may debilitate the core's drive into the periphery. Europe fits into this paradigm if one envisions a "collective hegemon," led by the US, but partnered with Europe, in which a certain division of labor is agreed in MENA, with the US specializing in hard power and the EU in soft power.

Indeed, this chapter will show that despite Europe's benign self-image, the distinction between the European and American projects was only ever one of degree. The asymmetric hub-and-spokes relations created by the Euro-Med project reproduced the power imbalance between core and periphery and served European interests first, much as structuralist approaches expect. The thrust of the Euro-Med partnership, namely the parallel export of neo-liberalism (with its associated inequalities) and the attempted export of "democracy," helped to precipitate the Arab Uprising. This "imperial overstretch" resulted in the spread of both failed and more repressive states, rather than a liberal peace, and led to a spillover (blowback) of the consequences—mass migration and terrorism—across European borders that threaten the very survival of the EU. What went wrong?

From European imperialism to Euro-Mediterranean Partnership

The heritage of European imperialism

If the Middle East's dysfunctions now afflict Europe, the origins of those dysfunctions go back to the profound reshaping of the region under the impact of European imperialism. Arbitrary boundary drawing by Britain and France permanently fragmented the region into a multitude of weak and insecure states, grossly violating regional identity, generating several enduring border conflicts and stateless peoples, sources of ongoing irredentism. Israel, a colonial settler state established under British auspices at the expense of indigenous people, was bound to be rejected; yet its unmatched network of strategic depth in the west made it the dominant regional military power. The region was incorporated into a global economic division of labor, as the break up of the large Ottoman market severed regional interdependencies, whilst its economic links were reoriented to the imperial core(s). The concentration of much of MENA's enormous oil wealth in tiny Western client states ensured those countries exported capital surpluses to the west while larger MENA states with the land and labour potential for diversified economies lacked capital.

The western powers faced nationalist resistance from the outset, but did not depart without a struggle. In the Suez war of 1956 Britain and France, together with Israel, attacked Nasserite Egypt; the standard-bearer of Arab nationalism that had led resistance to the west's attempt, under the Baghdad Pact, to sustain control of the region. But the war so aroused nationalism that it led, instead, to Europe's political recession from the region, ultimately culminating in Britain's 1974 military withdrawal from the Gulf. This left, from the viewpoint of the west, a "vacuum" which the US gradually began to fill.

The Euro-Mediterranean Partnership (EMP)

While withdrawing militarily from the region, European states, notably France and Britain, retained interests there and Europe as a whole was affected by growing interdependencies with MENA and needed, therefore, to remain engaged with it. The 1970s Euro-Arab Dialogue was a response to the oil crisis that threatened European economies and which several European states sought to alleviate through arms for oil trade. Energy security continued central to European relations with MENA: in 1995 of the 9.6 million barrels per day (bpd) of oil imported by Europe 5.5 bpd (57%) came from MENA (Marr 1998; Hollis 1997; Holden 2010).

Geographical proximity exposed Europe to flows of migrants from its southern Mediterranean neighborhood, thought likely to greatly increase if growing youth unemployment in the region was not addressed through economic development. In 2016 about 13 million foreign-born immigrants and over 20 million Muslims in total lived in Europe and made up 4 to 5 percent of its total population (Hackett 2016), and the EU sought to secure the cooperation of MENA governments in containing such flows. In the mid-1990s there was alarm at the anti-westernism aroused in the south of the Mediterranean but also among European Muslims by the 1990 Gulf war. The Algerian civil war precipitated European fears of a spillover of instability to the north: failed states, stagnant economies and civil wars were seen as a source of refugee flows, drug trafficking, and terrorism. As the EU gradually came into being as a collective actor with its own identity, it became ambitious to reassert Europe's influence over its MENA near neighborhood, both to enhance its economic advantages in the area against competitors, and to stabilize the region by projecting the "normative" power of a liberal peace (Tonra and Cavatorta 2007; Youngs 2004).

The centerpiece of Europe's effort was the Euro-Mediterranean Partnership (EMP), launched by the 1995 Barcelona Declaration between Europe and southern Mediterranean states, with the avowed aim of transforming the Mediterranean region into an area of shared prosperity, and hence stability. The heart of the scheme was a cross-regional free-trade zone that, in the EU's liberal paradigm, was expected to generate prosperity that would dilute radicalism and conflict. Security challenges emanating from the southern Mediterranean were seen as deriving from economic and political failures in MENA that could be pre-empted through socio-economic reforms launched in cooperation with MENA countries (Youngs 2003). It was also expected that economic and political liberalization would foster each other and the scheme, at least nominally, made aid and trade conditional on political reform.

The internal contradictions of the EMP

While the EMP was supposed to generate prosperity in the partner nations, in the immediate term, it actually worsened the conditions of trade for MENA (Joffe 1998: 66–8). Europe's trade agreements with MENA states in the pre-neo-liberal 1970s had granted them preferential access to European markets for some of their industrial and agricultural products (Salame 1998: 35), and MENA states were allowed, reflective of their lower levels of development, to protect their own industries. The EMP agreements not only required the opening of MENA markets to European industrial exports (and those of Europe-based US multinationals) but also committed MENA countries to the global trade regime, for example on services and protection of intellectual property rights, that favors the north. The only improvement for MENA was slightly increased EU quotas for its agricultural exports (Miller and Mishraf 2005; Marks 1998; Parfitt 1997; Nienhaus, 1999).

The EMP gave MENA partner countries 12 years to dismantle their tariffs and accorded them financial aid to upgrade their industries so they could compete on the wider market and also to ease the balance of payment deficit that was expected in the transition period when European exports to the region would be more competitive than indigenous production. The MENA economic takeoff would, it was argued, be facilitated by forcing its industries, through tariff reductions and technical assistance, to move from import substitution industrialization (ISI) to export strategies. Privatization of state owned industries was also encouraged. Both the requirement that MENA states increase administrative transparency and an investor-friendly regulatory framework were expected to encourage investment in the region. Nevertheless, the elimination of tariffs and barriers for EU industrial exports damaged MENA small and medium-sized businesses (60% of Morocco's and 30% of Tunisia's industries were not expected to withstand European competition) (Schumacher 2004). MENA exports to the EU did increase but Europe's exports to the region grew faster, at an annual average of 8 percent since the mid-1990s (Schumacher 2010); the EU ran a trade surplus with its southern partners in the years after 2000. As for investment, the EMP was expected to divert it to the EU since under the hub-and-spokes arrangement, investors in the EU hub now got access to MENA partners too (the spokes), while investing in the spokes would not give access to other spokes in the absence of a MENA free-trade zone, which the hub-and-spokes system discouraged. In practice, North Africa and the Gulf region together accounted for only 3 percent of European foreign direct investment (FDI) outside the EU in 2003–8 (Schumacher 2010: 13). In the first decade of the EMP, 1994–2005, the average income of the south as a percentage of the north *declined* slightly to 18.1 percent. As Joffe (1998: 66–8) observed, no economy has ever developed under the economic openness the EMP mandated.

Rather, its actual effect was to generate crony capitalism. Regimes used neo-liberal discourse and pressures from the EU and international financial institutions (IFIs) to legitimize privatization and structural adjustment as the inevitable responses to the demands of globalization. Privatizations of public sectors were used to legitimize appropriation of public assets by ruling elites and their families and cronies, thereby turning public monopolies into private ones. Tellingly, IFIs held up as models of good governance Egypt and Tunisia, where the cronies of Gamal Mubarak and the Ben Ali family took advantage of their pressures for privatization to turn public sector assets into private monopolies.

For Dostal (2009), the underlying problem of the Euro-Mediterranean project was the EU's post-Cold War adoption and export of neo-liberal ideology, with its stress on a market that favours corporations at the expense of the European Social Charter; this was a reflection, Grahl (2004) argued, of the dominance of business interests over the EU that was naturally replicated in EU external policy toward MENA. Arguably the EMP was an instrument through which Europe was acting, together with the US and IFIs, as part of a "collective hegemon," deploying a combination of incentives and pressures to force MENA states to open their economies to western capitalist penetration, and to extend the structural power of core capital over the periphery (Holden 2010: 15; Cavatorta and Durac 2010: 8).

MENA's acceptance of this suboptimal outcome reflected the process by which the partnership was constructed: the EU negotiated agreements individually with each southern partner rather than collectively (and separately from the Gulf countries, with their greater bargaining leverage). This reflected the fragmentation of MENA countries which, producing similar low-value-added products, saw each other as competitors and sought privileged individual bargains with the EU. As in other prisoner's dilemma games, all got worse deals than had they acted together. The effect of the EMP was therefore to reconstruct and institutionalize an economic regime reflective of the dominance of the world economic core and the dependence of the periphery.

This economic trajectory ensured that there would be a sharp disconnect between the rhetoric and reality of political reform. Hyde-Price (2006) argues that the EU operates as a realist actor, promoting its interests irrespective of the values it espouses in principle; hence, primacy is given to the economic side of partnership agreements while democratization and human rights are neglected. Indeed, the neo-liberal generation of crony capitalism in MENA had generated *less* inclusionary authoritarian regimes: ruling coalitions were restructured, with older populist (labor and peasant) constituencies marginalized. Democratization was deterred because the masses that pay the cost of neo-liberal policies could be empowered by it, possibly bringing Islamist governments to power (Guazzone and Pioppi 2009). Authoritarian regimes were needed to implement free-trade agreements and other neo-liberal policies against the resistance of MENA populations (Tonra and Cavatorta 2007; Cavatorta and Durac 2010: 7–8; Kienle 1998). And, Teti (2012) argues, the democratization ostensibly urged by the west was of the "thin" variety compatible with neo-liberal globalization—which had limited regional appeal—while Islamic versions and re-distributory forms of governance were discouraged.

The Atlantic partnership debilitates the Mediterranean partnership

If the economic provisions of the Mediterranean partnership explain part of what went wrong, the partnership was also spoiled at the political level by Europe's increasing complicity in US policy in MENA. In spite of the European origins of many of the current problems of the Middle East, regional opinion had seen Europe as benign compared to the US. However, the EU's regional image declined as its policies converged with those of the US.

As Europe's dominance of the region ended, the US increased its military presence, relying considerably on hard power against hostile states such as Libya under Qaddafi and Iraq under Saddam Hussein. Europe, although much more dependent than the US on MENA for trade and energy, relied on America's military power to provide regional security and protection of oil supply routes (Marr 1998). Yet the MENA policies of the US, specifically its bias toward Israel and its military interventionism, antagonized the region and stimulated or exacerbated the periodic regional crises from which Washington then claimed to protect its allies. Europe was seemingly "caught," according to Salame (1998), between MENA and the US. For example, the success of political cooperation among the Euro-Mediterranean Partnership countries was predicated on the resolution of the Arab–Israeli conflict—which was expected in the wake of the Oslo Accord; but the failure of the peace process blocked such cooperation (Aliboni 2010). There was widespread frustration in the Arab world that the EU could not balance the pro-Israeli bias in Washington that allowed Israel to evade a land-for-peace settlement. Another key episode was the 2003 US-mounted regime change in Iraq, in the face of opposition in much of Europe that, in destabilizing the region, inflicted high costs on Europe. And what made Europe's alignment with the US dangerous at home was America's unpopularity with some 12 million European Muslims. However, Europe lacked the cohesion to be a unified actor capable of tempering US policies, as was brutally exposed by its division over the 2003 Iraq war which made a shambles of Europe's common foreign and defense policy; on the contrary, Europe became ever more implicated in US MENA policy, with important consequences for European priorities toward MENA.

As a consequence of the blowback from US policy, democratization as an EU priority was increasingly eclipsed by security concerns, which led European states, particularly Britain and France, to sustain close alignments with pro-western authoritarian states, notably Egypt because of its peace with Israel and its self-representation as a bulwark against Islamic radicalism. After 9/11 and the bombings in London and Madrid, the stress shifted further toward security cooperation with southern Mediterranean regimes against the common "terrorist" threats from radical Islamists, despite rhetorical insistence that political reform was needed to attack the roots of terrorism (Seeberg 2010: 299–300; Hollis 2012). EU democracy promotion was seen in the Mediterranean south as a rhetorical tool selectively applied against regimes that defied the west: thus, rigged elections were accepted in Egypt and Algeria and condemned in Iran and a fair election in the Palestinian territories was rejected because it brought Islamists to power. This was widely seen as reflecting a preferential treatment of regimes that were friendly with the US and Israel or in which Europe had oil interests (Idriss 2010). Moreover, Europe was drawn, through its membership in NATO into American occupation regimes in Iraq and Afghanistan and enlisted in the US war on terror. Europe's remaining "soft power" appeared at risk owing to its involvement in what was seen as a war on Islam in Middle East public opinion. Generally, a dynamic was created wherein blowback resulting from US-led interventionism in MENA drove the US and Europe closer together over the resulting threats of terrorism (Schumacher 2010). Far from becoming more critical of the costs of US policy, Britain and France's 2011 intervention in Libya seemed to express a desire to imitate American-style regime change via hard power (air bombing at little risk of casualties for their own forces but substantial "collateral damage" in the target society).

Europe and the Arab Uprising

The Euro-Mediterranean Partnership was supposed to have helped prevent the instability in MENA's neighborhood that erupted with the Arab Uprising. But Europe bore some responsibility for encouraging the Uprising and its post-Uprising policies proved ineffective in containing its fallout. What might be called the EU's post-sovereignty outlook had a role in provoking the Uprising, while the destabilizing consequences of the Uprising has propelled a European move away from this outlook.

The European role in the Arab Uprising

In certain indirect ways, Europe, together with the US, played a role in encouraging the Arab Uprising. In spite of European security alignments with some of the region's authoritarian governments and the EU's actually very tepid push for democratization (as compared to their more robust insistence on economic neo-liberalism), the post-sovereignty discourse coming out of Europe, encouraged by the EU's own apparently successful move beyond sovereignty, greatly underestimated and devalued the indispensable role of states in a globalized world, even non-democratic ones, and lacked sufficient appreciation of the costs of state failure.

At both official and NGO levels the *rhetoric* of democracy promotion was unrelenting. Transnational advocacy networks for human rights proliferated in the Euro-Mediterranean area over the two decades of the EMP (Feliu 2005). Activists trained by US and EU government funded democracy promotion campaigns and western NGOs helped prepare the climate for the Arab Uprising. Although originating in America, the so-called non-violent resistance paradigm, popularized by Gene Sharp (Arrow 2011) publicized the techniques by which activists could use non-violent protest to provoke the collapse of authoritarian regimes; it played some role in inspiring the techniques of the Arab Uprising. Also, Europe, inspired by its own move away from national sovereignties, was in the vanguard of the normative shift away from an "international society" based on sovereign equal states to one wherein sovereignty was made conditional on "good governance" and on states' fulfilment of their "responsibility to protect," with human rights violations justifying intervention—all as judged and implemented by the western great powers. The "responsibility to protect," (R2P) doctrine conveyed the misapprehension to dissident activists in MENA that the west would be obliged to intervene should repression exceed certain limits and the Libyan intervention reinforced this illusion. These post-sovereignty discourses were spread within MENA civil societies via Internet technology, which played a key role in encouraging the middle class anti-regime political mobilization that spearheaded the Arab Uprisings. Thus, even as the neo-liberalism promoted by the west reduced MENA authoritarian states' ability to satisfy the welfare of mass publics and widened inequalities inside MENA societies, the parallel democratization and post-sovereignty discourses helped de-legitimize their authoritarian governance among many citizens. The immediate consequence of the contradiction between the neo-liberal economics and democratization sides of the Euro-Mediterranean Partnership produced the exact opposite of what the EMP ostensibly intended—the widespread de-stabilization of the MENA regional states system.

European policy toward the uprising states was quite inconsistent from the point of view of the values Europe claimed to promote (democracy, responsibility to protect), but perfectly understandable as a reflection of geopolitical interests. Thus, in pro-western Egypt and Tunisia European governments only abandoned presidents when it was clear they were on the way out and in Bahrain, they remained silent on the Saudi/Khalifa repression of protestors. By contrast, traditionally anti-western Libya, where the Qaddafi regime had no allies to protect it, was the target of military intervention while anti-western Syria, which did have powerful allies, was targeted with economic sanctions (Held and Ulrichsen 2014).

Libya. The Libyan intervention exposed cleavages within the EU as Britain and France ignored the objections of Germany and of Italy, which had seen Qaddafi as key to controlling migration. The rapid mission change from humanitarian protection of civilians to regime change, along with the rebuffing of the attempted African Union mediated political settlement, exposed the motives of London and Paris: the desire to empower friendly clients who would grant oil or reconstruction contracts. The 3,000 sorties flown by European states in Libya cost millions of euros but resulted in a failed state that gave jihadist al-Qaida avatars fertile ground to establish themselves in North Africa. The spillover of the crisis in Mali soon drew France into a policing operation from which it could not easily find an exit and which made it a target for terrorism. The Libyan civil war unleashed a massive migrant flow, but although Tunisia and Egypt opened their borders to some half a million refugees, the 45,000 headed for Europe precipitated attempts to stop the flow (Koser 2012); Italy and Malta, which had opposed the intervention, bore the costs for the ambitions of London and Paris. Libya had been a bulwark against immigration from Africa and had provided work opportunities that dried up after Qaddafi, diverting work seekers to Europe (BBC 2015). Finally, the intervention ruined the international climate for R2P since the western misuse of the UN humanitarian resolution that Russia and China had acquiesced in, to serve geopolitical interests, alienated these great powers, who had a strong interest in defending the norm of sovereignty against western expansion in MENA at the expense of the multi-polar world order they sought.

Syria. The Syrian Uprising began as a mobilization of protestors against a repressive authoritarian regime. The west's discourse of democratization (and financial support for dissidents) had helped generate exile groups that, at an early stage, promoted the uprising. Moreover, the possibility of external military intervention shaped both opposition and regime strategies as protests turned into an uprising: the discourse of humanitarian intervention encouraged the opposition to think that the regime could not bring the full force of its repressive capabilities against protestors without provoking foreign intervention, an expectation that kept alive both their resistance and their unwillingness to compromise. External activists told those on the ground, pointing to the Libya no-fly zone, that "the international community won't sit and watch you be killed" (Seelye 2011). This encouraged Syrians to risk their lives and to eschew the compromise with the regime needed for a pacted transition. The Libyan intervention gave further momentum to the revolt. The regime, for its part, accelerated its repression in the hope of denying the opposition control over parts of Syrian territory that could be used, as in Libya, as a staging ground for outside intervention.

The EU's response to regime repression was to slap sanctions on Syria, ostensibly to deter the regime from further repression, but which actually made things worse for Syrians. Western sanctions on Syria's oil sales helped debilitate the regime's capacity to fund state institutions and to maintain its control over wide swaths of the country but did not similarly debilitate the regime, per se, which found alternative funding sources, for example in Iran.

At the same time, as the west raised the discourse of the international criminal court, regime elites realized that, their bridges burned, there was no way back: they would have to stick together and do whatever it took to win. In parallel, Russia and China, antagonized by the west's use of a UN humanitarian resolution to promote regime change in Libya moved to protect Syria from a similar scenario. While the west in consequence proved unwilling to directly intervene militarily to end the war on western terms (exit of Asad), the US, with support from Britain and France continued to insist that Asad had to go and either directly or via the Gulf monarchies, provided large amounts of game-changing weaponry, notably anti-tank weapons, much of which was transferred to militant Islamist groups. They seized control of significant parts of Syrian territory and prevented the regime from recovering territorial control; the stalemate and failed state thus produced would otherwise have been quite unlikely.

This vacuum was soon filled by the Islamic State (IS) that incorporated territory from two states, Syria and Iraq, whose governments the western powers had directly or indirectly debilitated. Islamic State soon became a magnet for European Muslims who travelled to Syria to join jihadist groups fighting Asad. Ironically, this led the Syrian government's UN delegate to accuse the west of exporting terrorists to Syria.

> It's hard to believe that a terrorist who leaves Paris, London, Brussels . . . and arrives in Syria without a visa, without a passport, through dozens of states and the Turkish–Syrian border, has done so without intelligence services overseeing these operations.
>
> *(Bashar Ja'afari)*[1]

The well-grounded fear in European capitals was that their radicalized citizens would return home to carry out terrorist attacks at the bidding of IS and this fear was soon realized in Paris and Brussels. In parallel, a massive flow of Syrian refugees began to swamp Europe's borders.

Europe was split on how to respond to the Syrian crisis: while Germany and most other Europeans countries stressed the need to work with Russia to promote a political solution, London and Paris held to their demands for Asad to go; without having any means to effect such an exit, their stance only encouraged continued intransigence and stalemate in Syria. Given that they carried far less of the Syrian refugee burden than other European states, especially Greece and Germany, not to mention the fact that these two ex-imperial powers bear heavy responsibility for the initial creation of a dysfunctional Levant—their stand was bound to damage European unity.

European policy toward the post-Uprising crisis

The EU promised a major rethink of its policies toward MENA after the Uprising exposed their flaws. Past support for authoritarian regimes was acknowledged to have been a mistake and henceforth the "3Ms"—money, market access, and mobility for MENA states—were to be conditional on their movement toward democratization. In practice, this was overtaken by events such as the failure of Egypt's democratic transition. Little conditionality was enforced and, as a result of Europe's economic recession, little funding provided to assist democratization. More than this, western dominated IFIs set out to use the economic crisis in MENA countries such as Egypt, to reinforce demands for austerity, thereby undermining the conditions for democratization and, indeed, stability in the Mediterranean south. The EU had no alternative approach except more of the same combination of neo-liberal economics and exhortation of political democratization that had helped de-stabilize MENA in the first place (Teti 2012: Isaac 2012; Balfour 2012).

However, as what had begun as a Middle East crisis soon became a European one, as failed states in MENA generated massive refugees flows and became breeding grounds for terrorism, EU policy shifted to containment of the blowback in Europe. Initially, there was broad public sympathy in Germany, Sweden, and Austria for the plight of the refugees. However, in mid-2015 a mass inflow of asylum seekers threatened internal political stability. Europe's capacity for joint action to manage the crisis rapidly fell behind the surge in migrant numbers, sparking recriminations among EU members; front-line states such as Italy or Greece had to absorb the influx that Germany's Chancellor Merkel's public welcome to refugees had encouraged. Following the terrorist attacks in Paris and Brussels in 2015–16, fear that migrant flows would harbour terrorists led to further securitization of the refugee issue (Lehne 2016). The ability to control borders is a key attribute of sovereignty and nationhood, and, as Walt (2016) put it, if Europe cannot control access to its own territory, it will not be able to control its political fate either: "The danger is migration that alters local communities too rapidly and appears to be beyond the control of local, national, or EU-level authorities."

Faced with this threat, a new European consensus emerged that the flow of refugees had to be controlled by reinforcing the EU's external border. Funding increased for "humanitarian containment"—the use of aid to care for refugees in the Middle East, notably Syria's neighbours, to prevent a spillover into Europe. Border controls and coastguards were beefed up. Europe also sought agreements with bordering states to close migrant channels across their territory; in the most important such agreement, that of the EU and Turkey initialled in March 2016, Ankara committed to take back immigrants that transited Turkey to Greece and the EU to accept an equivalent number of asylum seekers up to 72,000 and to liberalize visas for Turkish citizens traveling to the EU (Youngs and Gutman 2015; Koser 2012; Lehne 2016).

Ironically, the crisis unleashed by the Arab Uprisings soon threatened the very survival of the EU. European states began trying to take back some of the sovereignty they had delegated to the EU, in the first place over borders, the main symbol of sovereignty. The migrant crisis threatened the Schengen Agreement on open borders, "one of the EU's singular accomplishments (as well as a tangible symbol of unity)," as Walt (2016) observed. It encouraged the growth of right-wing populist parties that so effectively tapped into and mobilized both anti-migrant and anti-EU sentiment across Europe that mainstream parties were also forced to take stands against mass migration. Growing Euroscepticism fuelled by the migration crisis was most extremely manifested in the campaign for Britain's exit from the EU, which seriously threatened the European project. The European states that had started by belittling the sovereignty claims of MENA states, now struggled to reclaim their own under pressures emanating from MENA.

Conclusion

Britain and France exported the Westphalian states system to the Middle East but in a flawed form that had conflict and instability built into it. As Europe shed its imperial past, the US assumed the role of world hegemon, deploying hard power to contain Middle East conflicts and to secure the region's oil. Europe sought, through the EMP, to export its experience of economic integration and democratization as an alternative solution to MENA's instability (Youngs 2004). In practice, the EMP aimed less at partnership than at assimilation of the south to the neo-liberal practices of the north, thereby promoting the reconstruction of the hub-and-spokes structure typical of imperialism. Increasingly, too, Europe became a partner in the project of US hegemony over the region.

The contradictions in European policy, between the fostering of crony capitalism and of regime de-legitimizing democratic discourses, and between partnership with MENA and with a Washington whose policies exacerbated MENA instability, largely nullified any stabilizing effect that EMP might have had. Moreover, the post-sovereignty discourse disseminated from Europe fundamentally misread the situation in the southern Mediterranean. The Arab Uprising showed that democracy (or more precisely democratic capitalism) can only be exported at great risk of destabilizing fragile states; that such social engineering is quite beyond the capacity of external powers; and that the regional state, authoritarian or not, is the only bulwark against anarchy—civil war, mass migration, and terrorism. Western policies were decisive in creating, within roughly a decade, three failed states in Iraq, Libya, and Syria. These failed states (as earlier in Afghanistan) then became the sites of "blowback," posing the dual threats of terrorism and mass migration—and in consequence threatening the very survival of the European project.

Note

1 Bashar Ja'afari cited in Euronews 19 April 2016: www.euronews.com/2016/04/19/we-re-victims-of-european-terrorism-says-syria-negotiator-basharja-afari/

Bibliography

Aliboni, Roberto (2010), *The Mediterranean and the Middle East: Narrowing gaps in transatlantic perspective*, Washington, DC: German Marshall Fund, Mediterranean Paper Series, March.

Arrighi, Giovanni and Beverly Silver (2001), "Capitalism and world (dis)order," in Michael Cox, Tim Dunne, and Ken Booth (eds), *Empires, systems and states: Great transformations in international politics*, (Cambridge: Cambridge University Press), pp. 257–79.

Arrow, Ruaridh (2011), "Gene Sharp: Author of the nonviolent revolution rulebook," 21 February, online article available at www.bbc.com/news/world-middle-east-12522848

Balfour, Rosa (2012), Conditionality after the Arab Spring, Barcelona: European Institute of the Mediterranean, PapersIEMED 16.

BBC (2015), "Mourning the death of the 'messiah of Africa'," 6 December, online article available at www.bbc.co.uk/news/magazine-35005828

Burbach, Roger and Jim Tarbell (2004), *Imperial overstretch: George W. Bush and the hubris of empire*, (Black Point, NS: Fernwood Publishing).

Cavatorta, Francesco and Vincent Durac (2010), *The foreign policies of the European Union and the United States in North Africa: Diverging or converging dynamics*, (London and New York: Routledge).

Clark, Ian (2001), "Another double movement: The great transformation after the Cold War," in Michael Cox, Tim Dunne, and Ken Booth (eds), *Empires, systems and states: Great transformations in international politics*, (Cambridge: Cambridge University Press), pp. 237–56.

Cox, Richard (1996), "Social forces, state and world orders," in Richard Cox with Timothy Sinclair, *Approaches to world order*, (Cambridge and New York: Cambridge University Press), pp. 85–123.

Dostal, J. M. (2009), "The European Union and economic reform in Syria," in J. M. Dostal and A. Zorob (eds), *Syria and the Euro-Mediterranean relationship*, (St Andrews: Center for Syrian Studies and Boulder, CO: Lynne Rienner Publishers).

Feliu, Laura (2005), "Global civil society across the Mediterranean: The case of human rights," *Mediterranean Politics*, 10, 365–84.

Finnamore, Martha and Kathryn Sikkink (1998), "International norm dynamics and political change," *International Organization*, 52(4), 887–917.

Fromkin, David (1989), *A peace to end all peace: The fall of the Ottoman Empire and the creation of the modern Middle East*, (New York: Avon Books).

Grahl, J. (2004), "The European Union and American power," in L. Panitch and C. Leys, *The empire reloaded*, (London: Merlin Press), pp. 284–300.

Guazzone, L. and D. Pioppi (2009), *The Arab state and neo-liberal globalization: The restructuring of the state in the Middle East*, (Reading, UK: Ithaca Press).

Hackett, Conrad (2016), "5 facts about the Muslim population in Europe," Pew Research Center, July 19, www.pewresearch.org/fact-tank/2016/07/19/5-facts-about-the-muslim-population-in-europe/

Held, David and Kristian Coates Ulrichsen (2014), "The Arab Spring and the changing balance of global power," 26 February, online article available at www.opendemocracy.net/arab-awakening/david-held-kristian-coates-ulrichsen/arab-spring-and-changing-balance-of-global-power

Holden, P. (2010), "Security, power or profit? The economic diplomacy of the US and the EU in North Africa," in Francesco Cavatorta and Vincent Durac (eds), *The foreign policies of the European Union and the United States in North Africa: Diverging or converging dynamics*, (London and New York: Routledge), pp. 10–31.

Hollis, Rosemary (1997), "Europe and the Middle East, power by stealth?," *International Affairs*, 73(1), 16.

Hollis, Rosemary (2012), "No friend of democratization: Europe's role in the genesis of the Arab Spring," *International Affairs*, 88(1), 81–94.

Hyde-Price, A. (2006), "Normative power Europe: A realist critique," *Journal of European Public Policy*, 13, 217–34.

Idriss, Admad (2010), "Europe and democracy in the wider Middle East," 5 December, online article available at www.europesworld.org

Isaac, Sally Khalifa (2012), *Europe and the Arab revolutions*, Berlin: KFG Working Paper No. 39.

Joffe, G. (1998), "Relations between the Middle East and the west: A view from the south," in B. A. Roberson (ed.), *The Middle East and Europe: The power deficit*, (London and New York: Routledge), pp. 45–73.

Johnson, Chalmers (2004), *Blowback: The causes and consequences of American Empire*, (New York: Henry Holt).

Kienle, E. (1998), "Destabilization through partnership? Euro-Mediterranean relations after the Barcelona Declaration," *Mediterranean Politics*, 3(2), 1–20.

Koser, Khalid (2012), "Migration, displacement and the Arab Spring: Lessons to learn," Brookings Institute, 22 March, available online at www.brookings.edu/research/opinions/2012/03/22-arab-spring-migration-koser

Lehne, Stefan (2016), "The tempting trap of Fortress Europe," Carnegie Europe, 21 April, available online at http://carnegieeurope.eu/2016/04/21/tempting-trap-of-fortress-europe/

Levitsky, Steven and Lucian A. Way (2005), "International linkage and democratization," *Journal of Democracy*, 16(3), 20–34.

Manners, Ian (2002), "Normative power Europe: A contradiction in terms?" *Journal of Common Market Studies*, 40, 235–58.

Marks, J. (1998), "High hopes and low motives: The new Euro-Mediterranean Partnership initiative," *Mediterranean Politics*, 1(1), 1–24.

Marr, P. (1998), "The United States, Europe and the Middle East," in B. A. Roberson (ed.), *The Middle East and Europe: The power deficit*, (London and New York: Routledge), pp. 74–104.

Marshall, Jonathan (2016) "Deadly blowback from neo-imperial wars," *Consortiumnewscom* 25 March, available online at https://consortiumnews.com/2016/03/25/deadly-blowback-from-neo-imperial-wars/

Michalek, J. (2005), "Economics in the Mediterranean: Common challenges," in A. Marchetti (ed.), *Ten years Euro-Mediterranean Partnership*, (Bonn: Center for European Integration Studies, Rheinische Friedrich-Wilhelms-Universität), pp. 59–81.

Miller, R and A. Mishraf (2005), "The Barcelona process and Euro-Arab economic relations: 1995–2005," *Middle East Review of International Affairs*, 9(2), 94–108.

Nienhaus, V. (1999), "Promoting development through a Euro-Mediterranean free trade zone?," *European Foreign Affairs Review*, 4, 501–18.

Parfitt, T. (1997), "Europe's Mediterranean designs: An analysis of the Euromed Partnership with special reference to Egypt," *Third World Quarterly*, 18(5), 865–81.

Salame, Ghassan (1998), "Torn between the Atlantic and the Mediterranean: Europe and the Middle East in the post-Cold War era," in B. A. Roberson (ed.), *The Middle East and Europe: The power deficit*, (London and New York: Routledge), pp. 20–44.

Schumacher, Tobias (2004), *Survival of the fittest: The first five years of Euro-Mediterranean economic cooperation*, EUI–RSCAS Working Paper, No. 14, Badia Fiesolana.

Schumacher, Tobias (2010), *Transatlantic cooperation in the Middle East and North Africa and the growing role of the Gulf states*, Washington, DC: German Marshall Fund, Mediterranean Paper Series, July.

Seeberg, Peter (2010), "Union for the Mediterranean: Pragmatic multilateralism and the depoliticization of EU–Middle Eastern relations," *Middle East Critique*, 19(3), 287–302.

Seelye, Kate (2011), "Syria unrest 'cannot be contained'," *The Daily Beast*, 28 March, online article available at www.thedailybeast.com/articles/2011/03/28/syria-unrest-cannot-be-contained-dissidents-say.html.

Teti, Andrea (2012), "The EU'S first response to the Arab Spring: A critical discourse analysis of the partnership for democracy and shared prosperity," *Mediterranean Politics*, 17(3), 266–84.

Tonra, Ben and Francesco Cavatorta (2007), "Normative foundations in the EU foreign, security and defence policy: The case of the Middle East peace process," *Contemporary Politics*, 42(4), 731–56.

Walt, Stephen M. (2016), "Europe can still save itself," 14 March, online article available at http://foreignpolicy.com/2016/03/14/europe-can-still-save-itself-migrants-borders-syria-iraq/

Youngs, R. (2003), "European approaches to security in the Mediterranean," *Middle East Journal*, 57(3), 414–31.

Youngs, R. (2004), "Normative dynamics and strategic interests in the EU's external identity," *Journal of Common Market Studies*, 42(2), 415–35.

Youngs, Richard and John Paul Gutman (2015), "Is the EU tackling the root causes of Middle Eastern conflict?," Carnegie Europe, 1 December, available online at http://carnegieeurope.eu/2015/12/01/is-eu-tackling-root-causes-of-middle-eastern-conflict/imi6

7

A NEW ERA IN EURO-MEDITERRANEAN RELATIONS

Richard Youngs

Contemporary Euro-Mediterranean relations have advanced through successive phases of development. In a first phase from 1995, the Euro-Mediterranean Partnership (EMP) promised a comprehensive framework for mutually shaped cooperation between the European Union, Arab states and Israel. In a second phase that began after 2001, the rise of terrorist concerns intensified tensions between security and the EMP's commitment to liberal cooperation. The Arab Spring heralded a third phase that swung back towards apparent optimism and the possibility of deeper and more values-based partnership across the Mediterranean. A fourth phase has now commenced, dominated by more geopolitical factors; the fate of this more eclectic and still half-formed phase remains uncertain.

The series of apparent turning points through which Euro-Mediterranean relations have passed leaves a profound but unsettling analytical legacy that questions several core assumptions about EU foreign policy. In laying out the broad trajectory of Euro-Mediterranean relations this chapter sets the overarching context for other parts of this volume that look at more specific policy questions. It provides a cautionary tale of EU inconstancy. Over the course of two decades the EU has shifted from one strategic approach to another, and flitted between engagement with and neglect of the southern Mediterranean. By examining Euro-Mediterranean relations over an extended time period and through successive phases, the chapter demonstrates that these relations do not have an entirely fixed, intrinsic identity but have been frequently remoulded in reaction to geopolitical changes.

The Union is currently embarked on a strategic recalibration that seeks to update its approach to the region in light of an unprecedented sweep of geostrategic crises. While in some ways the EU is right to do so, it risks subverting many erstwhile pillars of its signature approaches to foreign policy that are still relevant to the emerging geopolitical context. This matters for the Mediterranean itself but also in broader conceptual terms. This is because the EU now struggles to retain a quality of strategic engagement that keeps faith with its early promise to be a distinctive kind of foreign policy partner in the southern Mediterranean.

Three lives

In the twenty years between 1995 and 2015, Euro-Mediterranean relations went through three phases of development.[1]

Early hopes

The first phase began when the creation of the Euro-Mediterranean Partnership promised a quantitative and qualitative leap forward in relations between European states and twelve countries from the Middle East and North Africa (MENA) region. When the EU devised this new framework, the EMP was one of the EU's most comprehensive and forward-looking foreign policy initiatives. The EMP represented an ambitious and multilateral approach to Euro-Mediterranean relations. What at that stage was named the Barcelona Process indicated that the EU would not neglect the southern Mediterranean as the Union concentrated on preparing central and eastern European candidate states for accession. Its guiding philosophy was notable in rejecting realpolitik geopolitical strategies and basing itself on a progressive notion of cooperative security, joint decision-making, region-building, political reform and social integration. The very fact that the EU chose to focus on deepening a 'Mediterranean' rather than 'broader Middle East' policy suggested a preference for inclusive cooperation with the Union's most immediate neighbours. The EMP was not only an important policy milestone; it also nourished distinctive theoretical conceptualizations of EU foreign policy.

At a moment, in the mid-1990s, when the distorted spectre of a 'clash of civilizations' framed much analytical discourse, the EMP at least formally enshrined a firm rejection of exclusionary and defensive geostrategy. It was widely praised as one of the most significant examples of the EU's commitment to a distinctive type of liberal-cooperative foreign policy. While EU member states retained different and historically rooted perspectives on the southern Mediterranean, they compromised sufficiently to agree what was at least in formal terms a common approach to the region – even if many details of how the EMP commitments would be implemented still had to be defined.

Despite the elements of foreign policy innovation, the EMP's limitations gradually became apparent. Southern Mediterranean governments resisted cooperation in an increasing number of areas, pushing back against security cooperation, human rights initiatives and economic liberalization. The EU relied heavily on support for economic liberalization and the integration of markets spilling over to deliver security benefits, inter-regional harmony and political modernization. This approach may have worked in Europe but struggled to gain traction in the southern Mediterranean. Indeed, the nepotistic way in which regimes oversaw their selective processes of economic reform seemed to tighten rather than loosen their grip on power and nourish further strategic risk.

Far from exuding any warm glow of mutual partnership, southern Mediterranean governments signed up to the EMP without enthusiasm and largely because in the mid-1990s they saw few other strategic alternatives. They increasingly complained that the EMP provided a vehicle for the EU surreptitiously to impose its own – and not genuinely universal – values on Arab states. Paralysis in the Israeli–Palestinian peace process magnified tensions and brought many areas of Euro-Mediterranean cooperation stuttering to a standstill. The EMP had been conceived as a low-politics means of locking in the fragile signs of cooperation between Israel and Arab states; yet it was itself undone by the very tensions it was designed to soften. As civil conflict raged in Algeria and as Israelis and Palestinians resorted to violence once more, the EMP's lack of conflict resolution tools became painfully evident.

The analytical curiosity was that diplomats and analysts alike could not agree whether the EMP was just too different, too liberal, too post-modern to take root in a viscerally non-liberal MENA region, or conversely whether it was in fact not nearly different or partnership-based enough in the way it set out to pursue European interests and norms. The EU was criticized for being too traditional and foisting its own values hegemonically on the region. But it was in equal measure admonished for the precise opposite; for being strategically weak and insipid, naively thinking its liberal templates could work in a region that required a tougher use of geopolitical power. Regimes and many academic critics fumed against normative imperialism; conversely, civil society groups complained that the EMP's focus on liberal values such as human rights and democracy was far too weak, not too over-weaning (Hollis 1997; Joffe 1997).

The 9/11 jolt

The second phase of Euro-Mediterranean relations took shape in the aftermath of the inflexion point of 11 September 2001. The terrorist attacks in New York and Washington DC, and then later in Madrid and London, ushered in a period dominated by the dynamics of securitization. Under the EMP, cooperation in justice and home affairs gained prominence and member states put in place new de-radicalization initiatives. Counter-terrorist cooperation intensified across the Mediterranean Sea. The heightened concerns with security appeared to drag the EMP away from long-term political community building towards short-term threat-containment. While this policy shift may have been an understandable response to terrorist attacks, critics argued it was pursued in a way that compromised the EMP's geostrategic comparative advantage (Volpi 2004). The EU seemed to abandon its own liberal-cooperative ideals of shared identity building for uncertain and elusive strategic gain.

After 9/11, many EU leaders rhetorically recommitted themselves to the founding principles of the EMP. The EU introduced a number of new democracy and human rights initiatives. Leaders spoke frequently about the need finally to 'get serious' about political reform: giving citizens a genuine voice to hold their governments accountable would be the best way to address the social discontent driving the radicalization that was returning to haunt Europe. With such transformative aims in mind, the EU created the European Neighbourhood Policy (ENP). This would supplement the EMP with more tailored action plans in each partner state.

Yet, after a flurry of post-2001 activity, governments soon chose not to invest any significant effort to foster democratic reforms in the southern Mediterranean. Nor did they press for fully inclusive partnership that incorporated mainstream Islamist movements. The 9/11, London and Madrid attacks encouraged some European actors to engage more systematically with political Islam across the southern Mediterranean, invariably to the chagrin of regimes. Yet this engagement was less than wholehearted. Sceptics thought that most European governments were not genuine in their claim to have realized the importance of reaching out to Islamist parties. Some states' securitization of Islam sat uneasily with the EMP's founding tenets (Attina 2003).

Securitization dynamics sat uneasily with the notion of building a structure of EMP governance based on incorporating the southern Mediterranean into a range of EU multilateral cooperation. A plethora of links now existed between the northern and southern sides of the Mediterranean below the level of the state. The EMP was almost uniquely rich in this domain. It had facilitated dialogue between NGOs, municipalities, youth groups, journalists, unions, business actors, parliamentarians and artists. Yet the results of all this activity were disappointing and dialogue was increasingly distorted by security tensions.

Moreover, in the late 2000s, the EU seemed increasingly introverted. It was immersed in drawn-out internal, institutional reforms. As the threat of radicalism and international terrorism appeared to have plateaued, EU–Mediterranean relations lost some of their drive. As its own economic crisis hit hard, the EU needed buoyant export markets. It began to accord greater priority to rising economies, especially in fast expanding Asia. The more troublesome Middle East slipped down its list of priorities.

The French government proposed the creation of a new Union for the Mediterranean (UfM). After a number of diplomatic confrontations and a process of re-modelling, the UfM was effectively set up as a secretariat focusing on low-key, technocratic development projects. The new initiative was designed to focus on uncontroversial areas of cooperation and to take politics out of the policy equation – the kind of politics that were just about to erupt in spectacular fashion in Tunisia, Egypt and then elsewhere. For many, this represented a new low point (Schlumberger 2011). The EU's approach to the Mediterranean now suffered from neglect, institutional confusion and low priority technocracy – all features that were the very opposite of what governments had signed up to in the original EMP.

The cruellest spring

The Arab Spring of course marked the beginning of another, third phase in analytical debate. The EU responded to the social uprisings in MENA states in 2011 with a battery of new policy initiatives. It offered more incentives for political reforms, the prospect of deeper partnership, engagement with a wider range of actors in the region and policies more tailored to each Mediterranean country's specific circumstances. Yet as the hopes of reform cooled, most observers criticized the EU for a relatively lacklustre response to the Arab revolts (Balfour 2011; Merlini and Roy 2012; Peters 2012). These revolts to some extent returned the EMP to some of its original spirit, taking the focus away from the security narrative of the years before 2011. As reforms faltered, however, the impact on Euro-Mediterranean relations became more complex.

To some degree, aspects of the original liberal-cooperative ethos of the EMP gained a new lease on life. The EU's tools of external governance were certainly relevant in accounting for the way in which some more technical areas of EU rules were adopted by Arab states from 2011. But overall, resistance to the concept of importing EU governance grew across the Middle East. Indeed, popular control over decision-making in many areas tipped the scales against this technocratic vision of cooperation with Europe.

It gradually became clear that the Arab awakening would not open the door to entirely harmonious cooperation and community building across the Mediterranean, as many predicted. Indeed, many of the architects of Arab change insisted that they sought more autonomy from such deep Western entanglement. And differences widened between member states as they read the potential for Arab reform in different ways. This divergence militated against the prospect of a common Europeanized approach to cooperation and political reform in the post-2011 southern Mediterranean.

In juggling with the diverse political trends across the southern Mediterranean after 2011, the EU deployed a mix of policy dynamics.[2] The weight of member states' policies became more significant relative to EMP and UfM instruments. Governments' strategic calculations produced greater variation in policies towards different southern Mediterranean states, as these took divergent political paths. European governments sought to regain their sway in overall EU policies towards the Middle East. While some areas of deeper cooperation were pursued within the rubric of the UfM, in some parts of the Middle East the Arab Spring encouraged European governments to give greater priority to bilateral, national foreign policy action. This was particularly so as the process of reform stumbled in many states and instability erupted.

This emerging context challenged the analytical centrality of the EMP ethos. A pattern of governance centred on national governments' strategic calculations and actions was at least as relevant as Europeanized models of governance in structuring relations with the new Middle East. European responses were as much about national governments' high diplomacy as they were predicated on Brussels-centred policy instruments. European governments not only saw the fashioning of a new Middle East as a positive opportunity, but also sought to deploy national diplomatic means to protect against its risks and uncertainties. In some policy areas the balance between national foreign policies and common EU efforts shifted towards the former. This was seen particularly in Libya, where the divergence between member states was as fundamental as anything witnessed since the inception of the EU's common foreign and security policy.

Egypt was an important illustration of these shifts. After the Egyptian military seized back power in the 2013 coup, EU policy increasingly limited itself to a defensive protection of basic European interests. As Egypt headed toward a coarser and more unalloyed authoritarianism than existed under former president Hosni Mubarak, the EU reaction was tepid. Member states gradually moved back toward a policy of security-oriented engagement. Despite the increasingly extensive repression, the EU negotiated a significant new aid package for 2014–15 with the Egyptian regime. Member states restarted arms sales. Most spectacularly, the French government agreed a sizeable package of arms exports. The Egyptian regime had little interest in negotiating an EU free-trade agreement and stifled European support to civil society organizations. The EU's engagement with the Muslim Brotherhood dried up.

After 2011 a variation in European policies was driven by a combination of contrasting domestic political structures within different Arab states, on the one hand, and European governments' contrasting security-related calculations in different parts of the region, on the other hand. Both these variables sit uneasily with explanations of EU foreign policy that attribute most importance to common, Europeanized policy instruments (Damro 2015; Lavenex 2014). Academics have commonly criticized EU policies for being too uniform – and they have argued that this is because they proceed from entrenched institutional templates and elaborately designed external policy instruments. Some elements of the EU's response to the Arab revolts did indeed fit this institutionalist template. However, such inside-out explanations of EU foreign policy decisions failed to account for much of European policy variation in the immediate aftermath of the Arab revolts.

This has become even more evident as the momentum of the Arab spring has ebbed and the UfM, as well as member states' national diplomacy, has struggled to adapt to the complex political specificities of southern Mediterranean states. The faltering path of the Arab spring has posed serious questions for standard models of political transition – models upon which the EMP was heavily predicated. In a sense, European foreign policy became a dependent as much as independent variable – affected by, not just affecting, domestic constellations in southern Mediterranean states. The EU began to respond in a more flexible and even expedient fashion to the fluidity and specificity of domestic developments within different parts of the Middle East. The EU has supported different types and degrees of political reform in Arab states. It has pursued different mixes of bottom-up civil society support and top-down security cooperation. The EU's reform-oriented strategy in Tunisia looked radically different from its more defensive strategy in Egypt, and both in turn diverged from the humanitarian-security turn to policy in beleaguered Jordan.

A new phase?

By 2015, memories of the Arab Spring were fading and Euro-Mediterranean relations were centred on a very different set of issues. The challenges of the current political and strategic context are well known, and outlined in other chapters of this volume. A number of factors have coincided to raise far-reaching and searching questions for the EU's foreign policy approaches in the southern Mediterranean. The EU is now affected by its largest ever influx of refugees and migrants. Violent conflict has destabilized Syria and Libya. The rise of Islamic State and other radical groups wreaks havoc in the MENA region, menacing European security and interests in the region while sponsoring terrorist attacks within the EU itself. Except in Tunisia, political reform has stalled. Geopolitical rivalries have intensified across the region, driven by a combination of sectarian tensions and national power competition.

Buffeted by this vexing set of challenges, the EU has lost influence. Regimes increasingly resist European strictures on cooperative security, political and economic reform. It is clear that the EU's Mediterranean strategy has been insufficiently geopolitical to forestall the competitive power politics that now dominate the Mediterranean and the wider MENA region. In response to this chain of events, the EU and its member states have begun to adjust, and the shape of Euro-Mediterranean relations is undergoing significant change.

A key sign of and vehicle for such change has been the drawing up of a revised ENP. The EU published its much-debated 'ENP Review' document in November 2015 (European Union 2015). This promises 'new ways of working' and indicates that security and 'stabilization' will now be the EU's highest priorities in both the southern and eastern neighbourhoods. To allow deeper cooperation, the EU will encourage the principles of 'differentiation and greater mutual ownership'. The EU will strengthen its engagement 'with partners in the security sector' and on conflict prevention. Member states are to be more fully involved in selecting priorities and more ministerial meetings will be held. The EU will modernize its funding instruments, like twinning and technical assistance programmes to make these more strategic and targeted. A 'flexibility cushion' will allow for quick funding in response to crises on the ground.

EU diplomats explain what they see as the logic behind the new ENP: EU policy can no longer be based on the assumption that neighbouring states will smoothly align themselves with and into an EU sphere of governance. The EU has to start from a clear and disaggregated understanding of its geopolitical interests and build tailor-made strategies with each individual state from such an assessment. Johannes Hahn, Commissioner for European Neighbourhood Policy and Enlargement Negotiations, explains: 'Until now the ENP has relied almost exclusively on community instruments. This review offers the possibility to bring all our instruments together, to attempt a much more coherent approach to the key security challenges in the region.'[3] Diplomats concur that a more geostrategic logic is set to provide the ENP's new spine.

If the EMP's initial narrative was about creating a single, regional space and common polity, today the EU's focus is self-evidently on borders and barriers between itself and the southern Mediterranean. Many of the measures the EU has brought forward in 2015 and 2016 are the very antithesis of what the EMP originally stood for. The search for a more secure Europe now provides the EU's playsheet.

The EU has allocated funds to set up a European border and coastguard system; deploys Rapid Border Intervention Teams to deal with emergency situations on the EU's external frontiers; employs extra guards to control refugee movements; and has provided the border agency Frontex with new powers directly to eject arriving refugees. Member states are now pushing for full implementation of the border surveillance system Eurosur that was introduced in 2013 and that aimed to support border security through the use of drones, high-resolution cameras and satellite tracking systems.

Internally and at the EU's interface with the Mediterranean, European governments have increased funding for surveillance, policing, border control and intelligence, fearful of the Islamic State expanding its activities beyond its strongholds in Syria and Iraq. In February 2016 the EU brought forward plans for a closed border along Macedonia's border. Operations Sophia and Triton in the Mediterranean have been progressively beefed up to provide more extensive patrols. Overall, EU defence spending will increase in 2016 for the first time in a decade, as a response to security concerns emanating from the southern – as well as eastern – neighbourhood.

A total of over 9.2 billion euros was made available from the EU budget for 2015–16 to control the arrival of refugees and close down trafficking networks. EU member states promised an extra 200 million euros for multilateral agencies like the World Food Program and the UN refugee agency to care for refugees within the Middle East. A new Madad trust fund for initiatives involving Syrian refugees has 1 billion euros at its disposal – half of this from the European Commission, half from EU member states. Most high profile, of course, the EU has awarded 6 billion euros to the Turkish government to keep refugees in camps inside Turkey. Several member states have taken similar steps in their national policies. The UK, for example, has doubled humanitarian aid to Syria, to over 5 billion euros for 2015–19.

Border management and counter-terrorism appear to have increasingly fused as part of an overall EU response to the new context. Europol opened a European Counter-Terrorism Centre at the beginning of 2016. This new centre has dispatched experts to refugee arrival camps because of a perceived need to stop jihadis slipping into Europe. Member governments are pushing forward deeper cooperation between police and justice forces, through Europol and Eurojust. States are tentatively beginning to share more intelligence information with each other – by early 2016 all but three member states had signed up to an information sharing arrangement managed through Europol. The EU's Internal Security Fund has been increased to 3.8 billion euros for 2014–20 (European Political Strategy Centre 2016).

The EU's role in international counter-terrorism has become more notable. France has dramatically reinforced its counter-terrorism operation across five Sahel countries, known as Operation Bekrane. In early 2016, a group of EU donors pushed the OECD to change its definition of 'aid' to include some military spending and funds for refugee camps. A core focus of European strategy is to boost local actors' capacity to fight the Islamic State. Several EU member states are helping build the security capabilities of forces combating the group. Belgium, Denmark, France, Germany, Italy, the Netherlands and the UK have provided hundreds of military trainers to Kurdish peshmerga fighters and Iraqi security forces since late 2014. France and the UK have stepped up training for Syrian rebels since the summer of 2015.

In 2015, the EU diverted over 20 million euros to help Tunisia secure its borders and develop a national security strategy. The EU extended a Radicalisation Awareness Network centre of excellence to Tunisia and began a new dialogue on 'Security and the fight against terrorism' in late 2015.

The terrorist attacks in Paris in November 2015 and the refugee crisis have made most European governments more willing to reach a negotiated settlement with the regime of Bashar Assad in Syria. Even France and the UK that had held the hardest line against the Syrian leader have begun to acknowledge the need to enter into dialogue about some form of negotiated compromise solution to the country's civil conflict. A number of member states have recently increased their engagement in coalition actions against IS in Syria and/or Iraq. In late 2015, Germany joined the anti-ISIS coalition, after having previously ruled this out.

The EU and a number of member states have promised an upgraded security engagement in Libya – where they see terrorism and refugee challenges as two sides of the same coin. In May 2016, international powers – including EU member states – agreed to prepare for a Libya International Assistance Mission and to start arming the new Government of National Accord. Several EU governments now have small-scale special forces and intelligence operations up and running inside Libya, aimed at degrading IS.

Embracing a combination of strategic approaches, the EU is seeking to complement these direct security measures with initiatives more redolent of the familiar, core EMP rationale. In addition to incipient security-oriented changes, the EU has promised to tackle the underlying root causes of conflict and the refugee surge. In early 2016, the EU drew up a new investment plan for North Africa; its idea is that 4.5 billion euros of EU money will be used to leverage 60 billion euros of private investment, as a quid pro quo for MENA countries controlling migrant outflows. The UK has shifted 200 million pounds more of its aid budget toward tempering instability, including through conflict and stabilization initiatives specifically in the Middle East and North Africa. A number of European donors have increased support for governance initiatives within opposition-held territory in Syria. The UK and the European Commission are funding Tamkeen, a 20 million euro project aimed at building participative committees to provide local services like health, education and electricity in several Syrian cities on the basis of projects chosen by committees of local notables.

Uncertainties of the new era

While these developments represent an increased European engagement in the MENA region, there are significant limits to this policy upgrade – and doubts about how effective the EU's recalibrated strategic approach is likely to be.

Perhaps most obviously, despite all the security challenges now in play, European governments are still not inclined to engage in significant security interventions. Only five EU member states – Belgium, Denmark, France, the Netherlands and the UK – have participated in the coalition carrying out air strikes against the Islamic State in Iraq. Taken together, these states have contributed a small fraction of the level of airpower provided by the United States. Only France and the UK have been willing to undertake significant military action within Syria. No EU state has contemplated a large-scale military engagement involving ground troops. Germany has remained particularly adamant in its opposition to military engagement in Syria and Iraq. Moreover, EU member states in general still refuse to supply the Syrian opposition with arms.

More structurally, the EU is still finding its strategic footing in the way it envelops Euro-Mediterranean relations within a better developed wider Middle East policy. While the ENP review document promises to build bridges between the Euro-Mediterranean states and other parts of the MENA – recognizing that today it makes no sense to have a policy framework that separates Syria and Iraq, for instance – the EU has so far done little to follow through on this in any tangible sense. Indeed, the EU's engagement in Iraq remains strikingly limited. The EU has pressed for more inclusive governance and promised to support Iraqi Prime Minister Haider al-Abadi to the extent that he advances with democratic reform. The European Commission has opened some projects in Iraq on religious tolerance, media freedom, and human rights – each with around 1 million euros of funding. Yet such support remains on a limited scale. The EU still has a Mediterranean policy pursued in a way that diverts the Union from developing a broader MENA policy more in tune with geopolitical developments within the region.

Neither is it proving easy to strike an effective balance between short- and long-term strategic logics. In practice the EU's attempts to address the root causes of instability, through initiatives backing political reform and modernization in the MENA region, are becoming weaker not stronger. Not surprisingly, the EU has struggled to keep pace with shifts in MENA states' domestic politics and the lack of clarity about which way these trends may ultimately be heading. The policy challenge has shifted from how fully to engage moderate Islamists to how to respond to the reconstitution of statist models of political authority. The region's model of state–society relations has been upended without being reassembled in any clearly distinctive fashion. This militates against firm EU engagement.

Of all European donors, only the European Commission, Denmark, Germany, Sweden and the UK now give non-negligible amounts of governance and civil society aid to the region, with annual contributions of at least 100 million euros. Few member states have significantly increased their still limited funds in the region. French aid remains at a relatively low level even in the wake of the Paris attacks.[4] Most EU states are now spending far more on beefing up domestic capabilities in surveillance, policing, border control and intelligence than on the core, traditional strands of Euro-Mediterranean relations. The diplomatic leverage that the EU now expends with MENA countries to increase the return of illegal migrants displaces much of the focus on governance reform. Moreover, member-state arms sales have increased to key MENA states like Egypt, Algeria, Saudi Arabia and Jordan. In Bahrain, the UK has started to build its first permanent naval base in the region in forty years even as the Bahraini regime tightens repression against opposition forces.

Tunisian activists feel that, in league with the Nidaa Tounis government and remnants of the former regime, the EU is walking Tunisia backwards towards a soft version of a police state that draws its oxygen from the cross-Mediterranean counter-terrorism narrative. Democratization has become equated with a consensual regime battling against radicals and brooking little dissent in doing so. Many activists feel alienated from the 'insider', EU-supported NGOs that are lauded for having helped pilot this consensual transition (Aliriza 2016). They openly fear that a revived ethos of secular statism is creating tensions between the regime and the civic sphere once again. The decision of moderate Islamist party Ennahda to drop its religious identity seems to play into this – and because of this, is seen in a less positive light within Tunisia than by the European Union.

Analysts criticize the EU for being less willing now to take into account the views of local actors in the Mediterranean as it shifts – in the eyes of many in the MENA region – towards a classically defensive realist 'lifeboat' approach (Huber and Paciello 2015). In Morocco, Egypt and Tunisia governments are repressing NGOs with the argument that these hinder the 'war on terror', hassling the very NGOs funded by the EU, even as the Union works with the regimes on counter-terrorism. Through the southern Mediterranean, the state has increased its economic power, through the military in Egypt, the Makhzen in Morocco and regime-linked business elites in Tunisia. The size of the public sector has increased through the region. This means that even in the economic domain the EU's aims and basic approach have lost traction. These prevailing MENA economic models have widened inequalities and worsened social indicators.

In most MENA states evidence is mounting of diminished European influence. Morocco – preferred partner during twenty years of Euro-Mediterranean relations – suspended cooperation with the EU for nearly a year in mid-2015. In Egypt, the Sisi government is increasingly uninterested in any deep or broad partnership with the EU or European governments. Interlocutors in Cairo point out the irony that even parts of the Egyptian military now seem more circumspect in their backing for Sisi than are many European diplomats and governments. Discontent and instability are growing again as Sisi's decision to give two islands to Saudi Arabia looked like the price for the latter's financial largesse. As authoritarian rule is more arbitrary than under Mubarak, it does not even succeed on its own terms of bringing predictability. Indeed, political order is crumbling as a result of de-institutionalization. Sisi rules by decree on an increasingly wide range of measures. Egypt has the unenviable combination of a brutal but weak state. In this context, the basic premises of European support for state-delivered security and state-driven modernization look increasingly unconvincing.

Beyond humanitarian aid, the EU runs only a handful of projects related to Syria – on youth, civil society networks, education and the environment. Some European governance initiatives in Syria are facing difficulties as their local committee partners have fled to refugee camps at the

Turkish border and funding has been diverted into more basic humanitarian support (Boffey 2016). Shia militia are gaining power in Iraq as they battle IS and have blocked political reforms pushed by Western powers.

European involvement in Libya still awaits an invitation from the new unity government, which is reluctant to allow in outside forces. Neither of the two pre-existing governments has accepted the Government of National Accord. Several European special forces are nevertheless cooperating with the renegade Tobruk administration on pushing back against IS. This risks undercutting the broader strategy of supporting the unity deal. Meanwhile many existing EU projects are being wound down and no strategy to build better governance structures in Libya has begun. Indeed, the unity government still excludes the key actors in tribal areas and local administrations and is delaying the kind of decentralization that would give more autonomy to eastern parts of Libya and bring them into a political process (Toaldo 2016).

Conclusion

Euro-Mediterranean relations have not developed along a smooth, unilinear path. The EU has shifted between different strategic approaches. It has swung periodically from liberal to more realist foreign policy approaches and back again. Southern Mediterranean states have likewise moved between more and less cooperative approaches within the EMP. While the Euro-Mediterranean policy framework has accumulated some modicum of its own self-sustaining momentum, external events and trends have played a significant role in pushing and pulling European and MENA states' policies in contrasting directions at different moments of time. By breaking down the recent evolution of Euro-Mediterranean relations into its successive phases, this chapter shows how these relations cannot be described as having a particularly thick form of fixed or intrinsic identity. They have been shaped by as much as they have shaped regional events.

As the surge of refugees into Europe and the threat posed by Islamic State have come to dominate concerns since 2015, the EU has begun to adopt a tighter focus on security challenges emanating from the MENA region. National governments' diplomacy has taken more of a centre-stage role relative to common EU-level institutional channels. Within European foreign policies, the balance between common EU initiatives and national foreign policy has tilted towards the latter. Today EU foreign policy in the MENA region looks less qualitatively unique than when it set out its aspirations at the EMP's birth in 1995. The internal dynamics of EU foreign policy have begun to shift, with the EMP no longer the central pillar of European action and engagement to quite the same extent it was previously.

In many ways the EU's adjustment to new geopolitical realities is welcome, as it begins to fashion this fourth phase in Euro-Mediterranean relations. The challenge is for the EU to retain the best of its traditional foreign policy approach while it supplements this with more targeted strategic action. So far, the EU has sought to add geopolitical elements to its Mediterranean policy without adopting an overly dominant deployment of hard-power projection. Its incipient strategy for dealing with conflicts, instability and authoritarian resilience is not yet one of pure containment, but one that retains at least a notional concern with the structural drivers of conflict and instability. The issue is how well liberal and realpolitik approaches today mesh together.

In this, EU geostrategy is still clearly far from being successful. Indeed, Europe's apparent inability to shape Mediterranean events has become increasingly evident. For a long time academics were concerned with critiquing EU hegemony and neo-colonialism in the Mediterranean – as is evident from many chapters in this volume, this remains a widespread perspective. Today, the story is surely increasingly one of European impotence, more than of the EU's unacceptable degree of control over the southern Mediterranean. For their part, most MENA governments now attach less weight to their relations with the EU, while civic activists from the region express a sense of having been abandoned by European governments.

As the EU has moved away from its original policy designs, yet has declined to deploy significant hard power, its MENA strategy increasingly looks stranded in an ineffective in-betweeness – it lacks the virtues of both reform-oriented inclusion and classical geopolitical power. The fact that there is tension between geostrategy and the notion of equally balanced partnership is hardly news; it does seem analytically important to point out that the EU may be losing on both these fronts simultaneously. The danger is of the EU drifting towards a superficial form of strategic engagement, stepping back from far-reaching involvement in a region increasingly seen as a geopolitical headache to be tempered rather than a partner to be nurtured.

Notes

1 The following summary draws from a more detailed overview provided in Youngs (2016).
2 For a fuller account, see Youngs (2014).
3 Speech to European Parliament, 10 March 2015, http://europa.eu/rapid/press-release_SPEECH-15-4591_en.htm
4 For these aid figures, see www.oecd/dac.stats

References

Aliriza, F. 2016. 'Between Democracy and Police State: Tunisia's Troubled Transition', in I. Fakir, *The Middle East Unbalanced: Analysis from a Region in Turmoil*, Beirut: Carnegie Middle East Centre.

Attina, F. 2003. 'The Euro-Mediterranean Partnership Assessed: The Realist and Liberal Views', *European Foreign Affairs Review*, 8, 181–99.

Balfour, R. 2011. *The Arab Spring, the Changing Mediterranean, and the EU: Tools as a Substitute for Strategy*, Brussels: European Policy Centre.

Boffey, D. 2016. 'Gaziantep: Home to ISIS, Sex Traders . . . and a Quest to Rebuild Syria', *The Guardian*, 8 May, available at www.theguardian.com/global-development/2016/may/08/gazientep-turkey-tamkeen-quest-to-rebuild-syria

Damro, C. 2015. 'Market Power Europe: Exploring a Dynamic Conceptual Framework', *Journal of European Public Policy*, 22(9), 1336–54.

European Political Strategy Centre, 2016. *Towards a Security Union: Bolstering the EU's Counter-Terrorism Response*, European Commission.

European Union, 2015. Joint Consultation Paper: Towards a New Neighbourhood Policy, JOIN(2015)6, March, p. 8.

Hollis, R. 1997. 'Europe and the Middle East: Power by Stealth?', *International Affairs*, 73(1), 15–29.

Huber, D. and Paciello, M. 2015. *Overhauling EU Policy in the Mediterranean: Towards More Inclusive, Responsive and Flexible Policies*, Rome: IAI.

Joffe, G. 1997. 'Southern Attitudes towards an Integrated Mediterranean Region', *Mediterranean Politics*, 2(1), 12–29.

Lavenex, S. 2014. 'The Power of Functionalist Extension: How EU Rules Travel', *Journal of European Public Policy*, 21(6), 885–903.

Merlini, C. and Roy, O. (eds) 2012. *Arab Society in Revolt: The West's Mediterranean Challenge*, Washington DC: Brookings.

Peters, J. (ed.) 2012. *The European Union and the Arab Spring: Promoting Democracy and Human Rights in the Middle East*, Plymouth: Lexington.

Schlumberger, O. 2011. 'The Ties that do Not Bind: The Union for the Mediterranean and the Future of Euro-Arab Relations', *Mediterranean Politics*, 16(1), 135–53.

Toaldo, M. 2016. *Intervening Better: Europe's Second Chance in Libya*, London: ECFR.

Volpi, F. 2004. 'Regional Community Building and the Transformation of International Relations: The Case of the Euro-Mediterranean Partnership', *Mediterranean Politics*, 9(2), 145–64.

Youngs, R. 2014. *Europe in the New Middle East: Opportunity or Exclusion?* Oxford: Oxford University Press.

Youngs, R. (ed.) 2016. *Twenty Years of the Euro-Mediterranean Partnership*, London: Routledge.

PART II

Geopolitical perspectives

8

EU MEMBER STATES' REPRESENTATION AND POSITIONING AND THE NORTH–SOUTH DIVIDE IN EURO-MEDITERRANEAN AFFAIRS

Tobias Schumacher

Although the European Commission has displayed considerable agency over the last 25 years as far as the development of institutionalised EU-led cooperation frameworks with the southern Mediterranean is concerned, EU member states have played a crucial role in shaping, implementing and, at times, even obstructing EU policies towards this geopolitical space. In particular southern EU member states such as France and Spain, and to some extent Italy, have been leaving a strong imprint on EU–Mediterranean relations as a result of their policy entrepreneurship, which, in turn, is mainly a function of historical legacies and geographical proximity. In contrast, northern and eastern EU member states, i.e. those members that are not directly located at the Mediterranean shores, 'have traditionally been cast in a secondary role when it comes to shaping Euro-Mediterranean relations' (Behr and Tiilikainen, 2015b: 2). Thus, their traditional interests in, and more general foreign policy orientation towards, eastern Europe, as opposed to the Mediterranean EU member states' tendency to project power towards North Africa and the Middle East, has led scholars to speak of 'north–south differentiation' in EU foreign policy-making towards the southern Mediterranean, a notion coined by Gillespie in 1997 (Gillespie, 1997c: 72) – or even of a 'north–south split', a term employed rather widely ever since (Bicchi, 2007; Behr and Tiilikainen, 2015a). As is argued elsewhere (Schumacher, 2011; Schumacher et al. 2016), non-Mediterranean EU member states have indeed resorted for a long time to practices such as free-riding, opportunity-maximizing and issue linkage as well as veto playing. Yet, it would be misleading to argue that such practices are exclusively confined to the foreign policy toolbox of non-Mediterranean EU member states, as members of the EU's 'Club Med' – a much employed notion to depict southern EU member states' alleged cohesiveness – have, at times, not shied away from applying these themselves either.

Against this backdrop, this chapter provides an overview of EU member states' perspectives vis-à-vis the southern Mediterranean as a geopolitical space and analyses how Mediterranean, northern and eastern – i.e. non-Mediterranean – EU member states' representation and positioning have evolved over the last almost six decades in the framework of their EU membership. It is argued that the north–south divide in Mediterranean-related EU foreign policy-making is a function of EU enlargement and thus the incorporation of countries with differing and, at times, even conflicting foreign policy preferences and interests. The chapter demonstrates that throughout the first three decades of European integration, division lines between member states revolved around, by and large, a rather simplistic and supposedly antagonistic 'pro-Israel vs. pro-Arabs' dichotomy whereas the accession to the EU of Spain and Portugal – two countries with a distinct interest in Mediterranean affairs – in 1986 was the true starting point for the emergence and rather rapid manifestation of north–south divergence. In recent years, this divide has continued to underlie and thus impact Mediterranean-related EU foreign policy-making. However, some signs of a growing awareness of, and thus interest in, developments in the southern Mediterranean among non-Mediterranean member states can be identified that may hint at a potential weakening of this imbalance of preferences and interests.

Of historical legacies and path dependencies in the construction of the EU's Mediterranean policy

Since its inception in the 1950s, the European integration process has always had a Mediterranean dimension of sorts, which was – almost inevitably – bound to influence the EC's emerging external relations framework and thus, later on, shape its foreign policy orientation. Yet, this was not necessarily a matter of choice rather than, initially at least, the result of concrete political pressure and the salience of mainly French historical legacies. In the context of the negotiations leading to the Treaty of Rome, France forced the other founding members to include in the Treaty a protocol that, by taking into account Algeria's special status as a French Overseas Department (until 1962) as well as France's relations with its former colonies Morocco and Tunisia in the framework of the Franc Zone, committed the EC to engage in an economic association with North Africa. This was done with a view to regulating North African countries' access to the EC's emerging common market and to adjust individual member states' bilateral trade relations to the EC's evolving trade regime. More important, it was a function of France's objective to contribute to economic and social stabilisation in the Maghreb regardless of whether this was in line with the aims and preferences of the young Community or whether the latter possessed the political and legal basis for the pursuit of such an aim. This French *diktat* was a harbinger of the role historical legacies and path dependencies of individual member states were bound to play in the years to come, and it led observers to conclude that 'the evolution of the policy was accidental' (Pomfret, 1986: 18). Papa and Petit-Laurent already in 1976 even went so far as to argue that

> each Mediterranean country, considered separately, had a European policy well before the Community realised that it had a *de facto* Mediterranean policy. Indeed, each Mediterranean country had already worked out for itself exactly what the Community could mean for it in the various sectors of its development, well before the Community realised that it was building up bit by bit a mosaic which soon came to represent a Mediterranean totality of a far wider scope than the merely commercial context.
>
> *(Papa and Petit-Laurent, 1976: 266)*

This impression was reinforced as France, throughout the 1960s and 1970s, and inspired by the Gaullist ambition to reinforce the country's rank, both regionally and globally, continued to regard the Mediterranean space almost exclusively through the lens of its *rélations privilégiées* with the three Maghreb countries. It surely used its Community membership to work towards an intensification of relations with Spain, but opposed for example, as of 1967 and the outbreak of the Six-Day War, other member states' attempts at deepening EC–Israel ties, not least in light of its influential and self-proclaimed role as advocate of Arab Mediterranean countries' interests. In contrast, the Benelux countries favoured closer relations with Israel and, for many years, opposed France's aspirations to grant Franco's Spain preferential trade concessions. Italy, as the other Mediterranean member state and regarded by some as a 'non-neocolonialist country enjoying good relations with Arabs' (Aliboni, 1999: 75), assumed for quite a long time a cautious and at times even unfavourable attitude towards a further structuration of the Community's trade relations with Mediterranean non-member countries, as it feared competition in the citrus market – a sector it had dominated for years.

Although the EC-6 succeeded in leaving some of these differences aside when they collectively agreed in 1972 to institutionalise commercial, economic and financial relations with southern neighbours through the adoption of the Global Mediterranean Policy (Shlaim and Yannopoulos, 1976) and the subsequent conclusion of association agreements, this could not conceal the fact that already in the late 1960s and early 1970s, in the framework of the emerging European Political Cooperation (EPC), they had clashed repeatedly over the Israeli–Palestinian conflict and the Palestinian question. On one end of the spectrum was France, then accused by Israel of having a one-sided anti-Israel stance,[1] while on the other the three Benelux countries and Italy were even subjected to heavy Israeli lobbying 'not to succumb to the French position' (Miller, 2011: 20). This came at a time when France had just previously given up its opposition toward the conclusion of an EC–Israel agreement in return for the Netherlands' support for closer ties with the three Maghreb countries and the initiation of exploratory talks with Lebanon and the short-lived United Arab Republic, composed of Syria and Egypt. This diversity of positions and interests among the founding members of the EC became even more pronounced after the accession to the EC of Denmark, Ireland and the United Kingdom in 1973 and Greece, Portugal and Spain in 1981 and 1986, respectively.

As a matter of fact, it was the EC's southern, more than its first northern enlargement that changed the character of intra-EC divisions as far as the southern Mediterranean was concerned. At first, however, the accession of Denmark, one of the most pro-Israeli countries in Europe (Malmvig, 2015: 114), the United Kingdom, *de facto* one of the two architects of the contemporary state system in the southern Mediterranean and the Middle East in the early twentieth century (Hollis, 2010: 8), and Greece, under the then prime minister Andreas Papandreou, the only EC member state to grant full diplomatic status to an external Palestine Liberation Office (in December 1981) accentuated the 'pro-Israel vs. pro-Arab divide' further, thus reinforcing pre-existing divergences of interests within the Community. These divergences did still not run along explicit north–south lines. This was due to the fact that member states' interests in the southern Mediterranean continued to be limited, by and large, to the Israeli–Palestinian conflict and, as far as Denmark, the United Kingdom and other non-Mediterranean EC member states were concerned, the uninterrupted flow of oil supplies. Moreover, it was mainly France that continued trying to raise awareness among EC member states of the 'necessity to ensure the stability of the southern Mediterranean states' (Meyrede, 1999: 53), though these efforts subsided after the Global Policy was put in place during 1975–7. Interestingly, both Italy and Greece, until 1986 the only other two Mediterranean EC member states, abstained from utilising their membership to Europeanise their Mediterranean-related national interests, though Italy, under the then prime minister Bettino Craxi, who in the first half of the 1980s had developed a rather assertive national Mediterranean policy, attempted briefly 'to elaborate a regional security policy in which Italy was expected to play a prominent role' (Aliboni, 1999: 75).

The emergence of the north–south divide in Euro-Mediterranean policies and the beginning of southern EU member states' policy entrepreneurship

It was thus the accession to the EC of Spain, and indirectly of Portugal, in 1986 that truly widened the already existing imbalance of interests and preferences within the Community as their membership implied that the French objective of gradually inserting Maghreb-related (economic) cooperation initiatives into distinctly European frameworks – in particular since 1981 under President Mitterrand – was no longer the ideational prerogative of just one member state. Spain, whose recognition of Israel in January 1986 was a precondition for its accession to the EC, never conceived of the Mediterranean as a global space and Portugal – because of its geographical location on the edge of the Mediterranean and its proximity to Morocco – even less. Instead, due to its previous role as a colonial power in Western Sahara, Spain – determined to transmit to both its European and non-European neighbours that it was 'a European country in the Mediterranean region rather than a Mediterranean country in Europe' (Tovias, 1999: 218)[2] – was at the beginning of its membership predominantly interested in the western Mediterranean, focusing almost exclusively on its two North African enclaves Ceuta and Melilla.

The first signs of a true north–south divide thus emerged when Spain and France declared at the Strasbourg European Council in 1989 that the Community was in need of deepening its relations with the southern Mediterranean (Meyrede, 1999: 58), a plea that led the European Commission to adopt the Matutes report – named after the Spanish Commissioner in charge of the EC's Mediterranean policy – which envisaged a considerable increase in financial assistance for, and enhanced cooperation with, southern Mediterranean countries. French president Mitterrand himself contributed to the sentiment of suspicion among northern member states when only shortly after the European Council meeting he declared that the existing Global Policy approach was unrealistic and even harmful (ibid.). As a matter of fact, he was seconded by the Economic and Social Committee and the European Parliament's Committee for External Economic Relations, both of which criticised the global approach and subsequently its successor, the Renovated Mediterranean Policy (RMP) (Tovias, 1999: 223), for their lack of strategic objectives and financial endowment, but also for the continuous pursuit of individual member state interests at the expense of a truly common approach (Economic and Social Committee, 1989; European Parliament, 1991). Rather than fostering greater Community spirit, this critique was also the starting point for temporary, though considerable, southern Mediterranean-related policy entrepreneurship on the part of southern EC member states – a development that ultimately demonstrated that north–south divergence had become a pattern in Mediterranean-related Community foreign policy-making rather than just an occasionally emerging feature.

Of all the Mediterranean EC member states, France was first in acting as a policy entrepreneur. In 1989, with the support of Spain, Portugal and Italy, it aired the idea of an exclusive multilateral Western Mediterranean Forum, also known as the 5+5 initiative, destined to bring together Mediterranean EC member states with their counterparts from the Maghreb and Malta to engage in regular dialogue on economic, social and cultural matters as well as political, security- and migration-related issues. After the initiative was launched in December 1990 and followed up by another high-level meeting in October 1991, it was temporarily suspended as a result of the civil war in Algeria and major differences among the participants over Libya's involvement in, and support for, international terrorism. It was only resumed in early 2001 when the parties held a foreign ministers' meeting in Lisbon. Initially, the initiative was considered by non-Mediterranean EC member states as a French attempt 'to impose [France's] pre-eminence in the Western Mediterranean' (Meyrede, 1999: 60) and to co-opt other Mediterranean EC member states into a French-led sub-group of four Mediterranean member states. In recent years, non-Mediterranean member states have continued to monitor 5+5 deliberations suspiciously, but have become somewhat more cautious in their critique, also as the French government has repeatedly tried to reassure them that France is 'not trying to create a new structure for cooperation'[3] that would compete with existing ones. On one hand, the more cautious attitude of non-Mediterranean member states is due to the existence of intergovernmental and/or informal sub-regional initiatives that they themselves are participating in and that they have no interest in exposing to outside critique or even scrutiny. On the other hand, a number of non-Mediterranean member states have recently begun to even consider the initiative as a potentially beneficial instrument in the context of the EU's, and thus their own attempts, at curbing immigration, though these considerations have, so far at least, not impacted on their generally rather suspicious views vis-à-vis the 5+5 initiative.

French policy entrepreneurship at the time was complemented by what one observer dubbed Spanish 'Protagonismo' (Gillespie, 1997b). Drawing from a speech by Italian foreign minister Gianni De Michelis in December 1989 in Paris, during which he argued in favour of applying the principles that have been guiding the Conference for Security and Cooperation in Europe (CSCE) to the entire Mediterranean space, Spain in 1990 was instrumental in developing the idea of a Conference for Security and Cooperation in the Mediterranean (CSCM) (ibid.: 34).[4] This proposal, which envisaged the establishment of a CSCE-like pan-Mediterranean system that would provide security and stability and contribute to the easing of tensions through inter-regional, regional and sub-regional cooperation, was initially submitted to all EC member states in late February 1990 and, after consultations with Italy, France and Portugal, to all CSCE member states at a CSCE meeting in September 1990 and, then, in a more elaborated way also in March 1991. However, as soon as it became obvious that the entire initiative followed primarily the logic of Spanish interest- and thus security-related calculations (Aliboni, 1991: 33–4) – a fact that was even publicly admitted by a Spanish senior official[5] – the initiative was eyed with suspicion by Germany and, surprisingly, France itself, which in spite of its co-ownership, and mainly for reasons related to the envisaged involvement of non-Mediterranean countries such as the United States and Canada, regarded it as premature (Carle, 1992: 49). When, eventually, the United Kingdom and the Netherlands also pointed to the potential duplication effects of such a project with other existing security-related initiatives, the idea was quickly abandoned (Gillespie, 1997c: 70).

While Spain, France, Italy, Portugal and Greece were the only EC member states that participated in the short-lived Mediterranean Forum for Dialogue and Cooperation, which was initiated by Egypt in November 1991,[6] Malta, then not yet a member state, also engaged in temporary policy entrepreneurship with its proposal to create a Mediterranean Council. Whereas all the Mediterranean EC member states supported the Maltese proposal,[7] northern member states hardly paid any attention to it, not least as they considered it rather dismissively as just another supposedly desperate attempt to focus more strongly on the southern Mediterranean at a time when they, and Germany and the United Kingdom in particular, were preoccupied with the fallout of the end of the Cold War and the reordering of Europe.

Towards further institutionalisation of Euro-Mediterranean cooperation frameworks: the consolidation of the north–south divide and southern member states' policy entrepreneurship

In order to raise greater awareness among northern member states of Mediterranean-, i.e. Maghreb-related developments, and with a view to potentially diminish the north–south divide in Euro-Mediterranean relations, Spain, mainly through its foreign minister Francisco Fernández Ordóñez, understood these geostrategic dynamics and decided to intensify its lobbying efforts at the EC level just shortly after it had become clear that neither the CSCM nor the Mediterranean Forum and the 5+5 initiative would benefit from Community support. By pushing Commissioner Abel Matutes in early 1992 to develop a partnership concept that focused exclusively on North Africa, and by using a rather apocalyptic rhetoric which allowed him to depict the political and socio-economic situation in the Maghreb as a 'ticking time bomb',[8] Francisco Fernández Ordóñez – and after his death in June 1992, foreign minister Javier Solana – succeeded in obtaining the attention of other, non-Mediterranean member states. As Spain was able to instrumentalise the European Commission, northern member states could no longer afford to not address Mediterranean-related issues as they were for the first time presented as a common concern. This was further accentuated by Portugal's decision to align itself with Spain and devote the Lisbon European Council Summit in June 1992 exclusively to the creation of an EC–Maghreb Partnership (Aghrout and Geddes, 1995) which was eventually adopted by the member states (Economic and Social Committee, 1992; Dobrescu et al. forthcoming; Schumacher et al. 2016), all of which, while in Lisbon, declared that the 'Southern and Eastern shores of the Mediterranean as well as the Middle East are geographical areas in relation to which the Union has strong interests both in terms of security and social stability' (European Council, 1992: 40).

Though the Lisbon European Council was regarded by southern EU member states as a success, the Council conclusions did not rectify the imbalance of interests and preferences within the EU, nor did they offer greater clarity as to how the newly adopted EC–Maghreb Partnership would relate to the RMP.[9] This came particularly to the fore at the Essen European Council Summit in December 1994. In the run-up to this gathering, Spain was increasingly worried about two developments. First, it feared that a more concerted effort on the part of northern EU member states towards integrating former Soviet satellite states in central and eastern Europe into the EU would not only negatively affect the financial benefits it derived from EU cohesion funds, but also that a shift towards the east would inevitably diminish the newfound and fragile focus on the southern Mediterranean and lead to a decrease of financial assistance (Gillespie, 1997b: 68; Tovias 1999: 226–9). Second, the prospect of EU membership of Sweden, Finland and Austria – i.e. countries whose foreign policy priorities traditionally have not revolved around the southern Mediterranean (Behr and Tiilikainen, 2015a; Schumacher, 2001) – accentuated these fears as northern enlargement would not only widen the already existing north–south divide within Euro-Mediterranean relations, but also shift the EU's centre of gravity further north and, by extension, to the east, too (Tovias, 1999: 226). As a result of these considerations, Spain, drawing support from France, Italy and Portugal, and in close collaboration with the new Spanish Commissioner for the southern Mediterranean Manuel Marín and the Greek EU presidency in the second half of 1994, had prepared a proposal for the establishment of a Euro-Mediterranean Partnership (EMP) (Gillespie, 1997a; Joffé, 1999) which would merge the EU–Maghreb Partnership with the RMP and entail a considerable change of the hitherto existing financial distribution ratio between central and eastern Europe and the southern Mediterranean.

At the summit itself, all the features that until then had marked the north–south divide re-emerged with full force and for the first time in Euro-Mediterranean relations also openly. Spain, represented by Prime Minister Felipe González, decided to oppose Germany and thus Chancellor Helmut Kohl and threatened to block the EU's eastern enlargement unless both the EMP and a considerable increase in financial aid for southern Mediterranean countries were approved. Though a major agreement in favour of the Spanish position was reached, the way it came about was clearly marked by issue linkage and blackmailing, to which both northern and southern EU member states reverted (Gomez, 2003). In fact, this process of 'bluff, bluster, horse-trading and fudge' (Edis, 1998: 95–6) has been a key characteristic of southern Mediterranean-related intra-EU decision-making ever since, for literally each time northern and southern, and eventually also eastern, EU member states have had to revisit the distribution of financial aid or the granting of trade preferences, two diametrically opposed positions – free trade vs. financial assistance and partial trade liberalisation – have clashed with one another. Examples in this regard are manifold and range from the confrontations that occurred at the Cannes European Council in June 1995 to discussions revolving around the scope of Euro-Mediterranean association agreements and to the debate on whether southern Mediterranean countries were to be included in the European Neighbourhood Policy in 2002/3 and thus given the possibility to benefit from (partial) integration into the EU's single market.

The eastern enlargement and the emergence of the European Neighbourhood Policy: the north–south divide post-EMP

The north–south divide in Euro-Mediterranean policies widened considerably as a result of the EU's eastern enlargement in 2004–7. Cyprus and Malta, both of which were initially target countries of the EMP, and to a lesser extent Slovenia, only shortly after their accession to the EU began to align themselves with the 'Club Med' as regards Euro-Mediterranean issues more generally. In contrast, the remaining seven central and east European member states' positioning vis-à-vis what since 2003 came to be considered the EU's southern neighbourhood developed, if at all, at a much slower pace, not least due to the dominant objective in their respective foreign policies being to contribute to stability and democratic and economic transition first and foremost in eastern Europe.

When, in 2002, first the United Kingdom and then Sweden in anticipation of the upcoming enlargement proposed the establishment of a European neighbourhood policy that would address Ukraine, Belarus and Moldova – all of which rank highly on the respective foreign policy agendas of the Baltic countries, and of Poland, Hungary, Slovakia and the Czech Republic (the Visegrad-4) – this alerted southern EU member states to the fact that the already fragile balance of EU foreign policy priorities was about to tip in favour of eastern Europe. Rather than France or Spain, Italy was the first to react and, benefiting from the support of Commission President Romano Prodi, ensured that what eventually developed into the European Neighbourhood Policy (ENP) in March 2003 incorporated also all the southern Mediterranean countries (European Commission, 2003). However, understanding already before it had even joined the EU that the British and Swedish proposals presented an opportunity for Poland to shape the future course of EU foreign policy and thus possibly soften the hitherto rather strong focus on the southern Mediterranean, the Polish government also attempted to engage in policy entrepreneurship. In January 2003, it submitted the 'Polish proposals concerning the future shape of the enlarged EU towards the new eastern neighbours', in which it argued for a considerable strengthening of EU relations with the latter, the conclusion of new association agreements, as well as the inclusion of Russia in the European Economic Space in the medium term.[10] Though this rather premature activism was quickly dismissed by Germany out of fear that it would antagonise Russia, it signalled to all EU member states that EU foreign policy-making more generally, and Mediterranean-related decision-making in particular, would, once enlargement was completed, not only imply more time-consuming and probably even more sophisticated bargaining, but also be exposed to more favour exchanging and issue linkage, and most of all veto playing (Schumacher et al. 2016).

Though eastern member states have turned out to be passive and unenthusiastic, albeit loyal members of Euro-Mediterranean cooperation frameworks (Rozsa, 2005; Behr and Tiilikainen, 2015a) ever since they joined the EU, they have at the same time occasionally resorted to favour exchanging and issue linkage as well as in fact veto playing. As far as the latter is concerned, the Czech Republic (Najšlová, 2015) for example prevented a common EU position, or rather the notion thereof, being adopted when in 2012 it was the only EU member state that voted against a status upgrade of Palestine at the United Nations. Also, in early 2009 in the framework of its EU presidency, it was the only EU member state that explicitly defended Israel's unlawful actions in Gaza in the context of Operation Cast Lead (Bouris, 2014), insisting for quite some time that the initially planned upgrade of EU–Israel relations must not be affected.[11] With regard to the former, i.e. favour exchanging and applying issue linkage, the most prominent example is the creation of the Eastern Partnership (EaP) in 2009 (Schumacher, 2011), which was inseparably linked to the emergence of the Union for the Mediterranean (UfM) (Bicchi and Gillespie, 2012).

While the idea to strengthen the ENP's eastern dimension was first discussed in a Polish–Lithuanian proposal of December 2007 and a subsequent proposal by the Czech Republic in April 2008, Poland and Sweden developed these further and presented the EaP initiative in May 2008 to the Foreign Affairs Council. In so doing, they could rely on the support of even more non-Mediterranean member states, of which Romania, Bulgaria, the Czech Republic, Hungary, Slovakia and the three Baltic states, as well as Germany stood out. While the latter had already in early 2007 proposed the so-called ENP+,[12] the newly admitted central and east European EU member states participated in Polish–Swedish policy entrepreneurship – a development that culminated in the adoption of the 'Elaboration of the Eastern Partnership' paper in October 2008 and the 'Warsaw Joint Statement' in late November 2008, both of which eventually converged into the EaP initiative that was officially launched at the Warsaw Summit in 2009 (Wojna and Gniazdowski, 2009).[13] In particular, for France as well as other Mediterranean member states interested in seeing the UfM initiative go through the European Council, the prospect of an emerging EaP was almost impossible to prevent. It had become obvious already by December 2007, when the Polish–Lithuanian proposal was launched, that the advocates of enhanced cooperation with eastern neighbours were determined to link acceptance of the UfM with their plans to create a sub-regional cooperation framework for the east. In this regard, it did not come as a surprise that France even felt compelled to offer both Hungary and the Czech Republic symbolic side payments in the form of the conclusion of strategic bilateral partnerships, trusting that these would preclude the two governments from vetoing the UfM (Schumacher, 2011: 94). Thus, by promoting the UfM, France unintentionally but *de facto* generated a collective win set for a large number of southern, northern and eastern member states as their respective foreign policy interests and preferences in the Mediterranean or in eastern Europe could be Europeanised without generating negative distributional consequences. Moreover, the establishment of the UfM and the EaP respectively provided both France and Poland, and by extension their respective supporters in the European Council, with an opportunity to capitalise on their policy entrepreneurship also vis-à-vis their domestic constituencies as it allowed them to portray the establishment of these frameworks as examples of their leverage and thus allegedly considerable influence on EU foreign policy-making.

Conclusion: the north–south divide post-Arab Spring in perspective

The outbreak of what was widely and rather prematurely coined 'the Arab Spring' in early 2011 had a rather mixed impact on the north–south divide in Mediterranean-related EU foreign policy-making. Unsurprisingly, when the European Commission and the High Representative for Foreign Affairs and Security Policy (HR/VP) published in March 2011 the EU's 'partnership for democracy and shared prosperity with the southern Mediterranean' (European Commission and HR/VP, 2011a), which was destined to outline the EU's response to the Arab uprisings, central and eastern member states intervened almost immediately. Anxious that such a partnership might lead to a reinforced focus on the Mediterranean at the expense of the EaP, they demanded that the balance, carefully crafted in 2008–9, between the southern and eastern neighbourhood was kept and that such a partnership was not meant to be a precursor for a new and potentially costly policy initiative. This interventionism bore fruit quickly as the 'new response to a changing neighbourhood' that was presented by the Commission and the HR/VP in May 2011 (European Commission and HR/VP, 2011b), converged with the previous communication and no longer addressed just the southern Mediterranean but also eastern Europe.

Even though this underlines the continuously existing protective attitude of mainly eastern and southern EU member states vis-à-vis their respective neighbourhoods in recent years on the EU level, most recent developments in the southern Mediterranean, such as Islamist radicalisation, state collapse, violent inter- and intra-state conflict, the current refugee crisis and in particular their cross-regional fallout, have been somewhat narrowing the north–south divide to the extent that nowadays also many eastern and northern member states acknowledge the importance that the southern Mediterranean has not just for Mediterranean EU member states, but in fact for the entire EU. Some ideational convergence between northern, eastern and southern member states is thus emerging, as they increasingly share a growing number of threat perceptions and security concerns in regard to the southern Mediterranean, and as they unite seemingly more easily behind corresponding EU responses. This came particularly to the fore in the framework of the 2015 review of the ENP. On the one hand, eastern, northern and southern member states resorted to established coordination patterns and aligned their individual positions with those of other member states which are marked by similar path dependencies and which share similar foreign policy interests and preferences in either neighbourhood. For example, among the many non-papers that member states submitted to the European Commission and the European External Action Service, i.e. the two bodies that coordinated the review, several were co-authored by either most southern Mediterranean member states collectively, or by the Visegrad-4, or jointly by some eastern and northern member states (Furness et al., 2017). On the other hand, however, three non-papers were even drafted jointly by northern, eastern and southern member states, the most characteristic of which in this regard was the Presidency Trio paper, co-authored by Malta, Slovakia and the Netherlands (ibid.) – a development that hints at the fact that after years of considerable north–south antagonism over Mediterranean-related matters, even some sort of north–south joint policy entrepreneurship had finally become possible in a post-Arab Spring setting. This is underlined by the fact that even though some of the non-papers of 'like-minded' member states still argued along the lines of the hitherto existing north–south divide and advocated explicitly the strengthening of either the UfM or the EaP in the overall framework of a revised ENP, all non-papers expressed similar strategic concerns and focused more or less on the same priority actions (ibid.).

Nonetheless, it remains to be seen whether this recent ideational convergence was just a temporary development or in fact the beginning of a more systematic convergence of member states' foreign policy preferences and interests, and possibly policies, in and towards the southern Mediterranean. So far at least, the emerging ideational convergence has not translated into a more cohesive approach as the north–south divide continues to have a strong bearing on EU member states, with those directly affected by, for example, the current refugee crisis, pushing for collective action while particularly eastern member states refuse to submit to a unified approach.

One year after the new ENP has been adopted, and six months after the publication of the EU Global Strategy by the HR/VP (HR/VP, 2016), the EU and its member states are still in a process of elaborating how these overarching policy frameworks towards the southern Mediterranean and beyond can be linked to one another and subsequently implemented. But even if the member states – northern, eastern and southern alike – succeeded in developing such a roadmap, it seems rather likely that its operationalisation, and with it the potential reduction of the north–south divide in Mediterranean-related EU foreign policy-making, has become a function of the multi-faceted developments in the EU's neighbourhood itself and is, once more, dependent on the political will of EU member states, most of which, in times of growing Euroscepticism, have not necessarily displayed much appetite for collective and supposedly costly EU (foreign policy) action in recent years.

Notes

1 See statement to the Knesset by Prime Minister Golda Meir, 15 December 1969, in: *Israel Documents*, Vol. 2, p. 890.
2 Initially, as a non-EC member state linked to the EC through a preferential trade agreement, Spain until 1986 was for two years a target country of the EC's Global Mediterranean Policy before it then envisaged EC membership.
3 Briefing of the press by the spokesperson of the French Foreign Ministry on 23 January 2001.
4 Strictly speaking, the idea of a CSCM dates back to a proposal already made by Italian foreign minister Giulio Andreotti during a CSCE conference in Venice in October 1984 (see Schumacher, 2005).
5 See *New York Times*, 20 March 1991, interview with the then Deputy General Director in the North Africa Department of the Spanish foreign ministry, Miguel Ángel Moratinos (see also Schumacher, 2005).
6 See also *Al Ahram*, 10 November 1991 (in Schumacher, 2005).
7 See *Agence Europe*, 9 April 1993 (in Schumacher, 2005).
8 Ordóñez quoted in Gillespie (1997b: 36).
9 In particular southern Mediterranean countries outside the Maghreb voiced their concern, as was exemplified by the statement of the Egyptian foreign minister: 'I would like to express our serious preoccupations concerning the so-called Maghreb policy which we believe should be developed into a general Mediterranean initiative' (*Agence Europe*, 24 July 1992, in Schumacher, 2005).
10 See 'Non-paper z polskimi propozycjami w sprawie przyszłego kształtu polityki rozszerzonej EU wobec nowych wschodnich słsiadów' in: *Polityka rozszerzonej Unii Europejskiej wobec nowych sąsiadów*, Warsaw: Fundacja im. Stefana Batorego, 2003, pp. 93–107, available at: www.batory.org.pl/doc/nowi_s.pdf
11 See *EUobserver*, 27 April 2009, 'Czech EU Presidency Splits with EU Commissioner over Israel'. Eventually, Belgium, Sweden and Portugal opposed the Czech position and forced the Czech EU Presidency to postpone the upgrade. See https://euobserver.com/foreign/28012
12 See the German EU presidency's programme 'Europe Succeeding Together' 1 January–30 June 2007, available at: www.eu2007.de
13 The 'Elaboration of the Eastern Partnership' paper was drafted by Poland and Sweden with the support of the Czech Republic and published on 3 October 2008. See Joint Statement of the Foreign Ministers of the Visegrad Group Countries and of Bulgaria, Estonia, Lithuania, Latvia, Romania and Sweden, Warsaw, 24 November 2008.

References

Aghrout, A. and A. Geddes (1995), 'The Maghreb and the European Union: From Development Cooperation to Partnership?', *International Politics*, 33, 227–43.

Aliboni, R. (1991), 'European Security across the Mediterranean', Chaillot Paper 2, WEU Institute for Security Studies, Paris.

Aliboni, R. (1999), 'Italy and the Mediterranean in the 1990s', in: Stavridis, S., Couloumbis, T., Veremis, T. and Waites, N. (eds), *The Foreign Policies of the European Union's Mediterranean States and Applicant Countries in the 1990s*, Houndmills Basingstoke: Palgrave Macmillan, pp. 73–98.

Behr, T. and T. Tiilikainen (eds) (2015a), *Northern Europe and the Making of the EU's Mediterranean and Middle East Policies. Normative Leaders or Passive Bystanders?*, Abingdon: Routledge.

Behr, T. and T. Tiilikainen (2015b), 'Introduction', in: Behr, T. and Tiilikainen, T. (eds), *Northern Europe and the Making of the EU's Mediterranean and Middle East Policies: Normative Leaders or Passive Bystanders?*, Abingdon: Routledge, pp. 1–10.

Bicchi, F. (2007), *European Foreign Policy-Making toward the Mediterranean*, Basingstoke: Palgrave Macmillan.

Bicchi, F. and R. Gillespie (eds) (2012), *The Union for the Mediterranean*, Abingdon: Routledge.

Bouris, D. (2014), *The European Union and Occupied Palestinian Territories: State-Building without a State*, Abingdon: Routledge.

Carle, C. (1992), 'France, Mediterranean and Southern European Security', in: Aliboni, R. (ed.), *Southern European Security in the 1990s*, London and New York: Pinter, pp. 40–51.

Dobrescu, M., T. Schumacher and S. Stavridis (forthcoming), 'Southern Europe: Portugal, Spain, Italy, Malta, Greece, Cyprus', in: Hadfield, A., Manners, I. and Whitman, R. (eds), *Foreign Policies of EU Member States: Continuity and Europeanisation*, Abingdon: Routledge.

Economic and Social Committee of the European Communities (1989), *Opinion of the Economic and Social Committee on the Mediterranean Policy of the European Community*, Brussels, 12 July, CES(89) 835.

Economic and Social Committee of the European Communities (1992), *Opinion on Economic Cooperation with the Maghreb Countries*, CES(92)1041, Luxembourg, 24 September.

Edis, R. (1998), 'Does the Barcelona Process Matter?', *Mediterranean Politics*, 3(3), 93–105.

European Commission (2003), *Wider Europe – Neighbourhood: A Framework of Relations with our Eastern and Southern Neighbours*, Brussels, COM(2003) 104 final.

European Commission and High Representative for Foreign Affairs and Security Policy (2011a), *A Partnership for Democracy and Shared Prosperity with the Southern Mediterranean*, Brussels, 8 March, COM(2011) 200 final.

European Commission and High Representative for Foreign Affairs and Security Policy (2011b), *A New Response to a Changing Neighbourhood: A Review of European Neigbourhood Policy*, Brussels, 25 May, COM(2011) 303.

European Council (1992), *Conclusions of the Presidency*, Lisbon, 26/27 June. Available online at www.europarl.europa.eu/summits/lisbon/li1_en.pdf

European Parliament, Committee for External Economic Relations (1991), *Report of the Committee on External Economic Relations on a Revamped Mediterranean Policy*, Session Documents 1991, Brussels, 3 May.

Furness, M., T. Henoekl and T. Schumacher (2017), *Crisis, Coordination and Coherence: European Decision-Making and the 2015 European Neighbourhood Policy Review*, unpublished manuscript.

Gillespie, R. (ed.) (1997a), *The Euro-Mediterranean Partnership: Political and Economic Perspectives*, London: Frank Cass.

Gillespie, R. (1997b), 'Spanish Protagonismo and the Euro-Med Partnership Initiative', in: Gillespie, R. (ed.), *The Euro-Mediterranean Partnership. Political and Economic Perspectives*, London: Frank Cass, pp. 33–48.

Gillespie, R. (1997c), 'Northern European Perceptions of the Barcelona Process', *Revista CIDOB d'Afers Internacionals*, 37, 65–75.

Gomez, R. (2003), *Negotiating the Euro-Mediterranean Partnership: Strategic Action in EU Foreign Policy?*, Farnham: Ashgate.

High Representative for Foreign Affairs and Security Policy (HR/VP) (2016), *Shared Vision, Common Action: A Stronger Europe. A Global Strategy for the European Union's Foreign and Security Policy*, Brussels.

Hollis, R. (2010), *Britain and the Middle East in the 9/11 Era*, London: Wiley-Blackwell and Chatham House.

Joffé, G. (ed.) (1999), *Perspectives on Development: The Euro-Mediterranean Partnership*, London: Frank Cass.

Malmvig, H. (2015), 'Denmark: Between Clumsy Hans and Thumbelina?', in: Behr, T. and Tiilikainen, T. (eds), *Northern Europe and the Making of the EU's Mediterranean and Middle East Policies: Normative Leaders or Passive Bystanders?*, Abingdon: Routledge, pp. 109–30.

Meyrede, L. (1999), 'France's Foreign Policy in the Mediterranean', in: Stavridis, S. and Couloumbis, T., Veremis, T. and Waites, N. (eds), *The Foreign Policies of the European Union's Mediterranean States and Applicant Countries in the 1990s*, Houndmills Basingstoke: Palgrave Macmillan, pp. 40–72.

Miller, R. (2011), *Inglorious Disarray: Europe, Israel and the Palestinians since 1967*, London: Hurst.

Najšlová, L. (2015), 'The Czech Republic: Many Allies, One Friend', in: Behr, T. and Tiilikainen, T. (eds), *Northern Europe and the Making of the EU's Mediterranean and Middle East Policies: Normative Leaders or Passive Bystanders?*, Abingdon: Routledge, pp. 159–78.

Papa, G.-P. and J. Petit-Laurent (1976), 'Commercial Relations between the EEC and the Mediterranean Countries: An Analysis of Recent Trends in Trade Flow', in: Shlaim, A. and Yannopoulos, G. (eds), *The EEC and the Mediterranean Countries*, Cambridge: Cambridge University Press, pp. 265–304.

Pomfret, R. (1986), *Mediterranean Policy of the European Community: A Study of Discrimination in Trade*, Basingstoke: Palgrave Macmillan.

Rozsa, E. (2005), 'National Attitudes of New EU Member States towards the EMP: The Case of Hungary', EuroMeSCo Paper 42, Lisbon.

Schumacher, T. (2001), 'The Mediterranean as a New Foreign Policy Challenge? Sweden and the Barcelona Process', *Mediterranean Politics*, 6(3), 81–102.

Schumacher, T. (2005). *Die Europäische Union als internationaler Akteur im südlichen Mittelmeerraum: 'Actor Capability' und EU-Mittelmeerpolitik*, Baden-Baden: NOMOS.

Schumacher, T. (2011), 'Germany and Central and Eastern European Countries: Laggards or Veto-Players?', *Mediterranean Politics*, 16(1), 79–98.

Schumacher, T., D. Bouris and M. Olszewska (2016), 'Of Policy Entrepreneurship, Bandwagoning and Free-riding: EU Member States and Multilateral Cooperation Frameworks for Europe's Southern Neighbourhood', *Global Affairs*, 2, 259–72, DOI: 10.1080/23340460.2016.1216230.

Shlaim, A. and G. Yannopoulos (eds) (1976), *The EEC and the Mediterranean Countries*, Cambridge: Cambridge University Press.

Tovias, A. (1999), 'Spain's Input in Shaping the EU's Mediterranean Policies, 1989–1996', in: Raanan Rein (ed.), *Spain and the Mediterranean since 1898*, London: Frank Cass, pp. 216–34.

Wojna, B. and M. Gniazdowski (2009), *Eastern Partnership: The Opening Report*, Warsaw: PISM, April.

9

THE NORTH–SOUTH DIVIDE

Southern perceptions of the Mediterranean

Yahia H. Zoubir

The Mediterranean is one geographic entity; however, its divides are numerous. The north–south divide is the most noteworthy because it has had lasting effects on the identities and mutual perceptions of the peoples of both shores. This division is exacerbated in the southern Mediterranean's colonial history. While the southern Mediterranean displays close similarity to the problems that characterize the states that compose it, this region is not homogeneous and attempts at regional integration schemes (such as the Arab Maghreb Union [UMA] and the Agadir Agreement) have all but failed. Southern Mediterranean states suffer from similar socio-economic, political and security problems, namely, economic disparities, bad governance, poverty, corruption, authoritarianism, cronyism and domestic terrorism, problems which partly account for the upheavals that began in 2010 (Zoubir, 2012a). These domestic conditions have continuously resulted in the widening of the development gap with Europe and are thus reflected in the relations between the two shores of the Mediterranean.

This chapter deals with the perceptions that southern Mediterranean states and societies have of this complex zone characterized by conflicts and antagonisms but also by human and economic interactions among its inhabitants, thus creating interdependence between the shores of this unique sea. The chapter reviews the perceptions that Arabs[1] have of the Mediterranean. The largest part looks at the interactions between the southern Mediterranean governments and the European Union (EU) and their perceptions of the various political, economic and security proposals that the EU has put forth to establish a zone of stable neighborhood in the south. In the second part, the chapter looks at the perceptions that civil societies, which have been divided into four categories, have about the north. The main argument throughout the chapter is that there exists a perception of a permanent divide between the north and the south at all levels, a perception shared by both states and societies.

General Arab perceptions of the Mediterranean

In view of the conditions prevailing in the south, on the one hand, and of the various proposals put forth by the EU, on the other, what have been the southern perceptions of the Mediterranean? While it is not easy to gauge those perceptions, one can get a good sense of them from some opinions polls, newspaper articles, and interviews with officials and academics, as well as with members of civil society organizations. Before gauging southern perceptions, a few remarks should be made. First, there is no evidence that there is an Arab vision of the Mediterranean. The great Arab thinker, Ibn Khaldûn wrote about the importance of the Mediterranean for Muslim rulers; he discussed the strategy that these rulers had adopted in order to take control of the maritime space separating Muslims from their Christian enemies and the time of Muslim maritime greatness, as part of a long history of the Mediterranean, before the decline caused by the inability of the incumbent rulers (Picard, 2010). The vision of a maritime space separating Muslims in the south from Christians in the north of the Mediterranean has continued to this day. Arabs focus on the contradictions and conflicts that pervade this zone. Decades after their independence, Arabs still feel the effects of colonialism and perceived neocolonial approaches threatening the south. Indeed, independence has not resulted in an end of the dependence on the former colonial powers. For Arabs, conflicts dominate in the Mediterranean. During the Cold War, the United States and the Soviet Union vied for domination through proxy wars in Palestine, Western Sahara, Libya, Egypt, and Syria, to name but a few. For Arabs, the Mediterranean, regardless of the absence of a natural demarcation line, is a divided zone, where the Judeo-Christian north prevents the Arab-Muslim south from ever emerging as an equal power. In their minds, there is a clear line separating the developed north from the developing south on most issues. In Arab eyes, the north encompasses, at least at the popular level, not only the European countries, but also the United States and Israel, i.e., the western world. While Arabs continue to view the former colonial powers with great suspicion, they also perceive the United States and Israel as the main threat to Arab security.

Arab states' perceptions of the Mediterranean

Undoubtedly, Arabs perceive the Mediterranean as a zone of perpetual conflict and inequalities. The Arabs do not view the Mediterranean as a geopolitical entity, nor do they have a Mediterranean policy. True, they feel concerned by events in the Mediterranean, such as the threats of weapons of mass destruction, terrorism, the dominant presence of the US Sixth Fleet and sub-Saharan refugees, but they see them simply as threats taking place in a geographical space. Put eloquently, "Arab interest in the Mediterranean is a function of their interest in the EU rather than an interest in a Mediterranean standing by itself, independent of any other considerations" (Soltan, 2010, 69). To think that the southern Mediterranean leaders could conceive of the possibility of an integrated Mediterranean region is naïve at best, for in spite of sharing the same religion, a similar language and common history, the Mediterranean Arabs have failed in their own zone to form any type of integrated region (Labaronne, 2013), so how could they consider an integrated *Mediterranean* region, assuming that this is really the desired outcome?

The southern Mediterranean region is a fragmented region dominated by authoritarian regimes that view security mostly in terms of their own preservation. These regimes are faced with internal threats rather than with any external strategic menace, with the exception of the countries in the Levant that are confronted with the intractability of the Palestinian–Israeli conflict. The central Maghreb (Algeria, Morocco, and Tunisia), which can be considered as a Mediterranean sub-system, has the potential for building a security community; however, for historic and ideological reasons the regimes there have shown no willingness to build one, owing mostly to the rivalry between the two major powers, Algeria and Morocco. The suspicions between these two states can be observed in the constant, costly arms race (security dilemma), but also in the go-it-alone policies toward the multilateral organizations, such as the EMP, NATO's Mediterranean Dialogue (MD), or the 5+5 forum. The Western Sahara conflict is often used as the justification for the lack of regional cooperation and integration, but, in reality, even without this conflict, regional cooperation would be hampered due to long-lasting issues in Algerian–Moroccan relations (Zoubir, 2000). Yet it would be mistaken to blame the Maghrebi states alone for the failure to build an integrated Maghreb and/or a security community. One can hypothesize that the preferential treatment that external actors show vis-à-vis one of the Maghreb states, as for instance, granting Morocco Advanced Status in the EU (2008), a status which was extended to Jordan in 2010 and to Tunisia in the form of Privileged Partnership in 2011, or the US designation in 2004 of Morocco as a Major Non-NATO Ally, hinder the erection of a regional community in the southern Mediterranean, for those European and US decisions are precisely the type of actions that exacerbate tensions among Mediterranean Arabs and their competition with one another, but also, wittingly or not, they remove any incentive for the countries of the south to cooperate with one another or with the north as a bloc. This also reinforces the perceptions among individual north African perceptions that the north seeks to accentuate divisions in the south. The question worth asking, of course, is whether such bilateral agreements between the EU and individual Arab states contribute in any way to south–south cooperation and/or the building of a security community in the Mediterranean? The answer is self-evident; indeed, the EU's attribution of an Advanced Status to a particular state, for instance, in spite of the rhetoric, only serves limited objectives without producing any acceleration of community building.

In sum, these European bilateral policies and the multiplication of initiatives have the following consequences: i) they reduce the need for the states to build south–south security cooperation or a security community and consolidate the preference for bilateral relations with the EU and the Mediterranean Dialogue; ii) the preference for bilateral agreements provides the justification for the EU/MD not encouraging south–south cooperation; iii) they also aggravate south–south tensions because the privileged status they grant a given state in the EU/MD increases the perception of insecurity of its rival; iv) such policies result in the southern states seeking strategic partnerships with non-Mediterranean powers, not only with the United States but also Russia and China. For instance, Algeria has developed strong ties with the United States and entered strategic partnerships with both Russia and China. Undoubtedly, the contradictory policies expose the credibility of the EU with respect to its normative values, but they also put in question its real motivations in the region. Evidently, this also shapes the perceptions of states and civil societies in the southern Mediterranean.

In addition to these issues, it is important to emphasize the different security cultures between the two shores, differences which also affect the perceptions that southern Mediterranean rulers have of security. During the Cold War, for Arabs—both in the Mashreq and the Maghreb—Israel, seen as an expansionist and aggressive power, represented the biggest threat to their sovereignty and territorial integrity. However, in the post-Cold War era, the incumbent regimes have faced new, domestic issues that have become the main threats to their security and stability. Rulers in the Maghreb and in Egypt were confronted by the rise of Islamism in different forms, radical or otherwise. Challenged by a potent Islamist threat, the regimes created the UMA partly to respond collectively to this threat (Zoubir, 2012b). However,

> Security cooperation at the region level is still unfamiliar to the Arab security culture. Building regional security through cooperative means creates strong suspicions in governments attached to national military power and the traditional view of state strategic secrecy. The Arab countries never practiced cooperative security mechanisms as the European countries have been doing since the Helsinki Process started. Also comprehensive security is a suspicious concept to Arab political elite and

> policy-makers . . . The human and political dimension of comprehensive security . . . is still unaccepted by the Arab leaders who consider human and political measures of enhancing region security as true violation of the Arab political order.
>
> *(Attinà, 2004, 24)*

Therefore, while the sub-systems of the Mediterranean are interdependent in terms of security, making the Mediterranean "one integrated security region" (Soltan, 2004, 4), building a Mediterranean security community has been a much harder endeavor than its optimistic proponents imagined. The reasons for the obstacles to operationalize a Mediterranean security community have much to do with the different perceptions and expectations that the two shores of the Mediterranean hold.

Southern Mediterranean perceptions of Mediterranean security

The Euro-Mediterranean Partnership in 1995 was the culmination of previous southern European initiatives to engage with North Africa. Immigration, the rise of Islamism, the civil conflict in Algeria and terrorist attacks in Paris were among the concerns that led to its launch. Developments in the south also explain the EU's increased neoliberal economic policy (Joffé, 2016b, 30) and security engagement with the southern Mediterranean rather than an engagement on "co-development, regional integration or democracy promotion" (Khader, 2016, 6), although, in rhetoric, the EMP was predicated upon a commitment to good governance and respect for human rights, as well as the integration of the southern Mediterranean region (south–south integration). Essentially, for the EU, the gradual creation of a Euro-Mediterranean free-trade zone was a prerequisite if a Euro-Mediterranean zone of peace, stability and security had any chance of materializing. In other words, neoliberal economic development in the southern Mediterranean would produce positive effects because it would promote long-term stability due to enhanced job opportunities in the south, which would eliminate one of the roots of migration, increase the standards of living and reduce the appeal of extremist religious ideologies. Not only that, but economic liberalism would eventually result in liberal democratic institutions, prerequisites for cooperation and stability at home and globally. Unsurprisingly, France was an enthusiastic advocate of the EMP and decided to engage with its former colonies in the region so that it could undermine the old order in the southern Mediterranean (Volpi, 2016[2004]). But even though the southern Mediterranean states joined the EMP, they did so with different motivations and expectations. Thus, participation in the EMP was never a genuine commitment to European values given that the southern Mediterranean states were all authoritarian with no intent to change their domestic structures of power to accommodate what they perceived as interference in their internal affairs. They also were cognizant of the fact that the EU had no power to resolve the Arab–Israeli conflict and that neither Israel nor the United States were willing to allow the EU to have any say in the "peace process" and neither was the EU a neutral broker in the Western Sahara conflict (Darbouche and Zoubir, 2008). With respect to the Palestinian–Israeli conflict, Mediterranean Arabs also felt that Europe practically enticed them to participate alongside Israel in a Mediterranean partnership while the prospects for peace were quite remote. Furthermore, the prevailing perception was that the EU remained the main driver of the whole EMP process, which failed to differentiate between the southern Mediterranean countries as the EU adopted a "one-size-fits-all" approach (Joffé, 2016a, 313). In their view, the EU wished to impose its own approach to southern Mediterranean security without the south having any input into European security policy, which did not give enough consideration to interstate conflicts in the south (Soltan, 2004). For the southern regimes, security was seen as part and parcel of national security and their own stability. Access to EU markets and aid to development, not political reforms, were, and still are, perceived as the best means to help southern Mediterranean countries and stem the flow of illegal migrants to Europe.

From the start, southern Mediterranean leaders were not truly enthusiastic about the perceived EU interference in their domestic affairs and the violation of their sovereignty. Not only were they apprehensive about the EU's call for political reform, but they also sensed that the Barcelona Process aimed at erecting "fortress Europe," to secure Europe from the instability originating in the southern shores of the Mediterranean, particularly the threat of massive illegal immigration. While they were resentful of EU conditionality, they were aware that southern European states were less eager to impose this conditionality to extract political reforms because they needed cooperation from the southern Mediterranean governments in protecting the northern shores of the Mediterranean. This had become even more evident after 9/11 and the subsequent EU securitization policies which southern Mediterranean regimes used to circumvent the need to reform and to convince Europeans of the link between Europe's security and the durability of the incumbent regimes in the south. Under those circumstances, human rights, though inscribed in their association agreements with the EU, did not stop MEDA aid from being disbursed to autocratic regimes, such as Egypt, in spite of an appalling human rights record and dismal reforms.

The southern Mediterranean regimes perceived the Global War on Terrorism as a timely opportunity and the competing multilateral arrangements offered by the United States (Broader Middle East and North Africa Initiative, Middle East Partnership Initiative, Pan-Sahel Initiative, Trans-Saharan Counterterrorism Partnership, etc.) and NATO, whose public relations drive had succeeded in earning a more positive image, as a way of deflecting the EU's discourse on democracy promotion. The regimes paid lip-service to the calls from both the United States and the EU to promote democracy and the rule of law, but in reality they astutely made some cosmetic changes, which resulted in a new authoritarianism (King, 2009), which satisfied nonetheless the European demands for democratization.

Southern Mediterranean perceptions of the ENP, the new ENP and the UfM

The launch of the European Neighborhood Policy (ENP) in 2004, which offered a bilateral track, did nothing to assuage the generally negative perceptions of the southern Mediterranean partners. While the new policy offered eastern Europeans integration to the EU, no such proposition was extended to the south; all they were promised was "accession to everything but the institutions" of the EU. In addition, the perception in the southern Mediterranean countries was that this was yet another initiative dictated from the north. Besides,

> it added nothing to partner-state empowerment, nor did it improve access to the European labor market or reduce the securitization of the relationship across the Mediterranean basin. It also undermined the objective of removing the "hub-and-spoke" nature of the original agreement, with its implication of European hegemony over the EMP, for the new arrangement actually intensified the hierarchical characteristics of the relationship and made them permanent.
>
> *(Joffé, 2016a, 315)*

This observation captures accurately the perception that some southern Mediterranean states held regarding the ENP and their indifference toward the Mediterranean dimension of the European Security and Defense Policy (ESDP), which, too, was perceived as an asymmetrical partnership. For instance, while Morocco endorsed the ENP, Algeria, a major energy supplier to Europe less dependent on EU funding and which has always upheld an independent foreign policy (Zoubir, 2005), was reluctant to endorse another initiative deemed "Eurocentric." The Algerian government resented the fact that the ENP was initiated without consultation with the potential beneficiaries; in Algiers' eyes, the absence of such consultation undermined the claims of partnership that were supposed to constitute the foundations of cooperation between the two shores of the Mediterranean and thus prove that the notion of "shared European values" inscribed in the neighborhood policy were no less than an imposition of European hegemony in the ENP (Boumghar, 2013). Furthermore, for Algerians, the ENP's "carrot and stick" approach (conditionality), the "more for more" and "less for less" principles with respect to adherence to human rights, and, implicitly to cooperation on migration, reflected a European policy similar to a teacher (EU)–student (southern Mediterranean partners) relationship. Southern Mediterranean leaders in general resent what they perceive as a diktat on democratic change, which they argue should be internally driven and not subject to outside interference. Many southern Mediterranean partners have argued that their cultural values are different from those prevailing among eastern and central Europeans and that, therefore, differentiation should be acknowledged by the EU in dealing with the southern shore.

Whatever their reservations, and even though it was "classified as a low-credibility association policy because it explicitly excludes a membership perspective for the ENP countries and does not set high political standards for participation" (Schimmelfennig and Scholtz, 2009, 24), most southern Mediterranean partners adhered, not without suspicions, to the ENP and, eventually, to the New ENP launched in 2011. Adherence to the New ENP (NENP) was accepted more easily, although it still contained conditions on democracy promotion, because the southern Mediterranean partners felt that they were consulted and associated with the new conception and because NENP took into account the specificities of the various partners. With the so called "Arab Winter" and the eruption of serious conflicts, not only in the southern neighborhood (Libya and Syria) but also in Ukraine, the ENP Review of 2015 referred to the "ring of fire" which had replaced the "ring of friends" in its neighborhood. As a long-time observer of Mediterranean relations put it, the 2015 ENP Review was "a step back when compared to its two predecessors . . . as it invariably leads to the substantiation of and thus support for autocratic rule in the EU's Southern neighborhood" (Schumacher, 2016, 1) and practically put an end to the conditionality that had been one of the bases of the ENP in its relationship with the southern partners. Clearly, in view of the fallout from the "Arab Spring," stability of the regimes and the polities in the south has now taken precedence over the democratization promotion trumpeted hitherto.

The need for closer cooperation with the autocratic regimes in addressing problems such as terrorism, illegal migration, and drug trafficking compelled the EU to grant southern Mediterranean regimes a more equal position in the partnership ("ownership"), thus satisfying their long-standing demand for equal partnership. However, the satisfaction of the southern Mediterranean regimes does not derive from their ability to convince the EU to grant them ownership in the Mediterranean partnerships, but from the fact that they can preserve their autocratic rule—without, however, changing the structural north–south economic dependency. In fact, far from the constructivist, relatively optimistic, thinking about the erection of a security community in the Mediterranean (Adler and Crawford, 2002), the dominant EU approach is based on neorealism, the same paradigm that dominates the thinking of southern Mediterranean rulers; hence, "the EU has asserted itself as neither a strategic actor nor a normative power" (Noutcheva, 2015, 34). Worse still, the EU, and this is a strong perception among southern Mediterranean regimes, has failed to demonstrate any leverage in conflict resolution, the Arab–Israeli and Western Sahara conflicts being the best illustrations.

The new NEP was a welcome development for the autocratic leaders in the south, who are reluctant to conduct genuine political reforms, for they fear that such reforms would encourage political demands for change from domestic forces, primarily the Islamists. Given that autocratic regimes in the south attribute internal instability to socioeconomic weaknesses, and knowing that the EU is concerned that this instability can spill over onto European soil, the EU would undoubtedly provide the necessary funding in the south in order to preserve that stability, no matter how precarious. Thus, the abandonment of the EU's normative policy, coupled with the EU's financial assistance, will allow the southern regimes to keep a modicum of domestic political and social stability while providing southern Mediterranean governments with the legitimacy to maintain their autocratic rule.

Perhaps this was the intention behind the Mediterranean Union, which France's presidential candidate Nicolas Sarkozy launched in 2007. Indeed, the Mediterranean Union, renamed Union for the Mediterranean (UfM) in summer 2008, "offered" yet another approach to the relationship between the two shores of the Mediterranean, an approach whose main objective was France's ambition to regain its dominant position in the EU's Mediterranean policy. As Khader put it bluntly but accurately, Sarkozy's proposal could be summed up as: "EU policies towards the Mediterranean have failed, Turkey has no place in Europe and France's Arab policy is something of the past" (Khader, 2016, 37). Once again, the southern Mediterranean governments responded to this proposal with no single voice, but, regardless of their objections, they did nonetheless join because it offered a multilateral framework, without conditionality, and focused on six major regional projects. The UfM had basically started a new process that diluted the previous ambitions of a regional community construction. In fact, "the UfM's brand of multilateralism is based on inter-state conventional relations rather than a community-like model of relations" (Aliboni, 2010, 21). Even if the initiative emanated from a European country, the appealing aspect from the southern Mediterranean perspective is that the UfM was meant as a collective endeavor, hence alleviating the usual southern grievance regarding co-ownership of Mediterranean policy.

Indeed, the governance of the UfM is based on a professed equitable functioning and shared responsibility (e.g. the provision for a co-presidency). Regardless of the real motivations of its architects, the UfM is just another initiative that offers little in terms of regional community building. And this is exactly how the southern Mediterranean leaders see it, and the way it has been set up could not but please the autocratic regimes that have been effective "in shaping the Mediterranean framework and the EU policy in this regard" (Soltan, 2010, 70), especially since the framework imposes no conditionality. The UfM also provides a forum through which southern Mediterranean rulers can voice their views on the Arab–Israeli conflict, even though this will have no significant influence in practice. Given that the EMP, which did not deliver on its promises, is linked to the UfM, as wished by the southern partners in the hope of reinvigorating the EMP, the question is whether the EMP–UfM has any chance of creating effective instruments that help go beyond stability and securitization policies that preserve the status quo to the detriment of issues of good governance, human rights and the rule of law. A close look at the motivations of the southern Mediterranean countries demonstrates that each state promotes its own national interests (Driss, 2009) oblivious to collective endeavors to create a Mediterranean community. Undoubtedly, the design of the UfM as an inter-governmental organization based on a series of technical projects suited the interests of the southern states. Such preference was already evident in the 5+5, a regional forum for dialog regrouping five southern Mediterranean countries (Algeria, Libya, Mauritania, Morocco, and Tunisia) and five southern European countries (Italy, France, Portugal, Spain, and Malta). This forum, which came into existence in the early 1980s and was revived in 2001, focuses on stability and security, development and economic integration in the Maghreb, debt, food security, cultural dialog, technology, and migration. Unquestionably, the southern Mediterranean leaders have a positive perception of the 5+5, which does not include Egypt, not only because of its small format, but also because it shields the grouping from the Arab–Israeli conflict, a conflict which has poisoned the EMP on various occasions. But this forum is moribund; nothing much has happened since the last summit in Malta in October 2012.

Southern Mediterranean civil societies' perceptions of the Mediterranean

As suggested throughout this chapter, neither the regimes nor civil societies hold common perspectives on the Mediterranean, let alone a vision of the Mediterranean as a unified entity. On the contrary, both see it in terms of a north–south divide. Southern civil societies have different perceptions of and expectations from the northern shore of the Mediterranean. Yet, there is a common perception that revives whenever an Arab country is invaded, as was the case of Iraq in 2003 because of

> the trauma of the occupation of Arab land by the European colonial powers . . . [and] older historical traumas such as the Crusader invasions of the Arab East or the expulsion of the Arabs from Spain (Al Andalus) and Southern Europe.
>
> *(Corm, 2007, 217)*

Undoubtedly, the war on Iraq

> has reinforced the feeling that the divide between the Arab East and the West is in fact permanent . . . [and] has caused Westerners to be seen as essentially hostile to the Arabs, interested above all in dominating them.
>
> *(Corm, 2007, 213)*

Certainly, southern Mediterranean and Arab-Muslim public opinions in general explain the west's behavior in the Arab world and its unconditional support for Israel against the backdrop of "the last two historical traumas—the Crusades and, colonialism." In sum, the perception of a divide between the southern Mediterranean and Europe is an enduring one and is prevalent among states and societies alike; and certainly, "historical traumas can heavily influence future perceptions" (Jervis, 1968, 470).

This section divides civil societies in the south into four categories: Islamists, secular activists, jihadists, and the youth.[2] However, notwithstanding the ideological and political differences between these categories, with a few exceptions, they all perceive that the northern countries have wronged the inhabitants of the south, be it through colonial rule, military interventions (Iraq, Libya, Syria . . .) under the pretext of protecting human rights, unconditional support to Israeli occupation of Palestinian territories, attempts to impose western values on the south, distorted views of Islam, mistreatment of Muslims in Europe, support for southern dictatorial regimes serving western interests, and neglect of civil societies in the south. They also believe that western countries have little or no respect for Arab/Islamic values and do not show any objectivity toward Arab/Islamic countries, thinking that Arabs/Muslims cannot ever experience democracy. These perceptions are reflected in the media, as well. Another general perception, a more positive one, apparent through various opinion polls conducted in the southern Mediterranean region is that people there believe that "citizens of Western nations do have equal rights and duties," "admire the West for its scientific and technological expertise, particularly in the area of advanced technology," and value its "respect for human values, rights, freedom, and democracy," and its "high level of economic advancement."[3]

The fear of Islamist parties coming to power through free elections, as was the case in Algeria in 1991 with the Islamic Salvation Front's victory or with Hamas in Palestine in 2006, contributed to the perception in the south that Europeans are opposed not just to Islamist parties, but to Islam and its values, as well. There is some truth to this perception as there is no evidence that the EU has seriously engaged with even so-called moderate Islamist parties; if anything, there has been no real attempt to engage the Islamist political parties because "a persistent, often ill-defined uneasiness towards Islamist interlocutors in general appears to be stalling the EU's search for a common direction" (Kausch, 2009, 132). Islamist parties throughout the southern Mediterranean perceive that prejudices prevail among Europeans, governments, and public opinion alike, and have sought to change their image in order to dispel the relationship made between Islamism and terrorism. In doing so, they hope to show that their policies would in fact be more democratic than that of the incumbent regimes which the north rely on to maintain stability. But, Islamists run the risk of being accused of colluding with foreign powers, as has often happened. Indeed, secular intellectuals and government officials have accused Islamist political parties of conspiring with foreign powers; they also accused foreign governments of supporting Islamist parties to overthrow them. This was particularly evident during the Algerian civil conflict (Zoubir, 1996), even if the government itself was seeking to coopt moderate political parties to counter radical Islamists in order to provide a façade of democracy (Zoubir and Aït-Hamadouche, 2007). This was also the case much more recently in Tunisia, where many Tunisians the author interviewed in 2011–12 believed that Europeans supported the Islamist Nahda party to rule the country. Throughout the southern Mediterranean, Islamist parties are cognizant of the limits imposed by the secular regimes when allowing them participation in the political process and know that the regimes can resort to severe repression against Islamists should Islamist political parties be perceived as a serious challenge to their rule, as was the case in Egypt in 2013. The EU's support for the new autocratic regime in Egypt was a major disappointment for "moderate" Islamists.

Secular activists and NGOs admire the democratic values in the northern countries; however, the prevailing perception among them is that they have been abandoned by the European governments who prefer to deal with the authoritarian regimes in the south for the sake of stability. Following the Arab Spring, civil society organizations had great hopes from Europe (Krüger and Ratka, 2014). Yet, the fear of foreign interference subsists: "We want Europe to help us financially and economically, but at the same time, there is always this allergy that we keep because in our memory the colonial heritage is always present" (cited in Krüger and Ratka, 2014, 19). In sum, Tunisians, like most southern Mediterranean citizens welcome economic and financial aid from Europe, but reject any domestic interference. Those on the left side decry the north's neoliberal policies which, they believe, aggravate conditions in the south. But, secularists and democrats suffer from the west's actions in the Arab World and its "double standards" when dealing with Arabs and Muslims (imposition of sanctions on Iraq, Libya, Sudan, Iran; invasion of Iraq; overthrow of the Libyan regime . . .) as opposed to the west's behavior toward Israel or other non-Arab/Muslim countries:

> The Western powers preach democracy, reform and the rule of law, but their behavior in the region directly or indirectly contradicts these basic principles. Secularists and democrats in the region are thus looked upon with suspicion by conservative or Muslim radical fundamentalists . . .
>
> *(Corm, 2007, 219)*

This view of the west's double standards is shared across the Arab/Muslim world.

The perceptions of jihadist Islamists is quite different since they perceive the west in general as crusaders seeking to divide and undermine the Muslim world and the secular rulers in the Arab world as their accomplices. For them, the divide is permanent and it behooves committed Muslims to topple the secular regimes and weaken the forces of Zionism and Christian crusaders (Hafez, 2013). Therefore, cooperation of southern Mediterranean regimes with the European states is tantamount to treason toward Muslims. In this category, one can also include the north African immigrants in Europe, particularly in France, who feel confined to the lower ranks of society and that they are denied opportunities in spite of being citizens. In France, this perception and the rather poor conditions in which they live have generated their hatred for the country, a perception which enabled the extremists to transform it into a conflict between Muslims and Europeans, using a leftist, class struggle discourse more than a religious one. However, this is not the only reason jihadists justify their hate of the west. The latter's war on Iraq and Israel's attacks on Lebanon and Gaza strengthen the belief that these are wars against Muslims. These perceptions provide the justification for either joining the fight in Iraq or committing terrorist attacks inside the European countries where they live. They reject liberal democracy and its institutions which they believe serve only to confuse and corrupt Muslims. For instance, as a British sociologist put it, the

> Islamic State's political theology rejects all forms of democracy and denounces it as immoral. Islamic State's propaganda depicts the West not merely as bad but as evil. Its objective is to present the distinction between itself and the West in a language that morally polarizes and heightens the differences between the two. From the standpoint of Islamic State propaganda, the values of Islam and democracy are fundamentally antithetical to one another . . . It claims the threat that a secular society poses to Muslims residing in the West is, above all, a moral one.
>
> *(Furedi, 2015)*

Furthermore, radical Islamists—and Muslims in general for that matter—view the controversies arising in France over the banning of the veil in public places and the wearing of the "burkini" on beaches by Muslim women as corroborating the allegation of western bias against Islam.

Southern Mediterranean youth have an idyllic vision of the northern shores of the Mediterranean, perceived as an Eldorado separated by a sea that needs to be crossed, no matter the risk. The unemployment of even educated youth has also been a major problem and forced new graduates to migrate to Europe. Beyond the economic attractiveness of Europe, the youth in the south are attracted by the democratic values prevalent in the north (Tessler, 2016). It is quite conceivable that these views on democratic values are widespread throughout the southern Mediterranean; autocratic governance provides a plausible explanation of the desire of the youth to want to cross the Mediterranean to enjoy the freedoms that they believe are guaranteed in Europe and which cannot be obtained at home. This being said, it would be a mistake to think that the youth espouse uncritically western values in their totality. One should not underestimate the sociocultural differences that exist between the two shores of the Mediterranean.

Conclusion

This chapter sought to identify the main perceptions that southern rulers and populations hold regarding the Mediterranean. The major observation is that there exist collective perceptions shared by both states and societies, regardless of the nature and ideologies of the states and the categories within civil societies analyzed in this chapter. A sense of unity of the Mediterranean simply does not exist. All see the Mediterranean as a divided zone afflicted by conflicts and fractures (political, economic, cultural, and religious). In the south, the traumas caused by colonial policies have not subsided and there is a sense that the north seeks to continue its domination through interventions in Arab-Muslim lands, its imposition of neoliberal economic policies, and through political schemes, such as the promotion of democracy whose main objective is believed to be interference in the southern countries' domestic affairs and the violation of their sovereignty. Western support for Israel and sanctions imposed upon Arab-Muslim nations corroborate the perception that the north is hostile to the south. While the states in the south welcome cooperation with the north through the various mechanisms that have been advanced through different Mediterranean proposals, the states perceive their relationship with the north as one of dependency inflicted by the north precisely through the various initiatives or partnerships. The states are aware though that cooperation is necessary in order to obtain the badly needed financial support to maintain stability. But, it is precisely that support to the incumbent southern regimes that confirms the perception that the north maintains its dominance through the backing it gives to illegitimate, autocratic regimes in the south. Although the secular/democratic forces and even Islamists admire the scientific, technological, and democratic developments of the north, they nonetheless resent the north not only because of its support for those regimes, but also because of the double standards in its behavior toward Arabs and Muslims. An analysis of the views of the regimes and the four categories of social societies identified in this chapter, as well as the media, shows a disturbing common underlying perception that the north upholds a Huntingtonian view of a clash of civilizations, through which the north perpetually seeks to impose its diktat on the south.

Notes

1 The term Arab is used for lack of a better word that would encompass the Amazigh, Druze, and Copts, among others in the region. In his novel, *Les Anges meurent de nos blessures* Yasmina Khadra (2014), coined the term Araberbers to describe the inhabitants of the Maghreb.

2 One could add the media as a fifth category; it is not included here because the perceptions as conveyed through the media resemble those of state and civil society, with little variation.

3 These statements have been extracted or paraphrased from Gallup Polls, Pew Research Center's Global Attitudes and Trends, and Euromed Surveys of Experts and Actors (EuroMeSCo).

Bibliography

Adler, E. and Crawford, B. (2002), "Constructing a Mediterranean Region: A Cultural Approach," paper presented at the Conference on "The Convergence of Civilizations? Constructing a Mediterranean Region," Lisbon, Portugal, June 6–9, available at: http://ies.berkeley.edu/research/MeditAdlerCrawford.pdf (accessed 15 June 2003).

Aliboni, R. (2010), "Security and Cooperation on Security in Current Euro-Mediterranean Relations," in Aliboni, R. and Saaf, A. (Eds), *Human Security: A New Perspective for Euro-Mediterranean Cooperation* (Paris: European Institute for Security Studies).

Attinà, F. (2004), "The Building of Regional Security Partnership and the Security Culture Divide in the Mediterranean," *Institute of European Studies* (UC Berkeley), available at: http://escholarship.org/uc/item/7821m737#page-3 (accessed 10 March 2016).

Boumghar, L. (2013), "La Position algérienne à l'égard de la politique européenne de voisinage," *Annuaire IEMed de la Méditerranée 2013* (Barcelona: IEMed).

Corm, G. (2007), "The West versus the Arab World: Deconstructing the Divide," in Anheier, H. K. and Isar, Y. R. (Eds), *Conflicts and Tensions* (London: Sage Publications).

Darbouche, H. and Zoubir, Y. (2008), "Conflicting International Policies and the Western Sahara Stalemate," *International Spectator*, 43 (1), 91–105.

Driss, Ahmed (2009), "Southern Perceptions about the Union for the Mediterranean," EuroMeSCo Report, June, available at: www.euromesco.net/euromesco/media/UfM_Driss.pdf (accessed 20 July 2010).

Eurostat-Statistics Explained (2014), "Youth Statistics: North Africa and Eastern Mediterranean," available at: http://ec.europa.eu/eurostat/statistics-explained/index.php/Youth_statistics_-_North_Africa_and_Eastern_Mediterranean (accessed 12 September 2016).

Furedi, F. (2015), "Islamic State Propaganda Buys into Western Culture of Victimhood, *The Australian*, available at: www.frankfuredi.com/article/islamic_state_propaganda_buys_into_western_culture_of_victimhood (accessed 15 July 2016).

Hafez, M. (2013), "Illegitimate Governance: Roots of Radicalization in the MENA," in Khadim, A. (Ed.), *Governance in the Middle East and North Africa: A Handbook* (London and New York: Routledge), pp. 85–98.

Jervis, Robert (1968), "Hypotheses on Misperception," *World Politics*, 20, 454–79.

Joffé, G. (2016a), "Barcelona, Twenty Years On," in Zoubir, Y. H. and White, G. (Eds), *North African Politics: Change and Continuity* (London and New York: Routledge), pp. 309–28.

Joffé, G. (2016b), "Southern Attitudes towards an Integrated Mediterranean Region," in Youngs, R. (Ed.), *Twenty Years of Euro-Mediterranean Relations* (London and New York: Routledge), pp. 27–41.

Kausch, K. (2009), "Europe's Engagement with Moderate Islamists," in Emerson, M., Kausch, K., and Youngs, R. (Eds), *Islamist Radicalization: The Challenge for Euro-Mediterranean Relations* (Brussels, CEPS), pp. 129–50.

Khader, B. (2016), *Europe and the Arab World: An Assessment of European Policies, 1957–2015* (Louvain University, Belgium, unpublished manuscript).

Khadra, Y. (2014). *Les Anges meurent de nos blessures* (Paris: Pocket).

King, S. J., (2009), *The New Authoritarianism in the Middle East and North Africa* (Bloomington, Indiana).

Krüger, L.-T. and Ratka, E. (2014), "The Perception of European Policies in Tunisia after the Arab Spring," *L'Europe en Formation*, 1(371), 9–25.

Labaronne, D. (2013), "Les Difficultés de l'intégration économique régionale des Pays maghrébins," *Mondes en développement*, 3(163), 99–113.

Noutcheva, G. (2015), "Institutional Governance of European Neighborhood Policy," *Journal of European Integration*, 37(1), 19–36.

Picard, Christophe (2010), "Ibn Khaldûn, le pouvoir musulman et la Méditerranée," *HALAL Magazine*, 24 October, available at: www.halalmagazine.com/ibn-khaldun-le-pouvoir-musulman-et-la-mediterranee/ (accessed 17 May 206).

Schimmelfennig, F. and Scholtz, H. (2009), "EU Democracy Promotion in the European Neighborhood," *Challenges to Democracy in the 21st Century*, Working Paper No. 9, National Centre of Competence in Research (NCCR).

Schumacher, Tobias (2016), "Back to the Future: The 'New' ENP towards the Southern Neighborhood and the End of Ambition," College of Europe Policy Brief, No. 1.

Soltan, G. (2004), "Southern Mediterranean Perceptions and Proposals for Mediterranean Security," EuroMeSCo Brief, available at: www.euromesco.net/euromesco/media/euromesco08_final.pdf (accessed 20 July 2004).

Soltan, G. (2010), "Arab States and the UfM," *IEMed 2010* (Barcelona: IEMed), available at: www.iemed.org/anuari/2010/aarticles/Gawad_UfM_en.pdf (accessed 10 June 2011).

Tessler, M. and Miller-Gonzalez, J. (2016), "Maghrebi Youth in the Wake of the Arab Spring: General Observations and Evidence from Tunisia and Algeria," in Zoubir, Y. and White, G. (Eds), *North African Politics: Change and Continuity* (London and New York: Routledge), pp. 18–43.

Volpi, F. (2016[2004]) "Regional Community Building and the Transformation of International Relations: The Case of the Euro-Mediterranean Partnership," in Youngs, R. (Ed.), *Twenty Years of Euro-Mediterranean Relations* (London and New York: Routledge), pp. 73–90.

World Bank (2016), "International Comparison Program Database," available at: http://data.worldbank.org/indicator/NY.GDP.PCAP.PP.KD (accessed 12 September 2016).

Zoubir, Y. (1996), "The Algerian Political Crisis: Domestic, Regional, and International Repercussions," in Vasconcelos, Á., Zoubir, Y. H. et al. (Eds), *L'Islamisme Politique dans les Rapports entre l'Europe et le Maghreb* (Lisbon, Portugal: Friedrich Ebert Stiftung), pp. 10–36.

Zoubir, Y (2000), "Algerian–Moroccan Relations and their Impact on Maghrebi Integration," *Journal of North African Studies*, 5(3), 43–74.

Zoubir, Y. (2005), "The Resurgence of Algeria's Foreign Policy in the Twenty-First Century," in Bonner, M., Reif, M., and Tessler, M. (Eds), *Islam, Democracy, and the State in Algeria* (London: Routledge), pp. 169–83.

Zoubir, Y. (2012a), "The Arab Turmoil: An Exploratory Interpretation," *The Maghreb Review*, 37(3–4), 323–33.

Zoubir, Y (2012b), "Tilting the Balance toward Intra-Maghreb Unity in Light of the Arab Spring," *International Spectator*, 47(3), 64–80.

Zoubir, Y. and Aït-Hamadouche, L. (2007), "The Fate of Political Islam in Algeria," in Maddy-Weitzman, B. and Zisenwine, D. (Eds), *The Contemporary Maghrib* (Gainesville, Florida: University Press of Florida) pp. 103–31.

10

US OUTLOOK ON THE MEDITERRANEAN

Katerina Dalacoura

There is no unified US outlook on the Mediterranean. The 'Mediterranean' does not appear as a separate region on the State Department website and Washington's think tanks have few, if any, specialists or publications on the subject as such. Academic and policy output on 'US and the Mediterranean' is scant. The sea where Africa, Asia and Europe converge is crucial for the United States, not least because of the presence of the Sixth Fleet and the existence of close American allies along its north, south, east and west coasts, such as Spain, France, Italy, Greece, Turkey, Israel, Cyprus, Egypt, Tunisia and Morocco. Vital US interests intersect in the Mediterranean. However, no overarching unifying theme or concept has been offered by American strategists to connect US interests, concerns and policies within it as a geographical space.

Instead of an overarching unifying theme, US foreign policy has traditionally focused on the Mediterranean's sub-regions, namely the eastern Mediterranean, North Africa and southern Europe. It has also centred on a number of issue areas (security, geopolitics, energy, political economy, migration) which are also treated in relative isolation from one another – although I argue in this chapter that the ways in which they are beginning to interconnect may encourage, in future, a more unified US approach and outlook towards the Mediterranean. After a historical overview of US policy towards the Mediterranean, the chapter discusses US policy foreign policy under the Obama administrations. This sets the scene for the core sections of the chapter which examine the two sets or clusters of issues that have preoccupied US policy towards the Mediterranean between 2009 and 2016: security and geopolitics; energy, political economy and migration.

Historical overview

The United States has had a naval presence in the Mediterranean since the early nineteenth century but it was during the early Cold War years that the sea became a focus of US foreign policy and geopolitical concerns. Writing in 1948 on the role of the Mediterranean in American foreign policy, William Reitzel started one of the rare academic books on the subject by stating that 'until very recently the United States had no interest in the Mediterranean that it consciously asserted as vital' (Reitzel, 1948). World War II and the start of the Cold War changed that: Reitzel argues that oil reserves in the Middle East, the need to keep the Soviet Union out of the Mediterranean and the promotion of democracy, as well as the control of the spread of communism, may constitute the main elements of the definition of this interest, 'although there is no consensus on it in American opinion' (Reitzel, 1948: 3). The US Naval Forces Mediterranean were renamed the Sixth Fleet in 1950, with a focus on Africa and Europe. The Fleet was involved in the Lebanon intervention of 1958 and the Yom Kippur War of 1973. There was also a conventional US military presence in Portugal, Spain, Italy, Greece and Turkey (Lesser, 2013). Having said all that, there is a view that in the Cold War the Mediterranean as such was marginal in transatlantic strategic thinking (Lesser, 2013).

One geographical sub-division that prevailed in the US outlook during the Cold War and post-Cold War years was between the eastern and western Mediterranean, with the understanding that responsibility for the latter would be within the purview of US European allies individually or, later, under the guise of the EEC and the European Union. This is not to say that bilateral relations with the Maghreb countries did not or do not matter for the United States. It has a close and long-standing relationship with Morocco which includes a free trade deal entered into force in 2006; it has also been involved, directly and through the United Nations, in the Western Sahara dispute. Algeria, a Soviet ally during the Cold War, and Libya under the mercurial Muammar Gaddafi, preoccupied the United States because they fed into its Cold War geopolitical calculations. More recently, terrorism and energy have reattracted American interest in the Maghreb, as we shall see later (Lesser, 2009: 21). Nevertheless, there has been an understanding, particularly since the end of the Cold War that the Maghreb is more directly of European concern and 'it is most unlikely that the US will displace European influence in North Africa' (Lesser, 2009: 21).

The eastern Mediterranean is clearly within the purview of the United States, from among the western powers. After the debacle of the Suez War of 1956, Britain and France were ignominiously pushed out from their former areas of colonial influence in the Levant (their more recent involvement tends to be under the guise of the European Union and also in collaboration with Germany and/or other European powers). The Israeli–Palestinian conflict, which has dominated the eastern Mediterranean during the entire post-World War II period, has become during that time more directly of US, rather than European, concern. The US commitment to the defence of Israel is one of the bedrocks of its foreign policy but the Camp David Agreement of 1978 and the Agreement of Principles of 1993 also invested it, at least on one level, in conflict resolution between Israel and the Arabs, and the Palestinians.

Since the end of the Cold War, the Mediterranean has acquired further significance for the United States because of European security and because it is en route to the Gulf, to which it provides an important logistical link. In recent years, US relations with individual southern European countries, Portugal, Spain and Greece, with whom bilateral links used to be more important, have been 'Europeanized', in the sense of them being subsumed under the EU rubric (Lesser, 2009: 5–6). The end of the Cold War removed Soviet containment as one of the two axes of US policy towards the Mediterranean and led to profound changes in US policy towards Europe and the Middle East. Oil remained important but the invasion of Kuwait by Iraq in 1990 and the first Gulf War that followed caused a shift of attention in American policy towards the Gulf, away from the Mediterranean shores. At the same time, the wars of former Yugoslavia focused US activity back to the Mediterranean, with the Sixth Fleet supporting intervention in those wars. Northern and sub-Saharan Africa were part of EUCOM area of responsibility and were tied to the American security presence in Europe; since 2007, except Egypt, they are the responsibility of AFRICOM (Lesser, 2009: 11).

The attacks of 11 September 2001 transformed US foreign policy towards the Middle East by drawing the United States more directly into the region, with the focus again being the Gulf. Since the early 2000s the strength and capabilities of the Sixth Fleet have been reduced. The wars in Iraq and Afghanistan and the 'war on terror' under the influence of neo-conservative ideology defined US foreign policy for a generation and set the scene against which the two Barack Obama administrations constructed American global policies and outlook towards the Mediterranean.

The Obama administrations (January 2009–December 2016)

Barack Obama was elected to the American presidency with a promise to extricate the United States from the Iraq and Afghanistan wars. His pragmatic, realist stance, and his effort to align ends and means in US foreign policy, were in direct and explicit contrast to the idealism of George W. Bush. Obama aimed to 'externalize' the burden of war where vital US interests were not concerned. He chose what has been described as 'surrogate warfare' to deal with the Bush legacy and as an alternative means of maintaining US influence in the Middle East region (Krieg, 2016: 98). The resultant scaling down of the American presence has taken place in parallel with a growing expectation that US dependence on Middle Eastern oil will gradually decrease and enable the United States to further reduce its involvement in the region. The Obama 'pivot' (or rebalancing) to Asia, where more vital US interests lay as China rose, was both a cause and a symptom of the strategic shift away from the Middle East.

Barack Obama laid out in a speech to the United Nations in 2013 his vision of core US interests in the Middle East which he pledged to protect if necessary by military force: 'preventing the spread of nuclear weapons and other weapons of mass destruction; ensuring the unimpeded flow of energy resources to world markets; countering international terrorism; and supporting American allies' (Serwer, 2016: 1). A fifth longer-term objective to be sought through multilateral cooperation was 'promoting American values, including democracy, human rights, and open markets' (Serwer, 2016: 1).

For critics, Obama's Middle Eastern policy confirmed a sense of American decline and revealed 'Obama's inability to shape the Middle East' (Gerges, 2012: 11). It also meant the abandonment of US allies and demonstrated Obama's personal failings (timidity, prevarication) (Melhem, 2016). For supporters, it was a necessary readjustment following the destructive over-extension of the Bush years. Either way, US policy caused alarm and disquiet among US allies in the Middle East (notwithstanding the fact that a large part of political and popular opinion in the region had railed for decades against US interference there). It simultaneously disappointed the 'hawks' and the liberal interventionists in Washington who shared the illusion, derived from a fictitious past, that the United States would be able to shape or even control events in the Middle East.

In the course of the two Obama administrations, a series of events convulsed the Mediterranean and shaped US policies towards its sub-regions. The 2008–9 global economic crisis and in particular the Eurozone crisis profoundly affected the European Union as a whole and in particular its southern European, Mediterranean flank, Spain, Italy and Greece. The Greek crisis presented a potential existential threat to the Eurozone – and possibly the EU itself – which would have had implications for US foreign policy in Europe and beyond. The global and European economic crises were followed by (and to some degree may have contributed to) the eruption of the Arab uprisings of 2011 with their complex and varied impact on domestic and regional politics and a toxic mix of war and intervention in the cases of Libya, Bahrain, Yemen and Syria. The turmoil and vacuums of power that followed the uprisings especially in Syria and Libya, as well as the long-term problems in Iraq, led to an upsurge in Islamist extremism, with implications for the entire Middle East, Europe and beyond. With the exception of Tunisia, further authoritarianism, rather than the hoped-for democratization, has been the political outcome of the Arab revolts.

War, instability and repression contributed to a migration crisis of historic proportions in 2015–16, which vitally affected Europe and also drew in the North Atlantic Treaty Organization. Russia, having annexed Crimea and intervened militarily in Ukraine in 2015, continued in its bid for geopolitical ascendancy by moving southward and entered the Syrian civil war in September 2015 in support of the regime of Bashar al Assad. Last but not least, from 2009 the discovery of large gas reserves in the seabed of the eastern Mediterranean have had considerable geopolitical implications and affected conflicts and relationships between Israel and its neighbours, in particular Egypt and Turkey; but also the parties to the Cyprus conflict, Greece and Turkey.

Security and geopolitics

As suggested earlier, the Sixth Fleet is unique in giving a degree of unity to the Mediterranean in US foreign policy. Although the Fleet played a role in the Balkan wars in the 1990s and in particular in the Kosovo intervention in 1999, it has more recently concentrated on supporting American operations in the Middle East and Africa. During the Obama years, the Fleet participated in the Libya intervention of 2011 and carried out strikes and supported allied action against al Qaeda and so-called Islamic State (ISIS) in Syria and Iraq. Some of these activities of the Sixth Fleet took place under NATO command. In early 2016, NATO also became involved in salvaging refugees crossing from Turkey to Greece.

Within the context of the crisis unleashed by the post-2011 Syrian civil war, NATO has been called upon to support one its members, Turkey. In 2013 NATO deployed Patriot anti-ballistic missile batteries along the Turkish–Syrian border. NATO has also supported Turkey against Russia in the two countries' rivalry caused by their support of different sides in Syria. Turkey became involved in the Syrian civil war with the aim of removing Bashar al Assad's regime. It supported the Free Syrian Army but, as it was revealed that the FSA was not up to the task, allowed access to al Qaeda offshoot Jabhat al-Nusra to Turkish soil to bring in arms and fighters. In November 2015 the shooting down of a Russian jet by Turkey raised a worrying prospect of confrontation as NATO rallied to Turkey's support. However, despite US support of Turkey through NATO over Syria, there has also been tension between the two allies: the United States collaboration with the Syrian Kurdish Democratic Union Party (PYD) in the struggle against ISIS alarmed Turkey because of the close PYD–PKK links (Barkey, 2016: 28–9).

Russia's growing activities in the Mediterranean constituted a geopolitical concern for the United States. The Soviet Mediterranean Fleet was abolished in 1991 and Russia's Mediterranean Task Force was established in 2013; it is supported by the Black Sea Fleet, one of the four Russian fleets, based in Sevastopol. Russia's only naval base in the Mediterranean is in Tartus, Syria. Safeguarding it was given as one reason for the Russian intervention in Syria in support of the Bashar al Assad regime, but this was probably a side issue.

Syria was a long-standing Soviet and then Russian ally in the Middle East, a vestige of a more glorious past. Through it, Russia is 'returning to the Middle East', though its 'game' is probably being played on a bigger chessboard (Malashenko, 2015). As it is operating on the same side as Iran in Syria, Russia may be rebuilding a regional alliance with it, possibly in an attempt to recapture Cold War relationships (Salem, 2015: 2). The major purpose of Russia's Syrian intervention has been to bolster Russia's bid for global prestige and status and strengthen its geopolitical position in Ukraine, within Europe, against NATO. There is even a suggestion, reportedly by a NATO official, that following Russian intervention in Syria, the Mediterranean 'is a contested space again'. According to this analysis, Russia's presence south of the Bosphorus is a longer-term and bigger challenge than its intervention in Syria, with the prospect even of complicating US ability to project its naval power as far as the Gulf. NATO has admitted that it has no 'southern strategy' to match the one it has developed in eastern Europe (Jones, 2015).

The above is one perspective, however; for others, there is a possibility of Russian and US cooperation in Syria (Rachman, 2016), especially in the light of a common enemy in ISIS. One analyst at least, Thanos Dokos, believes that the return of Russia has been exaggerated as a threat and is doubtful that Russia can become a big player (Thanos Dokos, personal communication April 2016).

The Obama administration has resisted calls for direct intervention in the Syrian civil war but it has supplied arms to the opposition since 2013. From 2014, it has taken part in anti-ISIS strikes there (and in Iraq). The Sixth Fleet is in a supporting role in these attacks in Syria, which are also carried out by drones. The United States has also offered training and equipment to the Iraqi army since the debacle of the fall of Mosul in June 2014 (Dyer, 2016). Ironically, the presence of ISIS in Syria has placed the United States on the same side as Iran and Hizballah, long-standing US rivals in the region. The 2015 nuclear deal with Iran – Obama's major Middle Eastern achievement but a cause of alarm for Saudi Arabia and other regional US allies – has not resolved the confrontation but may help reduce and manage it in the long run.

Obama has tried to extricate the United States from the Iraq and Afghanistan wars with a view to scaling back its involvement in the Middle East, as we saw. This entails local regional powers assuming a bigger role which has indeed happened, with US allies Turkey and Saudi Arabia – as well as smaller powers Qatar and the United Arab Emirates – formulating and executing region-wide foreign policies in pursuit of their interests. Unfortunately, however, the US strategy has led, not to regional power management and stewardship of the problems of the Middle East, but to a power struggle, as Saudi Arabia has pitted itself against Iran and its allies, namely the Iraqi and Syrian governments and Hizballah of Lebanon. This has added fuel to the Syrian civil war and has impacted US concerns in the Levant negatively.

These concerns have ISIS at their core. It is unconvincing to claim that ISIS, since it emergence in 2014, constitutes an existential threat to the United States but it does directly threaten its citizens and assets, and those of its European and Middle Eastern allies. ISIS has the potential of drawing the United States back to the Middle East region, something that the Obama administration – having learnt the lesson from the Bush years – has resisted.

North Africa presents a different set of geopolitical and security challenges for US policy in the Mediterranean and the policies it is formulating there are distinct from its interventions in the eastern Mediterranean (although al Qaeda and now ISIS are providing an unwelcome connecting thread between the two sub-regions). 'Al Qaeda in the Islamic Maghreb', one of the al Qaeda 'franchises', has since the mid-2000s constituted a danger to Egypt and Tunisia, both American friends, and contributed to regional instability by attacking Algeria. Tunisia's democratic transition, the only successful outcome of the 2011 Arab revolts to date, is partly threatened by domestic and external Islamist terrorism, and the United States plays a role in supporting Tunis in this struggle (even though its security interests there are not substantial).

The terrorism phenomenon in North Africa is connected to terrorism in the Sahel, to its south. Boko Haram has been active with deadly effect in Nigeria and neighbouring states since the late 2000s. Turmoil and internal conflict in Mali triggered a French military intervention in 2013; Mali continues to be troubled by instability as the terrorist attack in Bamako on 20 November 2015 demonstrated. US concerns in North Africa are even connected, albeit tenuously, to the situation in Somalia, a failed state for a number of years, where the Islamist extremist al Shabaab movement has made a bid for control with an anti-western and anti-American agenda.

Egypt has conventionally constituted a central focus of US policy and it offers a connecting point in the US outlook between North Africa and the eastern Mediterranean, as it straddles both. Egypt has been unstable internally since the 2011 rebellion and this has affected the security situation in its most vulnerable area, which is the Sinai peninsula. A vacuum of power opened up in the Sinai following the overthrow of Mubarak, and fuelled a pre-existing conflict (Middle East Institute, 2014). The troubled Sinai peninsula threatens Egypt and indirectly, because of Sinai's proximity to Gaza, also Israel. It has also given ISIS a foothold and it has vied for power there with al Qaeda.

The issue in North Africa that has dominated the Obama policies there and in the Mediterranean as a whole has been Libya. Following the outbreak of the rebellion against the regime of Muammar Gaddafi in 2011, NATO (Britain, France, with the United States not taking a front role) intervened in support of the popular forces against the regime; Qatar, Jordan and the UAE also collaborated.

Subsequent to the overthrow of Gaddafi, Libya has become effectively a failed state, opening up the opportunity for Islamic extremism to take root. ISIS has found Sirte, in the east of the country, the easiest ground to populate and has sought to push out and dominate other Islamist extremist groups. Obama's complaint in 2016 that Britain and France did not carry their weight in assisting Libya's reconstruction after the Libya intervention of 2011 (Goldberg, 2016) is indicative of the point made earlier, that the United States considers Mediterranean issues, particularly North Africa, as being to a considerable extent the responsibility of Europe. It is illustrative of the general tone and direction of Obama's foreign policy, which rests on burden sharing with US allies. This is in contradistinction to the over-extension during the Bush years but it also has some continuities with past American views in the Mediterranean: one is reminded of Bill Clinton's criticism of Europe not assuming responsibility for the Balkans, its own 'back yard', in the 1990s. The difference is that ISIS has the potential of harming US interests more directly because its power base in North Africa adds to its 'global' presence, so to speak.

North Africa is important for the United States and the European Union because of its energy resources, in particular oil and gas. Alongside Syria and the Middle East, it is the second major route for migrants and therefore a source for the migration crisis which has been unfolding in the Mediterranean with renewed ferocity since 2015. These problems are important in themselves, and will be considered next, but what must be emphasized here is that they interlink with security issues, especially the threat of terrorism, and therefore shape the US geopolitical outlook on the Mediterranean.

Energy, political economy and migration

The United States does not really depend on the Mediterranean for energy. To put the matter in perspective: in 2014 the United States imported 27 per cent of its needed oil supplies, the lowest percentage since 1985. Twenty per cent of these imports came from the Gulf, primarily Saudi Arabia and Iraq. Having said that, the United States is vulnerable to oil price fluctuations, which are in turn affected by what happens in the Gulf. The American Fifth Fleet is headquartered in Bahrain with a view to safeguarding traffic through the straits of Hormuz (Serwer, 2016: 3). When it comes to the Mediterranean, the United States acts on the understanding that energy resources and their continuing flow are important to its allies, both Middle Eastern and European. Furthermore, energy sources are intimately linked with a number of conflicts which involve US allies in the Mediterranean.

US energy concerns in the Mediterranean can again be divided geographically into two major sub regions, the eastern Mediterranean and North Africa. With regard to the former, the Obama administration has been confronted with a rapidly changing situation, which presents both dangers and opportunities. In one analysis, the eastern Mediterranean region 'stands to become one of the world's most important sources of natural gas over the next half century' (Stocker, 2012: 579). The Tamar and Leviathan fields were discovered in 2009 and 2010 respectively in Israeli waters. The Aphrodite field was discovered in Cypriot waters in 2011. Israel and Cyprus stand to gain the most from these finds. Lebanon also has claims on the discoveries (Zhukov, 2013). Some analysts suggest that gas may offer an opportunity for cooperation and the resolution of conflict in the eastern Mediterranean (Gürel and Le Cornu, 2014: 11–33). However, this is an overly optimistic scenario in a sub-region where mistrust is profound and relations are still perceived as zero-sum. In another interpretation, energy resources may serve as objects of future conflicts, rather than a means to sustain old conflicts (Stocker, 2012: 580). Stocker distinguishes between two energy conflicts in the region, the borders of 'exclusive economic zones' of Cyprus, Turkey, Lebanon, Israel, Egypt and an emerging Palestinian state and the future of the pipeline infrastructure (Stocker, 2012: 580). The discovery of energy reserves and the possibility of discovering more has 'revived the question of delineating the exclusive economic zones (EEZs) of all littoral states in the Eastern Mediterranean and added one potential regional dispute' (Grigoriadis, 2014: 124).

The parties to the potential eastern Mediterranean conflicts involving energy, with the exception of the Syrian government, Hamas in Gaza and Hizballah in Lebanon, are US allies. Israel's discovery of the Leviathan gas field has strengthened the possibility of energy self-sufficiency by that country. Lebanon has a potential claim on the gas reserves and the strong position of Hizballah, an enemy of Israel and the United States, in that country complicates the picture. Egypt's discoveries have changed its own foreign policy calculations. The Israeli discoveries have the potential of strengthening its relationship with Cyprus and Greece. With regard to the delivery of gas and the positioning of the pipelines, the fraught relationship between Cyprus and Turkey may prove an obstacle although the possibility (in 2016) of a resolution of the Cyprus conflict may transform that particular situation.

The presence of al Qaeda and ISIS in North Africa has increased the risks to the supply of energy, an important consideration for US allies in Europe. Gas and oil reserves are prized possessions which terrorist groups seek to put their hands on. The terrorist attacks in In Amenas in Algeria in January 2013 (where an al Qaeda-linked group demanded the end of French activities in Mali) are an illustration of the interconnections between North Africa and the Sahel security concerns and of how energy and terrorism can become interlinked. ISIS disrupts oil production in Libya to increase the country's instability (in contrast to Syria where its control of oil adds to its coffers and ability to control territory) (Jones and Saleh, 2016).

In its consideration of energy issues in the Mediterranean, the United States has to take into account China's growing role. Christina Lin argues that China 'has entered the Eastern Mediterranean basin and MENA at large by expanding its economic, political, and military footprint'. In light of the perceived waning influence of the US, traditional allies such as Israel and Turkey are upgrading ties with China. In Syria, China supports the Assad regime and has even conducted joint naval war games in the eastern Mediterranean with Russia (Lin, 2014a). China's activities in the Mediterranean are propelled by its search for energy resources as well as its push for exports, especially in weapons systems (Turkey and Egypt have turned to China for such sales, which raised alarm bells in the United States). Although some analysts have proposed that China's interest in the Mediterranean may have geopolitical significance for the United States and its allies, China has no obvious strategic concern there. In an alternative interpretation, the presence of China in the Mediterranean can also offer an opportunity for cooperation, rather than strife, with NATO (Lin, 2014b).

War and conflict have caused an unprecedented migration crisis in the Mediterranean since 2015, ironically an event that has underlined the unity of the sea and the interdependence of its northern and southern, eastern and western shores. The origins of the crisis are not to be found only in the Mediterranean, as those who attempt the crossing come from as far east as Afghanistan and as far south as Somalia. But the Mediterranean is the point at which they all converge to reach Europe, with obvious implications for the European Union and particularly Greece and Italy which are the frontline states. The northern and southern shores of the Mediterranean, despite the Eurozone crisis, continue to be separated by a huge gap in living standards and this accentuates the migration crisis. This issue indirectly affects the United States, and NATO forces have played a role, since early 2016, in policing the sea and helping alleviate the humanitarian crisis and prevent the flow of people.

The migration crisis is not linked only to war but also to the wider problems of instability, lack of opportunity and undemocratic government in the Middle East and North Africa. All of these are of some concern to US policy makers, though their ability to shape domestic politics in those countries is in fact quite limited. For example, the role of the United States in the Egyptian uprising and its aftermath has been exaggerated: it did not help overthrow Mubarak or 'abandon' him; it did not support the Muslim Brotherhood in 2012–13. However, the American post-2011 contribution to what appears to be a successful case of democratic transition in Tunisia is a positive one, both bilaterally and through the International Monetary Fund and NATO, which named it major non-NATO ally in 2015.

Finally, the United States, involvement in the Mediterranean occurs within multilateral settings involving most importantly its European allies and partners. The Transtantlantic Trade and Investment Partnership (TTIP) negotiations between the United States and the European Union, whose successful conclusion was a major Obama foreign policy objective, are a reason why the Eurozone crisis and the economic situation in southern Europe were of concern to the United States. The United States is still involved in the Balkans through collective arrangements. At the time of writing, in 2016, 680 US troops are still deployed in Kosovo under NATO as part of Kosovo Force (KFOR). Other multilateral arrangements dealing with the Mediterranean which bring together the United States with individual European states and the European Union include NATO's Mediterranean Dialogue which was initiated by the North Atlantic Council in 1994 and involves seven non-NATO Mediterranean states, Algeria, Egypt, Israel, Jordan, Mauritania, Morocco and Tunisia.[1] The Organization for Security and Cooperation in Europe, which includes 55 states from North America, Europe and Central Asia (OSCE), also comprises a Mediterranean Partnership for Cooperation: the 1975 Helsinki Final Act makes special mention of security in the Mediterranean as being intimately linked to European security (Hauser, 2005: 2–11).[2] The French-led Union for the Mediterranean which was launched in 2008 as a continuation of the Euro-Mediterranean Partnership also known as the Barcelona Process[3] has 'attracted a surprising degree of attention in Washington' (Lesser, 2009: 8).

Conclusion

The US outlook on the Mediterranean continues to be fragmented, with Washington treating the various issues that arise in its sub-regions in an ad hoc manner. This is despite the understanding that the Mediterranean is an important strategic point for the United States, underpinned by the naval US presence there which provides the capacity for protecting vital US interests, should the need arise, and furthering its goals.

There is an argument (Lesser, 2016b) that terrorism and migration will give the Mediterranean in the near future more weight as compared to the Gulf, with both the EU and NATO looking south where transatlantic interests are engaged more and more. This may mean that the United States will see the Mediterranean increasingly through the lens of its European security interests. It is indeed the case that the growing threats from terrorism and the migration crisis provide a unity to the Mediterranean which has been lacking in the American outlook. The growing presence of Russia and China there may also force Washington to view the Mediterranean with renewed urgency. However, this view is convincing only up to a point.

Terrorism and migration do not threaten vital US interests in the Mediterranean. The Mediterranean would become crucial for the United States only 'by default', so to speak, were its military presence and the security of its allies there to come under threat. This is not likely, particularly given the re-definition of US interests and the scaling down of what constitutes its vital interests. The US policies towards the Mediterranean are affected by the decision in Washington to reduce its military presence in the Middle East 'to correspond to its reduced and shifting interests' (Serwer, 2016: 9). If the trend set by Barack Obama continues in the post-Obama years, we can expect both a 'leaner' US presence in the Mediterranean and a continuing expectation by Washington that its European and Middle Eastern allies should be more active in policing their common interests in the Mediterranean.

Acknowledgements

I would like to thank the editors of the volume, Richard Gillespie and Frédéric Volpi; and Thanos Dokos, Spyros Economides and Rachel George for their help. All errors are mine.

Notes

1 See www.nato.int/cps/en/natolive/topics_52927.htm (Accessed 12 September 2016).
2 See www.osce.org/networks/111472 (Accessed 22 September 2016).
3 See http://ufmsecretariat.org/page/2/?s=united+states&lang=en# (Accessed 23 September 2016).

Bibliography

Barkey, H. J. (2016) Syria's Dark Shadow Over US–Turkey Relations. *Turkish Policy Quarterly*, 14(4), 25–36.

Dyer, G. (2016) Iraqi Army Faces Tough Task to Repeat Ramadi Victory over ISIS. *Financial Times*. 2/3 January.

Gerges, F. (2012) *Obama and the Middle East: The End of America's Moment?* (New York: Palgrave Macmillan).

Goldberg, J. (2016) The Obama Doctrine. *The Atlantic*. April Issue. Available at www.theatlantic.com/magazine/archive/2016/04/the-obama-doctrine/471525/ (Accessed 16 September 2016).

Grigoriadis, I. (2014) Energy Discoveries in the Eastern Mediterranean: Conflict or Cooperation?, *Middle East Policy*, 21(3), 124–32.

Gürel, A. and Le Cornu, L. (2014) Can Gas Catalyse Peace in the Eastern Mediterranean?, *The International Spectator*, 49(2), 11–33.

Hauser, G. (2005) *The Mediterranean Dialogue: A Transatlantic Approach*. Arbeitspapiere zur Internationalen Politik und Außenpolitik. Available at: www.ssoar.info/ssoar/bitstream/handle/document/21843/ssoar-2005-hauser-the_mediterranean_dialogue_-_a.pdf?sequence=1 (Accessed 16 September 2016).

Jones, S. (2015) Mediterranean Alarm Bells Ring at NATO. *Financial Times*. 22 October.

Jones, S. and Saleh, H. (2016) ISIS in Libya: Stoking Conflict. *Financial Times*. 20 March. Available at www.ft.com/content/c06fb0d6-e1f7-11e5-8d9b-e88a2a889797 (Accessed 16 September 2016).

Krieg, A. (2016) Externalizing the Burden of War: The Obama Doctrine and US Foreign Policy in the Middle East. *International Affairs*, 92(1), 97–113.

Lesser, I. (2009) *The United States and the Mediterranean: A New Strategic Context*. Mediterranean Academy of Diplomatic Studies. MEDAC Publications in Mediterranean IR and Diplomacy. Summer. Available at www.um.edu.mt/__data/assets/pdf_file/0011/226883/Ian_Lesser_MedAgenda.pdf (Accessed 16 September 2016).

Lesser, I. (2013) Strategic Implications and Turmoil in Southern and Eastern Mediterranean: Energy Security and Transatlantic Cooperation. Henry Jackson Society. June 4. Available at http://henryjacksonsociety.org/2013/06/04/strategic-implications-and-turmoil-in-southern-and-eastern-mediterranean-energy-security-and-transatlantic-cooperation/ (Accessed 16 September 2016).

Lesser, I. (2016a) NATO Looks South. German Marshall Fund. Available at www.gmfus.org/blog/2016/02/16/natos-aegean-deployment-shape-things-come (Accessed 16 September 2016).

Lesser, I. (2016b) *Israel as a Mediterranean Security Partner.* Israeli Mission to the European Union. Available at http://embassies.gov.il/eu/NewsAndEvents/Newsletter/Pages/Israel-as-a-Mediterranean-Security-Partner.aspx (Accessed 16 September 2016).

Lin, C. (2014a) China's Increasing Role in the Mediterranean. Transatlantic Academy. April. Available at www.transatlanticacademy.org/node/697 (Accessed 16 September 2016).

Lin, C. (2014b) China's Mediterranean Presence is an Opportunity for NATO. Transatlantic Academy. April. Available at www.transatlanticacademy.org/node/702 (Accessed 16 September 2016).

Malashenko, A. (2015) Russia Returns to the Middle East: Putin's Syria Bet. *Le Monde Diplomatique* (English edition), 29 October.

Melhem, H. (2016) Obama's Tarnished Legacy in the Middle East. *The Cairo Review of Global Affairs.* Winter 2016. Essays. Available at www.thecairoreview.com/essays/obamas-tarnished-legacy-in-the-middle-east/ (Accessed 15 September 2016).

Middle East Institute (2014) Special Feature: A History of Terrorism in Egypt's Sinai, (an interactive guide). Available at www.mei.edu/sinai-terrorism (Accessed 15 September 2016).

North Atlantic Treaty Organization (2015) Mediterranean Dialogue. Available at www.nato.int/cps/en/natolive/topics_52927.htm (Accessed 15 September 2016).

Organization for Security and Cooperation in Europe (2016) Mediterranean Partners for Co-operation. Available at www.osce.org/networks/111472 (Accessed 15 September 2016).

Rachman, G. (2016) Russia and the US Can Deliver Peace in Syria. *Financial Times*, 3 May. Available at www.ft.com/content/4f3a1e5c-0e01-11e6-b41f-0beb7e589515 (Accessed 15 September 2015).

Reitzel, W. (1948) *The Mediterranean: Its Role in America's Foreign Policy* (New York: Harcourt).

Salem, P. (2015) Putin Comes to Syria: Contexts and Consequences. Middle East Institute, 21 September. Available at www.mei.edu/content/at/putin-comes-syria-contexts-and-consequences (Accessed 15 September 2015).

Serwer, D. (2016) Recalculating US Policy in the Middle East: Less Military, More Civilian. Middle East Institute. Scholar Series, 'The Middle East and the 2016 Presidential Elections', April. Available at www.mei.edu/sites/default/files/publications/Serwer.pdf (Accessed 15 September 2015).

Stocker, J. (2012) No EEZ Solution: The Politics of Oil and Gas in the Eastern Mediterranean, *Middle East Journal*, 66(4), Autumn, 579–97. Available at https://muse.jhu.edu/article/489422/pdf (Accessed 15 September 2015).

Union for the Mediterranean, (2016) Website. Available at http://ufmsecretariat.org/page/2/?s=united+states&lang=en# (Accessed 15 September 2016).

Zhukov, Y. (2013) Trouble in the Eastern Mediterranean Sea. *Foreign Affairs*, 20 March. Available at www.foreignaffairs.com/articles/cyprus/2013-03-20/trouble-eastern-mediterranean-sea. (Accessed 15 September 2016).

11

ISRAELI REGIONAL PERSPECTIVES AND THE MEDITERRANEAN[1]

Daniela Huber

The Mediterranean has been a point of reference for Israelis since the waves of immigration to Palestine began. It has passed from being framed and remembered as a place of drama (*Exodus 1947*), to a place of fear (being thrown into the sea by enemies),[2] to a recently more positive connotation, finding expression in the concept of 'Mediterraneanism' (Yam Tikhoniut in Hebrew) which enjoys more popularity in Israel since the 1990s as Alexandra Nocke (2009) and David Ohana (2011) have pointed out. The concept can serve as an internal bridge between Ashkenazi and Mizrahi Jews, but also as an external bridge between Israel and Europe in the northern Mediterranean, and Israel and Turkey and the Arab societies of the eastern and southern Mediterranean. Ohana sees Israel as a 'Mediterranean society in the making' (Ohana, 2011: 3). However, as Raffaella Del Sarto has suggested, while there is a general acknowledgement that Israel has some Mediterranean cultural features, most Israelis still consider that it does not really belong to any region (Del Sarto, 2006: 118).

This chapter seeks to contribute to this debate by examining Israeli regional perspectives in and on the Mediterranean through three linked lenses: the Israeli perception of the Mediterranean, its strategic vision for it, as well as resulting policy practices in the region. Despite the EU's Mediterranean agenda, Israel does not perceive the Mediterranean as one region but rather as comprising linked areas, that is Europe in the northern Mediterranean, the Middle East and North Africa in the eastern and southern Mediterranean, and Turkey somewhere between these areas. Even though Israel has geostrategically benefited from the Arab uprisings, uncertainty has increased threat perceptions. While the EU and Turkey are seen with renewed suspicion and the Arab eastern and southern Mediterranean as inherently unstable, the Shia crescent which stretches from the Gulf (Iran) to the Mediterranean (Syria and Lebanon) is perceived as an existential threat. This has informed Israel's strategic vision towards the Mediterranean. While in the early Oslo years, Israel hesitantly began to share parts of Europe's normative vision of the Mediterranean region, this tendency was abandoned with the breakdown of the peace process and the resurrection of the Iron Wall doctrine. As a result, Israel's policy practices are unilateral on the Palestinian front and bilateral on the regional front – where Israel also upholds a de-facto alliance system with Egypt, Jordan and Saudi Arabia, directed against a 'Shiite crescent' – while multilateral practices such as the Arab Peace Initiative, Palestinian statehood bid at the UN or the Iranian nuclear deal have so far been either evaded or rejected.

The Israeli perception of the Mediterranean

Self-image and perception of the other are mutually constitutive and enduringly so. A rather substantial literature of Israeli scholars has described an Israeli self-image that could be termed a 'prevailing sense of loneliness' (Amos Elon, *The Israelis: Founders and Sons*), 'Massada syndrome' (Bar-Tal, 1983), 'siege mentality' (Bar-Tal and Antebi, 1992) or 'people apart syndrome' (Arian, 1989). This self-image which came along with a substantial threat perception of its Arab neighboring countries existed throughout the string of Israeli–Arab wars (1948–9, 1956, 1967, 1969–70, 1973, 1982), but also survived the gradual decline of the Arab–Israeli conflict (Sela, 1997), as Israel entered a peace accord with Egypt in 1979 (seen as a 'cold peace') and as the regional Arab system moved towards the pursuit of collective diplomacy with Israel (embodied in the Fahd plan and the Fez summit) in the 1980s. This self-image did change in the 1990s not only as a result of the gradual lifting of the Arab boycott of Israel, the signing of the Oslo Accords with the PLO and of a peace treaty with Jordan; but notably also as a result of the active political leadership on tearing down this image by Yitzhak Rabin who, after having been elected prime minister, famously declared in his first address to the Knesset that

> No longer are we necessarily 'a people that dwells alone', and no longer is it true that 'the whole world is against us'. We must overcome the sense of isolation that has held us in its thrall for almost half a century. We must join the international movement toward peace, reconciliation and cooperation that is spreading over the entire globe these days – lest we be the last to remain, all alone, in the station.
>
> *(Rabin, 1992)*

However, with the advance of the Right to power, the breakdown of the so-called 'peace process', the onset of the Intifada and Israel's worldwide broadcasted violent response to it, the feeling of isolation bounced back and increased from 2009 onwards, as relations with Europe and Turkey soured in the wake of the war on Gaza. Thus, Israel entered the period of the Arab uprisings with a renewed sense of being a 'people apart'. How then have Israelis perceived the uprisings? This will be observed in the following for the three areas of the Mediterranean, that is the Arab world, Europe and Turkey.

As Magen points out, in 2011, Israeli officials saw the uprisings more as a 'Teheran 1979' than a 'Berlin 1989' (Magen, 2015: 117). An Israeli analyst referred to the events as an 'Arab Winter' instead of 'Arab Spring' (Lehrs, 2013). The eastern and southern Mediterranean were seen as imploding and unstable. Magen has distinguished three phases in the official assessment of the uprisings, that is a 'period of high anxiety' with the coming to power of the Muslim Brotherhood in Egypt and a perceived strengthening of the Shia crescent; a phase of 'reduced anxiety' with the coup against Morsi; and a third phase connected to the breakdown of statehood in Iraq, Syria and Libya (Magen, 2015: 118–21). Regarding this third phase, it should be noted, however, that the security establishment does not view ISIS as an existential threat to Israel (Yadlin, 2014), in sharp contrast to the consolidation of Iranian power in light of the regional turmoil which is seen as an existential threat as became clear in Netanyahu's sustained attempts to undermine the nuclear framework deal between Iran and the P5+1.[3] Israeli public opinion has been largely congruent with these views of the political establishment. According to survey data of the Israel Democracy Institute (2016) majorities of Israelis found that relations with Egypt suffered under the Morsi presidency and saw the coup as in Israel's interest, while ISIS is not seen as an existential threat to Israel. While a majority of Jewish Israelis (58 per cent) do not support a regional peace agreement (Israel Democracy Institute, 2016), relations with so-called 'moderate' Arab states are nonetheless seen as a foreign policy priority as data of the Mitvim (2015) foreign policy index indicate.

The same index shows a low prioritization of relations with the EU. While the EU is seen as an important economic partner according to the European Neighborhood Barometer (European Commission, 2016), a comparatively low proportion of Israelis perceive the EU as positive or fair (Israel Democracy Institute, 2016). This mixed perception of Europe has increased with the EU's settlement guidelines and labelling policy which Israel Prime Minister Benjamin Netanyahu likened to the boycott of Jewish businesses in Nazi Germany (in Beaumont, 2015). These survey results are supported by the academic literature on the issue. Harpaz and Shamis distinguish between three different political approaches in Israel towards the role of Europe: the antagonist approach according to which the EU follows its own material interest to gain hegemony in the region; the ideological-supportive approach which finds that Israel and Europe share common values; and the pragmatic approach, the middle ground, which displays some suspicion of the EU but favours enhanced relations, especially in the economic area (Harpaz and Shamis, 2010: 591–5).

Somewhere between Israel's perception of Europe and the Arab world lie perceptions of Turkey. The *Mavi Marmara* incident in 2010,[4] and the ensuing crisis were perceived in Israel as a Turkish attempt to cater to the 'Arab street', specifically in the early period of the uprisings. In a poll conducted in September 2012, however, a majority of Israelis thought that Israel should improve ties with Turkey (Mitvim, 2012). The importance given to Turkey notwithstanding, in 2013, a majority of Israelis saw Turkey as somewhat or very unfavourable – an attitude reciprocated in Turkey (Pew Research Center, 2013).

In conclusion, Israel does not seem to perceive itself as very much 'at home' in the Mediterranean region and this perception has increased in the wake of the Arab uprisings. The EU and Turkey in the northern/eastern Mediterranean are seen with renewed suspicion in light of the settlement guidelines and labelling policy on the EU part and the *Mavi Marmara* incident on Turkey's side. The eastern and southern Mediterranean are seen as inherently unstable and thus potentially dangerous, while the so-called Shia crescent which stretches from the Gulf (Iran) to the Mediterranean (Syria and Lebanon) remains a perceived existential threat with Iran consolidating its power as the Arab world is imploding. While this relative consolidation of power also applies to Israel, in terms of perceptions the Mediterranean is nonetheless seen as a more unpredictable, dangerous and threatening place which directly informs Israel's strategic vision of the Mediterranean.

Israel's strategic vision of the Mediterranean

There are diverse strategic visions which have been floated in the Mediterranean by its key actors and which can be distinguished along the lines of Alexander Wendt's three cultures of anarchy: the Hobbesian, Lockean and Kantian cultures, being based on images of enmity, rivalry and friendship respectively (Wendt, 1999). How has Israel's strategic vision related to them?

In the Arab world, an early vision which came close to envisaging a Kantian community for the Arab world on one hand, while being exclusionary of Israel, on the other, was pan-Arabism. Pan-Arabism, in fact, shows how a Kantian vision can serve to foster identification with a certain community at the expense of reinforcing enemy images with an imagined other. The common fight against Israel was one of the few issues that gave concrete expression to pan-Arabism in the 1950s and 1960s (Barnett, 1998). However, pan-Arabism has never translated into reality and instead, the Arab system of states has developed into a classical Lockean system based on the mutual acceptance of sovereignty (Barnett, 1998; Sela, 1997) – including the sovereignty of

Israel within the 1967 borders. The most recent Arab peace initiative, endorsed by the Arab League in 2002 and re-endorsed in 2007, is an almost classical example which seeks to uphold sovereignty of all states in the region, including the one of Israel and of a Palestinian state.

The EC/EU's strategic vision of the Mediterranean region – i.e. of its southern neighbourhood – has evolved over time from the Arab Dialogue (a form of inter-regionalism) and the Global Mediterranean Policy (based on almost exclusively economic bilateral agreements) to a Kantian approach which found expression in the early 1990s with the Euro-Mediterranean Partnership (EMP) and in the early 2000s in the European Neighbourhood Policy (ENP), both aiming at building a security community in the neighborhood in diverse ways. Both initiatives have, however, reached a dead end and the EU seems currently to be reverting to a more Lockean approach which is less informed by its values and the idea of building an identity community, and is honest about pursuing its interests and classical bilateral relations with its neighbouring states. The same can be said of Turkey, which has effectively abandoned its 'zero problem with neighbours' policy which came close to Europe's Kantian vision of a shared neighbourhood, inclusive of Israel (Huber, 2015).

As these diverse strategic visions have floated in the Mediterranean region, Israel has responded to them with its own vision that has been directly influenced by its self-image and perception of the neighbourhood. As Del Sarto has pointed out, 'since its establishment, Israel's cognitive boundaries between "us" and "them" were repeatedly reconfirmed, thus nurturing a defiant and basically "realist", foreign policy' (Del Sarto, 2006: 92). Towards the Arab world, this 'realist' foreign policy has been dominated by what Avi Shlaim has termed the 'Iron Wall' doctrine, which has been characterized by a unilateralism which included the language of force, territorial expansion and disregard for international law, and which was only temporarily abandoned in the early 1990s by the Rabin-led government (Shlaim, 2014: 599). This type of unilateralism has come close to a Hobbesian approach toward the Arab neighbourhood and the Palestinians specifically. However, Israeli foreign policy has also included Lockean elements, as may be most evident in bilateral relations established with Egypt and Jordan. Israel has, however, so far rejected a multilateral and comprehensive approach to peace in the region, which it perceives as an imposition of an international solution to the conflict (Huber and Kamel, 2015).

Thus, the EU's Barcelona process has represented a rather deep challenge to Israel's own strategic vision for the region, even though similar visions began to float in Israel in the early 1990s, notably in Shimon Peres' book *The New Middle East*, in which he argued for economic regionalization, for a 'regional community of nations, with a common market and elected centralized bodies, modelled on the European Community' (Peres and Naor, 1993: 62). The concept of 'Mediterraneanism' became somewhat more important in the Israeli discourse and – as Israeli journalist Zvi Barel termed it – the 'Mediterranean Sea ceased to be a place into which Jews could be thrown, and turned into a "basin" around which one discuss[es] common regional problems' (in Nocke, 2009: 27). The fate of this discourse was, however, bound to the peace process. As it failed, the Israeli political system has consistently moved towards the right,[5] and the Iron Wall doctrine has bounced back.

Israeli policy practices in the Mediterranean

Israel's perception of the northern, eastern and southern Mediterranean and its corresponding strategic vision of the Mediterranean can be seen as the background for its specific web of political, economic and societal relations across the Mediterranean which will be explored in the remainder of this contribution.

Israel's web of political relations in the Mediterranean

In its web of political relations in the Mediterranean, Israel's policies towards the Palestinians are characterized by unilateralism, while it maintains a de-facto bilateral alliance system with Egypt, Jordan and Saudi Arabia. Multilateral approaches such as the Saudi peace initiative, the Palestinian push to move towards statehood at the UN level, the recent French peace initiative or the US/EU-led nuclear deal with Iran have so far been either evaded or actively undermined.

Israeli–Arab relations

Israel's political relations with the Arab countries of the Mediterranean have gone through diverse phases since the 1948 war. The first phase – from 1948 through 1967 – commenced with Israel's bilateral negotiations on armistice agreements with Egypt, Jordan, Lebanon and Syria. While bilateral relations were initially not normatively prohibited, in 1950 the Arab League codified them as taboo as the Palestine issue crystallized as one of the focal points of pan-Arabism (Barnett, 1998: 85–6). After Israel's quick and resounding defeat of the Arab forces in the 1967 war, the essence of the conflict changed from a legitimacy/identity conflict to a territorial conflict as the Arab consensus against diplomacy with Israel fragmented (Sela, 1997: 111). While the leading confrontation state – Egypt – signed a bilateral peace agreement with Israel in 1979, leading to its temporary expulsion from the Arab state system, the Arab League under the leadership of Saudi Arabia embraced comprehensive peace with Israel as evident in the Saudi Fahd plan which was adopted in a revised version at the Arab League's Fez summit in 1982. Israel rejected the plan, increased settlement activity in the occupied Palestinian territories and engaged in one of the country's longest and most controversial wars in 1982.

The Intifada in 1987 heralded in a new phase in the conflict – a return to the Israeli–Palestinian dimension. This phase was dominated by the so-called 'peace process' which began with the Madrid Conference, initiated by the Bush administration in 1991, and intensified with the bilateral Oslo I and II Accords in 1993 and 1995 and the Israeli–Jordanian peace treaty in 1994. This first period of negotiations, however, entered into troubled waters when Benjamin Netanyahu was elected prime minister in 1996, and received a death-blow with the failed talks in Camp David in 2000. In the wake of the second Intifada which started in 2001, a second round of negotiations saw two main proposals: the international Quartet (which embodied the two-state solution) and the Saudi peace initiative. To evade both, Israeli Prime Minister Ariel Sharon unilaterally disengaged from Gaza and built the separation wall and fence. Both acts and the continued settlement expansion in the occupied West Bank constitute security practices which follow a strictly unilateral logic that has since dominated Israeli policies.

A fourth period started with the Arab uprisings and is still in the making, yet some key structural issues can already be highlighted. Firstly, in face of the explosion of its immediate neighbourhood, Israel seems increasingly unlikely to give up control of area C – which constitutes more than 70 per cent of the territory and according to Oslo II is under exclusive Israeli security control. The Palestinian Authority is trying to counter this trend by bringing the conflict back to the international level – to the United Nations – by seeking to become a member state based on the pre-1967 borders and possibly also to the International Criminal Court (ICC). This multilateralization of the conflict is, however, resisted by Israel and the US (Huber and Kamel, 2015). Secondly, as sectarian cleavages in the region are increasing, Israel finds its de-facto alliance system with Egypt, Jordan and Saudi Arabia consolidating against the so-called Shia crescent which spans from the Gulf to the Mediterranean (Iran, the Syrian regime and Hizballah in Lebanon). While Israel has so far evaded the Arab peace initiative, recently it has rhetorically supported Egyptian President Abdel Fattah Al-Sisi's role in it, probably as a tactical move to play it off against the French initiative which Israel rejects. Thirdly, while the conflict with the 'Shia crescent' seems currently frozen by the civil war in Syria, it is bound to revive, as the nuclear deal has not been anchored in a broader regional or international setting (which would imply addressing Israel's nuclear status as well). Finally, the increasing ethnic fragmentation of the region which might lead to a territorial fragmentation of the area based on ethnic groupings, sits well with the idea of a Jewish state in the region and the idea of fragmented Palestinian areas within this territory.

Israel–EU relations

Israel's relations with the EU have been bumpy from the very beginning, when the European Community tried to develop a common foreign policy role in the 1970s, by focusing on the Israeli–Palestinian conflict. While the EC has not been a major player in the conflict, the EU's role was boosted by the Oslo Accords, when it committed itself to build up the institutional structure of a future Palestinian state. This policy is seen as increasingly problematic as it is financing the occupation, thus releasing Israel from a financial burden, and as it operates within the parameters set by the occupying power (Khalil and Del Sarto, 2015: 144). Besides its aid, the EU has sought to establish a mediating role in the conflict, but this was in the 1990s and is still blocked by both Israel and the United States. Somewhat in competition with the US-led multilateral talks (Peters, 1998), the EU set up the Barcelona Process as a regional forum which would surround and anchor Israeli–Palestinian peace talks in an envisaged regional security community. In the framework of the Barcelona Process, the EU has signed an Association Agreement with both Israel (1995) and the Palestinian Authority (PA) (1997). Israel was reluctant, however, to be incorporated into the category of Mediterranean states in the Barcelona Process – claiming that it was more European in terms of its political and economic posture than its eastern and southern Mediterranean neighbours – and wanted to keep its special bilateral relations with the EU outside of the Barcelona Process (Peters, 1998). Furthermore, as the peace process deteriorated, the Barcelona Process too came to a halt. At the same time, the EU succeeded in being included in the main diplomatic forum established in 2002 during the second Intifada – the Middle East Quartet.

In 2004, the EU launched the European Neighbourhood Policy (ENP), which – as an example of 'differentiated bilateralism' (Del Sarto and Schumacher, 2005) – was more in line with Israel's own vision of the region and conducive to substantiating EU–Israel relations. In 2007, Israel asked for an upgrade in relations, which would have enabled it to participate in further community programmes besides the programmes in which it is already participating, such as the EU's R&D programme Horizon 2020, Tempus, Erasmus Mundus, etc. This was positively received at first by the EU, but then put on hold following the Israeli offensive in the Gaza Strip in late 2008 and the unwillingness of the Netanyahu government to commit to substantive negotiations. Nonetheless, relations in practice continued to deepen in areas not covered by the upgrade and trade has continued to increase.

Nonetheless, political relations have entered into more troubled waters in recent years. Triggered by the deadlock in peace talks and the unabated growth of Israeli settlements in the occupied Palestinian territories which are making the two-state solution supported by the EU increasingly unfeasible, the EU has become more assertive in three areas: the implementation of the rules of origin and labelling issue (see the section 'Israel's economic and energy relations in the Mediterranean') and the settlement guidelines published in 2013 regulating the eligibility for EU funding of Israeli entities working within Israeli settlements the territories occupied by

Israel in 1967. The Netanyahu government has reacted to these measures with condemnation and, in turn, passed a bill designed to target Israeli left-leaning NGOs that receive funding from the EU. It has also rejected the French peace initiative presented in Paris in early June 2016 without Israeli and Palestinian participation, which Israel perceives as an illegitimate outside imposition of a solution.

Turkish–Israeli relations

In 1949, Turkey was the first Muslim majority state to recognize the state of Israel, signalling its alignment with the west in the unfolding Cold War. In 1958, as a countermove to the establishment of the United Arab Republic (UAR) between Egypt and Syria, Turkey even embarked on a secret 'peripheral alliance' with Israel (Bengio, 2004). This was abandoned, however, in the 1960s when Ankara turned to a more balanced course between the western and Arab 'worlds' for various reasons related to energy, the economy and the Cyprus conflict. In the aftermath of the Cold War and with the commencement of the peace process between Israelis and Palestinians, Turkey's relations with Israel intensified, but this changed again in the early 2000s, after the peace process had broken down. With Israeli–Palestinian violence escalating, cooperation with Israel became more difficult to justify in Turkey, especially to the conservative constituency of the Justice and Development Party (AKP). The AKP government developed its 'zero problems with neighbours' policy, in the framework of which Turkey took on the role of a regional interlocutor. It acted as a mediator between Israel and Syria, as well as between Israel and Hamas. Turkish troops also participated in UNIFIL after the 2006 Lebanon War.

The caesura in Turkish–Israeli relations came with the Gaza War (Israeli Operation Cast Lead) in December 2008/January 2009 and the 2010 Gaza Flotilla raid, both perceived in Turkey as improper acts of aggression. Ankara requested an apology from Israel, which chose to express regret instead. In September 2011, after the leaking of the UN Palmer Report, Turkey downgraded diplomatic relations with Israel, which in turn interpreted this as a move to garner support from the Arab street and to boost Turkey's soft power in the region at Israel's expense. With the Syrian civil war, as common security interests between Turkey and Israel increased, Israeli Prime Minister Netanyahu apologized for the *Mavi Marmara* incident and an agreement on the normalization of relations was reached in June 2016.

Israel's economic and energy relations in the Mediterranean

Israel's most important trade partner is the EU. Thirty per cent of its total trade crosses the Mediterranean to Europe (European Commission, 2015) and also includes settlement products at values 20 times higher than the EU imports from the Palestinian authority (Palestine Trade Center, 2013). Furthermore, EU–Israeli trade comprises arms transfers: €200 million in terms of exports to Israel with France, Germany and Romania as the top three exporters (Phillips, 2009), and 1.63 billion USD in terms of imports of Israeli weapons to Europe (Cohen, 2016). Israeli–EU trade relations are based on the Association Agreement (AA), signed between the EU and Israel in 1995 in the framework of the Barcelona Process, under which Israeli exports to the EU were exempt from custom duties. As the EU signed a similar agreement with the Palestinian Authority, the territorial scope of both agreements was necessarily exclusive and goods produced in Israeli settlements therefore exempt from the territorial scope of the Israeli AA and not eligible for preferential treatment. While Israel agreed to differentiate between goods produced in Israel and in Israeli settlements in 2004 on all origin certificates, Israeli companies producing in settlements could continue to label their goods as 'made in Israel' (Gordon and

Pardo, 2015). The EU, however, published labelling guidelines in 2015, enabling European customers to decide whether to buy goods from settlements or not. This is only mandatory for some agricultural products and cosmetics, not for packaged foods or industrial products.

After the EU, Israel's second most important trading partner in the Mediterranean is Turkey which represents almost 4 per cent of Israel's total trade and is Israel's sixth most important trade partner. Also, here the arms trade plays an important role: after India with 24 per cent of deliveries, Turkey has been the second biggest recipient with 19 per cent of Israel's arms exports between 2004 and 2007 (Perlo-Freeman, 2009). While Israel stopped supplying military equipment to Turkey in the wake of the *Mavi Marmara* incident in 2010, this was resumed in 2013. Apart from this interruption to the arms trade, Israeli–Turkish trade has not suffered from the *Mavi Marmara* incident.

Trade with other Mediterranean countries is rather low. With the Arab League boycott in 1945, trade between the Arab world and Israel was blocked. However, this boycott was gradually abandoned not only with those Arab states that signed peace treaties with Israel (Egypt and Jordan), but also with Morocco, Tunisia, Qatar and Oman, which opened mutual trade offices in the 1990s (that have been closed down since the breakdown of the 'peace process'). Trade between Israel and Egypt, Jordan, Morocco and Tunisia all figure well below 1 per cent of Israel's trade today while there are no official numbers on trade with Qatar and Oman.

Finally, a key issue for Israel in the Mediterranean in the decades to come will be the Mediterranean gas finds. First natural gas was discovered offshore from Ashkelon in 1999 and the first field – Mari B – has been exploited since 2004. The more substantial fields were discovered in 2009 (Tamar, where production started in 2013) and 2010 (Leviathan, where production will start in 2017), while more discoveries might follow. These fields make Israel not only energy self-sufficient, but will also make it an energy exporter as soon as it finds an appropriate outlet for this gas (Henderson, 2013). While this complex issue creates new incentives for cooperation among eastern Mediterranean countries, the fact that maritime boundaries had not been clearly demarcated in the region has also led to conflict, most evidently maybe in the warmongering rhetoric between Turkey and Cyprus on the one hand, and Israel and Lebanon on the other. Regarding natural gas offshore from Gaza, which was discovered in 2000, exploitation has been blocked by Israel, specifically since 2006 when Hamas won parliamentary elections and subsequently seized power in the Gaza Strip.

Israel and societal relations in the Mediterranean

Israel is not only geographically located at the Mediterranean Sea, but in many respects it could be seen as a Mediterranean 'microcosm' given that parts of its population come from the northern, eastern and southern Mediterranean. This applies not only to the native population (Muslims, Christians, Druze and Jews) which remained within Israel's border after the 1948 war,[6] but also represents a heritage of Jewish migration to Israel. While the biggest immigration group comes from Russia, Ukraine and eastern Europe with more than 1.7 million immigrants since 1948, there has also been Jewish migration to Israel from Mediterranean countries, especially from North Africa (Morocco, Algeria, Tunisia, Libya, Egypt with almost 430,000 immigrants), Turkey (63,000 immigrants) and Syria (10,000 immigrants). The so-called 'Jewish exodus' from the Arab world took place in the 1950s and 1960s, supported by the state of Israel, but also as a result of unprecedented hostilities Jews experienced in their home countries during times of intercommunal violence in Palestine or Israeli–Arab hostilities and wars (Sachar, 2007: 396–403). Legally, this exodus was based on the 'law of return' and 'nationality law', enacted by the Knesset in 1950 and 1952 respectively, which enabled Jews from all over the world to 'return' to and become citizens of Israel. At the same time, the 'right of return' of the Palestinians who became refugees just before and during the 1948 war (anchored in UN resolution 194), and even more so that of their descendants, continues to be denied by Israel. As of today, according to the Israeli Central Bureau of Statistics, Israelis born in Israel represent 75 per cent of Jewish Israelis (Central Bureau of Statistics, 2015), while the latest big immigration wave has come from the Mediterranean: immigration from France reached a record high in 2015 (Reuters, 2015).

When it comes to the flows of refugees and asylum seekers which are crossing the Mediterranean today, Israel faces similar issues to other Mediterranean countries. There are currently more than 46,000 African asylum seekers in Israel, mainly from Eritrea (73 per cent) and Sudan (19 per cent) who have entered Israel through the Sinai border. The state policy toward asylum seekers (often referred to as 'infiltrators') is officially called 'group protection', which means temporary non-deportation (African Refugee Development Center, 2015). Since 2009, only 0.25 per cent of all asylum claims submitted have been successful in obtaining refugee status (Sabar and Tsurkov, 2015: 9). Israel has adopted a policy of 'prolonged detention without trial' with the aim to 'deter future "infiltrations"', policies which are in clear contravention of the Refugee Convention (Sabar and Tsurkov, 2015: 12).

A final issue which relates to Israel and societal relations in the Mediterranean are tourism flows. Regarding incoming tourism, the main visitor group are Europeans accounting for 60 per cent of all tourism inflows to Israel. From the Middle East and North Africa, only four countries are recorded, that is Turkey which makes up 0.8 per cent, Jordan with 0.6 per cent, Egypt with 0.2 per cent and Morocco with 0.1 per cent (Central Bureau of Statistics, 2015). Data on outbound Israeli tourism are more difficult to obtain, since Mediterranean countries such as Spain and France – key destinations for Israeli tourists – do not report numbers to the World Tourism Organization. Until 2009, Turkey was the top tourist destination of Israelis in the world with more than half a million visiting Turkey in 2008. This number dropped significantly after the *Mavi Marmara* crisis. Other key destinations of Israeli tourism in the Mediterranean are Greece, as well as Egypt and Jordan to which travel has, however, gone down since the Arab uprisings.

Conclusions

Mediterraneanism was introduced at the beginning of this contribution as a concept which revived in the early 1990s as a bridge between Israel's internal and external 'eastern' and 'western' orientations. However, Israel's self-image and perception of the Mediterranean do not currently sustain this concept. The Mediterranean is perceived as an untrustworthy (north-eastern Mediterranean with Europe and Turkey), unstable/dangerous (eastern and southern Mediterranean) and existentially threatening (the Shia crescent stretching from the Gulf to the eastern Mediterranean) place, as a result of which the Iron Wall doctrine has been re-erected. In its political web of relations, Israeli practices have been characterized by unilateralism on the Palestinian front and bilateral practices on the regional front, while multilateral practices such as the Arab Peace Initiative, the French initiative, the Palestinian statehood bid at the UN or the Iranian nuclear deal have so far been evaded or rejected. In its web of economic and social relations, Israel is most integrated with the northern Mediterranean and, to a lesser degree, Turkey in the eastern Mediterranean, but hardly with the Arab eastern and southern Mediterranean.

Putting these findings in another way, economically and socially Israel is more located in the northern Mediterranean in terms of trade or tourism. In the political and security area, however, Israel clearly finds itself in the eastern Mediterranean and has indeed been the dominant power in constituting the eastern Mediterranean as a security complex (Buzan and Waever, 2004) through its specific security practices in this area until the onset of the Syrian civil war. Today, the eastern Mediterranean is increasingly characterized by dynamics which are located beyond the state level. Nonetheless, the current disintegration of the eastern Mediterranean in terms of territorial sovereignty and ethnic fragmentation is falling in line with the idea of a Jewish state and fragmented Palestinian areas within this territory, and it might not be a mere coincidence that the discussion on one-state, two-state and parallel/overlapping-state scenarios – which deeply resonate with current debates on Syria – has been revived.

Notes

1 This contribution has been written in the framework of a research project, generously funded by the Gerda Henkel Foundation and pursued at LUISS University in Rome, which focuses on the role construction of key powers in the Middle East for the case of the Israeli–Palestinian conflict.
2 As Avi Shlaim recounts, Israel's former Prime Minister Yitzhak Shamir, for example, used the concept in his often repeated saying 'The Arabs are the same Arabs, and the sea is the same sea' (Shlaim 2014, 426).
3 P5+1 refers to the five permanent members of the United Nations Security Council (China, France, Russia, United Kingdom, United States) and Germany.
4 The *Mavi Marmara* was the Turkish ship of the so-called 'Gaza Freedom Flotilla' which according to its organizers attempted to break the Israeli blockade of Gaza, bringing humanitarian aid with it. The Israeli navy boarded the ships in international waters and in the ensuing fighting on the *Mavi Marmara* eight (eventually nine) Turkish citizens and one Turkish-American citizen were killed. Turkey withdrew its ambassador from Tel Aviv and requested an apology.
5 Since 1996, Israel's governing coalitions have been dominated by right-wing parties (Likud and Kadima), with the only exception of Ehud Barak (Labour) from 1999–2001. This trend is likely sustainable, as polls have shown that young Israelis have moved towards the right (Kashti, 2011).
6 At least 700,000 Palestinians became refugees during the 1948 Arab–Israeli war, while about 100,000 Palestinians remained within Israel's borders, see Morris (1988).

References

African Refugee Development Center (2015) Refugees in Israel, available at http://ardc-israel.org/en/content/refugees-israel (accessed 19 April 2016).

Arian, A. (1989) A People Apart: Coping with National Security Problems in Israel, *Journal of Conflict Resolution* 33(4), 605–31.

Barnett, M. (1998) *Dialogues in Arab Politics* (New York: Columbia University Press).

Bar-Tal, D. (1983) *The Masada Syndrome: A Case of Central Belief* (Napa, CA: International Center for Peace in the Middle East).

Bar-Tal, D. and D. Antebi (1992) Siege Mentality in Israel, *International Journal of Intercultural Relations* 16(3), 251–75.

Beaumont, P. (2015) EU Issues Guidelines on Labelling Products from Israeli Settlements, *The Guardian*, available at www.theguardian.com/world/2015/nov/11/eu-sets-guidelines-on-labelling-products-from-israeli-settlements (accessed 7 April 2016).

Bengio, O. (2004) *The Turkish–Israeli Relationship: Changing Ties of Middle Eastern Outsiders* (New York: Palgrave Macmillan).

Buzan, B. and O. Waever (2004) *Regions and Powers: The Structure of International Security* (New York: Cambridge University Press).

Central Bureau of Statistics (2015) Statistical Abstract of Israel 2015, available at www.cbs.gov.il/reader/shnaton/shnatone_new.htm (accessed 19 April 2016).

Cohen, G. (2016) Israel's Weapons Sales to Europe More than Double amid Refugee Crisis, *Haaretz*, available at www.haaretz.com/israel-news/.premium-1.713087 (accessed 7 April 2016).

Del Sarto, R. (2006) *Contested State Identities and Regional Security in the Euro-Mediterranean Area* (New York: Palgrave Macmillan).

Del Sarto, R. and T. Schumacher (2005) From EMP to ENP: What's at Stake with the European Neighbourhood Policy towards the Southern Mediterranean? *European Foreign Affairs Review* 10(1), 17–38.

European Commission (2015) European Union, Trade in Goods with Israel, available at http://trade.ec.europa.eu/doclib/docs/2006/september/tradoc_113402.pdf (accessed 9 August 2016).

European Commission (2016) EU Neighborhood Barometer, available at www.euneighbourhood.eu (accessed 9 August 2016).

Gordon, N. and S. Pardo (2015) Bordering Disputed Territories: The European Union's Technical Customs Rules and Israel's Occupation, in: R. Del Sarto (Ed.) *Fragmented Borders, Interdependence and External Relations: The Israel–Palestine–European Union Triangle* (New York: Palgrave Macmillan).

Harpaz, G. and A. Shamis (2010) Normative Power Europe and the State of Israel: An Illegitimate EUtopia? *JCMS: Journal of Common Market Studies* 48(3), 579–616.

Henderson, Simon (2013) Natural Gas Export Options for Israel and Cyprus, GMF policy paper, www.gmfus.org/publications/natural-gas-export-options-israel-and-cyprus.

Huber, D. (2015). *Democracy Promotion and Foreign Policy. Identity and Interests in US, EU and Non-Western Democracies* (Basingstoke: Palgrave Macmillan).

Huber, D. and L. Kamel (2015) The Multilateralisation of the Israeli–Palestinian Conflict: A Call for an EU Initiative, *IAI Working Paper*, available at www.iai.it/sites/default/files/iaiwp1502.pdf (accessed 18 May 2016).

Israel Democracy Institute (2016) The Peace Index, available at www.peaceindex.org/indexMainEng.aspx (accessed 7 April 2016).

Kashti, O. (2011) Poll: Young Israelis Moving Much Farther to the Right Politically, *Haaretz*, available at www.haaretz.com/poll-young-israelis-moving-much-farther-to-the-right-politically-1.353187 (accessed 7 April 2016).

Khalil, A. and R. Del Sarto (2015) The Legal Fragmentation of Palestine–Israel and European Union Policies Promoting the Rule of Law, in: R. Del Sarto (Ed.) *Fragmented Borders, Interdependence and External Relations: The Israel–Palestine–European Union Triangle* (New York: Palgrave Macmillan).

Lehrs, L. (2013) Egyptian Plague or Spring of Youth? The Israeli Discourse regarding the Arab Spring, available at www.mitvim.org.il/israel-and-the-arab-spring (accessed 9 August 2016).

Magen, A. (2015) Comparative Assessment of Israel's Foreign Policy Response to the 'Arab Spring', *Journal of European Integration* 37(1), 113–33.

MITVIM (2012) A Majority of Israelis Support an Israeli Apology to Turkey as Part of an Agreement to Mend Relations, MITVIM Public Opinion Poll, available at www.mitvim.org.il/images/Israel-Turkey_Poll_September_2012.pdf (accessed 9 August 2016).

MITVIM (2015) The 2015 Israeli Foreign Policy Index, available at www.mitvim.org.il/images/2015_Israeli_Foreign_Policy_Index_of_the_Mitvim_Institute_-_2.pdf (accessed 9 August 2016).

Morris, B. (1988) *The Birth of the Palestinian Refugee Problem, 1947–1949* (New York: Cambridge University Press).

Nocke, A. (2009) *The Place of the Mediterranean in Modern Israeli Identity* (Boston: Brill).

Ohana, D (2011) *Israel and its Mediterranean Identity* (New York: Palgrave Macmillan).

Palestine Trade Center (2013) EU Trade with Israeli Settlements, available at www.paltrade.org/upload/multimedia/admin/2014/06/53a01bc5a3de3.pdf (accessed 9 August 2016).

Peres, S. and A. Naor (1993) *The New Middle East* (New York: Henry Holt).

Perlo-Freeman, S. (2009) Arms Transfers to the Middle East, available at www.nonproliferation.eu/web/documents/other/samperlofreeman82324e9ea9f3af411.pdf (accessed 9 August 2016).

Peters, J. (1998) The Arab-Israeli Multilateral Peace Talks and the Barcelona Process: Competition or Convergence? *The International Spectator* 33(4), 63–76.

Pew Research Center (2013) Turkey–Israel Topline, Pew Research Center's Global Attitudes Project, available at www.pewglobal.org/2013/10/17/turkey-israel-topline/ (accessed 7 April 2016).

Phillips, L. (2009) Arms Exports to Israel from EU Worth € 200m, *EUobserver*, available at https://euobserver.com/foreign/27359 (accessed 7 April 2016).

Rabin, Y. (1992) First Address to the Knesset by Prime Minister Rabin Presenting his Government, available at www.mfa.gov.il/mfa/foreignpolicy/mfadocuments/yearbook9/pages/1%20%20address%20to%20the%20knesset%20by%20prime%20minister%20rabin.aspx (accessed 18 May 2016).

Reuters (2015) Israel Reports Record Immigration of Jews from France in 2015, *Ynetnews*, available at www.ynetnews.com/articles/0,7340,L-4744313,00.html (accessed 19 April 2016).

Sabar, G. and E. Tsurkov (2015) Israel's Policies toward Asylum-Seekers: 2002–2014, IAI Working Paper, available at www.iai.it/it/pubblicazioni/israels-policies-toward-asylum-seekers (accessed 9 August 2016).

Sachar, H. (2007) *A History of Israel: From the Rise of Zionism to Our Time* (New York: Alfred A. Knopf).

Sela, A. (1997) *The Decline of the Arab–Israeli Conflict: Middle East Politics and the Quest for Regional Order* (Albany: State University of New York Press).
Shlaim, A. (2014) *The Iron Wall: Israel and the Arab World* (New York: W. W. Norton).
Wendt, A. (1999) *Social Theory of International Politics* (Cambridge: Cambridge University Press).
Yadlin, A. (2014) ISIS is No Existential Threat to Israel, *Ynetnews*, available at www.ynetnews.com/articles/0,7340,L-4567128,00.html (accessed 7 April 2016).

12

TURKISH REGIONAL PERSPECTIVES AND THE MEDITERRANEAN

Bill Park

This chapter will seek to explore the importance of Turkey's various stakes and relationships in the Mediterranean region, the contradictions and connections between them, and the priority Ankara affords them. Above all, it will stress how the Mediterranean, in all its manifestations and variety, constitutes just one of a number of regions to which Turkey belongs, and with which it interacts. Turkey has a long Mediterranean, as well as Aegean and Black Sea, coastline. It exploits the natural resources that these seas have to offer, such as fishing and tourism. It has a growing interest in the energy resources of the eastern Mediterranean and in prospective Aegean reserves. Much of its trade is seaborne via the Mediterranean and Aegean seas, and trade is conducted with all littoral states in the region – predominantly with EU Mediterranean states, but at least until the 'Arab Spring' increasingly with the states of the eastern and southern Mediterranean shores too. Its security, and its relationships with its NATO partners, is highly dependent on developments there. However, these initial remarks do not capture the complexity of Turkey's geopolitics.

To put Turkey's Mediterranean status into perspective, it is first necessary to provide some political, geopolitical and historical perspective. A succession of electoral victories, the first of them in November 2002, combined with an impressive economic performance, allowed Turkey's Islamist Adelet ve Kalkinma (AKP) governments to bring about a paradigm shift in Turkey's worldview and in its foreign policy behaviour. For all its mistrust of the west the Turkish Republic's pre-AKP foreign policy had generally focused on what the Kemalist establishment hoped was Turkey's destiny to become integrated into the west, economically, politically and socially (Cetiner, 2015; Hale, 2012; Park, 2012: 1–156). In 1952 Turkey became, and remains, NATO's only majority Muslim member. From NATO's perspective, Turkey's key attribute was its geographical location, which was crucial to the containment of the Soviet Union and, as the Soviet navy began to appear ever more frequently in the Mediterranean, for the opportunity afforded by Turkey's control of the Bosphorus to monitor and, if necessary, bottle up the Soviet Black Sea fleet. Turkey has also long aspired to join the EU, becoming in 1995 the only country to have a Customs Union with the organisation. These western alignments encouraged Turkish interaction with the countries of the Mediterranean's northern shores, but Turkey adopted a generally distant approach towards the Middle East and North Africa (MENA). This was inspired in part by a distrust of Arabs that dated back to the circumstances of the collapse of the Ottoman empire in the region, and by a dim view of the political and economic prospects of the Arab world in particular. In any case, the former MENA Ottoman domains fell under the sway of the UK and France until the post-1945 decolonisation process. The Republic's official secularism further distanced Turkey from its Islamic neighbourhood. Of course Turkey's MENA relationships were never completely frozen, not least as a consequence of Turkey's growing energy needs and the obligation to cooperate, with Iran and Iraq in particular, with respect to their shared Kurdish problems, but taken together Turkey's foreign policy preferences limited its interaction with much of the MENA region. However, Ankara did opt to develop an economic, military, intelligence and strategic relationship with Israel during the 1990s that brought it much closer to the Jewish state than it was to any of its Muslim neighbours, which further indicated the tenor of Kemalist Turkey's regional alignments and preferences (Inbar, 2001; Bengio, 2010). Cold War divisions had also served to alienate Turkey from much of its MENA neighbourhood, and had obstructed political and economic access to much of the Balkans, as well as to the Caucasian, Turkic central Asian and other states of what was then the Soviet Union.

Turkey's eastern Mediterranean location was also deemed useful to its Cold War western allies, but here Ankara had interests and perspectives of its own that were not always a close fit with Washington's or Europe's. Ankara did permit the US to use the Incirlik air base near Adana to reinforce Lebanon during the 1958 crisis there, and a year earlier had itself massed forces on the Syrian border in response to a feared communist coup. More generally, however, Turkey was reluctant to permit the US access to Incirlik and other facilities in Turkey whenever Middle Eastern crises have occurred – for example during the 1967 and 1973 Arab–Israeli wars (Bolme, 2007). Turkey's stake in Cyprus, and the difficult relationship with fellow NATO (and since 1981 EU) member Greece has been the most enduring regional thorn in the side of Turkey's western relationships. The outbreak in 1963 of intercommunal violence on the island raised the prospect of a Turkish military intervention in defence of the Turkish community there. This prompted the famous 'Johnson letter' in which the then US president warned Turkey that it could be left to its fate by its NATO allies in the event of Soviet support for the Greek side. This was the first serious blow to Turkey's faith in its western alignment (Bolukbasi, 1993). Turkey's 1974 invasion of Cyprus, and its subsequent creation of the Turkish Republic of Northern Cyprus (TRNC), led to a US congressional embargo on military supplies to Turkey, followed by Turkish restrictions on US use of military facilities in the country. To this day the failure to resolve the island's division, and the continuing Turkish military presence in the TRNC, constitutes a major obstacle to Turkey's EU accession (Diez, 2002; Ker-Lindsay, 2011). Even during the Cold War and under Kemalist governments, Turkey's perceptions of its interests in its neighbourhood, including those in the eastern Mediterranean, did not always fit comfortably with those of its western allies.

A 'central' country, again?

Turkey had already begun to adjust to post-Cold War realities even before the AKP came to power. The US-led invasion of Iraq in 2003, which Turkey opposed, added further impetus to the AKP government's foreign policy shift (Hale, 2007). These changed circumstances offered new opportunities that, as in Ottoman times, raised the issue of Turkey's place in the region. When the Turks, and particularly the Osmanli tribes, arrived in Anatolia hundreds of years ago it was not at all clear what the boundaries of their expansion should be. Confronted with a weak Byzantium they quickly moved into the Balkans and north of the Black Sea until they reached points of resistance or suffered overreach. Conquest of the generally fragmented and weak MENA littorals also came easily. Ottoman control was cemented further by the establishment of an Istanbul-based Caliphate, which fused imperial power with a degree of religious unity that bound together at least the Muslim parts of the empire. In the Mediterranean, Ottoman expansion involved naval battles with the fleets of Venice, Genoa, Spain and Portugal, and by the mid-fifteenth century the Ottomans were militarily dominant in the Mediterranean and, soon after, in the Black Sea too. Ottoman ships even conducted raids against the British Isles and Scandinavian coastlines. At their peak the Turks of Anatolia were indeed at the centre of a vast region covering the Middle East, North Africa and the Balkans, though they were still acutely conscious of their central Asian origins.

The Turkish Republic that emerged in 1923 from the defeat and dismemberment of the Ottoman empire was an entirely new state, and one far more constrained in every respect than its Ottoman predecessor. The expulsion of millions of Greeks from Anatolia broke littoral Anatolia's centuries-old and integral interaction with and contribution to Mediterranean developments. The regional foreign policy of the new republic was – by choice, circumstance, and capacity – broadly isolationist and self-sufficient. However, the eventual termination of the European colonial presence in the region, and then the end of the Cold War, raised the novel question of how Turkey should relate to those adjacent regions it had once dominated. Could its preoccupation with becoming 'western' survive the new pressures and opportunities that confronted Ankara? Or would it rediscover its Balkan, or Eurasian, or Middle Eastern, or wider Islamic, or Mediterranean, or even more distant Eurasian and Turkic, past(s)? The emergence of the Islamist, post-Kemalist, less exclusively 'western' AKP enabled Turkey to confront these dilemmas head on.

Turkish foreign policy under the AKP became increasingly associated with the thinking of Ahmet Davutoglu who was promoted to the position of foreign minister in 2009, from his previous position as the prime minister's foreign policy advisor. In August 2014 he became prime minister, although in May 2016 he was obliged to step down as President Recep Tayyip Erdogan took increasing control of the country's political scene. Davutoglu's foreign policy ideas contrasted significantly with the approach to external relationships that had been associated with the Republic's past Kemalist governments. Turkey now sought to emerge as a determined actor on the world stage. Under Davutoglu's guidance, Turkish foreign policy became associated with catchy phrases such as 'strategic depth', 'soft power', and 'zero problems with the neighbourhood' (Aras, 2009; Grigoriadis, 2010; Murinson, 2006; Ozkan, 2014; Stein, 2014a). It has also been described as 'Turkish Gaullism' (Taspinar, 2011), as the foreign policy of a rising trading state (Kirisci, 2009), and as 'pan-Islamist' (Ozkan, 2014). It was, and still is, perhaps all of these things. It has also been regarded as 'neo-Ottoman' (Taspinar, 2008). Turkey under the AKP aspired to put itself once again at the centre of a vast and complex region that would incorporate much of the MENA region, the Balkans, the Caucasus and central Asia. Davutoglu's guiding and highly geopolitical concept was that of 'strategic depth'. Turkey is, or should be, a 'central' rather than a peripheral country able to exploit its history, geography, culture, religion, and increasing economic prowess to put itself at the heart of a region that roughly corresponds to the former Ottoman empire and, increasingly, beyond, into sub-Saharan Africa to the south and eastwards into Asia. For Davutoglu (2007: 78–9), 'Turkey's geography gives it a specific central country status . . . it should be seen neither as a bridge country which only connects two points, nor a frontier country'. Thus, 'Turkey is a middle eastern, Balkan, Caucasian, central Asian, Caspian, Mediterranean, Gulf, and Black Sea country' simultaneously. This central location meant that Turkey could function as a linking mechanism between diverse regions. Combined both with Turkey's economic dynamism relative to most of its neighbours and with its Ottoman legacy, Turkey's role should be 'one of providing security not only for itself, but also for its neighbouring regions . . . by taking on a more active, constructive role'

(Davutoglu, 2007: 78–9). The 'zero problems with the neighbours' approach and an activist regional foreign policy were expressions of this mindset.

This is – or was, when it was initially enunciated – a plausible and attractive argument, but it did not really take into account the question of whether Turkey has the capacities – political, economic, military, diplomatic – to seriously address the problems of and Turkey's relationships with so extensive and diverse a set of neighbouring regions. Nor does it indicate how Turkey should prioritise relationships with its various neighbourhoods. Furthermore, it is difficult to achieve 'zero problems with the neighbours' when the neighbours have so many problems with each other – Israel with its Palestinian neighbours and the Arab world more widely, Azerbaijan with Armenia, Russia with Georgia and Ukraine, Greek Cypriots with Turkish Cypriots, Sunnis with Shias, and so on. Furthermore, in its own responses to various regional tensions, Ankara did not always play the mediating role that Davutoglu promised it would, but instead often took sides. Turkey also has some problematic neighbourhood relationships of its own, some of them enduring – as with Greece, Cyprus and Armenia – and others that wax and wane – with Iran, Iraq, Israel, Syria and Russia. With the 'Arab Spring', Ankara was additionally confronted with choosing between neighbouring regimes and neighbouring peoples, or between various ethnic and sectarian factions in neighbouring countries. This has caused it difficulties with the governments of Syria and Egypt, and with Libya and Iraq too, and led Turkey to sponsor factions in the intercommunal conflicts that have bedevilled Syria, Iraq and Libya in recent years. Added to these problems are the roles of external actors – the US, the EU and of course Russia. In short, the clumsiness of Turkey's foreign policy behaviour, the complexities of the multiple and criss-crossing neighbourhoods in which Turkey is located, and Turkey's own limited capacities, meant that the 'zero problems with the neighbours' approach was soon supplanted by problems in all directions. Furthermore, Turkey's relationship with the states and peoples of the Mediterranean littoral date back to Ottoman times, which have sometimes left behind a legacy that is not invariably viewed positively by many of Turkey's Mediterranean neighbours. Although Turkey under the AKP initially sought to revive and enrich these ancient relationships via trade, cultural exchange and religious affinity, as turmoil emerged in Turkey's various neighbourhoods, so did some unhappy memories of Ottoman rule. This observation applies to the Balkans and the Caucasus as well as to MENA.

Turkey as a Mediterranean power

One of the regions to which Turkey belongs is of course the Mediterranean. Turkey's interests in the region are diverse and substantive. They include the divided island of Cyprus and the developing energy fields off its coasts; the offshore Greek islands to which thousands of mainly Syrian refugees have migrated from Turkey; the maritime differences with Greece in the Aegean; the Bosphorus and Marmara Sea route for substantial volumes of trade to and from the Black Sea; and the economic significance of Mediterranean tourism to the Turkish economy. Izmir is the base for a NATO command HQ, and Turkey shares a stake in Mediterranean security with other NATO countries in the region – Greece, Italy, Spain, France and of course the US in particular. Turkey has a significant NATO-affiliated naval and aerial presence in the region, and the long-standing NATO base at Izmir currently functions as the alliance's Allied Land Command (LANDCOM).[1] Other NATO military facilities include the airbase at Incirlik, currently used by but for long withheld from US bombers in their engagement with Islamic State (IS) forces in Syria. Turkey's Black Sea status and its responsibility for implementing the Montreux Convention that regulates use of the Bosphorus are important factors in Russia's access to the Mediterranean region. Turkey's Aegean or Fourth Army, also based in Izmir, is not NATO-assigned, was formed in 1975 to address Turkey's Aegean dispute with fellow-NATO member Greece, and incorporates the sizeable Turkish military presence in the TRNC, which consists of somewhere between 17,500 and 30,000 Turkish troops (International Crisis Group, 2011).

Turkey is also an EU accession candidate. Turkey is currently the only country to enjoy a full customs union with the EU and the EU is Turkey's most important trading partner. Although Germany leads the way, France and Italy are in fourth and fifth places respectively as destinations for Turkish exports. Iraq is Turkey's leading non-European export market, much of this accounted for by the Kurdistan region of Iraq – which exports its oil via the Turkish Mediterranean port of Ceyhan. Italy leads the way among Mediterranean countries as a source of imports into Turkey, but China, Germany and Russia – the latter as Turkey's major source of energy imports – are all ahead of any Mediterranean trade partner.[2] Turkey's is by far the biggest non-EU economy in the Euro-Mediterranean Free Trade Area, designed to liberalise trade between the EU and southern Mediterranean countries, and between the southern Mediterranean countries themselves.[3] Although Turkish trade has diversified in recent years, the political instability and weak economies of the Mediterranean's non-European countries limits the scope for significant enhancement of Turkey's trade relations with them. It can be seen from this that Turkey's Mediterranean geography has only a limited impact on its trade patterns, and has mixed consequences for its security concerns and arrangements. However, Turkey's location, diplomatic alignments and military capacities have significance for overall Mediterranean security.

Islam first?

Turkey, with much of the Mediterranean region, is a Muslim country, and a member since 1969 of the Organisation of Islamic Cooperation (OIC). In 2005, a Turkish citizen, Ekmeleddin Ihsanoglu, became the OIC's first ever elected secretary general. The OIC has provided a multilateral forum via which Ankara has been able to cultivate other Muslim states of the Mediterranean region, and a platform where it could lobby for its own interests and perspectives – for example, with respect to the Turkish Republic of Northern Cyprus (TRNC). Turkey under the AKP has at times presented itself as a 'model' or 'source of inspiration' to Muslim states seeking to combine Islam with modernity and democratisation, and as a country with a foot in both the Muslim and the western camps it has engaged in diplomatic initiatives designed to bridge the gap between them. Thus, in 2002 and in the wake of the 9/11 attacks it hosted an inter-civilisational EU–OIC forum, and in 2005 co-sponsored with Spain an 'Alliance of Civilisations' initiative. Turkey was also active in enlisting western support for the beleaguered fellow Muslims, the Bosnians and Kosovars, in the Balkans during the 1990s. Turkey's own Islamic identity led it to play a key peacekeeping role in Afghanistan, but as part of NATO, and in Lebanon, alongside both European and Muslim partners (Park, 2012; 122–42). What all this conveys is that Turkey is perhaps uniquely part of both the northern and European, and the southern and primarily Islamic, Mediterranean worlds.

Even so, some have detected a pan-Islamism, especially of the Sunni variety, in the AKP government's foreign-policy approach. This seemed to strengthen with the emergence of the 'Arab Spring' and with the AKP's consolidation of power domestically (Ozkan, 2014). It sometimes appeared to stray towards anti-western sentiment (Park, 2015). This thinking merged with Ankara's faith that it could reshape the region, and encouraged Ankara's supportive policy towards the pro-Islamist and especially Muslim Brotherhood forces in Tunisia, Libya, Egypt and Syria. Given Turkey's location, it has been events in the eastern Mediterranean that have proved most compelling. Ankara turned against its erstwhile (and Alawite) friend in Damascus, Bashar al-Assad, and sponsored the formation in August 2011 of the Syrian National Council (SNC), which, with the Turkey-backed Free Syrian Army (FSA), was initially hosted in Turkey. The FSA, along with Turkmen and more jihadi elements of the opposition to the Syrian regime, continued to receive training and arms from Turkey – whether to fight regime forces, Syria's Kurdish fighters, or more recently the IS presence in Syria (Stein, 2014b, 2015a,b; Tur, 2015). Turkey initially held itself aloof from an anti-IS coalition of Arab and western countries that Washington had assembled, refusing to allow US bombers to use Incirlik in its anti-IS campaign (Stein, 2015c). Washington was obliged to air drop military supplies to Kobane's Kurdish defenders against their IS besiegers from further afield, while the Turkish military looked on and Erdogan loudly criticised Washington's action (*Today's Zaman*, 2015). Erdogan offered an insight into Ankara's thinking with his comment that 'for us, the PKK [Kurdistan Workers' Party] is the same as ISIL. It is wrong to consider them as different from each other' (*Today's Zaman*, 2014). Turkey's November 2015 shooting down of a Russian plane, and Moscow's fierce reaction, served as an additional reminder of Ankara's limited capacity to shape Syrian events in the face of the preferences of the major powers. On the other hand, its August 2016 military intervention in Syria, accompanied by FSA elements, and its rapprochement with Moscow, also indicated that Ankara is a key factor in the Syrian crisis. That the intervention clearly highlighted the link between Syria's Kurdish issue and Turkey's also served as a reminder of Turkey's profound domestic and regional vulnerabilities.

Similarly detrimental to Turkey's position in the region has been its spat with the Egyptian government of Abdul Fattah al-Sisi. Ankara emerged as a fervent supporter of Egypt's Muslim Brotherhood president Mohamed Morsi, and a much more unrelenting critic of the 'coup' that ousted him than either its western allies or most of the Gulf states, the Arab League or the OIC. The Turkish position added grist to the sense that its approach to the region was now driven by pro-Muslim Brotherhood and even neo-Ottoman inclinations, although Ankara argued that it was simply keeping faith with the democratically elected leader of Egypt. Cairo withdrew its ambassador due to Ankara's stance (Gursel, 2013; Idiz, 2013) and in November 2013 expelled Turkey's ambassador. Turkey's willingness to host exiled Egyptian Muslim Brotherhood groups and their media outlets, which conduct an incessant campaign against the al-Sisi government, prompted Cairo to accuse Turkey of encouraging Egypt's escalating round of violence (Tastekin, 2015).

Turkey became embroiled in the events of the 'Arab Spring' further west in Libya too. In the increasingly violent crisis in Libya that broke out in 2011, Ankara again adopted a position somewhat at odds not only with the majority of its Muslim regional neighbours but with its NATO and EU partners too (Stein, 2015d). Ankara's initial response to the prospect of a western intervention to stem the bloodshed was indicated by President Erdogan's rhetorical question, 'What does NATO have to do with Libya?', which somewhat overlooked Libya's geographical proximity to and economic entanglement with the countries of the northern Mediterranean coastline. Although Turkey soon adopted a more cooperative stance, Ankara's own sympathies were at best neutral as between the western and Arab-supported Operation Dignity coalition and the opposition Operation Dawn. Ankara had supported the establishment in 2012 of the Muslim Brotherhood-rooted Justice and Construction Party, based in rebel-held Misrata. Furthermore a number of Turkish ships allegedly carrying weapons to the Libyan opposition and even jihadi groups were intercepted by Greek and Libyan navy units, and Egypt intercepted containers of allegedly Turkey-supplied weapons on its border with Libya. In December 2014 Egypt also imposed restrictions on males travelling to Libya or Turkey, at around the same time that the commander of Operation Dignity's air force apparently threatened to shoot down

Turkish aircraft that entered Libyan airspace without permission. In 2014 Abdullah al-Thinni, head of the 'government' faction, accused Turkey of interfering in Libya's domestic affairs and withdrew the Libyan ambassador from Ankara. The Libyan General Khalifa Haftar declared Turks 'unwelcome persons' in Libya, which prompted Ankara to advise its remaining citizens there to leave. Although Ankara threw its weight behind the internationally supported Government of National Unity that emerged at the end of 2015, the Libyan crisis demonstrated how distant Ankara could be from both its Arab neighbours and its western allies.

The Syrian, Egyptian and Libyan episodes demonstrated the peculiarities of Turkey's regional position as it had evolved up to mid-2016. Ankara's determination to engage with the Muslim world hit up against the complexities of the 'Arab Spring'. Turkey's reactions to these dramatic developments led to a falling out with most Muslim countries bordering the Mediterranean. Short of a total Sunni victory in Syria, re-establishing trust between Damascus and Ankara will surely prove difficult in the future. Nor are anti-Muslim Brotherhood elements in Egypt, such as those currently in power, likely to forgive Ankara's stance towards the overthrow of Morsi any time soon. Turkey's western allies, Moscow, the region's Shia states and even some of the Sunni Arab regimes such as those in Cairo and Amman are suspicious of Ankara's links with jihadi elements in the region. In 2015 even Tunisia's foreign minister voiced his concern about Ankara's apparent role in facilitating the movement of jihadi elements passing to and through Libya.[4] Perhaps a post-Davutoglu, post-Erdogan or post-AKP government would find it easier to repair the damage that has been done, but in the meantime what has become most evident is Turkey's inexperience in dealing with the Arab world, its misunderstanding of regional perceptions of the Ottoman past, the ideological basis of the AKP's approach to MENA, and its limited capacity to shape the region to its own design. Turkey is not the regional power it had thought it was, and is more echo chamber for the region's ills than engineer of the region's destiny. The failed July 2016 coup attempt reinforces that observation.

Turkey and the eastern Mediterranean's non-Islamic states

Interestingly, the AKP government's growing identification with the Muslim and Arab world was a significant factor in its falling out with Israel. The May 2010 Israeli commando raid on the *Mavi Marmara,* a ship carrying humanitarian aid to Gaza and which resulted in nine Turkish deaths, had been preceded by a public display of anger by Erdogan in Davos in 2009, during which he stormed off a platform he was sharing with Israeli president Shimon Peres. Israel's late 2008 military campaign in Gaza had prompted increasingly anti-Israel and pro-Palestinian utterances from various government figures (Park, 2015: 588–9). In the wake of the *Mavi Marmara* incident, ambassadors were withdrawn and a war of words ensued. US attempts to restore the relationship failed, with Ankara holding out for a more fulsome apology than Israel felt inclined to offer, compensation, and a lifting of the siege of Gaza. The military relationship between the two countries was also formally frozen. Trade between them continued to prosper, although Israeli tourism to Turkey fell dramatically. There seems little doubt that Hamas was generally grateful to Turkey, as it represented Ankara's preferred faction in Palestinian politics vis-à-vis the more generally recognised Palestinian Authority. Indeed, an Israeli condition for the normalisation of relations with Turkey was that it should curtail its relationship with Hamas. In mid-2016 the Turkey–Israel relationship was restored. The deal did indeed involve curtailing Hamas activities in Turkey, but also permitted the resumption of Turkish humanitarian assistance to Gaza. It is unlikely that the formerly close security-based relationship between the two countries will be re-established, but both are uneasy about Iranian influence in the region and need to limit their respective diplomatic isolation (Tastekin, 2016).

In any case, the Arab world, much of which prefers the Palestinian Authority to Hamas, had not been much moved by Turkey's break with Israel. Arab concern with the plight of the Palestinians and with the existence and behaviour of Israel has become more rhetorical than actual, some Arab countries – notably Egypt and Jordan – long ago arrived at an accommodation with the Jewish state, and many are more concerned about the IS threat and by Iranian activity than they are by Israel's behaviour. Once again, Ankara's position appeared ideological and lacking in nuance, and suggested another misreading of the regional mood. Turkey had been prepared to sacrifice its Israeli friendship, but had not at all strengthened its position in the Arab world as a consequence.

Turkey's relationships with Nicosia and Athens remain troubled and politically interconnected, but recent major gas finds off the Israeli, Cypriot (and Egyptian) coasts offer an additional impetus to improved relationships between Turkey on the one hand and Cyprus, Greece and Israel on the other (Carlson, 2016; Tanchum, 2015). The finds have led to closer security cooperation between Jerusalem and Nicosia, as both have a stake in protecting their gas fields, and new understandings relating to energy and security with both Egypt and Greece. Ankara's initial response was to contest Nicosia's right to exploit its new-found energy resources, to quibble over the demarcation of waters between the two halves of Cyprus, and to send its own seismic research vessel to the waters off the northern Cypriot coast. Once again Turkey found itself isolated, as Washington expressed its displeasure with Ankara's provocative approach by withholding the transfer of two decommissioned US frigates to the Turkish navy. However, Turkey – which relies on Russia and Iran for 75 per cent of its gas imports and would prefer to reduce that dependence – is the more natural export market and transit route for Israeli and Cypriot gas. Energy issues might also help explain the optimism surrounding talks over Cyprus too, which resumed in mid-2015 following a hiatus caused by the tiff over offshore gas. In mid-2016 the talks were still rumbling on, with familiar claims to optimism tempered by the fact that the stumbling blocks to agreement were also familiar – not least the size, role and status of the Turkish force still stationed on the island (Arisan and Eralp, 2016; Tzimitras and Gurel, 2016).

Nor has progress been made on the perennial differences between Ankara and Athens on delineation of the waters and air space in the Aegean. Although there is a constant risk of incident between the militaries of the two NATO states, they have managed to compartmentalise the issue and to conduct more or less normal relations for some time now (International Crisis Group, 2011). However, the refugee crisis, in which hundreds of thousands of refugees, mostly but not exclusively Syrian, found their way to Greek Aegean islands from the Turkish mainland in the hope of eventually making it to the more affluent EU countries further north, revealed the geographical complexity of the Turkey–Greece border and highlighted that it serves as the border between EU and non-EU territories in the Mediterranean. It also served as yet another reminder of how Anatolia has long functioned as a major east–west route in the region, for people as well as for ideas and trade. The crisis impelled a deal between Turkey and the EU in early 2016 by which those Syrian refugees that did not qualify for asylum would be returned to Turkey. In return for each refugee returned, one would be settled in Europe. In addition to concerns about the deal's compatibility with international law, there was also consternation in Europe with the vague suggestion that in return for Ankara's cooperation Turks might be granted visa-free access to the EU and that Turkey's stalled accession negotiations might be reinvigorated. Indeed, Brussels agreed to re-open talks with Ankara on a controversial budgetary accession chapter – Ankara had sought the opening of five accession 'chapters' – and suggested that visa-free entry might be achievable within months (Karnitschnig and Barigazzi, 2016). In fact it soon became evident that Brussels was demanding the implementation of 72 conditions for visa-free entry that had been agreed back in 2013.[5] Fudging on this issue continued throughout the year. In any case, in the wake of the failed July 2016 coup attempt and its aftermath, Turkey's EU accession appeared as distant a prospect as it had ever done. The deal, or the realisation on the part of would-be Syrian migrants that their prospects of reaching Europe were dim, did lead to a fall in the number of people crossing into Greece. It also stranded many refugees there, and of course in Turkey, where there were doubts about whether its treatment of refugees met internationally agreed standards (European Stability Initiative, 2016). Greece and Turkey also agreed to permit a NATO maritime task force to track the movement of migrants in their Aegean waters, although there were reports of difficulties in implementation stemming from the Greek–Turkish territorial differences there (Neuger, 2016; Stamouli, Peker and Barnes, 2016).

Observations

What general observations can be made about Turkey's Mediterranean role? First, it is clear that Turkey is connected with the states, institutions and issues of the region in multiple and frequently overlapping ways, and that its various bilateral and multilateral relationships do not always align well. Second, Turkey's peculiarities – as a northern littoral and NATO and EU associated but Muslim state; as a Eurasian and continental as well as a maritime state; as a regionally powerful state in a part of the world in which external actors play key roles; and occupying a geographical corridor that links east to west and, to a degree, north to south – mean that few states in the Mediterranean region or beyond are burdened with so heavy a foreign policy agenda and are tempted by so wide a range of policy choices. Third, both the domestic turbulence of recent years and the longer-term discontinuities in Turkey's historical evolution have served to intensify the tendency towards what could be regarded as 'paradigm shifts' in the country's relationships with other Mediterranean states, both those that are immediate neighbours and those that lie further afield. The failed coup attempt of July 2016 and its uncertain ramifications accentuated doubts surrounding Turkey's consistency and continuity. Somehow the fact that the Turks were latecomers to the Mediterranean shores still shapes its neighbourhood relationships. Although Islamic, it is not part of the Arab world that predominates in the region and is often seen by it as a former coloniser, outsider and Trojan horse for external interests rather than as a natural partner. Although a member of NATO and an accession candidate to the EU, it is not invariably regarded as European due to its religion, democratic failings, level of development, geography and foreign policy choices. Although Eurasian, its links with its northern and eastern neighbours have suffered periods of rupture, and – with Tsarist and Soviet Russia especially – traditional enmity. Perhaps its potential is as a 'central' country that links its various neighbourhoods to each other, as envisaged by Ahmet Davutoglu and as implemented by the republic's Ottoman predecessors. For the time being, however, the reality is less grandiose. Turkey has a foot in many camps but is not truly integral to any of them. Its chief strategic partners in the Mediterranean region are neither its main trading partners nor its immediate neighbours, nor even – in the case of Greece – its natural allies. Its major trading partners are not its 'natural' allies (Russia, Israel) or even Mediterranean at all (Russia, Germany). Turkey is not simply an odd fit in the Mediterranean region, it is an odd fit in all the regions it abuts. This 'loneliness' could in principle be addressed by the adoption of a clearer and more focused prioritisation of its foreign policy agenda, and in the immediate post-Davutoglu period the signs were that Ankara was seeking to repair some of its damaged relationships in the region. However, a degree of mistrust of Turkey's reliability and its true intentions will surely endure. Thus, it seems that the best Turkey can hope for, in the Mediterranean region and beyond, is to build a set of functioning transactional bilateral and multilateral relationships. A deeper 'belonging' to any of the political and cultural constellations and states that surround it will, however, surely remain elusive.

Notes

1 See www.lc.nato.int/index.php (accessed 23 May 2016).
2 See http://atlas.media.mit.edu/en/profile/country/tur/ (accessed 23 May 2016).
3 See http://ec.europa.eu/trade/policy/countries-and-regions/regions/euro-mediterranean-partnership/ (accessed 23 May 2016).
4 'Tunisia accuses Turkey of facilitating jihadists' transit', 2 April 2015, www.yahoo.com/news/tunisia-accuses-turkey-facilitating-jihadists-transit-212556482.html?ref=gs (accessed 22 June 2016).
5 Roadmap towards a visa-free regime with Turkey, http://ec.europa.eu/dgs/home-affairs/what-is-new/news/news/docs/20131216-roadmap_towards_the_visa-free_regime_with_turkey_en.pdf (accessed 4 September 2016).

References

Aras, Bulent, 2009. 'The Davutoglu era in Turkish foreign policy', *Insight Turkey*, 11(3), 127–42.

Arisan, Nilgun, and Eralp, Atila, 2016. 'Critical juncture in Cyprus negotiations', Istituto Affari Internatzionale, 13 May, www.iai.it/sites/default/files/iaiwp1613.pdf (accessed 22 June 2016).

Bengio, Ofra, 2010. *The Turkish–Israeli relationship: changing ties of Middle Eastern outsiders*, New York: Palgrave Macmillan.

Bolme, Selin, 2007. 'The politics of Incirlik air base', *Insight Turkey*, 9(3), 82–91.

Bolukbasi, Suha, 1993. 'The Johnson letter revisited', *Middle Eastern Studies*, 29(3), 505–25.

Carlson, Suzanne, 2016. 'Pivoting energy relations in the Eastern Mediterranean', *Turkish Policy Quarterly*, 15(1), 67–78.

Cetiner, Yusuf Turan, 2015. *Turkey and the west: from neutrality to commitment*, Lanham, Maryland: University Press of America.

Davutoglu, Ahmet, 2007. 'Turkey's foreign policy vision: an assessment of 2007', *Insight Turkey*, 10(1), 77–96.

Diez, Thomas, (eds), 2002. *The European Union and the Cyprus conflict: modern conflict, postmodern union*, Manchester: Manchester University Press.

European Stability Initiative, 2016. 'Sailing in the dark', 19 March, www.esiweb.org/pdf/ESI%20newsletter%20-%20Sailing%20in%20the%20dark%20-%20visa%20terror%20and%20refugee%20agreement%20-%2019%20May%202016.pdf (accessed 22 June 2016).

Grigoriadis, Ioannis N., 2010. *The Davutoglu doctrine and Turkish foreign policy*, Working Paper 8, Hellenic Foundation for European and Foreign Policy (ELIAMEP), April, www.eliamep.gr/en/all-publications/working-papers/the-davutoglu-doctrine-and-turkish-foreign-policy/ (accessed 10 December 2013).

Gursel, Kadri, 2013. 'How did Turkey lose Egypt?', *Al Monitor*, 13 September, www.al-monitor.com/pulse/originals/2013/09/turkey-egypt-policy-setback-cause.html (accessed 5 March 2015).

Hale, William, 2007. *Turkey, the US and Iraq*, London: SAQI.

Hale, William, 2012. *Turkish foreign policy since 1774*, (3rd edition), London and New York: Routledge.

Idiz, Semih, 2013. 'Turkey's Middle East policy lies in shambles', *Al Monitor*, 3 September, www.al-monitor.com/pulse/originals/2013/09/turkish-middle-east-policy-shambles.html, (accessed 5 March 2015).

Inbar, Efraim, 2001. *The Israeli–Turkish entente*, KCL Mediterranean Studies.

International Crisis Group, 2011. 'Turkey and Greece: time to settle the Aegean dispute', Europe Briefing n.64, 19 July, www.crisisgroup.org/~/media/Files/europe/turkey-cyprus/turkey/B64-%20Turkey%20and%20Greece-%20Time%20to%20Settle%20the%20Aegean%20Dispute.pdf, (accessed 23 May 2016).

Karnitschnig, Matthew, and Barigazzi, Jacopo, 2016. 'EU and Turkey reach refugee deal', *Politico*, 20 March, www.politico.eu/article/eu-and-turkey-finalize-refugee-deal/ (accessed 4 September 2016).

Ker-Lindsay, James, 2011. *The Cyprus problem: what everyone needs to know*, New York: Oxford University Press.

Kirisci, Kemal, 2009. 'The transformation of Turkish foreign policy; the rise of the trading state', *New Perspectives on Turkey*, 40, 29–57.

Murinson, Alexander, 2006. 'The strategic depth doctrine of Turkish foreign policy', *Middle Eastern Studies*, 42(6), 945–64.

Neuger, James G., 2016. 'NATO warships to track Aegean refugee flow after Merkel plea', 11 February, www.bloomberg.com/news/articles/2016-02-11/nato-warships-to-monitor-aegean-refugee-flow-after-merkel-plea (accessed 3 July 2016).

Ozkan, Behlul, 2014. 'Turkey, Davutoglu and the idea of pan-Islamism', *Survival*, 56(4), 119–40.

Park, Bill, 2012. *Modern Turkey: people, state and foreign policy in a globalized world*, London and New York: Routledge.

Park, Bill, 2015. 'Turkey's isolated stance: an ally no more, or just the usual turbulence?', *International Affairs*, 91(3), 581–600.

Stamouli, Nektaria, Peker, Emre and Barnes, Julien E., 2016. 'Turkey blocks expansion of NATO's Aegean mission', *Wall Street Journal*, 15 June, www.wsj.com/articles/turkey-blocks-expansion-of-natos-aegean-mission-1466020162, (accessed 3 July 2016).

Stein, Aaron, 2014a. 'Turkey's new foreign policy: Davutoglu, the AKP and the pursuit of regional order', *Whitehall Papers*, Royal United Services Institute, 83, no.1, December.

Stein, Aaron, 2014b. 'The origins of Turkey's buffer zone in Syria', 11 December, http://warontherocks.com/2014/12/the-origins-of-turkeys-buffer-zone-in-syria/ (accessed 9 February 2015).

Stein, Aaron, 2015a. 'Turkey's evolving Syria strategy', *Foreign Affairs*, 9 February, http://www.foreignaffairs.com/articles/143023/aaron-stein/turkeys-evolving-syria-strategy (accessed 5 March 2015).

Stein, Aaron, 2015b. 'Turkey's role in a shifting Syria', Atlantic Council, 13 May, www.atlanticcouncil.org/blogs/menasource/turkey-s-role-in-a-shifting-syria (accessed 18 June 2015).

Stein, Aaron, 2015c. 'The Incirlik expansion and the US-Turkish strategy to fight ISIS', Atlantic Council, 8 October, www.atlanticcouncil.org/blogs/menasource/the-incirlik-expansion-and-the-us-turkish-strategy-to-fight-isis?utm_content=bufferd61d6&utm_medium=social&utm_source=twitter.com&utm_campaign=buffer#.Vhdk1P-Enzs.twitter (accessed 26 October 2015).

Stein, Aaron, (2015d) 'Turkey's proxy war in Libya', *War on the Rocks*, 15 January, http://warontherocks.com/2015/01/turkeys-proxy-war-in-libya/ (accessed 21 June 2016).

Tanchum, Michael, 2015. 'A new equilibrium; the Republic of Cyprus, Israel and Turkey in the eastern Mediterranean strategic architecture', Friedrich-Ebert-Stiftung and Peace Research Institute Oslo (PRIO), http://file.prio.no/publication_files/cyprus/OP1%20A%20New%20Equilibrium.pdf (accessed 22 June 2016).

Taspinar, Omer, 2008. 'Turkey's Middle East policies: between neo-Ottomanism and Kemalism', Carnegie Endowment for International Peace: Carnegie Papers no. 10, 7 October.

Taspinar, Omer, 2011. 'The rise of Turkish Gaullism: getting Turkish–American relations right', *Insight Turkey*, 13(1), 19–25.

Tastekin, Fehim, 2015. 'Turkey accused of escalating violence in Egypt', *Al Monitor*, 6 February, www.al-monitor.com/pulse/originals/2015/02/turkey-egypt-muslim-brotherhood-escalating-violence.html (accessed 8 February 2015).

Tastekin, Fehim, 2016. 'How Erdogan will spin his deal with Israel', *Al Monitor*, 28 June, www.al-monitor.com/pulse/originals/2016/06/turkey-israel-palestine-normalization-hamas-erdogan.html?utm_source=Boomtrain&utm_medium=manual&utm_campaign=20160629&bt_email=william.h.park@kcl.ac.uk&bt_ts=1467219171225 (accessed 4 July 2016).

Today's Zaman, 2014. 'PKK, ISIL are the same, says Erdogan', 4 October, www.todayszaman.com/national_pkk-isil-are-the-same-says-erdogan_360766.html (accessed 5 March 2015).

Today's Zaman, 2015. 'Erdogan: I don't understand why Kobane is so strategic for the US', 22 October, www.todayszaman.com/national_erdogan-i-dont-understand-why-kobani-is-so-strategic-for-us_362331.html (accessed 6 March 2015).

Tur, Ozlem, 2015. 'Turkey and the Syrian crisis: deepening regional and domestic challenges', *Orient*, 1, 23–8.

Tzimitras, Harry and Gurel, Ayla, 2016. 'Cyprus settlement negotiations: from euphoria to reality', *Turkish Policy Quarterly*, 15(1), 51–63.

PART III

Peace and conflict

13

THE MEDITERRANEAN OBSERVES THE WORLD, THE WORLD OBSERVES THE MEDITERRANEAN

Conflict and peace in the Mediterranean

Stephan Stetter

Introduction

In this chapter I look at conflicts and peacebuilding in the Mediterranean region. I will address both the southern and the northern parts of the Mediterranean with a view to both the colonial and the post-colonial eras. Today, as a result of major political events, such as de-colonization (starting with Greece in the 1820s, reaching its peak with the de-colonization of Arab states mainly from the 1920s to the 1970s) and state break-up (e.g. the former Yugoslavia during the 1990s) a record number of twenty-two states border the Mediterranean Sea, while almost the entire north of the Mediterranean – a total of eight states – is part of the supranational European Union (EU).[1]

By analysing conflicts and peacebuilding in this region, this chapter is conceptually guided by a historical international political sociology (HIPS) of modern world society (Buzan and Lawson 2013; Hobden and Hobson 2002; Stetter 2008). A HIPS perspective allows understanding conflicts and peacebuilding in the Mediterranean as world societal phenomena that are simultaneously shaped by interlacements between the region's internal and external dynamics. This world societal embedding unfolds within a densely integrated, yet highly differentiated and hierarchical global political order – i.e. what the English School of international relations (IR) theory, from which I will conceptually draw in this chapter, refers to as international society (Bilgin 2012). The central contours of international society were established during the European-dominated nineteenth century and have been subject to evolutionary change in world society since then. The key argument I pursue in that context is that both conflicts and peacebuilding in the Mediterranean are shaped by dynamics related to the evolution of international society, in particular the evolution of discourses and practices that legitimize both violent conflict *and* non-violent conflict resolution in world politics. The English School concept of primary institutions of international society then offers an intriguing vantage point from which to study such patterns of conflict and peacebuilding (Buzan 2004; Buzan and Gonzalez-Pelaez 2009). Primary institutions are, in a nutshell, powerful ideas, or constitutional principles (Reus-Smit 1999), that shape global imaginaries of global order and legitimize practices, e.g. notions of self-determination, sovereignty, de-colonization, human rights, regional integration, great-power politics and (economic) progress. I will look at these narratives and practices to which primary institutions relate from two angles.

The first angle is about how the Mediterranean observes the world, thereby stressing the agency of region's internal dynamics. This is in particular about how actors from the region appropriate, use, and adapt primary institutions of international society, thereby legitimizing both conflict and peacebuilding. This relates to national, sub-national and transnational actors, both governmental and non-governmental. The second angle then discusses how the world observes the Mediterranean and how external interventions from outside the region – mainly but not exclusively from the west – contribute to both conflicts and peacebuilding in the region.[2] This relates to various forms of external interventions and securitization practices, that can take the form of political, societal, military or economic interventions by great powers, international organizations (IOs) and societal actors, mainly international non-governmental organizations (INGOs). Such external interventions are shaped by an underlying perception of global interconnectivity that nurtures a securitization of regional politics. This chapter is divided in three main sections. First, I offer a short introduction into the HIPS perspective, focusing on the concepts of international society and how the notion of primary institutions informs my analysis of Mediterranean conflicts and peacebuilding. The following section then studies conflicts and peacebuilding from the aforementioned 'inside-out' perspective, i.e. how the Mediterranean observes the world. The final section looks at how the world observes the Mediterranean, thus focusing on the 'outside-in' angle.

Conflicts and peacebuilding in the Mediterranean: a HIPS perspective

Given the introductory character of this chapter, I do not wish to overburden it with theoretical baggage. Instead, I concentrate on a few central parameters that will structure and guide the subsequent mapping exercise of conflicts and peacebuilding in the Mediterranean. I will highlight in particular the concept of primary institutions of international society, as originally set out by the English School, as a useful analytical tool for the study of conflicts and peacebuilding (Buzan 2004; for an application of the concept of primary institutions to the Middle East see Buzan and Gonzalez-Pelaez 2009). The main advantage of such a theoretically guided roadmap is that it allows linking the study of conflict and peacebuilding in the region to a (sociologically and historically) informed discussion on how conflict and peace in the region relate to broader political and social dynamics in the modern, globalized world, and how we can explain change and continuities over time. In short, it allows studying conflicts and peacebuilding in the Mediterranean as phenomena in a strongly interconnected, yet at the same time highly diversified and unequal global political order (Eisenstadt 2000; Rosenberg 2007; Wimmer 2002). That is why in the following sections I will look at conflict and peacebuilding through the prism of the broader constitutional/institutional structure of world politics, or international society rather than focusing exclusively on conflict themes, the interests and identities of conflict actors or concrete peacebuilding compromises.

International society is a concept that originates in the English School, one of the few IR theories with strong historical and sociological credentials that relates to a broader school of thought currently gaining ground in IR and that can be referred to as a historical international political sociology (Bigo and Walker 2007; Stetter 2013). The concept of international society is based on the idea that the interaction between states (but also non-state actors) over time engenders shared discourses and practices that define the relations between units and ultimately define the very idea of actorhood in the international system. In other words, the very identity of and the relations between states and non-states actors such as IOs, civil society, INGOs, business actors, religious leaders or armed groups are not taking place in a social vacuum but are shaped by an evolving institutional order. A central element of this order is what Barry Buzan (2004) calls primary institutions of international society. In his definition, primary institutions are the quasi-constitutional principles that underpin interactions in world politics and that legitimize specific forms of actorhood and action in international society. Primary institutions are, for example, principles such as sovereignty, the territorial ordering of political rule, international law, great power prerogatives, self-determination, nationalism and popular rule (e.g. various forms of democracy), diplomacy (including bi- and multilateralism), war/violent interventions, human rights, market regulation and others (e.g. environmental custodianship). The interplay between all these primary institutions shapes, in myriad ways, the expansion of the modern state-based system, including the numerical increase of nation states in the context of de-colonization but also the remarkable quantitative increase in the number of IOs and INGOs over the course of the last two centuries (Meyer et al. 1997; Reus-Smit 2011). But this global outreach of international society should not lead to the conclusion that world politics is a homogenizing project. First, while primary institutions are highly legitimized, they also are contested, think of global protest movements against what many perceive as a neo-liberal and unjust global economic order. There also are tensions between different primary institutions, for example between sovereignty and human rights. Moreover, specific primary institutions, such as war, legitimize violent conduct in international affairs (but also think of how human rights legitimize the use of force in the context of the responsibility to protect), while others, such as great power politics, privilege some states over other. Thus, second, and as in particular post-colonial and post-Eurocentric theories in various HIPS traditions highlight, the expansion and deepening of international society unfold within a deeply unequal and hierarchical global political order (Buzan 2014; Hobson 2012). There is a lot of path dependency to this inequality. Thus, historical legacies bear strongly on international politics, such as the long shadow cast by European imperial rule, including European imperial outreach to the Mediterranean. This also relates to the power of external (super-)power(s) in regional politics in the Mediterranean during and after the Cold War. The same holds true for how European integration at the northern shores of the Mediterranean affects the region as a whole. Thus, as students of the Euro-Mediterranean Partnership (EMP), which was formally established during the 1990s, are well aware, it is the north (i.e. the EU) that likes to sit in the driver's seat when it comes to region building, whereas southern co-ownership, for various reasons, tends to stand more on paper than defining political realities (Gillespie 2013).

The Mediterranean region is no exception to this embedding into the broader structures of international society. Of course, a HIPS approach on the Mediterranean could easily start prior to the consolidation of modern international society in the nineteenth century, take only Fernand Braudel's (1996) seminal studies of the region in early modernity. However, for the purpose of sketching out conflicts and peacebuilding in the contemporary era a focus on the region since the nineteenth century is in my view warranted. This is due to the fact that key political and social parameters that shape the region's integration in the contemporary global political and social order as well as the power gaps between the north and south that persist until today emerged during this period. This relates to European imperialism since the Napoleonic military expeditions to the southern Mediterranean and the colonial outreach of European powers to the southern Mediterranean in the context of the creeping demise of the Ottoman Empire. It also covers the process of de-colonization as well as the integration of the region into a global economic market (e.g. migration of Tunisian or Egyptian workers to European and Gulf state labour markets, or the integration into the global energy market, e.g. in relation to producer states such as Algeria, transit states such as Turkey or huge consumer markets such as the EU and Turkey) as well as the spread of discourses about economic development, education, human rights, democracy, good governance, gender equality and other ideas closely linked to a world culture that emerged globally in the nineteenth century too. Drawing from this historically and sociologically sensitive perspective on the integration of the Mediterranean region in world politics and modern world society, the following two sections now study the aforementioned role of regional as well as outside actors in shaping conflicts and peacebuilding in the region.

The Mediterranean observes the world: conflict and peacebuilding inside-out

In this section, I will focus on the significance of the region's internal dynamics for conflicts and peacebuilding in the Mediterranean. More specifically, I look at how actors from the region appropriate, use, adapt and struggle with primary institutions of international society such as sovereignty, self-determination, democracy, diplomacy, human rights and others. From the outset, it has to be noted that regional actors do not act in a political and societal vacuum, neither when engaging in intra-regional dialogues nor when relating to outsiders. In other words, conflict and peacebuilding in the Mediterranean are embedded in larger social ontologies of an unequal global political and social order in which hierarchies prevail, in particular those from which 'the west', however defined, still stands to profit. This focus on global hierarchies makes a historical perspective particularly useful. Thus, nineteenth-century European colonialism leaves its mark on regional politics, even after the gradual demise of the colonial order that led, for example, to Egypt's and Algeria's independence in 1922 and 1963 respectively. The heritage of colonialism in the Mediterranean manifests itself not only because there are until today colonial left-overs such as the British sovereign military bases in Cyprus, Gibraltar or the Spanish possessions in Ceuta and Melilla, surrounded by Morocco. Add to this what is often referred to as settler colonialism (Elkins and Pedersen 2005) from within the region, such as the Moroccan occupation of the Western Sahara or the Israeli occupation of the West Bank, the Gaza Strip and East Jerusalem – or historically the Ottoman imperial outreach to North Africa, the Levant and the western and southern Balkans (including the Adriatic Sea).

What matters in addition are the long-term ideational and structural consequences of colonialism and how this leaves an imprint on conflict and peacebuilding in the region. That is why many scholars refer to regional politics in the Mediterranean as being shaped by 'post-colonial' dynamics (Slater 2004). Think, for example, of the 'visible' marks left by colonialism such as the way boundaries in the regions were once drawn by European powers and how conflicts ensuing over these borders inform conflicts today. The Sykes–Picot agreement of 1916, the Balfour Declaration of 1917 or the San Remo conference of 1920 are cases in point. The boundary demarcations envisioned in the early twentieth century continue to play a role in contemporary conflicts such as Greco-Turkish relations, the Syrian war, the Israel–Palestine conflict or the Kurdish–Turkish conflict. There also is some continuity in how European and other outside powers lent support to specific ethno-national-religious groups in the eastern Mediterranean at the expense of others – in the nineteenth century European powers justified their outreach into the region by claiming to 'protect' specific, often Christian, groups in the region. This history of an experience with European divide-and-rule-tactics shapes political debates in the southern Mediterranean until today, and underpins the widespread suspicion about the 'real' motives behind western interventions in the region. Post-colonial dynamics then also have a 'subjective' dimension. More specifically, there is a deep-seated 'post-colonial anxiety' that shapes political debates in many states in the region (Bilgin 2011). This anxiety is based on the belief that outside powers, in particular those from the west, until today meddle in regional and national affairs, with the prime objective of weakening the south and denying regional actors real agency in shaping their destinies while pretending to pursue universal goals, such as protecting human rights. The 2011 military intervention in Libya, justified largely on the grounds of the responsibility to protect (R2P) but serving western powers' national interest too, is a good example here (while it has the be borne in mind that this intervention also was actively supported by the Arab League and Arab states). Another showroom case is Turkey. There, post-colonial anxieties shape the deep-seated suspicion that the west has always aimed to undermine Turkey and still attempts to do so. This is a fear dating back at least to the Treaty of Sèvres of 1920 in which western powers planned a partitioning of the Turkish heartlands of the Ottoman Empire. Sèvres has ever since become a powerful symbol in Turkish politics for alleged western conspiracies and unfair treatment of Turkey, for example a suspicion that European support for Kurds is not about human rights or other universal principles, but is meant to weaken and divide Turkey. Or the suspicion that the EU likes to promise Turkey membership in the club, but ultimately has no interest in allowing Turkey in, using membership negotiations as a fig leaf to appease Turkey. Post-colonial anxieties can be found in many other states in the region, too. Take Israel, where memories of centuries of European anti-Semitism, the Holocaust and decades of severe hostility by Arab states and people vis-à-vis Israel are regularly invoked in order to legitimize the Othering of Palestinians and the settlement of 'Judea and Samaria', as the Occupied Palestinian Territory is increasingly referred to in Israeli debates. Post-colonial anxieties also figure in Arab countries and nurture powerful narratives in these countries about all possible western, American or 'Zionist' conspiracies. It would, however, be wrong to limit post-colonial anxieties to the south, thereby reifying a Eurocentric concept of a bifurcated world, consisting of a 'rational' west and an 'irrational' south that allegedly has a monopoly in adhering to strange conspiracy theories (Hobson 2012). In fact, conspiratorially thinking and post-colonial anxieties about the 'Other' also shape the widespread emotional fear in the north about Islam and migrants. And it also can be found in EU member states that have, historically speaking, a strained relation with the west. Consider here Greece, where a deep-seated suspicion, pervading domestic political debates, about hypocritical and sinister 'western' intentions prevails. This was visible, for example, in the widespread public opposition and calls for resistance in Athens and other Greek cities against 'the west' during NATO's (of which Greece is a member) intervention in Kosovo in 1999.

The imperial outreach of western powers to the Mediterranean in the nineteenth century was not only pursued by non-Mediterranean states, such as Britain, Czarist Russia or the German Empire and, particularly after World War II, the US and the Soviet Union. It also comprised *European* Mediterranean states – in particular France – which attempted to fill the power vacuum created by the slow retreat of the Ottoman Empire. By doing so, European Mediterranean powers somewhat re-invoked millennia-old ideas of a Europe-centred *mare nostrum*, a term originally coined by the Romans, that views the Mediterranean as a sea that links rather than divides its northern and southern parts, but this under the premise that the power to shape regional affairs ultimately resides at the northern shores. This thinking underpinned the colonial outreach of Spain in parts of Morocco, Italy's ambitions in Libya, but most importantly France's imperial project from the Maghreb to the Levant and it can also be said to guide, in a post-colonial world, the EU's thinking about region building in the context of the EMP.

In the light of this history of manifold interventions from the north, states and people in the Mediterranean's south thus regularly had to affirm their agency – this is their claim to self-determination, sovereignty, and human rights – through open political resistance to western powers, including recourse to violence (or counter-violence for that matter). The Algerian uprising against France is probably the most prominent case here, but anti-imperial mobilization occurred also in Egypt as early as the 1800s and later on in the nineteenth century, triggered by pan-Arab nationalism, in Arab territories in the eastern Mediterranean (of what later became Lebanon and Syria) as well as in Mandate Palestine, where since 1923 Jewish and Palestinian nationalists rose up against British rule, and indeed against each other. To be sure, outside interventions by European Mediterranean powers and others did not stop after the major wave of de-colonization since the end of World War II. Take the intervention of France and Israel, together with Great Britain, in the Suez Campaign of 1956 or the interventions in the Syrian war by Russia, on the one hand, and the US-led coalition, on the other – the US and Russia of course not being Mediterranean states, save Russia's naval facility in the port of Tartus that was leased by Syria to the Soviet Union already in the early 1970s – and, of course, the strong military presence of the US around the Mediterranean Sea, both in its role as supreme power of NATO and in its bilateral relations with selected Mediterranean states. And, as far as the dominance of the north in regional governance beyond security more narrowly defined is concerned, one has to add to this the various policies through which the EU, including Mediterranean EU member states, aim to shape the region's political, economic and societal outlook under the stated objective to foster (peaceful) region building. This ranges from the EMP to the dysfunctional Union for the Mediterranean to the heavily security-related EU military naval missions in the Mediterranean Sea in the context of refugee migrants' movements.

The way regional actors relate to, adapt and use primary institutions of international society such as sovereignty, territorial borders, human rights and self-determination has thus to be seen in the context of larger historical trajectories that are to a considerable degree shaped by postcolonial dynamics. But this should not lead to the conclusion that the south lacks agency, quite to the contrary. Thus, nationalist and independence movements in the southern Mediterranean – e.g. the Tanzimat reform movement in Turkey in the nineteenth century, the moderate branch of political Islam in the tradition of Muhammad Abduh, Atatürk in Turkey, Venizelos in Greece, Zionism and pan-Arabism – shared with the west a belief in key modern ideas such as self-determination, nationalism and sovereignty, as well as a belief in societal and economic progress and the need for a 'strong' state. The agency of actors from the southern Mediterranean is also evident with a view to political relations between states and people in the south. Thus, Egypt under President Nasser and up until the 1967 war against Israel skilfully manipulated, through effective recourse to the idea of Arab unity, public discourse in other Arab countries thereby fostering Egyptian regional hegemony. One could also refer to the status of Israel and Turkey as regional powers that today possess more political, military and economic clout than all other states in the southern Mediterranean. But also the status as an underdog can be quite potent a resource in political struggles. That was a lesson not only in the colonial era but, for example, also figures prominently in Palestine's approach to garner political support in the region and the west by emphasizing the asymmetric character of its conflict with Israel.

Actors from the southern Mediterranean are thus not on the sidelines when games of sovereignty and self-determination are played (Aalberts 2010). And it often is competition and conflict between ethno-national groups and states in the region that fuels conflicts. Many regional conflicts directly relate to key primary institutions of international society such as sovereignty and territoriality, Israel–Palestine being the most prominent case here. But this also comprises other cases, ranging from the communal tensions in Cyprus that during the 1970s led to the division of the island that continues today, to secession movements in the northern Mediterranean, both in the past (Yugoslavia in the 1990s) and the present (Catalonia). Also consider the complex border conflicts between Greece and Turkey and, more recently, in the context of the discovery of large offshore gas resources in the eastern Mediterranean, the merging of long-existing geopolitical conflicts between states in the region and new conflicts about the delineation of Exclusive Economic Zones in the territorial waters of or close to Cyprus, Egypt, Israel, Lebanon, Palestine and Turkey.

Notwithstanding the ubiquity of regional internal conflicts in the southern Mediterranean there have been instances in which diplomacy has been able to mediate conflict dynamics, sometimes more enduring (as in the post-war order in Lebanon) sometimes short-lived (such as the Oslo Agreements between Israel and Palestine). While all these endeavours arguably do not amount to encompassing peacebuilding, for example in the form of a southern Mediterranean security community, the Turkish–Israeli reconciliation agreement of 2016 is another example of at least rudimentary forms of regional cooperation that actors seek. However, this hardly ever takes the form of sustainable multilateralism. Cooperation rather builds on logics of (temporary) alliance building and balancing between regional powers. Take the recent attempt by Cyprus, Greece and Israel to foster a tripartite alliance that in many ways responds to what these three states perceive as threats from Turkey. The perseverance of alliance building and great power thinking in intra-regional affairs also explains the saliency of the primary institutions of war and (military) intervention in regional politics in the southern Mediterranean. Thus, not only outside powers intervene by military means in the region but so do regional powers, either directly or indirectly, take for example Turkey's support for Hamas, Israel's backing of Christian militias during the Lebanese civil war or the large-scale interventions in the Syrian war by Turkey (and many other powers from the region and beyond). This centrality of war as a primary institution is also evident in relation to the various wars between Israel and Arab states from 1948 to 2006 as well as the three 'Gaza wars' between Israel and Hamas since 2008 (with a view to the centrality of war as a primary institution in the region see also Buzan and Gonzalez-Pelaez 2009). As Halliday (2011) argued with a view to the wider Middle East (including the Maghreb, Turkey and the Levant) external military interventions into other states are a highly legitimized and often practised strategy in regional politics, the aforementioned examples attest to this. And it, of course, relates to the violent territorial conquests by Islamist groups in Libya, the Sinai and Syria – and the counter-insurgencies by international alliances and national governments (e.g. the Egyptian military in the Sinai).

Conflict and peacebuilding in the southern Mediterranean are, though, not only shaped by recourse of regional actors to those primary institutions that tend to put states in the centre, such as sovereignty, territoriality, war, diplomacy and others. Equally important is recourse to primary institutions such as human rights and democracy that legitimize both states and individuals as meaningful political actors (Reus-Smit 2011). A case in point is the current transformation process in Arab countries, the short-lived Arab Spring that started with the uprisings in Egypt and Tunisia in 2010/11. In both countries the protest against long-term autocratic and corrupt rulers was largely society-driven. Through the streets of Tunis and Cairo resonated a call for greater equality and dignity – in short: a demand for meaningful citizenship and a more inclusionary system. Yet, this longing for human rights and democracy – and less corruption – cannot straightforwardly be associated with peacebuilding, and not only because democracy can be a divisive affair as the election and military ouster of Egyptian president Muhammad Mursi from the Muslim Brotherhood attested. Elections and debates over equal citizenship rights turn out to be a highly divisive affair in many southern Mediterranean countries, in particular Arab countries, mainly because there is a historical heritage and constitutional institutionalization of zero-sum politics. More specifically, in many states in the region, from authoritarian states such as Egypt and Syria to Lebanon's consociational democracy and Israel's ethnic democracy, the domestic political system is organized along ethno-national lines and if this is not the case, as in

Egypt, the political system is organized in a way that privileges specific social groups, as for example the military class in Egypt (Stetter 2008). To be clear, carefully designed institutions of ethno-national representation have played a positive role in mediating conflicts and institutionalizing political mechanisms for reaching consensus, take again Lebanon. But the downside is that it tends to reinforce and reify entrenched and often highly conflictive group identities rather than overcoming such divisions, for example in the context of Lebanon between Maronites, Druze, Shia and Sunni. The same patterns of inclusion and exclusion can be found on the regional level, where entrenched and antagonistic national identities have largely prevented the emergence of a regional security architecture and regional peacebuilding, with the exception of lukewarm attempts by outside powers, such as the EU in the context of the EMP to create such a security umbrella. However, many observers actually argue that notwithstanding its noble ambition the practice of the EMP tends to reinforce conflicts rather than overcoming them, mainly because its neo-liberal economic outlook fails to tackle the underlying socio-economic grievances that de-stabilize states in the southern Mediterranean. Finally, in the context of the European sovereign debt crisis, several EU member states in the northern Mediterranean have witnessed grave domestic conflicts as well, while the EU as a whole struggles with intra-European solidarity, thereby putting the entire European peace project at risk. Thus, European integration – that for decades served as an anchor of stability in the northern Mediterranean – has turned into a conflictive and divisive endeavour that alienates states, elites and people within the EU as a whole and within many member states, including Cyprus, France, Italy, Greece and Spain.

The world observes the Mediterranean: conflict and peacebuilding outside-in

The previous section has addressed conflicts and peacebuilding in the Mediterranean through an inside-out perspective. While highlighting the agency of regional actors I have, however, emphasized the importance of outside actors within this regional arena. In line with the HIPS approach that informs this chapter conceptually, an outside-in perspective is thus most evident with a view to how (post-)colonial dynamics and primary institutions interrelate. This relates in particular to the ways in which western powers intervene into the Mediterranean, in particular its southern shores, through political, economic, cultural and, indeed, military means – the bulk of these outside powers not being Mediterranean states, France being the most significant exception here. Since this type of intervention, and how it has simultaneously hampered *and* enhanced the agency of Mediterranean actors, has already been addressed above, I will focus in this section on other, but by no means less pervasive external interventions and discuss their relevance for conflict and peacebuilding.

The key argument pursued here is that the Mediterranean – the south more than the north – tends to be observed by the world as a 'problematic' region that engenders insecurity (Richmond 2007). As a result of this perception and the fear of spill-overs stemming from risks and threats attributed to Mediterranean politics, the region becomes securitized on several levels from culture and politics, to security and economics (Buzan et al. 1997). These securitization dynamics then justify external interventions through aid, reform programmes, military assistance, technocratic advice, democracy promotion and support of local NGOs. These interventions transcend a classical great power perspective, yet they do include interventions by global powers such as the US, the EU, Russia and more recently China. All these powers intervene in the region through diplomatic, developmental and military channels, thereby resembling a more than century-old competition between outside actors, which strive for geo-political and geo-economic impact in the region. But the aforementioned securitization dynamics transcend this state-based competition logic insofar as the Mediterranean has become a space of intervention for other political actors too, such as IOs (including the [illegible] 1997; Meyer et al. 2006). These interventions mainly affect the south of the Mediterranean, although in recent years, in particular since the crises that shook most southern European economies and gave way to interventions by European [illegible] institutions in these states, massive outside interventions also occur in the north [illegible].

Outside interventions by non-state actors relate, first, to interventions in the context of the so-called liberal 'peacebuilding consensus' (Richmond and [illegible]) [illegible] IOs, in particular the UN and some of its sub-organisations [illegible] conflicts in the region. This takes various forms and ranges from deliberations at the UN Security Council to tailor-made missions and institutions that deal with specific conflicts, for example the UN Special Rapporteur for Syria, the Middle East Quartet (consisting of the UN, the US, Russia and the EU and that was established in 2002 in order to [illegible] the moribund Israeli–Palestinian peace process) or the Baker Plan for the Western Sahara. The UN/peacebuilding approach also comprises the work of the United Nations Relief and Work Agency (UNRWA) that deals with Palestinian refugees in the region to the United Nations High Commissioner for Refugees (UNHCR) that has become a central player in the context of the refugee movements triggered by the war in Syria. Moreover, there are a range of more classical UN-peacekeeping missions currently under way in the Mediterranean, namely in Bosnia Herzegovina, Cyprus, off the Lebanese coast, Syria (the Golan) and the Western Sahara (i.e. in relation to Morocco's occupation of the Western Sahara) or the Multinational Force and Observers Mission in the Sinai. As I have already highlighted earlier, such interventions of course also comprise external interventions that aim to preserve 'stability' in the region such as the massive military assistance of the US to states such as Egypt, Israel and Jordan, the assistance by Iran and Russia to Syria or the support lent by Saudi Arabia and Qatar to Lebanese and Syrian actors. It also relates to the financial and training support the Palestinian police force gets from the United States and the EU. And it also entails military interventions by outside powers to which I have alluded earlier and which sometimes occur in the name of preserving stability, sometimes under the banner of universal norms, such as R2P.

But rather than further enlisting these various forms of external interventions and in order to avoid focusing exclusively on military interventions and peacekeeping missions, it is paramount to understand the broader mentality to which these and other forms of intervention adhere. More specifically, I refer to here to a broader, global construction of the Mediterranean region as an area that 'exports' risks and threats of various sorts. This threat perception in turn legitimizes a securitization of the Mediterranean and a construction of the region as the source of various insecurities, governance problems and even state failure. While traditionally these discourses and practices of intervention relate mainly to southern Mediterranean states and their forms of more or less pronounced ineffective bureaucratic authoritarianism (Hinnebusch 2006), the focus has in recent years increasingly shifted to the Mediterranean's north, too, for example in relation to dysfunctional party systems, neo-patrimonial clientelism and entrenched corruption in states such as Cyprus, Greece, (south) Italy and Spain. It is in relation to such securitization dynamics that political, security-related, economic and cultural interventions into the region unfold. The HIPS perspective then reminds us that contemporary interventions cannot be properly understood without taking into consideration the long history of external interventions by mainly western powers that perceive the global south as a realm of insecurity in need of 'civilizational' tutelage. This historical perspective, to be clear, alerts us to both similarities and differences in such long-term temporal trajectories. While, for example, overt racism largely disappeared from political discourse, the same cannot be said about a deeply ingrained sense of the alleged superior civilizational standards of western governance. The observation of such governance problems – and the fear of spill-overs to Europe or the wider world – have during the last decades legitimized manifold interventions by IOs and INGOs into regional politics. Let me highlight by closing this section with four key realms of outside intervention.

There is, first, the political level. Political interventions relate first and foremost to democracy promotion as well as developmental and technical assistance, the latter being geared to state bureaucracies in the south. With regard to democracy promotion, the US and the EU have in recent decades played the most central role, both through official government programs and civil society initiatives by INGOs. Scholars have identified here a democracy–stability dilemma that results in western governments usually preferring the stability of autocratic regimes when compared with too swift a democratic transformation. For example, while the EU has included negative conditionality clauses in its Association Agreements (AA) with states in the southern Mediterranean, it has avoided suspending agreements even in light of documented grave human rights violations, for example in Egypt or Tunisia prior to the short-lived Arab Spring of 2011. Increasingly, in states such as Egypt, Israel and Turkey external support for local NGOs is, moreover, framed as illegitimate outside interference and local NGOs are branded as 'foreign agents', a sign of authoritarian revival in the region. A second type of intervention, more closely related to the military interventions referred to earlier can be found in the wider field of security-related affairs. This relates to the envisaged fortification of the EU's external border that comprises EU/NATO naval missions in the Mediterranean, a more robust future mandate for Frontex, the EU external border agency and repatriation agreements of the EU with southern Mediterranean states, including EU-sponsored refugee camps in the Maghreb region.

A third level of external interventions then relates to the economic sphere. Central here is, of course, the EMP and the AA the EU has concluded with most non-member states in the Mediterranean, that tie these countries to the European market – as critics argue not necessarily to the advantage of southern economies and welfare states. Economic interventions also relate to the so-called 'austerity policy' of the Troika institutions (European Central Bank, European Commission and International Monetary Fund (IMF)) in the context of the economic crises that hit Cyprus and Spain and, in particular, Greece. Economic interventions, however, transcend Euro-Mediterranean relations. They are embedded in an international society that is based on what critics refer to as a neo-liberal market approach. Under what became known as the Washington Consensus (named after the international financial institutions located in Washington, DC, namely the IMF and the World Bank), neo-liberal structural adjustment programmes (SAPs) were designed during the 1980s and 1990s to intervene, and continue to strongly intervene, in the national economics of states such as Egypt, Morocco and Tunisia. As critics emphasize, these SAPs had their share in weakening welfare structures, a political vacuum filled for example by Islamist organizations such as those affiliated with the Muslim Brotherhood (on political Islam see Volpi 2010). Finally, external interventions relate to the regional diffusion of what can be termed 'world cultural' principles. This relates to interventions by states, IOs (in particular the UN and the EU) but in particular countless INGOs that design and implement programmes and activities, often in liaison with local partners, that aim to spread universal ideas such as human rights, gender equality, environmental protection and others. Cultural interventions, however, do not only promote notions of global unity. They also highlight difference, either through negative Othering (e.g. the fear that exists in wide parts of Europe about Islam or in parts of southern Mediterranean societies about 'corrupt' western values) or through a celebration of cultural difference (e.g. dialogue of religions or civilizational dialogue programmes that became en vogue during the 1990s).

Concluding remarks

What probably is one of the lasting observations that can, over time, be made with regard to conflicts and peacebuilding in the Mediterranean region is the degree to which this region, both institutionally and in political narratives, does not figure as a region at all. The difference between the region's north and south, in particular against the background of an international society that evolved in the colonial era and has strong post-colonial credentials until today, has been emphasized throughout this chapter. Against this larger matrix of a strongly interconnected, yet highly unequal global political order conflicts and peacebuilding in the Mediterranean still reinforce the 'Othering' of the south as a realm of insecurity and threats – and a parallel 'Othering' in the south of the north being hypocritical and possessed by a lust for intervention. That is why, in addition to all the challenges brought about by contemporary conflicts in both the south and the north of the Mediterranean – such as the lack of a just and stable security architecture between states and a renewed social contract that fosters good governance and meaningful citizenship in the south, but also renewed efforts to foster European integration in the north – an effective transformation of conflicts and sustainable peacebuilding arguably require a more integrated view of the Mediterranean as one region more than ever.

Notes

1 Mediterranean states (UN member states that have a land border with the Mediterranean Sea) are Albania, Algeria, Bosnia and Herzegovina, Croatia, Cyprus, Egypt, France, Greece, Israel, Italy, Lebanon, Libya, Malta, Monaco, Montenegro, Morocco, Palestine (which is a UN observer state), Slovenia, Spain, Syria, Tunisia and Turkey. Croatia, Cyprus, France, Greece, Italy, Malta, Slovenia and Spain are Member States of the EU. Albania, Bosnia-Herzegovina (which has a 15 kilometre border with the Adriatic Sea), Montenegro and Turkey are four Mediterranean states that are currently Candidate Countries.

2 The notion of observing the world and being observed by the world is a concept from Jan Busse's forthcoming PhD thesis on governmentality in Palestine.

3 It has to be noted, though, that European integration – in particular through the supreme status of European law – limits national sovereignty not only in southern European Member States, but across the Union – and indeed establishes EU sovereignty.

Bibliography

Aalberts, Tanja E. (2010): 'Playing the Game of Sovereign States: Charles Manning's Constructivism avant-la-lettre'. *European Journal of International Relations* 16(2), 247–68.

Bigo, Didier and Walker, R. B. J. (2007): 'International, Political, Sociology'. *International Political Sociology* 1(1), 1–5.

Bilgin, Pinar (2011): *Regional Security in the Middle East: A Critical Perspective*. London: Routledge.

Bilgin, Pinar (2012): 'Globalization and In/Security: Middle Eastern Encounters with International Society and the Case of Turkey'. In: Stephan Stetter (ed.): *The Middle East and Globalization: Encounters and Horizons*. New York: Palgrave Macmillan, pp. 59–76.

Boli, John and Thomas, George M. (1997): 'World Culture in the World Polity: A Century of International Non-Governmental Organization'. *American Sociological Review* 62(2), 171–90.

Braudel, Fernand (1996): *The Mediterranean and the Mediterranean World in the Age of Philip II*. Berkeley: University of California Press.

Busse, Jan (2015): 'Observing Power as Governmentality in Palestine: De-Constructing the Dynamics of World-Societal Order'. *Middle East Critique* 24(2), 161–89.

Buzan, Barry (2004): *From International to World Society? English School Theory and the Social Structure of Globalisation*. Cambridge: Cambridge University Press.

Buzan, B. (2014): 'The "Standard of Civilisation" as an English School Concept'. *Millennium Journal of International Studies* 42(3), 576–94.

Buzan, Barry and Gonzalez-Pelaez, Ana (eds) (2009): *International Society and the Middle East: English School Theory at the Regional Level*. Basingstoke: Palgrave Macmillan.

Buzan, Barry and Lawson, George (2013): 'The Global Transformation: The Nineteenth Century and the Making of Modern International Relations'. *International Studies Quarterly* 57(3), 620–34.

Buzan, Barry, Wæver, Ole, Wilde, Jaap De (1997): *Security: A New Framework for Analysis*. Boulder: Lynne Rienner.

Eisenstadt, Shmuel N. (2000): 'Multiple Modernities'. *Daedalus* 129(1), 1–31.

Elkins, Caroline and Pedersen, Susan (eds) (2005): *Settler Colonialism in the Twentieth Century: Projects, Practices, Legacies*. New York: Routledge.

Gillespie, Richard (2013): 'The Challenge of Co-ownership in the Euro-Mediterranean Space'. *Geopolitics* 18(1), 178–97.

Halliday, Fred (2011): *The Middle East in International Relations: Power, Politics and Ideology*. Cambridge: Cambridge University Press.

Hinnebusch, Raymond (2006): 'Authoritarian Persistence, Democratization Theory and the Middle East: An Overview and Critique'. *Democratization* 13(3), 373–95.

Hobden, Stephen and Hobson, John M. (2002): *Historical Sociology of International Relations*. Cambridge: Cambridge University Press.

Hobson, John M. (2012): *The Eurocentric Conception of World Politics: Western International Theory, 1760–2010*. Cambridge: Cambridge University Press.

Meyer, John W., Drori, Gili S. and Hwang, Hokyu (2006): 'World Society and the Proliferation of Formal Organizations'. In: John W. Meyer, Gili S. Drori and Hoyku Hwang (eds): *Globalization and Organizations: World Society and Organizational Change*. Oxford: Oxford University Press, pp. 25–49.

Meyer, John W., Boli, John, Thomas, George M. et al. (1997): 'World Society and the Nation-State'. *American Journal of Sociology* 103(1), 144–81.

Reus-Smit, Christian (1999): *The Moral Purpose of the State: Culture, Social Identity, and Institutional Rationality in International Relations*. Princeton: Princeton University Press.

Reus-Smit, Christian (2011): 'Struggles for Individual Rights and the Expansion of the International System'. *International Organization* 65(2), 207–42.

Richmond, Oliver P. (2007): *The Transformation of Peace*. Basingstoke: Palgrave Macmillan.

Richmond, Oliver P. and MacGinty, Roger (2015): 'Where Now for the Critique of the Liberal Peace?' *Cooperation and Conflict* 50(2), 171–89.

Rosenberg, Justin (2007): 'International Relations: The "Higher Bullshit": A Reply to the Globalization Theory Debate'. *International Politics* 44(4), 450–82.

Slater, David (2004): *Geopolitics and the Post-Colonial: Rethinking North–South Relations*. Malden: Wiley-Blackwell.

Stetter, Stephan (2008): *World Society and the Middle East: Reconstructions in Regional Politics*. Basingstoke: Palgrave Macmillan.

Stetter, Stephan (2013): *Ordnung und Wandel in der Weltpolitik: Konturen einer Soziologie der internationalen Beziehungen*. Baden-Baden: Nomos.

Volpi, Frédéric (2010): *Political Islam Observed*. London: Hurst.

Wimmer, Andreas (2002): *Nationalist Exclusion and Ethnic Conflict: Shadows of Modernity*. Cambridge: Cambridge University Press.

14

MILITARY AND POLITICS IN THE MEDITERRANEAN

Aurel Croissant and Tanja Eschenauer

Introduction

The Mediterranean is home to a bewildering variety of different regimes and patterns of political–military relations. The region includes established (e.g. Israel, Italy, France), post-socialist (e.g. Albania, Croatia, Slovenia) and emerging democracies (Tunisia), hybrid regimes that combine democratic and autocratic features such as Turkey and Lebanon, and closed autocracies in Algeria, Morocco, and Syria (see Table 14.1).

In the mid-1970s, in the early 1990s, and, again, since 2010, many autocracies in the region had come under pressure to respond to public demands for political liberalization. Authoritarian regimes were replaced with democracies in Spain and Greece after 1974/75. The downfall of the Soviet Union and the breakdown of the multinational Federation of Yugoslavia triggered a wave of state-building in the Balkans which eventually resulted in transitions to (minimal) democracy in Albania, Bosnia and Herzegovina, Croatia, Montenegro, and Slovenia. Lately, the Arab Uprisings of 2010 onwards witnessed the fall of dictators in Egypt, Libya, and Tunisia. But only in Tunisia has this led to a fragile and limited democracy. Finally, with Turkey, the region is host to a paradigmatic case of the recent "rollback of democracy" (Diamond et al., 2016), as the political regime transitioned from electoral democracy to electoral authoritarianism under the government of Prime Minister and later President Recep Tayyip Erdogan.

In this chapter, we will argue that in the different polities in the Mediterranean, militaries fulfill varying roles in politics. While the armed forces (interchangeably also army or military) are always part of the ruling coalition in authoritarian regimes, there are different ways in which they contribute to the inner workings and survival of these regimes. In Egypt and Algeria, for example, the military's influence has traditionally been extensive, whereas in Tunisia and Libya it remained in a more subaltern position. Despite its prominent role in the former regime and during the transition, in Spain and Greece the military today is under firm democratic control. In the former socialist republics, democratic governance in the security sector may be deficient and fragile, nevertheless, the militaries seem to have accepted their role as a "nonpolitical" servant of civilian governments.

The rest of this chapter is structured as follows. We start with a conceptual framework for analyzing military roles in the Mediterranean from the early post-World War II era until the recent wave of anti-regime uprisings during the Arab Spring. This framework distinguishes three dimensions of military roles in the Mediterranean: i) state- and nation-building;

Table 14.1 Freedom House status of Mediterranean countries in 1973, 2010, and 2016

	Freedom House status 1973	*Freedom House status 2010*	*Freedom House status 2016*
Albania	not free	partly free	partly free
Algeria	not free	not free	not free
Bosnia-Herzegovina	—	partly free	partly free
Croatia	—	free	free
Egypt	not free	not free	not free
France	free	free	free
Greece	not free	free	free
Israel	free	free	free
Italy	free	free	free
Lebanon	free	partly free	partly free
Libya	not free	not free	not free
Montenegro	—	free	partly free
Morocco	partly free	not free	partly free
Slovenia	—	free	free
Spain	not free	free	free
Syria	not free	not free	not free
Tunisia	not free	not free	free
Turkey	partly free	partly free	partly free

Source: Freedom House 2016.

ii) the exercise and organization of political power; and iii) revolutions and transition processes. We then present a comparative analysis of the development of political–military relations on the basis of these three types of military roles. Finally, we summarize our arguments and present conclusions so as to bring to the fore (sub-)regional trends.

Three types of military roles in the Mediterranean region

The differentiation of military roles in politics into three types, which we propose in this chapter, is a descriptive tool based on three assumptions. First, there is no linear and evolutionary succession of military roles that begins with state-building and ends with a transition process to a democratic regime. Instead, roles merge or alternate and sometimes are even intertwined. Second, the role of a military in a given historical phase depends on the role it played during a previous phase.[1] A specific role during a transition, for example, is highly influenced by the military's previous role in exercising and organizing political power (Agüero, 1998; Barany, 1993). Third, the types of military roles are not linked to a specific regime type. State- and nation-building as well as the exercise and organization of political power, for instance, can occur in both autocracies and democracies.

The military's role in state- and nation-building

Especially when armed forces are involved in a struggle for decolonization or in a war for independence, they regularly emerge as *state-* and *nation-builders* that have a special relationship to the state and the nation and identify strongly with its values and principles (Koonings and Kruijt, 2002: 20; Perlmutter, 1969). Such militaries often assume a leading role in the formulation and the defense of the national identity. Therefore, they do not only strengthen and secure the state with their repressive capacities but also fulfill social functions to develop and guide the young nation (Janowitz, 1964; Koonings and Kruijt, 2002: 3). In particular, military conscription and education are thought of as enhancing state- and nation-building (Simonsen, 2007). Besides its socializing function, military state- and nation-builders regularly steer political processes and engage in economic activities to push forward modernization and development (Cronin, 2014; Koonings and Kruijt, 2002).

The military's role in exercising and organizing political power

The varying, multifaceted possibilities for militaries to contribute to the exercise and organization of political power can be arranged along a continuum. At the one extreme, we allocate regimes in which the military itself is the overt or hidden carrier of political power and is the political decision-maker. At the other extreme, there are regimes in which political control over the armed forces is intact and the military willingly restricts its role to the assistance of the political leadership (Croissant et al., 2010; Croissant et al., forthcoming). In between these extremes, we can find militaries that do not appear as ruling actors themselves but nonetheless fulfill a crucial regime-supporting role and, therefore, maintain a tight grip on decision-makers. To describe the roles of Mediterranean militaries, we adopt the concepts "ruling militaries" and "supporting militaries" by Basedau and Elischer (2013) and add a third type—the military as servant of a civilian principal.

Military ruler constitutes the most obvious, dominant role a military can fulfill in the exercise and organization of political power. A military ruler emerges if coup leaders or former rebels assume leading executive positions such as the post of the regime leader after a military coup or a civil war (Basedau and Elischer, 2013: 363; Croissant et al., forthcoming). Following the takeover, the military dominate the ruling coalition and steer the political process—either overtly or behind a civilianized façade. Because of the military's control over the political process, elections, which might be held in these regimes, lack real competition and do not follow a democratic logic (Basedau and Elischer, 2013: 360).

Military supporters, in contrast, do not govern, but support and assist the political leadership in exercising and organizing political power. By deterring political opposition, military supporters ensure the regime's survival and become one of its stabilizing pillars. In return, the military receives concessions in terms of impunity from juridical persecution and veto power to influence policies (Basedau and Elischer, 2013: 361). What distinguishes supporting from ruling militaries is that rulers carry governing qualities themselves, whereas supporters exert extensive influence on those holding political power (Croissant et al., forthcoming).

Lastly, a military can assume a role as the *servant of the civilian authorities*. Here, "the military has no autonomous decision-making power outside those areas specifically defined by civilians" (Croissant et al., 2010: 955). Political authorities decide and implement national policies without military inference and can independently choose to delegate power and tasks to the military (ibid.). Even though the military may have a crucial role in providing security for the regime, it does not autonomously decide the extent of this engagement and exerts neither formal nor informal veto rights in political affairs. Political control over the armed forces is not bound to a specific regime-type since democracies and autocracies alike can succeed in subordinating the armed forces to civilian decision-makers (Croissant and Kuehn, 2015).

The military's role in regime transitions and anti-regime mass protests

Regime transitions sometimes start with mass mobilization. In situations of anti-incumbent mass contention, the political survival of an autocrat ultimately depends on the military's loyalty

(Skocpol, 1979). However, military roles during such "dictators' endgames" (Pion-Berlin and Trinkunas, 2010; Pion-Berlin et al., 2014) vary considerably across dictatorships. Some militaries impede the initiation of a democratic transition by defending the dictator's survival, whereas others side with the opposition or stage a coup d'état (Croissant et al., 2016). Whether a military takes the role of the *defender of the dictator*, an *ally of the opposition*, or a *coup plotter* depends on the dictator's ability to secure the military's interest in the persistence of the regime. In general, a dictator who succeeds in ensuring the military's loyalty through economic concessions and political prerogatives can count on its support during times of crises. In contrast, an autocrat who fails to persuade the military that staying loyal is the most beneficial choice will likely face political downfall (ibid.). However, military institutions can also be important actors in transitions that occur without mass mobilization, i.e. transitions initiated from above or pacted transitions. In this regard, Agüero (1998) argues that the stronger the military's influence is during the transition, the better able it is to maintain its prerogatives and stifle post-authoritarian reforms. At least in Latin America, southern Europe, and Asia, military leaders were the better able to safeguard their prerogatives the longer the regime had existed, the deeper the military's rule was institutionalized, and the greater was the military's internal cohesion (ibid.; Croissant et al., 2010; Croissant and Kuehn, 2015).

Mediterranean militaries in state- and nation-building

Most of the state- and nation-building in the Mediterranean has to be situated within the nineteenth and twentieth centuries' historical context of Europe, as well as the Middle East and North Africa (MENA). Expansionist adventures by European powers, the demise of the Ottoman Empire, and the wave of decolonization following World War II marked historic watersheds for state- and nation-building. During this phase of radical change and political turmoil, the region's armed forces emerged to different extents as catalyzers of state- and nation-building.

State-building in Algeria and Israel, for example, was accompanied by armed conflicts that were fought by paramilitary forces that would later be incorporated into the regimes' regular militaries. Since Israel's formation as an independent state was sealed through military power in 1948, the Israel Defense Forces (IDF) have traditionally been viewed as the key actor in early state-building and a guarantor of the nation's survival. Furthermore, Israel's first Prime Minister, David Ben-Gurion, enhanced nation-building by actively applying the military as an "agent of socialization and education" (Lissak, 1971; also Ben-Eliezer, 1985). Consequently, Israel's military became "the first structure to be successfully transformed from an autonomous pre-independence organization into a truly national institution" (Perlmutter, 1969: 59). In Algeria, the National Liberation Army (ALN) laid the foundation for the post-war regular armed forces that justified their influential role in post-colonial politics due to their important contribution to the struggle for independence (Cook, 2007: 29–30).

Egypt, Tunisia, and Syria all established "monarchical-style presidential systems" (Owen, 2014: 61) after independence. Yet, the countries' militaries emerged to varying extent as driving forces of this process. The Tunisian military played neither a central role in the founding of the modern republic nor in designing the post-independence regime (Ware, 1985). Civilians and party functionaries, not the military, managed Tunisia's transformation from a protectorate to a republican system in the 1950s (Perkins, 1989).

Egypt's armed forces, in contrast, played a key role in the emergence of the modern republic. Disillusioned by King Farouk's policies and continued British interference, the Free Officers Movement ousted the king on 12 July 1952 (Hashim, 2011: 67). Once in power, the military launched profound land and property reforms, increasingly penetrated society, and dominated the executive and political process (ibid.: 67; Cook, 2007: 64). Due to its crucial role as state- and nation-builder after the 1952 revolution, the military has perceived itself as 'the guardian of the nation' ever since.

Like in Egypt, the Turkish political order established by Mustafa Kemal Ataturk was formed, led and guarded by political soldiers and reflected their own understanding of a modern nation-state (Söyler, 2015). It was not until the government of the Justice and Development Party (Adalet ve Kalinma Partis, AKP) took over in 2003 that this long period of military tutelage came to an end.

The trajectories of political–military relations in other Mediterranean countries differ from these MENA experiences. In southern Europe, the armed forces played an important role in state- and nation-building in the nineteenth and twentieth centuries, for example in the Greek and Italian independence and unification wars and the civil wars in Spain (1936–39) and Greece (1946–49). Although the armed forces made a strong contribution to national consciousness-building (see, for example, Carforio, 1997: 45, on the case of Italy), the *société militaire* did not possess a permanent hegemony over the *société civile* (for France, see Vogel, 1997). Rather, the military as the "school of nation" was an agent of state-building promoted and spearheaded by civilian and cultural elites. Nevertheless, there were occasionally frictions between civilian and military powers, even to the extent that soldiers staged coups (Spain 1936, France 1958 and 1961) or took over government (Greece 1967–74).

The southeast European countries share two similarities. First, political–military relations in Albania and Yugoslavia from the end of World War II until 1990 followed the universal model of party–army relations in communist single-party regimes, although differences between the individual cases remained (Herspring and Volgyes, 1978). The military acknowledged the supremacy of the party, although no clear division between party and military elites existed. While neither party nor military elites supported the idea that the military ought to be apolitical, the dual-elite model was the source of the military's politicization and the guarantor of party supremacy. Second, the military only had a marginal role in the process of state- and nation-building that followed the collapse of the multiethnic Federation of Yugoslavia in the early 1990s, even when the armed forces were involved in a war for independence, as in Croatia and Slovenia (cf. Danopoulos, 1996).

Mediterranean militaries in organizing and exercising political power

Until the mid-1970s it was only in France and Italy that the political–military relations conformed to the normative model of democratic civil–military relations in which the military as an institution is fully under political control by elected institutions (Carforio, 1997; DeVore, 2009). While the colonial war in Algeria negatively affected French civil–military relations, symbolized by the mutinies of segments of the colonial forces in Algeria (1958, 1961), political and military reforms in the Fifth Republic created the basis for long-term stable and democratic civilian control (Vennesson, 2003; Ruffa et al., 2013).

Regarding Spain and Greece and the five (post-)socialist countries of southeast Europe, one has to differentiate between an earlier pre-democratic and a later post-authoritarian period. In Greece and Spain, the armed forces had a major role in the creation, exercise, and defense of authoritarian rule until the mid-1970s. In post-civil war Greece, a "restrictive democracy" had emerged, which was controlled by the political triarchy of the conservative-dominated institutions of parliament, monarchy, and military. When this alliance crumbled, colonels of the armed forces organized a putsch on 21 April 1967. The emerging "nonhierarchical" military regime did not enjoy broad support from either civilian elites or military elites (Linz and Stepan, 1996: 131; Gürsoy, 2009: 56). The growing social discontent erupted into a wave of student demonstrations that were brutally suppressed by the military junta. To close the ranks in the military and strengthen nationalist support for the colonels, the regime launched an attempt to bring the whole of Cyprus under Greek control in the spring of 1974 (Karabelias, 2003: 62). Given the impending war with Turkey, the "military as institution" defected from the "military as government" (Linz and Stepan, 1996). Within days, the military regime imploded. The transition to democracy was accompanied by institutional reforms that abolished the veto power of the military permanently and simultaneously reestablished the institutional integrity of the armed forces (Gürsoy, 2009: 63–4). Today, civilian control is well established, institutionalized, and effective (Duman and Tsarouhas, 2006).

The Franco regime in Spain, unlike the authoritarian regime in Greece, was a civilian dictatorship. Following the Franquists victory in 1939, the authoritarian order evolved into a personalist dictatorship which coopted various traditionalist, royalist, conservative, and clerical elements in society (Linz and Stepan, 1996). Although the armed forces were well represented in the state apparatus and in the government, it did not have the means to control access to government positions or public policy-making (Agüero, 1995). Following the political opening in 1975, many military officers still identified themselves with the Franquist order but did not try to veto the transition process. However, the breakthrough for the radical transformation of political–military relations came with the failed military coup of 1981. The failure of the coup provided civilian elites with the opportunity to get rid of the last remnants of military opposition. The balance of power between the government and armed forces was now definitively shifted in favor of the democratic forces (Agüero, 1995; Serra, 2010).

In the socialist southeast Europe, the military was the final guarantor of regime security. The socialist soldier was politically dependent upon the vanguard party, but this dependence was incomplete. The armed forces retained the right to limited institutional autonomy in which their own structural integrity was maintained as a necessary condition for performing the designated functions of maintaining regime security or waging war. Yet, the structural integration of military elites into the party apparatus was combined with political dependency and unequal partnership (Remington, 1978). The transition from the socialist dictatorship to parliamentary democracy came along with the abolition of this model in favor of the western model of democratic control over the military, although this is perhaps more strongly institutionalized in Croatia and Slovenia than in Bosnia, Albania, and Montenegro (cf. Fluri et al., 2005).

Armed forces' roles in the MENA countries vary both across regimes and over time. The Tunisian military, for example, had been under civilian supremacy ever since independence from France in 1956 (Sorenson, 2000). The prerequisites for the military's marginal political role were set by the first President Habib Bourguiba, who excluded its members from the political sphere, limited military capabilities and kept the military widely out of internal repression (Ware, 1985: 37–8; Sorenson, 2000: 106–7). His successor Zine El Abidine Ben Ali pursued Bourguiba's way of depoliticizing the armed forces and relied heavily on police, paramilitary forces and secret services (Sorenson, 2000: 107). After the downfall of Ben Ali's regime in 2011, the military did not strive to attain extensive political power. However, the transition process of 2011 has not left the structure of political–military relations completely untouched. As a reaction to increased security threats and, possibly, as an attempt to reverse the armed forces' marginalization during the previous regime, the military's budget, capabilities and equipment were boosted after 2011 (Grewal, 2016).

The Egyptian military constituted the actual ruler of the regime for nearly two decades after the 1952 revolution. Only after their military defeat in 1967, did President Gamal Abdel Nasser start to sideline the armed forces (Harb, 2003: 269–70). Nasser's successor, Anwar Sadat, continued the civilianization of the regime and curtailed the military's political representation and personnel capabilities (Hashim, 2011: 71). In exchange for lost political privileges, the military received extensive prerogatives in the economic sector (Springborg, 2011). The military remained influential under Hosni Mubarak (1981–2011) but fulfilled a supporting rather than a ruling role. In return, Mubarak turned a blind eye to the military's nontransparent business practices and approved regular military interference in security and foreign policy related domains (Cook, 2007). After ousting Mubarak in February 2011, the military reassumed the influential role of a military ruler it had already fulfilled following the 1952 revolution. It led the country for a transitional period until Mohamed Morsi was elected president in June 2012. This civilian interlude came to a sudden end when only a year later the military staged another coup to remove Morsi from office. The coup leader, General Abdel Fattah el-Sisi, set up an interim government and in 2014, after his military retirement, became president himself.

Like in Egypt, the Libyan monarchy was overthrown in a coup. In September 1969, a group of young, mid-ranking soldiers led by Captain Muammar al-Qadhafi deposed King Idris I. Unlike the Egyptian armed forces, however, Libya's conventional military could not become a leading political force in the new regime (Gaub, 2013: 226). Qadhafi intensely fractured the regime's coercive institutions and fostered the development of dual structures within the coercive apparatus. Whereas he maintained regular army units for the regime's external defense, he additionally established multiple paramilitaries for the repression of internal political dissent and to deter potential military coup plotters. Key leadership positions were allotted to members of his own family and tribe. As Qadhafi appreciated loyalty and tribal kinship more than military performance, the armed forces suffered a lack of military effectiveness and professional training (Lutterbeck, 2013: 40).

In Syria, the army assumed a highly politicized role after independence from France in 1946, and competing military factions regularly staged coups to oust the political leadership (Kamrava, 2000: 77). When air force general and defense minister Hafiz al-Assad took over power in a military coup in 1970, Syria was among the most coup-ridden countries in the world (Quinlivan 1999: 133). Yet, Assad prevented Syria from sliding into another heyday of coups by privileging Alawites within the armed forces and filling key positions in the military and security apparatus with trusted loyalists (Nassif 2014: 169–86). Beginning under Hafiz and continued under his son, Bashar al-Assad, the military started to support rather than directly rule the regime. Both Assad presidents forged the creation of a so-called *mukhabarat* state (police state) in which both civilian and military units encounter domestic threats (Al Hendi, 2011). Whereas the military at large has not been involved excessively in everyday repression, military intelligence and elite army units constitute important pillars of the regime's internal repressive apparatus (ibid.).

Turkey has also witnessed a number of military coups. In the eyes of Turkey's military leaders, these interventions, launched in 1960, 1971, 1980, and 1997, were designed to "correct deviations" from the path outlined by Mustafa Kemal Ataturk. During each of these coups, the military's leadership replaced the incumbent civilian government with another government that was more acceptable to the military (Barak, 2016). The military then returned to the barracks but its leaders kept a close eye on civilian politicians. However, under the AKP government since 2003, there has been a deep and far-reaching shift in civil–military relations. The AKP leader, Erdogan, set out to curtail what he regarded as the excessive influence of the military in the state (Söyler, 2015). Yet, not all segments of the armed forces seem to have been willing to accept their new role, as indicated by the failed coup d'état by segments of the Turkish military in July 2016. The case of Turkey under AKP rule also demonstrates that there is a difference between political control and democratic control of the military.

Israel is a unique case. It is widely considered to be the only functional and stable democracy in the Near East. However, since 1948, and even more so since 1967, the predominance of security issues in the state, the lack of meaningful separation between its civilian and security spheres, and its powerful security sector gave rise to powerful security networks composed of acting and retired security officials and their partners in the state's civilian spheres (Sheffer and Barak, 2013). The prevalent practice known as "parachuting," in which former military leaders join the top echelons of political parties and cabinets (Etzioni-Halevy, 1996), means that high-ranking officers in the IDF frequently transition from military service to various civilian spheres following their retirement from military service (Barak and Tsur, 2012).

Mediterranean militaries in regime transitions and anti-regime mass protests

In the past four decades the Mediterranean experienced three consecutive waves of regime transitions and anti-regime mass mobilizations: A first southern European wave (Portugal, Spain, and Greece) in 1974–5; a second southeast European wave from 1990 until 1992; and the third wave of mass contention in North Africa and the Middle East ("Arab Spring") from December 2010 onwards.

Unsurprisingly, the differences in types of authoritarian rule, levels of socioeconomic modernization, the role of armed forces as ruler and/or supporter of authoritarian rule and the degree of "robustness" of the coercive apparatuses (Bellin, 2012) correlate with the role armies played in uprisings and transitions from authoritarianism toward "something else" (O'Donnell and Schmitter, 1986).

In Greece and Spain, the transition to democracy was primarily organized, dominated, and (in the Spanish case) negotiated by civilian elites. The limited influence of the military on the course and contents of the transition reflected the fact that in Greece, the ruling colonels had lost any credibility or bargaining power after their Cyprus adventure had failed. In addition, civilian elites remained unified in their opposition to the continuation of military rule and their preference for democracy and civilian control over the armed forces. This prevented the military from shaping the course of democratization or the contents of the new constitution of 1975 (Gürsoy, 2009: 62–5).

In Spain, most high-ranking officers accepted democratic reforms as inevitable and even beneficial for the modernization of the military (Agüero, 1995). Although sympathy in the officer corps for the attempted coup of February 1981 might have been widespread, most military officers stayed quartered. Similar to what happened in Turkey in July 2016, the failed coup in Spain offered the political parties and the civil government a chance to initiate a profound transformation of the military. However, this took place in Spain—unlike probably in Turkey—with the explicit goal of strengthening democratic accountability and parliamentary oversight of the armed forces (Serra, 2010).

In southeast Europe, the military played a minor (Croatia, Bosnia and Herzegovina) or marginal role (Albania, Montenegro, Slovenia) in the transition process. That had certainly to do with the fact that the civilian elites in these countries (except Bosnia and Herzegovina) had at their disposal a well-established set of effective instruments to control the military. Therefore, the military's coup potential was all but irrelevant and the militaries did not interfere with the institutionalization of democracy. A second aspect that helped establish civilian control over the military in eastern Europe was the civilians' interest in joining NATO and the EU, which provided a powerful incentive to reform civil–military relations (Croissant and Kuehn, 2015). With the exception of Croatia and Bosnia and Herzegovina, the peaceful nature of the political transition further facilitated civilian control because civilians did not have to rely on the military in order to establish the new politico-economic order. Finally, the civilian institutions continued to enjoy high degrees of legitimacy throughout the transition process, such that the military could not have justified an autonomous political role for itself. Yet, in Bosnia and Herzegovina (and to some extent, in Albania) the institutionalization of democratic governance in the security sector (including police, intelligence services, and former pro- or anti-government militias) remain deficient and challenging (Fluri et al., 2005; Ebnöther et al., 2008).

In contrast, the role of the military in the Arab Uprisings of 2010 onwards has been a central one. Due to the strength of the popular upheavals, dictators all over the MENA region had to fall back on the repressive capabilities of their militaries to secure their survival (Pion-Berlin et al., 2014). Despite their alleged robustness (Bellin, 2012), however, the region's armed forces reacted differently to the mass protests with military behavior ranging from brutal repression as in Syria to siding with the protesters as in the Tunisian case.

In Tunisia, the same mechanisms that were intended to prohibit the military from intervening in politics lastly hampered its interest in intervening on the regime's behalf. For fear of a military intervention, Ben Ali had turned the military into a small, apolitical but relatively professionalized institution and instead strengthened the internal security apparatus (Hanlon, 2012: 5; Ware, 1985). Lacking the incentives to ensure Ben Ali's regime, the military became an ally of the opposition and smoothed the way for a democratic transition (Springborg, 2014).

Why Egypt's military assumed the role of a coup plotter can be explained by looking at its changed role during the last years of Mubarak's presidency. The once symbiotic relationship between the president and the military had suffered deep cracks because Mubarak allowed the advance of two potential rivals to the military's privileged position. On the one hand, Mubarak leaned on a mighty internal security apparatus and changed the power balance to the disadvantage of the armed forces (Barany, 2011: 32). On the other hand, his son Gamal and the new economic business elite posed a serious challenge to the military's economic activities (Nepstad, 2013). During the uprising, the military sensed a chance to retaliate against Mubarak for favoring Gamal's business elite and the internal security apparatus at its expense.

The Libyan coercive apparatus was as fragmented in its response to the uprising as it had been prior to the Arab Spring. Whereas parts of the military refused to crack down on protesters, joined the ranks of the opposition, or aligned with rebellious revolutionary brigades, other parts tried to secure the regime with brute force (Haddadt, 2011: 2; Gaub, 2013: 233–7.). After months of bloody civil war, Qadhafi was lynched in his birth town of Sirte in October 2011. However, a successful democratic transition regime could not be initiated. The disintegration of the armed forces and the flourishing of a wide range of militias created a nontransparent, highly fragmented security landscape (Mattes, 2014). The resulting power vacuum has left room for various insurgent activities, including those of the so-called Islamic State.

Syria's military took the role as defender of the regime. Nonetheless, a significant number of troops, mainly Sunni Muslims, defected into the ranks of the opposition and founded the Free Syrian Army (Nepstad, 2013: 344). One of the reasons for the military's decay is its highly disproportional religious composition compared to the majoritarian Sunni population. Besides ascriptive selection, the Syrian regime has used a mix of political concessions and material cooptation to buy the military's loyalty (Nassif, 2014). For fear of losing these privileges, vast parts of the Alawite-dominated military stayed loyal to Assad (Nepstad, 2013: 344).

Conclusions

What can be learned from this overview? Our study suggests four crucial conclusions. First, as in other parts of the world, the post-World War II period has seen significant transformations in the roles of military institutions in national politics across the region. While in the past there were basically three models of military in politics—ruler, supporter and servant—today it seems that the ruler model is nearly extinct: As of 2016, only two out of seventeen cases in the region remain fully praetorian ("military ruler"); in another three countries, the military remains politically powerful and assertive ("military supporter"). However, in the remaining twelve countries, the military is the servant of the civilian authorities—a sharp contrast to just a quarter of a century ago. Moreover, most of the servant-style military roles in the organization and execution of political power can be found in democratic political systems (see Table 14.2).

Second, while the military in many Mediterranean countries has played an important role in state- and nation-building, only in parts of northern Africa and the eastern Levant did the military shape these processes well into the post-World War II era. Furthermore, politically powerful militaries arose where civilians had to rely heavily on the military's coercive and organizational means for eking out state sovereignty and ensuring their hold on power. However, while in socialist party regimes (Albania, Yugoslavia) the organizational machinery of the ruling party ensured the military's subordination, weak political organization and ongoing elite conflict resulted in the emergence of the military as the pre-eminent political force in parts of southern Europe and, especially, across the southern shores of the Mediterranean Sea. However, Israel is a deviant case. A comparative glance across and beyond the region suggests that this is not only due to the remarkable stability of the institutional foundations of Israel's democracy, but also because of the absence of those problems that elsewhere have led to the appearance of praetorian armies, such as bitterly divided elites and domestic challenges to the legitimacy of civilian politicians. Yet, we believe that Israel also does not neatly fit the parameters of liberal democratic political–military relations. While certainly not a praetorian military in the classical sense of the concept, the pattern of interaction between the military and the nonmilitary sphere is more similar to the type of civil–military convergence that can also be found, for example, in Singapore (see Croissant and Kuehn, 2015).

Third, despite the recent wave of mass contention and anti-regime protests, a closer glance at the role of the military in regime crises reveals that the recent episodes of "dictators' end-games" in which the dictator's political survival depends on the loyalty of the armed forces are an exception. During the south and southeast European revolutions in the 1970s and 1990s, the armed forces did not play such a decisive role, nor did they have a strong impact on the mode and outcomes of the transitions from authoritarianism towards democracy.

Finally, the single most important determinant of radical changes in the political role of Mediterranean militaries after World War II has been the onset of the third wave of democratization since the early 1970s which has opened critical windows of opportunity for civilians to re-align civil–military relations and establish civilian control. Yet, the contrast between Greece and Spain in the 1970s and Egypt since 2011 strongly suggests that democratizers will not succeed and might be ousted by the military if they attempt to curtail the military's political privileges without the necessary political and civic backup (Serra, 2010; Croissant et al., 2013). But just as democratization is neither a necessary nor a sufficient condition for the establishment of civilian control over the military, changes in political–military relations can also take place without an outright transition of the political regime.

Table 14.2 Summary of military roles and regime types

	Regime type (2016)	*Freedom rating (2016)*	*Exercising and organizing political power as of 2016*	*State- and nation-building (after World War II)*	*Regime transition and mass protest*
Albania	electoral democracy	3.0	servant	marginal	joined intra-regime elite defection (1990), but marginal role
Algeria	autocracy	5.5	ruler	yes	blocked transition and organized coup d'état (1992)
Bosnia-Herzegovina	electoral democracy	3.5	servant	marginal	no unified national armed forces before 2006
Croatia	liberal democracy	1.5	servant	marginal	marginal (1991)
Egypt	autocracy	5.5	ruler	yes	joined anti-incumbent mass movement by coups d'état (2011/2013)
France	liberal democracy	1.0	servant	no	—
Greece	liberal democracy	2.0	servant	marginal	joined opposition (1974)
Israel	liberal democracy	1.5	servant	yes	—
Lebanon	autocracy	4.5	supporter	yes	marginal (2007)
Libya	civil war	6.0	no unified national armed forces	marginal	collapse of military organization (2011)
Montenegro	electoral democracy	3.0	servant	no	marginal (1991/2006)
Morocco	autocracy	4.5	servant	marginal	—
Slovenia	liberal democracy	1.0	servant	no	marginal (1991)
Spain	liberal democracy	1.0	servant	marginal	stayed quartered (1975–81)
Syria	civil war	7.0	supporter	marginal	loyal to regime (2011)
Tunisia	liberal democracy	2.0	servant	no	joined anti-incumbent mass movement (2010)
Turkey	electoral democracy	3.5	supporter	yes	transition from above (1983)

Note: Liberal democracy: combined political rights and civil liberties score of 2 or less on a scale from 1 to 7 (as suggested by Diamond, 2008); electoral democracy: combined freedom score of more than 2 but listed as electoral democracy by Freedom House.

Source: Freedom House (2016).

Note

1 We define military role as an interface of the two dominant concepts in military research: political–military relations and political control over the armed forces. 'Political–military relations' refers to "the structures, processes and outcomes of the interactions between the political system and its actors on the one hand, and the military on the other" (Croissant and Kuehn, 2015: 259). "Political control" more specifically refers to the extent of control that political decision-makers exercise over the armed forces. In a state of complete control, the "military is subordinate enough to do only what civilians authorize them to do" (Feaver, 1996: 14). Since we understand a military role as an intersection of political–military relations and political control, analyzing a military's role means assessing the armed function vis-à-vis the political sphere and the extent of authority the political decision-makers possess.

References

Agüero, F. (1995) *Soldiers, Civilians, and Democracy: Post-Franco Spain in Comparative Perspective* (Baltimore: Johns Hopkins University Press).

Agüero, F. (1998) Legacies of Transitions: Institutionalization, the Military, and Democracy in South America, *Mershon International Studies Review*, 42(2), 383–404.

Al Hendi, A. (2011) The Structure of Syria's Repression: Will the Army Break with the Regime? *Foreign Affairs*, 3 May.

Barak, O. (2016) Security Networks, Deep States, and the Democratic Deficit in the Middle East, unpublished manuscript.

Barak, O. and E. Tsur (2012) The Military Careers and Second Careers of Israel's Military Elite, *Middle East Journal*, 66(3), 473–492.

Barany, Z. (1993) *Soldiers and Politics in Eastern Europe, 1945–90* (Basingstoke: Macmillan).

Barany, Z. (2011) The Role of the Military, *Journal of Democracy*, 22(4), 24–36.

Basedau, M. and S. Elischer (2013) Auf dem Rückzug in die Kasernen? Autoritäre Herrschaft und Militär im subsaharischen Afrika, in: S. Kailitz and P. Köllner (Eds), *Autokratien im Vergleich* (Baden-Baden: Nomos).

Bellin, E. (2012) Reconsidering the Robustness of Authoritarianism in the Middle East: Lessons from the Arab Spring, *Comparative Politics*, 44(2), 127–49.

Ben-Eliezer, U. (1985) A Nation-in-Arms: State, Nation, and Militarism in Israel's First Years, *Comparative Studies in Society and History*, 37(2), 264–85.

Carforio, G. (1997) The Italian Military: Between Fascist Dictatorship and Democracy, in: A. Bebler (Ed.), *Civil–Military Relations in Post-communist States: Central and Eastern Europe in Transition* (Westport: Praeger).

Cook, S. A. (2007) *Ruling but not Governing: The Military and Political Development in Egypt, Algeria, and Turkey* (Baltimore: Johns Hopkins University Press).

Croissant, A. and D. Kuehn (2015) The Military's Role in Politics, in: J. Gandhi and R. Ruiz-Rufino (Eds), *Routledge Handbook of Comparative Political Institutions* (London: Routledge).

Croissant, A., D. Kuehn and T. Eschenauer (2016) The "Dictator's Endgame": Explaining Military Behavior in Nonviolent Anti-Incumbent Mass Protests, unpublished manuscript.

Croissant, A., T. Eschenauer and J. Kamerling (forthcoming) Militaries' Roles in Political Regimes: Introducing the PRM Dataset, *European Political Science*.

Croissant, A., P. W. Chambers, D. Kuehn and S. O. Wolf (2010) Beyond the Fallacy of Coupism: Conceptualizing Civilian Control of the Military in Emerging Democracies, *Democratization*, 17(5), 948–78.

Croissant, A., D. Kuehn, P. Lorenz and P. W. Chambers (2013) *Democratization and Civilian Control in Asia* (Basingstoke: Palgrave Macmillan).

Cronin, S. (2014) *Armies and State-building in the Modern Middle East: Politics, Nationalism and Military Reform* (London: I. B. Tauris).

Danopoulos, C. P. (Ed.) (1996) *Civil–Military Relations in the Soviet and Yugoslav Successor States* (Boulder: Westview Press).

DeVore, M. R. (2009) Armed Forces, States and Threats: Civil–Military Institutions and Military Power in Modern Democracies, PhD thesis, Massachusetts Institute of Technology, Department of Political Science.

Diamond, L. (2008) *The Spirit of Democracy: The Struggle to Build Free Societies throughout the World* (New York: Holt).

Diamond, L., M. F. Platter and C. Walker (Eds) (2016) *Authoritarianism Goes Global: The Challenge to Democracy* (Baltimore: Johns Hopkins University Press).

Duman, Ö. and D. Tsarouhas (2006) "Civilianization" in Greece versus "Demilitarization" in Turkey: A Comparative Study of Civil–Military Relations and the Impact of the European Union, *Armed Forces and Society*, 32(3), 405–23.

Ebnöther, A. H., P. H. Fluri and P. Jurekovic (Eds) (2008) *Security Sector Governance in the Western Balkans: Self-Assessment Studies on Defence, Intelligence, Police and Border Management Reform* (Vienna and Geneva: Geneva Centre for the Democratic Control of Armed Forces).

Etzioni-Halevy, E. (1996) Civil–Military Relations and Democracy: The Case of the Military–Political Elites' Connection in Israel, *Armed Forces and Society*, 22(3), 401–17.

Feaver, P. D. (1996) The Civil–Military Problematique: Huntington, Janowitz, and the Question of Civilian Control, *Armed Forces and Society*, 23(2), 149–78.

Fluri, P. H., G. E. Gustenau and P. I. Pantev (Eds) (2005) *The Evolution of Civil–Military Relations in South East Europe* (Geneva: Physica).

Freedom House (2016) Freedom of the World 2016 Data. Available online at: https://freedomhouse.org/report/freedom-world-2016/table-scores.

Gaub, F. (2013) The Libyan Armed Forces between Coup-proofing and Repression, *The Journal of Strategic Studies*, 36(2), 221–44.

Grewal, S. (2016) *A Quiet Revolution: The Tunisian Military after Ben Ali* (Washington: Carnegie Endowment for International Peace).

Gürsoy, Y. (2009) Civilian Support and Military Unity in the Outcome of Turkish and Greek Military Interventions, *Journal of Political and Military Sociology*, 37(1), 47–75.

Haddadt, S. (2011) *The Role of the Libyan Army in the Revolt against Gaddafi's Regime* (Doha: Al Jazeera Centre for Studies).

Hanlon, Q. (2012) *Security Sector Reform in Tunisia a Year after the Jasmine Revolution* (Washington: United States Institute for Peace).

Harb, I. (2003) The Egyptian Military in Politics: Disengagement or Accommodation? *Middle East Journal*, 57(2), 269–90.

Hashim, A. S. (2011) The Egyptian Military, Part One: From the Ottomans through Sadat, *Middle East Policy*, 18(3), 63–78.

Herspring, D. R., and I. Volgyes (Eds) (1978) *Civil–Military Relations in Communist Systems* (Boulder: Westview Press).

Janowitz, M. (1964) *The Military in the Political Development of New Nations: An Essay in Comparative Analysis* (Chicago and London: University of Chicago Press).

Kamrava, M. (2000) Military Professionalization and Civil–Military Relations in the Middle East, *Political Science Quarterly*, 115(1), 67–92.

Karabelias, G. (2003) A Brief Overview of the Evolution of Civil–Military Relations in Albania, Greece, and Turkey during the post-WWII Period, *Journal of Political and Military Sociology*, 31(1), 57–70.

Koonings, K. and D. Kruijt (2002) Military Politics and the Mission of Nation Building, in: K. Koonings and D. Kruijt (Eds), *Political Armies: The Military and Nation Building in the Age of Democracy* (London and New York: Zed Books).

Linz, J. J. and A. Stepan (1996) *Problems of Democratic Transition and Consolidation: Southern Europe, South America, and Post-Communist Europe* (Baltimore: Johns Hopkins University Press).

Lissak, M. (1971) The Israel Defence Forces as an Agent of Socialization and Education: A Research in Role-Expansion in a Democratic Society, in: M. R. van Gils (Ed.), *The Perceived Role of The Military* (Rotterdam: Rotterdam University Press).

Lutterbeck, D. (2013) Arab Uprisings, Armed Forces, and Civil–Military Relations, *Armed Forces and Society*, 39(1), 28–52.

Mattes, H. (2014) Rebuilding the National-Security Forces in Libya, *Middle East Policy*, 21(2), 85–99.

Nassif, H. B. (2014) Generals and Autocrats: Coup-Proofing and Military Elites' Behavior in the 2011 Arab Spring, PhD thesis, Indiana University.

Nepstad, S. E. (2013) Mutiny and Nonviolence in the Arab Spring: Exploring Military Defections and Loyalty in Egypt, Bahrain, and Syria, *Journal of Peace Research*, 50(3), 337–49.

O'Donnell, G. and P. C. Schmitter (1986) *Transition from Authoritarian Rule: Tentative Conclusions about Uncertain Democracies* (Baltimore: Johns Hopkins University Press).

Owen, R. (2014) *The Rise and Fall of Arab Presidents for Life: With a New Afterword* (Cambridge: Harvard University Press).

Perkins, K. J. (1989) *Historical Dictionary of Tunisia* (Metuchen: Scarecrow Press).
Perlmutter, A. (1969) *Military and Politics in Israel: Nation-building and Role Expansion* (London: Cass).
Pion-Berlin, D. and H. Trinkunas (2010) Civilian Praetorianism and Military Shirking during Constitutional Crises in Latin America, *Comparative Politics*, 42(2), 395–411.
Pion-Berlin, D., D. Esparza and K. Grisham (2014) Staying Quartered: Civilian Uprisings and Military Disobedience in the Twenty-First Century, *Comparative Political Studies*, 47(2), 230–59.
Quinlivan, J. T. (1999) Coup-Proofing: Its Practice and Consequences in the Middle East, *International Security*, 24(2), 131–65.
Remington, R. A. (1978) Civil–Military Relations in Yugoslavia: The Partisan Vanguard, *Studies in Comparative Communism*, 11(3), 250–64.
Ruffa, C., C. Dandeker and P. Vennesson (2013) Soldiers Drawn into Politics? The Influence of Tactics in Civil–Military Relations, *Small Wars and Insurgencies*, 24(2), 322–34.
Serra, N. (2010) *The Military Transition: Democratic Reform of the Armed Forces* (Cambridge: Cambridge University Press).
Sheffer, G. and O. Barak (2013) *Israel's Security Networks: A Theoretical and Comparative Perspective* (New York: Cambridge University Press).
Simonsen, S. G. (2007) Building "National" Armies—Building Nations? Determinants of Success for Postintervention Integration Efforts, *Armed Forces and Society*, 33(4), 571–90.
Skocpol, T. (1979) *States and Social Revolutions: A Comparative Analysis of France, Russia and China* (Cambridge: Cambridge University Press).
Sorenson, D. S. (2000) Civil–Military Relations in North Africa, *Middle East Policy*, 14(4), 99–114.
Söyler, M. (2015) *The Turkish Deep State: State Consolidation, Civil–Military Relations and Democracy* (New York: Routledge).
Springborg, R. (2011) Economic Involvement of Militaries, *International Journal of Middle East Studies*, 43(3), 397–9.
Springborg, R. (2014) Arab Militaries, in: M. Lynch (Ed.), *The Arab Uprisings Explained: New Contentious Politics in the Middle East* (New York: Columbia University Press).
Vennesson, P. (2003) Civil–Military Relations in France: Is there a Gap? *Journal of Strategic Studies*, 26(2), 29–42.
Vogel, J. (1997) *Nationen im Gleichschritt. Der Kult der Nation in Waffen in Deutschland und Frankreich 1871–1914* (Göttingen: Vandenhoeck & Ruprecht).
Ware, L. B. (1985) The Role of the Tunisian Military in the Post-Bourgiba Era, *Middle East Journal*, 39(1), 27–47.

15

STALLED CONFLICTS IN THE MEDITERRANEAN

Neophytos Loizides

Introduction

This chapter examines contemporary conflicts and stalemates in the broader Mediterranean region. While emphasizing there is no single uniform model of a 'Mediterranean' conflict or stalemate, it points to a number of shared patterns and commonalities in such regional ethno-political issues as the Arab–Israeli, Balkan, Spanish/Catalan, Cypriot, Greek–Turkish, Kurdish and post-Arab Spring conflicts. Specifically, it asks why most peacebuilding projects have failed despite the visible involvement of European and international organizations and despite historical legacies of tolerance and accommodation in the Mediterranean region. Focusing on intra-state conflict, it argues that dominant groups have been reluctant to accommodate diversity, preferring to maintain mutually hurtful and destructive stalemates. To shed light on this puzzling pattern, the chapter cites recent failures to accommodate diversity, showing how dominant nationalisms have used negative demonstration effects and false analogies from the past to constrain attempts at political accommodation.

Political accommodation and stalled conflicts

Stalled conflicts in the Mediterranean particularly intra-state conflicts are explicitly linked to failures in embracing political accommodation including for instance federal or consociational models.[1] This is a paradox as historically the region, even its most conflictual eastern part, has hosted a multiplicity of popular federal movements and nationalist ideologies, for example, among the Balkan nations (Stavrianos 1959), the southern Slavs (Banac 1983, 1984), Macedonians (Rossos 2008), Greeks and Turks (Anagnostopoulou 1997; Veremis 1989), Israeli and Palestinians (Yiftachel 2006) and pan-Arab nationalists (Ajami 1978; Dawisha 2003).

Looking at the devastating civil wars in the post-Arab Spring era, it is difficult to imagine today the strength of pan-Arab nationalism a few decades earlier. The United Arab Republic was a popular but short-lived manifestation of this failed project. Other potentially federalizable Mediterranean sub-regions have also failed, as for instance, the long-dreamed-of federation among the Balkan people, or more specifically, among South Slavs, including Habsburg and Ottoman Štokavian speakers; the latter dialect 'united' the Serbo-Croat Bonsiak linguistic world and set the stage for the political union of the South Slavs. Nonetheless, when the former

Yugoslavia fell apart, this particular section did not manage to maintain its 'federal unity' despite a shared language and rich intellectual traditions. While western media initially pointed to its ethnic diversity as a cause of its violent breakdown, this argument seems limited. For instance, federalism was equally short lived among the 'ethnically related' Serbs and Montenegrins (Ramet 2006). Likewise, the attempt to federalize Libya in three main provinces lasted only for about a decade (1951–63). Following Muammar Gaddafi's takeover in 1969, federal options between Libya and its neighbours were negotiated, first with Egypt and Syria and then with Tunisia, but both attempts ended in acrimony (Dawisha 2003).

Meanwhile, early consociational attempts in the Mediterranean region's smaller multiethnic states, including Cyprus (Kyriakides 1968; Markides 1977) and Lebanon (Zahar 2005; Dekmejian 1978) led to similarly violent breakdowns. Both cases commonly feature as major examples of unsuccessful consociationalism in the relevant literature (Schneckener 2002; Lijphart 1996). The Cyprus stalemate is particularly puzzling, as reunification talks have failed to reach a comprehensive settlement despite a signed agreement on bicommunal administration since 1977–9, strong pro-federalist positions embraced by at least three main political parties in the island (i.e. AKEL, DISY and CTP), and the proactive involvement of international and regional organizations including the United Nations and the European Union (Richmond 2005; Anastasiou 2008; Ker-Lindsay 2011).

In another telling case, Turkey could have mitigated its own stalled conflict with its Kurdish minority through political accommodation in the form of decentralization. In the Turkish as well as the Egyptian cases, we could point to the large population as an important pre-existing enabling condition for decentralization. Both current stalemates could, in theory, be addressed by introducing 'informal' federal or consociational arrangements, as in South Africa, Singapore or Spain, to regulate conflict with territorial and non-territorial minorities. Instead, the AK Party has governed Turkey with little formal or informal power-sharing with either Kurds or rival Kemalist political parties. Likewise, in post-Mubarak Egypt, the choice of a (majoritarian) presidential system has deepened the conflict between supporters of the Muslim Brotherhood and the military, reversing the brief achievements of the Arab Spring. Tunisia, on the contrary opted for proportional parliamentary democracy in accordance with the prescriptions of the consociational school, so far effectively mitigating the conflict between political Islam and secularism.

Perceptions of stalemates and political accommodation

In addressing stalled conflicts, 'hawks' usually draw from grievances, hatred, and security dilemmas (Jervis 1976; Kaufman 2011; Petersen 2011), while 'doves' point to mutually hurting stalemates and opportunities for compromise through some form of political accommodation (Zartman 1989; McGarry 2011; Heraclides 2001). Perceptions are central in evaluating the claims of each camp. A prevalent perception in the region is that power-sharing is unnecessary because people have been living in peace and harmony for ages. Integrationist and assimilationist programmes downplaying ethnic differences are common, particularly in left-wing political movements. By emphasizing a 'mythical peaceful past' and 'unity over minority rights', leftist movements have restricted, even undermined, federal and consociational prospects. Perceptions challenging the very existence of minorities, let alone their rights, are fundamental to the region's protracted conflicts and stalemates. Even if individuals are welcome as equals in nation-building, cultural rights are violated.

Historically, the failure of the Arab unity project could be attributed to its emphasis on 'unity' rather than 'diversity'; in principle, diversity could have been accommodated using federal and consociational devices. This is also true for Turkey and its Kurdish minorities but applies equally well to Shiite versus Sunni conceptions of Arab unity (and their respective fears). Other cases in the region, particularly those in Spain (Catalans and Basques) and Italy (South Tyrol) suggest the viability of an alternative route. By way of contrast, the failure to mediate a two-state solution in Israel/Palestine suggests the absence of credible alternatives even under conditions where partition has emerged as the only visible alternative (Yiftachel 2006).

Mediating power-sharing requires explicit (constitutional) commitments to minorities that the achievement of 'national unity' will not preclude diversity. Credible constitutional arrangements should aim to safeguard minorities from the loss of autonomy or representation while majorities should be protected from dysfunctional constitutional provisions and secession. The major advantage of federal and consociational arrangements is that they frequently offer the most credible way to address security, financial or identity risks, while combining shared goals with separate spheres of government for majorities and significant minorities. Likewise, power-sharing, either through guaranteed group representation in the central government or through territorial decentralization and federalism, could be understood as a form of 'compensation' for groups likely to resist a 'hegemonic' or assimilationist state, as they will now have a vested interest in the power-sharing structure.

In both Yugoslavia and the Arab-speaking world, attempts at state-building have failed to balance the tensions between unity and diversity, leading to disintegration and conflict. In the case of Iraq, Dawisha argues these tensions became evident during the peak of Arab nationalism in 1958 following the July 14 coup and the emergence of rival parties. For the 'Iraq First Group', issues of preserving diversity across ethnic and religious lines were critical: 'Arab Unity was seen as a Sunni project designated to ensure the ultimate subjugation of the non-Sunni communal groups' (Dawisha 2003: 219). Dawisha adds that the Iraqi First group 'was not necessarily averse to some form of union, but theirs was a much looser conception than that held by the nationalists, at most a federal arrangement in which Iraq would retain considerable autonomy' (ibid.: 216). A similar pattern emerged in Syria, eventually resulting in the failure of the larger Arab unity project (ibid.).

For their part, South Slav federal/state-building projects fell short of balancing regional/federal autonomy with national solidarity. Using the term 'flawed unification', Banac (1984: 13) says Yugoslavia failed to meet the promise of its intellectual founding fathers. This was particularly true in interwar Yugoslavia, originally called the Kingdom of Serbs, Croats and Slovenes. According to Ramet (2006: 37), its component peoples 'came to the kingdom with rather different expectations and for different reasons'. Like Kurds in Iraq today, Croats and Slovenes sought security, aligning with the new kingdom to protect themselves from further territorial losses to Italy but also hoping for a federal constitution (ibid.). But Serbian elites assumed political, economic and cultural hegemony within the new state, adopting strict centralism. And as in the pan-Arab case, 'the policy of monopolizing the top posts in the country for Serbs was, at a minimum, politically insensitive, likely to give provocation, and short-sighted' (Ramet 2006: 37).

The general insistence on integration/assimilation largely explains the conflict trajectory in the Mediterranean region. For instance, Iraqi centralists downplayed crimes against Kurds by attributing these exclusively to the Saddam Hussein regime. Turkish nationalists, mostly on the left, voice similar arguments when discussing their own Kurdish national minorities, attributing crimes to previous regimes. Yet since the mid-1990s, the Turkish left has found limited support among the Kurdish minority. Even after the election of a moderate leader from the region, Kemal Kılıçdaroğlu, as president, the main opposition party, CHP (Republican People's Party), won only a tiny fraction of its votes in Kurdish regions, thus failing to create a new platform from which to transcend the stalemate.

Stalemates and failing political settlements

A second dominant perception of stalled conflicts is that multi-ethnic states are prone to failure. This is particularly true of (but not limited to) those espousing right-wing nationalisms, which frequently see any recognition of ethnic or religious diversity as a stepping stone to secession. Right-wing nationalisms have a particularly strong attachment to power, authority and territory, frequently treating sovereignty in a non-negotiable manner while attributing conflicts with their minorities to external interference.

In the narratives of most Middle East and Balkan nationalisms, territories 'won or kept with blood' are not in any sense renegotiable through federal or consociational arrangements. Unsurprisingly, then, remembrance of fallen soldiers is a central theme in the region's official discourses, as demonstrated, for instance, in Turkey's stance on PKK casualties in the 1990s (Navaro-Yashin 2002: 118). Parliamentary debates are telling; for instance, in his 1995 speech to the Turkish Grand National Assembly, conservative President Süleyman Demirel remembered with compassion all Turkey's 'martyrs and our teachers who have become victims of terrorism while trying to educate our children through great self-sacrifice' (Loizides 2016: 216). And even though Recep Tayyip Erdoğan initially attempted to accommodate Kurdish minority rights, he eventually adopted the major principles of Turkish conservative nationalist ideology.

Elsewhere in the region, various contemporary political parties have drawn their inspiration from national liberation movements, as in Croatia (HDZ), the Republic of Macedonia/FYROM (VMRO-DPMNE), Cyprus (DISY among Greek Cypriots, UBP among Turkish Cypriots) and Lebanon (Kataeb party), to mention only a few. Yet these political parties have shown elements of adaptation in the past decade, suggesting that power-sharing is not necessarily incompatible with right-wing (or left-wing) ideologies. Centre-right political actors have often developed effective and credible ties with external peace actors, such as the European Union, although admittedly this has not happened in the Israeli case due to the predominantly unconditional US support. Yet processes of positive adaptation towards moderation have also occurred in leftist political traditions. For instance, in Spain, the left has traditionally supported power-sharing arrangements with Catalans and Basques, often against the wishes of right-wing opposition, while in Cyprus, several impressive mobilizations by the Turkish–Cypriot left have demonstrated a clear desire to transcend the Cyprus stalemate.

While encouraging, such breakthroughs remain few and far between. Political parties seldom reach consensus in issues of power-sharing, as moderate parties frequently face ethnic outbidding by intra-ethnic rivals. In the presence of dominant nationalist perceptions, it is easier for the masses to adopt political views uncritically and act in ways that strengthen existing elite consensus, thus creating a vicious cycle between public expectations and the viability of federal or consociational projects. Even moderate elites may shy away from promising peace settlements, if they perceive them as politically risky or unfeasible. Arguably, a reassuring international environment for political accommodation might enable domestic actors to reassess their positions. In the end, one might be left wondering whether power-sharing fails because external actors actively work against it or because domestic forces have not acted pre-emptively to neutralize destructive outside influences – or both.

'Power-sharing is destructive'

A third common perception is that power-sharing cannot resolve issues of multi-ethnicity. A core understanding, for instance, driving the current Syrian crisis is that federalism and consociationalism have devastating effects and could worsen ethnic and religious conflicts. For the most part, critics say power-sharing in various forms has failed in the region. The relatively recent examples of Lebanon, the former Yugoslavia and post-1960 Cyprus have consolidated the view of federalism and consociationalism as dysfunctional, if not catastrophic. Sadly, the region lacks an indisputably successful consociational or federal model which could inspire others to follow suit. Looking at the period between World Wars I and II, Ramet points out that while Norway and Finland in Europe provided models of what newly independent states could be, there was no similar model for the Balkans (2006: 3). More recently in Iraq, external and domestic critics alike have emphasized the absence of a relevant federal example. For instance, Muslim religious leaders, as well as 'liberal and democratic' politicians, have stressed the need to preserve the country's unity and have frequently 'urged the Kurds not to rush into formulae like federalism and confederalism with which *the region is not familiar*' (*Mideast Mirror* 2004; emphasis added). As argued elsewhere (Loizides 2016), Ottoman institutions and religious legacies of tolerance preserved cultural diversity for centuries; despite their embedded hierarchical nature, they could have provided the political and cultural antecedents for federal and consociational arrangements. But the reading of the Ottoman past is frequently limited to brief references in national history books and is highly selective.

In fact, how elites publically frame the *millet* legacy in post-Ottoman successor states makes the public endorsement of federal and consociational arrangements difficult, if not impossible. Through a series of false analogies, contemporary critics compare recent minority accommodation proposals in the form of power-sharing or community recognition to the *millet* system and its role in the violent collapse of the Ottoman Empire (Berkes 1963). One example is Sonyel's *Minorities and the Destruction of the Ottoman Empire* (1993), published by the Ataturk Culture, Language and History Foundation, an institution devoted to the preservation of Kemalist thought in Turkey. Such perceptions preclude any discussion of federalism, in either the official Turkish Republican ideology or the broader majority discourses in the country, including AKP's counter-hegemonic positioning. Thus, despite the general liberalization since the 1990s of Turkish discourse on domestic and regional identity representation (Somer 2005; Fokas 2008), institutional transformation through power-sharing does not feature in the political discourse. Instead, Turkey has moved towards an increasingly majoritarian (semi-presidential) system and will fully endorse presidentialism in the near future.

State institutions play a central role in maintaining hegemonic perceptions on political accommodation, particularly when confronted with contrary examples from other parts of the world, including Spain, as mentioned earlier. After visiting Spain in 1993, for instance, Turkish PM Tansu Çiller allegedly proposed the use of the Basque model to solve the conflict in Kurdish regions, something she later denied (Pope 1993: 14). Her rival and ANAP successor Mesut Yilmaz rejected the idea of federation with the Kurds and stated that regional cultures in Turkey must be allowed to exist through their own means (TRT TV 1992). On another occasion, Yilmaz said the Kurdish language should become the second official language in Turkey, but this proposal was eliminated before any debate could take place (McDowall 1997: 428).

More recently, in early 2007, a Turkish prosecutor initiated a criminal inquiry against former president and coup leader Kenan Evren for even suggesting Turkey should become a federation. Drawing on his early proposal for administrative regions, Evren had spoken openly in the media, suggesting Turkey would one day decide on federalism; otherwise, 'there will be no peace', he said, adding that the 10 per cent election threshold obstructed Kurds from getting into parliament (*Turkish Daily News* 2007). Not surprisingly, reactions were overwhelmingly negative, with some attributing the former general's comments to insanity.

Protracted stalemates: alternative explanations

Lack of political accommodation and stalled conflicts in the Mediterranean region are also driven by structural conditions. There is, for instance, significant variation in external intervention strategies and other structural conditions across historical and contemporary conflicts in the Mediterranean region, including size, regime type, natural resources and level of economic development. Structural factors certainly contribute to the emergence and implementation of federal and consociational settlements, but no easily identifiable set of structural conditions is shared by most cases presented here.

As noted earlier, alternative accommodation formulas have failed despite historical institutional precedents, ethnic or linguistic affinities, and major external incentives, as demonstrated in the last few decades by the European Union's intervention in 2004 in Cyprus. Another factor in understanding stalemates and political accommodation in the Mediterranean region is the impact of colonial rule. While acknowledging this factor, it is important to consider the experience of other countries before reaching any conclusions. For one thing, the success of federal arrangements is not confined to industrial nation-states among which no federation has failed since World War II (Bermeo 2002). For another, in much of the developing world, successful federations and consociations have survived and even thrived in volatile regional environments. These include a number of former colonies, such as India, Nigeria, Brazil, Ethiopia, South Africa and Indonesia, whose socioeconomic and political conditions, arguably, are similar to those in the Middle East or the post-Ottoman Balkans. Thus, explanations emphasizing colonial effects might not adequately account for the nature of stalled state-building in the region. Faced with comparable challenges, other post-colonial leaders, for example, in India, have successfully countered colonial legacies by embracing political secularism and federal accommodation that offered symmetrical treatment to the various religious and ethnic communities across the country (Kohli 2004). In contrast, it could be argued that in the eastern part of the Mediterranean, coercive power-sharing has turned the region's 'early advantage' of tolerance into an unfortunate demonstration of how federalism and consociationalism can lack prospects or viability.

Finally, it is useful to draw comparisons with post-communist societies in the Balkans as well. Critics of power-sharing in the region claim ethno-federalism facilitates nationalist mobilization and state disintegration (Bunce 1999). For Bunce, the design of these systems puts into place virtually all of the building blocks necessary for the rise of nationalist movements (ibid.: 49). This process seems confined to communist federations, although a similar argument could be made for authoritarian regimes in the Middle East. In Yugoslavia, Stefanovic (2009) identifies the problem as the country's centralism, not federalism. He argues that 'despite its formal federal character, the centralized organization of the Communist Party, which wielded political and economic power, insured that Yugoslavia was a unitary state' (ibid.). He concludes: 'Communist Yugoslavia was *not a genuine federation* as the communist federations were federal in form but unitary in content' (ibid.; emphasis added; see also Connor 1984; McGarry 1998).

Transcending stalled conflicts

Despite their 'federal and consociational failures' some of the successor states of the former Yugoslavia, including Bosnia, Kosovo and the Republic of Macedonia/FYROM (like Lebanon) returned to such arrangements in the absence of alternatives and in the search for more genuine and viable forms of power-sharing. These states are already seeing some success: decreased violence, reduced international involvement in peacekeeping commitments, and return in some areas of internally displaced persons. Admittedly, federalism and consociationalism are difficult to effectuate in prolonged stalemates, especially as these areas might resort to federalism or power-sharing when it is too late – too much blood has been shed in the past, and any central authority or shared institutions including political parties have been absent.

Yet a supporting international intervention could be the key in transcending the obstacles facing these renewed power-sharing projects. To cite a couple of examples, Bosnia has at least partially avoided the fate of other post-conflict societies in the region where lines of division were perpetuated with almost zero returns. And power-sharing provisions in the Republic of Macedonia/FYROM prevented renewed violence after the short 2001 war despite predictions to the contrary.

A key lesson from these cases, for instance a potentially federal or decentralized Syria, is that the latter should combine decentralization with power-sharing at the centre (consociationalism). A consociational arrangement will ensure that the future government of Syria would be fully representative of the country's ethnic, linguistic and religious identities. A government of national unity inclusive of all democratically elected groups will prevent secessionist demands as all legitimate groups will feel represented in decision-making. Power-sharing will prevent situations where a territorially significant group becomes consistently excluded/ostracized from the central government. Such groups often respond with secession following attempts by others to ostracize them politically during negotiations to form a government. In environments of low inter-ethnic trust as in Syria, a constitutional formula has to be in place to ensure inclusivity, proportionality and functionality.

External peace allies and credible incentives are also critical in socializing undecided actors to overcome stalemates and accept a peace settlement compromise. Yet external mediation and power-sharing institutions could be designed to better accommodate domestic political parties and their needs. And as demonstrated in the broader literature, external intervention works best in areas where indigenous leadership has been extensively engaged in decision-making and implementation (Dahlman and Ó Tuathail 2005; Bieber 2006; Belloni 2008; Stefanovic and Loizides 2011).

Conclusions

This chapter reaches three conclusions in its analysis of stalemates in the Mediterranean region. First, it identifies the core features that have marked the protracted and stalled conflicts in the Mediterranean countries pointing to the role of majority nationalisms and dominant ethnicities. Majority nationalisms in the region have confronted ethnic and religious diversity not only by eliminating differences through ethnic cleansing and genocide (commonly associated with both the southern European and the post-Ottoman countries) but also by incorporating, even glorifying, diverse 'folklore' traditions provided these are adjusted to fit within the parameters of the dominant state nationalism (Hobsbawm 1992; Triandafyllidou 1998: 606). In a nutshell, it is not surprising that the roots of many contemporary stalled conflicts from Morocco (Western Sahara) to southeast Turkey and the former Yugoslavia lie not in exclusion and oppositional state-building programs but in ambitious efforts to forcibly integrate and assimilate unwilling 'half-brothers and sisters' (Stefanovic 2005).

Second, the chapter argues that traditions of elite accommodation and past legacies matter. On the one hand, they can sustain power-sharing arrangements (Daalder 1974; Lijphart 1977), but on the other, they can act as barriers to such arrangements if negative memories, nationalist narratives and false analogies prevail in the public discourse. Although contemporary federal and power-sharing models differ greatly from the Ottoman Empire's *millet* system, the communist Yugoslavia or the post-colonial arrangements created for Cyprus and Lebanon, these cases sustain discourses negating contemporary attempts for political accommodation; they also constrain recent institutional innovations which could potentially overcome the stalled Mediterranean conflicts.

In the cases of both Lebanese and 1960s Cypriot consociationalism a serious constraint has been the ethnicization of power-sharing arrangements by allocating specific positions to candidates according to their ethnicity. Yet power-sharing does not necessarily need to over-emphasize ethnicity. Even in the cases of ethnic federations, political systems could protect local minorities through generous human rights provisions even local power-sharing securing veto rights to local minorities. As to the central government, an alternative to the corporate ethnic Lebanese approach is the liberal d'Hondt process employed in the all-party cabinet of Northern Ireland and elsewhere (Loizides 2016). A d'Hondt style executive is generally easier to present and defend across the Mediterranean region because of its liberal elements compared to other ethnic corporate alternatives known historically mainly through the Lebanese, South Tyrol and Cypriot examples. Such alternative power-sharing systems are inclusive of all political parties on the basis of their electoral strength nation-wide; they could broaden the participation of opposition groups effectively encouraging power-sharing among the larger ethnic and religious groups without excluding other minorities or liberal non-ethnic political affiliations.

In conclusion, power-sharing and federalism could be appropriate antidotes to ongoing conflicts in this volatile region. This is particularly important for the current debates on the 'day after' in Syria and Iraq. The Arab and South Slav unification projects discussed earlier are not the only cases in point. The essence of the Macedonian or Kurdish conflict in the twentieth century does not lie in the exclusiveness of neighbouring nationalisms, but in the involuntary incorporation of 'brotherly communities' into narrowly defined centralized nationalist programmes. In fact, recent examples from post-war Yugoslavia and elsewhere suggest that the appropriate institutional design could overcome ideational and structural barriers. As mentioned elsewhere, in *most conflictual environments*, the relative success of power-sharing should be understood in relation to previous records of civil strife (Loizides 2016). Following this reasoning, post-Franco Spain, post-Taif Lebanon and more recently, post-Arab Spring Tunisia could be considered so far as 'relative success' stories (Zahar 2005; Bieber 2006; O'Leary 2005; Belloni 2008). These cases and their individual successes or failures also suggest that there is no uniform pattern of conflict or stalemate in the Mediterranean region.

Admittedly, re-introducing power-sharing in difficult cases where previous experience has been negative might require major investment and support from outside actors, at least for a transitional period. In addition, related peace mediations require a deep understanding of the arguments of critics. It is essential to confront the arguments of those who oppose power-sharing and to design institutional arrangements that ease potential defects. Besides analysing stalled conflicts and failures, we need to identify conflict-mitigating institutions that have been most effective under 'least likely' conditions. The 'transferability potential' of such institutional arrangements lies in their capacity to mitigate 'most difficult' conflict situations, setting the stage for comparable arrangements in similar or less complicated environments. A challenge for future research is identifying the key aspects of peace processes that could offer inspiration, especially in the most troubled countries in the Mediterranean region.

Note

1 Consociationalism, among other key features, stipulates that power be shared by majorities and minorities, and it implies formal or informal veto rights for all parties (Lijphart 1977; McGarry and O'Leary 2005). Consociationalism involves power-sharing at the centre, for instance, through the collective presidency in Bosnia or the allocation of certain key posts to members of specific groups as in Lebanon.

Federalism refers to situations where authority is territorially divided between central and provincial governments, with both enjoying constitutionally separate competencies. Federations could be also consociations, as in Belgium and Switzerland, but not all federations are consociations, as in the United States and Australia. In addition, it could be argued that some federations function as semi-consociations, as in Canada and India. Semi-consociations include some elements of consociations but not others, for instance proportionality and community autonomy but no guarantees for long-term power-sharing or fully effective veto rights. There are also consociational agreements with territorially intermingled populations that do not take a federal form, such as post-1960 Cyprus, Lebanon and Northern Ireland after the 1998 Good Friday Agreement. Power-sharing could take either territorial or non-territorial forms through the inclusion of ethnic minority parties in the central government and guaranteed veto rights (see also Loizides 2016).

Bibliography

Ajami, Fouad. 1978. 'The End of Pan-Arabism', *Foreign Affairs*, 57(2): 355–73.

Anagnostopoulou, Sia. 1997. *Asia Minor, 19th Century–1919: The Greek Orthodox Communities. From the Rum Millet to Greek Nationhood* (in Greek). Ellinika Grammata, Athens.

Anastasiou, Harry. 2008. *The Broken Olive Branch: Nationalism, Ethnic Conflict and the Quest for Peace in Cyprus: The Impasse of Ethnonationalism*. Syracuse, NY: Syracuse University Press.

Banac, Ivo. 1983. 'The Confessional "Rule" and the Dubrovnik Exception: the Origins of the "Serb-Catholic Circle" in the Nineteenth-Century Dalmatia', *Slavic Review*, 42(3): 448–74.

Banac, Ivo. 1984. *The National Question in Yugoslavia: Origins History, Politics*. Ithaca: Cornell University Press.

Belloni, Roberto. 2008. *State Building and International Intervention in Bosnia*. London: Routledge.

Berkes, Niyazi. 1963. *The Development of Secularism in Turkey*. New York: Routledge.

Bermeo, Nancy. 2002. 'The Import of Institutions', *Journal of Democracy*, 13(2): 96–110.

Bieber, Florian. 2006. *Post-war Bosnia: Ethnicity, Inequality and Public Sector Governance*. New York: Palgrave Macmillan.

Bunce, Valerie. 1999. *Subversive Institutions: The Design and the Destruction of Socialism and the State*. Cambridge: Cambridge University Press.

Burgess, Michael. 2006. *Comparative Federalism in Theory and Practice*. New York: Routledge.

Connor, Walker. 1984. *The National Question in Marxist–Leninist Theory and Strategy*. Princeton: Princeton University Press.

Daalder, Hans. 1974. 'The Consociational Democracy Theme', *World Politics*, 26(4): 604–21.

Dahlman, Carl and Gearóid Ó Tuathail. 2005. 'The Legacy of Ethnic Cleansing: The International Community and the Returns Process in Post-Dayton Bosnia–Herzegovina', *Political Geography*, 24(5): 569–99.

Dawisha, Adeed. 2003. *Arab Nationalism in the Twentieth Century: From Triumph to Despair*. Princeton: Princeton University Press.

Dekmejian, Richard Hrair. 1978. 'Consociational Democracy in Crisis: The Case of Lebanon', *Comparative Politics*, 10(2): 51–65.

Fokas, Effie. 2008. 'Islam in the Framework of Turkey–EU Relations: Situations in Flux and Moving Targets', *Global Change Peace and Security*, 20(1): 87–98.

Heraclides Alexis. 2001. *I Ellada ke o Ex Anatolon Kindynos* [Greece and the Eastern Threat], (in Greek). Athens: Polis Publishers.

Hobsbawm, Eric. 1992. 'Introduction: Inventing Traditions', in Eric Hobsbawm and Terence Ranger (eds), *The Invention of Tradition*. Cambridge: Cambridge University Press, pp. 1–14.

Hutchinson, John and Anthony Smith (eds) 1994. *Nationalism*, Oxford: New York: Oxford University Press.

Jervis Robert. 1976. *Perception and Misperception in International Politics*. Princeton, NJ: Princeton University Press.

Kaufman, Stuart J. 2011. 'Symbols, Frames, and Violence: Studying Ethnic War in the Philippines', *International Studies Quarterly*, 55: 937–58.

Ker-Lindsay, James. 2011. *The Cyprus Problem: What Everyone Needs to Know*. Oxford: Oxford University Press.

Kohli, Atul. 2004. 'India: Federalism and the Accommodation of Ethnic Nationalism', in Ugo Amoretti and Nancy Bermeo (eds), *Federalism and Territorial Cleavages*. Baltimore: Johns Hopkins University Press, pp. 281–301.

Kyriakides, Stanley. 1968. *Cyprus: Constitutionalism and Crisis Government*. Philadelphia: University of Pennsylvania Press.
Lijphart, Arend. 1977. *Democracy in Plural Societies: A Comparative Exploration*. New Haven: Yale University Press.
Lijphart, Arend. 1996. 'The Puzzle of Indian Democracy: A Consociational Interpretation', *The American Political Science Review*, 90(2): 258–68.
Loizides, Neophytos. 2016. *Designing Peace: Cyprus and Institutional Innovations in Divided Societies*. Philadelphia: University of Pennsylvania Press.
McDowall, David. 1997. *A Modern History of the Kurds*. London: I. B. Tauris.
McGarry, John. 1998. 'Orphans of Secession: National Pluralism in Secessionist Regions and Post-Secession States', in Margaret Moore (ed.), *National Self-Determination and Secession*. Oxford: Oxford University Press.
McGarry, John. 2011. 'Centripetal Theory and the Cyprus Conflict', paper presented at the Workshop on Power-Sharing, organized by the Ethnicity and Democratic Governance Project, Munk Centre, University of Toronto, 17 November.
McGarry, John and Brendan O'Leary. 2005. *Federation as a Method of Ethnic Conflict Regulation*, Forum of Federations (available at www.forumfed.ca accessed online 18 October, 2012).
Markides, Kyriakos. 1977. *The Rise and Fall of the Cyprus Republic*. New Haven: Yale University Press.
Mideast Mirror. 2004. 'The Challenge of Federalism in Iraq', January 23, accessed online through Nexis UK, 14 November, 2011.
Navaro-Yashin, Yael. 2002. *Faces of the State: Secularism and Public Life in Turkey*. Princeton NJ: Princeton University Press.
O'Leary, Brendan. 2001. 'An Iron Law of Nationalism and Federation? A (Neo-Diceyian) Theory of the Necessity of a Federal *Staatsvolk*, and of Consociational Rescue', *Nations and Nationalism*, 7(3): 273–96.
O'Leary, Brendan. 2002. 'In Praise of Empires Past: Myths and Method of Kedourie's Nationalism', *New Left Review*, 2(18): 106–30.
O'Leary, Brendan. 2005. 'Power-sharing, Pluralist Federation, and Federacy', in Brendan O'Leary, John McGarry and Khaled Salih (eds), *The Future of Kurdistan in Iraq*. Philadelphia: University of Pennsylvania Press, pp. 47–92.
Petersen, Roger D. 2011. *Western Intervention in the Balkans: The Strategic Use of Emotion in Conflict*. Cambridge: Cambridge University Press.
Pope, Hugh. 1993. 'Turkish Army Blocks Moves to Kurdish Reform', *The Independent*, 15 October, p. 14.
Ramet Sabrina. 2006. *The Three Yugoslavias: State-Building and Legitimation, 1918–2005*. Bloomington: Indiana University Press.
Richmond, Oliver. 2005. 'Shared Sovereignty and the Politics of Peace: Evaluating the EU's "Catalytic" Framework in the Eastern Mediterranean', *International Affairs*, 82(1): 149–76.
Rossos, Andrew. 2008. *Macedonia and the Macedonians: A History*. Stanford: Hoover Institution Press.
Schneckener, Ulrich. 2002. 'Making Power-sharing Work: Lessons from Successes and Failures in Ethnic Conflict Regulation', *Journal of Peace Research*, 39(2): 203–28.
Somer, Murat. 2005. 'Resurgence and Remaking of Identity: Civil Beliefs, Domestic and External Dynamics, and the Turkish Mainstream Discourse on Kurds', *Comparative Political Studies*, 38(6): 591–622.
Sonyel, S. R. 1993. *Minorities and the Destruction of the Ottoman Empire*. Ankara: TKK.
Stavrianos S. Leften. 1959. *The Balkans since 1453*. New York: Rinehart.
Stefanovic, Djordje. 2009. 'The Unintended Consequences of Ethnic Federalism: How Yugoslav Communists Dug Their Own Graves', unpublished paper presented at the Regular Session of Historical Sociology Section, at the Annual Meeting of the American Sociological Association, San Francisco, August 10.
Stefanovic, Djordje. 2005. 'Seeing the Albanians through Serbian Eyes: The Inventors of the Tradition of Intolerance and their Critics, 1804–1939', *European History Quarterly*, 35(3): 465–92.
Stefanovic, Djordje and Neophytos Loizides. 2011. 'The Way Home: Peaceful Return of Victims of Ethnic Cleansing', *Human Rights Quarterly*, 33(3): 408–43.
Triandafyllidou, Anna. 1998. 'National Identity and the "Other"', *Ethnic and Racial Studies*, 21(4): 593–612.
TRT TV. 1992. 'Motherland Party Leader Rejects Idea of Federation for Kurds', September 7, cited in *BBC Summary of World Broadcast*, September 9.
Turkish Daily News. 2007. Week in Review, March 10, accessed online through Nexis UK, 14 November, 2011.

Veremis, Thanos. 1989. 'From the National State to the Stateless Nation 1821–1910', *European History Quarterly*, 19(2): 135–48.

Yiftachel, Oren. 2006. *Ethnocracy: Land and Identity Politics in Israel/Palestine*. Philadelphia: University of Pennsylvania Press.

Zahar, Marie-Joelle. 2005. 'Power Sharing in Lebanon: Foreign Protectors, Domestic Peace, and Democratic Failure', in Donald Rothchild and Philip Roeder (eds), *Sustainable Peace: Power and Democracy after Civil Wars*. Ithaca: Cornell University Press, pp. 219–40.

Zartman, William. 1989. *Ripe for Resolution: Conflict and Intervention in Africa*, Oxford: Oxford University Press.

16

INSURGENCIES, TERRORISM AND POLITICAL VIOLENCE IN THE MEDITERRANEAN REGION

Krista E. Wiegand

Terrorism and insurgency, two common types of political violence, occur in many states worldwide, but the Mediterranean region has experienced a particularly high amount of such violence in recent decades. In particular, armed resistance pursued by Islamist groups has wreaked havoc in states all across North Africa and up to Lebanon (Hizballah), Syria (Islamic State of Syria (ISIS)) and Turkey (ISIS), even spreading into western Europe. At the same time, secular groups including the PKK (Turkey) and PLO (Palestine) have also been active in pursuing political violence in the region for several decades, though they have been fewer in number compared to Islamist groups. Compared to other regions of the world where terrorism and insurgency occur, the Mediterranean region has experienced much more religious political violence than secular violence.

Much of the Mediterranean region, particularly North Africa and the eastern part of the Mediterranean where the 'Middle East' begins, is commonly considered to be a region fraught with sectarian violence, terrorist attacks and unending civil wars. Unfortunately, there is some truth to this perception; political violence, particularly religiously motivated violence, has been a longstanding feature of this region for many decades, especially since the early twentieth century (Wiegand 2012). This region is not necessarily a region specifically prone to violence, nor are its religious traditions, mainly Islam, fundamentally violent. Nevertheless, over the past four decades in particular, both nationalist and radical Islamic groups have pursued violence on a level not experienced before. Though there has been some amount of political violence in this region since the end of colonialism in the mid-twentieth century and the creation of the state of Israel in 1948, it has only been in the past 40 years that religiously motivated violence has dominated the region as a result of the rise of radical Islam. In particular, with the rise of radical Islam in the latter part of the twentieth century, it is not surprising that the Mediterranean region has experienced high levels of political violence influenced by Islamic radicals. Such religiously motivated violence, rooted in zealous religious ideology, can range from riots to engaging in full scale civil war – as ISIS is currently pursuing in Syria.

This chapter begins with a discussion of the types of political violence pursued by non-state actors and the similarities and differences of Islamist and secular armed groups. It then moves on to discuss the status of such groups in the Mediterranean region. The remainder of the chapter provides explanations for the motivations of such groups, and includes a discussion of ISIS as an Islamist terrorist and insurgency group and Hamas as a nationalist Islamist terrorist and insurgency group.

Political violence

According to Honderich (1976: 98), political violence can be viewed as the 'use of considerable or destroying force against persons or things, a use of force prohibited by law and directed to a change in the policies, personnel or system of government, and hence to changes in society'. Under this definition, political violence is mostly the result of actions by non-state actors, such as that seen in riots, revolutions, terrorism and in insurgencies. Though these types of political violence are used around the world, when it comes to Islamists and some secular groups based in the Mediterranean region, the tactics of choice have been terrorist violence and insurgency.

Political violence generally occurs when a group of citizens are strongly dissatisfied with a particular issue, which is disputed, and either or both parties are unable or unwilling to resolve the dispute through peaceful means. Egypt's people's revolution in 2011, the 1990s *intifadah* and terrorism by the PLO up to the 1980s and attacks by Islamic Jihad, Hamas, and several other Palestinian groups more recently exemplify the use of political violence by those extremely dissatisfied with the status quo. It is the very inability of non-state actors to achieve much from the political status quo, and their status as outcasts can lead certain non-state actors to threaten governments through types of political violence like terrorism and insurgency. In many cases non-state groups are deliberately or indirectly excluded from the political system by being banned or repressed by the government. When non-state actors are not provided any legitimate channels through which to express their grievances, such actors could likely turn to political violence instead (Neumann 2005).

If the political system works effectively, governments and dissatisfied non-state actors should be able to bargain or negotiate demands and frustrations of each party, resulting in a resolution of disagreements over resources, territory, identity, ideology and other similar disputed issues. In many states, governments and non-state actors are able to peacefully resolve disagreements through debates, legislatures, regulations and if necessary through the use of mediators, arbitration or adjudication through a court system. Yet there are occasionally disagreements over disputed issues that are either perceived by one or both parties as indivisible, or non-negotiable, or either or both parties refuse to provide concessions or negotiate certain demands. The result is either stalemate with the maintenance of the status quo, or if the non-state actors are dissatisfied with the status quo enough, the likelihood of them pursuing political violence against the government or others in society increases significantly.

When it comes to understanding the root causes of these disagreements, those that are most common include disputes of territory, ideology and identity, particularly as ethnic and religious identities are tied to territory (Wiegand 2012). Even though economic gains often lie at the root of the use of violence by non-state actors, peaceful settlement is, in general, the option that most often results in successful settlement of these disputes as the resources are divisible (Huth 1996). This is due to the fact that it is far easier for the parties involved to negotiate shared use of these resources via a division of them, such that both sides gain the resulting access to things like the economic resources, food, utilities and tax revenue. Conversely, when it comes to issues of an indivisible nature that are impossible to divide, like identity or ideology, peaceful resolution through political means tends to be far more difficult. For an example illustrating this, one need not look any further than the Palestinian–Israeli conflict over territory, which is based on both religious and ethnic identity. Conflicts based on ethnic or religious issues between two distinctly different sides tend to more often see the usage of terrorism and insurgencies in excess of what would be expected in other disputes, and the Mediterranean region is no exception (Wiegand 2010).

When non-state actors lack legitimacy, they also lack power, unless they use force to gain leverage (Jost and Major 2001). This is why political violence is attractive for non-state actors that perceive their status as discriminated against, banned or repressed. The result is often that violent non-state actors believe that the ends justify the means of violence. Even the worst acts of political violence can be perceived as justified if the ends are justified. This is particularly the case

> where a campaign of violence is successful in achieving its political objectives, perceptions of the campaign will tend to hinge on the legitimacy of the objectives rather than the means employed. Typically the winners will label the campaign a war, a liberation struggle, or a revolution, as they think appropriate, but will dwell more on the outcome than the process.
>
> *(Guelke 1995: 27)*

In situations when specific groups living in a state hold the government to be illegitimate as compared to the group's own principles, norms, values and practices, violence is often the means with which they pursue their own agenda. Thus, one perspective of these uses of terrorism and insurgencies might be that it is a violation of the legitimate social contract between the state and its people (Underwood 2007).

Insurgency and terrorism

When it comes to those that are labelled as terrorists or insurgents, they tend to be non-state actors that reject the laws, rules and morals of states and those in power, while in some cases, terrorist and insurgency groups seek specific changes to certain issues but do not reject the status quo political system (Wiegand 2010). Terrorism here is understood as generally unconventional violence that is pursued by non-state actors who are targeting non-combatants in order to achieve some type of political objective. Insurgency is similar, but mainly different regarding the targets, which are not non-combatants, but instead military or security forces that are representing the government.

Insurgency groups can also be referred to as guerrillas, militias, rebel movements or armed opposition groups, and if they also pursue the targeting of non-combatants, they can simultaneously be categorized as terrorist groups. Examples of these dual action groups are Hamas in Gaza and Hizballah in Lebanon (Wiegand 2010). Insurgents are often confused with terrorist groups, mainly because they too are non-state actors that use violence to achieve their political objectives. As a result, the terms terrorism and insurgency tend to sometimes be used interchangeably, mainly because they share many features, particularly the make-up of the groups as violent non-state actors, the means used and the objectives. Because terrorism and insurgency only refer to types of tactics, the same non-state actors can often be labelled as both terrorists and insurgents, the main distinction being only the type of target focused on at the time. For example, Hamas acts as a terrorist group when a suicide bomber blows up a bus of Israeli non-combatants, but it acts as an insurgency group when it targets IDF soldiers on posts in the West Bank. Therefore, insurgency and terrorism can sometimes overlap, meaning that some groups use both tactics and sometimes there is a grey area where it is difficult to define which tactic is being used.

Generally, both terrorists and insurgents are comprised of non-state actors who are not part of the state in any manner and are not condoned by the government. Terrorists are hard to identify, as they do not wear uniforms, they operate out of sight in underground cells, and they are far fewer in number than the militaries of states. Insurgency groups which conduct attacks on military targets, on the other hand, tend to be better organized, and are thus able to maintain a higher degree of public status, where terrorist organizations must operate underground to survive. An insurgent is generally comprised of a non-state actor 'with clear political objectives that contests a government's authority and legitimate monopoly on violence and uses force in order to reform, overthrow or secede from an existing state regime or control a specific geographical area' (de Zeeuw 2008: 4). The level of organization of insurgency groups varies extensively. Some groups are highly organized, well disciplined and centralized like Hamas and Hizballah, while other groups are more decentralized with scattered cell groupings such as factions of al-Qaeda and ISIS.

The most significant difference between terrorism and insurgency is who they each target. Insurgents mainly target combatants – militaries, security forces, or police, deliberately selected because of their role as security forces for the state. Unlike with insurgency, victims of terrorism are generally non-combatants, oftentimes referred to as civilians. Non-combatant status means they are not involved in combat and are bystanders in a war zone or regular citizens during peacetime. Another distinction between terrorism and insurgency is that targets of terrorism are mainly selected at random rather than being targeted for particular reasons. Overall though, most terrorism, including the terrorism conducted in the Mediterranean region, targets random people who are supposed to symbolize the suffering of greater society. Targets of terrorism are not the primary targets, but are instead targets of opportunity or representative or symbolic targets, serving as generators of a message (Schmid 1988).

When it comes to the means of conducting warfare, terrorists almost always use unconventional violence, while insurgents can use both conventional and unconventional methods. Further, insurgents are often well trained in the conduct of war, and use weapons similar to their professional military opponents, though these weapons are often obtained illegally. A key tactic of insurgency groups is to 'wear down governmental forces, while avoiding set-piece battles with the state's regular army units, since guerrilla groups are inferior in size to regular armies and poorly equipped compared to them' (Art and Richardson 2007: 8). Among the most common means that insurgents use in conducting attacks are roadside bombs against armed convoys, suicide bombings against government or military buildings, sniper attacks against soldiers and even random rocket attacks into otherwise secure military bases and outposts. Even when it comes to more conventional attacks, insurgents will often ambush their military opponents, attack at nightfall or other unexpected timeframes, and take advantage of friendly non-combatants to serve as suppliers, homes for insurgent forces and even using property like schools and hospitals as points from launching attacks against soldiers. One well known group that uses these tactics is Hamas, which is based in Gaza.

On the other hand, terrorist groups use suicide bombings, roadside bombings, beheadings and other brutal methods to gain attention for their objectives. Since the purpose of terrorist attacks is to surprise non-combatants to create fear and anxiety, most terrorist attacks occur during peacetime, not during wartime. Attacking when least expected is the typical strategy, though there are certainly times when terrorists attack non-combatants in the middle of a civil war, such as in Iraq or Syria. Like insurgents, rules of conventional war do not apply to terrorists since they are non-state actors, and therefore, they ignore norms and rules typical in the use of force pursued by conventional forces (Wiegand 2010).

All terrorist and insurgent groups by definition have political objectives, generally considered more important than the violence pursued. Indeed, terrorist attacks and targeted killings against both combatants and non-combatants are meant to be an intermediate step in attaining the attention for a greater grievance or demand by the group. Individuals who become terrorists generally maintain major grievances they wish to express to those they perceive as the cause. Such objectives for these groups might include the release of prisoners in an enemy state (Palestine, Lebanon), or outright independence under which the group of people they represent might attain recognized statehood (Hamas, PKK). Liberation movements tend to focus specifically on attaining independence or political autonomy, or at the very least desired changes in leadership, government or the regime in power itself. Also known as self-determination movements, these groups were relatively common in the colonial period, during which militias represented larger political movements that sought full independence from their colonial overlords.

The result of terrorism or insurgencies can be a shift in the type of the government or regime in the state. Typical examples of these cases have led to the end of long-term colonial regimes, such as when the British left Palestine or when the French left Algeria (Crenshaw 1983). That being said, outright changes in government or regime type as a result of these tactics by non-state groups is relatively rare, even when they are used over a long period in time. Indeed, the typical result is more minor changes, such as a simple redistribution in power within the targeted government. One example of this is the change that occurred after the civil war in Lebanon, 'as well as minor shifts in the balance of power between the terrorist challengers and the regime' (Crenshaw 1983: 8).

Islamist and nationalist terrorism and insurgency

There are three distinct types of terrorism and insurgency in the Mediterranean region – Islamist transnational, Islamist nationalist and secular nationalist (see Tables 16.1 and 16.2). Both types are non-state actors, they both use similar violent tactics, and their targets are both the same, whether non-combatants or combatants. The primary difference between these two types is their political objectives and more specifically, how practical or realistic their goals are (Wiegand 2012).

The first category, Islamist, is purely influenced by the religious ideology of radical Islam, which is transnational in nature. These transnational Islamic groups, also referred to as jihadist, *takiri* or *Salifiya* groups, do not necessarily act within one state's boundaries and their objectives are generally idealistic and purely ideological, such as the goal of ISIS – the creation and expansion of an Islamic caliphate and the destruction of sovereign states. The defining feature of this

Table 16.1 Terrorist groups in the Mediterranean region

Group name	*State*	*Years active*	*Islamist or nationalist*
Al-Qaeda in the Islamic Maghreb	Algeria	2007–present	Islamist
Ansar al-Sharia in Libya	Libya	2012–present	Islamist
Army of Islam (Gaza Strip)	Palestine	2006–present	Islamist
Fatah	Palestine	1959–present	Nationalist
Hamas	Palestine	1987–present	Islamist
Islamic Jihad Movement in Palestine	Palestine	1987–present	Islamist
Islamic State of Iraq and the Levant	many states	1999–present	Islamist
Izz ad-Din al-Qassam Brigades	Palestine	1993–present	Islamist
Libya Revolutionaries Operations Room	Libya	2013–present	Islamist
Libya Shield Force	Libya	2012–present	Islamist
Muslim Brotherhood	Egypt	1928–present	Islamist
Popular Resistance Committees	Palestine	2000–present	Islamist

Tabel 16.2 Insurgency groups in the Mediterranean region

Group name	*Country*	*Years active*	*Islamist/secular*
Ajnad al-Sham Islamic Union	Syria	2013–present	Islamist
Anti-Coup Alliance	Egypt	2013–present	Islamist
Army of Mujahedeen	Syria	2014–present	Islamist
Authenticity and Development Front	Syria	2012–present	Islamist
Brigade 93	Libya	2012–present	Nationalist
February 17th Martyrs Brigade	Libya	2012–present	Islamist
Free Syrian Army	Syria	2011–present	Nationalist
Islamic Front (Syria)	Syria	2013–present	Islamist
Jabhat al-Akrad	Syria	2013–present	Nationalist
Jabhat Ansar al-Din	Syria	2014–present	Islamist
Libya Shield 1	Libya	2012–present	Islamist
Muhajirin wa-Ansar Alliance	Syria	2014–present	Islamist
Muslim Brotherhood of Syria	Syria	1940–present	Islamist
People's Protection Units	Syria	2011–present	Nationalist
Rafallah al-Sahati Brigade	Libya	2011–present	Islamist
Shura Council of Benghazi Revolutionaries	Libya	2014–present	Islamist
Toubou Front for the Salvation of Libya	Libya	2007–2011 2012–present	Nationalist
Zintan Brigades	Libya	2011–present	Nationalist
Al-Qaeda	many states	1988–present	Islamist

type of group is that their objectives do not affect one state or political system, but instead, they maintain broader objectives related to the expansion of radical Islam, fighting against perceived heretics, apostates or those perceived as interfering in politics in states in the Islamic world (Wittes 2008). Because the objectives of transnational Islamic groups are not at all moderate or feasible in the view of most governments, these groups are truly outcasts who can play no actual role in working within the status quo political systems in the Mediterranean region. Al-Qaeda and its affiliates, and ISIS fit into this category of transnational Islamic terrorist groups.

The second type of terrorist and insurgency groups is nationalist and localized, and can be secular or still based on religious tenets. Most terrorist and insurgency groups in the region fall into the category of nationalist and religious. All of these groups focus on nationalist objectives within their state boundaries. Islamist nationalist groups include Hamas in Palestine, Shura Council of Benghazi Revolutionaries in Libya and the Islamic Front in Syria, all of whom are rooted in Islamic ideology, but also mainly limit their political objectives to influencing the politics within one state. This type of Islamist based violence is therefore as nationalist as it is religious.

A third type, which is not Islamic at all, is the secular group, which is much smaller in number in the Mediterranean region. These groups maintain strong nationalist objectives, also focusing on one particular political system, but they are not rooted in Islamist or other religious tenets. Nationalist groups in the region include Fatah in Palestine, Brigade 93 in Libya and the Free Syrian Army in Syria. Their objectives are generally more tangible and practical, such as improving rights for their nation or ethnic group, gaining more territorial autonomy or seeking sovereign territorial rights and political control. Another major distinction is the level of practicality of their political objects. Generally, these secular groups seek political goals that are actually attainable, unlike the political goals of transnational Islamic groups. Because of this status, nationalist groups have the ability to reform and transition into political parties, or at least maintain political branches of the organization, sometimes ceasing all violent action such as Muslim Brotherhood of Egypt.

There are several conditions that could make violence attractive and effective for terrorist and insurgency groups in the Mediterranean region. One perspective is that political violence is attractive as a strategy when non-violent strategies are ineffective or fail, a government is perceived as illegitimate, and violence is more appropriate to achieve goals such as inciting fear (Martin et al. 2008). Another general argument is that democratization provides greater opportunities for political participation of such groups, therefore making political violence less likely (Huntington 1968). By providing opportunities for political participation, this would prevent political groups from claiming exclusion. This exclusion or grievance displacement explanation focuses mainly on the lack of access that Islamist groups have. Non-state actors can turn to terrorism and insurgency because they feel excluded, and their use of violence 'depends to a large extent upon the access one has to the communication channels and institutions already available in any given society' (Crelinsten 1987: 419). Similarly, Burgat (1997) argues that such exclusion has driven some Islamist groups to turn to force and that given the circumstances of severe repression, political violence would be the best means to defend themselves and attempt to influence politics. Therefore, from this view, the use of political violence is a reaction to the political conditions in which such groups find themselves, not an inherent characteristic of Islamist groups. Hafez (2003) similarly argues that Muslims rebel due to institutional exclusion and indiscriminate repression by the state. Based simply on common sense, in these circumstances, Islamist groups do not have an option about whether to use non-violent political participation, meaning that their options for political influence are limited.

When radical Islamist groups are banned, such as in Egypt, Algeria and Tunisia, moving underground may be the only option available. In some circumstances, electoral laws may be designed to minimize the influence of radical Islamist parties, so that such partial inclusion does not really allow Islamist groups to actually have real political influence. A related problem for Islamist groups is that electoral politics frequently involves corruption, minimizing the probability of winning. Even when Islamist parties are able to gain political influence, they generally only receive minor ministries, are limited in pushing policies through parliamentary committees, and lack the ability to veto policies pushed by the majority parties (Sivan 2003).

Turning to violence as an alternative to political participation to get the attention of the government and influence the likelihood of shifting policies related to Islamic principles may be the best option. Specifically regarding terrorism, Crenshaw (1981: 384) asserts that the main catalyst for terrorist tactics is the lack of opportunity for political participation: 'where paths to the legal expression of opposition are blocked, but where the regime's repression is inefficient, revolutionary terrorism is doubly likely, as permissive and direct causes coincide'. Perhaps the best example of such violence due to severe repression and exclusion from the political system is the experience of the Islamic Salvation Front (FIS), which won the 1992 election in Algeria, only to be banned as a party and informed by the military that the election results were nullified. Fearing the potential power of the FIS, the military then proceeded to arrest and repress FIS members, directly provoking the FIS to turn to violence and use both terrorist tactics and insurgency against the military. The result was a civil war in Algeria that led to tens of thousands of deaths.

The exclusion or grievance displacement theory is useful to explain the strategy to use violence. One problem with the exclusion argument is that violent Islamist groups do not always target the governments that exclude them, targeting non-combatants through terrorism instead (Blom, Bucaille and Martinez 2007). Further, many radical Islamist groups use violence when they have not experienced exclusion or repression. In a study of Islamist terrorist groups,

Dalacoura (2006) found that state repression and exclusion were not generally related to Islamist terrorism. For example, Hamas actually increased its terrorist activity after the 1996 Palestinian election, an election in which Hamas leaders actually had an opportunity in which to participate, though they chose to not do so. Weinberg (1991) also found no evidence of state repression and exclusion from the political system leading to terrorism. Rather, elections can actually generate violent attacks (Rapoport and Weinberg 2001). The implication here is that even in democracies, fledgling democracies or states with elections that cannot really be considered democracies which are so common in the Mediterranean region, terrorism and insurgency are just as common.

Islamic State of Iraq and Syria

Perhaps no group has tried so hard to step into the limelight of international terrorist activity as the Islamic State of Iraq and Syria (ISIS), also variously known as the Islamic State of Iraq and the Levant (ISIL) and *Daesh* in Arabic, though since June 2014 the group has referred to itself as Islamic State (IS). ISIS is the most extreme of the Islamic terrorist and insurgency groups in the region. Proclaiming itself the only true Islamic caliphate under its caliph Abu Bakr al-Baghdadi, it claims authority over all Muslims worldwide, and has acted violently to enforce its version of Sharia law. When one examines efforts against the group, conventional counterterrorism strategies have clearly proven to be ineffective.

ISIS found its start under the label of *Jama'at al-Tawhud wal-Jihad* (The Organization of Monotheism and Jihad) in 1999 under Abu Musab al-Zarqawi (Weiss and Hassan 2015). Several years later in 2004, the group went on to pledge allegiance to al-Qaeda and Osama bin Laden, and changed the name of their group to Tanzin Qa'idat al-Jihad fi Bilad al-Rafidayn (The Organization of Jihad's Base in Mesopotamia), which became more commonly known as al-Qaeda in Iraq (AQI). Gaining notoriety as AQI, the group would go on in the coming years to merge with other terrorist groups, thereby increasing its reach and power. In 2006, they merged with several other Sunni groups and renamed themselves as the Mujahideen Shura Council (MSC).

Following the death of their leader al-Zarqawi in 2006, the MSC again merged with several other organizations to create the Islamic State of Iraq (ISI), though it was not until the death of al-Zarqawi's successors, Abu Omar al-Baghdadi and Abu Ayyub al-Masri, that the current leader who has made ISIS the preeminent terrorist organization in the world, Abu Bakr al-Baghdadi came to power (Weiss and Hassan 2015). Since expanding to Syria in 2013, and adopting the revised label of ISIS, the organization pushed back both rebel and government forces in Syria. Worse, since 2015, ISIS's control over vast territories in Syria has resulted in forcing a population of between 2 and 8 million people to adhere to their ideals of Islam.

Since the start of their struggle to seize control of the Muslim world, ISIS has followed a number of clearly articulated goals. Their primary objective is the restoration of the Sunni Islamic caliphate of early Islam, wherein they revive the original Wahhabi project of the restoration of the caliphate governed by strict Salafist doctrine, which will eventually spread to all corners of the Earth. Under this objective, all innovations in religion since those days are rejected, and those who follow secular law are condemned as disbelievers, and so a major priority of ISIS is to purify Islamic society. Ultimately, they hold with the belief of the final day of judgment by God being near, which will be heralded by the arrival of one Imam Mahdi, and that they will defeat an army of Rome at the town of Dabiq in fulfillment of this prophecy.

Since its ascendance to the world stage, ISIS has conducted terrorist attacks outside Syria and Iraq in several Mediterranean states. In Tunisia, ISIS forces have previously infiltrated the country to carry out attacks against security forces, likely taking advantage of the continued upheaval in neighboring Libya. Further, attacks have been directed against foreign tourists, though the forces of ISIS in the country are not yet strong enough to take and hold territory of their own. In Libya itself, ISIS has divided their claims in the country into three provinces: Cyrenaica in the east, Fezzan to the south and Tripolitania in the west. Forces in Libya affiliated with ISIS have been the most successful outside the main branches in Iraq and Syria, particularly around Derna and the former dictator Gaddafi's hometown of Sirte. In 2014, a large portion of the Egyptian group Ansar Bait al-Maqdis swore loyalty to ISIS, with the result that the Sinai province of ISIS was created. The most notable attack that they have claimed to have perpetrated was the bombing that took down Russia Metrojet Flight 9268, which claimed 224 lives in 2015.

Perhaps the most startling attacks were those that occurred in Paris in November 2015 the Brussels bombing of 2016 and the wedding bombing in Turkey in the summer of 2016. As it currently stands, ISIS continues to operate despite widespread opposition from states around the world. Getting support in the form of finances from the occupation of territory, kidnappings for ransom, donations from Saudi Arabia and other Gulf states, material support brought in by foreign fighters enlisting with the cause, and fundraising through modern communication networks, it is entirely likely that ISIS will remain a threat for some time to come.

Hamas and Hizballah

Hamas is a nationalist movement rooted in religious ideology, operating within the context of the Palestinian–Israeli conflict, based on a major disagreement between the Palestinians and the government of Israel about the existence of a Palestinian state, the boundaries of the Palestinian West Bank and Gaza Strip, the status of Jerusalem, the right of return of Palestinian refugees and reparations for Palestinian refugees. Hamas – *Harakat al-Muqawama al-Islamiya* (Islamic Resistance Movement) – was founded in 1987 as a militant outgrowth of the non-violent Palestinian Muslim Brotherhood by Sheikh Ahmad Yassin and his followers, who believed violence was an effective means to challenge Israel in the intifada. Within a few years of its creation, Hamas had surpassed the Brotherhood as the more influential Islamist political movement in the Palestinian territories. By the early 1990s, the leadership of Hamas restructured the organization, creating three separate wings – political, social and resistance, resulting in the creation in 1991–2 of the militant Izz al-Din al-Qassam Brigades. The al-Qassam Brigades are estimated to have about 1,000 active members (Council on Foreign Relations 2009).

Overall, Hamas's objectives can be considered a combination of Islamist ideology and nationalism. The group's original objectives were to liberate and 'Islamicize' Palestine, better known in rhetoric as the dismantling of the state of Israel. In its 1988 charter, Hamas leaders declared that 'It [Palestine], or any part of it, should not be squandered: it, or any part of it, should not be given up' (Covenant of the Islamic Resistance Movement 1988). Though the charter has not been amended, in recent years, leaders have indicated willingness to accept the state of Israel with pre-1967 borders (Hroub 2006: 20). Other objectives cited in its charter are prevailing justice for oppressed people and the spread of Islam.

At its founding, Hamas did not pursue terrorist tactics, only becoming more radical as the intifada wore on and the Oslo peace accords failed to decrease Israeli settlements in the West Bank and Gaza Strip, and Israeli military occupation, closures, checkpoints, curfews and other limitations on rights of Palestinians were increased. Hamas's military wing, Izz al-Din al-Qassam Brigades, has used several different violent tactics, including insurgency attacks on the Israeli army, attacks on Israeli settlers, suicide bombings within Israel against non-combatants, uprisings and rocket strikes on Israeli villages.

Hamas is not only a militant terrorist group, but also a political, cultural and social grass-roots organization (Hroub 2006: 19). Hamas provides significant social services to its constituents, ranging from sports clubs to schools and hospitals. Its political wing, known as National Islamic Salvation Party, also referred to as Change and Reform, put up candidates for the first time in the 2006 Palestinian legislative elections. Hamas won the election with 44.5 per cent of the vote compared to Fatah's 41.4 per cent, providing it with just over the majority of seats in the legislature (Central Elections Commission, 2006), and therefore, control of the Palestinian government. Infighting among Palestinian factions throughout 2007 led to a political crisis and what some refer to as a Palestinian civil war in which Hamas took control of the Gaza Strip in June 2007. Since then, the government has been split and Hamas continues to demand political reform before it will again cooperate with other Palestinian factions, mainly the secular party Fatah. Fatah refuses to recognize Hamas's rule of Gaza Strip, although Hamas continues to act as the governing body in Gaza. In 2014, the Israeli military and Hamas fought fierce battles that resulted in the deaths of more than 1,000 Palestinians, and recently in 2016, Hamas has retaliated against Israeli air strikes by striking Israeli forces with mortars.

Hizballah, which means Party of God, is comprised of Lebanese Shi'a Muslims, most of whom have been marginalized in Lebanese society, even though they account for more than a third of the population. Most members of Hizballah tend to come from the urban underclass, who initially founded Shi'a social and political movements in defence of the 'downtrodden masses'. The group is a powerful political entity in Lebanon, backed by Syria and Iran, a supporter of Palestinian political violence, and an influential player in Lebanese politics. Since the early 1980s, when Hizballah was founded as a Shi'a militia during the Lebanese civil war, the group has pursued a steadfast objective of destabilizing the state of Israel. With this objective in mind, Hizballah has actively challenged the Israeli military, the Israeli Defense Forces (IDF), both in Lebanon and Israel, for more than two decades, leading to the 34 day Lebanon War fought between Hizballah and Israel in the summer of 2006. Prior to this war, Hizballah conducted numerous armed attacks on the Israeli military along the disputed Lebanese–Israeli border.

Hizballah has achieved many of its stated objectives, all through terrorism and insurgency attacks on military personnel. The US government withdrew troops from Lebanon in the spring of 1984 after the 1983 US Embassy and Marine Forces bombings. Israel withdrew its troops from occupying south Lebanon in May 2000 after years of militant pressure by Hizballah. Hizballah has been able to incorporate Islamic principles into the Lebanese political system by achieving political representation in the Lebanese parliament, and they have improved the lives of Lebanese Shi'a. Hizballah has shifted from a terrorist group itself to a sponsor of terrorism, spreading the 'Hizballah model' to groups including Hamas, Islamic Jihad and other Palestinian extremist groups. Sponsorship and support involves guerrilla-style combat training, tactical training on the building and use of bombs and mines and funding. Throughout the 1990s, Hizballah's members transformed themselves into an efficient insurgency group with several hundred well trained soldiers, known as Islamic Resistance (*al-muqawamah al-Islamiya*) fighters who maintained a large arsenal of weapons provided primarily by Iran, funnelled through Syria. By the early 1990s, Hizballah had become an elite, highly skilled militia. From 1992 to 2000, Hizballah's armed wing primarily fought Israeli ground troops in the occupied area of south Lebanon and launched rocket attacks into northern Israel, claiming to be in retaliation for Israeli attacks in Lebanon. Since 2000, the government continued to allow Hizballah to actively engage with the Israeli military, including the 2006 war, over a small disputed territory, Shebaa Farms. Today, Hizballah devotes most of its efforts to being an active member of the recently reformed Lebanese government, though it still maintains arms. It is an active and key political party in the March 8 Alliance of opposition parties, with members in the parliament and cabinet. In the most recent election, the March 8 Alliance won 47 per cent of the seats in the parliament, indicating that Hizballah and its allies have a significant influence on Lebanese politics.

Conclusions

Islamic terrorism and insurgency have been exceedingly common in the Mediterranean region since the latter twentieth century. Despite accusations that Islam is a violent religion, this is not the reason, but it is instead because several radical and extremist Islamic groups have chosen violence as a means to achieve their political and religious objectives. Though less common, secular groups have also pursued political violence in the region, mainly and most recently as participants in the civil wars of Libya and Syria. Though it is impossible to eliminate all forms of terrorism and insurgency in the region, it is possible to work toward managing such violence and preventing further uses of force. A useful place to start for policy makers is to more carefully recognize the differences between terrorism and insurgency, and the differences between Islamic transnational groups, Islamic nationalist groups and non-Islamic nationalist groups. Attempting to pursue conflict management with al-Qaeda or ISIS is a difficult, if not impossible task due to the transnational character of the groups, their intangible objectives and their unwillingness to negotiate. Yet nationalist groups, whether Islamic or not, tend to have more moderate objectives and though they pursue violence, there is the potential for reformation into non-violent political parties, as demonstrated by groups such as the Muslim Brotherhood in Egypt, the Palestine Liberation Organization and the FLN in Algeria. Working with nationalist terrorist groups like Hamas is feasible as past ceasefires and political negotiations have demonstrated, despite returns to violence.

Although states in the Mediterranean region are rife with terrorism and insurgency, this does not mean that such political violence is inevitable, nor unmanageable. With different strategies, governments inside and outside the region can work to prevent future conflicts and non-state actors' involvements in such conflicts, as well as considering compromise and negotiations. This is a long-term problem in the region and without more unified agreement by governments in the region, such violence will continue. Fortunately, in recent years there have been strong attempts to collaborate counterterrorism and counterinsurgency movements, as well as talking with nationalist groups, both secular and Islamic.

Bibliography

Art, Robert J. and Louise Richardson. (2007). *Democracy and Counterterrorism: Lessons from the Past.* US Institute of Peace Press.

Blom, Amelie, Laetitia Bucaille and Luis Martinez. (2007). *The Enigma of Islamist Violence.* Columbia University Press.

Burgat, F. (1997). Ballot boxes, militaries, and Islamic movements, in *The Islamism Debate*, edited by M. Kramer. Tel Aviv: Moshe Dayan Center for Middle Eastern and African Studies, pp. 35–50.

Central Elections Commission, Palestine. (2006). The final results of the second PLC Elections. Retrieved on July 30, 2009 from http://www.elections.ps/template.aspx?id=291.

Council on Foreign Relations. (2009). Backgrounder: Hamas. Retrieved on September 18, 2009 from http://www.cfr.org/publication/8968/.

Covenant of the Islamic Resistance Movement. (1988). Hamas Covenant 1988. Retrieved on July 5, 2009 from http://avalon.law.yale.edu/20th_century/hamas.asp.

Crelinsten, R. D. (1987). Power and meaning: terrorism as a struggle over access to the communication structure, in *Contemporary Research on Terrorism*, edited by P. Wilkinson. Aberdeen: Aberdeen University Press, pp. 419–50.

Crenshaw, M. (1981). The causes of terrorism. *Comparative Politics* 13(4): 379–99.

Crenshaw, M. (1983). Introduction: reflections on the effects of terrorism, in *Terrorism, Legitimacy, and Power: The Consequences of Political Violence*, edited by M. Crenshaw. Middletown, CT: Wesleyan University Press, pp. 1–37.

Dalacoura, K. (2006). Islamist terrorism and the Middle East democratic deficit: political exclusion, repression, and the causes of extremism. *Democratization* 13(3), 508–25.

de Zeeuw, J. (2008). *From Soldiers to Politicians: Transforming Rebel Movements after Civil War*. Boulder: Lynne Rienner Publishers.

Guelke, A. (1995). *The Age of Terrorism and the International System*. New York: I. B. Tauris Publishers.

Hafez, M. M. (2003). *Why Muslims Rebel: Repression and Resistance in the Islamic World*. Lynne Rienner Publishers.

Honderich, Ted. (1976). *Political Violence: A Philosophical Analysis of Terrorism*. Cornell University Press.

Hroub, K. (2006). *Hamas: A Beginner's Guide*. Ann Arbor: Pluto Press.

Huntington, S. (1968). *Political Order in Changing Societies*. New Haven, CT: Yale University Press.

Huth, P. K. (1996). Enduring rivalries and territorial disputes, 1950–1990. *Conflict Management and Peace Science* 15(1): 7–41.

Jost, J. T. and B. Major. (2001). *The Psychology of Legitimacy: Emerging Perspectives on Ideology, Justice, and Intergroup Relations*. Cambridge University Press.

Kydd, A. and B. F. Walter. (2002). Sabotaging the peace: the politics of extremist violence. *International Organization* 56(2): 263–96.

Martin, Susanne, Ami Pedahzur, Aria Perliger and Leonard Weinberg. (2008). Choosing Violence or Nonviolence: Attractiveness and Unattractiveness in Strategic Decision-Making, paper presented at Annual National Conference of the Midwest Political Science Association in Chicago, IL, April 5.

Neumann, P. (2005). The bullet and the ballot box: the case of the IRA. *The Journal of Strategic Studies* 28(6): 941–75.

Rapoport, D. and L. Weinberg. (2001). *The Democratic Experience and Political Violence*. Portland, OR: Frank Cass.

Schmid, A. (1988). Terrorism and related concepts, in *Political Terrorism: A New Guide to Actors, Authors, Concepts, Databases, Theories, and Literature*, edited by A. P. Schmid and A. J. Jongman. New Brunswick: Transaction Books, pp. 1–38.

Sivan, E. (2003). Why radical Muslims aren't taking over governments, in *Revolutionaries and Reformers: Contemporary Islamist Movements in the Middle East* edited by Barry Rubin. Albany: State University of New York, pp. 1–9.

Underwood, L. (2007). *Terror by Consent: The Modern State and the Breach of the Social Contract*. New York: Peter Lang Publishers.

Weinberg, L. (1991). Turning to terror: the conditions under which political parties turn to terrorist activities. *Comparative Politics* 23(4): 423–38.

Weiss, M. and H. Hassan. (2015). *ISIS: Inside the Army of Terror*. New York, NY: Regan Arts Press.

Wiegand, K. E. (2010). *Bombs and Ballots: Governance by Islamic Terrorist and Guerrilla Groups*. Burlington, VT: Routledge.

Wiegand, K. E. (2012). Religiously motivated violence in the Middle East, in *The Middle East: Its History and Culture* edited by Jason Tatlock. College Park, MD: University of Maryland Press.

Wittes, T. C. (2008). *Freedom's Unsteady March: America's Role in Building Arab Democracy*. Washington, DC: Brookings Institution Press.

17

DO REGIONAL ORGANIZATIONS CONTRIBUTE TO SECURITY?

Perspectives on Euro-Mediterranean cooperation

Niklas Bremberg

Introduction

Seen from the perspective of international security, the Mediterranean region paints an ambiguous picture. On the one hand, none of the regional powers have waged large-scale conventional wars against each other since the 1973 Yom Kippur war. On the other hand, few observers would probably dare to characterize the region as peaceful since the Arab–Israeli conflict is still unresolved and various 'frozen conflicts', such as Cyprus–Turkey and Morocco–Algeria–Western Sahara, heavily affect regional security dynamics. While the northern Mediterranean can nowadays be characterized as forming a security community resting on tightly integrated and peaceful inter-state relations (Deutsch et al. 1957, Adler and Barnett 1998), the southern Mediterranean is beleaguered by growing instability in the wake of the Arab uprisings with the devastating civil war in Syria as the most tragic example to date. The Mediterranean region as a whole is moreover affected by a host of non-military threats and trans-boundary risks such as international terrorism, failed states as well as man-made and natural disasters, but thus far region-level cooperation to counter these challenges seems to be lacking. Although not necessarily a security challenge *per se* the refugee crisis as of 2015 adds yet another item to the list of issues that call for enhanced cooperation among states in the Mediterranean region.

In the light of these circumstances, this chapter addresses the questions of why, how and under what conditions regional organizations, such as the European Union (EU), contribute to security in the Mediterranean. Indeed, the international community's inability to reach an agreement on Syria due to the persisting conflict between the US and its western allies, and Russia and its allies in the Middle East, might prompt us to answer such questions squarely with 'no, they do not'. However, here the questions are posed in order to theoretically discuss the conditions under which such organizations would be successful in promoting security as well as explore the changing meaning and practice of security in international politics. Drawing upon insights from established perspectives and innovative approaches to international relations (IR), highlighting the limits and possibilities of security cooperation, this chapter seeks to put the question of the EU's role in Mediterranean security in a new light. The EU is of special interest since it can be understood as functioning as a security community-building institution.

Perspectives on Euro-Mediterranean security

The question on how to achieve security, often understood as explaining and understanding the causes of war among states and the possibility of inter-state peace, has fundamentally shaped IR as an academic discipline (Schmidt 2002). Indeed, to realist and liberal scholars alike, inter-state war has long been the 'acknowledged problem, to be both explained and overcome' (Holsti 1985: 17). However, what usually sets apart the proponents of realism and liberalism IR – the two dominant perspectives – is how they conceive of the nature and possibility of cooperation and conflict under conditions of international anarchy.

A basic assumption of realist thinking in IR is that states must always strive to ensure their survival, and that balance of power is an inescapable outcome under conditions of international anarchy.[1] Kenneth Waltz eloquently argued that 'if there is any distinctively political theory of international politics, balance-of-power is it' (Waltz 1979: 117). Indeed, cooperation on security in the guise of inter-state alliances are understood as a key mechanism of balance of power but even the most institutionalized alliance is in the end an intrinsically unstable arrangement that will wither away as soon as the underlying conditions turn unfavourable (Walt 1987; Mearsheimer 2001). Weaker states might engage in 'band-wagoning' with stronger ones for the sake of survival but this kind of cooperation often attempts at balancing some other state from becoming too threatening (Kaufman et al. 2007). International organizations are thus thought to ultimately reflect underlying power relations among the most powerful states. The hegemonic stability theory suggests that the political and economic order necessary for the emergence of international organizations is provided by the most powerful state around, i.e. the hegemon. The hegemon performs several functions as to the maintenance of the order, not for the sake of order as such, but because it maintains the position of the hegemon *qua* hegemon.[2]

Realists would explain security cooperation in the Mediterranean during the Cold War as determined by the US interest in keeping international trade routes open and containing Soviet influence in the region, together with the European powers' (mainly France and the UK) interests in retaining influence over former colonies in North Africa and the Middle East. Adrian Hyde-Price furthermore asserts that 'the structural arrangements of balanced multipolarity . . . shapes and shoves the post-Cold War European security system' (Hyde-Price 2007: 5). The EU can at best aspire to pursue 'milieu-shaping goals' aiming at stabilizing the southern Mediterranean, goals which in turn are set up and defined by the most powerful member states to meet their national interests (ibid.: 107–16). In a realist reading this helps explain why little progress has been achieved when it comes to the security-related aspects of Euro-Mediterranean cooperation since the 1990s, and even though security issues figure much more prominently in the latest revisions of the EU's flagship initiative towards the region – the European Neighbourhood Policy (European Commission 2015) – we should perhaps not expect too much to happen on that front.

Liberalism, especially its institutionalist strand, answers the questions on why, how and under what conditions international frameworks contribute to security differently from realism.[3] This is first and foremost because it relaxes a realist core assumption, namely that states must always care more about relative gains than absolute gains from international cooperation in order to assure survival. State–society relations, i.e. the relationship of states to the domestic and transnational social context in which they are embedded, are thought to be more important to explain state behaviour rather than state–state relations (Moravcsik 1997). Multiple channels connect states and societies ranging from informal governmental ties, multinational corporations and organizations. Hence, there are more possibilities for inter-state cooperation under international anarchy than realism admits, and the configuration of state preferences through societal ideas, interests and institutions matters as much, or more, than international power structures.[4]

Already in the 1970s, Robert Keohane and Jospeh Nye observed that 'Security, in traditional terms, is not likely to be the principal issue facing governments. Insofar as military force is ineffective on certain issues, the conventional notion of power lacks precision' (Keohane and Nye 1977: 8). This notion underlies the theory of complex interdependence which posits that the level of transgovernmental and transnational ties between states and societies determines conflict and cooperation in the international system (ibid.). International organizations are here understood to function as devices that states create in order to enhance the gains from cooperation, and even though powerful states might often play an important role when these organizations are first created they need not be essential for their functioning and development over time (Keohane and Martin 1995).

Moreover, the transformative power of economic interdependence is often put in the forefront by liberal scholars. In a Euro-Mediterranean context it is typically suggested that 'the single most powerful policy instrument for promoting peace and security . . . is the ultimate in market access: admission to or association with the EU trading bloc' (Moravcsik 2003: 85). Based on the argument that state–society relations set preferences which shape state behaviour, Euro-Mediterranean security cooperation would be facilitated by changes in domestic preferences favouring economic growth and prosperity rather than balance of power and sovereignty.[5] However, entrenched interests among societal actors within many EU member states, together with poor governance capacities and non-inclusive political structures in many countries in the southern Mediterranean have hampered the potential effects of economic integration envisioned in the Euro-Mediterranean Association Agreements crafted during the 1990s (Pierros et al. 1999; Dawson 2009).

Constructivism in IR tackles the questions on why, how and under what conditions international frameworks contribute to security quite differently from both realism and liberalism. Not necessarily a distinct theory of international politics, more of a social theory, constructivism has gradually made it into the mainstream of IR, and various constructivist approaches have been developed since the 1980s.[6] What distinguishes constructivist approaches from realist and liberal ones is the explicit recognition of the 'social construction of knowledge and the construction of social reality' (Adler 2002: 95). This carries both ontological and epistemological consequences which lay the foundation for a distinct constructivist style of scientific reasoning (cf. Searle 1995).

Alexander Wendt early on made a remark that has come to serve as a central tenant of constructivism in IR; namely that 'anarchy is what states make of it' (Wendt 1992). For example, purely structural and materialist conceptions of international politics have a hard time explaining why US military power is threatening to Cuba but not to Canada. Moreover, realist accounts at the end of the Cold War soon predicted a return of balance of power practices in Europe and the disintegration of NATO once the external threat of the Soviet Union had vanished (Waltz 1993). Instead, both NATO and the EU expanded. From a constructivist perspective, the fundamental lesson here is that the distribution of power may always affect states' calculations 'but *how* it does so depends on the intersubjective understandings and expectations, on the "distribution of knowledge," that constitute their conceptions of self and other' (Wendt 1992: 397, emphasis added). Moreover, shared convictions and social practices confront actors as social facts, even though they are not external to actors seen collectively. To put it differently, the 'building blocks of international reality are ideational as well as material' (Ruggie 1998: 879).

What do constructivist insights bring to the questions on why, how and under what conditions international frameworks contribute to security? Emanuel Adler and Beverly Crawford have suggested that the EU since the end of the Cold War has promoted a region-building process in the Mediterranean, or rather 'the invention of a region that does not yet exist [and] the social engineering of a regional identity that rests, neither on blood nor on religion, but on civil society voluntary networks and civic beliefs' (Adler and Crawford 2006: 19).[7] The long-term aim would be to construct in the Mediterranean region a pluralistic security community, although in the short and middle term the aim was to achieve a less ambitious regional security partnership (ibid., see also Volpi 2004). The means to achieve this aim were, for example, creation of multilateral partnerships, transnational security dialogues and consultations around a focal point (e.g. the Mediterranean) to a large extent embodied in the Euro-Mediterranean Partnership (EMP) (see also Adler and Greve 2009). However, this meant that the EU drew heavily on a repertoire of security practices developed in Europe during the Cold War (i.e. the CSCE/OSCE model), without necessarily adapting it to local circumstances in the southern Mediterranean (Bicchi 2006). Adler moreover suggests that the EU is failing to promote security community-building in the Mediterranean because 'a majority of Muslims have no or little ground for identification and negotiating meanings with Westerners; thus no learning can take place' (Adler 2008: 215). Although the statement might be questioned on empirical grounds, it holds the merit of showing that constructivist insights do not only lend themselves to benign notions of progress and change in international politics.

The changing meaning and practice of security

What do we make of this theoretical discussion on international security? First of all, it might be useful to take a step back and ask what we mean by security. In its simplest conceptual form, security can be said to deal with existential threats to a given community. In the twentieth century and especially in the period after the Second World War, societal survival was mostly equated with securing the territorial integrity of the nation-state by military means against the threat of foreign invasion.[8] The perceived threat of inter-state war not only performed an order-creating and order-sustaining function in Euro-Mediterranean region; it also lent a particularly strong military connotation to the concept of security as such. However, what happens to states' security policies when ingrained connotations of territorial defence and military deterrence are challenged by the acknowledgement of an increasing number of non-military threats and trans-boundary risks (such as e.g. international terrorism, pandemics, climate change, failed states) (cf. Vedby Rasmussen 2006)?

In a by now well-established conceptualization, fixating the meaning of security at any given time is described as 'securitization'. The concept is meant to capture a process through which an intersubjective understanding within a political community is construed, so as to treat something as an existential threat to a valued referent object, while moving the issue at hand from normal politics through enabling calls for urgent and exceptional measures (Buzan et al. 1998).[9] Securitization can be said to have pinned down the 'grammatology' of security. As such, it holds the merit of directing analytical focus on threat construction, instead of deductively trying to establish what security actually 'is' or essentially 'means' (cf. Baldwin 1997). Stressing the social construction of threats is to reiterate the almost tautological – but still important – insight that no security threat presents itself as such by itself. It has to be interpreted and intersubjectively understood within a political community as being a threat.

The concept of securitization has been widely used to show how the southern Mediterranean has been construed as a region of instability by the EU and many of its member states (see among others Malmvig 2005; Haddadi 2006). At the end of the Cold War, European diplomats and EU officials had started to depict the geographical proximity and the 'closeness of all types of relations' between EU member states and non-members in the Mediterranean as something that made the stability and prosperity of Europe ultimately dependent on the stability and prosperity [illegible] 2007). The European Commission even stated that [illegible] roadest sense' (European Commission 1990: 2). While [illegible] in the US, those attacks are often described as having [illegible] region even further towards strengthening counter- [illegible] and away from other goals such as democracy promotion [illegible] Wolff 2012).

[illegible] uthern Mediterranean might at first sight suggest that [illegible] regional organizations such as the EU to promote secu- [illegible] ant finding in the constructivist literature on security [illegible] ization might be a means for security communities to [illegible] lusion of its periphery (Acharya 2001). But if we as [illegible] presentations of security threats we might not capture [illegible] ore, the concept of securitization has been duly criticized [illegible] exceptional aspects of security practices (Williams 2003). Focusing exclusively on urgent measures as being the prime indicator of ongoing security dynamics runs the risk of losing sight of more low-key and routine-based security practices that nonetheless are important for the formation of intersubjective understandings of what constitute a security threat and, more importantly, *how* to deal with it.

In line with insights derived from practice approaches in social sciences we rather need to focus on the 'praxeology' of security in order to better understand why, how and under what conditions international frameworks contribute to security.[10] This is because the meaning of security cannot primarily be established deictically but rather by becoming aware of the pragmatic context and social practices in which actors are embedded (Kratochwil 2011). But focusing analytically on practices is not simply to stress the difference between ideas and behaviour. Practices should rather be understood as meaningful patterns of socially recognized activity (Bicchi and Bremberg 2016). As such 'practices are general classes of action, which although situated in social context, are not limited to any specific enacting' (Adler and Pouliot 2011: 5). Practices are not outside of or apart from discourses, and unlike habits, they can be learned from others and can be performed well or badly, and correctly or incorrectly (ibid.). Drawing upon Pierre Bourdieu's work, Vincent Pouliot suggests that the social power of practices relies on the establishment of ways-of-doing-things that appear self-evident. Indeed, the 'order of things is established through the iterated practices performed by capital-endowed agents, because their doing something in a certain way makes the implicit but powerful claim that "this is how things are"' (Pouliot 2008: 282).

Building on this notion of practice, Adler and Pouliot argue that security communities should be seen as constituting communities of practice defined as 'like-minded groups of practitioners who are informally as well as contextually bound by a shared interest in learning and applying a common practice' (Adler 2008: 196). Hence, states form security communities to the extent that the people representing them practise self-restraint on a daily basis so that conflicts are handled through compromises, and 'peace exists in and through practice when security officials' practical sense makes diplomacy the self-evident way to solving interstate disputes' (Pouliot 2008: 279). Understanding security communities as communities of practice also provides substance to constructivist explanations as to how security communities expand through processes of socialization, although it should be noted that 'socialization, learning, and persuasion follow rather than precede practice: at best, they co-evolve' (Adler and Pouliot 2011: 23). For example, NATO's eastward expansion can be explained by its adoption of cooperative security practices (Adler 2008). This also gives us clues as to how to conceive of the EU in relation to the questions on how, why and under what conditions international frameworks might contribute to security in a Euro-Mediterranean setting.

The EU as a security community-building institution in the Mediterranean

The popular uprisings in North Africa and the Middle East in 2011 and the subsequent breakdown of the incumbent order in the southern Mediterranean have not only put into question previously held understandings about regional stability but also the EU's relations with countries in the region. Political transition in Tunisia, modest reforms in Morocco, instability in Libya, the re-establishment of military rule in Egypt, civil war in Syria, the emergence of ISIS and the ongoing refugee crisis, present the EU with several challenges and apparently few opportunities. The predominant notion among practitioners and academics seems to be that if the Arab uprisings have revealed anything it would be the extent to which the EU is unable to shape events in the southern Mediterranean (e.g. Balfour 2011; Peters 2012).[11]

There are several suggestions as to what explains the EU's inability, ranging from deadlock between EU institutions, post-colonial prejudices, cognitive uncertainty and past practices shaping current responses (Tömmel 2013; Pace 2014; Del Sarto 2015; Natorski 2015; Bremberg 2016b). These accounts can be said to be more or less in line with institutionalist and constructivist insights in IR but there are analyses that draw on realism as well. For example, Assem Dandashly argues that the EU has sought to tailor its policies and instruments in the wake of the Arab uprisings primarily in order to promote security for the EU and its member states, in line with realist expectations (Dandashly 2015: 53). Scholars have also noted that the recent EU Global Strategy from 2016, to a higher degree than its predecessors, emphasizes the need for democratic reforms as a means to build resilient societies in the southern Mediterranean (EEAS 2016). Authoritarian regimes are seen as inherently unstable and a threat not only to their citizens but also to the EU, and this way of framing the need for reforms 'hints at the securitization of (the lack of) democracy in the region' (Bremberg and Britz forthcoming).

However, a recent study on security cooperation in the western Mediterranean from the end of the Cold War and until the Arab uprisings suggests a somewhat different understanding of the EU's role in the region (Bremberg 2015, 2016a). Even though the study does not cover the most recent developments it presents a number of theoretical insights that are highly useful in relation to the questions of why, how and under what conditions the EU can be said to contribute to security in the Mediterranean. The study suggests that the EU functions as a *security community-building institution* in that it provides cooperative frameworks that otherwise would not have been available, and that especially Spanish and Moroccan diplomats and officials have become increasingly embedded in them. The findings shed new light on how collective identity, power and cooperative practices relate to Euro-Mediterranean security.

First, in relation to collective identity, the study shows that the role that the EU plays in Spanish–Moroccan relations is of course dominated by, but certainly not limited to, the gravitational force of the internal market (cf. Moravcsik 2003). Importantly, this structural power is translated into a process in which habits of consultation are fostered (Bremberg 2016a: 52–5). That Spain and Morocco are involved in an increasing number of EU policy areas has served to lessen bilateral tensions on a range of contentious issues (e.g. trade and migration), although territorial disputes are left unresolved and are even seen as a latent source of distrust and conflict on both sides of the Strait of Gibraltar (see also Gillespie 2006). The findings suggest that practice precedes identity, and perhaps more interestingly, practices usually identified with tightly coupled security communities (e.g. reciprocity and self-restraint) might actually develop under conditions when the collective identity among a given set of states is weak or even absent, provided that there are already established venues for cooperation together with cooperative practices that can be emulated in new settings (see also Bremberg and Rieker 2016).

This potentially carries theoretical implications because it implies that collective identities should not necessarily be seen as a precondition for the spread of cooperative security practices. The EU has, ever since the 1990s, been promoting a Euro-Mediterranean region-building exercise with admittedly few successes. But it seems strange to argue that this failure is primarily due to a lack of a collective identity in the Mediterranean (cf. Adler 2008). The emergence of a collective identity that would embed various national, ethnic and religious identities in the region would be the result of a long and necessarily multifaceted process. It cannot be the precondition for the process to start. Even more important, there seems to be no good reason to assume that such an identity, if it ever would emerge, would have to be stronger than a common European identity. According to Jeffrey Checkel and Peter Katzenstein what actually characterizes the European security community is a relatively thin conception of collective identity that is lacking in emotional strength, to the extent that 'Europeans have made peace in . . . a community of strangers' (Checkel and Katzenstein 2009: 12).

Second, in relation to power, there seems to be consensus among a majority of states in the western Mediterranean on the goal of protecting people, property and the environment in the Mediterranean from natural and man-made disasters (Bremberg 2016a: 107–16). Of course, this can be seen as mainly reflecting convergence of political discourse, but there are numerous examples of practical cooperation taking place in the field of civil protection.[12] Regional cooperation in the Mediterranean as a whole has benefited from the creation of EU instruments such as the Union Civil Protection Mechanism. Instruments such as these do not only serve as a means for EU member states to assist each other, they are also increasingly important as tools to involve non-members. Importantly, they provide a social venue in which capital-endowed agents iteratively are doing things in a certain way (cf. Pouliot 2010). The EU supports a regional network-based community in the field of civil protection that builds upon, as well as transcends, already existing bilateral relations. This is important in relation to the overarching questions of this chapter since it indicates that a nascent community of practice is taking shape in the western Mediterranean, fostered by a shared interest in learning and practising civil protection.

Such communities might perform important, yet often poorly understood, functions in international security, in that they transcend national boundaries and bring together practitioners from various states on a regular basis. Indeed, this would not contradict the notion that security cooperation emerges around economically and politically powerful actors (cf. Hyde-Price 2007). But it shows that power, in terms of military capacity or economic strength, does not explain the outcome of the interactions in the multilateral venues and transgovernmental networks identified here. If we were to characterize the EU as a hegemon, its power seems to rest primarily in its capacity to continually provide funding and institutional 'hard-ware' for multilateral frameworks for cooperation.

Third, in relation to cooperative practices, the absence of conventional military threats to Spain has meant that the Spanish armed forces' role has expanded from having a primary focus on territorial defence to instead focusing on crisis management in order to enhance the Spanish state's capacity to handle such security threats as international terrorism and natural disasters (Bremberg 2016a: 70–9). Spain actively seeks to promote military cooperation outside of the EU, especially in the western Mediterranean and in the so called 5+5 framework, since it is seen as a means to also secure Spain. Morocco, so far, is the only Arab country to have participated in an EU-led operation under the Common Security and Defence Policy (CSDP) (i.e. EUFOR Althea in Bosnia) and the Moroccan regime shows a persistent interest in deepening its cooperation with the EU, besides its already quite close cooperation with the US and NATO. Enduring tensions with Algeria and the ongoing occupation of Western Sahara imply that territorial defence is still a major concern for the Moroccan armed forces, but the Moroccan elite is beginning to embrace notions of security similar to the EU and NATO, not least because this serves to promote Moroccan interests vis-à-vis its western allies.

Of course, it could be argued that cooperating on non-military threats and trans-boundary risks (such as terrorism and natural disasters) does not require any deeply held trust to begin with. The cost of not cooperating to counter such threats could be deemed too high or the benefits received from granting support to a powerful ally could be equally high. Indeed, this would be entirely consistent with a realist reading in IR that would also stipulate that as soon as common threats vanish, states go back to the way things were before (cf. Waltz 1993). But this kind of explanation fundamentally misses the point, because the way in which non-military threats and trans-boundary risks are perceived and, more importantly, the way in which the proper means to deal with them are perceived, has less to do with the distribution of material capabilities or balance of power practices. Instead, it has more to do with the gradual hollowing out of the notion of military deterrence in favour of a notion of crisis management that encompasses both military and civilian means to counter security threats. What is important to note here is that as Spain and Morocco are increasingly embedded in frameworks for cooperation provided by the EU, their shared repertoire of cooperative security practices broadens considerably.

Concluding remarks

This chapter has sought to show the possibilities and limits provided by the mainstream perspectives in IR when it comes to analyzing why, how and under what conditions regional organizations such as the EU can contribute to security in the Mediterranean, and it has suggested alternative ways to understand the EU's role in this regard by drawing on a recent study on security cooperation in the western Mediterranean. To be sure, the results would most likely have been different had another set of states been included, and a focus on other policy areas such as border control, asylum, migration, energy or environmental protection would probably have led to other results as well. For example, taking into account that the link between climate change and security has been increasingly acknowledged by international and regional organizations (Dellmuth et al. forthcoming), and not least by the EU (Youngs 2015; Sonnsjö and Bremberg 2016), it seems promising to further explore whether this has had an impact on environmental cooperation with non-members in the Mediterranean.

However, the main point here is that focusing analytically on practices and asking to what extent the EU can be said to provide cooperative frameworks and support transgovernmental networks that otherwise would not have been available opens up a whole new range of research avenues that could also encompass other policy areas and other sets of members/non-members. This way of conducting research also suggests new avenues for comparative studies that could include regional organizations in other parts of the world, such as for example southeast Asia and western Africa. Although we might assume that there are differences in how such organizations work, a focus on practices rather than only formal institutions would help to compare the nature and shape of such interactions in terms of how security is practised among groups of states in various regional settings, as well as to trace cross-regional diffusion patterns.

Nonetheless, there is no doubt that the issue of migration towards Europe and the failure on behalf of the EU to respond coherently and efficiently in the wake of the refugee crisis in 2015 provide quite a different and deeply disturbing piece to the puzzle of how the EU works as a security community-building institution in the Mediterranean region. Following upon the brutal response by many regimes in North Africa and the Middle East to the Arab uprisings, the normative dilemmas involved in Euro-Mediterranean security cooperation are also placed front and centre. For example, Moroccan officials acknowledge that it is hard to make a distinction

olicy, mainly because terrorist attacks might cause pol-
ers typically associated with civil protection. Moreover,
nd Coordination can also be used to monitor potential
or even protests (quoted in Bremberg 2016a: 119). This
cooperative security practices to deal with non-military
n liberal democracies and authoritarian regimes actually
political activities that these regimes do not approve of.
s well as normative dilemmas will probably play an even
on international security provided that more regional
ement to tackle non-military threats and trans-boundary
the Union will be facing a much more fragmented and
near future, but it is still uncertain whether the EU will
e rapidly changing Mediterranean region.

Notes

1 For examples of classical realism, see Morgenthau (1993 [1948]); structural realism or neo-realism, see Waltz (1979); neo-classical realism, see Rose (1998).

2 During the Cold War, the US guaranteed a range of international public goods, such as an open trading system and a stable international monetary regime, essential for the construction of the post-war economic order, but the ultimate political aim was to consolidate the Atlantic alliance against the Soviet Union (Gilpin 1981).

3 For examples of liberalism, see Doyle (1986), Russett (1993); for liberal institutionalism, see Keohane (1984), Ikenberry (1998).

4 Liberalism in IR can thus be said to draw upon neo-functionalist notions as well as theories of economic integration. On neo-functionalism in IR, see Haas (1958). For an introduction to regional integration studies, see Choi and Caporaso (2002).

5 This notion has been further developed in the literature on EU external governance, see Lavenex and Schimmelfennig (2009).

6 Constructivism in IR encompasses both mainstream and critical (post-structuralist) versions which are first and foremost distinguished from each other in relation to positivist and post-positivist epistemologies (however, see McCourt 2016). For examples of mainstream constructivism, see Katzenstein (1996), Wendt (1999). For examples of critical constructivism, see Ashley (1987) and Campbell (1998).

7 Peter Haas' work on the politics of international environmental cooperation is also interesting here. It points to the importance of governmental and non-governmental professionals acting as 'scientific knowledge-brokers' in order to get states around the Mediterranean to adopt a plan to fight marine pollution despite conflicting economic preferences and large power asymmetries (Haas 1990).

8 On the development of the concept of security in theory and practice, see Buzan and Hansen (2009).

9 On the other hand, 'de-securitization' denotes the process by which a political community downgrades or ceases to treat something as an existential threat to a valued referent object, either by rearticulating the issue at hand or by shifting the political focus whereby the relative importance of a previously securitized issue decreases (Waever 1995).

10 In social theory, practice implies 'a distinct social ontology: the social is a field of embodied, materially, interwoven practices centrally organized around shared practical understandings' (Schatzki 2005: 12). On practice approaches in IR, see Neumann (2002), Adler and Pouliot (2011), Adler-Nissen (2014), Bueger (2014), Bueger and Gadinger (2014), Bicchi and Bremberg (2016). For critical discussions on practice approaches in IR, see Hopf (2010), Ringmar (2014).

11 However, for a different take on the EU's response to the Arab uprising and the sources of its power vis-à-vis countries in its southern neighbourhood, see Borg and Bremberg (2015).

12 Major disasters in the Mediterranean region to which the EU has offered support include earthquakes in Algeria (2003), Morocco (2004) and Italy (2009); forest fires in Portugal (2003, 2004, 2005), Spain (2006), Albania (2007), Italy (2007) and Israel (2010); and floods in Algeria (2006). The Union Mechanism for Civil Protection was used to coordinate the assistance sent by several EU member states to

Morocco after the Al Hoceima earthquake in 2004. The EU also received requests for assistance from both Cypriot and Lebanese authorities to assist them in handling the humanitarian crisis and the environmental damages caused by Israel's offensive in southern Lebanon in 2006, and several EU member states contributed with personnel and equipment. EU civil protection teams assisted civilians both in Libya and at its borders during the crisis in 2011 (Bremberg 2016a: 107–8, 130).

Bibliography

Acharya, A. (2001). *Constructing a Security Community in Southeast Asia: ASEAN and the Problem of Regional Order*. London: Routledge.

Adler, E. (2002). 'Constructivism and International Relations', in: Carlsnaes, W., T. Risse and B. Simmons (eds) *Handbook of International Relations*. London: Sage.

Adler, E. (2008). 'The Spread of Security Communities: Communities of Practice, Self-Restraint, and NATO's Post-Cold War Transformation'. *European Journal of International Relations*, 14(2), 195–230.

Adler, E. and M. Barnett (eds) (1998). *Security Communities*. Cambridge: Cambridge University Press.

Adler, E. and B. Crawford (2006). 'Normative Power: The European Practice of Region-Building and Case of the Euro-Mediterranean Partnership', in: Adler, E., F. Bicchi, B. Crawford and R. Del Sarto (eds) *The Convergence of Civilizations: Constructing a Mediterranean Region*. Toronto: Toronto University Press.

Adler, E. and P. Greve (2009). 'When Security Community Meets Balance of Power: Overlapping Regional Mechanisms of Security Governance'. *Review of International Studies*, 35(S1), 59–84.

Adler, E. and V. Pouliot (eds) (2011). *International Practices*. Cambridge: Cambridge University Press.

Adler-Nissen, R. (2014). *Opting Out of the European Union: Diplomacy, Sovereignty and European Integration*. Cambridge: Cambridge University Press.

Ashley, R. (1987). 'The Geopolitics of Geopolitical Space: Toward a Critical Social Theory of International Politics'. *Alternatives*, 12(4), 403–34.

Baldwin, D. (1997). 'The Concept of Security'. *Review of International Studies*, 23(1), 5–26.

Balfour, R. (2011). 'Changes and Continuities in EU–Mediterranean Relations after the Arab Spring', in: Biscop, S., R. Balfour and M. Emerson (eds) *An Arab Springboard for EU Foreign Policy*. Egmont Paper no. 54. Gent: Academia Press.

Bicchi, F. (2006). '"Our Size Fits All": Normative Power Europe and the Mediterranean'. *Journal of European Public Policy*, 13(2), 286–303.

Bicchi, F. (2007). *European Foreign Policy Making toward the Mediterranean*. Houndmills: Palgrave Macmillan.

Bicchi, F. and N. Bremberg (2016). 'European Diplomatic Practices: Contemporary Challenges and Innovative Approaches'. *European Security*, 25(4), 391–406.

Bremberg, N. (2015) 'The EU as Security Community-Building Institution: Venues, Networks and Cooperative Security Practices'. *Journal of Common Market Studies*, 53(3), 674–94.

Bremberg, N. (2016a). *Diplomacy and Security Community-Building: EU and Crisis Management in the Western Mediterranean*, London: Routledge.

Bremberg, N. (2016b) 'Making Sense of the EU's Response to the Arab Spring: Foreign Policy Practice at Times of Crisis'. *European Security*, 25(4), 423–41.

Bremberg, N. and M. Britz (forthcoming). 'From region-building to crisis management: EU security strategies towards the Southern Mediterranean', in: Sperling, J. and S. Economides (eds) *The EU's Security Strategies*. London: Routledge.

Bremberg, N. and P. Rieker (2016). 'Security Community-Building in Times of Crisis: Morocco, the ENP, and Practices of Mutual Responsiveness', in: Rieker, P. (ed.) *Security Communities and External Governance*. Houndmills: Palgrave.

Borg, S. and N. Bremberg (2015) 'Ambigious Power Europe: A Relational Approach to How the EU Exercises Power in Global Politics'. Paper presented at the workshop 'Powerless EUrope: Exploring the EU's power towards the southern neighbourhood', Swedish Institute of International Affairs, 3–4 December, Stockholm.

Bueger, C. (2014). 'Pathways to Practice: Praxiography and International Politics'. *European Political Science Review*, 6(3), 382–406.

Bueger, C. and F. Gadinger (2014). *International Practice Theory: New Perspective*. Basingstoke: Palgrave.

Buzan, B. and L. Hansen (2009). *The Evolution of International Security Studies*. Cambridge: Cambridge University Press.

Buzan, B., O. Waever and J. de Wilde (1998). *Security: A New Framework for Analysis*. London: Lynne Rienner Publishers.

Campbell, D. (1998). *Writing Security: United States Foreign Policy and the Politics of Identity* (2nd and revised edition). Manchester: Manchester University Press.
Checkel, J. and P. Katzenstein (eds) (2009). *European Identity*. Cambridge: Cambridge University Press.
Choi, Y. and J. Caporaso (2002). 'Comparative Regional Integration', in: Carlsnaes, W., T. Risse and B. Simmons (eds) *Handbook of International Relations*. London: Sage.
Dandashly, A. (2015). 'The EU Response to Regime Change in the Wake of the Arab Revolt: Differential Implementation'. *Journal of European Integration*, 37(1), 37–56.
Dawson, C. (2009). *EU Integration with North Africa: Trade Negotiations and Democracy Deficits in Morocco*. London: Tauris.
Dellmuth, L., Gustafsson, M. T., Bremberg, N. and M. Mobjörk (forthcoming). 'International Governmental Organizations and Climate Security: Advancing the Research Agenda'. *Wiley Interdisciplinary Reviews: Climate Change*.
Del Sarto, R. (2015). 'Normative Empire Europe: The European Union, its Borderlands, and the "Arab Spring"'. *JCMS: Journal of Common Market Studies*, 54(2), 215–32.
Deutsch, K., S. Burrell, R. Kann, M. Lee, et al. (1957). *Political Community and the North Atlantic Area: International Organization in the Light of Historical Experience*. Princeton: Princeton University Press.
Doyle, M. (1986). 'Liberalism and World Politics'. *The American Political Science Review*, 80(4), 1151–69.
European Commission (1990). 'Redirecting the Community's Mediterranean Policy: Proposals for the Period 1992–1996', SEC (90) 812 final, 1 June, Brussels.
European Commission (2015). 'Review of the European Neighbourhood Policy', JOIN(2015) 50 final, 18 November, Brussels.
European External Action Service (EEAS) (2016). 'Shared Vision, Common Action: A Stronger Europe. A Global Strategy for the European Union's Foreign and Security Policy' Available at: https://europa.eu/globalstrategy/sites/globalstrategy/files/eugs_review_web.pdf [accessed 10 October 2016].
Gillespie, R. (2006). '"This Stupid Little Island": A Neighbourhood Confrontation in the Western Mediterranean'. *International Politics*, 43(1), 110–32.
Gilpin, R. (1981). *War and Change in World Politics*. New York: Cambridge University Press.
Haas, E. (1958). *The Uniting of Europe: Political, Economic, and Social Forces, 1950–1957*. Stanford: Stanford University Press.
Haas, P. (1990). *Saving the Mediterranean: The Politics of International Environmental Cooperation*. New York: Columbia University Press.
Haddadi, S. (2006). 'Political Securitization and Democratization in the Maghreb: Ambigious Discourses and Fine-Tuning Practices for a Security Partnership', in: Adler, E., F. Bicchi, B. Crawford and R. Del Sarto (eds) *The Convergence of Civilizations: Constructing a Mediterranean Region*. Toronto: Toronto University Press.
Holsti, K. (1985). *The Dividing Discipline: Hegemony and Diversity in International Theory*. Boston: Allen & Unwin.
Hopf, T. (1998). 'The Promise of Constructivism in International Relations Theory'. *International Security*, 23(1), 171–200.
Hopf, T. (2010). 'The Logic of Habit in International Relations'. *European Journal of International Relations*, 16(4), 539–61.
Hyde-Price, A. (2007). *European Security in the Twenty-first Century: The Challenge of Multipolarity*. London: Routledge.
Ikenberry, G. (1998). 'Institutions, Strategic Restraint and the Persistence of the American Postwar Order'. *International Security*, 23(3), 43–78.
Joffé, G. (2008). 'The European Union, Democracy and Counter-Terrorism in the Maghreb'. *Journal of Common Market Studies*, 46(1), 147–71.
Katzenstein, P. (ed.) (1996). *The Culture of National Security: Norms and Identity in World Politics*. New York: Columbia University Press.
Kaufman, S., R. Little and W. Wohlforth (2007). *The Balance of Power in World History*. Houndmills: Palgrave Macmillan.
Keohane, R. (1984). *After Hegemony: Cooperation and Discord in the World Political Economy*. Princeton: Princeton University Press.
Keohane, R. and J. Nye (1977). *Power and Interdependence: World Politics in Transition*. Boston: Little, Brown.
Keohane, R. and L. Martin (1995). 'The Promise of Institutionalist Theory'. *International Security*, 20(1), 39–51.

Kratochwil, F. (2011). 'Making Sense of "International Practices"', in: Adler, E. and V. Pouliot (eds) *International Practices*. Cambridge: Cambridge University Press.

Lavenex, S and F. Schimmelfennig. (2009). 'EU Rules beyond EU Borders: Theorizing External Governance in European Politics'. *Journal of European Public Policy*, 16(6), 791–812.

McCourt, D. (2016). 'Practice Theory and Relationalism as the New Constructivism'. *International Studies Quarterly*, 60(3), 475–85.

Malmvig, H. (2005). 'Security through Intercultural Dialogue? Implications of the Securitization of Euro-Mediterranean Dialogue between Cultures'. *Mediterranean Politics*, 10(3), 349–64.

Mearsheimer, J. (1990). 'Back to the Future: Instability in Europe after the Cold War'. *International Security*, 15(4), 5–56.

Mearsheimer, J. (2001). *The Tragedy of Great Power Politics*. New York: Norton.

Moravcsik, A. (1997). 'Taking Preferences Seriously: A Liberal Theory of International Politics'. *International Organization*, 51(4), 513–53.

Moravcsik, A. (2003). 'Striking a New Transatlantic Bargain'. *Foreign Affairs*, 82(4), 74-89.

Morgenthau, H. (1993 [1948]). *Politics among Nations: The Struggle for Power and Peace*. New York: McGraw-Hill.

Natorski, M. (2015). 'Epistemic (Un)Certainty in Times of Crisis: The Role of Coherence as a Social Convention in the European Neighbourhood Policy after the Arab Spring.' *European Journal of International Relations*, 22(3), 646–70..

Neumann, I. (2002). 'Returning Practice to the Linguistic Turn: The Case of Diplomacy'. *Millennium: Journal of International Studies*, 31(3), 627–51.

Pace, M. (2014). 'The EU's Interpretation of the "Arab Uprisings": Understanding the Different Visions about Democratic Change in EU-MENA Relations'. *JCMS: Journal of Common Market Studies*, 52(5), 969–84.

Peters, J. (ed.) (2012). *The European Union and the Arab Spring: Promoting Democracy and Human Rights in the Middle East*. Lanham, MA: Lexington Books.

Pierros, F., J. Meunier and S. Abrams (1999). *Bridges and Barriers: The European Union's Mediterranean Policy, 1961–1998*. Aldershot: Ashgate.

Pouliot, V. (2008). 'The Logic of Practicality: A Theory of Practice of Security Communities'. *International Organization*, 62(2), 257–88.

Pouliot, V. (2010). *International Security in Practice: The Politics of NATO–Russia Diplomacy*. Cambridge: Cambridge University Press.

Pouliot, V. and J. Cornut (2015). 'Practice, Theory and Study of Diplomacy: A Research Agenda'. *Cooperation and Conflict*, 50(3), 297–315.

Ringmar, E. (2014). 'The Search for Dialogue as a Hindrance to Understanding: Practices as Inter-Paradigmatic Research Program'. *International Theory*, 6, 1–27.

Rose, G. (1998). 'Neoclassical Realism and Theories of Foreign Policy'. *World Politics*, 51(1), 144–72.

Ruggie, J. (1998). 'What Makes the World Hang Together? Neoutilitarianism and the Social Constructivist Challenge'. *International Organization*, 52(4), 855–85.

Russett, B. (1993). *Grasping the Democratic Peace: Principles of a Post-Cold War World*. Princeton: Princeton University Press.

Schatzki, T. (2005). 'Introduction: practice theory' in: Knorr Cetina, K., T. R. Schatzki and E. von Savigny (eds) *The Practice Turn in Contemporary Theory*. New York: Routledge.

Schatzki, T., K. Knorr Cetina and E. von Savigny (eds) (2001). *The Practice Turn in Contemporary Theory*. London: Routledge.

Schmidt, B. (2002). 'On the History and Historiography of International Relations' in: Carlsnaes, W., T. Risse and B. Simmons (eds) *Handbook of International Relations*. London: Sage.

Searle, J. (1995). *The Construction of Social Reality*. New York: The Free Press.

Sonnsjö, H. and N. Bremberg (2016). *Climate Change in an EU Security Context: The Case of the European External Action Service*. Stockholm: Stockholms Universitet.

Tömmel, I. (2013). 'The New Neighborhood Policy of the EU: An Appropriate Response to the Arab Spring?'. *Democracy and Security*, 9(1–2), 19–39.

Vedby Rasmussen, M. (2006). *The Risk Society at War: Terror, Technology and Strategy in the Twenty-First Century*. Cambridge: Cambridge University Press.

Volpi, F. (2004). 'Regional Community Building and the Transformation of International Relations: The Case of the Euro-Mediterranean Partnership'. *Mediterranean Politics*, 9(2), 145–64.

Waever, O. (1995). 'Securitization and Desecuritization', in: Lipschutz, R. (ed.) *On Security*. New York: Columbia University Press.

Walt, S. (1987). *The Origins of Alliances*. Ithaca: Cornell University Press.
Waltz, K. (1979). *Theory of International Politics*. Reading, MA: Addison-Wesley.
Waltz, K. (1993). 'The Emerging Structure of International Politics'. *International Security*, 18(1), 44–79.
Wendt, A. (1992). 'Anarchy is What States Make of It: The Social Construction of Power Politics'. *International Organizations*, 46(2), 391–425.
Wendt, A. (1999). *Social Theory of International Politics*. Cambridge: Cambridge University Press.
Williams, M. (2003). 'Words, Images, Enemies: Securitization and International Politics'. *International Studies Quarterly*, 47(4), 511–31.
Wolff, S. (2012). *The Mediterranean Dimension of EU Internal Security*. New York: Palgrave.
Youngs, R. (2015). *Climate Change and European Security*. New York: Routledge.

18

REGIME RESILIENCE AND THE ARAB UPRISINGS IN THE SOUTHERN MEDITERRANEAN

Four emerging approaches for explaining authoritarian persistence

Matt Buehler and Amnah Ibraheem

Scholarship on the Arab uprisings in the southern Mediterranean has emerged in three waves. The first wave of scholarship relayed fast-moving events to readers, who wanted minute-by-minute details on these democratic mobilizations. Almost journalistic in nature, this scholarship often followed closely one country—mostly Egypt or Tunisia—and described how protests began, intensified, and concluded. The main goal was to record and document the protests' storylines and chief organizers for readers. The second wave took on "big" theoretical issues of the uprisings, notably topics of regime continuity and change (Soliman, 2011; Stacher, 2012; Gengler, 2015). The third wave articulated either region-wide explanations for political change (Brownlee et al., 2015; Brynen et al., 2012) or focused on specific political actors, especially Islamist groups (Masoud, 2014; Al-Anani, 2012; Buehler, 2013), social movements (Beinin and Vairel, 2013), and labor unions (Lynch, 2014; Kamrava, 2014).

When the outcome of interest was exploring regime change or continuity, the analyst's empirical puzzle resulted in less variation than initially anticipated. Nearly all Arab autocracies experienced some unrest, yet only one—Tunisia—collapsed and produced democratization. Tunisia, moreover, continues to face major challenges in consolidating democracy after the ouster of its former autocrat, Zine el-Abidine Ben Ali. Other autocracies, notably Egypt, experienced leadership change—with the removal of Hosni Mubarak in January 2011—but not ultimately regime change. By 2013, authoritarianism resurged in Egypt by way of a coup. In Yemen and Libya, apparatchiks of the ousted regime became key leaders of the new state. This raised questions about how much change had actually occurred. Encouraged by the United States, Bahrain's Sunni monarchy initiated a "national dialogue" with Shia-led opposition groups. In less than a month, the dialogue collapsed. Other states—Morocco, Mauritania, and Jordan—implemented constitutional changes that did little more than rotate ministers or introduce tertiary reforms. This preserved the underlying structure of power. Whereas the media associated the Arab uprisings with regime change, the reality was regime continuity.

This chapter showcases four approaches that seek to explain this outcome of authoritarian persistence. Although these approaches have deep roots in studies completed before the Arab uprisings, they have been re-deployed in new, innovative ways to explain Arab regimes' surprising resilience. Discussing these four approaches has important implications for scholarship for two main reasons. First, the four approaches draw upon what are often termed institutional and structural explanations. Because these institutional and structural explanations are common to mainstream comparative politics, these four approaches carry great promise for helping research on the Arab uprisings contribute to major theoretical developments. Second, several of the approaches intersect two separate subfields of political science, notably comparative politics and international relations. Since processes involving the military, regime type, and foreign powers often include both domestic and international actors, they bridge these two traditionally distinct subfields. Research on these four approaches suggests such a stark division between comparative politics and international relations may be counterproductive for understanding authoritarian resilience of the Arab regimes in the southern Mediterranean.

Among the four approaches this chapter surveys, those related to institutional explanations include military loyalty, regime type, and foreign powers, while those connected to social structural explanations include center–periphery relations. By military sociology, we mean research on army internal politics—the likelihood of defection, status of officer benefits, and level of professionalization. This research explains why Tunisia's and Egypt's armies both turned against their *de jure* leaders, dictators Ben Ali and Mubarak, but only the former (and not the latter) defected from their *de facto* rulers, the underlying authoritarian regime. The section on monarchism examines formal regime type, specifically differences between Arab monarchies and presidencies. While initial studies on monarchies during the uprisings did not specify the mechanisms that made them more resilient than presidencies, recent ones have clarified their institutional advantage. Research on foreign powers concerns the role of external actors—the United States, France, or Saudi Arabia—in propping up Arab autocracies. Studies on center–periphery relationships analyze how urban–rural dynamics have bolstered some Arab autocracies. Where autocratic regimes could rally conservative forces of the rural countryside to their aid, it helped to counterbalance unrest boiling in urban cities. This chapter surveys these four approaches (military sociology, monarchism, foreign powers, and center–periphery relations), and proposes new future areas of inquiry extending from them.

Military sociology: understanding the "guys with the guns"

Since the 1990s, scholars have highlighted the centrality of military politics in the southern Mediterranean. A scholarly consensus deems that the loyalty of Arab regimes' coercive apparatuses is key to authoritarian resilience (Bellin, 2004; Kamrava, 2000). While many Mediterranean countries transitioned to more democratic armies post-1989, Arab militaries continue to be the penultimate guarantors of regime stability, as had been the case in the communist satellites of southeastern Europe (Croissant and Eschenauer, Chapter 14, this volume). When autocrats keep the "guys with the guns" loyal, their capacity to retain power increases (Barany, 2011). While early studies emphasized the importance of both the military's corporate interests and defections, research after 2011 has advanced these works by further detailing how the military forms interests and chooses whether or not to defect.

Early research after the 2011 uprisings compared how the Tunisian and Egyptian militaries' corporate interests differed from those of other Arab states, which motivated them to defect from autocrats. Zoltan Barany (2011) analyzed the behavior of military leadership in the six states where considerable bloodshed occurred (i.e. Tunisia, Egypt, Bahrain, Syria, Libya, and Yemen).

Egypt and Tunisia exhibited a high degree of military professionalization, meaning that the army had distinct corporate interests separate from dictators. Because the militaries of these states had autonomous corporate interests, they defected from dictators' coalitions to protect their own interests. Lower levels of military professionalization in other Arab states—especially Syria—encouraged these armies to remain loyal to dictators. Since these militaries' corporate interests intermeshed with those of dictators, they did not defect when protests erupted.

To understand the origins of the military's distinct corporate interests in Tunisia and Egypt, the first step is to break down the components of these regimes' coercive apparatuses to understand how they interact and compete with each other. It is unwise to presume that all units of a regime's coercive apparatus work in tandem to protect a dictator, without distinct (and sometimes mutually exclusive) interests. One major cleavage is between top-level officers and lower-level officers (Bou Nassif, 2015a: 65–87). The loyalty of the top leaders of the armed forces often differs from lower ranking officers, who pose a threat during uprisings (because they often choose to side with civilians) (Bou Nassif, 2015a: 66). Bou Nassif emphasizes, however, that the defection of the Tunisian and Egyptian military's top generals—and not their lower officers—forced Mubarak and Ben Ali into exile.

Bou Nassif argues that the origins of the Tunisian military's decision to defect from Ben Ali's side stems from conflict between different units of the coercive apparatus, especially between the army and the domestic intelligence agencies. Although Ben Ali served in the army, his regime did not forge symbiotic ties with it. Rather, it shifted massive benefits to domestic intelligence. This strategy emerged after a 1991 false coup, known as the Barakat al-Sahil affair, which domestic intelligence used to win Ben Ali's favor. Consequently Ben Ali did little to reward military leaders, leaving a professionalized and well-organized but underfunded bureaucratic army. Grewal (2015) has shown how Tunisia's post-revolutionary government has redressed the military's material concerns, enlarging its budget to compensate. Whereas the military's budget had been 5 percent of the national budget, it rose to 20 percent after democratization.

Conversely Egypt's dictators shifted benefits to the military, yet this also (ultimately) helped the latter develop autonomous corporate interests. Mubarak—and his predecessors, Anwar Sadat and Gamal Abdel Nasser—did much to enrich the military as a corporate unit. Nasser filled the bureaucracy with military officers, Sadat empowered the military economically, and Mubarak deepened the military's business involvement. Egypt's regime also created post-career financial rewards for officers to incentivize loyalty during their terms of active military service (Bou Nassif, 2013: 510, 519–29). Following retirement, many navy admirals became the chairmen of shipping companies, whereas air force officials became administrators of airports. Reports suggest that retired military officials could garner monthly salaries ranging between $16,670 and $166,670. Other sources estimate salaries of $83,000 per month (Bou Nassif, 2015b: 278). Military elites became powerful economically through managing public factories and enterprises, selling public lands, and running unregulated businesses (Bou Nassif, 2013: 278). Gradually, the army's participation in these economic activities became autonomous from the dictator, leading to the direct personal enrichment of officers outside the immediate scope of military service (Springborg, 2011).

Military opposition to Mubarak began to increase in the late 2000s. First, in the waning days of his regime, Mubarak paralleled Ben Ali by building up Egypt's police with bigger budgets and political attention rather than rewarding the military (Kandil, 2012: 5). Second, many military leaders opposed Mubarak's son and heir apparent, Gamal Mubarak. Collaborating with a group of private businessmen and investors, Gamal had pledged to privatize Egypt's economy. This would have threatened the public enterprises from which military officers profited handsomely. Hence, when protests rocked Egyptian cities beginning in 2011, the military turned against Mubarak and ousted him from power. Although for different reasons, both Tunisia's and Egypt's militaries developed autonomous corporate interests from autocrats that, ultimately, created propitious conditions for defection. What this meant, as Masoud writes, was that the Egyptian and Tunisian regimes had to rely on domestic intelligence and police to "mete out violence" on protestors, while their militaries maintained a "strangely neutral position between protestors and the regime's thugs" during conflicts (Masoud, 2011: 23).

Statistical large-*n* research has confirmed findings from qualitative studies of Egypt, Tunisia, and other Arab states. Analyzing a dataset of coups in the Arab world between 1950 and 2013, Albrecht (2014) examines whether dictators' coup-proofing strategies reduce coups and their success rate. Albrecht shows how when an autocrat's rule becomes excessively long, these leaders turn into "lame ducks" with an "accumulation of broken promises" which makes them vulnerable to other military leaders (Albrecht, 2014: 6).

While the military's corporate interests and those of autocrats diverged in Egypt and Tunisia, they intersected in other Arab regimes. Often, the military's corporate interests overlapped with the dictator's because the two had similar sectarian backgrounds. In Bahrain and Syria, for example, autocrats utilized their common sectarian traits to reinforce the loyalty of specific military units. Bahrain's Sunni king enhanced the loyalty of his Sunni-led army by importing Sunni troop reinforcements, notably from Saudi Arabia, the United Arab Emirates, and Pakistan.

The sectarian nature of Syria's regime has intermeshed the military's corporate interests with those of its autocrat. After the 1982 Hama uprising, Syria's regime moved to increase the number of Allawis—dictator Bashar al-Asad's religious sect—in the military. Through this "Alawiization" of the military, approximately 80–85 percent of every new graduating cohort of military officers came from the Allawi sect (Bou Nassif, 2015c: 6). Syrian dictator Bashar al-Asad deployed battalions constituted from the Allawi to fight crucial battles against Sunni rebels, especially the Free Syrian Army and armed Islamist groups. Asad rallied the Allawi military elite to his side, who feared that the former's ouster would cause their sect to lose the privileged positions it had acquired since the Allawi-led 1963 coup.

Although the military leadership—as a cohesive unit—chose not to abandon Syria's dictator Bashar al-Asad, recent research has sought to examine subnational instances of defection. By getting a bead on why soldiers have either deserted or defected from Syria's military, we can better understand why these abandonments have not toppled Asad's regime, as they did in the cases of Tunisia and Egypt (Ohl et al., 2015: 4). Whereas "desertions" occur when military officers or soldiers leave the army and flee the battlefield, "defections" occur when they leave the army and switch to fighting for the enemy. The former, in general, happens far more often than the latter. Reports estimate that up to 100,00 Syrian soldiers have deserted, which has lowered the number of active war fighters from 295,000 in 2011 to 120,000 in 2015 (Ohl et al., 2015: 4; Koehler et al., 2016: 441–2). An unknown percentage of these soldiers have returned to fight as rebels.

Some recent studies claim that these desertions relate to sectarianism, which may explain why they have not destabilized Syria's regime. Anti-Sunni discrimination within Syrian army ranks has caused deep resentment among Sunni officers (Bou Nassif, 2015c: 6). Compared with their Allawi counterparts, Sunni officers receive lower salaries, outdated equipment, and have poor-quality barracks. The Asads have, in effect, transformed Syria's military from a powerful national institution into a "family business," expressing little concern for modernizing its weapons or enhancing its internal organization (Bou Nassif, 2015c: 11–12). Additionally, an "aggressive, anti-religious ethos" pervades the military including public drinking and anti-Islamic jokes, which alienates socially conservative Sunni officers and soldiers. In fact, many Sunni officers perceive the military's purported secularism as merely a cover for the increasing "Allawi-ization" of the armed forces (Bou Nassif, 2015c: 15).

Because of discrimination, some Sunni officers' families have economic difficulties, which has encouraged them to leave Asad's army to fight with well-financed Sunni militant groups (Ohl et al., 2015: 5–7). Soldiers' "social ties" with "family, friends, and close home-town connections" inculcate moral beliefs persuading them "that desertion is an acceptable behavior" (Koehler et al., 2016: 239). These desertion dynamics have trapped the Syrian regime in an impasse in which a "militarization of the opposition" has been stalemated by a "militarization of loyalists" (Ohl et al., 2015: 3). Thus, Asad's regime is too weak to completely defeat its enemies, yet too strong to lose control. Although some Sunni officers have defected, Asad's reinforcement of Allawi officers' loyalty kept Syria's regime resilient, unlike Tunisia's during the 2011 uprisings.

The monarchical exception: specifying the advantage of kings

Although nearly a dozen Arab regimes witnessed major protests, the only Arab autocrats driven from power were presidents, not monarchs. Kings in Morocco, Jordan, and the Gulf retained power. Recent research has explored the institutional advantage of monarchical regimes in the southern Mediterranean region, especially Morocco and Jordan. The doyen of research on Arab monarchies—Michael Herb—first suggested that "monarchism matters" (Herb, 2012: 11). Monarchies like Morocco and Jordan are more stable than non-monarchies, because kings can maintain distance from political upheavals while they simultaneously promise reform. Monarchs also proffer more predictability and stability. Looking at the case of Morocco, kings' perceived predictability among citizens derives from their use of religious and traditional symbols to build legitimacy and project an image of historical continuity (Hammoudi, 1997). This predictability has empowered Arab monarchies to outperform Arab presidencies economically, a benefit that accrues to citizens who support kings. Yet Herb cautions that the stability of Arab monarchies may not endure future protests, especially if democratized Arab republics like Tunisia achieve economic growth (Herb, 2012: 11–12). Thus far such growth has not materialized, however.

A strategic explanation also exists for why Arab monarchies have remained more stable. Monarchical stability flows from strategies of coalition-building, which kings utilize to retain power (Gause, 2013). Specifically, monarchies can deter popular demands for reform through building a coalition of internal interest groups, regional allies, and foreign patrons (Yom, 2015). These coalitions are key to understanding how monarchies maintain stability. Many monarchies build domestic coalitions through wealth, paying for welfare and development programs (Yom and Gause, 2012: 75). That is, a king can draw potential opponents into his coalition through strategically deploying his financial resources (Gause, 2013: 24–6).

In Morocco and Jordan, kings have done this through providing development programs and subsidy benefits to residents of rural areas, especially among peasants or tribes who have historically supported the regime (Bergh, 2012). Morocco has also used state resources to buy the loyalty of oppositionists, including former leaders of the February 20th youth protest movement (Buehler, 2015). Likewise, Jordan has co-opted oppositionists through employing them in regime ministerial posts (Josua, 2016). Because many Arab monarchies have massive amounts of oil and gas revenue, especially Gulf kingdoms, these regimes are particularly adept at buying off internal opposition. Besides material patronage, both Morocco and Jordan have successfully co-opted some opposition into their coalitions through non-material concessions, especially major constitutional reforms promulgated in 2011 and 2012. One report called this Moroccan and Jordanian strategy "constitutions against revolutions" (Parolin, 2015).

Among the eight Arab monarchies, differences exist in their regime structures, shaping the strategies they employed to secure resilience during the 2011 uprisings. Extending the work of Herb (1999), Gregory Gause identifies two different types of Arab monarchies—individual and dynastic. To ward off opposition, individual monarchies like Morocco and Jordan—what Herb calls "linchpin" monarchies—responded to protests by introducing reforms, holding elections, and firing ministers. Dynastic monarchies rely on members of the royal family to control most important government posts and, hence, could not implement reforms such as firing key ministers without upsetting them (Gause, 2013: 15–18). Some "linchtier" monarchies—notably Oman—fall between these categories practicing both financial co-optation while also rotating ministerial leadership (Bank et al., 2014: 163). Some non-monarchical Arab autocracies—notably Syria—also follow the dynastic model, yet a dynastic structure has not reinforced its stability.

Sean Yom and Gregory Gause (2012: 76), also judged that powerful foreign allies—both western and Arab—furnished economic and military support to enhance the stability of Arab monarchies. The royal families of the Arab monarchies communicated transnationally, brainstorming amongst themselves about how to deal with protests (Yom, 2014a: 44–5). Yom discusses how Arab monarchies rallied as a united, regional community to support each other during the crises. Communications among the Arab royal families occurred by way of informal ties, especially marital relations and Sunni religious connections. They had common sectarian fears and beliefs of dynastic superiority (Yom, 2014a: 45). Such communication among the Arab monarchies led to shifts away from violent tactics to more tolerant ones, especially preemptive reform adopting the Moroccan and Jordanian models. For the domestic and international reasons, Arab monarchies have demonstrated the capacity to control and suppress opposition—a key dynamic that buoyed them during the uprisings.

Foreign powers and external intervention: black knights rescue regimes

One approach examines how foreign powers buttress regimes, what is known as the "black-knights" theory. While white knights of fairy tales rescue princesses from dragons, foreign powers act as "black knights" to save autocrats with whom they share national security interests. Western nations often gave lip service to democratization when popular uprisings broke out in Arab states in the southern Mediterranean but, in reality, supported the authoritarian status quo through policies of autocracy promotion.

Some of the seminal works on autocracy promotion come from Jason Brownlee (2011; 2012), who traces the historic origins of the strategic alliance between Egypt and the United States. This alliance began after the 1978 Camp David accords and continues through the 2011 uprisings until today. In the early 1970s, Sadat laid the groundwork for this future alliance by expelling Soviet advisors and increasing diplomatic communication with the United States. Through a new alliance with the United States after the 1979 Israeli–Egyptian treaty signed at Camp David, Sadat aimed to improve Egypt's economy and increase the military's technological capacity. The Egyptian economy experienced only a modest boost, however. Sadat could not curb spending among the generals, his core supporters who profited from new business opportunities after Camp David. While Sadat agreed to US and Israeli requests for a highly unpopular peace treaty, he responded to public opposition with new repressive laws to curb dissent. In a trade for peace with Israel, and massive financial benefits from the United States, Sadat enhanced the resilience of his regime (Brownlee, 2011: 649–51).

Although Egypt's regime benefited financially from its new alliance with the United States, the United States benefited strategically. Egypt became the US's "constable" or "gendarme" protecting US interests in regional conflicts (Brownlee, 2011: 657). Egypt, in effect, filled a role played by Iran's Shah before his ouster after the 1979 Islamic revolution. While successive

US presidents have stressed the need for democratization in the Arab world, the reality is that the United States works to promote the stability of autocracies. Hence, Brownlee concludes that Egypt's authoritarianism is an "international phenomenon . . . co-constituted by local and foreign actors" (Brownlee, 2012: 3).

While Brownlee centers on the United States as Egypt's "black knight" in the southern Mediterranean, other foreign powers—notably Saudi Arabia, the Gulf states, and France—shore up other Arab autocracies. An example emerges with the case of Saudi intervention in Bahrain (Ambrosio, 2014: 336). Seeking to stem the tide of Shia unrest, which it feared might spill over into its Eastern Province, Saudi Arabia intervened in the small island nation of Bahrain to prop up its Sunni-led monarchy in March 2011. The Gulf Cooperation Council (GCC), which had historically been an economic arrangement between the Gulf regimes, took an unprecedented action to authorize a military intervention in Bahrain to break up the standoff between Bahraini police and peaceful protesters. The GCC-led crackdown bolstered the region's Sunni monarchies, especially Saudi Arabia, which has become a force for "counter-revolution" in the Gulf (Kamrava, 2012: 96).

After successfully intervening in Bahrain, Saudi Arabia has moved to buttress other pro-Sunni Arab autocracies in the southern Mediterranean. After July 2013, Saudi Arabia played an active role in financially and diplomatically supporting General al-Sisi in Egypt after he overthrew Mohammed Morsi, the elected Islamist president. To reinforce a region-wide Sunni identity, Saudi Arabia also encouraged the GCC to make membership offers to Jordan and Morocco, which were declined. Curtis Ryan traces the GCC's evolution from an economic and cultural club into a force of military counter-revolution, cooperating to stabilize unrest during the Arab uprisings (Ryan, 2012: 28–9). By re-emerging as a leader in regional diplomacy, Saudi Arabia has aimed to reassert its dominance over Gulf states, especially Qatar (Kamrava, 2012: 98).

Two cases from the southern Mediterranean—Libya and Syria—complexify the "black-knights" approach, however. Western powers air bombarded Libya's regime to support democratization protests. In Syria, they have alternated between supporting secular rebels and bombing militants from the Islamic State, both of who fight Asad's army. Russia has directly supported Asad's forces, launching strikes against all opponents to his rule. But without a sustained commitment of post-intervention nation-building from foreign powers, Libya's and Syria's stability have collapsed. The fact that Libya, as Marc Lynch notes, had to "build a state largely from scratch" meant that little could be done to stop the "well-lubricated flows" of weapons that have fueled the civil war (Lynch, 2015). As of this chapter's writing in 2016, new US-led air strikes began aiming to unseat radical Islamists who have exploited the Libyan civil war to gain a strategic foothold in the country. Moreover, the United States and Russia have brokered a new accord to coordinate air strikes against the Islamic State, which will—inadvertently—reinforce the anti-US Asad regime's robustness. Although foreign powers' early interventions did not directly promote autocracy in Libya or Syria, which weakens the black-knights thesis, it ultimately rendered a far more dangerous, dysfunctional political order in the post-intervention environment for ordinary Libyans and Syrians.

Quantitative research also weakens the black-knights approach. According to Oisin Tansey's cross-national dataset, the United States has done far less than theorized to buttress authoritarian regimes. "Autocracy promotion," he explains, fails to show that there exists a US "intentional promotion of a particular type of regime abroad" (Tansey, 2015: 4–5). What appears as autocracy promotion from some foreign powers is not active promotion, but rather a passive "enabling" of authoritarianism in pursuit of another strategic objective. The upshot is that the United States bolsters autocracies but it also equally supports democracies, reflecting its own, idiosyncratic national security objectives.

Center–periphery tensions: urban–rural politics and regime resilience

Traditionally, studies of center–periphery politics examine how regimes geo-spatially organize power relations within their borders. During the state-building process, some Arab regimes of the southern Mediterranean region centered themselves upon the city, exhibiting an "urban bias" in the coalitions of support upon which they relied. By contrast, other regimes built themselves upon support from the countryside and made rural areas the pillars of their ruling orders. Following early state-building decisions, regimes chose either to orient state programs and benefits toward urban or rural areas, often contingent upon whether they had become strongholds of authoritarian support. New research has sought to utilize the center–periphery framework to examine issues of regime resilience and collapse during the Arab uprisings.

The 2011 uprisings followed a clear urban–rural divide, with some countries experiencing more unrest in rural areas than others. In Tunisia, the country in which the most democratic change has taken place, the uprisings moved gradually from the countryside—beginning in Sidi Bouzid—and concluded in the capital city, Tunis (Zurayk and Gough, 2014: 107). This unrest that became a revolution sprang from years of marginalization of rural areas, under the reign of Ben Ali (and Bourguiba previously). During his rule, Ben Ali favored the business elite, which flourished economically. They bought and profited from Ben Ali's neoliberal policies, which liberalized and sold off public industries (Gana, 2012: 201–3).

While Ben Ali's interests aligned with the businessmen, they contradicted those of rural citizens, which meant that levels of economic development were lower in rural areas. Indeed, most Tunisians living in the rural and southern provinces—54 percent—owned less than 5 hectares of land, while nearly 25 percent were landless tenant farmers. Poverty rates increased dramatically between rural and urban areas, with 13.9 percent in the former but only 3.8 percent in the latter (Zurayk and Gough, 2014: 113–15). Beginning in 2008, tensions in rural areas came to a climax with the Gafsa phosphate mine revolt (Allal, 2012). This labor unrest evolved gradually into broader "food protests," in which protesters sought to expose the neglect of the needs of rural citizens (Zurayk and Gough, 2014: 120–1). Gafsa transformed into a symbol of rural marginalization, presaging the successful 2011 revolution.

By contrast, unrest in Egypt, Morocco, and Mauritania concentrated in the cities, and never penetrated the countryside. Yet, like Tunisia, rural citizens of these states also suffered from prolonged underdevelopment. In the late 1990s, for example, approximately 80 percent of Egyptian farmers had to simultaneously hold non-farming jobs to make ends meet (El Nour, 2015). In part, this may explain why Egypt's "revolution" neither ultimately broke military control nor instituted full democracy. In both Morocco and Mauritania, regimes used similar co-optation strategies focused on rural areas to bolster their rule and counteract the urban unrest (Buehler, 2015).

Conclusion and future research

To secure the resilience of Arab regimes, the variables of military loyalty, monarchism, foreign powers, and urban–rural politics played a crucial role. While none alone had a determinative effect on regime resilience, they interacted to bolster Arab autocracies. The level of the military's loyalty, perhaps the most important factor, predicted whether or not the military would defect from authoritarian rulers. Whereas the army's defection from Ben Ali in Tunisia dovetailed with the collapse of the entire regime, it did not in Egypt, where the apparatus of the authoritarian state remained intact even after Mubarak left power. The Egyptian military's deep involvement in the country's political economy enhanced its loyalty to the authoritarian regime. Future research could examine the economic interests of Arab armies in other states to confirm whether they parallel these trends. Building off trends observed in Syria and Bahrain, future research could also examine how military sociology and minority politics interacted to either support or undermine authoritarianism in neighboring Arab regimes.

Studies identify the institutional advantages of Arab monarchies over republics. Yet, analytical complications persist. Because most Arab monarchies are also simultaneously oil *rentier* states, it is difficult to distinguish between advantages derived from monarchical institutions and those garnered from the *rentier* economy. Future research could better disaggregate these two areas, which would highlight which sources of regime resilience derive from monarchical institutions or, alternatively, flow from oil wealth. Interestingly, Frédéric Volpi has found that some Arab republics—notably Algeria—have not been "adversely affected by the wave of uprisings" by utilizing these same strategies (Volpi, 2013). He identifies Algeria's effective use of pseudo-democratic pre-emptive reforms, *rentier* patronage, and restrained security response (Volpi, 2013: 105, 111). Volpi's findings question whether such strategies of authoritarian resilience are limited to Arab monarchies or, alternatively, they may imply that they have gradually diffused to Arab republics also.

In the area of foreign powers, much research has focused on the United States and its allies in the southern Mediterranean, notably Egypt and Jordan. Indeed, both authoritarian regimes have reaped benefits from their peace treaty with Israel in terms of increased US military aid and technical assistance. Rather than constructing broad internal coalitions of support, these regimes have increasingly relied on foreign powers to prop up their rule. Future research, perhaps, may look at Arab regimes in which the United States has less direct geo-political interests, notably the north African cases. These states, long strongholds of French influence, have received backing from France, not the United States. French politicians had deep personal and strategic ties with Tunisia's regime, and such links remain especially strong with Morocco's regime. Future research might more deeply explore the security relations between France and its former colonies, comparing how such geo-political alliances differ from those between the United States and its Arab "gendarmes."

While the dominant discussion around regime resilience and center–periphery relations focuses on urban–rural cleavages, some have moved to redefine marginalized social groups as the "periphery" (artists, feminist groups, and LGBT citizens). Given the weight of variables such as military loyalty, monarchism, foreign powers, and the urban–rural conflict, the political role of such groups likely falls to secondary importance in explaining authoritarian robustness. For the above reasons, research related to Arab authoritarian resilience continues to attract scholarly attention and will provide new opportunities for research for students and scholars of the southern Mediterranean into the next decade.

Bibliography

Al-Anani, K. 2012. "Islamist Parties Post-Arab Spring." *Mediterranean Politics*, 17(3), 466–72.

Albrecht, H. 2014. "The Myth of Coup-Proofing: Risk and Instances of Military Coups d'État in the Middle East and North Africa, 1950–2013." *Armed Forces and Society*, 41(4), 659–87.

Allal, A. 2012. "Trajectoires 'Révolutionnaires' en Tunisie." *Revue Française de Science Politique*, 62(5), 821–41.

Allal, A. and Pierret, T. 2013. *Au coeur des révoltes arabes: devenir révolutionnaires*. Armand Colin.

Ambrosio, T. 2014. "Democratic States and Authoritarian Firewalls: America as a Black Knight in the Uprising in Bahrain." *Contemporary Politics*, 20(3), 331–46.

Bank, A., Richter, T., Sunik, A. 2014. "Durable, yet Different: Monarchies in the Arab Spring." *Journal of Arabian Studies*, 4(2), 163–79.

Barany, Z. 2011. "The Role of the Military." *Journal of Democracy*, 22(4), 24–35.
Beinin, J. and Vairel, F. (eds) 2013. *Social Movements, Mobilization, and Contestation in the Middle East and North Africa*. Stanford University Press.
Bellin, E. 2004. "The Robustness of Authoritarianism in the Middle East: Exceptionalism in Comparative Perspective." *Comparative Politics*, 36(2), 139–57.
Bergh, S. I. 2012. "'Inclusive' Neoliberalism, Local Governance Reforms and the Redeployment of State Power: The Case of the National Initiative for Human Development (INDH) in Morocco." *Mediterranean Politics*, 17(3), 410–26.
Bou Nassif, H. 2013. "Wedded to Mubarak: The Second Careers and Financial Rewards of Egypt's Military Elite, 1981–2011." *The Middle East Journal*, 67(4), 509–30.
Bou Nassif, H. 2015a. "A Military Besieged: The Armed Forces, the Police, and the Party in Bin 'Ali's Tunisia, 1987–2011." *International Journal of Middle East Studies*, 47(1), 65–87.
Bou Nassif, H. 2015b. "Generals and Autocrats: How Coup-Proofing Predetermined the Military Elite's Behavior in the Arab Spring." *Political Science Quarterly*, 130(2), 245–75.
Bou Nassif, H. 2015c. "'Second-Class': The Grievances of Sunni Officers in the Syrian Armed Forces." *Journal of Strategic Studies*, 38(5), 626–49.
Brownlee, J. 2011. "Peace before Freedom: Diplomacy and Repression in Sadat's Egypt." *Political Science Quarterly*, 126(4), 641–68.
Brownlee, J. 2012. *Democracy Prevention: Politics of the U.S.–Egypt Alliance*. New York: Cambridge University Press.
Brownlee, J., Masoud, T. E. and Reynolds, A. 2015. *The Arab Spring: Pathways of Repression and Reform*. Oxford University Press, USA.
Brynen, R., Moore, P. W., Salloukh, B. F., and Zahar, M. J. 2012. *Beyond the Arab Spring: Authoritarianism and Democratization in the Arab World* (Vol. 4). Boulder, CO: Lynne Rienner Publishers.
Buehler, M. 2013. "The Threat to 'Un-moderate': Moroccan Islamists and the Arab Spring." *Middle East Law and Governance*, 5(3), 231–57.
Buehler, M. 2015. "Continuity through Co-optation: Rural Politics and Regime Resilience in Morocco and Mauritania." *Mediterranean Politics*, 20(3), 364–85.
El Nour, S. 2015. "Small Farmers and the Revolution in Egypt: The Forgotten Actors." *Contemporary Arab Affairs*, 8(2), 198–211.
Gana, A. 2012. "The Rural and Agricultural Roots of the Tunisian Revolution: When Food Security Matters." *International Journal of Sociology of Agriculture and Food*, 19(2), 201–13.
Gana, N. 2013. *The Making of the Tunisian Revolution: Contexts, Architects, Prospects*. Edinburgh University Press.
Gause III, F. G. 2013. "Kings for All Seasons: How the Middle East's Monarchies Survived the Arab Spring." Brookings Doha Center Analysis Paper, 8.
Gengler, J. 2015. *Group Conflict and Political Mobilization in Bahrain and the Arab Gulf: Rethinking the Rentier State*. Indiana University Press.
Gerges, F. A. (ed.) 2013. *The New Middle East: Protest and Revolution in the Arab World*. Cambridge University Press.
Grewal, Sharan. 2015. "A Quiet Revolution: The Tunisian Military Post-Ben Ali." Regional insight paper prepared as part of the 2014–2015 Renegotiating Arab Civil–Military Relations: Political and Economic Governance in Transition Project, Carnegie Middle East Center.
Hamid, S. 2014. *Temptations of Power: Islamists and Illiberal Democracy in a New Middle East*. Oxford University Press.
Hammoudi, A. 1997. *Master and Disciple: The Cultural Foundations of Moroccan Authoritarianism*. University of Chicago Press.
Herb, M. 1999. *All in the Family: Absolutism, Revolution, and Democracy in Middle Eastern Monarchies*. SUNY Press.
Herb, M. 2012. "Monarchism Matters." *POMEPS Briefings*, 16(19), 11–12.
Hibou, B. 2011. *The Force of Obedience*. Polity Press.
Josua, M. 2016. "Co-optation Reconsidered: Authoritarian Regime Legitimation Strategies in the Jordanian 'Arab Spring'." *Middle East Law and Governance*, 8(1), 32–56.
Kamrava, M. 2000. "Military Professionalization and Civil–Military Relations in the Middle East." *Political Science Quarterly*, 115(1), 67–92.
Kamrava, M. 2012. "The Arab Spring and the Saudi-led Counterrevolution." *Orbis*, 56(1), 96–104.
Kamrava, M. (ed.) 2014. *Beyond the Arab Spring: The Evolving Ruling Bargain in the Middle East*. Hurst.

Kandil, H. 2012. *Soldiers, Spies and Statesmen: Egypt's Road to Revolt*. Verso Books.

Koehler, K., Ohl, D., and Holger Albrecht. 2016. "From Disaffection to Desertion: How Networks Facilitate Military Insubordination in Civil Conflict." *Comparative Politics*, 48(4), 439–57.

Lewis, B. 2000. "Monarchy in the Middle East." In Kostiner, J. (ed.), *Middle East Monarchies: The Challenge of Modernity*. Boulder: Lynne Rienner, pp. 15–22.

Lynch, M. 2013. "The War for the Arab World." *Foreign Policy: The War for the Arab World Comments,* 23 May, available at http://foreignpolicy.com/2013/05/23/the-war-for-the-arab-world/

Lynch, M. (ed.) 2014. *The Arab Uprisings Explained: New Contentious Politics in the Middle East*. Columbia University Press.

Lynch, M. 2015. *The Arab Uprisings Explained: New Contentious Politics in the Middle* East. New York: Columbia University Press.

Lynch, M. 2016. *The New Arab Wars: Uprisings and Anarchy in the Middle East*. New York: Public Affairs Press.

Masoud, T. 2011. "The Road to (and from) Liberation Square." *Journal of Democracy*, 22(3), 23.

Masoud, T. 2014. *Counting Islam: Religion, Class, and Elections in Egypt*. Cambridge University Press.

Ohl, D., Albrecht, H., and Koehler, K. 2015. "For Money or Liberty? The Political Economy of Military Desertion and Rebel Recruitment in the Syrian Civil War." Regional insight paper prepared as part of the 2014–2015 Renegotiating Civil–Military Relations in Arab States: Political and Economic Governance in Transition Project, Carnegie Middle East Center.

Parolin, G. 2015. "Constitutions against Revolutions: Political Participation in North Africa." *British Journal of Middle Eastern Studies*, 42(1), 31–45.

Ryan, C. 2012. "The New Arab Cold War and the Struggle for Syria." *Middle East Report*, 262, 28–31.

Sakr, R. 2013. "Rock the Casbah: Rage and Rebellion across the Islamic World." *British Journal of Middle Eastern Studies*, 40(4), 479–81.

Schulhofer-Wohl, Jonah. 2014. "Fighting between Allies and the Civil War in Syria." *Project on Middle East Political Science RSS*. POMEPS, 12 February. Available at http://pomeps.org/2014/02/12/fighting-between-allies-and-the-civil-war-in-syria/ [accessed 8 February 2016].

Soliman, S. 2011. *The Autumn of Dictatorship: Fiscal Crisis and Political Change in Egypt under Mubarak*. Stanford University Press.

Springborg, R. 2011. "Economic Involvements of Militaries." *International Journal of Middle East Studies*, 43(3), 397–9.

Stacher, J. 2012. *Adaptable Autocrats: Regime Power in Egypt and Syria*. Stanford University Press.

Tansey, O. 2015. "Questioning 'Autocracy Promotion'." *APSA Comparative Democratization Newsletter*, 13(1), 4–7.

Volpi, F. 2013. "Algeria versus the Arab Spring." *Journal of Democracy*, 24(3), 104–15.

Yom, S. L. 2011. "Oil, Coalitions, and Regime Durability: The Origins and Persistence of Popular Rentierism in Kuwait." *Studies in Comparative International Development*, 46(2), 217–41.

Yom, S. L. 2014a. "Authoritarian Monarchies as an Epistemic Community: Diffusion, Repression, and Survival during the Arab Spring." *Taiwan Journal of Democracy*, 10(1), 43–62.

Yom, S. L. 2014b. "Tribal Politics in Contemporary Jordan: The Case of the Hirak Movement." *The Middle East Journal*, 68(2), 229–47.

Yom, S., 2015. *From Resilience to Revolution: How Foreign Interventions Destabilize the Middle East*. Columbia University Press.

Yom, S. and Gregory Gause. 2012. "Resilient Royals: How Arab Monarchies Hang On." *Journal of Democracy*, 23(4), 74–88.

Zurayk, R. and Anne Gough. 2014. "Bread and Olive Oil: The Agrarian Roots of the Arab Uprisings." In Gerges, F. A. (ed.), *The New Middle East: Protest and Revolution in the Arab World*, Cambridge University Press, pp. 107–31.

PART IV

Political economy

19

BEYOND STATE AND MARKET

Development strategies in the Arab world

Amr Adly

Introduction

Sixty years after political independence, the Arab world is largely a case of unaccomplished economic, social, and political development. The region remains heavily dependent on exporting raw materials, namely oil and gas, with little ability to upgrade into higher value-added manufactured and service sectors. Strides in human development, especially in education, healthcare and life expectancy, have translated into the highest youth unemployment in the world (Achcar 2013). Politically, decades of top-down authoritarian modernization have led to the re-invention of primordial tribal, ethnic and sectarian identities amid increasingly failing nation-states and disintegrating societies. What went wrong?

This chapter aims at identifying the common features of the development strategies adopted and pursued by Arab states since independence. It examines their national, regional and international contexts and dynamics through which development choices were made and how they were implemented.

"Development strategy" is defined as state authoritative and concerted action over a period of time with the aim of transforming social and economic relations and structures in accordance with a certain notion of the public good (Evans 1995). The term hence applies to state agencies designing and implementing planned change. A development strategy is a point of intersection between the state, its political authoritative actions, and the economy. It may lean to the left with the state bureaucracy assuming a bigger role in the allocation and regulation of economic resources in a way that restrains or even completely displaces the market. It may conversely lean to the right where state action aims at clearing areas for market relations to thrive through trade, labor and capital liberalization, deregulation, and privatization or through a more proactive role in the institution of the market through robust private property rights protection, rule of law, and contract enforcement (North 1990, Amable 2003).

It could be stated that development strategies generally tackled the two issues of economic upgrading, referring to moving up the scale of the international division of labor into higher value-added goods and services (Evans 1995) and the improvement of the standards of living of the largest number possible of their people. Both goals have been practically interrelated having to do with the production of the economic cake and its distribution. This of course requires going beyond the description and analysis of state plans as expressed in official documents, laws, and regulations into a dynamic take on how the state has interacted with society and how it was (not) capable of achieving the end goals of transforming social and economic relations and structures over time.

State action, and hence politics as the authoritative allocation of economic value, is a central aspect in studying development strategies in general and especially in the Arab world. Since gaining political independence, the Arab state has become the principal agency shouldering the burden of economic modernization and socio-economic transformation. Arab bourgeoisies were either non-existent or too weak or made weak by the military, as in Egypt, Syria, and Iraq in the 1950s and 1960s. State dominance over development was only reassured by the access to easy oil rents since the 1970s. External rent flowing directly to state coffers made ruling elites more autonomous of their societies and less dependent on the overall performance of the economy. They also came to control the process of allocating state funds and defining the development priorities hence (Beblwai and Luciani 1987). Even for the non-oil-rich countries that were forced by the sheer pressure of fiscal crises and subsequent international conditionality to embark on economic liberalization in the 1980s and 1990s, the state remained central in the creation and sustenance of private big business (Heydemann 2004).

Almost all Arab states enjoyed vast mandates vis-à-vis their societies. They were marked by authoritarianism, unaccountability, and an effective control over massive economic resources be they financial, human, or physical. Yet, as authoritative as they may have been, Arab states were generally weak (Ayubi 1995; Soliman 2011). They were weak in terms of their inability to use their public authority in order to effect socio-economic transformation. They usually lacked the administrative and political capacities to penetrate and transform social and economic relations (Skocpol et al. 1985; Migdal 1988).

Arab states lacked absolute capacity, which refers to the ability of the bureaucracies to develop and implement coherent, cohesive, comprehensive, and long-term policies and regulations according to well-defined goals (Evans 1995; Adly 2012). Bureaucracies were used alternatively as means for cultivating support and distributing patronage by the generation of public employment and by staffing according to allegiance. The byproduct of this was bloated, inefficient, and expensive bureaucracies, which negated almost completely Max Weber's conception of a rational administration capable of pursuing public good.

Arab states have also lacked relative capacity, which refers to the ability of mobilizing societal partners that may augment or complement the capacity of the state in pursuing its development objectives (Shafer 1994). These states could cultivate bases of support. However, this was done through state distribution of resources along populist or clientelistic lines (Bianchi 1989) rather than through longer-term political engagement with supportive constituencies to socio-economic transformation. State legitimacy and most probably social stability and order required the state to use its resources to sustain distributive policies since independence. However, the state had little capacity to reshape social relations in a way that precluded any serious change at economic upgrading and the transformation of socio-political relations accordingly.

State-led industrialization (1950s–70s)

Following independence in the 1950s and 1960s, some Arab states adopted import-substitution industrialization (ISI). Modernization was equated with industrialization. The main challenge was perceived at the time to upgrade the economic structure from agriculture and to put an end to old patterns of dependency on the past colonial centers.

The state played a central role in ISI either through the establishment of large state-owned enterprises (SOEs) especially in heavy industries like iron and steel, petrochemicals, cement, and fertilizers or through the nationalization of private foreign as well as domestic enterprises. The public sector soon became the biggest employer. The push for state-led industrialization went hand in hand with land reform in Egypt, Iraq, Syria, and Tunisia that aimed at depriving the old landowning classes of their economic base of power. Land reform also allowed states more power in regulating agriculture and in the creation of a supportive middle-peasant class made up of beneficiaries of land redistribution (Abdel-Malek 1968).

Most ISI schemes were dependent on the transfer of the surplus from the agricultural sector to the industrialization efforts and from the countryside to emerging urban centers (Harik et al. 1992; Harik 1997; Richards and Waterbury 1996). Politically, the creation of a national market could not be separated from the process of nation building (Mitchell 1999). Authoritarian post-independence regimes in Egypt, Iraq, Syria, and Tunisia all relied on forging broad cross-class social coalitions that were centered on state-led industrialization. State-led modernization was portrayed as a project of national socio-economic transformation where social mobility was associated with industrial upgrading, bigger participation in the labor market, especially for women, and better chances at all stages of education. In the background, there was the great rural exodus and the movement into big cities working in industry and services.

State-led ISI was associated with some brand of nationalist socialism (Issawi 1980). Under Nasser (1954–70), Baathi regimes in Syria (since 1970) and Iraq (since 1968) it assumed a form of Arab socialism. Algeria followed suit after independence and especially under Boumedian (1965–78). Even in Tunisia, despite the rather reserved position vis-à-vis Arabism under Bourguiba (1956–87), the country underwent a phase of state socialism between 1960 and 1969. Agricultural collectivization coupled with an expanding public sector served as the policy basis for a left-leaning social coalition of unionized labor, middle peasants, and university students.

In conservative kingdoms, things developed somewhat differently. In oil-rich Libya, the monarchy (1951–69) depended on this extractive sector and an expatriate community of professionals and workers, in a way that enabled them to avoid industrial agitation and to suppress nationalist and socialist tendencies for a time. However, the question of how national oil wealth was being used in the broader context of left-leaning and populist military coups in the Middle East and North Africa (MENA) region led to the September takeover of 1969. Under Gadaffi, oil extractive deals were thoroughly renegotiated and more ambitious projects of infrastructure and rapid urbanization took place (Gurney 1996). However, the transformative impact of oil did not appear fully until the 1973 oil shock.

In Morocco, the kingdom lacked natural resources, with the exception of phosphates, which could hardly play the role oil could. Moreover, the country underwent an extended process of decolonization stretching from 1956 when the French withdrew until 1975 when the Spanish left the western desert. During that period, the monarchy was increasingly menaced by nationalist and socialist movements, both reformist as well as revolutionary. The monarchy was preserved by a strategy of strengthening the position of the king as the symbol of national independence and sovereignty (Owen 2002).

Like many other ISI models in the third world, industrializing Arab countries came to suffer from foreign currency shortages by the late 1960s and early 1970s. In fact, import-substitution proved to be import-intensive as most faced considerable problems with industrial deepening. Rather, the industrial sectors in most ISI countries were dependent on importing technology, capital, and in many instances intermediate goods. This translated into bigger pressure over their slim foreign currency earnings. In Egypt, these shortcomings revealed themselves as early as the mid-1960s, after the end of the first five-year plan (1960–5). The situation was dramatically worsened by the defeat of 1967 and the entry into a six-year period of military mobilization against Israel.

ISI models were left to struggle with little accessibility to much-needed inputs. Recession, deteriorating balance of payments, and external debt soon invited international conditionality as these countries started to negotiate loans with international financial institutions (IFIs) in return for accepting stabilization measures. Yet, this did not happen before the second half of the 1980s as many of these ISI-troubled models of development started to have direct and indirect access to oil rent after the first shock of 1973. Access to easy money allowed them to sustain failing industries and to overcome, albeit momentarily, their fiscal and economic problems and to go on with their populist distribution policies (Soliman 2011). The increase in oil prices breathed life in largely defunct ISI strategies and the social coalitions that were formed. Overall, ISI had little impact on these countries' position in the international division of labor (Adly 2012). They remained dependent on exporting raw materials in order to finance local industrialization.

Then came the oil

The first oil shock of 1973 constituted a turning point in the history of development and development strategies in MENA. Huge windfalls, thanks to the increase in international oil prices, redefined the economic structures, role of state, political regime dynamics as well as intra-regional relations. The increase in oil prices through the 1970s and 1980s reasserted the position of MENA in the global division of labor as a prime producer of energy.

The increase in oil prices had profound institutional and political–economic impacts that could not be easily undone by following rounds of oil price decline like the oil glut of 1986 that lasted till the early 2000s. The two oil shocks of 1973 and 1979 created permanent dependency on the supply of energy to the rest of the world. This dependency was by no means confined to the major oil and natural gas producers in MENA. It rather extended to minor producers like Egypt, Tunisia, Syria, Yemen, and Sudan, which found themselves tied to the oil rent cycles either directly by producing and exporting crude oil or indirectly through aid and workers' remittances from oil-rich countries.

For oil-rich countries, access to tremendously large rents enabled these governments to launch ambitious economic modernization projects that were state-led and that were translated into generous expenditure on infrastructure, primarily in cities and social expenditure especially on education and health together with subsidization of electricity, fuel and in some instances, the expansion in public sector employment (Hertog 2011). The result of this model was the recycling of most oil rent either externally in well-developed capital markets in the US, Europe and later on east Asia or internally in largely non-tradable sectors like construction, infrastructure and financial services (Beblawi and Luciani 1987). This model also encouraged the hyper-urbanization of the populations in these oil-rich countries, particularly in the ones with small populations like Libya and most GCC countries. These oil-rich countries could make huge strides in social development particularly education and healthcare.

Politically, the large resources that flowed directly to the state coffers enabled the rulers to tightly control the modernization process. Most of the national wealth flowed from state to society allowing ruling regimes to selectively allocate resources with the aim of cultivating bases of support among the populace. As most of these oil-rich countries had small populations, the spurt in economic and social modernization led to hosting large expatriate communities of workers and professionals. Currently, expats constitute more than 80 percent of the populations in Qatar and the UAE. Moreover, their share in the labor force in a relatively populated country like Saudi Arabia has never been less than 50 percent according to the minister of labor in 2013. Oil rents no doubt were crucial in the supporting of tribal-based systems in the GCC countries as well as in other "revolutionary" regimes like Gadaffi's in Libya and Iraq under Saddam.

Yet, despite the great benefits these societies, states and regimes could reap from oil-related rent, the dependency on oil has had its problems. These countries had to adapt to cycles of boom and bust on which they had little control, if any (Hertog 2011). The role OPEC could play in the early 1970s was bound to decline due to the deep political resentment between key members, especially against the background of the Iraq–Iran war (1980–8) together with the traditional problems of collective action and opportunism. The 1986 oil glut was one dramatic example. The Saudis contributed to bringing down oil prices mounting the pressure on the Iraqis and Iranians and effectively putting an end to the long war in 1988. However, this was the first time for many primary and secondary rentier states when they had to adapt to less revenue.

The problem henceforth was dealing with the fact that whereas oil prices, and thus oil revenue, were elastic, expenditure was not. For many Arab regimes, their ability to financially sustain populist distributive policies and patronage networks was critical for their survival. Cutting social spending, public sector employment and subsidies could prove politically very dangerous. The solution was mainly found in accumulating reserves from the times of boom to use during the times of bust. Countries with large oil production and relatively small populations, namely the GCC member states, could do that through the 1990s. Bigger countries, like Iraq or Algeria and even more critically minor oil producers like Egypt, Syria, and Tunisia, were caught between a rock and a hard place. Despite continued attempts to diversify their economies away from the utter dependency on oil, the vast majority of first- and second-tier rentier states failed.

The reasons for this persistent dependency are manifold. Some attributed it to the Dutch disease, where access to easy money and overvaluation of the national currency encourage investment in non-tradables and mainly in unproductive and speculative sectors that merely recycle oil rent. Others attributed the inability to diversify, not just amongst large Arab but also among all major exporters, to the overvaluation of wages in a way that precludes any chance of developing labor-intensive industries. A third group claimed that oil booms create certain institutional arrangements that link the state and the economy in a particular way during the times of boom. However, such arrangements generate vested interests and sticky institutional rules that linger even in times of bust depriving the state of any real regulatory or political capacity to aim at diversification (Karl 1997).

Things took an even more dramatic turn in Algeria. A major natural gas exporter, Algeria enjoyed massive windfall revenue throughout the 1970s. Ambitious public projects were launched and generous social spending could be sustained. As oil prices collapsed in 1986, the government found itself in an increasingly hard position. The introduction of austerity measures in 1988 led to widespread bread riots. The National Liberation Front (FLN) regime, in charge since independence in 1962, chose to deal with this by introducing political reforms, allowing free party formation and open elections. In the 1990 parliamentary elections, the Islamist Salvation Front (FIS) won the majority in the first round, triggering the military to intervene forcing the president to resign and annulling election results. Algeria fell into a prolonged civil war that lasted for over a decade. During the 1990s, the Algerian government could not undertake any serious fiscal or economic reforms given the general political and security situations.

The decline in oil prices had its negative impact also on non-oil rentier economies like Jordan, which witnessed its own bread riots in 1988 against austerity measures designed in reaction to the 1986 collapse in oil prices and hence the decline in external rents.

Not only did huge inflows of easy money impact oil-rich countries in MENA but they also created new intra-regional political, geopolitical, and economic dynamics. Many minor oil producers like Egypt, Tunisia, Syria, and Yemen and even some oil importers like Jordan became well integrated into regional rent-distribution mechanisms flowing primarily from the Gulf Cooperation Council (GCC) countries as well as Iraq and Libya.

Rent recycling was either intergovernmental or private. The first form was primarily aid flowing from oil-rich countries in the Persian Gulf to their poorer allies. The starkest example was during the Second Gulf War in 1990-91 where Egypt and Syria were handsomely rewarded for joining the international coalition against Iraq. They were rewarded in return with inflows of grants and investments from the GCC and western sponsors alike. Conversely, those who supported Iraq, explicitly or implicitly, like Yemen, Jordan, and Sudan were severely punished and were denied access to Gulf aid and in some instances their citizens were shunned by the GCC labor markets.

Beside intergovernmental aid, there existed private mechanisms for rent distribution in the form of workers' remittances from the GCC countries to labor-exporting countries like Sudan, Egypt, Syria, and Jordan. The case of Jordan was so dramatic as almost half of the labor force, mainly ethnic Palestinians, worked in the GCC countries in the early 1990s (Bouhga-Hagbe 2006). Workers' remittances stood for over 40 percent of the GDP making it a rentier state par excellence despite being an oil importer. Together with the GCC, Libya and Iraq hosted hundreds of thousands of Egyptian workers.

From ISI to state-controlled liberalization (1970s to 2011)

Tunisia and Egypt were the first non-oil Arab countries to embark on economic liberalization and private sector development. As the experiment with agrarian collectivization and import-substitution industrialization reached its limits in 1969, Bourguiba reversed most policies. In 1972, an investment law was issued with the aim of attracting foreign investment and mobilizing private domestic capital. Egypt followed suit by Anwar Sadat's (1970–81) open-door policy—*Infitah*—launched in 1974. The goal was to attract Arab and foreign investment so as to raise the growth rates and more importantly to fix the balance of payment deficit and foreign currency shortage. *Infitah* implied some partial import liberalization that altered somehow the consumption patterns of the new middle classes, especially those who had access to oil rent through remittances sent from the Persian Gulf.

However, neither Sadat's nor Bourguiba's policies were popular, especially among state-dependent constituencies of public sector workers and civil servants. In 1977, Egypt signed an IMF stabilization package according to which food subsidies were partly slashed. The result was the first "bread riots" in MENA that lasted for almost a week and led to the death of tens of protestors. Sadat was forced to reverse the austerity measures (Waterbury 2014). Tunisia was not far behind. In 1978, similar austerity measures led to widespread protests. The General Federation of Work (UGTT) played a central role in organizing the protests among its public sector followings. Bourguiba had to deploy the military and to reverse the early decisions (Erdle 2010).

Popular protests in 1977 and 1978 were quite significant for they marked the beginning of the end of the old state-dependent social coalitions once formed after independence and the beginning of a protracted legitimacy crisis for the (economically) liberalizing autocrats. Economic liberalization, austerity, and privatization of state owned enterprises meant the effective undoing of earlier privileges given to public sector employees and unionized workers. Both Sadat and Bourguiba were forced to back down, and further austerity measures did not materialize for years to follow. The governments could partly afford to avoid reforms thanks to the renewed access to oil-related rent following the second oil shock. This enabled the governments of

Tunisia, Egypt, and other MENA countries to sustain their public expenditure and to escape the political cost of austerity or privatization, but not for long.

In 1986, the oil glut dealt lethal blows to state finances in most of the MENA countries. In Egypt, state revenue plunged. The government signed a second stabilization package with the IMF in 1987 but due to the fear of a repetition of the 1977 riots, Mubarak shied away from implementing the agreed upon measures. The government instead opted for external borrowing, from international commercial banks. This pushed the country's external debt to a massive 45 billion dollars by 1989, which Egypt could no longer service by that time (Soliman 2011). In Tunisia, economic decline coincided with Bourguiba's failing physical and mental health. In 1987, Ben Ali deposed him in a palace coup. Soon, austerity measures were introduced with the aim of balancing the state budget.

It was Egypt, however, that first witnessed the most coherent and comprehensive liberalization and privatization attempt in MENA in the early 1990s. Following Egypt's decision to join the international coalition against Iraq, the country enjoyed one of the most generous debt relief packages in modern history. A massive 50 percent of total external debt was forgiven while the remaining half was rescheduled according to the Paris agreement club (Richards 1999). Egypt finally signed a stand-by agreement with the IMF in return for implementing a stabilization program. The program was initially successful and throughout the first half of the 1990s, the Egyptian government brought down significantly the budget deficit and inflation. In addition to the stabilization program, a twin-package was sponsored by the World Bank with the aim of supporting the restructuring of the Egyptian economy by privatizing SOEs and incentivizing the growth of the private sector through deregulation, export-led growth, and attracting FDIs.

Indeed, by the early 2000s, the bulk of the GDP in Egypt had passed into the hands of the private sector. According to World Bank (2009) an estimated around 75 percent of the non-hydrocarbon GDP and of employment belonged to the private sector in 2009. Big Egyptian business emerged through the process and dominated key sectors like telecommunications, heavy industry, and financial services. The situation in Tunisia did not differ much.

Through the 2000s, new economic teams rose to central positions in governments and central banks in Egypt, Tunisia, Morocco, and Jordan. These minsters and technocrats had a strong ideological commitment to neoliberalism and they often came from a private business or an IFI-professional background. These economies witnessed a considerable push towards privatization, FDI attraction, and export expansion through the 2000s and all the way until the global financial crisis of 2008. Most performed well in terms of annual growth rates. However, this economic expansion failed to generate jobs adequate in number and quality for new labor market entrants resulting in particularly high rates of unemployment and underemployment, mainly amongst educated youths (UNDP 2012). State–big private business relations were marked by high incidence of corruption and cronyism that proved liable on the legitimacy of the ruling elites, especially in the countries with the longest record of economic liberalization i.e. Tunisia and Egypt.

Overall, the process of economic liberalization remained heavily controlled by the state through the 2000s. The emergence of a big private sector meant the transformation of the role of the state rather than its withdrawal from the economy (Mitchell 1999). The state played a central role in the creation of big private business usually through the uneven distribution of property rights in favor of a politically connected few in Egypt, Tunisia, Syria, and Morocco (Adly 2009; Hibou 2009; Erdle 2010; Haddad 2011). Those who enjoyed asymmetrical access to political power and to insider government information were given privileged access to privatized SOEs, monopolistic positions in weakly regulated markets, public procurement and investment incentives and subsidies.

The end result by the 2000s was a kind of crony capitalism where big business operated in a blurred area where power generated wealth and vice versa. It came even close to state capture in a small economy like Tunisia under Ben Ali, where big business was to a great extent composed of family members and their allies. In Egypt, the Mubaraks and their associates enjoyed similar positions but they had to contend with other crony networks, especially the ones tied to the military, over access to public land and market shares. In Morocco, big business remained closely tied to the *Makhzen*. This of course meant that the liberalization process did not create a functioning market-based capitalism. Property rights remained unevenly distributed, rule of law weak, and contract enforcement unreliable.

The other feature was the subjection of the scope and pace of liberalization and privatization to "perceived" political requirements of authoritarian survival. Mubarak and Ben Ali regimes, as well as other liberalizing autocrats in Morocco, Jordan, and Syria were keen on avoiding the outbreak of popular protest or riots. They hence had to sustain large subsidy schemes for urban dwellers, large public employment in the state bureaucracy that translated into huge wage bills and pursued an inconsistent strategy of SOE privatization and trade liberalization. In Syria, no serious attempt at liberalizing the economy happened until the succession of Hafez Al-Assad by his son Bashar. However, the dynamics of economic liberalization and deregulation were completely subjected to political consideration of elite coherence and sectarian and regional balance of power (Haddad 2011). By the end of the first decade of the twenty-first century, Syria did not look much different from Egypt or Tunisia in terms of the wealth–power unity.

Libya under Gadaffi witnessed no relevant amount of economic transformation towards a market-based economy. This might have had to do with economic sanctions through the 1990s combined with oil abundance, which made it possible for the regime to avoid bearing political risks for economic transformation. There was rather some state privatization where Gadaffi and his sons, his bigger clan and his tribal allies came increasingly to enjoy the returns of oil (Owen 2014).

In the cases of Egypt and Tunisia, which witnessed the greatest extent of liberalization and private sector expansion, the ruling regimes were politically unable to undo the old social coalition inherited from earlier Nasserist and Bourguibist eras. They had to keep allocating ever-dwindling public resources to sustaining large subsidy, wage bills and debt interest. This disabled these states from servicing the burgeoning private sector through public investment in human and physical infrastructure. The political choices made then ushered the Mubarak and Beni Ali's regimes into a socio-fiscal trap and a spiral of legitimacy erosion and an economically exclusionary model.

The socio-fiscal trap resulted from a combination of stagnant, or even diminishing public revenues in both countries and an inflexible structure of public expenditure. On the revenue side, non-tax revenue (primarily external rents) dwindled consistently through the 1990s and the 2000s (Soliman 2011; Hibou 2009). However, the Tunisian and Egyptian states suffered from a generally weak capacity to collect taxes from property and capital holding classes due to a plethora of administrative and political factors. This resulted in an overall stagnation in tax revenue as a percentage of national income.

On the expenditure side, maintaining the old coalition of state-dependent employees, unionized labor, and urban middle classes was translated into an ever-inflated bill of wages, fuel and food subsidies, and other recurrent expenses. This curtailed the state capacity to invest in physical infrastructure and more importantly in education and vocational training causing major productivity problems to the emergent capitalist orders that limited their global competitiveness and their ability to grow, invest and to generate well-paid jobs (Achcar 2013). It also made the two authoritarian regimes too dependent on narrow bases of supporters with a general inability to include sizable strata of skilled and educated workers, especially youth, in formal, secure and productive jobs. In a sentence, the role the state played in the redistribution of income and wealth in Egypt and Tunisia since the 1980s perpetuated a non-developmental capitalist model that lacked socio-political legitimacy leading finally to the 2011 popular revolts that toppled the two longstanding dictators (Kandil 2012).

Development strategies after the Arab revolutions

The breakout of the 2011 Arab revolutions is the single most important turning point in MENA contemporary history. The revolutions unleashed complex and ongoing processes within and among states in the region and beyond. They resulted in the overall weakening or complete destruction of central state apparatuses in countries that underwent revolutions. In Syria, Libya, and Yemen, central governments were partly or totally overthrown. In Egypt and Tunisia, the state persisted but with a significantly reduced capacity to control all of the territory and population activities.

It is definitely too early to say what impact Arab revolutions will have on development strategies. On the one hand, central governments are in no position to realistically devise and implement plans with distributional consequences at this juncture. On the other, most are struggling with imminent and increasingly pressing economic, political, and security problems. In such a context, structural issues retreat to the background.

It can, however, be said that so far the revolutions have not caused any tangible change in the content of development strategies or in the institutional and policy tools used to forward them, not to mention the power relations that permeate them. This, however, does *not* dismiss chances of major changes in the long term. As a matter of fact, the quest for political stabilization after the most intense period of political and social turmoil in the modern history of the region is not likely to be achieved without the redefinition of the very foundations of the development models to be adopted. Most Arab countries, especially resource-poor ones are in need of development strategies that could generate inclusive growth and hence create legitimate and viable economic orders. Here, the process of economic inclusion is hardly separable from political integration as many of these countries are simultaneously reconstructing or reconstituting their national polities, on pluralist or authoritarian terms like Tunisia and Egypt respectively.

Even oil-rich countries that were largely spared the turmoil (with the marked exceptions of Libya and Iraq) have had to face plummeting international energy prices since mid-2014. Should this trend continue, future stability of these political economic models of development would become questionable. Most of these states have young populations, high unemployment due to the almost complete dependency on narrow oil-producing enclaves and high expectations for consumption and social mobility. What will these ruling elites do in case the world is heading towards an age of cheap energy is an open-ended yet increasingly pressing question that addresses the thorny issue of diversification away from raw materials.

How to develop is a simple yet hard question. As demographic, political and social pressure mounts on MENA governments, there has to be a general revision of all public policies that have distributional consequences ranging from public investment in infrastructure, education, and vocational training, economic regulation to subsidies and taxation. Beyond policies, change is also due for the institutions that govern state–society intercourse, which is subject to complex and multifaceted historical processes of transformation.

Conclusion

Development strategies touch upon the critical question of the capacity of states to transform socio-economic relations in their respective societies in accordance with a certain vision.

As Nazih Ayubi claimed, Arab states are overstated. They are indeed too big, too authoritative and with a very large mandate and claim over the resources of their societies. However, their capacity, both political as well as administrative, to penetrate and transform their economies and societies has proven limited. Arab states have adopted a great myriad of development strategies throughout their history. Some aimed at state-led industrialization through import substitution and targeting local markets. Others depended mainly on state-led development using abundant natural resources, namely oil and gas. A third group, mainly of non-oil economies, were forced or allured into economic liberalization and deregulation in the 1980s and 1990s.

However, most of the strategies failed to achieve the goal of having more inclusive economic systems that can generate growth, investment and employment for the great majority of their, rather young, citizens. They have also failed in making their economies less dependent on selling crude, and hence low-value-added, raw materials. The failure could be explained in political and institutional terms rather than in the particular content of the policies or strategies adopted.

Nowadays, and especially in the aftermath of the revolutions of 2011, the Arab region is undergoing a lengthy, complex, and multifaceted process of transforming state–society relations. The redefinition of the development model(s) in the region seems to hinge on these transformations that would be crucial in determining the mode of articulation between state and market and the distributional and re-distributional aspects of the economy.

Bibliography

Abdel-Malek, A., 1968. *Egypt: Military Society*. Random House, pp. 1805–92.

Achcar, G., 2013. *The People Want: A Radical Exploration of the Arab Uprising*. University of California Press.

Adly, A. I., 2009. Politically-embedded cronyism: The case of post-liberalization Egypt. *Business and Politics*, 11(4), 1–28.

Adly, A., 2012. *State Reform and Development in the Middle East: Turkey and Egypt in the Post-Liberalization Era*. Routledge.

Al-Rasheed, M. and Vitalis, R., 2004. *Counter-Narratives: History, Contemporary Society, and Politics in Saudi Arabia and Yemen*. Palgrave Macmillan.

Amable, B., 2003. *The Diversity of Modern Capitalism*. Oxford University Press.

Amsden, A. H., 1992. *Asia's Next Giant: South Korea and Late Industrialization*. Oxford University Press.

Ayubi, N., 1995. *Overstating the Arab State, Politics and Society in the Middle East*. London: I. B. Tauris.

Beblawi, H. and Luciani, G. (eds), 1987. *The Rentier State* (Vol. 2). Routledge.

Bianchi, R., 1989. *Unruly Corporatism: Associational Life in Twentieth-Century Egypt*. Oxford University Press.

Bouhga-Hagbe, M. J., 2006. Altruism and Workers' Remittances: Evidence from Selected Countries in the Middle East and Central Asia (EPub) (No. 6-130). International Monetary Fund.

Erdle, S., 2010. *Ben Ali's "New Tunisia" (1987–2009): A Case Study of Authoritarian Modernization in the Arab World*. Klaus Schwarz.

Evans, P. B., 1995. *Embedded Autonomy: States and Industrial Transformation*. Princeton, NJ: Princeton University Press.

Gurney, J., 1996. *Libya: The Political Economy of Oil*. Oxford: Oxford University Press.

Haddad, B., 2011. *Business Networks in Syria: The Political Economy of Authoritarian Resilience*. Stanford University Press.

Harik, I. F., 1997. *Economic Policy Reform in Egypt*. University Press of Florida.

Harik, I., Sullivan, D. and Patton, M. J., 1992. *Privatization and Liberalization in the Middle East*. Indiana University Press.

Hertog, S., 2011. *Princes, Brokers, and Bureaucrats: Oil and the State in Saudi Arabia*. Cornell University Press.

Heydemann, S., 2004. *Networks of Privilege in the Middle East: The Politics of Economic Reform Revisited*. New York: Palgrave.

Hibou, B., 2009. Le réformisme, grand récit politique de la Tunisie contemporaine, *Revue d'histoire moderne et contemporaine*, 56(5), 14–39.

Issawi, C., 1965. The Arab world's heavy legacy, *Foreign Affairs*, 43(3), 501–12.
Issawi, C., 1980. De-industrialization and re-industrialization in the Middle East since 1800, *International Journal of Middle East Studies*, 12(4), 469–79.
Kandil, H., 2012. Why did the Egyptian middle class march to Tahrir Square?, *Mediterranean Politics*, 17(2), 197–215.
Karl, T. L., 1997. *The Paradox of Plenty: Oil Booms and Petro-States*. University of California Press.
Migdal, Joel S., 1988. *Strong Societies and Weak States: State–Society Relations and State Capabilities in the Third World*. Pinceton, NJ: Princeton University Press.
Mitchell, T., 1999. Dreamland: The neoliberalism of your desires, *Middle East Report*, 29(210), 28–33.
North, D. C., 1990. *Institutions, Institutional Change and Economic Performance*. Cambridge University Press.
Owen, R., 2002. *State Power and Politics in the Making of the Modern Middle East*. Routledge.
Owen, R., 2014. *The Rise and Fall of Arab Presidents for Life: With a New Afterword*. Harvard University Press.
Richards, A., 1999. Dilatory reform vs. making a break for the market. In Phebe Marr (ed.) *Egypt at the Crossroads: Domestic Stability and Regional Role*, Washington DC. National Defense University Press.
Richards, A. and Waterbury, J., 1996. *A Political Economy of the Middle East*. Boulder CO: Westview Press.
Sfakianakis, J., 2004. The whales of the Nile: Networks, businessmen, and bureaucrats during the era of privatization in Egypt. In *Networks of Privilege in the Middle East: The Politics of Economic Reform Revisited*. Palgrave Macmillan US, pp. 77–100.
Shafer, D. M., 1994. *Winners and Losers: How Sectors Shape the Developmental Prospects of States*. Cornell University Press.
Skocpol, T., Evans, P. B., and Rueschemeyer, D., 1985. *Bringing the State Back In*. Cambridge University Press.
Soliman, S., 2011. *The Autumn of Dictatorship: Fiscal Crisis and Political Change in Egypt under Mubarak*. Stanford University Press.
United Nations Development Program (UNDP), 2012. *Arab Development Challenges Report: Towards the Developmental State in the Arab Region*, Cairo: UNDP.
Waterbury, J., 1970. *The Commander of the Faithful: The Moroccan Political Elite: A Study in Segmented Politics*. Weidenfeld & Nicolson.
Waterbury, J., 2014. *The Egypt of Nasser and Sadat: The Political Economy of Two Regimes*. Princeton University Press.
World Bank, 2009. *From Privilege to Competition: Unlocking Private-Led Growth in the Middle East and North Africa*, Washington DC: International Bank for Reconstruction and Development/World Bank.

20

THE POLITICAL ECONOMY OF ENERGY IN THE MEDITERRANEAN

Gonzalo Escribano

Introduction

During the last years, the global and Mediterranean energy landscape has been rapidly changing, with the emergence of new resources, like renewable energies and unconventional hydrocarbons, but also more ideational drivers such as sustainability and good energy governance to fight against climate change and the resource curse, respectively. The Arab Spring and its aftermaths have also altered the political economy of the region, within which energy plays a key role in producing and importing countries.

This chapter explores the political economy of energy in the Mediterranean from two complementary angles. Its first section addresses the main global and regional energy drivers of change for the southern shore of the Mediterranean, namely the abrupt decrease of oil (and gas) prices, the emergence of the US as an unconventional energy power, and the recently signed Paris Agreement. From a regional perspective, it focuses on a rapidly increasing energy demand and the deterioration of security conditions.

The second section argues that Mediterranean political economy balances are also shifting due to endogenous dynamics. Political economy considerations are becoming a fundamental aspect of Mediterranean energy realities, whether regarding the rejection of rentierism or opposing energy reform. This section also explores the international political economy of Euro-Mediterranean energy relations before concluding with a call for a renewed European energy narrative towards the Mediterranean.

Global and regional energy trends

From a global perspective, the most relevant recent energy trends for the southern Mediterranean are the oil price collapse that started in mid-2014 and the surge of US shale gas production that is transforming gas markets, together with a new energy policy framework after the Paris Agreement.[1] On the regional dimension, booming domestic energy demand and a worsened security context have prevented the region to benefit from enhanced Euro-Mediterranean energy relations in spite of the increasing Russian–EU rivalry.[2]

Oil price volatility is the key economic vulnerability of Mediterranean oil and gas producers (most gas contracts in the region are indexed to oil), like Algeria or Libya. The economy of energy importers in the region is also sensitive to oil prices, but Algeria and Libya completely depend on oil and gas income. In Algeria, the hydrocarbon sector represents around 30 per cent of GDP, 60 per cent of government revenues and over 95 per cent of exports. As a result of the oil price counter-shock, exports halved from almost US$73 billion in 2011 to US$37.5 billion in 2015, rapidly deteriorating the external balance. The current account deficit reached a 15.7 per cent record in 2015 and foreign reserves have plunged from 34 to 24 months of imports between 2012 and 2015, and the government expects the country's oil fund (*Fond de Régulation des Recettes*, FRR) to fall by the end of 2016 to a third of its 2014 level.[3]

In Libya, the oil sector accounts for over 60 per cent of GDP and 95 per cent of exports, and the public sector heavily depends upon the oil revenue. The decline in the oil price and the problems in restoring the level of production and exports after the fall of Gadaffi are causing a deep deterioration of the Libyan economy. The public deficit for 2015 exceeded 40 per cent of GDP, and the IMF believes that if the situation does not improve it may approach 70 per cent of GDP in 2016 (IMF, 2016). Fiscal imbalances of this magnitude are unheard of in modern economic history. Although the country benefits from two major buffers – its currency reserves and the assets of its sovereign wealth fund – the former are in free-fall and both have been subjected to the struggle between the two Libyan governments.

Low oil and natural gas prices will also further deter investments in exploration and production across the Mediterranean. In Algeria and Libya, the oil price fall will postpone already delayed energy projects due to energy policy or security concerns, worsening economic growth figures. Nevertheless, the geographical proximity to European markets and the relatively low cost of Algerian and Libyan resources places them in a better position than other high cost producers, for instance in the eastern Mediterranean. On the other hand, for oil and gas importers low prices are a positive economic supply side shock and the opportunity to rationalize energy subsidies. Several Mediterranean energy-importing countries have both renewables' deployment and efficiency targets, and are trying to better manage demand and to diversify energy mix and sources of supply. In this regard, low oil and natural gas prices also entail an internal shift in Mediterranean geopolitical balances in favour of importing countries.

The changing pattern of natural gas markets, both regarding its new geography and contractual terms, is precisely the second global driver affecting Mediterranean countries. The US shale revolution has altered the geographies of global and regional natural gas markets. According to some analysis, African natural gas exporters would be the main losers of US liquefied natural gas (LNG) exports to Europe, with a 35 per cent to 40 per cent reduction in their export gas revenues, compared with a 27 to 38 per cent reduction for Russia.[4]

Besides rebalancing gas resources worldwide, the emergence of an LNG global market constitutes a shift towards new contractual patterns and a more flexible and competitive market structure. While traditionally Mediterranean gas producers like Algeria (or in the past Libya and Egypt) have proved interested in participating in LNG markets, they have been reluctant to move away from oil-indexed long-term contracts to spot prices set at European gas trading hubs. The changes in LNG markets may force Mediterranean producers to accept some partial indexing to European hubs and more flexible contracts, and there are already signs of Algeria relaxing contractual terms in some recent deals. This is highly beneficial for regional gas importers, and is in fact incentivizing countries like Morocco to turn towards LNG.

At the same time, both Algeria and Libya hold vast untapped shale gas resources. The Ghadames Basin, encompassing eastern Algeria, southern Tunisia, and western Libya, is classified as a major shale gas basin; Turkey also has good potential in shale and tight gas resources (US EIA, 2015a). However, in spite of a favourable geology and a well-established gas industry, several obstacles (together with low oil and gas prices) hamper the development of unconventional gas in the region. In Algeria, popular opposition (including violent demonstrations in the south), water concerns, and long and bureaucratic procedures make the short-term development of Algerian shale gas reserves unlikely (Boersma et al., 2015). Similar concerns and a more complex security situation in Libya and southern Tunisia also prevent a rapid development of shale exploration in both countries.

However, the main global driver in the long run is climate change, which is projected to have very significant effects in the Mediterranean. According to the IPPC:

> [T]here is *high confidence* in model projections of mean temperature in this region. It is *very likely* that temperatures will continue to increase throughout the 21st century over all of Europe and the Mediterranean region. It is *likely* that winter mean temperature will rise more in NEU [northern Europe] than in CEU [central Europe] or MED [Mediterranean], whereas summer warming will *likely* be more intense in MED and CEU than in NEU. The length, frequency, and/or intensity of warm spells or heat waves are assessed to be *very likely* to increase throughout the whole region. There is *medium confidence* in an annual mean precipitation increase in NEU and CEU, while a decrease is *likely* in Mediterranean summer mean precipitation.
>
> *(Christensen et al., 2013)*

These projections have been worsened by more recent literature concluding that, in some scenarios, by the end of the century part of the region may become inhabitable for humans due to high temperatures related to more frequent and longer heat waves in summer (Lelieveld, 2016).

In spite of this, energy supply in the region is dominated by oil and gas, and fossil fuels are the region's main source of CO_2 emissions. Rapid demand growth implies a fast increase in CO_2 emissions from fuel combustion, which more than doubled between 1970 and 2013. There are however substantial north–south differences: in the northern Mediterranean, CO_2 emissions decreased by 0.1 per cent on average between 1990 and 2013; by contrast the average annual growth of CO_2 emissions in the south was 3.3 per cent. While in 2013 north Mediterranean countries represented 55 per cent of total CO_2 emissions in the region, by 2040 southern countries are projected to account between 64 and 68 per cent of Mediterranean CO_2 emissions (OME, 2015: 218). These trends call for a bigger effort in promoting proper adaptation and mitigation measures in the Mediterranean.

This leads us to Mediterranean regional energy drivers. Contrary to what happens in Europe, the southern shore of the Mediterranean faces a rapidly growing domestic energy demand. In the northern shore energy demand increased by only 0.6 per cent annually from 1990 to 2013, and it has actually decreased since the financial crisis. By contrast, in the South energy demand has boomed at an annual growth rate of 3.5 per cent since 1990, accelerating to 6 per cent from 2010 to 2013. According to OME, energy demand will grow in the southern Mediterranean 3.2 per cent annually until 2040 in their conservative scenario, or 1.3 per cent in the proactive scenario that contemplates stricter energy efficiency policies (OME, 2015).

For some gas producers, and coupled with the decline in domestic production, growing consumption has affected export potential. Egypt became a gas importer due to stagnating gas production and thriving demand. Political unrest and poor energy policies meant very low energy prices and bureaucratic delays, while foreign companies were not paid and were denied feedstock to export. The new government is trying to reform its energy policy to speed up the completion of delayed projects and the development of new fields, especially the promising super-giant Zohr gas field. The government has expressed its will to paying down its debt, reforming subsidies, adjusting natural gas prices and attracting foreign investment.[5]

Nevertheless, curbing domestic energy demand has become an imperative to keep fiscal deficits at manageable and financeable levels. Some countries in the region are among the bigger energy subsidizers in the world, especially regarding fossil fuels (Figure 20.1). Egypt, Jordan, Morocco and Tunisia have recently implemented energy subsidy reforms profiting from a low price environment (RCREE, 2015). Countries like Algeria are experiencing more difficulties in dealing with subsidy reform. In 2014, fossil-fuel subsidization rates were close to 80 per cent in Algeria and Libya, representing 9.4 per cent and 18 per cent of GDP, respectively; in Egypt, fuel subsidies amounted to 8 per cent of GDP (Figure 20.1).

The second regional trend is the deterioration of security conditions in the wider southern Mediterranean region, not only in the Mashrek and the Maghreb, but also in the Middle East and the Sahel. In the eastern Mediterranean, the Syria–Iraq crisis and its regional spillovers have disrupted the Mashrek energy landscape. While Syria was a minor oil producer, it was nevertheless the eastern Mediterranean's main oil and natural gas producer. The Syrian energy sector has suffered from the conflict itself and the sanctions imposed by the United States and the EU. Both have led its hydrocarbon production to a fraction of pre-conflict levels, delaying indefinitely exploration, development, production and transport. Even if the conflict were to subside, it would take years for the energy sector to return to pre-conflict operating conditions. Before the conflict, Syria produced almost 400,000 barrels per day (b/d) of oil and 316 million cubic feet per day of natural gas, accounting for one-fourth of government revenues (US EIA, 2015b). The rise of Daesh has also affected Egypt, which has suffered from several terrorist attacks targeting gas pipelines in the Sinai Peninsula and the Suez Canal, increasing the Egyptian energy sector risk premium.

Chaos has also spread to Libya, where oil production has endured a rollercoaster ride reflecting a succession of blockades, attacks, strikes and sabotages on oil and gas fields, pipelines and export terminals. Output in 2010 was close to 1.6 million b/d, but fell to 500,000 b/d in 2011, only

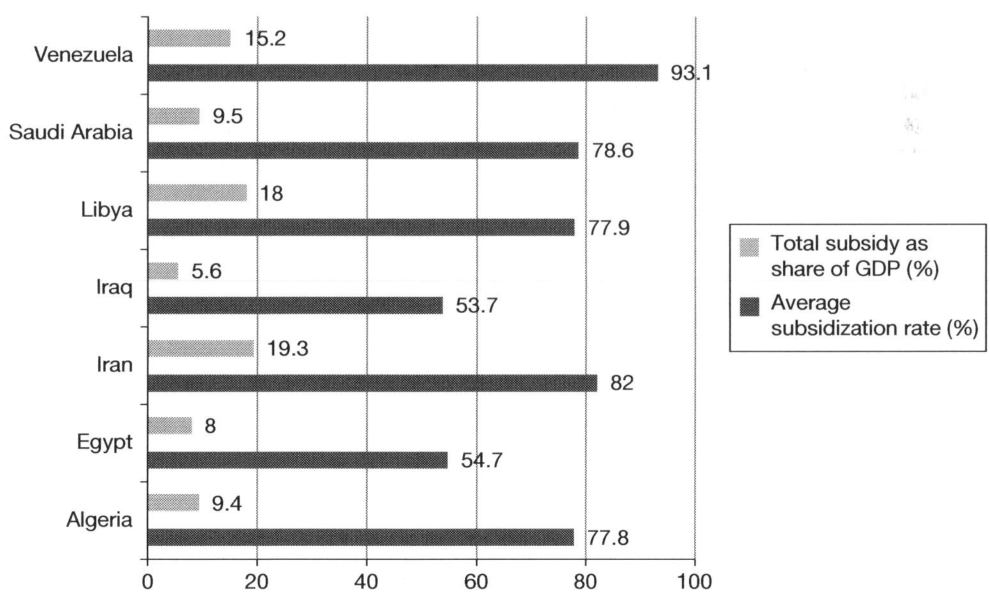

Figure 20.1 Fossil fuel subsidies in selected countries, 2014

Source: International Energy Agency, *Fossil-fuel Subsidies Database*, 2015 (available at www.worldenergyoutlook.org/resources/energysubsidies/fossilfuelsubsidydatabase/).

to recover to nearly 1.4 million b/d and subsequently to fall again below 400,000 b/d in 2015. The emergence of Daesh, with recent attacks on various installations, aggravates the problem and raises the question of whether this terrorist organization wants to replicate the strategy used in Iraq and Syria, where it used to derive significant income from the sale of oil (now in decline after the aerial attacks on its facilities). For the time being, in Libya, the attacks have focused on the destruction of targets to economically undermine the country's two governments as they inched towards unity, and possibly on the theft of fuel for replenishment or smuggling purposes. It is estimated that more than half the fuel sold in Libya at subsidized prices ends up in neighbouring countries where the prices are much higher.

However, existing conditions in Libya are not as conducive to contraband as those in Syria and Iraq, where the smuggling networks are much more consolidated and benefit from numerous local and Turkish intermediaries. Nor has the Syrian phenomenon of backyard refineries taken hold in Libya, because the population density is much lower, the penetration of ISIS has been relatively limited and the main oilfields are located a long way from the inhabited areas on the coast and the contraband networks on the borders (Reed, 2016). Nevertheless, the news that Daesh is seeking engineers and former workers in the Libyan energy industry could indicate a worrisome change of strategy.[6]

The Libyan chaos also threatens Algeria. While the Algerian internal security situation has greatly improved since the 1990s civil war, there still are several 'residual' terrorist groups active in the country. More importantly, Algeria has 5,500 km of complicated borders, including a 1,000 km border with Libya. In spite of the significant effort made by Algeria to increase border control, almost doubling its border police and increasing the security budget, terrorist groups have been able to operate in the Algerian territory from neighbouring countries.

The January 2013 jihadist attack against the In Amenas gas plant suddenly increased the risk perception of an energy supplier that to date had proved almost immune to seemingly harsher security conditions. The In Amenas facility produces about 10 per cent of Algerian gas, and the attack significantly reduced Algerian gas supplies to Italy through the Trans-Med pipeline, affecting Algerian gas production over almost two years. Security risks, costs and premiums have increased accordingly, further eroding foreign investment. More recently (March 18, 2016) AQMI conducted an unsuccessful missile attack against the Kherichba gas facility, forcing BP and Statoil to evacuate its personnel.[7] In a communiqué, AQMI threatened foreign energy companies and tried to link the attack to the In Salah population opposition to shale gas and the domination exerted by foreign companies on Algerian natural resources.[8]

All the previous drivers, global and regional, pose serious energy challenges for southern Mediterranean countries. However, a third striking regional development is the lack of capacity of southern Mediterranean hydrocarbon producers to profit from the window of opportunity that represents the European move to diversify away from Russia, and to project themselves (individually or regionally) as providers of energy security to the EU. Both the EU and its southern neighbours have missed such a positive and unexpected geopolitical external shock (for Mediterranean producers) to build a solid mechanism managing their energy interdependency. The last section of this chapter is precisely devoted to the shortcomings of Euro-Mediterranean energy relations, but before elaborating on that issue the next section explores the internal dynamics influencing the political economy of energy in the southern Mediterranean.

A political economy approach to energy in the southern Mediterranean

Political economy considerations are a key factor in analysing Mediterranean energy. Three aspects may be highlighted: the extent to which rentierism permeates the political economy balances of energy-rich countries, the political difficulties of removing energy subsidies in both producing and importing countries, and the international political economy of Euro-Mediterranean energy relations.

On the first aspect, perhaps the most significant divide is whether a particular country develops a rentier economy based upon hydrocarbon exports or diversifies its economic base to overcome rentierism. Some authors have argued that uncertainty over oil prices tends to exacerbate lobbying among conservative and reformist factions in oil exporting countries, making political economy balances more difficult to settle in times of high price volatility (Boucekkine et al., 2014). In the southern Mediterranean, Algeria and Libya are clear examples of rentier economies associated with political authoritarianism through centralized and opaque wealth management, rent-seeking elites, patronage and clientelism, and economic instead of political legitimization (Martínez, 2010; Volpi, 2013). Besides its political implications, rentierism also has significant economic effects. While in conventional, non-rentier economies, energy consumption almost always entails a positive contribution to economic growth, for Algeria this contribution has tended to be negative. In Egypt, where rentierism is lower, the diversification of the economy contributes to a more efficient allocation of resources, making energy consumption one of the fundamental drivers of economic growth (Fuinhas and Cardoso, 2013).

In Algeria, the political economy literature highlights the divide between the so-called 'affairistes' (business elites) and the conservatives (closer to the military). This cleavage has been in place since the mid-1980s, when conservatives thought that the economic recession that followed the oil counter-shock was temporary and that minor adaptations in economic policies would suffice. By contrast, those who saw a structural crisis in the making advocated the reform of the Algerian 'rentier' state (Martínez, 2010: 84). When oil prices started to rise again by the 2000s, the Algerian government had stabilized the Algerian economy, but did not accomplish a real modernization of its economic structure and institutions (Escribano and Lorca, 2008).

Things are not that simple today, with a business elite co-opted by the regime, favouring economic but not necessarily political reforms; a complex balance within the civilian and military branches of the 'revolutionary family'; a slow and frustrating pace of generational change and almost no elite renewal; and overall, the uncertainty over the capacity of the Bouteflika wing to continue to maintain a diversified network of alliances and balance between those actors given the president's poor health (Boubekeur, 2013; Zoubir, 2016). However, the fundamental cleavage regarding attitudes towards economic reform is still present in Algeria (Escribano and Lorca, 2012). For instance, the Forum des Chefs d'Entreprise (FCE, 2015) has openly expressed its criticisms towards the government's economic policies, pushing for unpopular reforms, like subsidy, fiscal, public administration and foreign investments reforms. On the other side, the political opposition and some influential figures have tried to discredit the reforms on the grounds that it is just another rent-seeking strategy from the economic elites.

In post-Gaddafi Libya, the political economy of energy has turned over a resource conflict among different factions, closer to that of Iraq or Sudan than to other Mediterranean cases. The struggle to control the assets of the central bank and the sovereign wealth fund are nothing but the backdrop to a more explicit fight over oil revenues, which manifests itself in the tug of war for the state oil company and its subsidiaries and for control of the energy infrastructure (oil and gas fields and export terminals). This magnifies existing political divisions and allocates resources to distribution for political patronage, exactly the same rental allocation mechanism at work under Gaddafi (Randall, 2015). Therefore, it has been argued that post-Gaddafi Libya's energy priorities consist in security, reconstruction and governance (Escribano, 2011). Furthermore, it has been pointed out that the need for an integrated infrastructure and single bureaucratic management to market the country's oil wealth has traditionally been a key factor in uniting Libya (Vandewalle, 2011).

The nature of the conflict is extremely complex, with political, territorial, ethnic and tribal divisions that only share the political economy of Libya's hydrocarbon resources. So extreme did the situation become that the security organization responsible for protecting energy facilities wrested control of them to extract political and economic advantages. The difficulties in forming a unity government have shown the hurdles that prevent resource governance pathways that may be acceptable to all sides in the conflict. In a clear illustration of the international repercussions of the east–west divide, the US navy even had to intercept the oil tanker *Morning Star* to prevent it being illegally sold by the government in the east.

The oil price collapse has aggravated the fiscal position of both Algeria and Libya. According to the IMF, the fiscal break-even oil price (the oil price that balances the budget) in 2014, when oil process started to collapse, was US$135/barrel for Algeria and US$206/barrel for Libya. Fiscal adjustment in Algeria is expected to reduce that figure to US$85/barrel by 2017, while in Libya IMF projections point to figures around US$195 for 2016, and US$150 for 2017 (IMF, 2016). Given that it is unlikely that prices will recover to that level, both countries will struggle to keep their budgets financeable and in spite of the significant foreign reserves accumulated over the last years their gradual depletion would make fiscal adjustments unavoidable.

A second issue is that both producing and consuming countries share the challenge of rationalizing energy subsidies, which constitute a key factor of southern Mediterranean political economy balances. The Arab Spring delayed the initial plans for subsidies reform, but countries like Egypt, Jordan or Morocco have profited from the window of opportunity of low oil prices to advance in reducing fossil-fuel price distortions and are working on reforming electricity subsidies. This suggests that it is better to reform energy subsidies before a serious crisis arises than embarking on a reactive, short-term fiscal oriented adjustment process under international pressure. Nevertheless, in the medium and long term, rationalizing energy subsidies will remain a key concern for political and economic stability (Fattouh and El-Katiri, 2015).

Moroccan efforts to advance subsidy reforms have been particularly praised by the International Energy Agency and supposedly constitute an example for other countries in the region (IEA, 2014). The high oil prices before 2014 seriously damaged public finances. In 2012 the Moroccan budget deficit reached 7.3 per cent of which 6.6 per cent was linked to the cost of energy subsidies and its reform become unavoidable. The government has since then reformed the system of subsidies for petroleum products. However, it has not been able yet to extend subsidy reform to the power sector by adopting a cost-based approach to the setting of electricity tariffs (Amegroud, 2015). A similar problem happens with subsidy reform in countries like Egypt or Tunisia: it remains quite gradual for fossil fuels, and lags behind regarding the electricity sector. In Egypt, for instance, there is the controversy on how to deal with the severe market distortions introduced by subsidies to liquefied petroleum gas (LPG). Liquefied petroleum gas is the most heavily subsidized energy product, but it was not targeted in the first cuts and is being excluded for removal at least for needy households (James, 2015). Without better political governance mechanisms, temporary fixes to the subsidy problem may be adopted, but a lasting solution is not in sight (Rohác, 2014).

This is also the case for energy-rich countries in the region. While the 2016 Algerian budget increased energy prices to large consumers and industry and introduced a new tax on fuels, such measures are insufficient to remove the distortions of one of the heavier energy subsidizers in the world. The government has repeatedly announced the need to reform the system of subsidies to make it less socially regressive and fiscally burdensome, and at the same time more efficient in satisfying the basic needs of the most vulnerable groups in society. However, unless a drastic change in policy unfolds over the next years, the most likely option is a gradual and incremental approach trying to avoid widespread social unrest (Escribano, 2016).

Finally, Mediterranean gas producers are missing the opportunity to profit from the increasing strategic rivalry between Russia and the EU. Well before the Russian annexation of Crimea in 2014, the 2005 gas dispute between Ukraine and Russia unfolded in the first gas crisis with the interruption of gas supplies in January 2006. By January 2009, continued disputes resulted in major supply disruptions in eighteen European countries. The European external energy policy goal has always been diversifying gas supplies from Russia, but the focus was almost exclusively in the Southern Gas Corridor towards the Caspian. This bet has delivered little success, with the Nabucco pipeline being abandoned and the Trans-Caspian pipeline facing an increasingly challenging environment. In spite of the difficulties in finding alternatives, when the EU looked around its neighbourhood, the Mediterranean was perceived as neither a credible nor a near-term solution (Chyong, 2015).

Instead, different European member states started to compete in promoting the alternatives to Russian gas fitting their preferences. Central and eastern member states insisted on continuing to privilege the Southern Corridor. Cyprus, supported by Greece, presented its newfound offshore gas reserves as a source of diversification from Russia. Italy favoured north African supplies from Libya and Algeria through the existing pipelines, while Spain stressed the potential of Algeria and the idle capacity in both the Algerian and Spanish pipeline and LNG system. Several European companies also started to think on how to develop the vast natural gas reserves discovered in the eastern Mediterranean. Newly discovered Israeli and Egyptian offshore gas fields, together with the possibility of using idle Egyptian LNG export capacity to market Cypriot and Israeli gas, have introduced a new geo-economic element in the Mediterranean energy landscape.

Algeria is a case in point. It holds the world's tenth largest proved natural gas reserves and the third largest technically recoverable shale gas resources, as well as the third largest proved crude oil reserves in Africa. However, natural gas production has been declining due to project delays resulting from bureaucratic problems, the inability to attract foreign investment, infrastructure gaps and other technical problems (US EIA, 2016). Furthermore, almost 90 per cent of gas export capacities in operation in the Mediterranean region are in Algeria. Without new investments in production and a improved demand management, Algeria may have in the future an even larger idle gas export capacity while holding the most significant available gas resources and the best established gas industry in the European neighbourhood after Russia.

Several authors have been warning about this worrying trend, asking for a comprehensive reform of the Algerian energy sector (Darbouche, 2011). The country's natural gas production had peaked in 2005 at 88 bcm/year before declining to an estimate of 85 bcm in 2015. The coming on-stream of the new south-west gas projects is expected to increase production to 100 bcm/year by 2020, but the same will happen with internal consumption. According to OME's conservative scenario, Algerian gas export potential is projected to be slightly more in 2030 than it was in 2010 (over 50 bcm; and only 35 bcm by 2040). In the proactive scenario Algeria's export potential could double by 2030 to over 70 bcm and remain above 60 bcm by 2040 (OME, 2015).

But there have also been criticisms of the lack of adaptation of European external policies towards Algeria, especially the design of an attractive model to integrate Algerian gas in the European energy market (Darbouche, 2008; Darbouche and Dennison, 2011; Escribano, 2010; Lebovich, 2016; Tagliapietra and Zachmann, 2015). The Algerians perceive a lack of clarity in the design of future European energy markets, especially the role of gas in the European energy mix, the impact of de-carbonization targets or the lack of intra-EU gas interconnections between Mediterranean Europe and the rest of the continent. Additionally, the existing Euro-Mediterranean framework is unable to address Algerian preferences or to incentivize energy reform in the country. Algeria is not interested in deepening its free-trade area with the

EU (it wants to renegotiate it), because contrary to what may happen in Morocco, Egypt or Tunisia, it does not provide any preferential tariff access to its exports, which are almost exclusively oil and gas. European energy policy together with new global realities could greatly influence Algerian policies, reducing or increasing the incentives for domestic energy reform.

Libya would be another candidate for future oil and gas supplies, but the current security context prevents the country from using its existing production and export capacity, not to mention attracting foreign investment (Darbouche and Hamilton, 2015; Seeberg, 2014). Other Mediterranean gas resources, like the new offshore eastern Mediterranean discoveries are years ahead of starting production. The global and regional drivers mentioned in the previous section, especially low gas prices, the uncertainty surrounding the evolution of global LNG markets, lack of infrastructures and geopolitical volatility may further delay significant volumes coming on stream (Zemach, 2016). The Egyptian case illustrates the uncertainties associated with global LNG market developments, geopolitics and energy policy reform. After becoming a net natural gas importer over the last years, it is expected that early in the next decade Egypt will start exporting gas again. In the OME's conservative scenario, its export potential will be some 17 bcm in 2030, but by 2040 Egypt will become a marginal gas exporter; under the proactive scenario, export potential could exceed 30 bcm by 2030 and decline to some 25 bcm in 2040.

Israel and Cyprus can also turn from energy importers to exporters developing their offshore gas fields. In Israel, 60 per cent of the electricity generated comes from gas produced from the Tamar field. The development of the Leviathan field has not started yet due to regulatory difficulties, which have made its development hardly competitive with cheap LNG imports. The companies controlling both fields have signed several agreements to export gas to Egypt, Jordan and Palestine, but geopolitical tensions, the lack of regional export infrastructure, low gas prices and unclear regulatory frameworks pose serious challenges (Tsafos, 2016). The OME's outlook projects Israeli gas export potential to peak in the second half of the 2020s at almost 20 bcm/year, but to decline sharply to insignificant levels by 2040. Cyprus could add another 5 bcm/year between 2025 and 2040 to the export potential of the region if the Aphrodite field were to be developed. However, for this to happen, the differences with Turkey should be settled. Some observers see a more balanced geopolitical order emerging in the eastern Mediterranean and project a Turkish–Israeli *rapprochement* that would achieve a breakthrough in exploiting its gas resources (Tanchum, 2015). Nevertheless, geopolitical complexities add to a depressed gas market situation in reducing companies' appetite for investing in regional offshore gas resources.

Turkey is a very special case, being the only Mediterranean country with which the EU has started accession negotiations involving accompanying reforms in the energy sector, including the right of establishment to provide services, competition policy and energy policy itself. The upgrading of the normative framework attracted significant foreign investments in the energy sector. Furthermore, while foreign investments have contracted since 2009, the energy and electricity sectors continue to receive significant FDI inflows due to the European interests in creating trans-national energy corridors through Turkey (Sánchez-Martín et al., 2015). Energy policy, and more precisely pipeline politics, has become a Turkish foreign policy tool (Bilgin, 2011).

The strategic vision in the Turkish Strategic Plan 2010–14 was to project the country as an energy hub. However, gas hubs are not a merely geographical feature: they need a liquid gas market, deep financial markets, arbitration procedures and other high quality institutions. As a whole, the net gas trade balance of the south-east Mediterranean will significantly deteriorate, with import requirements rapidly growing. There are several gas pipelines being decided and planned from Russia, the Caspian and the Middle East (OME, 2015: 91). For instance, the

Trans-Anatolian Pipeline (TANAP) is expected to transport Azeri gas through Turkey to connect with the Trans-Adriatic Pipeline (TAP) into the EU. The fate of the Turkish Stream pipeline replacing Russia's South Stream project would depend on the ups and downs of Turkey–Russia relations.

Going forward: the EU's role

To conclude on a Euro-Mediterranean note, it may be interesting to explore to what extent the EU is ready to adapt to the changes described in this chapter, which entail a different pattern of energy interdependence between Europe and the Mediterranean. There have been several Euro-Mediterranean energy initiatives, from the gas and electricity rings, the Mediterranean Solar Plan and now the three Euromed energy platforms for gas, electricity and renewables, coupled with the deployment of energy policy networks and other minor regulatory provisions in the respective European Neighbourhood Action Plans.[9] However, to date the EU and its southern neighbours have failed to use energy as a development and cooperation driver instead of securitizing it.

It has been argued that the EU should develop a credible and attractive narrative able to match the preferences of its southern Mediterranean neighbours (Escribano, 2015a). This could include developing regional and sub-regional narratives, managing energy interdependence rather than over-securitizing dependency, and a discourse shift towards democratic energy governance, which implies convincing southern producers to focus on development instead of rent by adopting transparent energy rules. The new political economy of the region means that energy wealth management in producing countries will be subjected to increased scrutiny (Escribano, 2015b). Emphasizing good governance allows for a compromise among different institutional elements that could serve as a focal point to energy policy reform. Finally, the Euro-Mediterranean energy discourse should include the fight against climate change, promoting sustainability through renewables' deployment and energy efficiency.

Offering improved access to the EU's energy market to oil and gas (but also renewable energy) southern Mediterranean producers in exchange for good energy governance and sustainability efforts can provide a more cooperative ecosystem to Euro-Mediterranean energy relations. In any case, and in spite of a rapidly changing global energy landscape, the Mediterranean remains a key energy partner for the EU. In fact, Mediterranean energy geopolitics are becoming more important and demanding for Europe, extending from traditional, narrow energy security concerns to the new challenges of climate change, sustainability and good energy governance. The political, socio-economic and environmental implications of the new southern Mediterranean energy landscape are prone to be increasingly relevant in the years to come.

Notes

1 For a more detailed analysis see the collective volume edited by Jalilvand and Westphal (forthcoming). Most contents on Algeria follow the author's chapter in that book (Escribano, forthcoming).

2 While the chapter focuses on the most recent drivers, energy in the region has experienced a rich and complex historical evolution. See for instance Darbouche and Hamilton (2015), Fuinhas and Cardoso (2013) and Martínez (2010).

3 IMF, IMF Staff Completes 2016 Article IV Mission to Algeria, Press Release No. 16/107, March 14, 2016.

4 Bordoff and T. Hauser (2014, figure 15) do not provide a breakdown by country, but given that North Africa is the main African region exporting gas to the EU it is assumed that the sub-region will bear most of such trade diversion.

5 'OTC: Egypt eyes free-market future as gas demand requires more development', *Oil and Gas Journal Online*, May 3, 2016.
6 *International Business Times*, 'Daesh vuole il petrolio della Libia', January 9, 2016.
7 *El Watan*, 'In Salah: les dessous de l'attaque de la base de Kherchba', March 19, 2016.
8 *Tout sur l'Algérie* (TSA), 'Aqmi dévoile des détails sur l'attaque du site gazier, menace les multinationales exploitant le gaz de schiste', March 19, 2016.
9 For a recent account of Euro-Mediterranean energy relations see Rubino et al. (2015).

References

Amegroud, T. (2015). 'Morocco's Power Sector Transition: Achievements and Potential', Istituto Affari Internazionali Working Paper 15/05, February.

Bilgin, M. (2011). 'Energy Policy in Turkey: Security, Markets, Supplies and Pipelines', *Turkish Studies*, 12(3), 399–417.

Boersma, T., M. Vandendriessche and A. Leber (2015). 'Shale Gas in Algeria: No Quick Fix'. Brookings Energy Security and Climate Initiative Policy Brief 15-01.

Bordoff, J. and T. Hauser (2014). 'American Gas to the Rescue?', Columbia Center on Global Energy Policy, September.

Boubekeur, A. (2013). 'Rolling Either Way? Algerian Entrepreneurs as Both Agents of Change and Means of Preservation of the System', *Journal of North African Studies*, 18(3), 469–81.

Boucekkine, R., F. Prieur and K. Puzon (2014). 'The Dynamics of Lobbying under Uncertainty: On Political Liberalization in Arab Countries', in J. Haunschmied, V. M. Veliov and S. Wrzaczek (eds), *Dynamic Games in Economics*. Berlin: Springer, pp. 69–87.

Christensen, J. H., K. Krishna Kumar, E. Aldrian et al. (2013). 'Climate Phenomena and their Relevance for Future Regional Climate Change', in T. F. Stocker et al. (eds), *Climate Change: The Physical Science Basis. Contribution of Working Group I to the Fifth Assessment Report of the IPCC*. Cambridge/New York: Cambridge University Press.

Chyong, C., L. Slavkova and V. Tcherneva (2015). 'Europe's Alternatives to Russian Gas', ECFR Commentary, April 9.

Darbouche, H. (2008). 'Decoding Algeria's European Neighbourhood Policy: Differentiation by Other Means', *Mediterranean Politics*, 13(3), 371–89.

Darbouche, H. (2011). 'Algeria's Shifting Gas Export Strategy: Between Policy and Market Constraints', Oxford Institute for Energy Studies, NG 48, March.

Darbouche, H. and S. Dennison (2011). 'A "Reset" with Algeria: The Russia to the EU's South', ECFR Policy Brief 46, December.

Darbouche, H. and J. Hamilton (2015). 'North Africa's Energy Challenges', in Zoubir, Y. and G. White (eds), *North Africa Politics: Change and Continuity*. Abingdon: Routledge, pp. 371–82.

Escribano, G. (forthcoming). 'Algeria: Global Challenges, Regional Threats and Missed Opportunities', in Jalilvand, D. R. and K. Westphal (eds), *Changing Dynamics of Energy: Political and Economic Challenges for the Middle East and North Africa Region*. Abingdon: Routledge.

Escribano, G. (2010). 'Convergence towards Differentiation: The Case of Mediterranean Energy Corridors', *Mediterranean Politics*, 15(2), 211–29.

Escribano, G. (2011). 'Una agenda energética para Libia: seguridad, reconstrucción y gobernanza', Análisis del Real Instituto Elcano no. 139, October.

Escribano, G. (2015a). 'Towards a Mediterranean Energy Community: No Roadmap without a Narrative', in Rubino et al. (eds), *Regulation and Investments in Energy Markets: Solutions for the Mediterranean*. Oxford: Academic Press, pp. 117–30.

Escribano, G. (2015b). 'The Political Economy of North African Political Transitions', in Y. Zoubir and G. White (eds), *North Africa Politics: Change and Continuity*. Abingdon: Routledge, pp. 3–17.

Escribano, G. (2016). 'Algeria Approves a Budget Right at the Brink', Elcano Royal Institute Analysis 3/2016, January.

Escribano, G. and A. Lorca (2008). 'Economic Reform in the Maghreb: From Stabilization to Modernization', in Y. Zoubir and H. Amirah-Fernández (eds), *North Africa: Politics, Region, and the Limits of Transformation*. Abingdon and New York: Routledge, pp. 135–58.

Escribano, G. and A. Lorca (2012). 'Modern Commercial and Social Entrepreneurship as a Factor of Change', in C. Merlini and O. Roy (eds), *Arab Society in Revolt: The West's Mediterranean Challenge*. Washington DC: Brookings, pp. 96–122.

Fattouh, B. and L. El-Katiri (2015). A Brief Political Economy of Energy Subsidies in the Middle East and North Africa (OIES paper MEP 11). Oxford: Oxford Institute for Energy Studies.

Forum des Chefs d'Entreprise-FCE (2015). *Pour l'Emergence de l'Economie Algérienne*. Algiers: FCE.

Fuinhas, J. A. and A. Cardoso (2013). 'Rentierism, Energy and Economic Growth: The Case of Algeria and Egypt (1965–2010)', *Energy Policy* 62, 1165–71.

International Energy Agency-IEA (2014). *Energy Policies beyond IEA Countries: Morocco 2014*. Paris: OECD.

IMF (2016). *Middle East and Central Asia Regional Economic Outlook*. Washington DC: IMF, April.

Jalilvand, D. R. and K. Westphal (eds) (forthcoming). *Changing Dynamics of Energy: Political and Economic Challenges for the Middle East and North Africa Region*. Abingdon: Routledge.

James, L. M. (2015). *Recent Developments in Egypt's Fuel Subsidy Reform Process*. Research Report, The International Institute for Sustainable Development, April.

Lebovich, A. (2016). 'Algeria: The Stirrings of Change?', in A. Dworkin (ed.), *Five Years On: A New European Agenda For North Africa*. ECFR, February, pp. 39–51.

Lelieveld, J., Y. Proestos, P. Hadjinicolaou et al. (2016). 'Strongly Increasing Heat Extremes in the Middle East and North Africa (MENA) in the 21st Century', *Climatic Change*, 137(1), 245–60.

Martínez, L. (2010). *Violence de la rente pétrolière: Algérie, Irak, Libye*. Paris: Presses de Sciences Po.

Observatoire Méditerranéen de l'Energie-OME (2015). *Mediterranean Energy Perspectives 2015*. OME: Paris.

Randall, E. (2015). 'After Qadhafi: Development and Democratization in Libya', *Middle East Journal*, 69(2), 199–221.

RCREE (Regional Center for Renewable Energy and Energy Efficiency) (2015). *Arab Future Energy Index (AFEX) Energy Efficiency 2015*. Cairo: RCREE, May.

Reed, M. (2016). 'Libya's Oil in ISIS' Crosshairs', Fuse blog, January 20.

Rohác, D. (2014). 'Policy Credibility and the Political Economy of Reform: The Case of Egypt's Commodity Subsidies', *Journal of Institutional Economics*, 10(2), 311–35.

Rubino, A., M. T. Costa, V. Lenzi and I. Otzurk (2015). *Regulation and Investments in Energy Markets: Solutions for the Mediterranean*. Oxford: Academic Press.

Sánchez-Martín, M. E., G. Escribano and R. de Arce (2015). 'Will Energy Save FDI Inflows to Turkey from the Cool Down of EU Accession Prospects?', *Turkish Studies*, 16(4), 608–38.

Seeberg, P. (2014). 'EU Strategic Interests in Post-Qadhafi Libya: Perspectives for Cooperation', *Middle East Policy*, 21(1), 122–32.

Tagliapietra, S. and G. Zachmann (2015). 'Reinvigorating EU–Algeria Energy Cooperation', Bruegel Blog, June 10. Available at http://bruegel.org/2015/06/reinvigorating-the-eu-algeria-energy-cooperation/

Tanchum, M. (2015). 'A New Equilibrium: The Republic of Cyprus, Israel, and Turkey in the Eastern Mediterranean Strategic Architecture', Peace Research Institute Oslo, Occasional Paper Series 1.

Tsafos, N. (2016). 'Israeli Gas: Too Soon to Declare Victory', German Marshall Fund Policy Brief, January.

US EIA (2015a). *Shale Gas Resources: An Assessment of 137 Shale Formations in 41 Countries outside the United States*, June 2013, updated September 24. Available at www.eia.gov/analysis/studies/worldshalegas/

US EIA (2015b). 'Syria: Country Analysis Brief', June 24. Available at www.eia.gov/beta/international/analysis.cfm?iso=SYR

US EIA (2016). 'Algeria: Country Analysis Brief', March 11. Available at www.geni.org/globalenergy/library/national_energy_grid/algeria/AlgeriaCountryAnalysisBrief.shtml

Vandewalle, D. (2012). 'After Qaddafi', *Foreign Affairs*, 91(6), 8–15.

Volpi, F. (2013). 'Algeria versus the Arab Spring', *Journal of Democracy*, 24(3), 104–15.

Zemach, S (2016). 'Toward an Eastern Mediterranean Integrated Gas Infrastructure?', German Marshall Fund Policy Paper, May.

Zoubir, Y. (2016). 'Algeria after the Arab Spring', *Foreign Affairs*, February 9.

21
GLOBALIZATION AND THE MEDITERRANEAN

Patrick Holden

This chapter applies different concepts of globalization to the evolution of the international relations and political economy of the Mediterranean in recent history. Globalization as an idea is related to numerous themes that are covered elsewhere in this volume, including neoliberalism, interdependence, the liberal peace and democratization as well as the role of the state and associated theories. Globalization is a highly nebulous concept, which can be used to denote a process and outcome (Rosenberg, 2005) and as a discursive tool as well as an explanation. The chapter explores the different senses in which the concept is relevant to the Mediterranean with particular relevance to the role of the state *vis-à-vis* transnational and global forces and dynamics. It takes a temporal approach in that it focuses on how the different forms of globalization interplay in the post-1989 conjuncture. A major fault line lies between the neoliberal template of globalization and the other geopolitical realities that obtain. The course of the chapter is as follows. First of all the various concepts, definitions and forms of globalization are outlined, including challenges and critiques of this concept, before moving on to a 'working definition' for the purpose of this chapter. Following on from this the core elements of the Mediterranean are introduced before an in-depth focus on socio-economic globalization and 'political globalization' in the region in recent history. Lastly the seemingly fading relevance of the globalization concept to the contemporary geopolitics of the region is discussed.

Globalization as phenomenon and concept

Globalization discourse entered the mainstream in the 1990s, inspired by the end of the Cold War, the intensification of transnational economic organization and interactions together with accompanying technological developments. Since the 1970s, reduced control over international financial movements has strengthened the growth of a global economy. The end of the Cold War reduced the primary geopolitical and ideological obstacle to this process. It is a fluid term, which itself embodies a large range of concepts, and there have been a vast range of definitions. A relatively banal definition was provided by the 'transformationalists' who noted the development of a new global space and a widening and deepening of global interconnectedness (Held et al., 1999). The 'transnational' is key to the concept; transnationalism referring to forces and institutions that cut across the inter-state, inter-national system. Globalization also built upon the much older (and more moderate) concept of interdependence. In both cases the concepts are scaled up to include the totality of planetary interactions. Jan Art Scholte (2000) also delineated another common meaning of globalization, referring to a-territoriality: the reduced importance of physical space in the contemporary world.

Mann (2013) writes of 'globalizations' (plural) to denote the different forms of globalizing tendencies. The different forms of globalization regularly delineated are:

- Economic/financial: the growth of transnational companies with transnational production structures (or supply chains) as well as markets, increased financial transactions and the increased integration of financial markets. This private sector led form of globalization can be labelled neoliberal globalization as it essentially tended to reduce the role of the state (public power) and privilege that of market forces (Holden, 2015).
- Social and cultural: new communications technology, the development of a global culture or at least the increase mutual influence and awareness of different cultures.
- Political: global governance (global institutions to manage common affairs), the growth of a global civil society (Kaldor, Selchow and Moore, 2012), and the development of common, laws, norms and values.

For many of course, at least in the 1990s, globalization essentially meant westernization, the spread of western economic, social and political laws, models, values and norms (Scholte, 2000). This is how globalization is perceived in the Mediterranean during the period in question. At its most extreme this form of globalization theory had a strong liberal teleological undertone, it was arguably a more subtle version of Fukuyama's (1992) ill-fated thesis of an end to 'History' and the triumph of liberal democratic capitalism. Some Marxists have also viewed globalization in quasi-teleological terms as the development of a truly global economy accompanied by transnational capitalist class and global institutions (Cammack, 2005). The Mediterranean as a region would challenge these assumptions (for better or worse).

Can globalization be objectively measured? There are a number of rankings and methodologies (Vujakovic, 2010). Many indicators are economic, including ways to measure different forms of trade and investment. Measuring the social and cultural dimensions of globalization is a more demanding task. Common indicators used include the flows of people for example migration and tourism (vital for many Mediterranean countries); as well as other cultural technological indicators such as internet bandwith speeds. On the other hand sociologists focused more on the reflexive nature of globalization; globalization as a state of mind as much as an actual fact (Giddens, 1990). Political scientists and critical social theorists have also explored how globalization discourse served to downplay the role of 'agency' in political and economic affairs and embodied all kinds of assumptions of inevitability (Fairclough, 2010; Rosamond and Hay, 2002).

Held et al. (1999) summarized the debate on the objective reality of globalization as divided between 'hyperglobalists', those who foresaw the end of the nation state and continued shrinking of space (Hardt and Negri, 2001), sceptics, who emphasized previous historical waves of globalization and the continued relevance of territorial power blocs (Hirst and Thompson, 1996) and 'transformationalists' who accepted the importance of globalization – the intensification of transnational connections – without assuming that this is denuding the power of the nation state (Held et al., 1999). Sceptics included some Marxists and other thinkers of a critical bent. Susan Strange (1998) decried 'globaloney' concepts which obfuscated the structural dominance of the United States. Of the globalization sceptics, a historical focus often underpinned their critique of the term. Rosenberg, writing in 2005, argued that the primacy of the nation state in the past has been exaggerated as has the power of 'global' forces and relationships in the contemporary era (Rosenberg, 2005). Globalization is a concept that has been reified (is used to explain both outcome and process) and fails to offer useful explanations of a range of different phenomena. Specifically he argued that economic and social changes of the 1990s had been over-interpreted.

This chapter takes the view that globalization, however problematic a concept, is a useful lens to apply to the Mediterranean. This region offers an obvious riposte to the more teleological assumptions of liberal (and some Marxist) globalization theory. The term is mostly applied through a critical political economy lens to understand the development of the state (in relation to global forces) and inter-state relations in the periods in question. It sees globalization as a plural phenomenon and a reflexive concept, which acts – and is understood to act – in different ways at different temporal conjunctures. The major landmark here is the move from the high-tide of globalization as pressure to westernize in the 1990s to a more chaotic form of globalization in the contemporary era.

The case of the Mediterranean

The relationship between globalization studies and the study of world regions is complex (Björn and Söderbaum, 2000; Higgott, 2000). This is certainly the case with a 'region' such as the Mediterranean which does not appear on most (non-geographical) templates. There is an obvious affinity in that regional studies also go beyond the nation state as a unit of analysis. 'Mediterranean studies' has a long pedigree and work was often rooted in concepts of interdependence and cyclical harmonies that are arguably analogous to some themes of globalization (Braudel, 1973). More commonly the Mediterranean is viewed as highly fragmented, the northern shore forming part of the core European/western capitalist bloc and the southern and eastern core forming part of culturally, economically, politically distinct regions. The striking aspect of the Mediterranean region is its role as a north–south microcosm or as a major global contact point between states at radically different levels of economic development, as well as a cultural and religious cross-roads. Global forces did not serve to unify the region but often had a fissile effect. The enlargement of the EU to include Spain, Portugal and Greece disrupted economic relations, and the pressures of global economic change threatened to shatter the economically weaker states of the other shores. Algeria's descent into civil war in 1992, after a botched political liberalization inspired by an economic crisis, was a case in point.

In the late twentieth century, under the auspices of European integration the southern European states experienced processes of globalization along the lines of the phenomena outlined earlier: increase in foreign investment, transnational/transregional economic organization (transnational companies and supply chains), social liberalization, political liberalization and increased interconnections with (in this case) European institutions and forces. At least until the Eurozone crisis this form of globalization was occurring in a managed fashion. In the years since 2009, popular resentment has increased against the European common currency and neoliberal globalization more generally. In its own highly peculiar environment Israel also experienced socio-economic globalization. However, the other Arab states of the southern and eastern Mediterranean, and Turkey, had a much cagier relationship to globalization. Most of these states had started to engage more with economic reform and neoliberal globalization (trade liberalization, increased efforts to attract foreign direct investment, shrinking of the state and so forth). This was partial and managed by the state although the state could not of course control the global economic forces which often buffeted these countries. Politically they were distinct and by the 1990s this area (together with the broader Middle East) stood out as an area immune from the third wave of democratization. Also, socially and culturally this formed part of an area viewed as one of the regions most immune to western social liberalization. The following sections will focus mainly on the southern and eastern shores as this is where the impact of globalization has been most debated and problematic.

The Mediterranean in the era of globalization

Socio-economic globalization

As noted earlier southern Europe (excluding the Balkans[1]) engaged with social and economic globalization within the framework of the EU. This confluence of globalization and European integration was most obvious in the case of Greece and the Iberian countries, which had transitioned from authoritarian rule in the 1970s. With liberal political and legal institutions they became increasingly globalized. These countries were able to reap a large increase in trade and foreign direct investment, mostly – but not entirely – from Europe. In the 1990s and early 2000s Europe was viewed as a shield or an instrument to control globalization, enabling, for example, sustainable reform of the welfare state (Guillen and Alvarez, 2001). Countries such as Spain and Greece maintained impressive growth rates in the late 1990s and early 2000s (although it later became apparent that this was fuelled by a dangerous boom in cheap credit). In older Mediterranean member states the problematic elements of globalization were more salient in political discourse (Gordon and Meunier, 2001), as witnessed, for example, by the strong showing of right wing parties in France.

Apart from Israel and Turkey, the states of the southern and eastern Mediterranean were classed as middle income countries in the 1990s. As with other states, globalization offered a mixed blessing. The optimistic thesis was that globalization offered massive opportunities for developing countries prepared to make use of them. An expanded world market offered new locations for them to sell their goods and services (European Commission, 2002). Growing transnational companies and supply chains offered foreign direct investment (FDI) which could spread technology and feed into the rest of developing country economies. In reality only a small number of states (mostly located in east Asia) had been able to profit from globalization to catch up with the west. Globalization in the Mediterranean and Middle East region had led to increased volatility in economic growth (Abed and Davoodi, 2003). Since the 1970s and particularly in the 1990s nearly all states in the region had to engage seriously with forces of neoliberal globalization (the exception being Libya due to its oil reserves and unique political system). Their essential task was to engage more with the global economy, in particular to reap foreign direct investment and new trading opportunities, without losing entire control over their political economies (Schlumberger, 2008). Smaller states, notably Israel and Tunisia or states without a lot of natural resources (such as Morocco) were most enthusiastic and proactive here, engaging in a series of reforms and proactive trade diplomacy (White, 2001). Henry and Springborg (2001) offered a crude but useful typology of states in the region:

- Bunker states: states that were authoritarian but allowed some political space (such as Egypt and Tunisia) and tried to engage with global economic actors on their own terms.
- Bully states: states that were more overtly oppressive (such as Ba'athist Syria) and were much more restrictive towards global economic forces.
- Globalizing monarchies: including Morocco (in particular) and Jordan. These states enthusiastically tried to attract trade and investment (while still keeping a grip on political change).
- Fragmented democracies: including Turkey, Lebanon and Israel.

Generally, as in other world regions globalization was used as rhetorical device to push for 'reform', although actual reforms were limited. Countries that were highly praised for their economic policies, such as Tunisia and Egypt, actually regressed politically in many cases.

Regional integration has been a common response to the pressures of globalization in other regions (see for example, Mercosur, ASEAN etc.). The basic logic is that regional integration can increase the weight of individual states, increase their attraction to outside investors and possibly create political resources to manage globalization. An attempt was made in the Maghreb to form a regional institution (the Arab Maghreb Union/AMU) which included a common market and customs union (Cammett, 1999). This was still-born due to political rivalry between Algeria and Morocco. In the early twenty-first century a more modest free-trade agreement was signed between Morocco, Tunisia, Egypt and Jordan. There was also a much broader Greater Arab Free-Trade Agreement (which has again been hamstrung by conflict). The dominant regional institution was of course the European Union whose role is discussed later.

Most of the states of the region were members of the WTO (but not Algeria, Lebanon, Libya or Syria). The first two of these countries now have observer status at the WTO but have not joined. In regard to the role of other global institutions, as in other developing regions the developing states of the region were interacting with the IMF and World Bank. These bodies, by persuasion or conditionality, attempted to support 'openness' in the region and can be understood as agents of globalization. After the attacks of 9/11 in 2001 there was a greater global focus on the region (the Middle East more broadly rather than the Mediterranean). The landmark Arab Human Development Report sought to put the 'Arab World' in a global context and castigated the relative failure of Arab states in different aspects of human development and the general closed nature of society (UNDP, 2002). The US itself launched a broad reform and modernization drive in the region. It signed free-trade agreements with Morocco and Jordan (it already had one with Israel) and signed many more (limited) trade and investment framework agreements (TIFAs) with Egypt, Lebanon, Libya and Tunisia.

The major single (if somewhat ambivalent) agent of globalization in the region was the European Union. As by far the dominant economic bloc in the region this was in a quasi-hegemonic position. In the 1990s it put itself into a leadership role as the partner to guide states of the region towards economic development and liberalization. The Euro-Mediterranean partnership committed all of the stakeholders (again except Libya) to further economic integration. The mode chosen by the EU was not (with the exception of Turkey) to form customs unions with states in question but rather to sign more open 'association' free-trade agreements. It also offered increase aid to modernize and reform the state (here it was linked with a range of other actors). The EU was not so enthusiastic about migration, however, as with the developed world in general its approach to globalization was schizophrenic in this respect (enthusiasm for liberalizing flows of goods and money coupled with extreme caution about flows of people). Neither the EU nor any of the other actors could secure for its Mediterranean partners a sustainable form of engagement with globalization. Countries such as Egypt, which had some success in attracting foreign investment and so forth continued to have very poor poverty and human development indicators (Amin, 2014). The food riots of 2008 (caused by a global spike in food prices) which engulfed much of North Africa were a sign of the continued volatility and vulnerability of these countries (Bush, 2009).

Political globalization

Political globalization is understood here as the spread of liberal democracy and other western political norms, combined with the increased influence of global and supranational institutions and laws (beyond the purely economic ones discussed previously). The non-European states of the region formed, in the 1990s, one of the redoubts against a global wave towards democratization (which in its recent iteration had spread across much of eastern Europe, South America and sub-Saharan Africa). Of the Mediterranean Arab states Libya and Syria were the most explicitly authoritarian. The others could be classified as different types of semi-authoritarian states, where a certain political space obtained but not full political competition. Lebanon had a unique consociational political system. Israel and Turkey could be classed as democracies but in both cases their treatment of minorities was highly controversial: in Israel's case it had ruled over millions of Palestinians without their consent for decades, and in Turkey's case the role of the military was also problematic. Apart from civil and political rights, other forms of human rights in the region were also notably problematic, including gender rights and minority rights. The non-European Mediterranean, as with many other world regions, experienced globalization as westernization in many respects, and often resisted it. The provisions of, for example, the Convention on the Elimination of Discrimination Against Women (CEDAW) were resisted and imperfectly implemented at best in the region (Kelly and Breslin, 2010). The dominant religious and cultural mores militated against a legalistic approach to formal gender equality. The secular rulers of countries such as Tunisia would claim to have improved, and the rulers of Egypt and Syria could generally be deemed to have maintained, minority rights at a reasonable level. The reaches of global civil society (which was overwhelmingly western in orientation) extended only feebly.[2] The Islamic nature of many local social movements and NGOs sat uneasily with the secularist trend dominant in Eurocentric civil society and western states and public institutions (Shakman Hurd, 2004).

The relevance of generic political principles to Arab states in the region has been fiercely debated with accusations of orientalism – assumptions as to the essential difference and non-modernity of Arab/Islamic culture (Sadowski, 1993) – on the one hand versus the danger of arrogantly imposing western templates and values on the other (Perry, 2006; Sadiki, 2004). The dominance of political Islam in the various opposition movements in these states led to serious tensions between basic concepts of democracy (political competition, majority rule) and broader liberal democratic norms of democracy and human rights. Religious parties and movements such as Ennahda in Tunisia, the Muslim Brotherhood in Egypt and Syria, the Front Islamique de Salut (FIS) in Algeria and Hamas in the Palestinian territories were much stronger than the generally weak (and often co-opted) secular opposition parties. However, there were real concerns over their respect for minorities (such as the Copts in Egypt) and no doubts as to their opposition to gender equality (as understood in the west). Generally, western actors found it hard to engage with indigenous (Islamist) forms of political participation (Volpi, 2009). Algeria provided a test case of this tension early on in this period when the military stepped in to cancel the elections after the FIS won the first round. Sectarianism is also viewed as having greatly shaped the political culture in the region – again some caution should be adopted towards the more essentialist and simplistic assumptions in this regard (Shakman Hurd, 2015) – notably in Egypt, Syria, Lebanon and Israel.

Ruling regimes felt the need to engage with the international human rights agenda, for example, signing up to support 'democratic principles and human rights' in their agreements with the EU but fiercely resisted any actual constraints on their power over their populations. Generally, the region remained a zone of 'realism' with regimes making limited concessions to global economic forces and global norms. In Ayubi's (1995) felicitous formulation they were generally 'fierce' (with powerful security apparatuses and ruling networks) if not 'strong' (in their real embeddness in society).

A variety of international actors promoted 'democracy' in different forms, though aid, dialogue, conditionality (theoretically) and other forms of interaction. The EU probably had the greatest institutional depth of democracy promotion, with legal agreements and association committees on human rights (with several countries) as well as extensive aid programmes. However, the EU's diffidence and incoherence in politically supporting its democratic values have been exhaustively analysed (Youngs, 2002). Writing in 2010, before the Arab Spring, Haynes's assertion that globalization had little impact on the political development of the region would have been widely accepted (Haynes, 2010). The major impact of globalization may well have been to nurture the growth of fundamentalist parties via the alienation caused by neoliberal economics and the spread of western culture and values.

It is noteworthy that the country which began the wave of popular uprisings across the Middle East (starting in late 2010), was Tunisia, the country which was most integrated into the European and global economy (Zank, 2011). Ben Ali's Tunisia was, superficially at least, a star economic performer with high levels of FDI and an extremely open economy (in terms of the role of international trade). The chain reaction of protests which followed was a prime example of contagion (Whitehead, 2001) another concept related to globalization and interdependence. As such the Arab Spring inspired much Eurocentric, liberal teleological commentary in the media. *Time* magazine's comparison of the events to the European year of revolution in 1848 was one case in point (Anderson, 2011). More astute observers were aware of the difficulties of real empowerment for the people of Arab states, given their location in the global economy and the historical trajectory of their institutions (Hinnebusch, 2014). As events transpired, the more authoritarian states (Syria and Egypt) were unable to accommodate any kind of peaceful transition and the resulting conflict destabilized the region. In a broader sense generic principles of 'democracy' conflicted with local specificities, such as the power of political Islam and the fear of sectarian conflict.

Globalization in the contemporary era of crisis

The Arab Spring unleashed a new wave of instability and conflict in the region. Globally the context had also changed and the inexorability of so-called neoliberal globalization was under pressure. The financial crisis of 2008 challenged both the economic power of the west and the prestige of neoliberalism as an ideology. In southern Europe, the Eurozone crisis led to great economic hardship, political and economic crisis and an inward turning of the European Union in general (Crum, 2013). Greece and Portugal suffered near financial collapses, and could only be 'rescued' by the EU institutions and the IMF. These bodies applied the kind of harsh structural adjustment that was normally only reserved for developing countries to these southern European states. Spain also suffered a shattering financial crisis, although it managed to avoid a formal bailout (Powell and Steinberg, 2012). Italy's economic growth and fiscal situation were also badly affected, while both Italy and Greece found themselves in the frontline of a heightened refugee crisis. A sharp division emerged between northern and southern Europe, as the Mediterranean states shared a massive unemployment problem and general malaise. This has led to a resurgence of political movements which, although not anti-globalization, called for a radically different form of globalization to the neoliberal version in force. 'Indignados' in Spain helped inspire a radical political party, while a radical left-wing party (Syriza) took power in Greece but was unable to extricate the country from its 'debtors' prison'.

European economic misery was coupled with the economic rise (perhaps over-hyped but still substantial) of emerging powers such as China, Russia, India and Brazil. In the early twenty-first century south–south trade increased strongly, amounting to over 50 per cent of global trade from 2006 (UNCTAD, 2012: 3).These countries (China and Russia in particular) are capitalist and engaged with global trade but they are not liberal capitalist (Stephen, 2014). In the case of

China, the social and economic (not to mention political) pluralism of the western model does not obtain. These countries and their elites are only partly integrated with the transnational global elite, as evidence by limited role in TNCs and in forums such as Davos (ibid.). All of this offered a different model to developing countries and different sources of capital and trade, which has altered the global geo-economic framework. Even bastions of economic liberalism such as the European Union have begun to take a more circumspect approach to global free trade (Holden, 2015). Meanwhile, the salience of territory and geopolitics (although it had never gone away) has grown more obvious as Russia reacted sharply to the western expansion in what it saw as its near abroad (leading to conflicts in Georgia and Ukraine). All of this meant that globalization is understood to be much less unidirectional in its form and detached from any teleological undertones.

Within the southern and eastern Mediterranean the instability caused by the Libyan, Syrian and Iraqi wars transformed the region. A new transnational phenomenon emerged in the form of massed refugee movements travelling to Europe (mostly from Syria and Iraq). Migration has always been the underside of globalization but has not been accepted by leading states as a quid pro quo. The ineffable horror of the Mediterranean crossings and the death of many thousands vividly illustrate the failure of managed globalization and managed interdependence in the region (Holden, 2016). Like Al Qaida before it (Gerges, 2005), Daesh or 'Islamic State' has availed itself of contemporary communications technology to mobilize and organize transnationally; and it has taken advantage of regional instability to challenge the conventional inter-state system. Meanwhile the Mediterranean as a political and economic entity remains absent from global governance templates. This was evidenced in the low priority given to mixed regions such as the Mediterranean in the preparation of the global Sustainable Development Goals (Holden, 2016).

Despite the economic fragility of states in the region, the influence of global and globalist institutions (such as the Bretton Woods institutions and the European Union) has waned rather than waxed. Once the military took back control of the Egyptian government, with a dramatic increase in repression the leadership was able to resist European pressure with massive financial support from Saudi Arabia and other Gulf states. Given the weakened geopolitical situation of the west, reforming/globalizing zeal took a back seat to realpolitik. This is most noteworthy in the EU's migration deal with Turkey (March 2016) which, in arranging a form of people swap, openly contravened international law regarding the individual rights of people seeking refugee status. It is also striking that the increasingly authoritarian government of Erodgan in Turkey was not a barrier to the EU in dealing with him. This deal was in turn precipitated by central European member states (notably Austria) and candidate states blocking the flow of refugees travelling by land from Greece, effectively creating a new border between the Mediterranean and the rest of Europe.

Conclusion

This chapter has reviewed the changing application and relevance of the globalization concept to the Mediterranean. It is evident that the hyperglobalist thesis of the 1990s has been comprehensively disproven, even in core western countries the state is being reconfigured rather than superseded. Such a vision never looked remotely feasible in the southern and eastern shores of the Mediterranean in any case. At the highpoint of neoliberal globalization in the 1990s, the states of this region were only cautiously engaging with global economic and social dynamics, while paying at best lip service to political globalization. Indeed there is a strong argument that the economic forces of neoliberal globalization countered the growth of political norms of equality, participation and human rights (Hinnebusch, 2015). In the current era, globalization has taken on a more anarchic quality. While the global economy continues to develop, efforts at substantial global governance are failing. This is most apparent in the poor response to the refugee/humanitarian crisis in Greece. Both global migration and global terrorism are facilitated by global communications advances, but political institutions and other mechanisms of civil society have not evolved apace. A grim realism pervades the region and the sense of globalization as a lever for 'reform' has faded as the agents of this form of globalization have seen their power wane. The concepts of transnationalism and interdependence are as relevant as ever to the region, as are global economic forces. However, the relevance of globalization as an overarching explanatory concept is increasingly tenuous.

Notes

1 The Balkan Mediterranean non-EU states are not included in this chapter for reasons of space.
2 There were significant civil society organizations in the region but their activity was restricted. The Euro-Mediterranean Human Rights Network was established in 1997 as a pan-regional institution to support the different NGOs in the region and link them in with global networks and organizations.

Bibliography

Abed, G. and H. Davoodi (2003) *Challenges of Growth and Globalization in the Middle East and North Africa* (IMF Publications).

Amin, K. (2014) International Assistance to Egypt after the 2011 and 2013 Uprisings: More Politics and Less Development, *Mediterranean Politics* 19(3), 392–413.

Anderson, K. (2011) 1848 vs 2011: In the Shadow of the Past, *Time*, available at http://content.time.com/time/magazine/article/0,9171,2058292,00.html accessed 6 July 2016.

Ayubi, N. (1995) *Overstating the Arab State* (London: I. B. Tauris).

Björn, H. and F. Söderbaum (2000) Theorising the Rise of Regionness, *New Political Economy*, 5(3), 457–72.

Braudel, F. (1973) *The Mediterranean and the Mediterranean World in the Age of Philip II*, Vol. 2 (London: Fontana).

Bush, R. (2009) Food Riots: Poverty, Power and Protest, *Journal of Agrarian Change*, 10(1), 119–29.

Cammack, P. (2005) The Governance of Global Capitalism: A New Materialist Perspective, in R. Wilkinson (Ed.), *The Global Governance Reader* (London: Routledge).

Cammett, Melani (1999) Defensive Integration and Late Developers: The Gulf Cooperation Council and the Arab Maghreb Union, *Global Governance*, 5(3), 379–402.

Crum, B. (2013) Saving the Euro at the Cost of Democracy?, *Journal of Common Market Studies*, 51(4), 614–30.

European Commission (2002) Trade and Development: Assisting Countries to Benefit from Trade, COM 513, 18 September.

Fairclough, N. (2010), Discourse and 'Transition' in Central and Eastern Europe, in Fairclough, N. (Ed.), *Critical Discourse Analysis: The Critical Study of Language*, (Harlow: Longman), pp. 503–26.

Fukuyama, F. (1992) *The End of History* (New York: Free Press).

Gerges, F. (2005) *The Far Enemy: Why Jihad Went Global* (New York: Cambridge University Press).

Giddens, A. (1990) *The Consequences of Modernity* (Cambridge: Polity).

Gill, Stephen (1995) Globalization, Market Civilization and Disciplinary Neoliberalism, *Millennium*, 24(3), 399–412.

Gordon, P. and S. Meunier (2001) *The French Challenge: Adapting to Globalization* (Brookings Institution Press).

Guillen, A. and S. Alvarez (2001) Globalization and the Southern Welfare States, in Sykes, R. Palier, B. Prior, P. and J. Campling (Eds), *Globalization and European Welfare States: Challenges and Change* (Palgrave).

Hardt, M. and A. Negri (2001) *Empire* (Cambridge MA: Harvard University Press).

Haynes, J. (2010) Democratization in the Middle East and North Africa: What is the Effect of Globalization?, *Politics, Religion and Ideology*, 11(2), 133–49.

Held, David, and A. McGrew (Eds) (2003) *The Global Transformations Reader: An Introduction to the Globalization Debate* (Cambridge: Polity Press).
Held, David, A. McGrew, D. Goldblatt and J. Perraton (1999) *Global Transformations: Politics, Economics and Culture* (Cambridge: Polity Press).
Henry, C.M. and R. Springborg (2001) *Globalization and the Politics of Development in the Middle East* (Cambridge: Cambridge University Press).
Higgott, R. (2000) Studying Regionalism: Old Lessons, New Lessons, *New Political Economy*, 5(3), 333–52.
Hinnebusch, R. (2014) Historical Sociology and the Arab Uprisings, *Mediterranean Politics*, 19(1), 137–40.
Hinnebusch, R. (2015), Globalization, Democratization and the Arab Uprising: The International Factor in MENA's Failed Democratization, *Democratization*, 22(2), 335–57.
Hirst, P. and G. Thompson (1996) *Globalization in Question* (Cambridge: Polity Press).
Holden, P. (2015) Neo-Liberalism by Default? A Critical Discourse Analysis of the European Union's Trade and Development Policy in an Era of Crisis, *Journal of International Relations and Development*. DOI 10.1057/jird.2015.10
Holden, P. (2016) The Mediterranean and the Global Sustainable Development Goals, (Review Article) *Mediterranean Politics*, 21(2), 292–300.
Kaldor, M., S. Selchow, and H. Moore (Eds) (2012) *Global Civil Society 2012: Ten Years of Critical Reflection* (Basingstoke: Palgrave Macmillan).
Kelly, S. and J. Breslin (Eds) (2010) *Women's Rights in the Middle East and North Africa: Progress amid Resistance* (New York/Lanham: Freedom House/Rowman and Littlefield).
Mann, M. (1986), *The Sources of Social Power: Volume I: A History of Power from the Beginning to A.D. 1760* (Cambridge: Cambridge University Press).
Mann, M. (2013), *The Sources of Social Power: Volume 4: Globalizations: 1945–2011* (Cambridge: Cambridge University Press).
Neaime, S. (2011), The Global Financial Crisis and the Euro-Mediterranean Partnership, in J. Costa-i-Font (Ed.), *Europe and the Mediterranean Economy* (London: Routledge).
OECD (2005) *OECD Handbook on Economic Globalization Indicators* (Paris: OECD).
Perry, G. (2006) Imperial Democratization: Rhetoric and Reality, *Arab Studies Quarterly*, 28(3/4), 55–87.
Powell, C. and F. Steinberg (2012) The Pain in Spain: Light at the End of the Tunnel?, *The International Spectator: Italian Journal of International Affairs*, 47(4), 57–63.
Robinson, W. (2004) *A Theory of Global Capitalism: Class and State in a Transnational World* (Baltimore: Johns Hopkins University Press).
Rosamond, B. and C. Hay (2002) Globalization, European Integration and the Discursive Construction of Economic Imperatives, *Journal of European Public Policy*, 9(2), 147–67.
Rosenberg, J. (2005) Globalization Theory: A Post-Mortem, *International Politics*, 42(1), 2–74.
Sadiki, L. (2004) *The Search for Arab Democracy: Discourses and Counter-Discourses* (New York: Columbia University Press).
Sadowski, Y. (1993) The New Orientalism and the Democracy Debate, *MERIP/Middle East Report No. 183*, Political Islam, pp. 14–40.
Schlumberger, O. (2000) Arab Political Economy and the European Union's Mediterranean Policy: What Prospects for Development?, *New Political Economy*, 5(2), 247–68.
Schlumberger, O. (2008) Structural Reform, Economic Order, and Development: Patrimonial Capitalism, *Review of International Political Economy*, 15(4), 622–49.
Scholte, J. (2000) *Globalization: A Critical View* (London: Macmillan).
Schwarz, R. (2008) The Political Economy of State-Formation in the Arab Middle East: Rentier States, Economic Reform, and Democratization, *Review of International Political Economy*, 15(4), 599–621.
Shakman Hurd, E. (2004) The Political Authority of Secularism in International Relations, *European Journal of International Relations*, 10(2), 235–62.
Shakman Hurd, E. (2015) Politics of Sectarianism: Rethinking Religion and Politics in the Middle East. *Middle East Law and Governance*, 7(1), 61–7.
Springborg, R. (2011) The Political Economy of the Arab Spring, *Mediterranean Politics*, 16(3), 427–33.
Stephen, M. (2014) Rising Powers, Global Capitalism and Liberal Global Governance: A Historical Materialist Account of the BRICs Challenge, WZB Berlin Social Research Center, Germany *European Journal of International Relations*, 20(4), 912–38.
Strange, S. (1998) Globaloney? (review essay), *Review of International Political Economy*, 4, 704–11.
UNCTAD (2012) Development and Globalization Facts and Figures, Available at http://unctad.org/en/PublicationsLibrary/webgdsdsi2012d2_en.pdf (accessed 6 July 2016).

UNDP (2002) Arab Human Development Report: 2002, Available at http://www.arab-hdr.org/publications/other/ahdr/ahdr2002e.pdf

Volpi, F. (2009) Political Islam in the Mediterranean: The View from Democratization Studies, *Democratization*, 16(1), 20–38.

Vujakovic, P. (2010) How to Measure Globalization? A New Globalization Index (NGI), *Atlantic Economic Journal*, 38(2), 237.

Wade, J. and S. Meunier (2010) Europe and the Management of Globalization, *Journal of European Public Policy*, 17(3), 299–317.

Wallerstein, I. (1979) *The Capitalist World Economy* (Cambridge: Cambridge University Press).

White, G. (2001), *A Comparative Political Economy of Tunisia and Morocco: On the Outside of Europe Looking In* (New York: State University of New York Press).

Whitehead, L. (2001) Introduction, in L. Whitehead (Ed.), *The International Dimensions of Democratization: Europe and the Americas* (Oxford: Oxford University Press).

Youngs, R. (2002) The European Union and Democracy Promotion in the Mediterranean: A New or Disingenuous Strategy?, *Democratization*, 9(1), 40–62.

Zank, W. (2011) North Africa under the Impact of African, Arab and European Integration: An Essay in Theoretical Synthesis. Paper at a Conference on Regional Integration in Europe and Africa: Models, Practices and Comparative Perspectives, University of Pretoria 16–18 February.

22

MINDING DEVELOPMENT GAPS IN EU MEDITERRANEAN POLICIES

A variegated neoliberalization thesis?

Karim Knio

Introduction

As a post-Second World War area of investigation, development studies (DS) is a multidisciplinary field which examines the nature and implications of developmental gaps within socially constructed global 'north-south' relations. While the field was understandably preoccupied with socio-economic development in the 1950s and 1960s, the range of thematic topics today has notably increased through the inclusion of issues such as environmental sustainability, human rights, governance, sexuality, gender, poverty and inequality to name a few. Similar to any field in social sciences, debates on the *nature* of development gaps are omnipresent and constantly contested. If some of the early developmentalist approaches (such as modernization and big push theories) believed in the instrumentality of development as a technique, a variety of structuralist approaches (such as dependency theories) linked the fate of development with the organization of global capitalism (Cypher and Dietz 2004; Todaro and Smith 2014). The recent advent of more relativist epistemologies to the field shifted the emphasis towards the social construction of reified entities such as security/development/core/periphery (Sörensen and Söderbaum 2012), while the proponents of Arturo Escobar problematized the practices of the 'development industry' and questioned the meanings of development itself and how the mere language of development gaps constitutes subjective yet dominant technologies of power (Escobar 2011).

Amidst these complexities, few scholars in DS today would disentangle these debates from the ascendancy and consolidation of neoliberalism as a global phenomenon. The extension of market logics into every single aspect of development, or even life, presents itself as a *mechanism* which intersects the myriad of thematic and theoretical classifications I referred to previously. In other words, the nature of development gaps is related to the nature of the mechanisms that cut across it. Simply put, a deeper understanding of global 'north-south' development gaps is intrinsically related to a deeper understanding of neoliberalism. Yet, the debates on the nature of neoliberalism[1] are equally complex and divisive. Is neoliberalism an ideology, a doctrine, a class project, a political movement or a discourse? Can it be an amalgam of these characteristics or not? If so, which ones? Does it exist in a singular form or is it polymorphic? Is it created and maintained by a structure, or is it only performed through the minds and activities of its players (Harvey 2007; Cahill, Edwards and Stilwell 2013)?

Clearly, the nature of these questions has direct implications for how the analyses of development gaps have been undertaken. So far, the dominant heterodox literature on neoliberalism has taken three divergent paths – varieties of capitalism (VoC) literature, historical materialism and post-structuralist governmentality-oriented approaches (Brenner et al. 2010: 185). While the VoC approach has stressed the endurance of institutional geographies on a national scale, historical materialist literature has dealt with the ways in which neoliberalism has developed in a globalized fashion as a transnational regime of governance led by market-based logics (ibid.: 206). Governmentality approaches on the other hand have focused on the ideationally sustained market logics which have fuelled the reproduction of entrepreneurial subjectivities and regulatory landscapes (ibid.).

Against this background, a group of scholars working within the intersection of political economy, sociology and geography sought to deal with the imprecise and elusive nature of the aforementioned definitions attributed to neoliberalism. In a series of widely received articles, Brenner, Peck and Theodore advanced what is now known as the 'variegated neoliberalization' argument or thesis (Brenner et al. 2010). Variegated refers to the 'systematic production of geo-institutional differentiation', while neoliberalization 'denotes a politically guided intensification of market rule and commodification' (ibid.: 184). As such, 'variegated neoliberalization' aims to capture the concomitant interaction between the systemic and the locally specific; the structural and the agentic, the patterning and the framing. In so doing, it seeks to demonstrate how tendential facilitations and intensification of commodification and marketization processes (systemic, structural and patterned) have been deepened by strategically reflexive players who seek to infiltrate and reshape regulatory contours situated in different and uneven geographical settings (locally specific, agentic and framed). In other words, it plots the *patterned incoherence* of neoliberalization processes.

In this chapter, I argue that my interpretation of the variegated neoliberalization thesis (VNLT) can comprehensively explain how the EU has been dealing with the various developmental gaps embedded in its Mediterranean policies. Stretched over a long time horizon, a succession of EC/EU–Mediterranean policies moved from being patchy and scattered (pre-Barcelona process) to exhibiting some signs of a consolidated model of development (post-Barcelona process) characterized by a conspicuous intensification of market logics. In parallel, this intensification process is then deepened within a widely stretched regulatory framework (from Morocco to Ukraine) whereby the EU deploys a similar regulatory logic against geographically differentiated institutions. From this perspective, the VNLT explains the patterned incoherence of neoliberalization processes embedded in these Mediterranean policies. To elucidate these points further, the next section will introduce the VNLT before I situate it within some cases taken from the EU–Mediterranean context. This will be followed by a section of reflection on the strengths and limitations of the VNLT.

VNLT: an overview

As highlighted in the introduction, any discussion on development and/or development gaps must take into consideration the sustained influence of neoliberal ideas and practices in contemporary policy debates. Nonetheless, the tasks of defining neoliberalism and tracing its geographical and historical trajectories remain a challenging proposition. Seeking to transcend these impasses, Brenner, Peck and Theodore (2010: 184) introduced the VNLT as a method of accounting for the systematic 'geoinstitutional differentiation of neoliberalization processes'.

Prior to Brenner et al.'s (2010) article, Peck and Tickell had previously situated neoliberalism as a process which is 'neither monolithic in form nor universal in effect', remaining 'institutionally variable, both across space and through time' (Peck and Tickell 2002; Tickell and Peck 2003). Hence, while there are 'family resemblances' to the discourses and practices of neoliberalism across different settings, according to Peck (2004: 395), it is important to note how these instruments are activated and deployed according to their local institutional contexts. Similarly, Brenner and Theodore (2002: 12) underlined a conceptualization of neoliberal restructuring as a struggle between defenders of the 'old space' and advocates of a 'new space', leading to a new regulatory arrangement which combines elements of an inherited geo-institutional landscape with the new 'projected spaces' embodied by neoliberal reform strategies. In other words, neoliberalization processes must confront and accommodate a pre-existing institutional order, which in turn must absorb and embed new spaces and strategies of neoliberal regulatory formations.

Building on these ideas, the VNLT was comprehensively outlined in the Brenner et al. (2010) article where the distinct yet relational constitutiveness between the 'uneven development of neoliberalization' and the 'neoliberalization of regulatory uneven development' concepts was at the core of the argument. In their own words,

> the problematic of variegated neoliberalization encompasses two foundational aspects of contemporary regulatory transformation: (a) *the uneven development of neoliberalization* – the differentiation and continual redifferentiation of market-oriented regulatory forms; and (b) *the neoliberalization of regulatory uneven development* – the constitution and continual reconstitution of marketized macrospatial institutional frameworks, or rule regimes, which govern processes of regulatory experimentation and cross-jurisdictional policy transfer . . .
>
> . . . The cumulatively transformative processes associated with these two dimensions of variegated neoliberalization cannot be represented through crude, stagist transition models. On a systemic level, neoliberalization processes are temporally discontinuous and spatially heterogeneous; and they produce (always mutating) macro-institutional frameworks that simultaneously intensify and exploit this constitutive spatio-temporal unevenness. It is for this reason that we adopt the terminology of unevenly evolving *neoliberalization processes*, rather than postulating the installation of some fully formed, coherently functioning, self-reproducing and 'regime-like' state of neoliberalism. The historical working out of neoliberalization processes has been aptly characterized as a 'wave-like' phenomenon, marked by an uneven but incrementally deepening form of diffusion and mutual interdependence.
>
> *(Brenner et al. 2010: 207–9)*

This 'wave-like' phenomenon proceeds in a succession of regulatory sequences which are market-oriented in nature, yet each distinctive in their own right (ibid.: 209). This means that, while the regulatory transformations are founded upon a range of already existing policy structures, they proceed to transform them and produce a range of inherently contradictory and paradoxical geoinstitutional formations (ibid.). As Brenner et al. (2010) argue, this understanding of neoliberalism suggests something drastically different from its traditional conceptualization as a linear, 'monolithic' entity with fully formed and consistent underpinning logics.

As such, Brenner et al. (2010) suggest that the 'uneven development of neoliberalization' entails a tendential facilitation and intensification towards commodification and marketization processes. This sentence needs some unpacking. Commodification processes here are used in a (neo) Polanyian sense and refer to some (as opposed to any) types of markets characterized by the treatment of essential factors of production as commodities. Hence, labour, land (or the environment) and money in these types of markets become commodities that can be bought and sold in their own right. They possess a price tag attached to them as opposed to markets characterized by administrative prices embedded in the legal, political, cultural, societal and ethical contours of the economy in question (Polanyi 1944; Block 2003). Marketization processes refer to the extension of these commodified markets into every single aspect of life (education, health, transport etc . . .).

The upshot argument relates the 'uneven development of neoliberalization' to 'disarticulated neoliberalization' (Brenner et al. 2010: 185). These neoliberalization processes were disarticulated because i) they were unevenly heterogeneous (extent of neoliberalization in the UK in the early 1980s, for example, was substantially different in scope and scale from West Germany and India); ii) they benefited from the continuous crises of their previous regulatory predecessors (Keynesian and/or state led demand management type of public policy); iii) but ones which provided some opportunities (facilitation) for some social forces to push for their ideas about commodification and marketization (Adam Smith Institute in the UK under Thatcherism for instance). These facilitations were intensified in a path dependent manner via diverse rounds of networking and collaboration.

On the other hand, 'the neoliberalization of regulatory uneven development' concept is related to 'deep neoliberalization' (Brenner et al. 2010: 185). Hereby, Brenner et al. (2010), emphasize the strategic and reflexive institutional deepening or thickening where market-led regulatory reforms have been articulated and consistently relayed through prior institutional settings which are geographically and temporally specific. Hence, reflexive policy making is always possible, but it can neither completely 'go out of the box' nor completely question the conditions policy makers find themselves in since the relaying process in itself fuels constant contradictions between past and present situations. In other words, as neoliberalization processes are intensified, it is the actors' situated reflexivity and the inter-connectiveness between these reflexivities that recursively deepen neoliberalization processes across time and space. (The findings of the de Larosière advisory committee to the EU on financial supervision after the crisis, for instance, framed the solution in terms of institutional deepening and not a major rethinking of what constituted the root causes of the crisis, see Knio 2014.)

By taking the concepts of 'uneven development of neoliberalization' (disarticulated neoliberalization) and 'the neoliberalization of regulatory uneven development' (deep neoliberalization) together, Brenner et al. (2010) are able to link a path dependency argument embedded in the former concept to a path shaping argument embedded in the latter. In so doing, they demonstrate the patterned incoherence of neoliberalization processes by highlighting their systemic commonalities across their differences.

The following quotation neatly summarizes the distinct yet relational constitutiveness of these two concepts. In the following sections, I will draw on the two foundational concepts of the VNLT and embed them within the EU's Mediterranean Policies context. According to Brenner et al. (2010),

> we outline this approach to variegated neoliberalization with reference to the sedimented, uneven and crisis-propelled evolution of processes of marketized regulatory restructuring since the 1970s. An initial offensive of 'disarticulated' neoliberalization in the 1970s and early 1980s was characterized by the path-dependent differentiation of market-oriented restructuring strategies across diverse, crisis-riven institutional contexts. Subsequent rounds of neoliberalization were layered upon this marketized pattern of regulatory uneven development, signalling the consolidation of a transformed, tendentially market-disciplinary geoinstitutional context for both market-promoting and

> market-constraining forms of regulatory experimentation. Within this 'deepening' configuration of neoliberalization, market-oriented regulatory transformations were reflexively interlinked and interpenetrated; transnational relays of market-oriented policy reform were intensified and thickened; and the metaregimes governing policy development were increasingly (re)oriented towards market-based rules.
>
> *(Brenner et al. 2010: 211)*

Uneven development of neoliberalization and the path dependency of EU–Mediterranean policies

The distinct yet relational constitutiveness between the two concepts envisaged by the VNLT can provide a useful framework for understanding the history, nature and development of neoliberalization processes within EU–Mediterranean policies. In this section, I will focus on the 'uneven development of neoliberalization' since it allows us to distinguish between i) the disarticulated origins of these policies between the mid- to late twentieth century; ii) the tendential facilitation of neoliberalization around the enactment of the Global Mediterranean Policy (GMP) in the early 1970s; and iii) the intensification of these neoliberalization processes from the inauguration of the Barcelona process in 1995 until the present. I argue that this triple cumulative movement (from disarticulation to tendential facilitation to intensified neoliberalization) not only provides us with a systemic account of what the EU is doing in the region, but also grounds and resonates much of the policy prescriptions set by the academic literature on EU–Mediterranean policies.

A strong argument from scholars of historical institutionalism (HI), for example, posits that the historical trajectory of EU–Mediterranean policies has taken on a path dependent character, having been shaped and informed by a variety of institutional legacies (see Gomez 2003; Emerson et al. 2005; Zank 2009). While I concur with this argument, historical path dependence arguments can benefit from a 'variegated' analysis of these historical events.

Disarticulation

For most of the latter half of the twentieth century Euro-Mediterranean relations lacked cohesion, largely guided by regional relationships and a desire to secure national economic interests. At the same time, social and political factors often jumbled these mercantilist ties and forced patchy policy responses. After gaining independence in the 1960s, many Mediterranean partner (MP) countries maintained deep economic ties to their ex-colonial counterparts, who moved to reinstate economic advantages through preferential trade agreements (Gomez 2003). Divisions arose between European Community (EC) member states as some of the bilateral agreements with the MPs were perceived to distort the common market ideals projected in the Treaty of Rome (1957) and grant special advantages to countries which could profit from their former colonies.

In this vein, the initial stages of the Euro-Mediterranean policies could be characterized by what Brenner et al. (2010: 213) describe as 'a proliferation of relatively unconnected, conjunctural and contextually bound projects'. It should be clear here though that these disarticulations had nothing to do with neoliberalization processes, since they were market based but not necessarily geared towards commodification and increased marketization.

Tendential facilitation

The subsequent decade (1970s), however, saw more shifting political terrains that incited reactionary, short-term measures from the European Commission and its member states. At the expense of adhering to a long-term strategy, the EC decided to pursue diplomatic battles, aiming to quell Cold War alignments and navigate through peace processes in the Middle East after the 1973 oil crisis (Yesilada 1991). In line with this background, the Global Mediterranean Policy of 1972 envisaged the creation of the cooperation agreements which granted MPs restrictive and preferential free-trade agreements.[2] It is within this specific context that a tendential facilitation of neoliberalization processes can be observed given that the language and practice of free trade, albeit restricted, was used for the very first time by the EC.

These facilitations nonetheless remained tendential since the implementation of these cooperation agreements took a long time to materialize amidst a wide discontent from MPs who only signed the agreements for lack of alternatives (ibid.). During the 1980s, EC–Mediterranean relations deteriorated as symbolized by the ineffectiveness and paralysis of the Renovated Mediterranean Policy (Clairet 1994).

Intensification

Approaching the 1990s, as trade relations between the EC member states and their MPs grew ever more interdependent, policy responses began to coalesce in the newly formed European Union. Proposals for implementing a common framework began to take shape with the establishment of the Euro-Mediterranean Partnership (EMP) in 1994, which emphasized free trade, economic growth and cooperation on democratic reforms and legal frameworks. The Barcelona Process in 1995 then came to constitute something of a 'critical juncture' in historical institutionalist terms, i.e. a watershed period ushering in a new era in Euro-Mediterranean relations. Namely, the EC's tentative experimental precedents gave way to a new direction following a cohesive strategy. The EMP and the Barcelona Process sought to institute a broad set of principles and objectives for the region. These included ordinary proclamations of 'shared prosperity' and 'building peace and stability', as well as specific organizational and legal blueprints laid out to foment economic, social and political development (Knio 2013: 67).

In practice, the EMP – and later the European Neighbourhood Policy (ENP) – privileged the economic realm over the social and political; as many scholars have illustrated, the EU development strategy prioritized trade liberalization and market deregulation at the expense of increased wages and public services[3] (see Khader 2001; Gallina 2006). Additionally, the EU maintained great leverage in its relationship with the MPs as its agricultural sector remained insulated from liberalizing forces and preserved its subsidies. As a formative model, the Barcelona Process has frequently resorted to market-based rule regimes and privatizing regulatory adjustments, integrating and intensifying a neoliberalized architecture into EU–Mediterranean relations. The last decade has witnessed further attempts to reinvigorate the objectives of the Barcelona Process through the 2005 Barcelona initiative and the Union for the Mediterranean (UfM) in 2008; these responses act to institutionally embed the free market as the central organizing apparatus of EU–Mediterranean relations. The post-Barcelona moment until the present can thus be understood as the intensification phase of neoliberalization.[4]

The recursive neoliberalization of uneven development in EU–Mediterranean policies

What follows from this intensification period is the cyclical infiltration and recursive development of new 'spaces' and 'strategies' of deepened neoliberalization. As Brenner et al. (2010: 215) have put it, the market-friendly experiments and regulatory reforms 'now [begin] to reconstitute the host organism itself'. The logic and design of neoliberalization now pervades the EU-Med area, having been reinforced through contemporary reforms which undermine social and political institutions in favour of promoting a market-centred agenda. The other dimension to this process is its articulation within an unevenly developed regulatory landscape, and the persistent drive to deepen neoliberalization has also consistently confronted resistance and complications as it expands across different contexts. A recent example serves to illustrate this phenomenon: the push to deepen trade relations in the region through the Deep and Comprehensive Free Trade Area (DCFTA) and its implications for MPs.

DCFTA and its implications for MPs

The DCFTA is an association agreement signed in 2014 between the EU, Ukraine, Moldova and Georgia gradually taking effect over 2016. While the language and terms can vary slightly between countries, the agreement broadly aims to establish a free trade area between the EU and those neighbouring states by liberalizing markets 'via the progressive removal of customs tariffs and quotas, and by an extensive harmonization of laws, norms and regulations in various trade-related sectors' (European Commission 2016: 2). An outline of the deal with Ukraine expounds upon the 'unprecedented level of integration' through deregulating both the services and non-services sectors of the Ukrainian economy, and allowing firms and capital based in Ukraine to access the EU's internal market (ibid.: 5). Inasmuch as norms and rights are mentioned, they are chiefly elaborated in the economic sphere – the agreement stipulates that decreasing commodity prices and expanding market opportunities should be the determinant of success (ibid.: 7).

Unsurprisingly, the drive for market-led 'rules of the game' and competition-driven regulatory regimes is never void of political resistance. In fact, various Ukrainian business associations expressed hostility to the implementation of the DCFTA (Shumylo-Tapiola 2012). What is remarkable, however, is how the EU aimed to extend trade liberalization across the rest of the European neighbourhood *in spite of* the institutional impediments and incongruent regulatory systems that frequently disrupt and disorganize this process.

After negotiations began with Ukraine, the EU explicitly indicated that the enhanced trade arrangement 'can serve as a model for other ENP partners in the future' (Council of the European Union 2007: 3). Once negotiations started with Tunisia and Morocco, civil society players in those countries called for key changes to the DCFTA from the EU in order to tailor any agreement to their sectoral demands (Van der Loo 2016: 334). The Arab NGO Network for Development, gauging the potential impact of the DCFTA in Tunisia, demanded that any agreement 'should not perpetuate this flawed system' which is prone to 'harm certain sectors and can lead to disappearance of important sectors such as manufacturing or mining industry'; they also expressed concerns for how the DCFTA 'can breach human rights in practice, mainly at the level of economic and social rights' (ANND 2016).

In Morocco, a number of industries which have heretofore remained principally under the ownership of the state – including gas, oil, mining and electricity – have also resisted privatization in staunch opposition to DCFTA provisions (Dimitrovova and Novakova 2015). Elsewhere, assessments and prognoses of an expanded DCFTA in the Mediterranean states have concluded that 'partner countries will not equally benefit', and that the effects on countries like Turkey and Tunisia would be insignificant, even close to zero as a percentage of GDP (Rau 2014: 2; ECORYS 2013: 16).

Is this a case then of norm/standard imposition and regulatory flattening with its subsequent resistance repercussions? Or is this a classical case of policy implementation failure?

Clearly, the EU's approach towards deep trade integration is consistent with the rational choice institutionalist literature advocating for greater structural incentives and enforcement mechanisms in EU–Mediterranean reforms (see Müller-Jentsch 2005; Montanari 2007). In fact, the EU has incrementally structured its ENP according to this logic by arranging financial rewards for countries that make progress on mandated reforms via the slogan of 'more for more and greater differentiation' (European External Action Service 2011). The DCFTA arrangements are a continuation of this rationale, as they are 'based on far-reaching market access conditionality, which links additional access to the EU's internal market to the progress in implementation' (Gstöhl 2015).

From the EU's perspective however, the push for the DCFTA is a reflexive innovation and not a straitjacket imposition of neoliberalized market led reforms. In reaction to the critiques against the DCFTA, and in line with streamlining the structure of incentives, the EU recently revised its discourse and practice on conditionality. It now focuses instead on 'ownership in partnership', highlighting the potential for cooperation à la carte through pragmatic flexibility and more differentiation in economic development and job creation, cooperation on energy, security and migration and mobility partnership (European Commission and European External Action Service 2015).

Going beyond simplistic debates on regulatory convergence/ divergence and policy failure, a 'variegated' analysis allows us to see how the recent discourses and practices on pragmatic flexibility and differentiation (2015) were cumulatively a reaction to 'more for more and greater differentiation' (2011). 'More for more' itself was a reaction to the joint ownership discourse embedded in the 'Joint Action Plans' of the ENP in 2007.[5] The 'action plans' themselves were the embodiment of ideas and practices around 'shared values and ring of friends' of 2004. The latter concepts/practices were a reaction to two things: the 2004 enlargement (where the EU was keen to prevent the emergence of new dividing lines between the enlarged Union and its new neighbours) and the paralysis of the EMP (whose one size fits all economic philosophy was the most dominant dimension within this tripartite partnership).

All of these discourses and practices were innovative and reflexive in relation to their own contexts. Nonetheless, the VNLT allows us to observe a couple of things here. On one hand, the *origins* of these discourses and practices were embedded within a neoliberal approach to economic development intensified with the EMP and embryonically facilitated by the cooperation agreements of the mid-1970s. They have never existed prior to these agreements. On the other hand, the *present* interdependence and cumulative aspect of these discourses and practices is now taking on a life of its own (consciously or unconsciously), where reflexive policy makers are constantly reacting to immediate layered problems but seem unable or perhaps unwilling to question both the origins and content of these problems. Ironically then, it is the situated reflexivity of these actors which is deepening neoliberalization policies in EU–Mediterranean policies.

Neoliberalization processes have tendencies towards commodification and marketization. This is clear. However, these tendencies are only iteratively activated through the actions, intentions and reflexivity of the actors involved. This is why the VNLT is well equipped to explain the patterned incoherence of the EU's Mediterranean policies. It simultaneously explains why it is internally logical, consistent and coherent for the EU to continue deepening its reforms in the Mediterranean, and why this deepening across different regulatory regimes is inherently unstable and conflictual.

Towards a variegated approach?

Clearly, the VNLT can bring a fruitful contribution to the EU Mediterranean policy literature from a variety of thematic and theoretical points.

First, it brings back important concepts such as neoliberalism and neoliberalization to the forefront of academic debates about policy implementation and deliberation. Second, it offers a robust analytical treatment of neoliberalization, where the term definitely denotes a process and not a conspiratorial monolithic entity. From a VNLT perspective, neoliberalization processes neither exist independently of our minds, nor exist only through our minds. Instead, it offers a complex articulation of these seemingly opposite propositions. Third, the VNLT can systemically ground and complement a welter of neoinstitutionalist accounts which have studied the repeated failures of EU Mediterranean policies. By bringing forward the patterned incoherence of neoliberalization processes, the VNLT can holistically relate the rational choice institutionalist argument pertaining to incentive structures (Müller-Jentsch 2005; Montanari 2007), to the normative/sociological argument about norm appropriateness (Johansson-Nogués 2006; Jonasson 2013), to the historical institutionalist accounts of path dependency[6] (Gomez 2003; Emerson et al. 2005; Zank 2009).

Theoretically, the distinct yet relational constitutiveness between disarticulated and deepened neoliberalization is explicitly inspired by more contemporary debates on structure–agency that are post-structurationist in their analysis. The VNLT clearly draws on Jessop's (2001) strategic relational approach where agency is deeply conditioned by the social contours and temporal horizons it inhabits, and is reflexively reorganized throughout. Agents, through this process, are subject to 'structurally inscribed strategic selectivities', while structures select such strategies based on 'individual, collective, or organizational learning capacities' and the resulting 'experiences' of the implicated actors (Jessop 2001: 1224).

This treatment of structure–agency clearly benefits from the critical realist concept of 'emergence'[7] where the existence of social structures cannot be reduced to the people who made them. Therefore, while social structures exist *in potentia*, they are activated by the iterative interaction of agents who recursively reorganize these structures. This is in contradiction to Giddens' structuration theory whose mutual constitutiveness thesis defines structures as 'chronically reproduced rules and resources instantiated by knowledgeable, practically skilled and reflexive human agents' (Giddens 1984). Structures in this theorization then act as 'memory traces' or the 'organic basis of human knowledgeability', providing actors with rules and resources which they might use, reproduce or change (ibid.). Therefore, while the relation between structure and agency for Giddens is internal and always inter-subjective, this relation is both external and internal, independent and dependent on our minds for Jessop (1996). Building on the latter's ontological and meta-theoretical insights, the VNLT is able to chart how tendentionally existing intensified neoliberalization processes can only be deepened through actors' interconnected reflexivity and intentionality.

Yet, these strengths do not mean that that VNLT is free of limitations. To my mind there are three important critiques to be made here. First, the facilitation and intensification tendencies of disarticulated neoliberalization processes seem to me to be a clear strength since the concept allows researchers to be specific about the nature of the processes they are dealing with without being deterministic in their overall analysis. However, the VNLT tells us nothing about the conditions under which these tendencies came about and what kind of interactions they sustained. As it stands, the argument can only be made by looking back at historical events retrospectively provided that one is theoretically wedded to the approach of course. Yet, to be more analytically rigorous, one needs to theoretically explore why these neoliberalization processes were selected in the first place, in relation to what other processes and why at that specific time. In a nutshell, the disarticulated neoliberalization concept seems to be more historically situated than theoretical.

Second, the theory of change advocated in this thesis is cumulatively incremental as the analysis is predicated upon successive rounds of variegation. Although this is a highly plausible argument, it simply comes at the expense of excluding explanations pertaining to abrupt changes. Although they are rarer, abrupt changes can and do actually happen. It is not clear, however, how the VNLT would be able to deal with such scenarios.

Third, the critical realist concept of emergence implicitly deployed in this thesis is 'light' in its usage. If one takes emergence to its logical conclusion, then both structure (material and ideational context or setting) and agency (social action) cannot be reduced to the people who made them. It also follows that structure and agency do not exist in the same temporal domain. Structure (context) then precedes agency (social action) while actors' elaboration postdates social action (see Archer 1995). From this perspective, actors' reflexivity (not be conflated with their conscious or unconscious actions) are always temporally specific and not omnipresent as the VNLT suggests.

In sum, the strong analytical and historical components of the VNLT can be further developed through a greater theoretical engagement with critical realism, especially the literatures on stratified emergence, structure–agency and causality. Despite its limitations, however, the VNLT provides us with a valuable repertoire of concepts and tools to help us study worldwide neoliberalization processes and their interaction with policy making The EU–Mediterranean policy context is hardly an exception.

Conclusion

It is the contention of this chapter that in order to fully understand existing development gaps today, it is necessary to employ a thorough understanding of neoliberalism and neoliberal processes. While these neoliberal processes have come to be understood in a wide variety of ways, the VNLT approach has become one of the dominant interpretations of this particular topic. If we apply the VNLT thesis in relation to the Euro-Mediterranean context, it is possible to understand that development gaps are a result of a decades-long process instantiated through EU–Mediterranean policies that have systematically created a variegated and inherently contradictory geoinstitutional framework. From the tendential facilitation of neoliberalization processes through the Global Mediterranean Policy of 1972 to the Barcelona Process of 1995 and the establishment of the EMP in 1994, development gaps were a result of the intensification of free market logics which gradually came to dominate Euro-Mediterranean relations. These gaps were further accentuated by a subsequent deepening of neoliberal logics embedded within the DCFTA – an agreement crafted in response to the uneven development in the region perpetuated by the existing regulatory system.

In sum, I argue that the VNLT approach makes a substantive contribution to explaining development gaps articulated by EU Mediterranean policies. By offering a comprehensive understanding of the neoliberalization of Euro-Mediterranean relations, the VNLT bridges a gap in the existing development literature and calls for an analytical reconceptualization of certain themes within it. Through an understanding of the initial disarticulation, tendential facilitation and intensification of the neoliberalization of Euro-Mediterranean relations, it is possible to formulate an understanding of the policy framework and institutional landscape that fostered development gaps over time and space within the region.

In parallel, I offer a set of critiques to the VNLT approach and propose a threefold reevaluation of its analytical apparatus – a deeper understanding of the conditions facilitating the development of neoliberal processes, a deeper application of 'emergence', as well as an analytical accommodation of abrupt change. Namely, in order to solidify its standing and offer a more comprehensive picture of the construction and re-construction of development gaps in EU–Mediterranean policies, the VNLT approach would benefit from a more thorough engagement with critical realism literature. In this sense, the VNLT approach should be an integral part of any DS scholar's analytical toolbox.

Acknowledgements

I would like to thank Jack Mullan and Aleksandra Piletic for their assistance in preparing this chapter.

Notes

1 Neoliberalism, in its simplest and uncontested meaning, refers to market-led regulatory frameworks usually codified in a set of policies which prioritize privatization, deregulation, trade liberalization and restrictive fiscal and monetary policies (see Harvey 2007, Cahill, Edwards and Stilwell 2013).
2 These restrictive preferential free trade agreements gave one-way free access to manufactured and semi-manufactured industrial goods to the EC, partial tariff exemptions on specific agricultural goods, limited amount of financial aids in the form of financial protocols, and some financial development assistance either through grants or long-term interest rates loans from the European Investment Bank (EIB). See Yesilada (1991).
3 The economic chapter of the EMP removed the one-way access agreement and institutionalized reciprocal free trade relations.
4 For an overview of the economic strategy of these policies see Knio 2009 and 2013.
5 The Joint Action Plans were introduced in 2003–4. However, the first wave of these plans were only fully implemented by most MPs by 2007, hence the date indicated here.
6 For an overview of these literatures, see Knio 2013.
7 Emergence in critical realism refers to 'situations in which the conjunction of two or more features or aspects gives rise to new phenomena, which have properties which are irreducible to those of their constituents, even though the latter are necessary for their existence' (Sayer 2000: 12).

Bibliography

Arab NGO Network for Development (ANND) (2016) 'On the Way to the DCFTA Tunisia Full Round Negotiations'. Available at http://www.annd.org/data/item/pdf/399.pdf (accessed 20 May 2016).

Archer, M. (1995) *Realist Social Theory: The Morphogenetic Approach* (Cambridge: Cambridge University Press).

Block, F. (2003) Karl Polanyi and the writing of 'The Great Transformation', *Theory and Society* 32(3): 275–306.

Brenner, N. and N. Theodore (2002) Cities and the geographies of 'actually existing neoliberalism', *Antipode*, 34(3): 349–79.

Brenner, N., J. Peck and N. Theodore (2010) Variegated neoliberalization: geographies, modalities, pathways, *Global Networks*, 10(2): 182–222.

Cahill, D., L. Edwards and F. Stilwell (2013) *Neoliberalism: Beyond the Free Market* (Cheltenham: Edward Elgar Publishing).

Clairet, P. (1994) EC–Med Relations: The Peace Process and Revisions to the Community's Mediterranean Policy, in: P. Ludlow (Ed.) *Europe and the Mediterranean* (London: Brassey's Centre for Policy Studies), pp. 147–89.

Council of the European Union (2007) Strengthening the European Neighbourhood Policy: Council Conclusions, Available at http://register.consilium.europa.eu/doc/srv?l=EN&f=ST%2011016%20 2007%20INIT (accessed 10 May 2016).

Cypher, J. M. and J. L. Dietz (2004) *The Process of Economic Development* (London: Routledge).

Dimitrovova, B. and Z. Novakova (2015) Re-Thinking the EU's Development Paradigm: Views from Morocco and Tunisia. EPC Policy Brief: 12 January.

ECORYS (2013) Trade Sustainability Impact Assessment in Support of Negotiations of a DFCTA between the EU and Morocco: Final Report. Available at http://trade.ec.europa.eu/doclib/docs/2013/ november/tradoc_151926.pdf (accessed 20 May 2016).

Emerson, M. (2005) *Democratisation in the European Neighbourhood* (Brussels, Belgium: Centre for European Policy Studies).

Escobar, A. (2011) *Encountering Development: The Making and Unmaking of the Third World* (Princeton: Princeton University Press).

European Commission (2015) Programme for the European Neighbourhood Policy (2014–2017): the EU's Single Support Framework to Tunisia (2014–2015). Available at http://ec.europa.eu/enlargement/neighbourhood/pdf/key-documents/tunisia_2014_2015_programming_document.pdf (accessed 10 May 2016).

European Commission (2016) EU–Ukraine Deep and Comprehensive Free Trade Area. Available at http://trade.ec.europa.eu/doclib/docs/2013/april/tradoc_150981.pdf (accessed 3 May 2016).

European Commission and European External Action Service (2015) Joint Communication to the European Parliament, the Council, the European Economic and Social Committee and the Committee of the Regions. Review of the European Neighbourhood Policy. SWD (2015) 500 final. Available at http://ec.europa.eu/enlargement/neighbourhood/pdf/key-documents/151118_joint-communication_review-of-the-enp_en.pdf (accessed 2 June 2016).

European External Action Service (2011) A New Response to a Changing Neighbourhood. A Review of European Neighbourhood Policy. Available at http://eeas.europa.eu/enp/pdf/pdf/com_11_303_en.pdf (accessed 2 June 2016).

Gallina, A. (2006) From Partnership to Friendships: Flows and Flaws in the Mediterranean Region, Federico Caffè Centre Research Reports No. 4/2006, Roskilde: Roskilde Universitet, 1–14.

Giddens, A. (1984) *The Constitution of Society* (Cambridge: Polity).

Gomez, R. (2003) *Negotiating the Euro-Mediterranean Partnership: Strategic Action in EU Foreign Policy?* (Aldershot: Ashgate).

Gstöhl, S. (2015) Models of external differentiation in the EU's neighbourhood: an expanding economic community? *Journal of European Public Policy*, 22(6): 854–70.

Harvey, D. (2007) *A Short History of Neoliberalism* (Oxford: Oxford University Press).

Jessop, R. (1996) Interpretive sociology and the dialectic of structure and agency, *Theory, Culture & Society*, 13(1): 119–28.

Jessop, R. (2001) Institutional re(turns) and the strategic–relational approach, *Environment and Planning*, 33(7): 1213–35.

Johansson-Nogués, E. (2006) Civil Society in Euro-Mediterranean Relations: What Success of EU's Normative Promotion? EUI Working Papers, RSCAS No. 2006/40. Italy: European University Institute (EUI) Robert Schuman Centre for Advanced Studies.

Jonasson, A.-K. (2013) *The EU's Democracy Promotion and the Mediterranean Neighbours: Orientation, Ownership and Dialogue in Jordan and Turkey* (Abingdon: Routledge).

Khader, B. (2001) The Economic, Social and Political Impact of the Euro-Mediterranean Partnership, in M. Maresceau and Erwan Lannon (Eds), *The EU's Enlargement and Mediterranean Strategies* (Basingstoke: Palgrave), pp. 269–82.

Knio, K. (2009) Governance, Politics and the European Mediterranean Partnership (EMP): Problems of Implementation or Policy Design?, in W. Hout and R. Robinson (Eds), *Governance and the Depoliticisation of Development* (London: Routledge), pp. 77–91.

Knio, K. (2013) *The European Union's Mediterranean Policy: Model or Muddle? A New Institutionalist Perspective* (Basingstoke: Palgrave Macmillan).

Knio, K. (2014) Role of Experts and Financial Supervision in the EU: The de Larosière Commission, in Monica Ambrus, Karin Arts, Ellen Hey and Helena Raulus (Eds), *The Role of 'Experts' in International and European Decision-Making Processes: Advisors, Decision Makers or Irrelevant Actors?* (Cambridge: Cambridge University Press), pp. 341–60.

Montanari, M. (2007) The Barcelona Process and the political economy of Euro-Mediterranean trade integration, *JCMS: Journal of Common Market Studies*, 45(5): 1011–40.

Müller-Jentsch, D. (2005) *Deeper Integration and Trade in Services in the Euro-Mediterranean Region: Southern Dimensions of the European Neighborhood Policy*. Vol. 311. World Bank Publications.

Peck, J. (2004) Geography and public policy: constructions of neoliberalism, *Progress in Human Geography* 28(3): 392–405.

Peck, J. and N. Theodore (2007) Variegated capitalism, *Progress in Human Geography*, 31(6): 731–72.

Peck, J. and A. Tickell (2002) Neoliberalizing space, *Antipode*, 34(3): 380–404.

Peck, J., N. Theodore and N. Brenner (2012a) Neoliberalism, Interrupted, in D. Cahill, L. Edwards, F. Stilwell (Eds), *Neoliberalism: Beyond the Free Market* (Cheltenham: Edward Elgar Publishing), pp. 15–30.

Peck, J., N. Theodore and N. Brenner (2012b) Neoliberalism resurgent? Market rule after the great recession, *South Atlantic Quarterly*, 111(2): 265–88.

Polanyi, K. (1944) *The Great Transformation: The Political and Economic Origins of Our Time* (Boston: Beacon Press).

Rau, M.-L. (2014) Conquering the EU Market with New Comprehensive Trade Agreements: Simulating DCFTAs between the EU and Neighbour Countries, The Hague: Agricultural Economics Research Institute.

Sayer, A. (2000) *Realism and Social Science* (London: Sage).

Shumylo-Tapiola, O. (2012) Ukraine at the Crossroads: Between the EU DCFTA & Customs Union, Russia/NIS Center, Russie Nei Reports No. 11.

Sörensen, Jens. S and F. Söderbaum (2012) *The End of the Development–Security Nexus? The Rise of Global Disaster Management* (Uppsala: Dag Hammarskjöld Foundation).

Tickell, A. and J. Peck (2003) Making Global Rules: Globalization or Neoliberalization, in J. Peck and H. Yeung (Eds), *Remaking the Global Economy* (London: Sage), pp. 163–81.

Todaro, M. and S. C. Smith (2014) *Economic Development* (New York: Pearson Series in Economics).

Van der Loo, G. (2016) *The EU–Ukraine Association Agreement and Deep and Comprehensive Free Trade Area: A New Legal Instrument for EU Integration without Membership* (Leiden: Brill).

Yesilada, B. (1991) The European Community's Mediterranean Policy: 1989–1990, in L. Hurwitz and C. Lequesne (Eds), *The State of the European Community: 1989–1990* (Boulder: Lynne Rienner Publishing), pp. 359–72.

Zank, W. (2009) The Modest Progress of Arab Integration, or Why Some Arab Countries have Integrated More with Europe than with their Neighbours. CCIS, Center for Comparative Integration Studies, Aalborg University.

23
CLIMATE CHANGE, ENVIRONMENTAL DEGRADATION AND RENEWABLE ENERGY

Michael Mason

Introduction

Since the early 1970s, shared concerns about marine pollution and other threats to the Mediterranean have motivated cooperation between countries in the region. The evolution, over 40 years, of the United Nations (UN) Mediterranean Action Plan attests to a growing body of rules seeking to prevent and mitigate ecological degradation in the marine environment and coastal areas. More recently, and outside this UN process, there have been multiple efforts to coordinate national actions on climate change, freshwater resources and renewable energy, much taking place under the aegis of Euro-Mediterranean cooperation, including the Barcelona Process, the Union for the Mediterranean and the Mediterranean Component of the European Union Water Initiative (MED EUWI). A complex, confusing array of overlapping processes has fostered institutional fragmentation and diluted political commitments to joint action.

At the same time, the ecological challenges facing Mediterranean countries' societies are severe: rapid population growth, urbanisation and economic development are feeding rising demands for water and energy, threatening to overwhelm the modest gains in environmental quality achieved by regional cooperation over the management of natural resources. Climate change in the Mediterranean basin is forecast to intensify the ecological disruption of human lives and livelihoods, particularly for vulnerable populations in the southern and eastern Mediterranean countries. While these impacts of regional warming have been acknowledged by the majority of Mediterranean states – evident in their carbon mitigation and adaptation commitments under the 2015 Paris Agreement of the UN Framework Convention on Climate Change (UNFCCC) – there are also countervailing geopolitical forces undermining multilateral action on low-carbon development, notably the securitisation of fossil fuel resources and population flows fuelled by violent conflict in north Africa and the eastern Mediterranean.

In this chapter I offer an overview of major transnational environmental challenges facing Mediterranean countries, highlighting projected climate change impacts, issues around water pollution and scarcity, and the emergent, uncertain transition to renewable energy. The collective environmental concerns of Mediterranean societies over urbanisation and economic development (e.g. ecological impacts arising from a shared economic dependence on tourism), typically linked to basin-wide biogeographical and climatological processes, have invited the scholarly labelling of a 'Mediterranean syndrome' (Eder and Kousis 2001: see also Marquina 2004) to capture a distinctive regional dynamic in environmental politics. To be sure, as noted later, there are recurrent institutional forms and effects, above all from the European Union (EU), both harmonising environmental policy in those member states bordering the Mediterranean, and also projecting environmental governance norms onto non-member states seeking to benefit from greater economic cooperation with the EU. Yet, the fractured political geography of the Mediterranean starkly reveals the shortfalls of EU soft power and the wider security interdependencies that, I claim, have slowed or stalled efforts to build basin-wide cooperation over freshwater and energy resources. I turn first to climate change as the issue with arguably the highest level of salience in recent public and policy discourses on environmental threats to the Mediterranean basin.

Climate change

The Mediterranean basin is projected to receive significant impacts from climate change. Regional climate modelling indicates generally a warming trend for the Mediterranean, more pronounced in summer and autumn, alongside a rise in high temperature events (Giannakopoulos et al. 2009; Jacobeit et al. 2014). Precipitation is projected to decrease across all seasons, contributing towards an increased frequency and intensity of drought (IPCC 2013: 7; Cook et al. 2016). A decline in soil moisture in all seasons, but especially in summer, is greatest in the southern and eastern Mediterranean, but the European states bordering the northern Mediterranean are also face drier growing conditions (Dubrovský et al. 2014). In coastal regions there are also concerns over sea-level rise, an increase in seawater temperature and rising acidity (Santos et al. 2014). Significant uncertainty remains regarding local climatic changes, in part because the Mediterranean is a climatic transition zone between temperate North Atlantic and tropical African atmospheric processes, and because even regional climate model simulations are unable to incorporate the physical geographic variation of the basin.

A number of EU-funded research projects have examined the projected impacts of climate change on Mediterranean countries. While focused on EU states, the PESETA II project, addressing sector-based economic impacts of climate change, projects for the Mediterranean region falling crop yields as a result of declining water availability and a truncated growing season. Under a business-as-usual scenario, agricultural yields for southern Europe are estimated to fall by 20 per cent in the 2080s with more severe yield reductions in the southern Mediterranean (Ciscar et al. 2014: 54–8). The PESETA II project also records, by 2071–2100, a major increase in the risk of meteorological forest fires in the Mediterranean coastal regions of Algeria, Morocco and Tunisia. By mid-century, coastal zones around the Mediterranean are projected to experience a decrease in summer tourism as a result of heatwaves and competing water demands. All Mediterranean coastal zones are also projected by PESETA II to face mounting costs from sea-level rises and sea-storm surges, which will impact on productive land and infrastructure (Ciscar et al. 2014: 71–81).

The southern and eastern Mediterranean is a region particularly exposed to climate change on account of water scarcity, rapid urbanisation and a reliance on rain-fed agriculture. The Climate Change, Hydro-conflicts and Human Security (CLICO) project, which included case studies in Egypt, Morocco, Palestine and Turkey, concluded that populations in the EU Mediterranean countries were generally less vulnerable to climate change than southern and eastern Mediterranean countries due to more advanced welfare and social security systems in the former states. Nevertheless, CLICO research also identified in southern Mediterranean countries examples of communal socio-economic systems (e.g. Bedouin drought management practices in the Egyptian Sinai) and governance structures (e.g. basin-level cooperative water management in Morocco) which demonstrate proven means for reducing vulnerability to climate change impacts (Gerstetter and McGlade 2012). Informed by these and other project insights, CLICO research has served as a necessary corrective to media and policy reports forecasting political instability and conflict as a result of hydro-climatic changes in the eastern Mediterranean and the Middle East (Kallis and Zografos 2014).

The UNFCCC Paris Agreement, which entered into force in November 2016, serves as the key international driver for the climate mitigation actions of Mediterranean states. To limit the rise in global temperatures to below 2 degrees Celsius above pre-industrial levels, the Paris Agreement invites parties to issue suitably ambitious 'nationally determined contributions' (NDCs) in greenhouse gas emission reductions, which have major implications for economic development and energy investment choices. The Mediterranean member states of the EU are bound by the union's commitment to a binding target of at least a 40 per cent domestic reduction in greenhouse gas emissions by 2030 compared to 1990, with national efforts delivered through participation in the EU emissions trading system (ETS) and tailored emissions targets for non-ETS sectors, such as agriculture, surface transportation and waste. These emission commitments are part of an energy and climate strategy for 2030 that includes targets for 27 per cent share of renewable energy consumption and 27 per cent energy savings compared with a business-as-usual scenario. Phase III (2013–20) of the ETS prioritises carbon trading with least developed countries (including UNFCCC Clean Development Mechanism credits), which serves as a disincentive to integrated Mediterranean-wide action on climate mitigation, although there is also an opportunity under the EU Renewable Energy Directive (2009/28/EC) for southern and eastern Mediterranean countries to export renewable energy-sourced electricity to Europe. Thus, Euro-Mediterranean carbon mitigation is steered more through EU energy trading interests than the UNFCCC process.

In contrast to unconditional EU climate mitigation commitments, the NDCs of the southern and eastern Mediterranean countries are, aside from Israel and Turkey, conditional on receiving significant financial, technological and administrative support from the international community. This is consistent with the Paris Agreement and the continued application of a 'common but differentiated responsibility and respective capabilities' norm in UNFCCC decision-making (UNFCCC 2015: Article 2), where industrialised countries are expected to exercise more ambitious emission reduction targets; and, despite a trend of declining CO_2 emissions, the EU still accounts for 9.6 per cent of the global total (PBL Netherlands Environmental Assessment Agency 2015: 23–5). For southern and eastern Mediterranean states, NDCs are incorporated into national strategies for sustainable development (e.g. Egypt and Morocco), clean energy transitions (e.g. Morocco, Tunisia), and donor-led climate adaptation planning (e.g. Jordan, Lebanon). In their NDCs, both Israel and Turkey cite strong demographic and economic growth as reasons qualifying their emissions reduction commitments.

The NDCs of most southern and eastern Mediterranean countries include statements on adaptation to climate change, and the Paris Agreement includes as an explicit goal 'increasing the ability to adapt to the adverse impacts of climate change and foster climate resilience and low greenhouse gas emissions development, in a manner that does not threaten food production' (UNFCCC 2015: Article 1(b)), requesting also that parties strengthen regional cooperation on climate change adaptation. However, recent attempts to craft Mediterranean-wide cooperation on climate change adaptation have largely been symbolic. A Mediterranean Climate Change Initiative, launched by the Greek government in October 2010, aimed to develop a regional strategy on climate change adaptation and low-carbon development: its modest networking gains were incorporated in the energy and climate change programme of the intergovernmental

Union for the Mediterranean (UfM), which brings together 28 EU member states and 15 countries from the southern and eastern Mediterranean. The first ministerial meeting on environment and climate change convened by UfM took place in May 2014: both an expert group and working group established by this meeting have yet to generate a coordinated agenda for climate change adaptation in the Mediterranean.

In the absence of a major institutional platform for Mediterranean climate cooperation, the EU remains the lead player for Euro-Mediterranean climate relations, skewing this interaction towards EU priorities and interests. The Interreg MED Programme (2014–20), which promotes territorial cohesion between the Mediterranean regions of ten member states and three pre-accession countries (Albania, Bosnia-Herzegovina and Montenegro), features a commitment to climate change adaptation under a priority programme priority on low-carbon and energy efficiency. EU dialogue with nine southern and eastern Mediterranean states (Algeria, Egypt, Israel, Jordan, Lebanon, Libya, Morocco, Palestine and Tunisia) on climate change adaptation and mitigation is fostered by financial and technological assistance under the separate ClimaSouth programme (2013–17), part of the European Neighbourhood Policy. ClimaSouth interventions are designed to be consistent with the overall EU goal of advancing democratic governance and market economy norms – a 'good governance' prescription that has struggled to implement a technical-managerial climate planning model across governance contexts directly and indirectly affected by political insecurity and conflict. Furthermore, the NDCs of the southern and eastern shore countries are either conditional or qualified: they are an expression of sovereign rights to economic development in which climate mitigation (and adaptation) commitments rest on the receipt of external financial, technological and administrative assistance and/or an expectation that the EU and international community recognise that demographic trends and priorities for economic growth can trump environmental constraints in these countries. As noted later, clean energy is an exception to this perceived tradeoff insofar as it is seen as supportive of economic development.

Marine environmental degradation and water management

The Mediterranean was the first marine area subject to international cooperation under the UN Regional Seas Programme. Established in 1975 to reduce and mitigate marine pollution, the Mediterranean Action Plan was followed a year later by the adoption of the Convention for the Protection of the Mediterranean Sea against Pollution (Barcelona Convention). Over time this regional environmental regime has expanded in scope and membership, facilitated by the United Nations Environment Programme (UNEP). In 1995 the Barcelona Convention was amended, renamed as the Convention for the Protection of the Marine Environment and Coastal Region of the Mediterranean: it now has seven protocols, including agreements on land-based sources of pollution, special protected areas and hazardous wastes. Phase II of Mediterranean Action Plan, launched in 2005, consolidated the shift in focus from marine pollution prevention to a broader concern with the sustainable management of Mediterranean natural resources and integrated coastal zone governance. To this end, in 2016 the 22 contracting parties of the Barcelona Convention adopted the Mediterranean Strategy for Sustainable Development (2016–25) as a framework to guide ecosystem-based decision-making at regional, sub-regional and national scales.

According to a seminal study by Haas (1990), the Mediterranean Action Plan represents a successful institutional design for coordinating international rule-making on pollution control, distinguished in part by the effective integration of scientific research and assessment. Indeed, at least in terms of its growing scientific command of the state of the Mediterranean environment and the comprehensive regulatory scope of the Barcelona Convention and protocols, this regional environmental regime has fostered improved governance of the Mediterranean Sea (Frantzi 2008; Skjærseth 2001). At the same time, there are concerns at the lack of effectiveness of the Mediterranean Action Plan in addressing land-based sources of pollution, which are responsible for 80 per cent of the pollution in the Mediterranean Sea. The modest progress made in the treatment of wastewater and solid waste management threatens to be overwhelmed by the rapid urbanisation and population growth in southern Mediterranean countries, as well as increasing industrial pollution from energy-intensive industries, such agro-foods, cement production, chemicals and metalworking (Massoud et al. 2003; Sauzade 2015).

Regional efforts to develop a joint freshwater management strategy have largely taken place outside the Mediterranean Action Plan, beginning with a Mediterranean Charter for Water adopted in Rome in 1992 at a meeting of water ministers from Mediterranean basin states. This charter informed a chapter on water in a wide-ranging Barcelona Declaration signed by Euro-Mediterranean foreign ministers in November 1995. Under the Barcelona Declaration, water scarcity is seen as an increasing problem in Mediterranean countries: regional collaboration on water is deemed necessary to ascertain current and future needs, to identify ways of reinforcing regional cooperation, and to make proposals for rationalising the planning and management of water resources (SEMIDE/EMWIS 2016). Little progress was made in these areas until Euro-Mediterranean cooperation was re-energised by the creation, in 2008 of the UfM. Bolstered by a permanent secretariat, the UfM water and environment programme created a Euro-Mediterranean Water Expert Group which, informed by the Barcelona Process, finished drafting in March 2010 a long-term Strategy for Water in the Mediterranean.

In April 2010 the draft Strategy for Water in the Mediterranean was presented to a Euro-Mediterranean conference hosted by the Spanish presidency of the UfM. There was consensus from UfM countries over the challenges facing water resources in the region, particularly in the south, where over 180 million people were classified as water poor (access to less than 1000 m^3 of renewable water per capita per year) and over 60 million were classified as facing a water shortage (access to less than 500 m^3 of renewable water per capita per year). In addition, there was common recognition of water abstraction pressures from agriculture, industry and domestic use, with rising levels of seawater intrusion in coastal aquifers due to overexploitation of groundwater resources (Union for the Mediterranean 2010: 4; see also Holst-Warhaft and Steenhuis 2010). Differences between EU and non-EU Mediterranean countries over implementation targets saw the latter secure more relaxed deadlines on the adoption by states of river basin planning and management. However, there was a failure to reach consensus agreement on the water strategy after Israel objected to references in the draft plan to the occupied territories.

After the deadlock in 2010, the UfM has continued to promote the development of a regional water strategy, but its framing of cooperation according to European norms of water governance has provoked sovereignty sensitivities from other non-EU Mediterranean states. Egypt and Turkey have objected to recommendations that cooperation on transboundary water resources in the Mediterranean should be in conformity with international water law, notably the Convention on the Protection and Use of Transboundary Watercourses and International Lakes (1992) and Convention of the Law of the Non-Navigational Uses of International Watercourses (1997). Both countries are not party to either convention, claiming prior use entitlements to major transboundary waters crossing their territories. In anticipation of a proposed UfM Ministerial Conference on Water, in 2016 the Water Expert Group renewed work on a revised Mediterranean water strategy, highlighting technical areas of joint concern rather than political–legal parameters for international cooperation.

For southern and eastern Mediterranean countries, the UfM water agenda for Euro-Mediterranean cooperation has a dominant European presence, despite region wide consultation and the parallel UN Barcelona Convention process. In 2005 the EU launched a Horizon 2020 Initiative to accelerate pollution reduction in the Mediterranean, seeking synergies between UN, UfM and EU regional programmes. Horizon 2020 also overlaps with the Mediterranean component of the EU Water Initiative (MED EUWI), launched in 2003 under the sponsorship of the government of Greece with a focus on integrated water resources management, and more recently supported by the Swedish International Development Cooperation Agency. Hampered at least initially by cumbersome governance (Terry Lawrence Associates 2007), MED EUWI has carried out regional and bilateral activities, including country dialogues with so-called partner countries (Lebanon, Egypt, Palestine, Syria and Tunisia), encouraging water management practices consistent with the EU Water Framework Directive.

Given the plurality of regional initiatives on water management in the Mediterranean, it is not surprising that concerns have been raised, particularly by eastern and southern shore states, at a lack of institutional efficiency and complementarity. Efforts have been made to address these shortfalls in coordination; for example, MED EUWI now provides technical and administrative support to efforts to revitalise the Strategy for Water in the Mediterranean. Nevertheless, the shift in gravity in Mediterranean water cooperation from UN-led hard law to EU-driven soft law processes has at the same time imported the slow, hesitant pace of European Neighbourhood Policy in the region, favouring a lowest common denominator of (technical) collaboration and not challenging regional wielders of geopolitical power (e.g. Israel, Turkey) who are generating transboundary inequities in freshwater allocation. These procedural complexities have hampered joint efforts to address marine environmental degradation in the Mediterranean Sea, but the biggest constraint to environmental effectiveness remains the rapidly increasing scale of land-based pollution sources – a result largely of urbanisation, industrialisation and population growth in southern Mediterranean countries. For the ruling elites of these states, there is currently no major economic or political incentive, or indeed capacity, to curb growth.

Renewable energy

Across the Mediterranean region a shared political commitment to an increased use of renewable energy derives from a convergence of interests between, on the one hand, EU goals for a low-carbon economy and, on the other, the need for southern and eastern shore Mediterranean states to invest in new energy infrastructure in the face of rapidly growing per capita energy consumption. As noted earlier, a priority axis for Interreg MED 2014–20, the EU territorial cohesion plan for member states and pre-accession countries in the Mediterranean region, is the promotion of low-carbon strategies and energy efficiency, including increasing the share of renewable local energy sources in the energy mixes of Mediterranean territories. The regional and bilateral mechanisms of the European Neighbourhood Policy extend these goals to the non-EU Mediterranean states, fostering their efforts to produce low-carbon energy, both for domestic use and also the future possibility, under the Renewable Energy Directive of exporting renewable energy-sourced electricity to Europe.

Since Euro-Mediterranean foreign ministers signed the Barcelona Declaration in 1995, the EU has viewed energy cooperation with southern and eastern Mediterranean countries as a matter of energy security and geopolitical stability. The EU Energy Diplomacy Action Plan (2015) defines Euro-Mediterranean cooperation as a means of strengthening the diversification of EU energy sources, supplies and routes, favouring the export of European expertise on low-carbon technologies and systems measures (Council of the European Union 2015: 6). Thus far, these has been limited interest from the net energy exporting states of the southern

Mediterranean (Algeria, Egypt), where interest in renewable energy (and energy efficiency) is seen as a means to preserve state rents on fossil fuel sales by reducing domestic oil and gas consumption. The EU has had more success through bilateral cooperation with net energy importing Mediterranean countries, signing memoranda of understanding with Jordan, Lebanon and Morocco, as well as deepening pre-accession energy cooperation with Turkey: in all these cases, the promotion of renewable energy and energy efficiency is conjoined with support for regulatory changes consistent with a greater role of private investment and energy trading.

In southern and eastern Mediterranean countries, a scaling up of commitments to renewable energy expresses a common governmental goal for the diversification of national energy mixes. Most of these countries have national renewable energy targets as a percentage of domestic electricity generation: while policy aspirations rather than legal obligations, these targets vary between 10 per cent (Israel) and 42 per cent (Morocco) by 2020 (REN21/MOFA/IRENA 2013: 18). The share of renewable energy in total energy consumption exceeds 5 per cent in four of these countries (Israel, Morocco, Tunisia and Turkey). In order to encourage new investment in energy infrastructure, the southern and eastern Mediterranean states are inviting foreign investors (public and private) in renewable energy. Regulatory incentives for renewable energy investment include the adoption of feed-in-tariffs (Algeria, Egypt, Israel, Jordan, Palestine and Turkey) and net-metering (Egypt, Israel, Jordan, Lebanon, Morocco, Palestine and Tunisia). The 500 MW Noor–Ouarzazate solar energy complex in Morocco, attracting US$3 billion financing from foreign and multilateral investors, is currently the most significant of these renewable energy developments. Further regional investment in clean energy is constrained by subsidies for domestic energy consumption and geopolitical instability.

While the European Union is due to meet its target of 20 per cent final energy consumption from renewable sources by 2020, staying on track also to meet the EU-level target of 27 per cent final energy consumption by 2030, there are concerns that renewable energy is not effectively integrated into the internal energy market (European Commission 2015: 4). The Mediterranean region is identified as a priority area for enhancing member state uptake of renewable energy and fostering network integration, with projects, for example, to increase transmission capacity between Portugal, Spain and other Mediterranean states. In September 2016 the first summit of Mediterranean EU countries (Republic of Cyprus, France, Greece, Italy, Malta, Portugal and Spain) issued a declaration identifying low-carbon energy projects and energy interconnections among a number of sectors justifying a doubling of European strategic investment. EU political commitments to the upscaling of renewable energy in the Mediterranean region are tempered by the recognition that, with the development of major gas fields in Egypt and Israel, European market access to these new reserves would make a significant contribution to energy security.

The same tensions between new fossil fuel development and clean energy commitments are expressed in wider Euro-Mediterranean cooperation on energy (Rubino 2016). In 2014 a ministerial conference of Euro-Mediterranean energy ministers launched three platforms for cooperation: (i) the development of a regional electricity market; (ii) the promotion of renewable energy sources and energy efficiency; and (iii) the creation of a Mediterranean gas hub. Under the administrative support of the UfM, initial efforts on the integration of transmission networks have focused on the southern and eastern Mediterranean countries, with the longer-term aim of fostering energy trading with the EU. The most ambitious cooperation initiative under the renewable energy platform is the Mediterranean Solar Plan, which has the long-term goal of incentivising investment in solar photovoltaic technology in the southern and eastern Mediterranean states by physically connecting to, and therefore allowing access to, EU clean energy markets. This draws in part on the idea of a Mediterranean clean energy community, the DESERTEC Initiative, developed since 2003 by a global civil society coalition (Mason 2009). In 2015 the UfM joined with the European Commission, European Investment Bank and the KfW Development Bank to establish a Mediterranean Solar Plan–Project Preparation Initiative to cover preparation costs for clean energy in selected partner countries (Algeria, Egypt, Jordan, Lebanon, Morocco, Palestine and Tunisia).

There has been a sustained effort under the European Neighbourhood Policy to engage with subnational authorities and civil society in the Mediterranean region, including projects promoting renewable energy and energy efficiency. Foremost amongst these is the Cleaner Energy Saving Mediterranean Cities Project (CES-MED), which, since 2013, has funded sustainable energy action plans covering 23 cities/regions in 8 target countries (Algeria, Egypt, Israel, Jordan, Lebanon, Morocco, Palestine and Tunisia). This CES-MED network is served by regional focal points in Rabat (Maghreb region) and Beirut (Mashreq region). The EU also encouraged participating local authorities to join the Covenant of Mayors for Climate and Energy – a separate European Commission initiative inviting local governments to issue voluntary energy and climate mitigation commitments consistent with EU policy. Due to its successful growth across and beyond the EU, the Covenant of Mayors has become the favoured EU platform for promoting scaling the adoption of European energy and climate goals in the southern and eastern Mediterranean countries. To this end, in 2016 the European Commission proposed a separate Mediterranean section of the Covenant of Mayors.

Some CES-MED participating municipalities have reported major governance challenges in aligning with EU norms on clean energy and climate change mitigation. In Algeria, Jordan and Palestine, CES-MED cities have declared as problematic high energy prices and/or supply dependence on a state utility. For Palestinian municipalities in the West Bank dependence on Israel for energy is part of a matrix of occupation-related restrictions on local self-determination: the CES-MED network avoids addressing conflict-related pressures on clean energy development. Where municipalities are granted more autonomy in energy choices, with the support of national authorities, the prospects for improved energy efficiency and use of renewables are enhanced. This is particularly noteworthy in Tunisia. At a CES-MED supported event in May 2015, the National Agency of Energy Efficiency in Tunisia launched an Association of Municipalities for Energy Transition, with over 200 Tunisian municipalities participating. Sousse, one of the Tunisian cities selected under CES-MED has, for example, received support from this national agency to adopt solar powered water heating for sports facilities (Cleaner Energy Saving Mediterranean Cities Project 2016).

Across the Mediterranean region, national commitments to renewable energy seemingly express a convergence of interests on clean energy development, though there are different political drivers: EU binding targets on renewable energy reflect a climate and energy agenda that attempts to square energy security with international climate mitigation commitments, while for the southern and eastern Mediterranean countries, investment in renewable energy is a promising vehicle for meeting rapidly expanding energy demand. Euro-Mediterranean cooperation on low-carbon energy, fostered principally by the EU and the UfM, anticipates a growing integration of the Mediterranean energy network. Nevertheless, this vision also accommodates a major role for the development of a regional gas hub given the development of substantial gas reserves in the eastern Mediterranean. Furthermore, with a supply glut in oil production and weak economic growth, there is little short-term prospect of a sustained recovery in global oil prices following their collapse at the end of 2015. Low fossil fuel prices have tempered the ambition of Euro-Mediterranean plans for the regional upscaling of renewable energy.

Conclusion

As noted in the introduction, the notion of a 'Mediterranean syndrome' (Eder and Kousis 2001) was coined to capture a distinctive regional dynamic in environmental politics, with basin-wide biogeographical and climatological processes shaping, and being shaped by, shared socio-economic development paths in the Mediterranean – notably urbanisation and tourist-oriented economic growth. There has also been distinctive regional cooperation in response to these social and ecological interdependencies, generating a diverse range of more or less developed institutional structures. In broad terms, the contrast is between, on the one hand, the legally binding obligations imposed on participating Mediterranean countries by the Barcelona Convention and the UNFCCC Paris Agreement and, on the other, the soft law norms imparted mainly by the EU and the UfM in a series of initiatives furthering Euro-Mediterranean cooperation over climate, environment and energy issues. While there are clear thematic overlaps between the UN-led and EU/UfM institutional pathways, there has been no meaningful orchestration or institutional clustering of Mediterranean environmental governance.

Established under the Barcelona Convention process, and administered by UNEP, the Mediterranean Action Plan continues to be the most stable governance platform for addressing the environmental protection of marine areas and coastal zones across the Mediterranean basin. Over time, with the adoption of successive protocols to the Barcelona Convention, the Mediterranean Action Plan has broadened its terms of reference. In 2016 this resulted in the adoption of a Mediterranean Strategy for Sustainable Development, embracing an ecosystem-based management philosophy. It is instructive that efforts to build Mediterranean cooperation over freshwater management, taking place outside the Barcelona Convention process, have struggled; for example, UfM attempts to draft a Strategy for Water in the Mediterranean have, as discussed earlier, provoked sovereignty sensitivities over the incorporation of norms from international water law (Egypt, Turkey) and international humanitarian law (Israel).

In the face of scientific observations and projections pointing to significant climate change in the Mediterranean area, there are growing efforts to integrate climate change considerations in the Mediterranean Action Plan. The favoured vehicle is the Protocol on Integrated Coastal Zone Management (2008), with the intent to integrate climatic variability and change into national strategies on integrated coastal zone management: these efforts are coordinated by a Regional Climate Change Adaptation Framework for the Mediterranean Marine and Coastal Areas, adopted at a Conference of the Parties to the Barcelona Convention in 2016. Locating this regional cooperation initiative within the UN-led Mediterranean Action Plan reflects the recognition, notably by southern and eastern Mediterranean states, that UfM and EU climate cooperation efforts have not yet effectively addressed the climate mitigation and adaptation priorities of these countries. Notwithstanding the valuable contribution of EU-funded research on climate change, water availability and other environmental pressures in the Mediterranean region, there is a perception that, outside the Barcelona Convention process, Euro-Mediterranean climate relations are skewed by European geopolitical interests.

Renewable energy is a policy domain where there is currently a significant, if contingent, overlap between EU climate mitigation goals (expressing UNFCCC obligations) and the energy diversification strategies of most southern and eastern Mediterranean states. Euro-Mediterranean energy cooperation rests on an EU drive to promote low-carbon economic development across the region. EU Mediterranean member states are locked into an energy and climate strategy that includes a target of a 27 per cent renewable energy share of final energy consumption by 2030. To support this, an upscaling of renewable energy use is promoted also in non-EU Mediterranean states through EU agreements with adjoining pre-accession territories and, further afield, a diverse set of projects delivered through the European Neighbourhood Policy. EU external energy policy in the region reinforces Euro-Mediterranean energy cooperation under the auspices of the UfM: higher levels of renewable energy and energy efficiency are seen as critical to the resilient functioning of an integrated energy network across the Mediterranean. At the same time, however, there are countervailing economic and geopolitical incentives in favour of new fossil fuel investments, particularly the current development of substantial natural gas reserves in the eastern Mediterranean. EU concerns over climate change are constrained by the paramountcy of energy security in Euro-Mediterranean energy cooperation: by themselves, for the time being, low-carbon energy sources are seen as insufficient for baseload electricity generation in Mediterranean countries.

The framing of regional environmental politics according to a Mediterranean syndrome of shared ecological risks slipping into a geographical determinism unless other political–economic forces and interests, operating at different scales, are admitted into the analysis. Some of these political–economic processes – European integration, energy securitisation, urbanisation, demographic growth – are registered above, though these longer-term trends are also altered and disrupted by unforeseen pressures, such as the recent migration crisis featuring hundreds of thousands of asylum seekers crossing the Mediterranean Sea to reach Europe: in 2015 and 2016 thousands died or went missing during these desperate journeys. The migration crisis is itself a symptom of a fractured political geography across the Mediterranean region, where shared security interdependencies have yet to generate a coordinated, effective response to conflict and political instability. Measured against the ambition that environmental cooperation should serve as a vehicle for peaceful coexistence and normative integration in the Mediterranean (e.g. European Neighbourhood Policy, UfM environment initiatives), the shortfall of European soft power is telling. While its ecological effectiveness is at best mixed, the more measured, managerial scope of the Mediterranean Action Plan suggests that environmental regime building in the region is best developed by UN institutions.

Bibliography

Ciscar, J. C., Feyen L., Soria A., Lavalle C. et al. (2014) *Climate Impacts in Europe: The JRC PESETA II Project*: EUR Number: 26586 EN, pp.54–59. Available at http://ipts.jrc.ec.europa.eu/publications/pub.cfm?id=7181

Cleaner Energy Saving Mediterranean Cities Project (2016) Tunisia Municipality of Sousse Sustainable Energy Action Plan. Rabat: CES-MED. Available at www.ces-med.eu/publications/tunisia-municipality-sousse-sustainable-energy-action-plan-seap-french

Cook, B. I., Anchukaitis, Kevin J., Touchan, Ramzi et al. (2016) 'Spatiotemporal drought variability in the Mediterranean over the last 900 years', *Journal of Geophysical Research: Atmospheres* 121: 2060–74.

Council of the European Union (2015) *Outcome of Proceedings: Council Conclusions on Energy Diplomacy* 10995/15, Brussels: General Secretariat of the Council. Available at http://data.consilium.europa.eu/doc/document/ST-10995-2015-INIT/en/pdf

Dubrovský, M., Hayes, M., Duce, P. et al. (2014) 'Multi-GCM projections of future drought and climate vulnerability indicators for the Mediterranean region', *Regional Environmental Change* 14(5): 1907–19.

Eder, K. and Kousis, M. (2001) 'Is there a Mediterranean syndrome?', in: Eder, K. and Kousis, M. (eds), *Environmental Politics in Southern Europe: Actors, Institutions and Discourses in a Europeanizing Society*. Dordrecht: Springer, pp. 393–406.

European Commission (2015) *State of the Energy Union*, COM/2015/0572 final. Brussels: European Commission.

Frantzi, S. (2008) 'What determines the institutional performance of environmental regimes? A case study of the Mediterranean Action Plan', *Marine Policy* 32(4): 618–29.

Gerstetter, C. and McGlade, K. (2012) 'Climate change, water conflicts and human security in the Mediterranean, Middle East and Sahel', CLICO Policy Brief, Available at www.clico.org/policy-briefs-sp-21028/

Giannakopoulos, C., Sager, P. le, Bindi, M. et al. (2009) 'Climatic changes and associated impacts in the Mediterranean resulting from a 2 °C global warming', *Global and Planetary Change* 68: 209–24.

Haas, P. M. (1990) *Saving the Mediterranean: The Politics of International Environmental Cooperation*. New York: Columbia University Press.

Holst-Warhaft, G. and Steenhuis, T. (eds) (2010) *Losing Paradise: The Water Crisis in the Mediterranean*. Farnham: Ashgate.

IPCC (2013) 'Summary for policymakers', in: Stocker, T. F., Qin, D., Plattner, G.-K. et al. (eds), *Climate Change 2013: The Physical Science Basis. Contribution of Working Group I to the Fifth Assessment Report of the Intergovernmental Panel on Climate Change*. Cambridge: Cambridge University Press.

Jacobeit, J., Hertig, E., Seubert, S. et al. (2014) 'Statistical downscaling for climate change projections in the Mediterranean region', *Regional Environmental Change* 14(5): 1891–906.

Kallis, G. and Zografos, C. (2014) 'Hydro-climatic change, conflict and security', *Climatic Change* 123: 69–82.

Marquina, A. (ed.) (2004) *Environmental Challenges in the Mediterranean 2000–2050*. Dordrecht: Springer.

Mason, M. (2009) 'Conclusion: towards a renewable energy transition in the Middle East and North Africa?', in: Mason, M. and Mor, A. (eds), *Renewable Energy in the Middle East*. Dordrecht: Springer, pp. 219–35.

Massoud, M. A., Scrimshaw, M. D. and Lester, J. N. (2003) 'Qualitative assessment of the effectiveness of the Mediterranean action plan: wastewater management in the Mediterranean region', *Ocean and Coastal Management* 46(9/10): 875–99.

PBL Netherlands Environmental Assessment Agency (2015) *Trends in Global CO_2 Emissions: 2015 Report*. The Hague: PBL.

REN 21/MOFA/IRENA (2013) *MENA Renewable Status Report*. Paris: REN 21. Available at http://www.ren21.net/Portals/0/documents/activities/Regional%20Reports/MENA_2013_lowres.pdf

Rubino, A. Costa Campi, M. T., Lenzi, V., Ozturk, I. (eds) (2016) *Regulation and Investment in Energy Markets: Solutions for the Mediterranean*. London: Academic Press.

Santos, F. D., Stigter, T. Y., Faysse, N. et al. (2014) 'Impacts and adaptation to climate change in the Mediterranean coastal areas: the CIRCLE-MED initiative', *Regional Environmental Change* 14(1): 1–3.

Sauzade, D. (2015) 'Assessment of pollution reduction programmes in the Mediterranean region', in: IEMed. *Mediterranean Yearbook 2015*. Barcelona: Institut Europeu de la Mediterrània, pp. 271–5. Available at http://www.iemed.org/publicacions/historic-de-publicacions/quaderns-de-la-mediterrania

SEMIDE/EMWIS (2016) Euro-Mediterranean Partnership and Water. Sophia-Antipolis: L'Office International de l'Eau. Available at www.emwis.org/overview/fol101997

Skjærseth, J. B. (2001) 'The effectiveness of the Mediterranean Action Plan', in: Miles, E., Andresen, S., Carlin, E. M. et al. (eds), *Environmental Regimes Effectiveness: Confronting Theory with Evidence*. Cambridge, MA: MIT Press, pp. 311–30.

Terry Lawrence Associates (2007) *Review of the European Water Initiative: Volume 1: Main Report*. Brussels: DG International Cooperation and Development.

UNFCCC (2015) *Decision 1/CP.21: Adoption of the Paris Agreement*, FCCC/CP/2015/10/Add.1. Bonn: UNFCCC Secretariat. Available at http://unfccc.int/paris_agreement/items/9485.php

Union for the Mediterranean (2010) *Strategy of Water in the Mediterranean*. Barcelona: Union for the Mediterranean.

24

POLITICS AND TOURISM IN THE MEDITERRANEAN REGION

Raoul Bianchi and Tom Selwyn

Tourism, colonialism and conflict

From its earliest times the expansion of travel in the Mediterranean basin has either been overshadowed by or indeed been closely implicated in acts of war, conquest and colonialism. Despite John Mason Cook's proclamation that theirs was a 'business of peace', both the opening of the Suez Canal in 1869, a key strategic asset ever since, followed by British imperial subjugation of Egypt by the late 1880s were the platform for the expansion of Thomas Cook & Son's operations further into Egypt and throughout the wider Middle East (Brendon 1991: 189). In north Africa, Hussey (2015: 77) notes how during the first bombardments of Algiers by French forces during in 1830, well-to-do visitors from French high society watched events unfold on board pleasure ships moored offshore. In the wake of the French conquest of Algeria in 1834 tourists became increasingly frequent visitors to Algiers while a few accompanied military expeditions into the interior commenting upon 'the savage beauty of the countryside and the people' (Hussey 2015: 105). Before we consign such distasteful forms of entertainment to a time pre-dating international human rights and political ethics, more recently, the Israeli bombardment of Gaza during 'Operation Protective Edge' in 2014, was observed from roof-top chairs and sofas by residents of adjacent Israeli towns (Mackey 2014). As Lisle (2007) remarks, the geopolitics of the tourist gaze is rather more complex and fuzzy than conventional juxtapositions of tourism and politics would suggest as evinced by the propensity of, admittedly, small numbers of tourists, to visit sites of conflict, including in the Balkans and Occupied Palestinian Territories.

During the nineteenth century the struggle for territorial control and resources to supply the growth of capitalist industry amongst the rising state powers of Europe led to the eventual invasion, annexation and integration of the southern and eastern Mediterranean shore into the orbits of metropolitan European power. Whilst this comprised a series of militaristic imperial ventures the European penetration of the southern shores also gave further impetus to manifold economic, social and cultural connections between northern and southern Mediterranean shores that were to mark the cross-fertilization of identities and language across the region as well as shape intra-Mediterranean movements of people (Tarrius 2002). More significantly, in terms of the representational politics and the trans-Mediterranean architecture of travel that was to follow, the rise of belligerent nationalisms of the late nineteenth century and the world wars of the first half of the twentieth century was to disrupt and suppress the historic cosmopolitanism of Mediterranean ports and cities. Increasingly, Mediterranean societies became absorbed into the territorial containers of emerging nation-states and their ethnic, cultural, linguistic and confessional fluidity and heterogeneity variously absorbed into post-colonial narratives of nationalism and economic modernization, albeit expressed in varying politico-cultural idioms (see Hourani 2005: 308–10).

Although the arrival of Thomas Cook signalled the end of privilege and with it the expansion of travel throughout the Mediterranean for emerging north European middle classes from the late nineteenth century onwards, he was merely following in the footsteps of earlier pilgrimage flows from Europe to the Middle East. Moreover, it was the French company Club Méditerranée that was to revolutionize the mass package holiday model and launch it as a key driver of capital accumulation throughout the Mediterranean and beyond after the Second World War. Founded in Paris in 1950 by two veterans of the French and Belgian resistance, Club Méditerranée in fact started as a non-profit organization before it later evolved into the billion dollar Chinese-owned multinational corporation it is today. While states played a significant role in the financing and operation of tourism facilities in post-war Mediterranean economies, Club Méditerranée provided the launching pad for a model of affordable tourism for a generation scarred by war without the need for government assistance, built around a network of low cost vacation villages (Furlough 2009: 175).

The Mediterranean has long served as a byword for hedonism, pleasure and sensuous delights while simultaneously being home to some of the most conflictual and unequal regions in the world. Moreover, nowhere else on Earth, perhaps the US–Mexico border notwithstanding, does the wealth and power of the advanced industrialized world press up quite so closely and at times, aggressively, against the impoverished south, as so starkly demonstrated by the current large-scale movements of refugees northwards through the region. Nevertheless, the pull of its ancient archaeological sites, pilgrimage centres and historic towns and myriad cultural events and festivals, and more recently, its islands, beaches and glitzy resorts has provided the bedrock upon which many Mediterranean states particularly on the north shore, have engineered a transition to modern capitalist economies albeit with varying degrees of success. This has provided a livelihood for literally dozens of businesses and trades encompassing long-standing local merchant families, foreign 'lifestyle' entrepreneurs, migrants from Africa, south Asia and the Middle East selling cheaply produced wares on the beaches, to the larger-scale capitalist enterprises and foreign corporations that have frequently absorbed the lion's share of tourism revenues in the major mass beach destinations across the Mediterranean basin.

In terms of their macro-economic standing there is a significant gulf in both the levels of economic development as well as the volume of tourist arrivals that continues to divide Mediterranean Europe from its counterparts on the southern and eastern shores where per capita incomes are on average around half or less than the north shore with the exception of Cyprus and Israel (see UNWTO 2016). In addition to the problems of chronic unemployment, poverty and indebtedness southern Mediterranean states also face mounting challenges associated with population growth. While in 1985 the approximately 350 million inhabitants of the Mediterranean basin were distributed relatively evenly between north and south, by 2025 the southern shore will account for two-thirds of the expected 600 million inhabitants that will reside in the region (Buades 2014: 22). The distribution of tourist arrivals across the Mediterranean basin is also highly uneven, ranging from 68 million arrivals in Spain, the world's third highest recipient, and nearly 40 million in Turkey, to figures that are considerably lower in areas of the war torn east of the region. And as for Turkey, situated at the cross-roads of Europe and the Middle East in more than mere geographical sense, its historically high volume of tourist arrivals has been significantly reduced since the arrival to its south of Daesh/ISIS, the refugee crisis, and other features of political instability. There are significant regional variations too in the competitiveness of the tourism sectors, as measured by the World Travel and Tourism Competitiveness Index, currently topped by Spain (World Economic Forum 2015).

At a conservative estimate given the unreliability of national statistics, the Mediterranean region receives approximately 250 million international tourists each year. Three-quarters of these arrivals are concentrated in just five countries (in order of importance: Spain, France, Italy, Turkey and Croatia) not all of which can be strictly speaking considered as part of the Mediterranean basin given their substantial touristic offer in the hinterland. Given such volumes, which of course does not account for the considerable movements of domestic tourists, as well as the various other, often overlapping flows of labour migration and refugee movements, it is perhaps unsurprising that the political dimension of tourism has been ignored in favour of an emphasis on tourism's economic and development potential.

Tourism and the building of states and nations

During the period of European colonial rule, travel to the Middle East was predominantly framed by Orientalist discourses through which travellers imagined themselves witness to a cultural landscape that remained essentially unchanged since biblical times (Daher 2007: 7). But throughout the Mediterranean processes of state formation in the nineteenth and early twentieth centuries became intertwined with periods of autocratic rule and the embrace of economic liberalism, often at the same time. Additionally, there was widespread adoption of tourism both as source of economic growth, contributor to political legitimacy, and the construction of more or less uniform narratives of the normalcy of the 'nation'. Indeed tourism was embraced as an instrument of nationalist propaganda in several Mediterranean states for the purposes of constructing and projecting a particular image of the 'nation' both outwards as well as inwards towards the domestic populations, particularly where strong regional and sub-national identities were seen by central government as 'problematic', as in Spain. During the dictatorial rule of Metaxas (1936–41), for example, Greece embraced the potential of tourism as an instrument of nationalist propaganda and in so doing celebrated Greece's plethora of ancient sites, monuments and national costumes as emblematic of the (young) nation's 'eternal national glory' (Dritsas 2009: 52). In Spain, although initial steps to promote tourism had already commenced at the beginning of the twentieth century, after the Second World War the authoritarian regime led by General Franco (1939–75) saw tourism as means to bolster a reinvigorated patriotic nationalism, less tainted by the legacy of the Civil War (1936–9) and as a means through which to 'siphon political capital from the putative market value of Spanish national identity' (Crumbaugh 2009: 11). Modern mass tourism thus became, as indeed it did elsewhere in the Mediterranean, a powerful symbolic cultural setting in which authoritarian regimes and state technocrats sought to define and remake the image of the nation and to integrate their economies into the wider circulation of capital.

Examples of the power of tourism related discourse to shape nationalist sentiments are readily to be found throughout the region, particularly clearly in Cyprus and Israel/Palestine. Thus, for example, in her examination of the Canbulet museum in Famagusta, Scott (2002) has shown the ways in which narratives about the Turks as enemies and potential colonial occupiers of Cyprus in the Ottoman period, have become transformed since the Turkish military intervention in the island in 1974, into stories and cartographic representations of the Turkish nation as saviour of the Turkish-speaking part of the island's population. In the Israeli case Selwyn (1996) has shown how tours for both internal and external tourists organized by the Society of Protection of Nature in Israel (SPNI) are specifically designed to inculcate amongst its followers feelings of deep connection between the landscape and the Israeli nation. By contrast the tours organized by institutions such as the Alternative Tourism Group (ATG) and the Jerusalem Tourism Cluster (JTC) are composed quite specifically to draw out a version of the symbolism of landscape that stresses the cosmopolitan nature of Jerusalem and the region more generally. Whilst this chapter was being written an initiative was announced by the (Israeli) Kfar Etzion field school to map out a hiking trail in what the Israeli authorities term 'Judea and Samaria', that is the occupied Palestinain territories, to supplement Israel's National Trail, which runs inside the country's internationally recognized frontiers. The SPNI has confirmed that it will consider how to support this so-called 'Eastern Trail'.

Tourism, uneven regional development and spread of capitalism

Prior to the emergence of the modern Egyptian state (1953) and the creation of the 'post-mandate' states of Syria, Lebanon, Jordan, Israel and the Palestinian Territories, travel to such ancient archaeological sites as Palmyra, Baalbek and Ephesus, as well as pilgrimage centres such as Bethlehem and Jerusalem in the eastern Mediterranean and the great cosmopolitan towns and cities of Aleppo, Alexandria and Constantinople was already well established. In both Greece and Turkey, the inter-war period saw attempts by their respective authoritarian and statist regimes to stimulate the development of hotels and tourist activity focusing in the main on ancient archaeological sites. Nevertheless, tourist numbers remained low and the infrastructure inadequate. It was only after the Second World War, following unsuccessful attempts by modernizing elites across the region to establish competitive industrial sectors during the late nineteenth and early twentieth centuries, that Spain, Greece, Turkey and Tunisia in particular began to look to mass beach tourism in order to compensate for weak and uncompetitive industrial sectors and as an effective short-cut to economic modernization. In Tunisia, a country whose only other major export at the time of independence was phosphates, President Bourguiba (1956–87) mobilized the resources of the newly independent state to drive economic modernization and integrate Tunisia into the post-war world economy. Hazbun (2008: 6) recounts how, in addition to an instrument of economic development, tourism was perceived as a demonstration of Tunisia's commitment to 'modernity' and 'openness'.

The precipitous post-war expansion of tourism within the Mediterranean region was not simply an outcome of the timely intersection between rising disposable incomes in the industrialized capitalist states of the north and endogenous statist interventionism in the south. In the cases of Greece and Spain, the influence of the United States was felt in the form of substantial inflows of foreign aid and private capital channelled into the construction of tourist facilities. Between 1968 and 1970 over 50 per cent of all foreign investment in tourism was US capital (Leontidou 1998: 106). Since the war, US tutelage of post-war Greece was strongly motivated by a fear of the communist 'threat', one that had been shared by Churchill. Despite the illiberal nature of Franco's regime, Spain too was the recipient of US loans and was critical to the post-war balance of power in the Mediterranean given its strategic location at the crossroads of the Atlantic, Europe and North Africa (Crumbaugh 2009: 24; Pi-Sunyer 1979: 58).

In the eastern Mediterranean, the waning influence of the European colonial powers was supplanted by the growing influence of the United States in the post-war politico-economic order in the Middle East. United States government backing for the expansion of international US hotel consortia and its major commercial airlines into the Mediterranean and beyond – Pan American Airways and TW – was integral to the emergence of Beirut and Cairo as regional transit hubs (Hazbun 2015). More importantly, as Hazbun notes, the closure of Israeli airspace to Arab carriers after 1948 followed by Nasser's programme of nationalization in Egypt after

1953, in conjunction with US backing for Lebanon's Middle East Airlines (MEA), were key factors helping to establish Beirut as a cosmopolitan centre of tourism and commerce in the 1950s and 1960s before this was overshadowed by the rise of international air piracy and the Lebanese civil war in the mid-1970s.

The impressive rates of growth and annual increases in per capita income experienced in the major mass beach destinations of Spain, Greece, Turkey and Tunisia during the 1960s and early 1970s is often seen as evidence of mass tourism's profound capacity to bring about 'transformative economic development in southern European and Mediterranean states, in the absence of viable economic alternatives' (Butcher 2003: 24) In addition it has also been argued that tourism laid the foundations for the dissolving of existing social hierarchies and was a catalyst for democratization of Mediterranean societies (Pack 2006: 191–5). Yet, not only has tourism prospered alongside authoritarian regimes in Egypt, Greece, Tunisia and Turkey, but also Spain's transformation from statist autarky and dictatorship to a modern capitalist economy was part of an explicit state-managed programme of economic liberalization designed to enhance the political legitimacy of Franco's dictatorial regime and smooth Spain's peaceful integration into the international liberal order of 'democratic' states – as documented by Crumbaugh (2009) and Pack (2006). Rather than herald the disintegration of the regime the 'iron fist of the Franco dictatorship was usually well hidden from tourists' (Löfgren 1999: 174). The democratic deficit associated with the centralized direction of tourism was keenly felt in Catalonia, where hostility to tourism amongst Catalan regionalist parties was premised on precisely Franco's support for tourism as well as the regime's attempt to annihilate all traces of regional cultural-linguistic difference (Pi-Sunyer 1979).

By the early 1980s, despite the transition to democracy in Spain and Greece, and the electoral victory of modernizing social democratic parties in both countries there was a remarkable ideological consistency with regard to the state's attitude towards the promotion of tourism. This period was concomitant with the accession of Greece and Spain, along with Portugal, to the European Community and the deepening integration of Mediterranean states into global capitalism and the intensification of tourism as instrument of capital accumulation. Although the 1970s witnessed increased social unrest and the transition to democratic rule across the European Mediterranean, the consistency with which tourism has been promoted by all political parties has hardened as indeed have attempts to foreclose popular critiques of tourism and its increasingly problematic consequences.

By the 1970s the shortcomings of the state-led development of tourism in the southern Mediterranean were becoming all too apparent. The failure to upgrade ageing hotels and resort stock together with the growing influence of integrated, transnational tour operators whose ability to amalgamate suppliers across different countries enabled them to squeeze profit margins, precipitated a transition towards a greater role for markets and private enterprise in the political economy of Mediterranean tourism. In Egypt and Tunisia policies of *infitah* or economic liberalization were implemented within a year of each other in 1970 and 1971 (Hazbun 2008: 11; Steiner 2006: 947). The principal effect was to increase the volume of private capital (domestic and foreign) investment channelled into the development of integrated luxury resort enclaves in previously undeveloped coastal locations. The onset of the oil crisis in 1973–4 triggered a downturn in tourism as arrivals and receipts momentarily fell (offset by increased oil revenues and remittances from workers in the Gulf). The aftermath of the energy crisis was marked by two further factors of significance – the recycling of 'petro-dollars' into luxury real estate and resort developments in Tunisia (Hazbun 2008: 28), and the opening up the Sinai Red Sea coast to tourism investments as a result of the cessation of hostilities between Egypt and Israel (Richter and Steiner 2008). Significantly, however, state policies of privatization and economic liberalization not only provided a much needed boost in tourism revenues, throughout the region, autocratic Arab states have sought to embrace globalization and stabilize their economies through tourism while simultaneously ensuring that the 'neo-patrimonial structure of power' remains unchallenged (Steiner 2006).

Despite the important role played by developmental states and the prevalence of autocratic governments along the southern Mediterranean shore, top-down policies of tourism development have always co-existed alongside spontaneous and unregulated private initiative. Despite what often appears to be an emphasis on large-scale tourism capital and international consortia in many parts of the Mediterranean, in reality there is great deal of variability and a diversity of ownership arrangements in which the vast majority of hotel/tourism firms are made up of small, family-run businesses and informal traders.

Class, liberal democracy and persistence of patron–client networks

In both the eastern Mediterranean, as well as Greece and Spain, wealthy families, networks of kin, prominent expatriate capitalists (including elite shipping and oligarchic-dynastic families in the Greek case, landed bourgeoisie in the Spanish case) and/or rich expatriate capitalists (often linked closely with one or both of the above familial categories) have been involved in the financing and running of iconic luxury hotels and other tourism businesses from an early period (Daher 2007: 25). In Spain, two of the most powerful transnational hotel and resort corporations originating in the Balearic Islands, Barceló and Riu, grew to prominence as a result of close links that were cultivated between their owners and the Franco regime in the 1950s (Buades 2009: 28–39). In Lebanon, a country that is heavily dependent on tourism and trade, a 'consortium' of thirty oligarchic families with business interests spanning finance, industry, construction, transport import–export agencies and public sector contracts came to prominence in the late 1940s and 1950s and controlled a range of tourism assets including the iconic St George's and Bristol Hotels as well as Air Liban and MEA (Traboulsi 2012: 116–17).

However, a salient feature of a number of many such dynastic families is their commitment to philanthropic causes. While the Barceló family have close ties to the Catholic order of Opus Dei, Daher (2007: 19–20) notes how a number of elite/notable families in the Middle East have supported a range of philanthropic ventures, financing heritage conservation and museums dedicated to the preservation of local cultural traditions, including the Saida Soap Museum and Bsous Silk Museum in Lebanon. Capitalism (as it exists within the tourism and hospitality spheres) in parts of the Mediterranean is thus not so much a coherent system of economic and political relations (as it is claimed to be in western/northern states) but more one aspect of uneven systems of relations interlaced with principles of patronage and clientage.

The transition to democracy experienced by the tourism-dependent economies on the north shore and the transformation of deficit-led state-run economies into liberal capitalist ones did little to uproot entrenched systems of patronage and clientelist practices. Rather than bring about far-reaching democratic political institutionalization they merely adapted and reconfigured the state to their own needs co-opting key interest groups and upwardly mobile fractions of the bourgeoisie into their networks of patronage and influence (Kurth 1993: 53). Despite concerted attempts by newly elected social democratic parties in Greece and Spain to introduce measures to constrain excessive urban expansion and reconfigure tourism towards a more sustainable model with more equitable distributive outcomes, resistance to the imposition of land use and conservation planning measures remained strong amongst both the rent-seeking bourgeoisie as well as an emergent class of small entrepreneurs (Briassoulis 2003: 106). In Greece, the electoral victory of PASOK in 1981 promised a radical restructuring of the economy towards those who had been excluded from the economic gains of the past but in fact, the emphasis on small to medium-sized tourism enterprises resulted in the indiscriminate expansion of urban construction and unregistered accommodation as small-scale entrepreneurs sought to cultivate ties with local party officials in order to access state funds, much of which was then channeled into speculative real-estate investments (Petras *et al.* 1993: 182).

In Spain, where the transition to democracy was more associated with a forceful implementation of neoliberal economic reforms the result was nevertheless not dissimilar. In this case the closure of protected state industries and rise in unemployment was followed by the precipitous expansion of finance, construction, real estate and low-wage/low-productivity tourism services throughout the 1980s and into the 1990s. Particularly in those regions where tourism makes up the predominant share of the economy (Andalusia, Balearic Islands, Canary Islands, Catalonia, Valencian region) an upwardly mobile rent-seeking urban/landed bourgeoisie colluded with public authorities, fueling the spectacular growth of untrammeled, speculative real estate/ tourism developments throughout the 1990s and into the twenty-first century (López and Rodríguez 2011: 17).

As numerous ethnographic studies have shown the arrival of mass tourism in the Greek islands, in a process also witnessed in parts of rural Spain, Portugal and southern Italy, helped to precipitate the transition from agrarian to capitalist societies during the 1950s and 1960s (e.g., Kousis 1989; Stott 1973; Zarkia 1996). The rapid insertion of tourism into these societies paved the way for upward social mobility and the emergence of new strata of small-scale entrepreneurs from amongst the peasant and fishing communities, as well as returnee migrants from the mainland in the case of the Aegean islands (Kenna 1993), who opened and operated a large number of small to medium-sized tourist enterprises. Futhermore, a small but upwardly mobile class of capitalist entrepreneurs grew out of what often began as small tourism businesses that later grew into large domestic consortia which were highly influential in the political sphere such as the Grecotel-Daskalontakis and Sani Groups in Greece (Dritsas 2009: 64).

Despite the rapid economic modernization and undoubted improvements in living standards and state revenues brought about by the considerable scope and scale of tourism development across the region since the 1950s, tourism has intensified rather than weakened many of the structural deficiencies of Mediterranean political economy (see Charnock *et al.* 2014: 48–9). In the absence of industrialization, tourism has accentuated the flow of investments into easier and more profitable avenues, including construction and real estate, and thus intensified speculative over productive investments. In what are often described as '*rentier*' or indeed 'semi-rentier' systems (Steiner 2006: 171), the accumulation of capital is generated predominantly through exploitation of access to land and other strategic resources (e.g., raw materials, leases, remittances and aid transfers) or else the manipulation of tightly controlled markets (monopolies) at the expense of productive investments in enterprise, innovation and improved labour productivity (Richter and Steiner 2008: 942–3). Where tourism is a strong feature of local economies, profits are mainly generated by capturing rents from the anticipated future returns on strategically placed land and other property assets.

Such rentier systems of accumulation have been prevalent throughout the Mediterranean since the nineteenth century (Sapelli 1995: 66–7). However, the role of tourism has often played an important part in accentuating their predominance, both in authoritarian states as well as in those states that have experienced a transition from oligarchic and authoritarian rule to various forms of parliamentary democracy. In the absence of industrialization tourism has often been a major force of urbanization, especially so where mass beach tourism is predominant. In so doing it has helped to shape the class character of those regions, as noted earlier in relation to entrepreneurship. Families that migrated to large-scale resort areas for work often maintained a foothold in agrarian economies thereby reinforcing the continuity of family-based networks of patronage and clientelism inhibiting the affirmation of democratic political values characteristic of mass-industrial societies (see Bianchi and Santana Talavera 2004).

Heritage marketing and the Euro-Mediterranean Partnership

So far we have identified a number of economic and political factors and processes (including the uneven path of capitalist development, the continuing salience of patron–client relations, the imperfect passage to democratic governance) that, taken together, help us understand an initiative of considerable politico-economic importance undertaken by the European Parliament and Commission in 1995. The so-called 'Barcelona Process' launched in that year consisted of complex strategic agreements between the EU and Mediterranean states. EC spokespersons explained that the main purpose of the 'Euro-Mediterranean Partnership' set up in Barcelona was to further the efficacy of the 'market' in the region thus raising the economic level of those countries, including Greece, which had joined the EU 1981, Spain/ Portugal (acceded in 1986) and the partner states on the Mediterranean's southern shore (cf. CEC, 2002: 13). The EMP would thus not only raise living standards and spread democracy (or both) but, by so doing, also make a substantial contribution to greater security in the EU itself. But the EMP was also important for strategies and agreements having to do with education, cultural heritage, and (thus) tourism.

The Barcelona Process thus combined and interwove politico-economic designs with cultural ones. 'Culture' thus came to be subsumed within the overall scheme. What is now referred to as 'cultural heritage' was brought into the marketplace – to be bought and sold like other products. A number of EC research and development programmes of work by academic partnerships of universities and research centres in Europe and partner Mediterranean states were undertaken to demonstrate the fundamental cultural unity of the region. These programmes were underpinned by a dual and contradictory set of philosophical and historical principles. On the one hand they reflected, as we have implied in various ways earlier, a certain cultural unity in the region that had existed for millennia. On the other hand they were part of a wider EU based project to impose neoliberal restructuring on southern Mediterranean states. The main aim, according to the EC, of the EMP was, and remains, to enhance competitiveness and stimulate economic development in the Mediterranean region and to integrate the southern shore further into orbits of European capital accumulation – remaking Mediterranean cities and neighbourhoods into suitable avenues of profitable accumulation for mobile transnational capital.

This is the background against which urban spaces and historic sites across the Mediterranean are being converted into ensembles of attractions and commodities to be consumed by a growing market of high-spending cultural tourists – a process accentuated in the case of 'flagship' heritage development projects orchestrated and financed by international donor agencies – further dismantling the dense social mix/socioeconomic diversity of such communities and disrupting long-standing ties between diverse resident communities and the urban fabric of historic Mediterranean quarters and 'heritage' sites as they are integrated into a globalized commodity economy for tourism (see Daher 2007: 27–41).

Tourism, refugees and regional re-bordering

Despite the rich legacy of antiquity, the abundance of archaeological ruins and cultural heritage across North Africa and the Middle East, the imbalance in the volume of tourist arrivals and distribution of revenues from tourism between the northern and southern shores, can partly be attributed to the region's 'fragmented geopolitics' (Hazbun 2008: xxxix).

Thus, to point to one historical moment as an example, there was a brief window of geopolitical stability in the wake of the fall of the Berlin Wall in 1989 and the peace agreements between Israel, Jordan and Egypt as well as the Oslo Accords of 1994. But by the end of the twentieth century, after a period of more or less uninterrupted expansion of mass travel, terrorist bombings and violent civil conflicts disrupted the eastern Mediterranean tourist trade and threatened to reconfigure the political and economic geography of contemporary Mediterranean tourism. Direct and indirect attacks on civilian targets and sites of cultural significance resulted in a reduction of tourist numbers in parts of the region as a result of heightened perceptions of risk and insecurity. The most dramatic collapse has of course been experienced by Syria, whose numbers and revenues have all but disappeared after reaching a high of 8.5 million arrivals and US$6.2 billion in tourism receipts in 2010 (UNWTO 2016). The origins and motives of the attackers are quite diverse despite most being attributed to 'militant Islamic' groups, although it is important to bear in mind the violent attacks on tourism installations that have also been perpetrated by more 'conventional' separatist movements, ETA (Spain) and the PKK (Turkey). In addition, southern European resorts are not immune from the violence associated with the spread of global terrorism as the 2016 'Bastille Day' attack by a disaffected youth from the *banlieux* of Nice demonstrated.

Events of these kinds have seen the Mediterranean increasingly transformed into a militarized frontier between the impoverished migrants and persecuted refugees from the global south seeking refuge in Europe, and those fully entitled to 'the collective fiction of universal rights' that comes from being a European citizen, including the right to the freedom of movement and travel, and those who are not (Calori 2015).

The terrorizing of tourists and tourism spaces and concomitant securitization of travel and border politics is underpinned by a discursive framing of the 'tourist' in contra-distinction to 'migrants', 'refugees', and 'terrorists' (often seen as interchangeable categories) further reinforcing tangible economic cleavages and forms of political exclusion that define and shape the militarism and securitization of Europe/European resorts. Border fences have been erected in Bulgaria, Hungary and Macedonia. The EU has made an agreement with Turkey to detain refugees in exchange for visa-free travel and a payment of €6 billion. The EU has also instructed Greece, a country already buffeted by years of economic crisis exacerbated by EU/troika-mandated austerity, to contain refugees within its borders. The re-territorialization of state power and concomitant re-bordering of the Mediterranean, together with EU political backing for the violation of one of the most fundamental codes of maritime conduct – the obligation to assist those in peril at sea – threatens to rupture long-standing ties of culture, exchange and trade between peoples along the Mediterranean shore and to further atomize and fracture the tentative unity and openness upon which decades of mass travel throughout the Mediterranean basin have depended.

Despite the many atrocities that seek to turn local communities against tourists, there have also been notable demonstrations of bravery shown towards tourists during such attacks (e.g., see Stephen 2015), as well as touching acts of compassion and solidarity between locals and tourists in the aftermath of the violence. Although thousands of tourists left in the immediate aftermath of a fatal terrorist attack on the Tunisian resort of Sousse in June 2015, which left 38 people dead (30 of whom were tourists), there have been notable acts of defiance and solidarity shown towards Tunisian hosts by tourists (Marlowe 2015). In addition, neighbouring Algeria, a country that has experienced its fair share of political violence, expressed its full solidarity with Tunisia and promised to launch a solidarity campaign to boost the already substantial flow of Algerian tourists to Tunisia (Traboulsi 2015).

Additionally, despite the often hostile and xenophobic reactions displayed towards refugees by populist nationalists throughout Europe and in some sections of the media, residents on the

Greek island of Kos and a number of visitors and tourists have rallied to lend humanitarian assistance to as many of the hundreds of thousands of refugees who have arrived on the island since the summer of 2015. One resident stated: 'This is hospitality. People with nothing understand more than people who have everything', alluding to the collective memory of past hardship and the more recent experiences of struggle related to the Eurozone crisis (cited in McVeigh 2015).

Tourism as resistance

The previous paragraphs lead us into our penultimate section. Our direction of travel so far in the chapter has stressed the extent to which tourism has been incorporated into the broader global and regional project of bringing the Mediterranean region further into the orbit of organized capitalism, the free market, and ideological and symbolic emphases on the centrality of state and nation (rather than images and ideas that stressed cultural unities within a cosmopolitan region). As we have pointed out this has involved the simultaneous marketization and nationalization of cities and tourist related heritage sites. Moving towards a conclusion we return to observations we have made earlier about those tourism initiatives that are self-consciously critical of the ways in which tourism has been used in this way.

To start with there have been diverse forms of civil society resistance against speculative real estate and excessive tourism developments (Cavo Sdero in Greece, Nivica in Albania, Save Beirut Heritage in Lebanon, for example). On the island of Malta, since the early days of tourism development the focus of environmental protests has shifted from concerns to do with the protection of flora and fauna from excessive urban development to social justice and the democratic use and organization of space (Boissevain 2004). More recently a wave of anti-austerity movements (e.g., Indignados, Spain) arising in the wake of the Eurozone crisis, have engaged in increasingly direct and forceful acts of resistance against speculative real estate-driven tourism. In Barcelona, the radical new mayor and former anti-eviction activist, Ada Colau, has galvanized local neighbourhood groups and activists in the former working class neighbourhood of Barceloneta, and has offered support and solidarity to what have become increasingly frequent protests targeted at the US-based online booking agency, Airbnb.

There are other examples of movements of resistance to tourist related developments. The political and legal actions of those groups opposed to the Hilton project in Malta described by Boissevain (2004) may be compared to the activities of the Mallorca based institution Arca which has led demonstrations against the eviction of poor (and often gypsy) residents in the centre of Ciutat de Mallorca at the same time as celebrating the extent to which this capital city has been shaped by its mixture of Christian, Arab and Jewish residents.

In Palestine the success of such groups as ATG and JTC (see earlier) has been powerfully (and equally successfully) complemented by such Israeli groups as Zochrot and Emek Shaveh, the former running tours to destroyed Palestinian villages in Israel, the latter taking tours to the disputed neighbourhood in Jerusalem of Silwan with the aim of challenging the idea, put forward by the Israeli authorities, that this largely Palestinian neighbourhood was, and should be seen to be part of the (Jewish) 'City of David'.

Conclusion

The geographical placing of the Mediterranean involves taking both a regional and a global view. The former suggests that the Mediterranean may be defined in relation to the sea itself whilst the latter takes the global passage through the region of traders, pilgrims, diplomats, refugees, tourists and others, as evidence that the region is pre-eminently a central part of a much wider world.

Mindful of this, and noting that the politics of tourism in the Mediterranean have been relatively under-studied, this chapter has suggested that there are several good and interconnected reasons for pursuing the topic. We have thus pointed out the extent to which tourism and the main political and politico-economic currents in the region have been interwoven since the early days. We have described how tourism has been put to use in the interests of spreading capitalism as well as to the advancement and promotion of ideas and practices having to do with state and nation being foundational principles of social and cultural solidarity. But we have also noted the use to which operators of 'alternative' tours have been using tourism to resist these notions in the name of regionalism and cosmopolitanism. We have described the 'unevenness' of tourist related capitalist development, pointed out that patron–client relations continue to cut across emergent class structures, and that the economic gap between the north and south of the region continues to widen. One implication here is that any attempt to explain violent attacks on northern tourists in the south would need to start from such regional economic inequality as well as the complex political fissures that cross-cut the region.

We have argued that these political, economic, and politico-economic features necessarily form backgrounds to explanations and explorations about of the place of 'cultural heritage' in the region. Thus we have identified contradictory tendencies. Whilst mainstream tour operations (typically flowing from private sector initiatives aided and supported by national and international government) sell commodified versions of heritage to tourists and international media, alternative versions (sometimes involving different sites and spaces) of heritage are being used to construct more critical narratives. We identified some of the many issues raised by the deployment of tourism related cultural heritage, particularly questions about who decides what heritage to display to whom – in other words, about the nature of the political and institutional processes engaged in the heritage project.

We may conclude by framing the Mediterranean in terms of the contradictory social facts of cosmopolitanism and multi-cultural coexistence, on the one hand, and narratives about the primacy of 'ethnic' and/or 'national' identity, on the other. The question that arises for students of the politics of Mediterranean tourism concerns the relationship between these alternative social and cultural orders and a cultural heritage shaped increasingly (and increasingly uniformly) by an emboldened market economy and the febrile politics to which it is bound.

References

Bianchi, R. V. and A. Santana Talavera (2004) Between the land and the sea: exploring the social organization of tourism development in a Gran Canaria fishing village, in J. Boissevain and T. Selwyn (eds), *Contesting the Foreshore: Tourism, Society and Politics on the Coast*. Amsterdam: Amsterdam University Press, pp. 83–108.

Boissevain, J. (2004) Hotels, tuna pens and civil society: contesting the foreshore in Malta', in J. Boissevain and T. Selwyn (eds), *Contesting the Foreshore: Tourism, Society and Politics on the Coast*. Amsterdam: Amsterdam University Press, pp. 233–60.

Brendon, P. (1991) *Thomas Cook: 150 Years of Popular Tourism*. London: Secker & Warburg.

Briassoulis, H. (2003) Crete: endowed by nature, privileged by geography, threatened by tourism? *Journal of Sustainable Tourism*, 11(2–3): 97–115.

Buades, J. (2009) *Do not disturb Barceló: Viaje a la entrañas de un imperio turístico*. Barcelona: Icaria Editorial.

Buades, J. (2014) *Exportando Paraísos: La colonización turística del planeta*. Barcelona: Alba Sud Editorial.

Butcher, J. (2003) *The Moralization of Tourism: Sun, Sand . . . Saving the World?* London: Routledge.

Calori, A. (2015) From Mare Nostrum to Triton, Europe's response to the Mediterranean crisis is little more than another budget cut, *Open Democracy*, 17 February, Retrieved, www.opendemocracy.net/can-europe-make-it/anna-calori/from-mare-nostrum-to-triton-europe%E2%80%99s-response-to-mediterranean-crisis, 12 October 2015.

Charnock, G., T. Purcell and R. Ribera-Fumaz (2014) *The Limits to Capital in Spain: Crisis and Revolt in the European South*. Basingstoke: Palgrave Macmillan.

Commission of the European Communities (CEC) (2002) *Dialogue between Cultures and Civilizations in the Barcelona Process*. Luxembourg: Office for Official Publications of the European Communities.

Crumbaugh, J. (2009) *Destination Dictatorship: The Spectacle of Spain's Tourist Boom and the Reinvention of Difference*. Albany: State University of New York Press.

Daher, R. F. (2007) Reconceptualizing tourism in the Middle East: place, heritage, mobility and competitiveness, in R. F. Daher (ed.), *Tourism in the Middle East: Continuity, Change and Transformation*. Clevedon: Channel View Publications, pp. 1–69.

Dritsas, M. (2009) Tourism and business during the twentieth century in Greece: continuity and change, in L. Segreto, C. Manera and M. Pohl (eds), *Europe at the Seaside: The Economic History of Mass Tourism in the Mediterranean*. Oxford: Berghahn, pp. 49–71.

Furlough, E. (2009) Club Méditerranée 1950–2002, in L. Segreto, C. Manera and M. Pohl (eds), *Europe at the Seaside: The Economic History of Tourism in the Mediterranean*. Oxford: Berghahn, pp. 174–95.

Hazbun, W. (2008) *Beaches, Ruins and Resorts: The Politics of Tourism in the Arab World*. Minneapolis/London: University of Minnesota Press.

Hazbun, W. (2015) Jet Set Frontiers: Tourism, Hijackings, Petrodollars, and the Politics of Aeromobility from Beirut to the Gulf. Talk given to the Anthropology of Tourism and Travel Colloquium Series, London, School of Oriental and African Studies. 13 October.

Hourani, A. (2005) *A History of the Arab Peoples*. London: Faber and Faber.

Hussey, A. (2015) *The French Intifada: The Long War between France and its Arabs*. London: Granta.

Kenna, M. E. (1993) Return migrants and tourism development: an example from the Cyclades. *Journal of Modern Greek Studies*, 11: 75–95.

Kousis, M. (1989) Tourism and the family in a rural Cretan community. *Annals of Tourism Research*, 16(3): 318–32.

Kurth, J. (1993) A tale of four countries: parallel politics in southern Europe, in J. Kurth and J. Petras (eds), *Mediterranean Paradoxes: The Politics and Social Structure of Southern Europe*. Providence, NJ: Berg, pp. 27–66.

Leontidou, L. (1998) Hesitant policy and uneven tourism development in the 1990s, in A. M. Williams and G. Shaw (eds) *Tourism and Economic Development: European Experiences*. Chichester: John Wiley, pp. 101–23.

Lisle, D. (2007) Defending voyeurism: dark tourism and the problem of global security, in P. M. Burns and M. Novelli (eds), *Tourism and Politics: Global Frameworks and Local Realities*, Oxford: Elsevier, pp. 333–45.

Löfgren, O. (1999) *On Holiday: A History of Vacationing*. Berkeley: University of California Press.

López, I. and E. Rodríguez (2011) The Spanish model. *New Left Review*, 69: 5–28

McVeigh, T. (2015) Sympathy and solidarity for migrants on Kos beaches as two worlds collide. *The Guardian*, 6 June. Retrieved, www.theguardian.com/world/2015/jun/06/kos-migrants-tourists-greece-traffickers-sympathy-solidarity, 10 August 2016.

Mackey, R. (2014) Israelis watch bombs drop on Gaza from front-row seats. *New York Times*, 14 July. Retrieved, www.nytimes.com/2014/07/15/world/middleeast/israelis-watch-bombs-drop-on-gaza-from-front-row-seats.html?_r=0, 17 October 2016.

Marlowe, L. (2015) Tunisia: holidaymakers express solidarity with locals. *Irish Times*, 29 June. Retrieved, www.irishtimes.com/news/world/africa/tunisia-holidaymakers-express-solidarity-with-locals-1.2266094, 11 August 2016.

Pack, S. D. (2006) *Tourism and Dictatorship: Europe's Peaceful Invasion of Franco's Spain*. New York: Palgrave.

Petras, J., E. Raptis and S. Sarafopoulos (1993) Greek socialism: the patrimonial state revisisted, in J. Kurth and J. Petras (eds), *Mediterranean Paradoxes: The Politics and Social Structure of Southern Europe*. Providence, NJ: Berg, pp. 160–224.

Pi-Sunyer, O. (1979) The politics of tourism in Catalonia. *Mediterranean Studies*, 1(2): 47–69.

Richter, T. and C. Steiner (2008) Politics, economics and tourism development in Egypt: insights into the sectoral transformations of a neo-patrimonial rentier state. *Third World Quarterly*, 29(5): 939–59.

Sapelli, G. (1995) *Southern Europe since 1945: Tradition and Modernity in Portugal, Spain, Italy, Greece and Turkey*. Harlow: Longman.

Scott, J. (2002) Mapping the past: Turkish Cypriot narratives of time and place in the Canbulat museum, northern Cyprus. *History and Anthropology*, 13, 3: 217–30.

Selwyn, T. (ed.) (1996) *The Tourist Image*. Chichester: Wiley.

Steiner, C. (2006) Tourism, poverty reduction and the political economy: Egyptian perspectives on tourism's economic benefits in a semi-rentier state. *Tourism and Hospitality Planning and Development*, 3(3): 161–77.

Stephen, C. (2015) Tunisia beach attack: local heroes now face unemployment. *The Guardian*, 5 July. Retrieved, www.theguardian.com/world/2015/jul/05/tunisia-beach-attack-local-heroes-unemployment?CMP=Share_AndroidApp_Gmail, 12 August 2016.

Stott, M. (1973) Economic transition and the family in Mykonos. *Mediterranean Studies*, 17: 122–33.

Tarrius A. (2002) *La mondialization par le bas: Les nouveaux nomades de l'économie souterraine*. Paris: Editions Baland.

Traboulsi, F. (2012) *A History of Modern Lebanon*. Second Edition. London: Pluto.

Traboulsi, K. (2015) Algerians vow to 'invade' Tunisia after Sousse massacre. *The New Arab*, Retrieved at: www.alaraby.co.uk/english/blog/2015/7/7/algerians-vow-to-invade-tunisia-after-sousse-massacre, 11 August 2016.

UNWTO (2016) *World Tourism Barometer*. Volume 14, January 2016. Madrid: UNWTO.

World Economic Forum (2015) *World Travel and Tourism Competitiveness Index: Growth through Shocks*. Geneva: World Economic Forum. Retrieved, www3.weforum.org/docs/TT15/WEF_Global_Travel&Tourism_Report_2015.pdf, 1 August 2016.

Zarkia, C. (1996) *Philoxenia*: receiving tourists – but not guests – on a Greek Island, in J. Boissevain (ed.), *Coping with Tourists: European Reactions to Mass Tourism*. Oxford: Berghahn, pp. 143–73.

PART V

Non-state actors and social movements

25

DEBATES ON CIVIL SOCIETY IN THE MEDITERRANEAN

Benoit Challand

The object of a vast aid industry and academic production, civil society has been and remains a topic of profound theoretical divides. Some sustain that, as a distinct sphere of activism and engagement autonomous from the economy, the realm of family and from the state, it is a buffer zone of debates that can help undo autocratic regimes. Others object to this irenic and idealized interpretation and consider its origins to lie in the political liberalism of the eighteenth and early nineteenth centuries (Keane, 1988), a mark of close association with capitalist, bourgeois theories of action. Such critical views towards the theme explain why, in an era of neoliberal policies, civil society fares so well. This negative connotation for most Marxist intellectuals is obvious in the German rendering: from *bürgerliche Gesellschaft*, the phrase that Marx used, German intellectuals and practitioners have used a more neutral *Zivilgesellschaft*. Away from a Marxist–liberal divide, the notion has also polarized the views of postcolonial scholars working on the historical relations in the Mediterranean region. For some, civil society is a western concept with no history on the southern shores of the Mediterranean or is used as an instrument of neo-colonial policies. Others disagree and point to one of the classical Arab philosophers, al-Farabi, and his embrace of the concept in his *Virtuous City* to demonstrate that, at least in Arabic, civil society has a local meaning and significance.

Recent political events, in particular the Arab Uprisings of 2011, have shelved the culturalist and essentialist accounts of Arab-Muslim societies that prominent scholars like Ernest Gellner (1991, 1996) relayed, and which argued about the impossible emergence of a "modular man" as a path toward the formation of civil society in the Arab world.

Current research can be subtler and has tried to avoid such binaries. One promising trend points to the *relational* nature of civil society in the Mediterranean basin, that is, efforts to consider the two, northern and southern, parts of the Mediterranean *not* as hermetically closed and culturally distinct areas, but as a place of *continuous interactions* where values, ideas and practices are constantly reinterpreted and reassembled in *relation* to the specific context of domination, resistance, or cooperation. For example, Tocqueville's (1981[1840]) contribution to a political theory of civil society though his journey in America is considered insufficient. New research points to his problematic analyses of colonial Algeria of the 1840s where he openly argued for some forms of racist practices (Kohn, 2008; Pitts, 2000). Put differently the "bright" side of civil society emerged in *relation* to the "darker" and simultaneous ideological justifications, made by Tocqueville, to racial segregation, states of emergency and imperial ideas. Additional work, placing a focus on constant large cultural interactions, has convincingly shown that the self-perception of Europe, here understood as the northern Mediterranean area, as secular polities was made possible by an imagined oppositional relation to the southern Mediterranean shores, imagined and reconstructed as "Islamic" and therefore automatically religious,[1] and thus hostile to "civil society." Thus, rather than arguing that Muslim society *is* or cannot be civil, a relational sociology tries to assess how the surge of Islamic associations might be connected to a politics of promoting secular organizations, or asks why some Islamic civil society activists might have campaigned in the 2013 and 2015 World Social Forums in Tunisia, despite the fact that such forums tend to be monopolized by secular-leftist civil society activists.

Barrels of ink have been poured to feed debates about civil society. More will join. One should never forget, however, that even if (*a priori*) hostility towards the concept is couched in a critique of its vague definitions and for teleological expectations (civil society as a democratizing panacea) (Camau, 2002), civil society has a life of its own: many actors, from left to right, religious or not, democratic or defender of conservative positions embrace and speak its language. The focus for social research is therefore an empirical one, and the challenge for scholars is to be aware of the fluidity and evolution, both of the concept and of its practices.

To demonstrate some of the most relevant and salient themes of civil society, this chapter offers a chronological overview of the debates surrounding it. Artificially, we will tackle four ideal types of civil society covering four different decades: civil society as a matter of political theory (1980s); civil society as an object of aid and political engineering (1990s); critical studies questioning some of the assumptions behind civil society (2000s); and new debates on civil society, particularly in the wake of the Arab Uprisings of 2011 (2010s). This periodization is not to be taken as automatically coherent phases. If the focus for the 1980s is on theory, it is because the most salient aspect of the theme of civil society is the intellectual debate, both in the Arab and European public spheres, where one sees the crystallization of a vulgate, or common understanding.

Let us first clear the ground with regard to the terminology, first with a couple of common or widespread definitions of civil society, and then with a brief discussion of how the concept is conveyed in Arabic, the most important language of the southern Mediterranean.

One generally accepted definition is that of Habermas (1996). The institutional core of civil society

> comprises those non-governmental and non-economic connections and voluntary associations that anchor the communication structures of the public sphere in the society component of the lifeworld. Civil society is composed of those more or less spontaneously emergent associations, organizations and movements that, attuned to how societal problems resonate in the private life spheres, distil and transmit such reactions in the amplified form to the public sphere. The core of civil society comprises a network of associations that institutionalizes problem-solving discourses on questions of general interest inside the framework of organized public spheres. These "discursive designs" have an egalitarian, open form of organization [. . .] All the same, they do form the organizational substratum of the general public of citizens.
>
> *(Habermas, 1996: 366–7)*

Cohen and Arato (1992: xxii) insist on the fact that civil society is not just a passive intermediary field, but a space for vigorous collective debates and pluralist communication. Based in part on Arato's own work in central and eastern Europe, they adhere to a pluralist vision of society, in which civil society is a potential strength to fight against the illiberal corporate economy and the extension of administrative state apparatuses (or the ruling one-party apparatus, as was the case in central and eastern Europe under Stalinism).

Note that these definitions that are now widely replicated in various forms, are based on European history. Habermas' definition which nests civil society as a specific institutional realm within the public sphere, stems from his study of communicative action in nineteenth and twentieth century western Europe, while Arato and Cohen's *opus magnum* is informed by a broader eastern and western European history. Other, more abstract definitions have been offered to reflect on the possible limitation of these foundational approaches. In order to find common ground between European and non-European manifestations of civic collective engagement as a means to propose solutions to political problems, i.e. civil society, I have proposed considering civil society a "source for collective autonomy" (Challand, 2009: 34–6).[2] In this, autonomy entails a political and cognitive dimension, namely the capacity for a social group (not mere individuals) to adopt the best institutional forms for this civil engagement, but also to choose the vocabulary to express this desire for collective engagement geared at defining a common good. One does not need to say "civil society" to be part of it. This definition also has the advantage of not being trapped in a domestic setting: increasingly civil society is transnational (think of the hundreds of thousands of euros or dollars allocated by foreign aid agencies for civil society promotion). Thus when adopting this definition as a way to define whether "there is a genuine civil society" in country X or Y, one has to assess whether local civic forms of collective engagements are genuinely independent of state or one-party systems, are autonomous in their capacity to choose the form and content of their engagement, and are free to respond to priorities set by external actors, typically foreign donors. In addition to autonomy, one also needs to add respect for pluralism (a violent group wanting to impede others from voicing their opinion should not be included, even if they constitute an autonomous project), and some forms of voluntary participation to the checklist of civil society. Only if all ingredients are accumulated can one expect civil society to play its part in a more democratic polity.

What about Arabic understanding of the concept of civil society? There are two main phrases used. The most current term is *mujtama' madani*, which is a direct equivalent of civil society, with the same connotation for civil—civilization—city (*madani—tamaddun—madina*). The alternative is *mujtama' ahli* or *'amal ahli*, for civic society or civic work. The use differs from one country to the other. In Tunisia, *mujtama' madani* has become part of daily language, while in Syria or Palestine, it can be perceived as exogenous and is thus eclipsed by the term *mujtama' ahli*. Some have observed (Carapico, 1998: 4–8) that Islamists prefer to use *ahli*. Some openly rebuke the phrase of *mujtama' madani* which demonstrates how civil society is also a battlefield for political and intellectual forces in Arab countries (Challand, 2008: 240).

One last semantic observation. The stress in Arabic on *'amal ahli*—civic work—hints at a further trap or frequent failure when talking about civil society. Too often the phrase has become synonymous with non-governmental organization, or NGO. While it is true that one specific type of organization, a formal institution such as an NGO, with a board of directors, an office, and maybe a website, are 99 percent of what European donors would see of say Yemeni or Tunisian civil society, this reduction of civil society to formal institutions, civil society organizations (CSOs), is problematic for at least two reasons. First, it replaces abstract principles (civic *work*, autonomy, independence, pluralism) with numbers and lists of NGOs. Second, it expects civil society to be made of professional associations, most frequently secular ones, when in reality the role and presence of small, local charitable associations (*khayriaat*, in Arabic) is often perceived as much more attuned to local priorities, and often with a much higher presence of women in their midst (MAS 2001; Browers 2006). Let us now look at the moment where debates about civil society started in earnest.

The 1980s

Civil society was subject to broad and complex theoretical elaborations throughout the nineteenth century, with Gramsci[3] as the main figure concluding this cycle of debates in the early twentieth century. Then, for most of the twentieth century, civil society was a non-topic (Keane, 1988). One had to wait until the 1980s to see its re-emergence, in the early part of the decade in Europe and the USA, while the Arabic turn came slightly later towards the end of the decade.

In the west, after Gramsci, the concept of civil society gradually disappeared, even though some authors explored the idea of state–society relations using a different vocabulary, such as the Habermasian "public sphere" (Habermas, 1989). Its massive return to centre stage is strongly indebted to European history and more precisely to Polish history, with the well-described proto-example of Solidarnosc. In its efforts to resist the state's authoritarianism, the Polish trade union represented an "incarnated" form of civil society. The concept was made fashionable again by the new left, in its search for a theoretical background to attack Stalinist and bureaucratic degeneration of the Soviet bloc in the east and to undermine state coercion in the west. In another anti-statist understanding,[4] the use of civil society could justify new social movements, which emerged after the troubled last years of the 1960s. In that sense, Gramsci's view of civil society proved to be a valuable ally, because of the notion of voluntary and cultural hegemony bestowed upon civil society. It finally gained ground because of the so-called "third wave of democratization" and the alleged role played by non-state actors in the series of post-Soviet and national liberations.

Among Arab intellectuals, the theme started generating critical scrutiny in the second part of the 1980s. The topic first concerned academic circles, in Egypt in 1988 and in Lebanon in 1990.[5] From 1990 onwards, the topic proliferated both in academic circles[6] and in public debates. A series of discussions in the most important international Arabic newspaper, *Al-Hayat*, a London-based daily provided confirmation of this budding trend. In August and September 1993, *Al-Hayat* published various articles demonstrating the need for the development of civil society in the region (Moussalli 1995: 79–80). The concept *mujtama' madani* (civil society) became a common topic and was widespread in day-to-day parlance, not just in academic circles. In Palestine, local NGOs began using civil society in pamphlets in 1995 (Challand, 2009). This gradual emergence coincides with the re-emergence *en force* of the concept in social sciences in general, in particular in the USA and in Europe. "Civil society" was therefore a matter of interest for political theory, both on the northern and southern shores of the Mediterranean.

The 1990s

Contrary to many views, Arab societies were not lagging (or if so, not substantially) vis-à-vis their European counterparts. The culturalist argument was however widespread. Gellner's writings (e.g. 1991 and 1996) are emblematic of these views, which recycled old ideas from the Cold War about the existence of homogeneous cultural blocs with opposing values, but now with Islam's crescent replacing the symbolism of the hammer and sickle of the communist flag.[7] Huntington's infamous book (1996) is just a continuation of this essentialist reading. Many studies in the 1990s discussed the alleged cultural incapability of Arab societies to align with liberal, individual values that propel western understanding of civil society.[8]

In the 1990s, interest in civil society became more practical and policy-oriented, following similar trends connected to the collapse of the communist bloc in 1989, renewed Mediterranean relations with the European Union and the so-called peace process in Palestine. As a result of a new agenda of "good governance," large international donors invested in the theme of civil society, which became increasingly associated with NGOs as an agent of political change. Studies of regime changes became staples for social scientists, in particular with studies of the third (or fourth) wave of democratization (Pridham, 2000: 1; Huntington, 1991). Attention in political science switched from debates about the constitutive elements of *democracy* to the study of *democratization* with all the necessary pre-conditions, influences, sequencing, and outcomes of a process generally moving from one end (non-democratic) of an imagined continuum to the other (democratic). With concern for democratization coinciding with the dominant neoliberal paradigm of the 1980s, civil society became an appealing topic throughout the 1990s. Because of its pluralist definition, understanding of individual action as constitutive of a space for control of the state, and anti-statist assumptions, 1990s' civil society was the poster child of good governance. Matched with Putnam et al.'s (1993) work on social capital, aid earmarked for civil society support was widely used by large developmental organizations and international financial institutions, such as the World Bank and the IMF. In exchange for financial support, "developing" countries engage in the dangerous path of conditionality, which

> has increasingly been tied to issues of governance and democratization, and support for those organs of "civil society" that are most amenable to market-friendly policies—a far cry from the earlier presumption that authoritarian regimes are more suitable because of their greater powers of resistance to populist agitation against the impact of adjustment.
> *(Fine et al., 2001: 11)*

The literature also underlines lasting contributions made by joint Mediterranean activities in the name of civil society, with very active networks in the realm of human rights activism, activities favored by the Barcelona Process launched in 1995, and efforts to turn the page in the Balkans after years of fratricidal conflicts that followed the collapse of former Yugoslavia. By the end of the decade, civil society was on everybody's lips, and civil society institutes, or semi-public entities such as the Anna Lindh Foundation (established 2004) and numerous "Houses of the Mediterranean"[9] emerged on its shores, particularly in Italy, France, and Spain. This can be seen as a direct extension of Barcelona's third pillar or third basket, which envisions increased cooperation between the two shores of the Mediterranean in the field of human rights, governance and cultural exchanges via a strengthened civil society.

The 2000s

If the last decade of the twentieth century was disposed to propagate a culturalist north–south divide, with an associationism-prone northern shore of the Mediterranean and a southern space where civil society had to be created and supported, more critical scholarship amended such views. The main direction of criticisms emerged to correct this false dichotomy: i) a more nuanced literature on democratization (Camau 2002); ii) new research showing the possible contribution of Islam; and iii) critical literature pertaining to aid for civil society and its role in conflict transformation.

With regard to democratization, Brynen, Korany, and Noble (1995) were among the first to express skepticism about the automatically benevolent view of civil society as an agent of democratic transformations. Inspired by critical "transitology" studies, Schlumberger offered an incisive criticism, free from culturalist explanations, about the limits of democratization in the Arab world (2000). Jamal (2009) noted that civil society could easily be recuperated by one of the many autocratic regimes among Arab states. Another strand of the literature criticized the effect of the NGO-ization of civil society, which was first visible in the former Yugoslavia (Hemment, 1998), and later in Palestine and other neighboring Arab countries (Hammami, 1995). While western actors supporting civil society insisted on individual rights, local Arab and southern Mediterranean actors preferred a defense of collective rights (such as self-determination in Palestine or Western Sahara; trade union rights in Egypt or Tunisia). Recent comparative work on civil society under authoritarian conditions has helped break new ground (Cavatorta and Durac, 2010).

Second, the view of Islam as an all-pervasive faith and political doctrine opposed to anything secular was gradually replaced by better informed empirical research about the multiple contributions by Muslim actors and even Islamic organizations to the realm of civil society. Numerous studies suggested that, historically, Muslim actors, male and female, and Islamic institutions have actively shouldered pluralistic engagements within the public sphere (Levine and Salvatore, 2005; Deeb, 2006). Critical of the view that Islamists were uncivil and therefore a barrier to democratization, scholars inspired by social movement literature, demonstrated that Islamist associations have a proven capacity for political learning (Cavatorta, 2006; Wegner, 2011) and coalition building with other segments of Arab societies (Schwedler, 2007). Within civil society itself, Islamic associations, such as charitable organizations, or *zakat* committees, have also made frequent contributions to cross partisan socialization and provided vital services that Arab states ceased to provide for a variety of reasons (Clarke, 2003; Browers, 2006). Because of the massive presence of Islam in public discourses, Muslim-majority societies might have a different moral coating for civic activism, but civil society and deep engagement for citizenship cannot be considered only the contribution of secularist groups and activists.

Third, sustained criticism coalesced and expressed skepticism that social and political engineering of regime change, externally driven democratization and conflict transformation could be a panacea for Arab politics, plagued by violent repression, corruption, and resilient dictatorships (Carapico, 2013). The fiasco of the 2003 war in Iraq is the latest evidence of such views. In Palestine, various authors suggested that the millions in aid that poured in to support the peace process were compensation for political guilt towards Israel (Le More, 2007) and only reinforce dynamics of intra-Palestinian contention and alienate Palestinians from their political elites (Wilderman and Tartir, 2014; Challand, 2009). Nathalie Tocci's (2007, 2011) substantial work, first around the Cyprus crisis and then in comparing the European Union's specific policies in support of civil society in conflict cases offered new comparative perspectives that have been most helpful for Mediterranean scholars. From the late 1990s onward, the EU equipped itself with numerous and potentially meaningful instruments in support of civil society.[10] Yet pragmatism led the EU to turn a blind eye to regular violations of freedom of association in Arab partner countries. Civil society appeared to be more of a fancy word to use, at times cynically. Despite promises to be more supportive of civil society and to abandon the policy of collaboration with Arab dictators when the Arab Uprisings broke out in 2011, the EU did not alter profoundly its approach to civil society in the southern countries (Bicchi, 2014). In the last ten years, the abstract concept of civil society became increasingly reduced to CSOs. Just like social movement being equated with social movement organisations, there exists a danger of acritical and elitist assumptions in much of the policy-oriented use of the phrase civil society. Put in Habermasian terms, speaking of CSOs evokes the possibility of the lifeworld (civil society) having been colonized by economic transactions underpinning foreign support for "civil society."

The Arab Uprisings and their meaning for civil society

Acclaimed as the triumph of bottom-up forms of participation, akin to some ideas of civil society, the 2011 Uprisings generated new debates on civil society. Mainstream media as well as rather shallow academic analyses represented these historical events as having emerged out of the blue, as a surprising or unexpected burst of citizens' activism. While there was a spontaneous dimension to some of the protests, the 2010 and early 2011 calls for large protests and the actual occupation of large city squares (Tahrir in Egypt, Qasbah in Tunis) were the results of rather long-term, or at least sustained, activism. A majority of analysts simply did not take this into account because the groups that spearheaded these early protests were understudied and/or underfunded civil society groups. This is particularly true of the trade union movements, which played a key role in Egypt and Tunisia (Beinin, 2015; Yousfi, 2015). They shouldered earlier waves of protests in the Gafsa basin in 2008. In Egypt, the collective strikes of 2006 in the textile sector, in particular in Mahallah Al-Kubra, nourished sustained calls for the formation of independent trade unions. The actual model of the Tahrir occupation was put in practice by a small Egyptian trade union, the real estate trade union which encamped until they gained support for their demand (Lachapelle, 2012). Trade unions became the mouthpiece of socio-economic grievances, both long standing (unequal territorial development in Tunisia) and more short term, related to neoliberal reforms. Their demands fused with political slogans (around political freedoms and elections) that had been repeated by other groups of activists (in Egypt, the Kefaya movement, or in Tunisia by the Bar Association) (Clark, 2013; Gobe and Salaymeh, 2015).

A comparative analysis of these historical events reveals new insights about civil society. First, 2011 confirms the convergence between southern and northern civil societies. Tahrir, but also the Libyan and Tunisian ousting of dictators coupled with demands for democratic reforms inspired similar occupation movements in Spain and Greece. Second, the Arab protests were genuinely domestic in their demands and were not connected to injustices in Palestine nor did they condemn, unlike earlier mass events in the region (think of the Iranian revolution in 1979), external meddling or western imperialism in the Middle East. Third, youths and other disenfranchised groups spoke with one strong voice against neo-patriarchy, using not only social media but also their forms of counter-culture (music, rap, or graffiti) to convey their grievances. Fourth, the Arab Uprisings have generated a trend towards self-reflexivity with a burst of reports, gray papers, and new academic publications.

Despite the violent turn taken in most Arab countries (especially in Syria, Libya, and Egypt), one can list a lasting effect for each of these developments. For the first (convergence) one can list willingness to discuss return migration initiatives, or formal representation for Tunisians living abroad through a National Council of civil society associations (*NAWAAT*, 2016). Second, there is a much more sustained wave of south–south and intra-Arab coordination among civil society actors. In Libya, Tunisia. Morocco, and Algeria a space for civic activism, albeit under threat or control, has emerged.[11] Third, youth networks have seen the light, but the challenge to sustain this burst of creativity and call for more political and economic inclusions remains a tall order. In Tunisia, for example, graduate youth unemployment is stuck at very high levels and the demand of young people for formal quotas in party lists has been largely unheard. Fourth and last, the consequence of sustained academic interest is too early to assess. A significant initiative has been taken by the Arab Council for Social Sciences (ACSS), a regional non-profit organization headquartered in Beirut and created in 2008, which has organized high profile conferences since the 2011 uprisings.[12] In an extensive report written by Mohammed Bamyeh, the ACSS put a particular focus on the links between academia and civil society and encouraged local studies of Arab social sciences, rather than relying on foreign studies which do not help build critical and institutional knowledge among Arab universities.[13]

An overview of this regional and international academic focus confirms the vitality of civil society as a theme for intellectuals and activists around the Mediterranean, despite the violent downturn in Egypt, Syria, and Libya. This catalog is a partial list of academic or NGO events that were organized since the Arab Uprisings and which entailed a focus on civil society (see Table 25.1).[14]

Table 25.1 List of Mediterranean conferences and workshops pertaining to civil society (2012–16)

Event	*Date*	*Location*	*Organizers*
Arab Uprisings: Challenges during Political Transitions and Comparative Lessons for Civil Societies in the Middle East and North Africa	18–20 April 2012	Amman	Graduate Institute, Geneva, with Arab Reform Initiative, Fr. Ebert Stiftung and GCSP
Citizenship and Minorities in the Muslim World	19–20 November 2012	Tunis	ISNA, Islamic Society of North America
Religion et citoyenneté dans le monde arabe	14 January 2013	Paris	Institute du Monde Arabe
Civil Societies in Transitions: Facing Current Challenges in Tunisia and Egypt	9–10 February 2013	Cairo	Graduate Institute, Geneva, with American Uni in Cairo and the Geneva Centre for Security Policy (GCSP)
Arab Transformations: Interrogating the Social Sciences	19–20 March 2013	Beirut	Inaugural ACSS Conference, Arab Council for the Social Sciences
Démocratie, Liberté et Religion	12–13 April 2013	Tunis	Observatoire Tunisien de la transition democratique, with Hanns Seidel Stiftung
Women Political Participation in Tunisia (1) and Youth and Citizenship in Tunisia (2)	March 2014	Tunis	FACT: Arab Forum for Citizenship in Transition
NGO-ization, Disciplining Dissent and Increasing Inequality within Palestinian Popular Resistance	6–10 May 2014	Tunis	Arab Council for the Social Sciences ACSS, Research Forum
Workshop on Women's Citizenship in Yemen	June 2014	Sana'a	FACT, with the Human Rights Information and Training Center in Yemen
The Impact of Arab Uprisings on Citizenship in the Arab World	12–14 November 2014	Balamand, Lebanon	Balamand Univeristy
Exploring an Agenda for Active Citizenship	February 2015	Beirut	Asfari Institute for Civil Society and Citizenship (AUB), with Arab Studies Institute
Policy-Institutional Factors of Youth Exclusion-Inclusion in Morocco, Tunisia, Egypt, Occupied Palestinian Territory, Lebanon and Turkey	24–27 February 2015	Beirut	Power2Youth, with American University in Beirut

Table 25.1 (continued)

Event	*Date*	*Location*	*Organizers*
Questioning Social Inequality and Difference in the Arab Region	13–15 March 2015	Beirut	Arab Council for the Social Sciences ACSS
Alternatives politiques pour une transformation socio-éccnomique et démocratique réussie en Tunisie et dans les pays sud de la Méditerranée	10–12 October 2015	Tunis	Rosa Luxemburg Stiftung
Political Parties in the Middle East: Past, Present and Future Perspectives	28–29 January 2016	Manchester	Center for the Advanced Study of the Arab World, with Manchester University
Citizenship Rights since the Arab Revolutions: The Cases of Tunisia and Egypt	9 February 2016	Tunis	Observatoire Tunisien de la Transition Democratique, with EUSpring (University of Napoli)
State–Societies Relations and Socio-Economic Rights in North Africa since 2011: Increasing Divergences?	19 February 2016	Tunis	El-Manar 1 University with EUSpring
The Shia Arabs: Questions of Citizenship	27–28 February 2016	Doha	Arab Center for Research and Policy Studies
Academia and Social Justice	11–13 March 2016	Beirut	Asfari Institute for Civil Society and Citizenship, with Arab Studies Institute
Youth Civic and Politic Engagement in the South East Mediterranean	4 April 2016	Napoli	POWER2YOUTH, with University of Naples "L'Orientale"
Rethinking Social Movements in the Digital Age: Activism: Dissent and Rebellion in the Post-Arab Spring	29 July 2016	Beirut	Orient-Institute Beirut OIB
Rural Women Cooperatives and the Quest for Empowered Citizenship in the Arab World	September 2016	Beirut	AUC, Asfari Institute for Civil Society and Citizensip, with Environment & Sustainable Development Unit
Politiques Migratoires en Méditerranée: Quel impact sur la sécurité?	22–23 April 2016	Tunis	CEMI with Konrad Adenauer Stiftung

Table 25.1 is not an exhaustive list: it entails only international events held in French or English, and does not include dozens of other academic workshops that analyzed the dynamics and outcomes of the Arab Uprisings without reference to civil society. But the existence of conferences on citizenship or minorities organized by Islamist organizations (November 2012), or the numerous regional meetings with people from Libya, Yemen, Tunisia, and Egypt (FACT activities), from Bahrain, Yemen, Libya, Tunisia, Algeria, and Morocco (Graduate Institute),[15] or regular meetings organized by the ACSS, an institution which had been mostly dormant until 2011, are all signs of intense cross-Mediterranean civil society and intellectual collaboration.

To this we can add the usual suspects of European or joint south–south Mediterranean research and academic projects. Publications by two large research clusters deserve attention. One is "Power to Youth" (2014–17), a Mediterranean research cluster led by Daniela Pioppi, and Maria Cristina Paciello analyzing issues of youth marginalization and migration youth policies in Tunisia, Egypt, Palestine, Morocco, Lebanon, and Turkey.[16] The second network, called "EUSPRING: Democracy and Citizenship Rights in North Africa after the Arab Awakening: Challenges to US and EU Foreign Policy" (2013–16) was hosted jointly by the University of Warwick and the University of Naples. It produced five publications entitled "Arab Citizenship Review,"[17] and organized numerous workshops and academic publications (some listed in Table 25.1).[18]

One salient novelty is the very rich south–south collaboration, which takes different forms. An intra-Arab platform on citizenship, called FACT (the Arab Forum for Citizenship in Transition) was created with "aims to be a regional exchange platform on the exercise of equal citizenship in Arab countries in transition, with a particular focus on gender equality."[19] It concentrates on Libya, Yemen, Egypt, and Tunisia, with thematic clusters around conceptions of citizenship, political participation, constitutions, and media. One could also mention an increased flow of aid across the Mediterranean that is not EU-based, such as the Turkish Cooperation and Coordination Agency (TIKA) which has offices in most Arab Mediterranean countries. Thus, there is multi-directional civil society cooperation.

The theme of citizenship makes frequent appearances in Table 25.1. Might it be that civil society associations, in the post-2011 context, concentrate their efforts on cementing the basis for formal political participation? This might also be connected to a surge in citizenship studies, which has attracted much of the scholarly attention in the last decade. In relation to citizenship, one can also underline the connected theme of civility, which has been suggested as an alternative, or complementary concept to civil society (Volpi, 2011; Salvatore, 2016). Are these new directions in the always evolving and contentious topic of civil society? More research is needed, and the future will tell whether the current connections to the theme of citizenship is not simply a new iteration of the liberal positive expectation attached to civil society

Conclusion

This chapter has tried to cover the most important evolutions and debates that can be identified in the last four decades of engagement with the concept of civil society. The rich Arab debates around civil society and the sustained collaboration across the two shores of the Mediterranean remain encouraging signs of the relevance of the themes, probably also revivified by the dramatic protests of 2011.

Two main stumbling blocks have been identified on the road toward an Arab civil society. The first, an essentialist one, posits that Islam is an unsurpassable barrier for civic engagement. This chapter has discussed many empirical examples that discard such views of cultural incompatibility. The debate will of course remain open, and analysts will be able to cherry-pick from the "successful" example of rather extensive integration of Islamic factions (*Ennahda*) in Tunisia to the collapse of the first democratically elected Egyptian president, Mohammed Morsi, deposed by a military coup in July 2013.

The second set of objections to civil society consists of a Marxist reading of international politics. Criticisms of the liberal predisposition of the theme remain: inspired by Marxist readings, Hanieh's influential text *Lineage of Revolt* (2013) is a perfect example of the current reticence in the use of "civil society" in internationalist Marxist writings. Instead, faithful to studies of various modes of production, Hanieh prefers analyzing flows of commodities. A dose of realist criticism has also emerged after a couple of years of die-hard enthusiasm in 2011 and 2012 about the symbolic significance and political achievement of the Arab Uprisings, often seen as an instantiation of the power of civil society. Recent studies have been critical of the expectations that civil society can contribute to "democratic transition,"[20] chiefly in an epoch where neoliberal reforms still feature prominently on the agenda. This agenda will certainly sustain both positive and critical appraisal of civil society in the Mediterranean basin.

Notes

1 These are vast debates in which Talal Asad's formation of the secular features prominently. Others have taken a more relational position. See Kilani (2005).

2 This is the short version. Civil society's autonomy is asserted when there is the "capacity of auto-institution." This vision of autonomy is not only understood in a Rousseauian sense that a group can chose its own laws or its collective orientation (the social contract) but also in Castoriadis' sense. To be autonomous, a society must have the capacity to call "into questions their own institution, their representation of the world, their social imaginary significations" (Castoriadis 1997: 18). Independence *of* and *from* is also present in a standard political science definition, that of Philippe Schmitter, who offers this definition: "Civil society can be defined as a set or system of self-organised intermediary groups that: a) are relatively independent of both public authorities and private units of production and reproduction, that is, of firms and families; b) are capable of deliberating about and taking collective actions in defence or promotion of their interests or passions; c) do not seek to replace either state agents or private (re)producers or to accept responsibility for governing the polity as a whole; d) and agree to act within pre-established rules of a 'civil', i.e. mutually respectful nature" (Schmitter 1997: 240). Note that this definition assumes the existence of a state. My own definition is also operational in the context of non-state politics, for example Palestine or Kurdistan. There can be a civil society in the absence of a sovereign state.

3 For Gramsci, civil society is not just a bourgeois creature, but can be the place for the creation of a counter, revolutionary alternative to bourgeois rule. Thus civil society becomes a potentially emancipatory realm, a place for cultural and hence later political hegemony. See Bobbio (1988: 87).

4 It is not just anti-statist. Civil society, in the eyes of the new left, can be a tool for attacking economic and neo-corporatist institutions. See Edwards et al. (2001: 3).

5 Reconstruction offered by Professor Mustafa Kamal Sayyid, during the conference "Civil Societies in Transitions: Facing Current Challenges in Tunisia and Egypt" Cairo, February 2013. Professor Sayyid is one of the contributors to a very important book for a critical discussion of democratization in the Arab world. See Brynen, Korany, and Noble (1995).

6 To name three influential texts: Sa'id Bensaid al-'Alawi et al. (1992), *Civil Society in the Arab Nation, its Role in the Realisation of Democracy*, Beirut; Sa'ad Ed-Din Ibrahim (1993), *Civil Society and the Democratic Transformation in the Arab Nation*, Ibn Khaldoun Center for Study and Research, Cairo; and Mohammed Abed al-Jaabari (1993), "Ambiguities of democracy and civil society in the Arab nation," *Al-Mustaqbal al-Arabi*, 197. Hisham Sharabi's controversial book *Neopatriarchy* (1988) expressed a negative assessment of the topic, saying that the conditions for the emergence of civil society are not met in Arab societies. There, because of the resilience of patriarchal structures and their mingling with state structures in the form of neopatriarchy, genuine equality among citizens was not likely to emerge in Arab societies (Sharabi, 1988: 35).

7 Fred Halliday (1996) is one of the first to draw the parallel. See also Challand 2010 in relation to the debate about Turkey's accession to the EU.

8 For a debunking of such views see e.g. Zubaida (1992, 1995), Norton (1995), or Moussalli (1995).
9 For example, the Fondazione Mediterraneao in Naples (www.fondazionemediterraneo.org/) or the Institut Europeu de la Mediterrània (IEMed) in Barcelona. On the Anna Lindh Foundation, see www.annalindhfoundation.org/
10 For example, one can cite the European Instrument for Democracy and Human Rights, or the Civil Society Facility as part of the ENPI revamped after 2011. See http://europa.eu/rapid/press-release_MEMO-11-638_en.htm.
11 Author's interview in Tunisia, January and May 2016.
12 See www.theacss.org/
13 For the full report entitled *Social Sciences in the Arab World: Forms of Presence,* see www.theacss.org/uploads/WEB-ASSR-Report-Arabic-2015.pdf.
14 Source: author's compilations of events identified through mailing lists (Socio of Islam), calls for paper, web announcements, and personal research. I am grateful to my two research assistants, Zoe Carey and Lebogang Mokwena for their help.
15 For an extensive report, see http://graduateinstitute.ch/files/live/sites/iheid/files/sites/ccdp/shared/Docs/Publications/Amman%20Conference%20Report01102012.pdf.
16 See www.power2youth.eu/project#sthash.hIGDi008.dpbs
17 Nos. 5 and 3 on Tunisia (by Ahmed Driss, Centre for Mediterranean and International Studies), Nos. 4 and 1 on Egypt (by Moataz El Fegiery and Ragab Saad, Cairo Institute for Human Rights Studies), and No. 2 on Morocco (by Ward Vloeberghs and Youssef Benkirane, CERAM/Ecole de Gouvernance et d'Economie de Rabat, Morocco).
18 See www2.warwick.ac.uk/fac/soc/pais/research/researchcentres/irs/euspring/.
19 See www.muwatana.net/about-us/.
20 See http://nachaz.org/blog/peut-on-penser-dans-la-transition-jocelyne-dakhlia/.

Bibliography

Abu-Sada, C. and Challand, B. (2011) *Le développement, une affaire d'ONG? Associations, Etats et bailleurs de fonds dans le monde arabe* (Paris: Karthala OFPO: IREMEAM).

Beinin, J. (2015) *Workers and Thieves: Labor Movements and Popular Uprisings in Tunisia and Egypt* (Stanford: Stanford University Press).

Bicchi, F. (2014) The Politics of Foreign Aid and the European Neighbourhood Policy Post-Arab Spring: "More for More" or Less of the Same?, *Mediterranean Politics* 19(3), 318–32.

Bobbio, N. (1988) Gramsci and the Concept of Civil Society, in: J. Keane (Ed.), *Civil Society and the State* (London and New York: Verso).

Browers, M. (2006) *Democracy and Civil Society in Arab Political Thought: Transcultural Possibilities* (Syracuse, NY: Syracuse University Press).

Brynen, R., Korany, B. and Noble, P. (Eds) (1995) *Political Liberalization and Democratization in the Arab World* (Boulder, CO: Lynne Rienner Publishers).

Camau, M. (2002) Sociétés civiles "réelles" et téléologies de la démocratisation, *Revue Internationale de Politique Comparée* 9(2), 213–32.

Carapico, S. (1998) *Civil Society in Yemen: The Political Economy of Activism in Modern Arabia* (Cambridge: Cambridge University Press).

Carapico, S. (2013) *Political Aid and Arab Activism* (Cambridge: Cambridge University Press).

Castoriadis, C. (1997) *World in Fragments: Writings on Politics, Society, Psychoanalysis, and the Imagination*, David Ames Curtis (ed. and trans.), (Stanford: Stanford University Press).

Cavatorta, F (2006) Civil society, Islamism and democratization: the case of Morocco, *Journal of Modern African Studies* 44(2), 203–22.

Cavatorta, F. and Durac, V. (2010) *Civil Society and Democratization in the Arab World: The Dynamics of Activism* (London: Routledge).

Challand, B. (2008) A nahda of charitable organisations? Health service provision and the politics of aid in Palestine, *International Journal of Middle East Studies* 40(2), 227–47.

Challand, B. (2009) *Palestinian Civil Society: Foreign Donors and the Power to Promote and Exclude* (London: Routledge).

Challand, B. (2010) From Hammer and Sickle to Star and Crescent: The Question of Religion for European Identity and a Political Europe, in: L. Leustean and J. T. S. Madeley (Eds), *Religion, Politics and Law in the European Union* (London: Routledge).

Clark, K. (2013) Aish, Hurriya, Karama Insaniyya: framing and the 2011 Egyptian Uprising, *European Political Science* 12, 197–214.
Clarke, J. (2003) *Islam, Charity, and Activism: Middle-Class Networks and Social Welfare in Egypt, Jordan, and Yemen* (Bloomington: Indiana University Press).
Cohen, J. and Arato, A. (1992) *Civil Society and Political Theory* (Cambridge and London: MIT Press).
Deeb, L. (2006) *An Enchanted Modern: Gender and Public Piety in Shi'i Lebanon* (Princeton: Princeton University Press).
Edwards, B., Foley, M. and Diani, M. (Eds) (2001) *Beyond Tocqueville: Civil Society and Social Capital in Comparative Perspective* (Hanover, NH, and London: University Press of New England).
Fine, B., Lapavitsas, C. and Pincus, J. (Eds) (2001) *Development Policy in the Twenty-first Century* (London: Routledge).
Gellner, E. (1991) Islam and Marxism: some comparisons, *International Affairs* 67(1), 1–6.
Gellner, E. (1996) *Conditions of Liberty: Civil Society and its Rivals* (New York: Penguin Books).
Gobe, E. and Salaymeh, L. (2015) Tunisia's "revolutionary" lawyers: from professional autonomy to political mobilization, *Law and Social Inquiry* 41(2), 311–45.
Habermas, J. (1989) *The Structural Transformation of the Public Sphere: An Inquiry into a Category of Bourgeois Society* (trans. Thomas Burger), (Cambridge MA: MIT Press).
Habermas, J. (1996) *Between Facts and Norms* (Boston: MIT Press).
Halliday, F. (1996) *Islam and the Myth of Confrontation: Religions and Politics in the Middle East* (London and New York: I. B. Tauris).
Hammami, R. (1995) NGOs: the professionalization of politics, *Race and Class* 37(2), 51–63.
Hanieh, A. (2013) *Lineages of Revolt: Issues of Contemporary Capitalism in the Middle East* (London: Haymarket Books).
Hemment, J. (1998) Colonization or liberation: the paradox of NGOs in postsocialist states, *Newsletter of the Eastern European Anthropology Group* 16(1). Available at www.depaul.edu/~rrotenbe/aeer/aeer16_1.html
Huntington, S. P. (1991) *The Third Wave: Democratization in the Late Twentieth Century* (Norman and London: University of Oklahoma Press).
Huntington S. (1996) *The Clash of Civilizations and the Remaking of the World Order* (New York: Simon & Schuster).
Jamal, A. A. (2009) *Barriers to Democracy: The Other Side of Social Capital in Palestine and the Arab World* (Princeton: Princeton University Press).
Keane, J. (Ed.) (1988) *Civil Society and the State* (London and New York: Verso).
Kilani, M. (2005) Il faut déconfessionnaliser la laïcité: Le religieux imprègne encore les imaginaires, *Journal des Anthropologues* 100–1, 37–48.
Kohn, M. (2008) Empire's law: Alexis de Tocqueville on colonialism and the state of exception, *Canadian Journal of Political Science* 41(2), 255–78.
Lachapelle, J. (2012) Lessons from Egypt's tax collectors, *MERIP, Middle East Report*, 264 (Fall), available at http://www.merip.org/mer/mer264/lessons-egypts-tax-collectors-0
Le More, A. (2007) *International Assistance to the Palestinians after Oslo: Political Guilt, Wasted Money* (London: Routledge).
Levine, M. and Salvatore, A. (Eds) (2005) *Religion, Social Practice, and Contested Hegemonies: Reconstructing the Public Sphere in Muslim Majority Societies* (New York: Palgrave Macmillan).
MAS, 2001. *Ta'dâd al-Munzhamât Ghayr al-Hukumiah al-Filasteeniah fil-Dhifah al-Gharbiyah wa Qita' Ghazzah* [Mapping of Palestinian Non-Governmental Organizations in the West Bank and Gaza Strip], (MAS Ramallah: Palestine Economic Policy Research Institute).
Moussalli, A. S. (1995) Modern Islamic Fundamentalist Discourses on Civil Society, Pluralism and Democracy, in: A. R. Norton (Ed.), *Civil Society in the Middle East*. Vol. I (Leiden and New York: E. J. Brill).
NAWAAT, 2016. Tunisians abroad dissatisfied with proposed representative authority, *NAWAAT*, online magazine available at http://nawaat.org/portail/2016/06/06/tunisians-abroad-dissatisfied-with-proposed-representative-authority/ (accessed 20 July 2016).
Norton, A. R. (Ed.) (1995) *Civil Society in the Middle East*. II Vol. (Leiden and New York: E. J. Brill).
Pitts, J. (2000) Empire and democracy: Tocqueville and the Algeria question, *Journal of Political Philosophy* 8(3), 295–318.
Pridham, G. (2000) *Dynamics of Democratization: A Comparative Approach* (London and New York: Continuum).

Putnam, R., Leonardi, R. and Nanetti, R. (1993) *Making Democracy Work: Civic Traditions in Modern Italy* (Princeton: Princeton University Press).

Roy, S. (2011) *Hamas and Civil Society in the Gaza Strip* (Princeton: Princeton University Press).

Salvatore, A. (2016) *Sociology of Islam: Knowledge, Power, and Civility* (Malden, MA: Wiley-Blackwell).

Schlumberger, O. (2000) The Arab Middle East and the question of democratization: some critical remarks, *Democratization* 7(4), 104–32.

Schmitter, P. C. (1997) Civil Society East and West, in: L. Diamond et al. (Eds), *Consolidating Third Wave Democracies*, Vol. II (Baltimore: Johns Hopkins University Press).

Schwedler, J. (2007) *Faith in Moderation: Islamist Parties in Jordan and Yemen* (Cambridge: Cambridge University Press).

Sharabi Hisham, (1988) *Neo-Patriarchy: A Theory of Distorted Change in Arab Society* (Oxford: Oxford University Press).

Tocci, N. (2007) *The EU and Conflict Resolution: Promoting Peace in the Backyard* (London: Routledge).

Tocci, N. (2011) *The European Union, Civil Society and Conflict* (London: Routledge).

Tocqueville, A. de, (1981) [1840]. *De la démocratie en Amérique*, Vol II (Paris: GF Flammarion).

Volpi, F. (Ed.) (2011) Political civility in the Middle East, *Third World Quarterly* 32(5), 827–43.

Wegner, E. (2011) *Islamist Opposition in Authoritarian Regimes: The Party of Justice and Development in Morocco* (Syracuse, NY: Syracuse University Press).

Wilderman, J. and Tartir, A. (2014) Unwilling to change, determined to fail: donor aid in the Occupied Palestine in the aftermath of the Arab Uprisings, *Mediterranean Politics* 19(3), 431–49.

Yousfi, H. (2015) *L'UGTT, une passion tunisienne: Enquête sur les syndicalistes en révolution 2011–2014* (Paris: Karthala).

Zubaida, S. (1992) Islam, the State and Democracy, *MERIP: Middle East Report* 179 (Nov.–Dec.), 2–10.

Zubaida S. (1995) Is there a Muslim society? Ernest Gellner's sociology of Islam, *Economy and Society* 24(2), 151–88.

26

TRANSNATIONAL ADVOCACY NETWORKS AND HUMAN RIGHTS ACTIVISM

Laura Feliu

Introduction[1]

The number and visibility of the transnational advocacy networks (TANs) linking the European area with the southern and eastern Mediterranean countries (SEMCs) has increased considerably in the last few decades. This form of transnational activism is driven by political and social agents organised into networks with different levels of jurisdiction and governance (Hooghe and Marks, 2011). The study of these TANs has aroused the interest of social scientists, particularly since the end of the 1990s. The influential work of Margaret E. Keck and Kathryn Sikkink (1998) identifies the formation of networks whose members are united by shared values, have a common discourse and establish a dense exchange of information and services (Keck and Sikkink 1999: 89). In particular, analysis has developed based on the constructivist literature, focused above all on the capacity of TANs to create and disseminate norms and their impact on state policies (Risse 2007: 263–4).

The most common characterisation of these networks highlights their non-profit, voluntary, reciprocal and horizontal nature. Their main aim is to promote causes, ideas and norms based on principles shared by their members (denouncing the policies towards immigrants in the north, authoritarianism and repression in the south, etc.). This basis in principles differentiates them from other forms of hierarchical or market-based social organisation (Mitchell and Schmitz 2012). Some of these aspects have been questioned by the more critical literature which assimilates these forms of organisation with other political and social actors competing for resources, which can lead them to put their own interests ahead of certain principles (Cooley and Ron 2002; Bob 2005).

In the Euro-Mediterranean area, these non-profit advocacy networks appear in very different forms, with different components and characteristics, ranging from the most institutionalised transnational NGOs acting as umbrella organisations for many other NGOs to forums held with varying regularity that bring together non-state actors, and networks focused on campaigns on specific themes. It is a conglomerate of complex relationships with a variable geometry, in which the components may overlap.

The formation of TANs in this region has been hampered by many factors. These include internal ones, especially the weakness of civil society in the SEMCs due to the difficulties in creating autonomous organisations and the limits imposed by repression, regional ones (the obstacles to the free circulation of people due to the hermetic frontiers of the European Union, the existence of a deep socio-economic fracture separating the north and south of the Mediterranean or the difficult political relationship between the SEMCs) and international factors, including support by western governments for the autocracies of the SEMCs.

This chapter analyses some of the principal TANs that include the protection of human rights on their agendas, either as a central focus of their activity or as another component of it. Specifically, networks linking the northern shore of the Mediterranean to the south and east are analysed, ignoring the south–south ones. These pages also include the study of a series of forums designed as spaces for creating and promoting advocacy networks in the Euro-Mediterranean region. These forums do not have the promotion of human rights as their exclusive theme, but this issue forms part of their agenda, sometimes linked to the question of democratisation. These aspects are developed in four sections. The first explains the impact of the Barcelona process in creating transnational forums and networks. The second deals with other initiatives critical of the Euro-Mediterranean Partnership and its liberal approach. The third analyses the impact of the Arab Spring on existing TANs and the new dynamics created. In the fourth and concluding section, the main challenges faced by these networks are evaluated and a brief assessment of the Euro-Mediterranean TANs is offered.

Transnational advocacy networks and the Barcelona process

According to Keck and Sikkink (1998: 90), the origin of TANs can be found in the questioning by NGOs and local actors of international networks seeking support to alter state behaviour in an authoritarian context. These authors also stress the importance of the prior existence of international networks and standards to facilitate their emergence. Since the establishment of new independent states in the southern and eastern Mediterranean, members of opposition parties, activists for different causes, representatives of ethnic and religious minorities and small associations linked to human rights have sought support from other militants and activists and associations already established in Europe. On other occasions, support for specific activists or causes was coordinated on European territory between different groups or associations. This was encouraged by the exile of activists, by organic contacts between parties and trade unions, particularly left-wing ones, and by associations of immigrant workers. Along these lines, transnational networks with a clearly bilateral stamp were set up. These networks sketched a degree of geographical specialisation depending on historical, political and geographical factors. In Germany, human contacts and actions were developed with respect to Turkey and the Kurdish issue; in Spain with the Sahrawi cause, in the United Kingdom with Palestine and in France with the North African countries. These transnational defence networks established sporadic, precarious communication channels; they lacked resources and were strongly dependent on a few personalities. Despite this, these networks were connected on the ground with political and trade union movements of significant size and with relevant tools for a conceptual and strategic struggle. In the 1960s and for nearly 20 years, Amnesty International was one of the few international NGOs active in the region and was particularly important for achieving visibility for situations of the violation of rights.

Euromed Civil Forum (ECF)

The launch by the EU of the Euro-Mediterranean Partnership (EMP) at the Barcelona Conference in November 1995 provided a considerable stimulus for the establishment of more formal networks, based particularly in the liberalised autocracies of the region. It must be remembered that the strengthening of the civil society of the SEMCs was an important component of what is known as the 'third basket' of the EMP. In fact, accompanied by the liberal plan to set up a free-trade area (FTA), the EU has considered the strengthening of the respective civil societies (and the promotion of networks linking them) as a way of encouraging the democratisation of the respective regimes in the long term. This low-political-cost process was adopted in preference to strong policies of denunciation and direct pressure on authoritarian rulers. It must be remembered at this point that the predominant concerns of European governments have been more to do with other issues, such as security, immigration control or the economic liberalisation of SEMCs. For this purpose, the European Union has offered its financial support to this civil society through different generations of programmes (MEDA, later the European Neighbourhood and Partnership Instrument (ENPI), and the European Instrument for Democracy and Human Rights, EIDHR) and has financed transnational networks like the Euromed Civil Forum (ECF), the Euromed Non-Governmental Platform (ENGP) or the Euro-Mediterranean Human Rights Network (EMHRN).

The Euromed Civil Forum (ECF) was a space for meetings and exchanges between representatives of the civil societies of EU countries and SEMCs taking place alongside the Barcelona process conferences of foreign ministers (Oliván 2001: 168).[2] The forums were not institutionally incorporated into the structures of the Euro-Mediterranean process, so their final recommendations had limited effect. Their establishment was promoted above all by Spain during the preparation of the 1995 Barcelona Conference (Hernando de Larramendi 2009: 53). This was an initiative involving a strong intervention by the organising states and the European Commission itself, which were the main sources of finance, and this explains the great variability of its format and content.

These annual meetings constituted an opportunity for their participants to make their voices heard and establish useful contacts. The participants were very diverse: NGOs, economic actors, trade unions, foundations, research centres, government representatives, etc. The lack of permanent structures meant that the same associations did not always take part in the different events and the agenda was not cumulative, as everything largely depended on the national organisers of the event. For this reason, and related with the decline of this activity,[3] reflection began after the Marseille summit in 2000 in order to consider reforms (Feliu 2014: 24), and this process continued at the Valencia Civil Forum in April 2002 (ACSUR-Las Segovias 2002). By 2003, they were working on the creation of the ENGP, in an attempt to establish a permanent interface between Euromed civil society and governments. At the Euro-Mediterranean ministerial conference in November 2004 in The Hague, the Euromed Non-Governmental Platform (ENGP) was recognised as the organising body of the ECF. The founding statutes of this regional-level umbrella organisation for civil society cooperation were adopted in April 2005, during its first general assembly in Luxembourg. The platform presented its demands to the Euromed Committee in Brussels for the first time in 2005 (Hernando de Larramendi 2009: 55).

The Euromed Non-Governmental Platform takes the form of national platforms coordinated with one another which must act independently in the respective states.[4] To these are added organisations and thematic platforms. Overall, it counts more than 80 organisations plus individuals coordinated from France (Mueller 2014: 105). In recent years, the activity of these platforms has been uneven due mainly to the economic crisis (which has reduced their own capital and funds coming from official institutions).[5]

We will also refer here to an initiative not directly linked to the European Union which is presented by its promoters as an improved format in relation to the Euromed civil forums: the Mediterranean Citizens' Assembly (MCA).[6] This formula was launched in 2008 by the Centre for Rural Studies and International Agriculture (CERAI) in Valencia, the European International

Movement and the European University of Tirana, and was financed by the Charles-Léopold Mayer Foundation for the Progress of Humankind (FPH) in Switzerland. The aim is to create a Mediterranean community of peoples and improve regional governance. As with the approaches we have already mentioned, its composition is mixed, including both members of civil society and intergovernmental organisations (EU, Arab League and so on) and state representatives. The Assembly consists of a Mediterranean coordination unit of organisations from civil society and a consultative council. Its operation is based on creating so-called 'local citizen circles' (about 20) in different areas of the region. Once a year, a major assembly is held with the participation of the citizens involved in the project.[7] At the assembly held in Tirana (Albania) in July 2015, faced with difficulties encountered by the organisational model, it was decided to convert it into a foundation with headquarters in Valencia.[8]

The Euro-Mediterranean Human Rights Network

The Euro-Mediterranean Human Rights Network (EMHRN) is a TNGO financed by the European Commission.[9] This is undoubtedly one of the most solid initiatives and it has achieved a greater international presence. The network was set up in 1997 as a transnational umbrella organisation promoted by the Danish Institute for Human Rights. In 2000, the EMHRN became independent thanks to the signing of a finance contract with the European Commission, which provides one-third of its budget, to which another third must be added by the Swedish and Danish governments and another third by private organisations (most of them Scandinavian). It currently includes more than 60 associations, as well as regional,[10] associate and honorary members from 25 countries.

The EMHRN is an organisation largely devoted to social lobbying actions vis-à-vis European institutions and develops only limited direct action on the ground (carried out largely through its member NGOs). The network monitors the European Union agenda and acts as a bridge between European governments and institutions and the countries where there are human rights violations (Jünemann 2003). To do this, the network draws up and disseminates information about the human rights situation in the SEMCs, although it has begun drawing up reports on specific subjects in European countries. One of the main aims is to promote network cooperation between its members. For countries on the southern and eastern shore, the network allows them visibility, access to the European political authorities and training possibilities.

The network has a stable structure formed by a general assembly meeting every three years and an executive committee (EC). Its agenda has largely focused on civil and political rights and is currently working via four thematic and geographical working groups.[11] It has offices in Copenhagen (headquarters), Brussels, Paris and Tunis (the latter being its Maghreb office since the Arab Spring).

The Barcelona process has promoted other sector platforms and TNGOs linked to specific dimensions of the human rights agenda.[12] Finally, there is the Anna Lindh Euro-Mediterranean Foundation for Intercultural Dialogue (ALF),[13] set up in 2005 at the Euro-Mediterranean Conference in Valencia as a network of national networks, coordinated by focal point institutions (heads of network), with 42 Euro-Mediterranean networks and 4,000 affiliated associations.[14] Although its activity focuses on intercultural dialogue, its fields of work are very diverse, including issues relating to democracy and civil society, aimed particularly at young people. The Foundation has organised two Anna Lindh Mediterranean Forums on Intercultural Dialogue (Barcelona in 2010 and Marseille in 2013).[15] Once again the composition of these meetings was very heterogeneous, bringing together youth leaders, civil society in general, non-state actors, parliamentarians and elected officials.

An alternative to transnational networks linked to the European Union?

The literature on TANs has analysed the disagreement between different groups or networks concerning their respective contexts and strategies (Hertel 2006; Bob 2005). At the 1995 Barcelona Euro-Mediterranean Conference, two models of meeting confronted one another: one linked to, although not dependent on, the authorities and another 'alternative' one entirely self-managed by associations. The latter approach was based on the denunciation of the Barcelona process as the spearhead for a neoliberal imposition promoted by the states and elites of the north, with the connivance of those in the south, leading to the deepening of the region's economic and social inequalities. With this perspective, a few days before the Barcelona summit of 2005 some 50 NGOs organised the Alternative Mediterranean Conference (AMC), which attracted the participation of about 1,400 people from almost 20 countries. From the AMC emerged the Council for an Alternative Mediterranean, made up of six organisations, but it did not last long. The fact that an alternative conference was organised at all, however, shows both the existence of different models of activism (organic relationship with institutions) and the existence of different visions, diagnoses and approaches relating to the Euro-Mediterranean order being demanded.

Both the continuity and the visibility of alternative conferences held parallel to the official Euro-Mediterranean conferences has been difficult to ensure. In 1999, some of the most critical sectors eventually took part in the Stuttgart Civil Forum, but an alternative forum was organised again in 2000 alongside the Civil Forum in Marseille. Since then, these meetings have been strongly influenced by the anti-capitalist movement fighting neoliberal globalisation (Echart Muñoz 2008: 229, 243).[16]

This coincided with the emergence of the World Social Forum (WSF) in Porto Alegre (Brazil) in 2001, which was considering the establishment of new international links between organisations and social movements through a series of meetings characterised by their non-hierarchical nature, self-management of activities and the absence of a final document. The participation of activists from the SEMCs in the WSF came late, as did the transfer of the Porto Alegre spirit and methodology to the region. The first social forums in the region were organised on the basis of national representation, and the most important were those devoted to Palestine (the Palestinian Thematic Social Forum, held in Ramallah in December 2002) and Morocco (the Moroccan Social Forum, held in 2002 and 2004).

During the World Social Forum in Porto Alegre in 2005, a call was made for the organisation of a North African Social Forum,[17] and its preparatory assembly was held in Bouznika (Morocco) in January 2006, with the participation of 500 activists from the different countries of the region.[18] However, the governments of various North African countries then blocked the holding of the forum, and it had to be delayed. Faced with this situation, it was decided to hold separate forums in each of the North African countries and Morocco was again the venue for a new social forum in January 2008. Finally, the first North African Social Forum took place in July 2008 in Al Jadida (Morocco), with the presence of around 2,300 participants.

Meanwhile, the holding of a Mediterranean Social Forum (MedSF) attempting to promote social participation and debate in the region took place in 2005, after two busy years of preparation.[19] It was promoted by a few Catalan organisations forming part of the international council of the World Social Forum, including the regional forums (Vivas 2005). More than 5,000 people attended this forum, which took place in Barcelona in June 2005 in a context of counter-celebration of the tenth anniversary of the Euro-Mediterranean process, under the slogan 'The Mediterranean: a sea of rights' (Sabata 2006).[20] The need to continue expanding the

MedSF in the region was a demand repeated at the different international meetings (including one in Malmö in September 2008). In May 2009, the International Council of the WSF met in Harhoura/Rabat (Morocco) and the same year seven thematic forums were held, most of them in that country. As will be seen in the next section, the Arab Spring was decisive for bringing the region centre stage in the 'another world' movement.

In parallel with these developments, other cause networks with shared values and visions with the previous ones have been established.[21]

The Arab Spring and transnational activism

The popular revolts that shook the SEMCs from the end of 2010 have become crucial points of reference for the analysis of transnational activism. It is worth asking how far the Arab revolts themselves arose as elements of a non-institutionalised transnational social movement. The literature in this respect warns us of the difficulty of developing processes of this kind that require sustained joint activity (Khagram, Riker and Sikkink 2002: 8) and capacity to alter the social order (Tarrow 2005). In the case of the Arab Spring, different revolutionary movements appeared with different national bases, and some largely south–south transnational components developed, not necessarily linked to the TANs analysed here. These transnational elements are visible in their rapid spread and contagious effect (successful experiences are emulated and failures observed and learnt from), in the important role played by exchanging information through social networks, and in the journeys of some leading figures to other locations to explain and mobilise, where they meet with other activists.[22] There are also clear components of transnational Arab public opinion (Cavatorta 2012: 80), and a space with shared norms that facilitates synergies.[23] All these are elements contributing to the transnationalisation of slogans, aims and experiences. Moreover, these events transformed the civil society of the SEMCs, shaking up existing groups and organisations and encouraging the creation of new ones.

As for the organisations previously forming part of the Euro-Mediterranean TANs, they are so different that no generalisation can be made about their contribution to the revolts. These groups were nowhere to be seen at the start of the revolts and, when they participated, their contribution was disparate. Some groups were central to the development of events; in other cases they were overtaken by demands going beyond their own programmes, or limited themselves to verbally supporting the mobilisations without going on to the streets, or even remained sceptical of them.

In this context of political and social struggle, the policy of cooperation and support by the member states of the European Union of the various autocratic regimes in the region, varying in degree of directness from case to case, was crudely exposed. It was difficult for support programmes for civil society not to be affected. For the TANs, networks like the EMHRN show that more notice is taken of them following the revolts and they are finding it easier for NGOs from the SEMCs to gain access to international institutions. Afterwards, the blocking of change in the majority of countries seems to have reinforced the old organisational formulas. The ENGP held its fourth general assembly in 2013 in Amman (Jordan) in a difficult situation for its continuity. A Euromed Civil Forum on gender issues was held in Brussels in September 2013 before the ministerial conference of the Union for the Mediterranean. The subsequent launching of a Foundation of Women for the Mediterranean has created conflict between members of these networks.[24]

Meanwhile, the EU–Southern Neighbourhood Civil Society Forum was launched,[25] with important involvement of European institutions in its design (including the European Parliament) and participation by the highest authorities. A smaller group of associations (between 100 and 150) took part in the preliminary work and meetings, where the space for debate was limited.

The creation of networking spaces with other organisations or the authorities continued to take priority. The idea was to promote dialogue between governments, EU institutions and civil society organisations, with the security agenda indirectly present.[26]

The Arab Spring has also placed the region at the centre of the debate and made its problems visible, with repercussions for the networks. These events brought a shake-up for existing organisations and platforms. The fact that it coincided with the acute world economic crisis, particularly affecting the European countries, neutralised some of the suggested initiatives. A reading of the minutes of the EMHRN council meetings shows an initial bewilderment at the events, followed by a search for new interlocutors representing the rebellious populations.[27] New strategies were suggested such as a direct presence on the ground and the introduction of economic and social rights onto the agenda (an aspect that has not yet been developed).

Because of its transversal and non-hierarchical nature as a mass movement, the Arab Spring reopens the debate on whether a good part of the initiatives to encourage and support civil society promoted from within the European Union are appropriate or have any impact. Aspects like the elitist nature of the initiatives, work focused on lobbying actions aimed at EU institutions or an agenda directed almost exclusively towards civil rights are among the most problematic aspects. There was inevitably a degree of questioning of the more institutionalised 'Euromed civil society', while other models of organisation (such as social forums) appeared to be perhaps a better match for the dynamics of the Arab Spring. In January 2011, the international council (IC) of the WSF considered holding the next forum in Egypt or Tunisia. Moreover, the secretariat of the World Social Forum moved from Brazil to Tunis in 2013. In 2013 and 2015 various WSFs were held in the Tunisian capital.[28] Meanwhile, the sector-based social forums continued.[29] The context facilitated the establishment of new sector-based networks.[30]

Major challenges facing the Euro-Mediterranean TANs

The observation of the aforementioned initiatives calls into question the characterisation of TANs as patterns for horizontal exchange. The direction of transnational links basically takes a vertical configuration and there are serious difficulties in setting up unmediated horizontal transnational networks from the centre of the system. The northern NGOs and associations begin in an advantageous position, giving them a degree of control over the processes. Their headquarters are in European countries or at least most of their meetings are held there, the majority of their budgets are controlled from Europe and the working languages established are usually English and/or French.[31] The technical/training issue is also an important one: the northern organisations provide southern ones with knowledge, giving them guidance on how to work with the big IGOs or on which 'technical' instruments to use. The issue of control of highly technified repertoires becomes crucial and serves to include or rule out organisations. This apparent superiority takes no account of the fact that political struggle in the south has a long history of revolution and opposition, with its own repertoires concerning much bigger and more difficult problems than those faced by the northern organisations.

Despite the difficulties, it must be stressed that the networks studied have made efforts to become more horizontal. In the case of the EMHRN, for example, this has come through balanced (north–south) representation of its members and on its bodies and in the decision-making processes. But, inevitably, the bulk of the processes take place on the northern shore, with all that implies. Even more horizontal structures, like the WSF, cannot escape structural factors linked with the international system cleavages: at the MedSF in 2005, the majority of participants were European (many from Spain), while non-Europeans represented only around 13 per cent (65 per cent of the more than 700 visa applications were rejected, Vivas 2005: 14).

The process of NGO-isation of human rights struggles, particularly but not exclusively in Europe, entails greater professionalism, but also bureaucratisation. Besides, the budgetary dependency on outside resources leads to a degree of adjustment to the lines laid down by the providers of funds; the strengthening of more consolidated associations with greater technical knowledge to the detriment of smaller initiatives, and greater self-control of criticism in order not to annoy donors. It can also promote a more mercantilist mentality associating action with visible results.

The members of networks and platforms have differentiated profiles depending on the type of initiative concerned. The respective founding charters give clues about the members' profiles. The discourse and work of these social actors show ideological differences involving different diagnoses of the situations, diverging proposed strategies and differences over the instruments to be applied. At the centre of the debate is how much and how the political power can be transformed, and using which forms of struggle. This inevitably brings out different views of the Euro-Mediterranean process itself and its derivations (Morera Herrera, 2008: 96).

But, on the ground, the classification of TANs and platforms is more complex, as there are important areas of convergence between groups or activists taking part in conceptually dissimilar forums. Participants in the networks associated with the Euromed process bluntly criticised European foreign policy and Euro-Mediterranean relations, especially the expulsion of human rights from the agenda after the launch of the Union for the Mediterranean. Clearly, the overlapping of activists is very considerable between the Euro-Mediterranean networks promoted or supported by the European Union, but also between networks on different axes.[32] There are different logics but with areas of intersection where participants, and eventually programme points, can coincide. Particularly for activists in the south, networks – notwithstanding ideological orientations – clearly represent an opportunity in a closed political and social field. It should be noted also that organisations associated with political Islam mostly are excluded from these forums.

The TANs act as communication networks, political spaces where meanings are negotiated (Keck and Sikkink 1999: 90). As has been said, the networks are involved in disseminating norms at different levels, both through declarations and documents as well as framing activities. In addition, the networks develop their own agenda-setting processes and contribute to national and international ones. A continuous process of choice takes place among a range of possible emerging claims depending on the political culture, the relations within the network and external factors including the programmatic lines established by the institutions, particularly if they finance projects and activities.

From a communication point of view, the most important value of TANs is their capacity to mobilise political information quickly and credibly where it could have the greatest impact (European institutions, social movements at international level, etc.) acting as sounding boards, raising the awareness of the EU and public opinion with regard to specific issues. As the academic literature recalls, one of the main functions of TANs is to publicly criticise and shame states for human rights abuses (Murdie and Davis 2012).

The transnational links created by associations for the protection of human rights on the southern shore of the Mediterranean are still weak if compared with those in other regions such as Latin America. This fact is understandable considering the difficulties in creating independent associations in authoritarian political contexts before the Arab Spring (Jünemann 2003: 98), but also in the current context of uncertainty (ECEM 2012: 289). Mediterranean NGOs and transnational networks also have a relatively small presence in international forums or wider global networks. Compared to Latin American or Asian NGOs, those from the southern and eastern Mediterranean have taken longer to become active in engaging with large IGOs such as the

United Nations, which are crucial in the promotion of human rights.[33] However, the impulse given by the European Union to the development of civil society in the SEMCs has contributed to creating institutionalised mechanisms which are now quite stable (Echart Muñoz 2008: 221).

Notes

1 I would like to thank Isaías Barreñada and Laurence Thieux for their contributions to the ideas of this chapter through our conversations.

2 The first meetings took place in: Barcelona (Spain) in 1995, La Valetta (Malta) in 1997, Naples (Italy) in 1997, Stuttgart (Germany) in 1999, Marseille (France) in 2000, Brussels (Belgium) in 2001, Valencia (Spain) in 2002, Naples (Italy) in 2003 and Limassol (Cyprus) in 2004.

3 The number of participants in this event had dropped from about 1,000 in the Barcelona FCE (1995) to about 400 in the early 2000s; this reduction in participation was more marked in the case of attendees from the SEMCs (Oliván 2001: 169).

4 Euro-Mediterranean Civil Meeting (EMCM) in Spain, Network of Palestinian NGOs (in Ramallah), Euromed Non-Governmental Platform (Casablanca), Ittijah-Union of Arab Community Associations (Haifa), Lebanese Euromed Platform (Beirut), and Euromed Non-Governmental Platform in Egypt.

5 The platform has a profile on Facebook 'EuroMed Non-Governmental Platform', www.facebook.com/EuroMed-Non-Governmental-Platform-470983486407490/?hc_ref=SEARCH&fref=nf accessed 28 May 2016.

6 See: http://acimedit.net/, accessed 17 May 2016.

7 Meetings have taken place in Valencia (Spain) in 2010, Tunis (Tunisia) in 2011, Volos (Greece) in 2012, Istanbul (Turkey) in 2013, Marseille (France) in 2014, Tirana (Albania) in 2015.

8 http://ceeivalencia.emprenemjunts.es/, accessed 12 May 2016.

9 See www.euromedrights.org/eng/, accessed 17 May 2016.

10 The regional members are: European Association for the Defence of Human Rights (AEDH), Arabic Network for Human Rights Information (ANHRI), Arab Institute for Human Rights (AIHR), Collectif 95 – Maghreb Égalité, Cairo Institute for Human Rights Studies (CIHRS), African and Middle East Refugee Assistance (AMERA).

11 These are: gender equality and women's rights; justice and law; migration and asylum, and Palestine, Israel and the Palestinians.

12 Among them we might mention the Euromed Trade Union Forum, the Euro-Mediterranean Environmental NGO Monitoring Committee, the Euromed Cultural Forum (FEMEC), the International Mediterranean Women's Forum or the Euromed Youth Platform.

13 Website: www.annalindhfoundation.org/, accessed 29 May 2016.

14 Co-financed by these 42 countries of the UfM and the European Commission, the ALF is run by a board of governors composed of representatives of those countries.

15 The number of participants has ranged between 1,000 and 1,500 participants, from more than 40 countries.

16 In April 2002 in Valencia, the parallel meeting was held under the significant name 'International meeting against the Euro-Mediterranean project and capitalist globalisation in the Arab world'.

17 See http://base.d-p-h.info/fr/fiches/dph/fiche-dph-8694.html#2, accessed 7 May 2016.

18 An informal North African network of human rights activists was instigated on this occasion, concerned by all the WSF themes (globalisation, democracy, the condition of women, migration and regional conflicts). See interview with Kamal Lahbib, *Jeune Afrique* (6 February 2006), www.jeuneafrique.com, accessed 16 September 2016.

19 Six preparatory international assemblies were held: the first one took place in May 2003 in Rabat, followed by one in July 2003 in Naples; Cyprus, in March 2004; Malaga, in September that year, and Marseille and Turkey in April 2005 (Echart Muñoz 2008: 256).

20 There were three main themes: denouncing the process of economic liberalisation in the Mediterranean, the protection of human rights and democratic freedoms, and the rejection of military occupation and imperialist strategies.

21 Including the network for solidarity against the occupation of Palestine and the BDS (boycott, disinvestment and sanctions) movement, among others.

22 For example, various members of the Moroccan 20-F movement made various tours in Europe (interview with Omar Brouksy, of the 20 February Movement, Rabat, April 2012). Also in 2012 and 2013,

ACSUR-Las Segovias organised meetings of young people linked to the popular revolts in the SEMCs in Bouznika (Morocco).

23 See, for example, the creation of national platforms for supporting revolts in other countries. This is the case of the Moroccan Democratic Network for Solidarity with Peoples, supporting the demands of the activists in Tunisia and Egypt (ECEM, 2012: 54).

24 See the joint statement by the Euro-Mediterranean Human Rights Network (EMHRN), the Euro-Med Non-Governmental Platform (ENGP) and the European Feminist Initiative (IFE-EFI), http://euromedrights.org/publication/setting-up-of-a-foundation-of-women-for-the-mediterranean-what-autonomy-what-independence/, accessed 17 May 2016.

25 The Forums take place in Brussels and have been held since 2014.

26 One of the central themes of the second meeting is civil society's role in de-radicalisation efforts.

27 EMHRN, 'EC meeting minutes', http://euromedrights.org/publication-type/meetings-minutes/, accessed 12 May 2016.

28 In 2013, the presence of 60,000 people was calculated. In 2015 there were 48,600 people, 4,398 organisations from 119 countries, and 1,079 activities proposed.

29 Social forum monitoring the North African Social Forum prepared its assembly in Spain for November 2013; the North African Forum for the fight against unemployment and insecure employment, was held in Algiers from 20 to 21 February 2013; the second North African Social Forum on migrants, took place in Uchda (Morocco) in October 2012; and the Free Palestine–World Social Forum in Porto Alegre from 28 November to 1 December 2012.

30 Once again, the International Citizen Debt Audit Network set up in April 2012 to supervise public debt in Europe and North Africa; the Euro-Mediterranean Forum against imposed and unnecessary large-scale works also set up in 2012; or various initiatives related to immigrants as the Watch the Mediterranean Sea campaign.

31 It was not until 2009 that the EMHRN used a communication officer in Cairo responsible for relations with the Arab media and created the version of the website in that language.

32 To quote some examples: the Algerian association Youth Action Group (RAJ), for example, takes an active part in the MSF, the EMHRN and the Euromed Human Rights Foundation; or the Moroccan association for Human Rights (AMDH) is member of the EMHRN and has been very active in the WSFs.

33 Along these lines it is surprising to see that in a network as important as the EMHRN the need to promote activism with respect to the United Nations has not been seriously raised.

Bibliography

ACSUR-Las Segovias (2002) *El proceso del Foro Civil Euromediterráneo. Revisión Crítica 1995–2000*, Madrid: ACSUR-Las Segovias.

Barreñada, I. and Martín, I. (2005) 'La sociedad civil y la Asociación Euromediterránea: De la retórica a la práctica', *Papeles* 92, 78–89.

Bob, C. (2005) *The Marketing of Rebellion: Insurgents, Media, and International Activism*, Cambridge: Cambridge University Press.

Cavatorta, A. (2012) 'Arab Spring: The Awakening of Civil Society. A General Overview', *IEMED Yearbook*, Barcelona, pp. 75–81.

Cooley, A. and Ron, J. (2002) 'The NGO scramble: organizational insecurity and the political economy of transnational action', *International Security* 27, 1, 5–39.

ECEM, Euro-Mediterranean Civil Meeting (2012) *La sociedad civil y las 'primaveras mediterráneas': Encuentros internacionales*, Madrid: ECEM.

Echart Muñoz, E. (2008) *Movimientos sociales y relaciones internacionales: la irrupción de un nuevo actor*, Madrid: Los Libros de la Catarata.

Feliu, L. (2005) 'Global civil society across the Mediterranean: the case of human right', *Mediterranean Politics* 10, 3, 365–84.

Feliu, L. (2014) 'Redes transnacionales de derechos humanos en el Mediterráneo', *Revista CIDOB d'Afers Internacionals* 105, 19–45.

Hernando de Larramendi, M. (2009) 'The Mediterranean Policy of Spain', in: Schäfer, I. and Henry, J.-R. (eds), *Mediterranean Policies from Above and Below*, Baden-Baden: Nomos, pp. 52–74.

Hertel, S. (2006) *Unexpected Power: Conflict and Change among Transnational Activists*, Ithaca, NY: Cornell University Press.

Hooghe, L. and Marks, G. (2011) 'Types of multi-level governance', *European Integration Online Papers (EIoP)* 5, 11.

Jünemann, A. (2003) 'The Forum Civil Euromed: Critical Watchdog and Intercultural Mediator', in: Panebianco, S. (ed.), *A New Euromediterranean Partnership Cultural Identitiy*, London: Frank Cass, pp. 84–107.

Keck, M. E. and Sikkink, K. (1998) *Activists beyond Borders: Transnational Activist Networks in International Politics*, Ithaca, NY: Cornell University Press.

Keck, M. E. and Sikkink, K. (1999) 'Transnational advocacy networks in international and regional politics', *International Social Science Journal* 51, 159, 89–101.

Khagram, S., Riker, J. V. and Sikkink, K. (2002) 'From Santiago to Seattle: Transnational Advocacy Groups Restructuring World Politics', in: Khagram, S., Riker, J. V. and Sikkink, K. (eds), *Restructuring World Politics: Transnational Social Movements, Networks, and Norms*, vol. I. Minnesota: Minnesota University Press, pp. 3–23.

Mitchell, G. E. and Schmitz, H. P. (2012) *Principled Instrumentalism: A Theory of Transnational NGO Behaviour*, Syracuse, NY: Moynihan Institute of Global Affairs.

Morera Herrera, D. (2008) 'Crítica a la ambivalencia postmarxista', *Revista de Ciencias Sociales*, 120, 81–100.

Mueller, Johannes (2014) *Non-state actors in Euro-Mediterranean politics: regional convergence and pro-integration advocacy*, PhD Thesis, Budapest: Central European University.

Murdie, A. and Davis, R. (2012) 'Shaming and blaming: using events data to assess the impact of human rights INGOs', *International Studies Quarterly* 56, 1, 1–16.

Oliván, H. (2001) 'El Fórum Civil Euromed: balance, continuidades y cambios', *Quaderns de la Mediterrània = Cuadernos del Mediterráneo*, 2, 164–71.

Risse, T. (2007) 'Transnational Actors and World Politics', in: Zimmerli, Walther C., Richter, Klaus and Holzinger, Markus (eds), *Corporate Ethics and Corporate Governance*, Berlin: Springer Berlin Heidelberg, pp. 251–86.

Sabata, M. (2006) 'El Foro Social del Mediterráneo 2005: Un primer paso en el proceso', in: *Anuario IEMed del Mediterráneo 2006: el año 2005 en el espacio Euromediterráneo*, Barcelona: Instituto Europeo del Mediterráneo (IEMed), pp. 206–7.

Solera, G. (2015) 'Más allá de las fronteras: cuál es el siguiente paso para la sociedad civil Mediterránea', *Quaderns de la Mediterrània* 22, 242–55.

Tarrow, S. G. (2005) *The New Transnational Activism*, New York: Cambridge University Press.

Vivas, E. (2005) 'Foro Social Mediterráneo: un balance', *Mientras Tanto* (July), 13–15.

27

ISLAMIST MOVEMENTS IN THE MEDITERRANEAN

Modernist Islam, Islamism and Salafism

Roel Meijer

Islam in the modern era, starting in the nineteenth century, can be divided into five currents: traditionalism, Sufism, modernism, Islamism and Salafism. The traditionalist current consisted of the religious scholars (*'ulama*), their four schools of jurisprudence (Hanafi, Shafi'i, Hanbali and Maliki), going back to the ninth century, and their institutions of learning, the Azhar in Cairo, the Qarawiyyin in Fez in and the Zaituna in Tunis. Sufism, or mystical Islam, divided in countless mystical orders, has a history going back to the Middle Ages; the modernists, who were influenced by Europe emerged in the nineteenth century. The Islamists, who rejected the West, emerged in the twentieth century. Finally, the Salafis focused on the return to the founding texts of Islam, the Qur'an and the Hadith, but in their present form they are in many ways modern. The focus of this chapter will be on the last three currents, as they have dominated the modern era and can be considered movements in the sense that they mobilise wide support for religious and political goals. Traditionalism and Sufism, though by no means negligible in terms of influence and popular support, have increasingly found competition from the last three which in the modern era have grown at the expense of the first two. One of the main concerns of the modernists and Islamists was to formulate an answer to the western civilizational challenge.

Islamic modernism

Jamal al-Din al-Afghani (1838–97), an Iranian Shi'i, who posed as a Sunni, and the Egyptian Muhammad 'Abduh (1849–1905), an *'alim* who became Grand Mufti of Egypt in 1899, are usually regarded as the founders of Islamic modernism, or reformism in the Arab world. They believed that the Islamic world was ignorant and backward in comparison to Europe, whose scientific, technological and philosophical achievement they admired. The Islamic world could regain its former strength if it could push aside the scholasticism of the four schools of jurisprudence and return to the original sources of Islam, the Qur'an and the Hadith. Their assumption was that the sources of Islam did not contradict reason. Heavily influenced by European liberalism, Muhammad 'Abduh's reforms concentrated on the promotion of individual interpretation of the religious texts (*ijtihad*), the introduction of western (Enlightenment) rationalism, and the upholding of human freedom. He criticised blind imitation (*taqlid*) of the schools of jurisprudence and the un-Islamic practices of mysticism, which diverted attention from the reform and modernisation of society. Concepts like the 'general benefit' (*al-maslaha al-'amma*), which resembled the European notions of the 'common good', but also fell back on a strong Islamic tradition were important tools to promote human agency and stress the humanistic dimension of Islam. Although in his early years 'Abduh was politically active and favoured a constitutional monarchy, in later life his reforms concentrated on education and the reform of the curriculum of the Azhar in Cairo (Sedgwick 2009).

Islamic modernism, or 'balanced reformism' (going back to the foundational texts, while introducing modern reforms) (Lauzière, 2016), rapidly spread along the shores of the Mediterranean. In Syria, Islamic modernism would even become more deeply rooted than in Egypt (Commins 1990). 'Abd al-Rahman al-Kawakibi (1849–1902) and Jamal al-Din al-Qasimi (1866–1914) were important promoters of the Arab cultural renaissance at the end of the nineteenth century. In Morocco modernists like Abu Shu'ayd al-Dukkali (d. 1937), influenced the next generation of reformers who combined Islamic reform with nationalism, such as the *'alim* and leader of the Moroccan Istiqlal Party 'Allal al-Fasi (1910–74). In Algeria 'Abd al-Hamid Ben Badis (1889–1940), who in 1931 founded the Association des Oulemas Algériens, is also considered a reformist. The influence of Islamic modernism, however, was uneven. In Egypt it was supplanted by the secular nationalism of the Wafd Party, which dominated political life until the 1930s. In Syria, as well, the National Block also turned to secular nationalism. These movements often adopted the tolerant attitude of the modernists and gave equal rights to Christians and Jews. The tide against these often elitist movements started to turn at the end of the 1930s, with on the one hand the rise of radical Arab nationalism in the form of the Neo-Destour in Tunisia, the Ba'ath Party in Syria, Young Egypt in Egypt, and the communist parties, and, on the other hand, the emergence of Islamism. While in the short run, radical Arab nationalism would win out in most countries and lead the struggle for independence, Islamism would make a come-back after the eclipse of pan-Arabism and Arab socialism in the 1970s and 1980s.

Islamism

In 1928 the founding of the Muslim Brotherhood in Egypt by Hasan al-Banna (1906–49) marked the beginning of political Islam or Islamism as a political ideology. Typical for the times, it was a movement of the lower middle classes, not of the *'ulama*, al-Banna himself having been educated at the teacher training college, the Dar al-'Ulum, instead of the Azhar. Another difference was its stance towards the west. While the Islamic modernists had been open to European ideas, the Muslim Brotherhood rejected the European example and its notions of politics, economics, education, and especially culture. Islam was a 'comprehensive system', perfect in itself, embracing all aspects of life. The Brotherhood's main claim was that Islam did not recognise the separation between politics and religion, represented in such slogans as 'Islam, state and religion' (*islam, al-din wa-l-dawla*). The establishment of an Islamic state was regarded as essential for achieving the revival of the Muslim world. Its political ideas, however, remained vague. Although Hasan al-Bann was not in principle against a parliamentary system, he did warn against the divisiveness of the multi-party system as *hizbiyya*, partisanship, and emphasised Islamic unity in the face of the imperialist attempt to divide the Islamic nation (*umma*). But whatever form an Islamic political entity would adopt, it would impose a strict public morality and build an Islamic personality by means of a systematic *da'wa* (outreach, preaching) based on Islamic norms and values which it felt were threatened by European secularism, materialism and moral decadence (Commins 1994). Activism and self-sacrifice were the hallmarks of the Muslim Brotherhood. On the other hand, its doctrine was quite open and inclusive. Hasan al-Banna, for instance, was heavily influenced by Sufism. Anyone who professed belief in God and Muhammad's message was considered to be a Muslim.

Above all, Hasan al-Banna was renowned for his charisma, activism and his capacity to build a vast organisation, called the Tanzim (literally 'the organisation'), and mobilise his followers for Islamic goals. Over the years, the Brotherhood established its own schools, orphanages and health clinics, built its own mosques and ran its own companies, becoming a state within a state. It rapidly expanded from its original base in Ismailiyya to Cairo and from there to all corners of the country. By 1948 it had half a million members. Hierarchical, with a top-down structure, the lowest unit, the so-called 'family' (*usra*), was a cell consisting of five to ten persons. Hasan al-Banna stood at the pinnacle of the organisation. He was the General Guide, or *al-murshid al-'amm*, a term adopted from Sufism indicating a master–disciple relation based on obedience, but also very much in the style of authoritarian movements in Europe at the time. Internal debate was discouraged, opposition suppressed, and dissension punished by expulsion, as several dissidents, some of them close to al-Banna, experienced. The Brotherhood appealed especially to the youth who were enrolled in Rovers and acquired military training in the so-called Battalions. After World War II it established the Secret Apparatus as its underground armed wing to wage the jihad.

It was its weight and capacity for mass mobilisation on the basis of a conservative moral programme of the movement that brought the Brotherhood into politics. To the monarchy and conservative politicians the Brotherhood was a tool to be used against the secularist Wafd and after World War II the communist movement. Hasan al-Banna was inclined to cooperate with the political powers, but followed his own agenda which in the end was incompatible with the established order. In 1948 the Brotherhood sent its Battalions to the front with Israel. In the chaotic last years of the monarchy it launched bomb attacks on official institutions and waged a campaign of arson and assassinations, killing the prime minister Mahmud Fahmi al-Nuqrashi. In retaliation, the regime had Hasan al-Banna assassinated one and a half months later and banned the Brotherhood. Deprived of its charismatic leader the Brotherhood had difficulty recovering. His successor, Hasan al-Hudaybi (1891–1973), a conservative, somewhat lacklustre judge, was unable to gain control over the movement and its armed wing. As result the movement was in a state of disarray when the Free Officers took over power in 1952. Although it welcomed the end of the 'old regime', it did not succeed in becoming the moral guidance of the Free Officers and in 1953 clashed with the military, which cleverly succeeded in dividing the opposition. Typical of the deep ambiguity of the movement towards politics, it accepted the dissolution of the parliamentary system in September 1953, and accepted its status as association (*jam'iyya*). However, this strategy would not save it from repression. After the democratic opposition was defeated the military turned on the Brotherhood. A failed attempted assassination on Jamal 'Abd al-Nasser in October 1954, was used to ban the organisation, hang those held responsible for the attack, and jail its followers for the next 20 years (Mitchell 1969).

The influence of the Brotherhood in the region was tremendous. It established branches in almost all countries of the Arab world, and its flexible somewhat ambiguous concepts allowed it to develop its own style, culture and ideological make-up in each country, sometimes in opposition to the 'mother' organisation in Cairo, which after 1954 was severely weakened. Like in Egypt, these organisations consisted mostly of laymen, not religious scholars. It was most successful in Syria, where, in contrast to Egypt, it continued the Islamic modernist tradition and adopted a moderate, democratic, anti-sectarian attitude, supporting constitutionalism. Its leaders Mustafa al-Siba'i (1915–64) and Isam al-Attar (b. 1927) represented a pragmatist streak in the Brotherhood. The Syrian Brotherhood was also more divided, having brought existing, regional 'societies' (*jam'iyyat*) with their local social, cultural and intellectual background together under its umbrella, rather than build a new organisation from scratch, as Hasan al-Banna had done. The movement actively participated in parliamentary elections and on several occasions took part in coalitions and produced several ministers, the last in 1963 (Lefèvre 2013). In Jordan it also developed in a different direction, becoming the main support of King Hussein against the pan-Arab forces, which in the 1950s threatened to overwhelm the kingdom. National education became the Brotherhood's stronghold and for years it produced the secretary general of the ministry of education. When the political parties were banned in 1957, it continued to operate legally as an association or NGO and build a nationwide infrastructure of schools, mosques, charitable and other social-religious institutions. In Palestine the Muslim Brotherhood remained weak during the ascendancy of the Palestinian Liberation Organisation (PLO) in the 1960s and 1970s, but emerged during the first intifada in 1987 when it established Hamas as its political branch. The Brotherhood's influence in the Maghreb in this period was indirect, as the secular movements in Algeria and Tunisia were in power after independence and the Moroccan Istiqlal Party dominated the Islamist scene. In Algeria Mahfoudh Nahnah (1942–2003) would establish an Algerian branch. In Lebanon the Muslim Brotherhood was restricted to the Sunni minority, that was for a long time dominated by notable families. However, despite its diversity, the Muslim Brotherhood had become a force to be reckoned with. Once established, it built vast personal and organisational networks of communication and channelled new ideas rapidly through the Mediterranean.

Radicalisation under authoritarian rule

Radicalisation of the Muslim Brotherhood and several of its branches is closely associated with Sayyid Qutb (1906–66). Qutb was born in Upper Egypt, enjoyed a semi-religious education at the Dar al-'Ulum and joined the liberal literary elite as a novelist, poet and journalist in the 1930s. His interest turned to Islamist themes after the World War II, writing, for instance, *Social Justice in Islam*. It was not until 1951 that he joined the Muslim Brotherhood and became editor-in-chief of their weekly publication, being arrested with its leaders in 1954 (Calvert 2010). He became radicalised in prison, where he was tortured and witnessed the slaughter of his fellow inmates. There he wrote *Milestones*, his most famous book, and his vast, 7,000 page long *In the Shadow of the Qur'an*. In these works he made two major theoretical steps that would leave a deep imprint on Islamism and Salafism. The first step was his comparison of Muslim society under Nasser and secular Arab socialism with the pre-Islamic period of barbarity/ ignorance (*jahiliyya*). As a writer Qutb was adept at using metaphors and his genius in using the term *jahiliyya* was not to limit it to a historical period, but to apply it to contemporary society, as it did not abide by the Quranic injunction 'to rule according to what God has sent down', that is, the *shari'ah*. His solution to contemporary challenges to Islam was the complete submission of Muslims to God's sovereignty (*hakimiyya*). With this theoretical move Qutb reversed Hasan al-Banna's tolerant stance that Muslims were Muslims as long as they claimed to be Muslims. The theory of *jahiliyya* opened the door to excommunication (*takfir*, derived from the word *kufr*, or unbelief) of Muslims who did not reject worldly power and man-made laws as idols (*taghut*). It also shifted the weight of activities from *da'wa* to jihad, or, alternatively, to the withdrawal from an impious society. The second step was Qutb's rejection of the rationalism of Islamic modernism. His radicalism stemmed from his claim that the sources of Islam were completely transparent and that his interpretation was not an interpretation but the truth. In this sense, Qutb's ideas were a major regression from the rationalistic approach of Muhammad 'Abduh, who tried to create room for human interpretation, agency and pluralism. Qutb's rejection of rationalism, his intuitive approach to Islam with its vitalist emphasis on jihad as an individual duty exerted by a vanguard, gave Islamism a single-minded, revolutionary direction, in many ways comparable to Leninism. However, like many ideologues of Islamism, Qutb did not elaborate on the structure of the Islamic state – it would constitute itself during the struggle to bring God's rule on Earth. Qutb was hanged in 1966 after he was accused of plotting against the state (Euben 1999).

Milestones opened a Pandora's box and played a crucial role in the radicalisation of the Islamist movement in the 1970s and 1980s. It became so important because it coincided with the collapse of Arab socialism and pan-Arabism and the defeat of the Arab armies during the Six Days War in June 1967. Not only were the authoritarian states gravely undermined ideologically, economically and politically, over the next years they were forced to release the Islamists from prison and accommodate the revivalist movement. This new trend was discernible in all the countries along the Mediterranean, but it was revealed in different countries in different periods, depending on the timing of the liberalisation process. Egypt was the first to witness the effects of Qutb's book. At first President Sadat, who succeeded Nasser in 1970, was to ride the tide and use the Islamist trend against the left by supporting the so-called *jama'at*, or Islamic groups, in the universities. He hoped that the newly released members of the Muslim Brotherhood would be able to contain this new generation and incorporate them in its disciplined organisation that it immediately started to rebuild after their release. This was only partially the case. In Lower Egypt, it succeeded in including many of the new generation in Cairo. Elsewhere, in Upper Egypt and Alexandria, the Islamic groups felt attracted to Qutbism and became an independent movement. Three trends developed in this period. The first trend, the Jama'at, operated against what they regarded as an impious society by means of the Islamic principle 'commanding good and prohibiting the bad' (*al-amr bi-l-ma'ruf wa-l-nahi 'an al-munkar*), for short *hisba* (Meijer 2009b). This strategy focused on the Islamisation of society by correcting people's private lives and demanding that they adhere to strict Islamic norms. While initially tolerated, by the end of the 1970s they had become a nuisance at the universities and neighbourhoods, encroaching upon the authority of the state and 'liberating' Islamic space. By that time, the Jama'at from Upper Egypt joined the second trend, the Jihad Organisation (Tanzim Jihad), which had evolved in Lower Egypt and focused on waging jihad against the impious ruler (*taghut*). On 6 October 1981, during a military parade they assassinated Sadat. The third trend called themselves the Society of Muslims, but they were called al-Takfir wa-l-Hijra (Excommunication and Migration) by the authorities. It drew a different conclusion from Qutb's theory of *jahiliyya* and following the example of the prophet who had migrated from Mecca (*hijra*) to Medina in 622 CE in order to conquer Mecca, it withdrew from society better to reconquer the centre of impiety. This group, as well, came into conflict with the state, after it kidnapped a minister of Awqaf (pious endowments) and its leader was hanged.

Qutb's ideas were highly influential in other countries as well. In Morocco student followers of Sayyid Qutb founded al-Shabiba al-Islamiyya or the Islamic Youth in 1969. It was banned, its leader Abd al-Karim Muti' (b. 1936) escaping to France after the assassination in 1975 of the left-wing trade unionist leader Umar ibn Jallun. In Algeria Mustafa Bouyali (1940–87) was the first to wage a jihad against the regime of Chedli Benjadid in the 1980s, withdrawing to the *maquis* where he was killed. Qutb was most influential in Syria, where the radical wing of the Brotherhood dragged the whole Syrian Muslim Brotherhood into a brutal confrontation with the Ba'ath regime which had taken over power in 1963 and disbanded the parliamentary system. As in Egypt, the clash with the secular minded authoritarian regime erupted almost immediately. The first uprisings in Hama took place in 1964, followed by demonstrations in 1967 against a secular article in a military magazine and another in 1973 in Aleppo against the secular constitution. The class dimension exacerbated the clash with the Ba'ath regime. Its land reforms and nationalisations targeted the notables, the urban middle classes, and the merchants of the souks, exactly those social groups that supported the Brotherhood. The regime was moreover dominated by Alawis, who had always been regarded by the Sunni majority as heretics. The turning point came in 1979 with the massacre by the jihadist Fighting Vanguard (*al-Tali'a al-Muqatila*), a group linked to the Brotherhood, of 83 Alawi cadets at the Artillery School in Aleppo. Based on Qutb's ideas of the impious state, this group called the regime 'godless' and 'apostate'. The subsequent escalation of violence and promulgation of Law No. 49 in 1980, making membership of the Brotherhood punishable by death, culminated in 1982 in the uprising and destruction of the provincial town of Hama, where between 20,000 and 40,000 of its inhabitants were killed (Lefèvre 2013). The Muslim Brotherhood was never able to recover from this onslaught. Its role was taken over by traditionalist *'ulama* and independent religious organisations, which absorbed the new upsurge in piety over the following decades (Pierret 2013).

Liberalisation under semi-authoritarian rule

Although the radical offshoots of the Muslim Brotherhood would catch the limelight, numerically and intellectually they remained marginal until the Arab Uprisings in 2011. The Muslim Brotherhood in its various forms in different countries would experience an unprecedented revival and become mainstream Islam in this period. Its re-emergence was due to the economic and political liberalisation that most authoritarian regimes were forced to implement in the 1970s and 1980s. It also took a major strategic step by openly rejecting violence. In Egypt, the more moderate leadership of the Muslim Brotherhood, even before its release from prison, had distanced itself from Qutb in Hasan al-Hudaybi's *Preachers not Judges* (*Du'a la quda*) (Zollner 2009). As a result, President Sadat, who succeeded Nasser in 1970, gradually released its members from prison in the following years, allowing the Brotherhood to operate as long as it did not interfere in politics. To ensure its survival in the long run, it recruited new members among university students. This second generation would give the Brotherhood a new profile in the 1980s and 1990s. Well-educated – the Brotherhood was strong in faculties of medicine, engineering and pharmacy – they were more open, not traumatised by Nasser's prisons, and became active in civil society, gaining political experience with other political currents in running the professional syndicates. During this process of 'political learning' they started to question the authoritarian nature of 'hearing and obeying' and started to break out of the narrow constraints of the Tanzim. In 1996 this led to the foundation of the Wasat Party, which in many ways took up the thread where the modernists had left off. Its leaders no longer propagated an Islamic state, the implementation of the *shari'ah* and the enforcement of *hudud* punishments. Nor did they use the populist slogan 'Islam is the solution'. Instead they referred to an inclusive, egalitarian 'Islamic civilisation', to which non-Muslims also belonged. Another important strategic decision was the acceptance by the Muslim Brotherhood of political participation and party politics (*hizbiyya*), a practice that had been condemned as divisive by Hasan al-Banna. Eventually, this liberal trend did not prove strong enough to carry the day in the Egyptian Brotherhood. None of the general guides, with perhaps the exception of Muhammad 'Akif (2004–10), were liberally inclined. The Brotherhood's road to full participation was also blocked by the regime. Although it was allowed to take part in general elections as coalition partners in 1984 and 1987 (winning 8 and 36 seats), it was not allowed to found a political party and from the 1990s onwards it was increasingly repressed, gaining only 1 seat in 1995 and 17 seats (of 444 seats) in the 2000 elections. When it gained 88 seats in 2005 the state clamped down and in 2010 it gained no seats at all in parliament. Liberals were mostly independent intellectuals, such as the lawyer Muhammad Salim al-'Awwa, the judge Tariq al-Bishri and the journalist Fahmi Huweidi. They had a certain sympathy for the Muslim Brotherhood but did not become members and belonged to the so-called Wasatiyya current which called for a democratic, reformed liberal Islam (Wickham 2013). One of its most prominent members was sheikh Yusuf al-Qaradawi (b. 1925), a Qatari based member of the Brotherhood who was able through Al Jazeera TV to become a global spokesman of this trend (Skovgaard-Petersen and Gräf 2009).

In other countries similar movements to the Brotherhood experienced the same (limited) opportunities to take part in politics. In Jordan the Muslim Brotherhood won 20 seats (Islamists in total won 34 seats) out of 80 seats in parliament in the general elections of 1989. In 1992 it founded a political party, the Islamic Action Front (IAF), but as it opposed the Jordanian peace treaty with Israel, its alliance with the monarchy ended and it was never able to win the same number of seats again. Newly established Islamist movements in other countries fared little better. In Tunisia the Islamic movement established the Mouvement de la tendence islamique, changing its name to Ennahda in 1989 in order to take part in elections. It won a limited number of seats by presenting independents. Two years later it was banned, and its leader Rachid Ghannouchi (b. 1941) fled to Great Britain, where he gradually adopted a liberal Wasatiyya programme over the next two decades. In Algeria the FLN regime of President Chadli Benjedid chose to liberalise after the riots of 1988 (500 dead) and installed a liberal constitution that allowed for a multi-party parliamentary system and free elections. In the municipal elections of 1990 the coalition of traditionalist, modernist, and Islamist forces, the Front Islamique du Salut (FIS), won control over most of the municipal councils, but when a year later it almost succeeded in winning the general elections the military stepped in and cancelled them, disbanded FIS and installed a dictatorship which would lead to a bloody civil war that continued until 1997 and would cost 150,000 Algerians their lives (Volpi 2003; Labat 1995). Where the regime blocked all forms of political liberalisation, such as in Syria, this did allow quietist Sunni piety movements to arise but under strong state control (Pierret 2013). Syria also sponsored the rise of Hizballah, a Shi'ite movement, which emerged after 1980 and was able to mobilise and emancipate the Shi'ite population of Lebanon.

It was in Morocco that the most substantial changes took place. There, over a period of 20 years, the Islamist trend traversed the whole trajectory from Qutbism in the 1970s to a Brotherhood organisation in the 1980s to a more pragmatic Wasatiyya trend in the 1990s. This fundamental change was initiated by King Hasan II, who at the end of the 1980s ended his reign of terror, known as the 'years of lead' (*les années de plombe*) of brutal repression, torture and disappearances, and made a pact with the Islamists. Initially, the Moroccan Islamist movement was allowed to organise itself freely as a civil society organisation and individuals were allowed to take part as candidates in elections. In 1997 the Mouvement unité et réforme (MUR) won nine seats in parliament. But the major step came when in 1998 it founded an Islamist party (the Parti du Développment et de la Justice under the leadership of first Saadeddine Othmani (b. 1956) and later Abdellilah Ben Kirane). Over the next years it became independent from MUR, and in 2002 and 2007 the PJD won 42 seats (out of 325 seats) in parliament. Equally important, it gained access to municipalities, winning in 17 localities in 2003 and later expanding its local power. Although within the party several tendencies have been discernible, the strong modernist trend of 'Allal al-Fasi is detectable in thinkers such as Ahmed Raysuni, who argues that politics should be based on 'pious citizens' and the 'community of the faithful' rather than an Islamic state and enforcing the *shari'ah* (Wegner 2011; Zeghal 2009).

Although the Arab Uprisings of 2010–11 were initially non-Islamic in inspiration but rather were geared towards gaining rights as citizens, at an early stage the Islamist trend would benefit from the eviction of the dictators. Rachid Ghannouchi returned to Tunisia after the fall of the Tunisian dictator Ben Ali on 14 January 2011. Later, Ennahda was legalised as a political party, winning 89 out of 217 seats in the general election of 2011 and forming a coalition government with two secular parties. Based on its previous pragmatic approach, it eventually overcame the strong secular inclination of the Tunisian elite and a constitution was adopted in January 2014. In Morocco, in exchange for its abstention from participation in the 20 February Movement, which was supported by al-'Adl wa-l-Ihsan movement, a Sufi (mystical inclined movement) which did not recognise the monarchy, in November 2011 the PJD for the first time won the elections (107 out of 395 seats) and provided the prime minister, forming a coalition government with three other parties. In Egypt, the Muslim Brotherhood benefited from the political opening after the fall of Mubarak on 18 February 2011, and established its own party the Freedom Justice Party in May 2011. In line with the reformist trend, it tried to form coalitions with the more secular parties, promising to abandon its populist slogan 'Islam is the solution'. In the end, however, its policies were not based on reform and dismantling the authoritarian state but on gaining power. After winning 235 of the 498 seats in parliament in the 2011–12 general elections, it formed a coalition government with the Salafi Nour Party, tried to draw up an Islamic constitution, and after Muhammad Morsi became president in 2012 (winning 51.7 per cent of the votes), aiming to impose its hegemony. On 3 July 2013 the military took over power, suppressed mass demonstrations and sit-ins and banned the Muslim Brotherhood, inaugurating a reign of brutal repression. The suppression of the Egyptian Muslim Brotherhood had wide-ranging implications for the Islamist movement throughout the Mediterranean world. The brief idea of creating an Islamic Mediterranean coalition based on Turkey, Egypt, Tunisia and Morocco, collapsed and the tide immediately turned against the legal and political participatory Islamist trend.

Salafism

Salafism has become one of the most important movements within Islam over the past four decades (Meijer 2009a). It has many roots, but the original idea, as in Islamic modernism, is to return to the original texts of Islam, the Qur'an and the Hadith and the ways of the pious forefathers (*al-salaf al-salih*), the first three generations of followers of Muhammad. The major difference is that modern Salafism is literalist, anti-rationalist and anti-hermeneutic; it argues that the text is transparent and there is a truth that the reader can discern without interpretation. The text is dominant, and Salafism is focused on the purification of doctrine and practice from unlawful innovations (*bid'a*). Its central concept is *tawhid* (the Oneness of God) and it focuses on the study of Hadith, which provides highly detailed instructions on correct daily conduct and rituals. Islamic modernists meanwhile argue that the text is for the benefit of humanity and that except for specified rituals, and specific issues, Islamic law only provides general guidelines for human conduct. It is the task of humankind to devise general principles from these guidelines. Concepts such as the 'general good', typical of modernism and Islamism, are not used by Salafism. In a sense, Salafism is the literalist correction of the rationalist tendency of modernism on the one hand and the political focus of Islamism on the other. The tendency in both movements to become more lax in doctrine, more pragmatic, giving more room for human agency, has opened space for the literalist Salafism to occupy and provide much stricter guidance and make claims to the truth. Salafism, in contrast to modernism and Islamism, is also vehemently anti-Shi'i, which it regards as non-Islamic, and therefore has a strong sectarian character. Its claim to belonging to the 'saved sect' reinforces it sectarian character (Wagemakers 2016).

However, despite its claims to authenticity, Salafism too has been affected by modern influences. It is divided into three currents: quietist Salafism which is completely focused on doctrine and purification of Islam and goes back to the ideas of the eighteenth century Hanbali reformer Muhammad ibn 'Abd al-Wahhab (1703–92), also called Wahhabism. This doctrine has been promoted by the religious establishment of Saudi Arabia and has been supported by the Saudi state since its foundation in 1932. It rejects politics and especially political parties as partisanship (*hizbiyya*) and critique of rulers is only allowed if it is done through discrete advice (*nasiha*). Many modernists felt attracted to Wahhabism since its claims to authenticity were stronger once the tide against the west had turned in the 1930s. Its influence grew again during the second Islamic revival of the 1970s. In contrast to the Muslim Brotherhood, it is strongly decentralised. Followers follow individual religious scholars because of their religious knowledge (*'ilm*) and are not members of a hierarchical organisation. Since the establishment of the University of Medina in the 1960s the number of students going to Saudi Arabia to study Salafism has grown exponentially, turning Salafi networks into one of the most dynamic transnational Islamic movements, stretching from Indonesia to Nigeria. Salafism acquired a further boost from the introduction of the Internet, becoming the dominant current on the net. Several scholars have become famous for their knowledge of the Hadith and the development of Hadith studies, such as Nasir al-Din al-Albani (1914–99), 'Abd al-'Aziz ibn Baz (1910–99) or Rabi' ibn Hadi al-Madkhali (b. 1931). Especially in semi-authoritarian regimes such as Tunisia, Morocco, Jordan and Egypt, the state supported the quietist current against the political threat of the Muslim Brotherhood. In Egypt the Salafi stronghold, al-Da'wa al-Salafiyya, was established in Alexandria in the 1970s. In Lebanon, it has spread since the 1980s in Tripoli. Elsewhere, the spread of quietist Salafism was later or limited. In Syria Salafism was weak and banned after 9/11. In Tunisia it has existed since the 1980s and was tolerated as long it remained focused on doctrine and *da'wa*.

Political Salafism combines the focus on the purification of doctrine with the political orientation of the Muslim Brotherhood. It stems from the so-called *Sahwa* movement that sprang up in Saudi Arabia in the 1980s. In the countries of the Mediterranean it remained limited until the Arab Uprisings when many of the quietist Salafi movements were forced to take part in politics. The most well-known example is the Egyptian Nour Party, which came out of al-Da'wa al-Salfiyya; founded in May 2011, it took part in the general elections of 2011–12 (winning 26 per cent of the votes) and in the presidential elections of 2012, producing a detailed political programme. It supported the military coup against the Muslim Brotherhood. But also in Morocco, Algeria, Libya and Lebanon political Salafism appeared in this period (Cavatorta and Merone 2017).

Jihadi Salafism, which is a combination of Sayyid Qutb's activist jihadism and the strict textual orientation of Salafism also experienced an upsurge in this period. The major difference from Qutbism is that it became a global movement, shifting its focus from the jihad against the 'near enemy' (impious authoritarian state or society) to the jihad in Afghanistan against the USSR under the leadership of Abdallah 'Azzam and then to global jihad against the 'far enemy' (also called 'Crusaders and Zionists' i.e, the west, especially the United States, and Israel) under the leadership of Osama bin Laden (Gerges 2005). For the Mediterranean countries Jihadi Salafism became crucially important because it attracted many of the Qutbist jihadis who had joined the jihad after the Soviet invasion of Afghanistan in 1979, the so-called 'Arab Afghans', who later returned to fight local battles in the 1990s. This was the case with the Groupe islamique armée (GIA) in Algeria, which terrorised the local population whom they regarded as 'unbelievers' (*kuffar*) during the civil war because they had taken part in elections, and the Libyan Fighting Forces, which operated in Cyrenaica. Since the American invasion of Iraq in 2003, Jihadi Salafism has been given an enormous boost. But it only became a powerful transnational force after the uprisings in Syria in March 2011. The brutal repression of the liberal uprisings eventually led to the rise of several jihadi movements in Syria such as Jabhat al-Nusra and in 2013 the Islamic State in Iraq and Syria (ISIS) (Lister 2015). Since its announcement of the caliphate in 2014, ISIS has been the first experiment to implement an Islamic state in the region.

That thousands of youths from Morocco, Tunisia and Egypt have joined ISIS as fighters shows the appeal jihadism has in the region.

Conclusion

Islamic modernism, Islamism and Salafism have played important roles in the Mediterranean basin since the end of the nineteenth century. They have expanded at the expense of Sufism and traditionalism. All three have turned Islam into an ideology (except for the quietists) because politics has been channelled through religion, but they have done this in different ways. Islamic modernism has left the most space to human agency on the basis of the principle of 'general benefit', laying emphasis on rationality and humanism. As a result, politics has been recognised as a separate field with its own laws and compromises. Over the past few decades Islamism has taken major steps in the direction of pragmatism, taking distance from the notion of the Islamic state as impractical and accepting democracy to give priority to the 'people's will' over 'God's sovereignty'. At the same time, this trend towards moderation has been undermined by the dogmatic literalism of Salafism, which gives priority to the holy texts and the purification of Islam from foreign accretions and innovation (*bid'a*). It finds solace in building separate, exclusive communities who live according to what they believe is 'pure' Islam. Finally, jihadism, either in its Qutbist or Jihadi Salafist version, still has a tremendous appeal for youth on the basis of its utopian character, combining violence, self-sacrifice and idealism. Based on these general trends, Islam is faced with four major challenges, all related to its modern totalising claims which are the product of the confrontation with the west. The first is related to claims to truth. The modernists have pointed the way by accepting that Islam is a divine truth but is subject to human interpretation that is fallible and subject to debate. The second is related to politics and the recognition that Islam presents a system of values and norms – also subject to debate – but not a political system and therefore should provide autonomous space for politics, which should be in the service of the Muslim community, not the other way round. The third challenge is related to the notion of history and the realisation that Islam has always been adaptable and there is no essential Islam. Modern Islam is largely a historical product formed in the confrontation with modernity and that should be recognised by Muslims and reflected upon. The last challenge is related to the political community and the realisation that it should be inclusive. The increasing need for a strong identity should be balanced by the realisation that it comes at a cost of exclusion of others and isolation.

Bibliography

Baker, Raymond (2003) *Islam without Fear: Egypt and the New Islamists* (Cambridge MA: Harvard University Press).

Calvert, John (2010) *Sayyid Qutb and the Origins of Radical Islamism* (London: Hurst).

Cavatorta, Francesco, and Fabio Merone (Eds) (2017) *Salafism after the Arab Awakening: Contending with People's Power* (London: Hurst).

Commins, David (1990) *Islamic Reform: Politics and Social Change in Late Ottoman Syria* (New York: Oxford University Press).

Commins, David (1994) 'Hasan al-Banna (1906–1949)', in Ali Rahnema (Ed.), *Pioneers of Islamic Revival* (London: Zed Books) pp. 124–53.

Euben, Roxanne, L. (1999) *Enemy in the Mirror: Islamic Fundamentalism and the Limits of Modern Rationalism. A Work of Comparative Political Theory* (Princeton: Princeton University Press).

Gerges, Fawaz A. (2005) *The Far Enemy: Why Jihad Went Global* (Cambridge: Cambridge University Press).

Gershoni, Israel, and James P. Jankowski (1995) *Redefining the Egyptian Nation, 1930–1945* (Cambridge: Cambridge University Press).

Labat, Séverine (1995) *Les islamistes algériens: Entre les urnes et le maquis* (Paris: Seuil).
Lauzière, Henri (2016) *The Making of Salafism: Islamic Reform in the Twentieth Century* (New York: Columbia University Press).
Lefèvre, Raphaël (2013) *Ashes of Hama: The Muslim Brotherhood in Syria* (London: Hurst).
Lister, Charles, R. (2015) *The Syrian Jihad: Al Qaeda, the Islamic State and the Evolution of an Insurgency* (London: Hurst).
Meijer, Roel (Ed.) (2009a) *Global Salafism: Islam's New Religious Movement* (London: Hurst).
Meijer, Roel (2009b) 'Commanding Right and Forbidding Wrong as a Principle of Social Action: The Case of the Egyptian al-Jama'at al-Islamiyya', in Roel Meijer (Ed.) *Global Salafism: Islam's New Religious Movement* (London: Hurst), pp. 189–220.
Mitchell, Richard, P. (1969) *The Society of the Muslim Brothers* (Oxford: Oxford University Press).
Pierret, Thomas (2013) *Religion and State in Syria: The Sunni Ulama from Coup to Revolution* (Cambridge: Cambridge University Press).
Sedgwick, Mark (2009) *Muhammad Abduh: A Biography* (Cairo: The American University in Cairo Press).
Skovgaard-Petersen, Jakob and Bettina Gräf (Eds) (2009) *Global Mufti: The Phenomenon of Yusuf al-Qaradawi* (London: Hurst).
Volpi, Frédéric (2003) *Islam and Democracy: The Failure of Dialogue in Algeria* (London: Pluto Press).
Wagemakers, Joas (2016) *Salafism in Jordan: Political Islam in a Queitist Community* (Cambridge: Cambridge University Press).
Wegner, Eva (2011) *Islamist Opposition in Authoritarian Regimes: The Party of Justice and Development in Morocco* (New York: Syracuse University Press).
Wickham, Carrie Rosefsky (2013) *The Muslim Brotherhood: Evolution of an Islamist Movement* (Princeton: Princeton University Press).
Zeghal, Malika (2009) *Islamism in Morocco: Religion, Authoritarianism and Electoral Politics* (Princeton: Markus Wiener).
Zollner, Barbara H. E. (2009) *The Muslim Brotherhood: Hasan al-Hudaybi and Ideology* (Abingdon: Routledge).

28

WOMEN'S MOVEMENTS WITHIN EURO-MEDITERRANEAN POLITICS

The need to go beyond 'the Arab woman'

Ali Bilgic

The image of the protesting Arab woman, once 'marginalized' and 'oppressed', but now 'emancipated', in Tahrir Square in January 2011 was only an episode, a moment, in a historical process that continues today with all its complexities. Europe has always been part of this complex historical process as a (neo)colonial power, a donor, a political ally of, and, sometimes, an obstacle to women's movements and their causes. These contradictory representations have intrinsically rendered southern Mediterranean women's movements 'Euro-Mediterranean'. This chapter is an examination of women's movements in the southern Mediterranean region (primarily in North Africa), placing them within wider Euro-Mediterranean political and economic dynamics.

The argument is that women's movements in all their heterogeneity as secular, nationalist, leftist, Islamist, feminist and non-feminist have been objects and subjects of Euro-Mediterranean politics since the colonial period. They have sometimes made uneasy alliances with states and 'Europe', and sometimes raised their critical voices against patriarchal/patrimonial practices originating from their societies, states or 'Europe'. This analysis starts with the discussion of women's movements during the colonial era. In this period, women took part in anti-colonial struggles as Islamists, socialists and nationalists. This is followed by a discussion of the second period when women's movements were banned, co-opted or instrumentalized by the post-colonial states. In this second period, women's movements continued their struggles, forming coalitions with both state and non-state level actors in order to advance their position. Europe was generally represented as a source of moral and political corruption whose colonial interests had never faded away. Towards the end of the period, Europe sometimes emerged as a new political ally, a donor, or sometimes as a neocolonial power. The second period ended with the Arab uprisings. Finally, the discussion will move to women's movements in the post-2011 Euro-Mediterranean region in order to analyse how the uprisings have affected the women in the region, and how 'Europe' has reacted to 'the awakening of Arab women'.

Women in anticolonial struggles

The emergence of the first women's movements in the southern Mediterranean occurred at a time not very different from that of their counterparts in the north. Those in the north were preoccupied with struggles for universal suffrage and/or equal wages, depending on their ideological orientation. In addition to those struggles, women's movements in the southern Mediterranean had to organize against colonialism and for national independence. In other words, 'Europe', by recourse to its colonialism, was a fundamental political dynamic for the first wave of women's movements. This anticolonial position has had recurring effects on the organizational structures and political alliances they have established, the strategies they have adopted, and the problems they have faced since the inception of women's movements. These effects are still echoed in contemporary Euro-Mediterranean politics.

The colonial period and the anticolonial struggles of southern Mediterranean countries resulted in two major modulations of Europe in particular and the west in general. The first one was the representation of Europe and colonial powers as the embodiment of political corruption, violent oppression of the colonized societies, and economic exploitation. This view, mainly shared by leftist, nationalist and/or Marxist groups, was countered by another modulation stemming from Islamist groups. While not completely abandoning the exploitative dimension of colonialism, this one mainly concentrated on a culturalist narrative. 'Europe' was represented as morally corrupt and as constantly attempting to spread its own cultural and political values such as secularism, materialism and individualism (Jad, 2004: 34–5).

These two modulations are vital not only to understand the major political dynamics in the following decades in the region, but also, and more importantly, to understand how the issue of 'woman' was appropriated according to contending political ideologies, regime forces and the opposition. It is also important for understanding what types of political activism women's movements had to pursue. Furthermore, women's movements developed diverse representations of Europe in their ideologies and activism. To put it differently, women, with their bodies and identities, found themselves at the uneasy junction of colonialism, anticolonialism, Islamism, nationalism and modernization as objects and subjects of politics.

In many southern Mediterranean countries, from Egypt to Tunisia, the modernization process and anticolonial (or pro-independence) struggles went in parallel in the late nineteenth and early twentieth centuries. Modernization of education, bureaucracy and the military to varying degrees in these countries led to the emergence of upper and middle class women who were politically conscious and economically (relatively) powerful enough to pursue their feminist political agendas, i.e. the Egyptian Feminist Movement (EFM) and the Modern Women Community in the Ottoman Empire. According to Hafez (2015: 48),

> the progression from Ottoman to European status symbols and shift in cultural norms brought about by modernization and colonialism caused many women to reflect on their contradictory plight as symbols of tradition and culture on the one hand, and as epitomising modernity and progress on the other.

Indeed, women were put at the centre of contestation between diverse political groups, whose representations of women varied.

In general, Islamists interpreted the increasing presence of women in the public space as another western, colonial and European infiltration to corrupt the Muslim society. This culturalist and essentialist view on society was not simply about women, but concerned the turbulence caused by modernization in society, and the political, economic and social reverberations of this process. Protecting Muslim women meant both fighting colonialism and conserving the Islamic essence of the society. As Kandiyoti (1991: 32) puts, Islamists were not against the adoption of the technology of the west, but its cultural infiltration had to be stopped, and this rendered discussions about polygyny and veiling central to political imaginations about what the society should be like. Surprisingly, modernist/nationalist/pro-left ideology was not immensely different from the latter. Duality marked their strategy of instrumentalization of women. On the one hand, the modernization of women was equated with that of society – the presence of women in the public space was represented as a signifier of being modern. On the other hand, an Egyptian or Algerian woman was represented as the keeper of the local values and traditions. Women of the nation were not simply those taking active part in public life as teachers, doctors, lawyers, politicians, but also and maybe more fundamentally, the wives and mothers who maintained the family and passed the nation's values to their children while preserving their honour in the public space (Hafez, 2015: 49–50). This dual role tailored for women had strong implications for women's movements in the following decades.

These complex dynamics in the region revealed gender to be one of the main determinants of politics, where women's movements developed diverse positions in relation to dominant political groups, Europe, and, also, to each other.

In many southern Mediterranean states, secular and Islamist women's movements emerged concomitantly. These movements made political alliances with dominant political groups depending on their position vis-à-vis Europe. For example, this division was observable in the EFM in Egypt, which was closer to secular/nationalist groups with membership of Muslims and Christian alike, and the Muslim Women's Society, founded in 1935 by Zeineb Al Ghazali. These movements developed alternative views about women, society and modernization in their countries, which can be summed up as a dichotomy between 'secular' and 'Islamist' women's movements. However, this dichotomy should be approached cautiously, since these movements shared commonalities. Al Ghazali's feminist activism matured within the EFM, finding that it was not as 'secular' as it was presented. For example, its journal had articles criticizing the Turkish women who justified their emancipation by reference to foreign laws (particularly the Swiss-based civil code adopted in Turkey in 1926), arguing that Muslim women should be under Shari'ah (Badran, 1991: 210). Furthermore, in their struggles against colonialism, the secular–Islamist binary was dissolved. The EFM was joined by the Muslim Women's Society MWS and the Muslim Sisters in Egypt; in Algeria, women's accounts about the Algerian war of independence were conglomerations of religion, culture, nation, country and independence. As discussed later, the postcolonial states developed similar positions towards these organizations in banning or co-opting them.

Lastly, in this period, southern Mediterranean women's organizations engaged with international and regional activities. The EFM had close relations with the International Women's Suffragette Alliance; the Turkish Women's Association hosted the International Women's Conference in Turkey in 1935. Women's movements from different Arab countries also organized the pan-Arab Women's Conference in Cairo in 1945. These activities were important reminders to their counterparts in Europe of their 'white feminism' by opening up possibilities of diversifying women's experiences in the Euro-Mediterranean region (Jad, 2004: 36). Their international and regional activities continued until the postcolonial regimes co-opted them. Islamist women's organizations, however, formulated a more critical position towards these activities, as Europe in its totality was considered to be a culturally imperialist formation that essentially contradicted Islam.

This period left two important legacies for the women's movements in the Euro-Mediterranean region. Firstly, the emergence of contending women's movements and their participation in anticolonial struggles in line with their ideological positioning not only signified women's activism and agency since their inception, but also revealed how women's movements lay at the centre of discussions about what type of society and political organization the country should aim for. Secondly, women's movements were 'Euro-Mediterranean' in character, as 'Europe' was integral to their ideologies and politics.

State feminism of postcolonial period in Euro-Mediterranean

Women actively took part in anticolonial struggles, from Algeria to Egypt. They organized movements in Egypt and Algeria to mobilize women and men against the colonizers; public preachers emerged from these movements to keep up the morality of the units; women also became active participants in public life as nurses, teachers and workers. Moreover, they joined active fighting individually or organized guerrilla groups, i.e. the Moudjahidines, the women fighters in the Algerian war of independence. However, it must be noted that this active participation in the fight did not necessarily lead to boosting gender equality, as in the case of the Moroccan liberation struggle. Women were considered as 'helpers' rather than fighters, in spite of the high risk they faced when transporting weapons, guiding soldiers through the mountains or carrying messages (Baker, 1998: 166). Following independence, both secular and Islamist parties in Algeria failed to promote the representation of women in politics (Abu Haidar and Amrane-Minne, 1999).

Feminist literature is rich in explaining the women who broke the patriarchal boundaries between the public and private during times of conflict; however, following the conflict, these women were expected to 'return' to the feminized private space. This pattern can be observed in the postcolonial states in the Euro-Mediterranean region. Most women's organizations were either banned, as in Egypt and Jordan, or co-opted, as in Syria, Algeria and Tunisia, 'despite the broad-based nature of independence struggles' (Jad, 2004: 37). As a similar trend emerged in the post-uprisings period from 2011 onwards, it is important to discuss how women's movements were positioned in the postcolonial states following the anticolonial struggles.

As discussed earlier, a dynamic emerged within the modernization discussions that were about the secularist and Islamist division in women's movements. This discussion was appropriated in the postcolonial period. The competition over women's bodies and identities became a question of what type of nation, society, individual and regime should be constructed. In postcolonial southern Mediterranean countries, different political projects capitalized on women's bodies and identities in order to justify and legitimize their own political agenda and marginalize the alternatives. In other words, divisions between Islamist and secularist women's movements with their crosscutting class hierarchies were reproduced by masculine political ideologies of nationalism/socialism, on the one hand, and political Islam, on the other, as the fundamental binary where the fate of the country lay.

This is the period of state feminism in the Euro-Mediterranean region. State feminism refers to a political ideology that appropriates some of the feminist objectives in the state's political agenda with the objective of increasing and consolidating the state's legitimacy internally and externally, and suppressing the domestic opposition by recourse to their criticisms of women's rights and freedoms. It should be noted that state feminism has not performed similarly across or within southern Mediterranean countries. Especially towards the end of this period, 'Europe', in the form of the European Union, became one of the actors that interacted with women's movements under the framework of state feminism and developmentalism.

Following Libyan independence in 1951, King Idris al-Sanusi launched a modernization process focusing on development, education and women's empowerment. The Women's Renaissance Society of Benghazi (1954) and Women's Society of Libya (1957) were two main women's movements that furthered women's empowerment in line with the modernizing regime's political agenda. General Gaddafi's coup and his dictatorship from 1969 to 2011 generated difficult implications for women's movements, most of which were co-opted by the state. The Gaddafi regime's main principles involved gender equality along with socialism, Arabism and anti-imperialism. He even took certain measures such as compulsory military service for women in 1979 in order to push women towards the public space. In 1989, Libya signed the

Convention on the Elimination of all Forms of Discrimination Against Women (CEDAW) with reservations. However, none of these led to more and equal participation of women in political, economic and social life, partly because of the patrimonial state's presence that did not allow pluralism, and partly because of the auxiliary status of women's movements, rather than them being strong alternatives (Bugaighis, 2014: 107). Whereas Gaddafi appropriated and instrumentalized women's movements to consolidate his regime and power domestically and internationally, this did not prevent the regime from disciplining women's bodies, sexualities and subjectivities in the name of 'Islamic identity', such as compulsory 'virginity tests' for girls and women accused of adultery (Alnaas and Pratt, 2015: 157–8).

A similar pattern can be observed in Tunisia as well. Tunisia became an independent state in 1956. Only five months after independence, the Family Code (CSP) was legalized, which promoted the status of women in public and social life. However, as Charrad (2001: 322) argues, the political agenda behind the CSP was nation-building by delegitimizing and dissolving loyalties based on kinship and Islam. As in Libya, women were once more represented as the 'bearers' of the new independent Tunisian nation: their bodies and identities were modulated as the carriers of the new political agenda. The postcolonial state claimed itself as the protector and promoter of women's rights. While secular feminist movements found themselves as part of the state feminist political agenda, Islamist feminist movements (e.g. an-Nahdha) started to gain strength in the 1980s. Following Bourguiba, Ben-Ali mobilized 'both autonomous and state-affiliated feminist organizations against the Islamist political opposition' against the backdrop of rising popularity of an-Nahdha (Khalil, 2015: 62).

The case of Egypt shows both resemblances and differences with Libya and Tunisia. As regards similarities, the Nasser regime in Egypt from 1952 onwards integrated modernization, nation-building, developmentalism and increasing women's participation in the new state policy agenda. The Nasser regime quickly passed legislation about the rights of work and employment for women. To counter the Muslim Brotherhood-supported *fatwa* that claimed that granting political rights for women was against Islam, the regime granted universal suffrage in 1956. Meanwhile, the Egyptian Feminist Union was banned. Feminists formed other organizations, such as the Women's Committee for Electoral Awareness and the National Feminist Union, although they were quickly banned along with the Muslim Sisters. In 1964, organizing women's political organizations was completely banned (Badran, 1991: 216–7). Anwar Sadat continued the practice of the Nasser regime to promote women's rights without provoking the rising political Islam in Egypt, all the while keeping an authoritarian grip on women's movements.

The Hosni Mubarak regime (1981–2011) was the period of neoliberalization, when the number of women's NGOs sharply increased. This was partly because 'the Mubarak regime sought to gain legitimacy in the international community as an arbiter of civil society' (Sika, 2014: 64). However, this meant that the state's coercive power on the women's movements partially decreased as the left-wing, Marxist, socialist, Islamist women's organizations increased in number, although this prevented them from forming a unified feminist movement (Sika, 2014: 64). Furthermore, the Mubarak regime successfully instrumentalized women's movements such as the National Council for Women. Important developments followed in the area of family law (such as the unconditional right for women to divorce) and in the public space (in 2003, the first female judges were appointed). In 2010, a quota for women in parliamentary elections was introduced (Hafez, 2015: 64). However, it must be noted that state feminism *par excellence* in Egypt defined women as 'proper' or 'improper' based on their political views. Some secular, Islamist, Marxist women's movements actively participated in the first strong anti-Mubarak movement in 2004–05, the Kifayeh (Enough!). The regime thugs harassed protesting women violently under the auspices of the police (Sika, 2014: 65).

Whereas Libya, Tunisia and Egypt were examples of state feminism where women's movements had to form uneasy alliances with the authoritarian regimes by constructing secular–Islamist women's movement binaries, Algeria (until the civil war in 1991) and Morocco were the countries where the modernizing state sacrificed women's rights to appease the Islamist opposition. After the war of independence, Algerian women's movements gained some advances in political, social and economic rights (Sinha, 2014, 35). However, the family law especially was a subject of disagreement among the conservative and modernizing elites, as the status of women was the backbone of their respective political agendas. In 1984, the family law was passed to appease the rising Islamist movement, including controversial clauses on polygamy, the husband's right to denounce marriage leaving the women and children unprotected and even forced marriages (Charrad, 2001: 199). The rise of the Islamic Salvation Front and the civil war following the cancellation of the election in 1991 witnessed increasing violence towards women by the Islamists. However, women's movements continued their resistance through forming autonomous organizations such as the National Women's Coordination, Women Living under Muslim Law and Collectif 95 Maghreb Égalité.

Following Morocco's independence, the main Moroccan political parties, namely the Istiqlal Party and Democratic Party, formed women's branches. However, neither of these party-affiliated movements nor Princess Lalla Aicha's support for women's rights generated any significant progress. At the beginning of the 2000s, the new king Mohamed VI gave signs of possible change in women's status in the family and personal status law, although he immediately retreated when the Islamist Justice and Development Party (Parti de la Justice et du Développement (PJD), after the similarly named Turkish party) organized a huge rally to halt the process (Touti, 2014: 123–4). When the Casablanca bombings (May 2013) forced political Islamists to the political margins, the women's organizations in Morocco seized the opportunity for new laws improving women's conditions. In October 2003, the king authorized a new nationality law granting some equality for women in family (Touti, 2014: 125).

The examples from different southern Mediterranean regimes highlighted that women's bodies and identities were a fundamental arena of contestation of opposing political projects. This was another area where the secular–Islamist binary was dissolved; that is, secular, nationalist and socialist regimes claimed the ownership of female bodies to be disciplined, and through these disciplining practices, protected the moral essence (Islamism) of the society. Meanwhile, secular–Islamist binaries between the women's organizations were constructed and consolidated by the regimes, while the 'proper' secular women's movements were to be heard by the regimes at the expense of other types of women's organizations. Notwithstanding the important improvements on women's rights in these countries, these improvements were instruments of regime consolidation (Ben Ali's Tunisia and Mubarak's Egypt), while women's organizations found themselves cooperating with the regimes in order to advance women's rights, given the existing legal constraints. However, this did not prevent secular and Islamist movements from uniting against misogynistic laws (Jünemann, 2013: 46). It must also be noted that women's movements that explicitly positioned themselves against the political and economic agenda of the regimes were persecuted by the regimes, which instrumentalized women's bodies and identities as a practice of appeasing the opposition, as in the case of Morocco and, especially, Algeria.

In the mid-1990s, women's movements in the southern Mediterranean were struggling with civil, family and citizenship laws that hindered gender equality. They were also struggling with political, economic and social marginalization of women, as well as authoritarian governments that either appropriated women's causes for the state political agenda, or instrumentalized women's issues in their relations with the opposition. The European Union made its first entry into this political struggle in 1995.

The EU's first articulation of gender equality was integrated into the Euro-Mediterranean Partnership, established in 1995. This was a novel initiative through which the EU adopted a proactive foreign policy in cooperation not only with southern Mediterranean states, but also with economic groups and civil society. According to one view, its holistic approach reflected a 'gendered human security' approach that extended the security policies from narrowly defined military security to human, economic and political security (Harders, 2003). However, in spite of this holistic approach, women's issues were incorporated in the second basket (the economic partnership) only to promote the increasing role of women in development and employment, while the other two baskets did not include any clause about women or women's movements (Orbie, 2006: 62). This reductionist approach was attempted to be fixed from 2001 onwards by gender-mainstreaming the EMP. In 2001, the Commission and the EU presidency organized a high-level forum on 'the role of women in economic development'. The conclusions of the forum were endorsed by the Euro-Mediterranean foreign ministers and in 2004 the 'Regional Programme on Enhancing the Role of Women in Economic Life' was launched to allocate €5 million to finance women entrepreneurs (Orbie, 2006: 63–4). The EU's approach shifted towards increasing gender equality through economic development, not vice versa.

In 2004 the European Neighbourhood Policy (ENP) was launched, through which the 'women in development' approach of the EMP was replaced by a 'gender and development' approach. The latter refers to 'the integration of a gender equality perspective and gender equality aim into all policies, in an effort to transform society and obtain social justice for all people' (Debusscher, 2012: 323). The European Neighbourhood Instrument (ENI), as the new financial tool, was introduced with a priority area of 'gender equality promotion'. However, a detailed analysis of the ENP has shown very little transformation on women's issues from an economic perspective (Debusscher, 2012: 333). Given the lack of improvement in gender equality in the southern Mediterranean, the Euro-Mediterranean ministerial conference in Istanbul in 2006 created the 'Istanbul Process', with an action plan of €4.5 million. However, the focus was again on increasing the role of women in economic life. The process was marginal to wider political relations (Euro-Mediterranean Human Rights Network, 2009).

How did the women's movements relate to the EU's proactive economy-focused actorness? One of the primary implications of the new EU role in boosting civil society, including women organizations, has been 'NGO-ization' of the women's movements. According to Islah Jad (2004: 40-2), Arab women's movements have been going through a process in which establishing an NGO, rendering it attractive of EU or UN funding, and using the funds to 'educate' women have become main parameters of political activism. However, this has resulted in certain political and ethical problems. For example, NGOs often act like top-down agents of modern institutions. In addition to this, the organization of NGOs with a board and a director with English language skills is less inclusive and egalitarian than women's movements.

The EU's approach, however, suffers from deeper problems. According to extensive research by Debusscher (2012: 335), civil society voices have been critical of the reductionism of the EU that assumes causality between the free market economy and gender equality, while extremely important issues even in economic spheres, such as harassment in work places and unequal wages, have been ignored. Furthermore, in spite of the focus on 'gender', the EU's insistence solely on women has ignored the role of men in the reproduction of gender inequalities; and therefore, women have been represented as the only group with responsibility for creating the conditions of equality (Debusscher, 2012: 336). The EU's developmentalist approach certainly matched the neoliberalization process in southern Mediterranean countries. However, what kind of women's movements and to what extent they have benefited from this developmentalism remains an open question.

Another issue is the mismatch between the EU's prerogative and its approach to gender equality and women's movements' historically constructed struggles in their countries. It goes without saying that the economic promotion of women has been part of the agenda of women's movements, although this agenda involves more than an economic objective. As discussed previously, women's movements in the southern Mediterranean have struggled with laws and social norms that obscure gender equality by silencing and marginalizing women. Family laws, citizenship laws and civic laws have always been part of their political agenda. In their activism they often conflict with authoritarian regimes or social forces, whose contending political projects are realized through disciplining women's bodies and identities. However, the EU's relations with women's movements have been shaped in a way that has sidelined these historical political struggles, by prioritizing the economic dimension at the expense of others. Whenever the EU makes a move towards promoting gender equality even in economic terms, it is always followed by a clause that the recommended measures should be in line with religious and cultural values, exactly those against which women's movements have fought (Orbie, 2006: 64). While doing this, and thus adopting a culturalist approach, the EU chose to exclude Islamist women's organizations as partners (Jünemann, 2013: 47).

During this period, which ended finally with the Arab uprisings, the EU actively participated in gender politics by interacting with women's movements, providing financial resources and offering certain agendas. 'Europe' was no longer a model to be followed, a colonialist to be fought or cultural imperialist. Women's political struggles have been influenced by the EU as a donor and source of funding. The latter's cautious approach can be explained by the political objective of not invoking the colonial memories of western cultural imperialism and the imposition of certain values. However, this led to two problems: firstly, in relation to development and EU funding, colonial presence 'echoed' in women movements (Jad, 2004: 35); secondly, the EU's economy-oriented gender equality agenda did not always match that of women's movements, who were fighting family laws, oppressive politics and social norms. The next section will discuss how the Arab uprisings have affected these relations.

Women's movements in the post-Arab uprisings period

The uprisings, which started in Tunisia in 2010 and spread almost to the entire MENA region, were a turning point for Euro-Mediterranean politics due to the fall of certain authoritarian regimes and changing geopolitical dynamics (Syrian civil war, competition between Saudi Arabia and Iran). The uprisings were also fundamental for women's movements in wider Euro-Mediterranean politics. This importance does not stem from the orientalist point of view that Arab women had finally 'awakened' and broken their chains of conservatism. The discussion has so far highlighted how women's movements in the Euro-Mediterranean region had actively performed politics at societal, state and regional levels. What renders the uprisings a turning point for women's movements was that, for the first time since the anticolonial struggles, women with different identities and subjectivities interacted with each other, resisted together and formed a collectivity in occupied squares and streets. Secular, Islamist, nationalist and socialist feminists as well as women who did not identify with any of these ideologies not only talked to each other, but also developed trust between themselves by blurring the dichotomies created in the previous decades (Bilgic, 2015).

The uprisings are one episode in the prolonged historical process of women's movements in the region, as the developments during and after the uprisings underline that the political dynamics that shaped previous decades' women's activism still continue to operate in the region. For example, in Egypt, following the fall of the Mubarak regime, women and men who came together to celebrate International Working Women's Day were severely harassed. When most of them were placed under custody by the interim military government, women were forced to have 'virginity tests'; a supporter of compulsory tests from the government even argued that 'these girls are not like mine or your daughters. They stay with men in their tents on the square' (Abouelnaga, 2015: 43–4). This practice was also one of the 'secular' Mubarak government's practices towards the dissident women in the name of preserving the moral identity of the society by disciplining women, whose 'honour' and body was embodied in society.

Tunisia was another example where the authoritarian regime's legacy shaped the interim period between the revolution and the first free elections. In spite of the wide participation of women in the revolution, women were marginalized during this period. Dissident women were excluded from power positions, where only a few women (three at ministerial level, two of whom proceeded to resign) were 'allowed' (Khalil, 2015: 62). In spite of this, secular/left-wing women's organizations, such as the Tunisian Association of Democratic Women, and urban Islamist women movements, such as En-Nour from Tataouine, have become politically active (Khalil, 2015: 66–7). In Libya, women's civil society activism, such as that of the Libyan Women's Platform for Peace, secured 16.5 per cent female representation in the new parliament (Langhi, 2015: 73). The M20 movement in Morocco successfully campaigned and achieved a gender equality clause in Article 19 of the constitution (Touti, 2014: 130). That said, in some post-revolution states such as Egypt, the previously gained rights of women came under threat. The Mursi-led Muslim Brotherhood regime in Egypt not only resulted in less representation of women in politics, but also the new constitution included elements in direct conflict with women's rights and freedoms. Meanwhile, the women's movements' struggle continued (Morsy, 2015: 90–6).

As in previous decades, state feminism, divisions between different women's movements, and patriarchal regimes' desire to discipline women were still shaping regional politics. A difference may be that Islamist women's movements increasingly performed political activism. In Libya, after the revolution, Islamist women's movements such as Harakat Qalam, joined by the Muslim Brotherhood, ran a campaign against CEDAW; their objective was to replace gender equality with gender complementarity (Alnaas and Pratt, 2015: 161). However, it can be misleading to put all Islamist women's movements categorically in the same basket. For example, in Egypt, while the International Islamic Committee of Women and Children has promoted an anti-feminist agenda, Women and Civilization has explored 'an Islamic, feminist epistemology and a discourse that is critical of both patriarchal interpretations of Islam and secular perspectives' (Abou-Bakr, 2015: 195). In Tunisia, radical, democratic, and Islamic women's movements also compete and interact with each other, having common goals such as addressing violence against women (Muhanna, 2015). These encounters and interactions can deepen the ideological differences among the movements, but also indicate healthy democratic competition. Moreover, as in previous decades, the interpretation of Islam has remained a platform where different feminist perspectives compete with one another.

While the region has been changing, how has the EU positioned itself vis-à-vis the women's movements? The EU's main reaction was the formulation of the New European Neighbourhood Policy (NENP). In 2013, the Commission (2013) stated that:

> Cultural and social discrimination against women remains a problem in the Southern neighbourhood. Women played an active part in the revolutions. Now it is crucial that the transition process and constitutional reform do not hinder progress on, or undermine the equality of women before the law and in society.

Does this statement mean that the EU will retreat from the position of 'being sensitive to cultural differences'? Not necessarily. However, there is an *intention* that the EU will take a more active role in increasing political participation for women and supporting women's movements working towards this end (Robinson, 2013). This would correspond to the political agendas of most of the women's organizations discussed earlier during the post-uprisings period. However, caution is in order here. In a 2011 document, political participation of women was related to economic growth and job creation objectives (European Commission, 2011). In addition, 'Spring for Women', launched in 2012 with UN Women allocated €7.2 millon, largely focused on the economic empowerment of women through micro-financing. The former EU High Representative for Foreign Affairs and Security Policy, Catherine Ashton, similarly highlighted the role of microcredit in women's empowerment, thus following the pre-uprisings trend; she also opened the door to the possibility that the EU would be more influential in social discrimination through civil society support (Kunz and Maisenbacher, 2015: 13).

It is clear that during the post-uprisings period, the EU has engaged in some attempts to release gender equality from the narrowly defined economic agenda, with the objective of adressing the issue in its complexity. However, its success is questionable. Against the backdrop of colonial history and cultural neoimperalism accusations, it is a challenging task for the EU to promote its own agenda on gender. Additionally, if the EU decides to become more active, it will need to work with local women's movements. Then, the question would arise of which movements the EU would like to work with, given the rise in Islamist women's movements, without invoking its culturalist approach that excludes 'certain' women's movements as partners (Jünemann, 2013: 53). Finally, a recently published report by International Cooperation and Development (2015) on the behalf of the EU Commission revealed that the EU has not been giving necessary institutional support to gender equality in partner countries.

Conclusion

In this chapter, it has been argued that women's movements have been a constitutive dynamic of Euro-Mediterranean politics since the colonial period. Three conclusions can be derived from the analysis. The first is that, in all three periods, the European political, ideological and economic presence in the region has been one of the determinants of gender politics. Women have often found themselves in a position where they must praise or condemn 'Europe' in order to advance their struggles. The second theme is Islam, which defies the orientalist reading thereof. Islam has been one of the most important platforms through which women's movements performed their politics. Thirdly, given the ongoing struggles in the field, Euro-Mediterranean politics will continue to be shaped by the dynamics of gender and sex. Women's movements will remain one of the main groups of agents shaping, and being shaped by, this regional politics.

References

Abou-Bakr, O. (2015) Islamic Feminism and the Equivocation of Political Engagement: fair is foul, and foul is fair, in: M. El Said, L. Meari and N. Pratt (Eds), *Rethinking Gender in Revolutions and Resistance: lessons from the Arab world* (London: Zed).

Abouelnaga, S. (2015) Reconstructing Gender in Post-Revolution Egypt, in: M. El Said, L. Meari and N. Pratt (Eds), *Rethinking Gender in Revolutions and Resistance: lessons from the Arab world* (London: Zed).

Abu-Haidar, F. and D. Amrane-Minne (1999) Women and Politics in Algeria from the War of Independence to Our Day, *Research in African Literatures*, 30(3), 62–77.

Alnaas, S. M. and N. Pratt, (2015) Women's Bodies in Post-Revolution Libya, in: M. El Said, L. Meari and N. Pratt (Eds), *Rethinking Gender in Revolutions and Resistance: lessons from the Arab world* (London: Zed).

Badran, M. (1991) Competing Agenda: feminists, Islam, and the state in nineteenth- and twentieth-century Egypt, in: D. Kandiyoti (Ed.), *Women, Islam, and the State* (Basingstoke: Macmillan).

Baker, A. (1998) *Voices of Resistance: oral histories of Moroccan women* (New York: State University of New York Press).

Bilgic, A. (2015) 'Real People in Real Places': conceptualizing power for emancipatory security through Tahrir, *Security Dialogue*, 46(3), 272–90.

Bugaighis, W. (2014) Prospects for Women in the New Libya, in: M. S. Olimat (Ed.), *Arab Spring and Arab Women: challenges and opportunities* (London: Routledge).

Charrad, M. (2001) *State and Women's Rights: the making of postcolonial Tunisia, Algeria, and Morocco* (Los Angeles: University of California Press).

Debusscher, P. (2012) Mainstreaming Gender in European Union Development Policy in the European Neighbourhood, *Journal of Women, Politics and Policy*, 33, 323.

Euro-Mediterranean Human Rights Network (2009) Gender Equality in the Euro-Mediterranean Region: From Plan to Action?, Istanbul, 24–25 October Conference Report. Available at http://afem.itane.com/DOCUMENTS/Francais/Publications/ISTANBUL%20CONFERENCE%20REPORT%20 2009.pdf

European Commission (2011) A New Response to a Changing Neighbourhood, COM(2011) 303, Brussels.

European Commission (2013) European Neighbourhood Policy, Working towards a Stronger Partnership, JOIN (2013) 4 Final. Available at http://www.eeas.europa.eu/archives/docs/enp/pdf/docs/2013_enp_pack/2013_comm_conjoint_en.pdf

Hafez, S. (2015) The Revolution Shall Not Pass through Women's Bodies: Egypt, uprising, and gender politics, in: A. Khalil (Ed.), *Gender, Women and the Arab Spring* (London: Routledge).

Harders, C. (2003) Gender and Security in the Mediterranean, *Mediterranean Politics*, 8(2–3), 54–72.

International Cooperation and Development (Ed.) (2015), *Evaluation of EU Support to Gender Equality and Women's Empowerment in Partner Countries* (April). Available at https://ec.europa.eu/europeaid/sites/devco/files/evaluation-cooperation-ec-gender-1338-summary_en.pdf

Jad, I. (2004) The NGO-ization of Arab Women's Movements, *IDS Bulletin*, 35(4), 34–5.

Jünemann, A. (2013) Facing a Dilemma: the EU's promotion of gender-democracy after the 'Arab Spring', in: J. Horst, A. Jünemann, D. Rothe (Eds), *Euro-Mediterranean Relations after the Arab Spring: persistence in times of change* (Farnham: Ashgate).

Kandiyoti, D. (1991) End of Empire: Islam, nationalism, and women in Turkey, in: D. Kandiyoti (Ed.), *Women, Islam, and the State* (Basingstoke: Macmillan).

Khalil, A. (2015) Tunisia's Women: partners in revolution, in: A. Khalil (Ed.), *Gender, Women and the Arab Spring* (London: Routledge).

Kunz, R. and J. Maisenbacher, (2015) Women in the Neighbourhood: reinstating the European Union's civilising mission on the back of gender equality promotion?, *European Journal of International Relations*, 23(1), 122–44.

Langhi, Z. (2015) Gender and State-Building in Libya: towards a politics of inclusion, in: A. Khalil (Ed.), *Gender, Women and the Arab Spring* (London: Routledge).

Morsy, M. (2015) Egyptian Women and the 25th of January Revolution: presence and absence, in: A. Khalil (Ed.), *Gender, Women and the Arab Spring* (London: Routledge).

Muhanna, A. (2015) Islamic and Secular Women's Acitivism and Discourses in Post-Uprising Tunisia, in: M. El Said, L. Meari and N. Pratt (Eds) *Rethinking Gender in Revolutions and Resistance: lessons from the Arab world* (London: Zed).

Orbie, J. (2006) Gender in the Euro-Mediterranean Partnership, in: M. Lister and M. Carbone (Eds), *New Pathways in International Development Gender and Civil Society in EU Policy* (Aldershot: Ashgate).

Robinson, E. C. (2013) The Arab Spring: A litmus test for the EU's women's rights policy in the Euro-Mediterranean area, Bruges Regional Integration and Global Governance Papers, available at http://aei.pitt.edu/44512/

Sika, N. (2014) An Egyptian Spring for Women?, in: M. S. Olimat (Ed.), *Arab Spring and Arab Women: challenges and opportunities* (London: Routledge).

Sinha, S. (2014) Gender Empowerment in Algeria, in: M. S. Olimat (Ed.), *Arab Spring and Arab Women: challenges and opportunities* (London: Routledge).

Touti, Z. (2014) The Struggle for Women's Rights in Morocco, in: M. S. Olimat (Ed.), *Arab Spring and Arab Women: challenges and opportunities* (London: Routledge).

29

YOUTH ACTIVISM AND PROTEST AROUND THE MEDITERRANEAN

Emma C. Murphy

The political landscape around the Mediterranean has been marked over the last decade by the increased visibility of youth-based social movements. Whether the scale and coherence of these movements has impacted in a transformational way upon specific political contexts or not, it seems fair to argue that any previous consensus on the 'de-politicization of the younger generations' (Benedicto, 2013: 712) now seems severely outdated.

The upsurge in activism reflects a set of shared and inter-linked experiences at a point in time when the problematic implications of neo-liberal orthodoxy on the distribution of wealth and prospects between generations have been foregrounded by profound economic crises and an era of austerity. Youth have exhibited declining levels of trust in the formal political structures and institutions of their national politics, which is hardly surprising since these appear to offer no effective avenues of resistance to the erosion of their prospects. Even so, their increased mobilization indicates that significant cohorts of youth are active political subjects, even if their engagement has not been through the formal electoral and party participation which marks conventional understandings of what it means to be political.

This chapter elaborates on the commonalities to be found in the youth experiences which have driven the wave of activism around the Mediterranean space. Subsequent analysis of the specific trajectories of youth-based social movements in southern Europe, the eastern and the southern Mediterranean countries illustrates, however, that – while the trigger events and consequent political participation were context specific – youth were often the most substantial and visible component of broader social movements, as defined by Della Porta and Diani (1999: 16): 'a collection of informal networks, based on shared beliefs of solidarity, which mobilize around conflictual interests through the frequent use of various forms of protest'. Often the vanguard, but profoundly intersected by other identities, youth assumed a symbolic role in social movements but neither their interests nor agency were necessarily distinct or exclusive.

Shared political exclusion

It might seem more intuitive to suggest that youth in democratic Europe should be studied separately from their southern Mediterranean peers in non-democratic environments – that youth in Spain would be better placed in an ordering category which included its northern EU partners like Germany rather than with north African Tunisia, Egypt or Morocco. However, evidence suggests that the Mediterranean is a shared (but by no means unique) space for youth in terms of the exclusionary experiences which are propelling them into political action.

In 2013, José Ignacio Torreblanca and Hélène Michou remarked on an 'unexpected Mediterranean convergence', a growing democracy deficit in southern Mediterranean countries which more closely aligned them with authoritarian or transition regimes in their north African and eastern Mediterranean neighbours than with northern Europe (Torreblanca and Michou, 2013: 148). They argued that the origins of this lay in part with the securitization of political institutions and agendas post 9/11 which side-lined democratic imperatives in favour of national security. For the populations of southern Mediterranean countries, this turned into increasingly repressive authoritarian rule, and a profound alienation from political institutions consumed by corruption and cronyism. Even when populations rose up and replaced their dynastic rulers, democracy found poor soil and a harsh climate. Institutions proved highly resistant to meaningful reform, external powers were preoccupied with issues of security, populations were polarized and fearful of political pluralism. The region thus continues to experience a freedom deficit.

In southern Europe the Eurozone financial crisis and the imposition of brutal austerity measures mired national governments, as well as the EU itself, in a crisis of democratic governance. The excruciating social costs of adjustment measures could not be resisted through democratic political systems: all were subordinate to the logic and demands of liberal capitalism and its banking elites.

> Forcing governments to systematically violate their own election promises and push through the same policies regardless of their political leaning also undermines the legitimacy of national political institutions. As witnessed in countries that have been bailed out, political systems are wearing out (as in Spain and Portugal) or breaking down (as in Greece and Italy).
>
> *(Torreblanca, 2013)*

Unsurprisingly then, Jover et al. (2014: 4) are able to refer to 'recent empirical literature, which has highlighted the links between the economic crisis and the erosion of trust in political institutions and representative democracy in different contexts'.

Young people suffer disproportionately from dysfunctional formal institutional arrangements which fail to deliver on their democratic promises. Unable to penetrate the tiers of political elites dominated by a previous generation, their specific agendas and interests do not find a hearing. For young people around the Mediterranean, this has become a growing source of frustration as a shared subordination of national economies to global liberal capitalism has impacted most intensely on themselves.

Socio-economic youth exclusion

Perhaps the most often highlighted aspect of this is the significantly higher levels of unemployment, under-employment and labour precariousness which young people suffer compared to older cohorts. This is true of both southern European and southern Mediterranean countries, albeit to differing degrees.

> Even before the economic crisis of 2008 each of those countries [France, Greece, Italy, Portugal and Spain] already had higher unemployment rates than the EU average. During and after the crisis youth unemployment increased sharply, especially in Greece

> and Spain. At the end of 2012 youth unemployment was above 50 percent in both countries, 55.0 percent in Spain and even 58.1 percent in Greece. The rate in Italy and Portugal was almost 40 percent.
>
> *(Eichhorst and Neder, 2014: 3)*

Young people in the 15–24 year old age group were particularly vulnerable, and NEET rates (those between 15 and 24 not in education, employment or training) rose to levels of 19 per cent in Spain by 2012, 21.1 per cent in Italy, and 20.3 per cent in Greece, all well above the EU average.

If Turkey and Israel exhibited relatively low rates of youth unemployment for 15–24 year olds, at 15.7 per cent and 10.7 per cent respectively, official figures for Egypt, Palestine and Tunisia stood at 18.9 per cent, 41.0 per cent and 31.2 per cent respectively. NEET rates were similarly high at 35.3 per cent (Egypt), 32.0 per cent (Palestine) and 25.4 per cent (Tunisia) (Bardak et al., 2015: 18). The realities of regional disparities and under-reporting, especially of females, meant that the real figures are likely to have been higher.

Analysts have attributed these figures not just to the impact of the financial crisis, but to deeper problems which create a mismatch between demand and supply in the labour markets. Education systems are rigid, offering low-quality education and poorly preparing young people for the demands of the workplace; active labour market programmes are under-developed and under-funded; minimum wages raise the payment costs of the least well-paid (usually young) workers making them relatively costly to employ, and the high costs of labour protection deter employers from moving new entrants to the labour market onto formally contracted work. As Castel puts it: 'Youth is at the epicentre of the expansion of precarious forms of labour' (Castel 2006, quoted in Sotiris, 2010: 204). The Arab countries of the southern Mediterranean undoubtedly fared worse in terms of long-term structural employment problems due to weak macroeconomic policies, poor governance, cronyism and poor integration into the global economy. Moreover, population growth rates in southern Mediterranean countries had been some of the highest in the world during the 1980s and 1990s, leading to a very substantial youth bulge such that they will require more than 1.5 million new jobs to be created every year for the coming decade (Ermsone, 2015: 6).

In all these countries, it is evident that unemployment and labour precariousness are not confined to the illiterate youth or those with only a few years of schooling. University graduates disproportionately experience high unemployment and under-employment, representing a poor return on national investments in education and illustrating further the structural features of economies which are unable to attract the high-added value investments which would enable them to move up the global ladders of production and exchange.

As the possibilities for secure, long-term employment appeared to be diminishing for the young, so too the neo-liberal retrenchment of the state and retreat from its welfarist commitments were eroding their potential to achieve financial independence, pushing them back into dependence on the family and informal solidaristic networks. The neo-liberal turn has created a fracture between the life experiences and expectations of generations, and a profound sense of inter-generational injustice marked by a narrative of systemic failure (Murphy, 2012).

To simply reproduce statistics is to miss the bigger picture for young people whose economic marginalization leads directly into a wider set of social exclusions. Hilary Silver, in a comparative analysis of European and Middle Eastern youth (Silver, 2007), set out even before the 2008 financial crisis the multiple ways in which youth from the two regions shared the lack of access to social opportunity. As well as unemployment and diminishing state support, young people experienced extended education, delayed marriage, prolonged dependence on the family and a delayed transition to a state of adulthood, with all its socially and geographically contextualized markers. Lacking the status of adults, they have been deprived of the non-material dimensions of social inclusion: they are unrepresented in social and political forums and their interests are given low value. The material aspects of unemployment, poverty and dependence are reinforced by multiple other exclusionary practices and vice versa, although individual youth experiences are intersected by other categories such as national or regional context, gender, class, race or religion.

This multi-dimensional social and economic marginalisation not surprisingly coincides with, and reinforces, political exclusion. This is not simply about distrust of political institutions that fail to recognize the needs and interests of young people. It is also a reflection of alterations in the political socialization processes instigated more or less globally in the late-capitalist era. Late modern life has witnessed the de-institutionalization of socialization processes. The role played by family, church (or mosque), school, trade union, political party and state in establishing the norms, expectations and behaviours of young people has been eroded by the fetish of individualism on the one hand and the logic of the market on the other. Consequently the young generation do not experience a relationship with politics in the way their parents did.

> The socialized individual who fulfilled demands derived from several roles has made way for the individual who is obliged to construct their own life through reflexivity and justify their behaviour and who maintains a critical distance with respect to groups, norms and role . . . By means of their action, the individual gradually builds themselves as a subject, learning to orientate themselves in an uncertain and fragmented world without clear reference points . . . In this new environment where the individual is obliged to be the author of socialization, relationships with politics do not constitute a component taken for granted of the integration process of young people into adult life.
>
> *(Benedicto, 2013: 714)*

One significant consequence of all this is the blurring of the boundaries of the social category of 'youth'. Biological criteria cease to be reliable since the social conditions of the stage between childhood and adulthood are not neatly determined by physical age. Youth is better understood as a state-of-being as much as transition, a social condition wherein an individual is no longer identified by surrounding society as a dependent child and yet full material independence and personal autonomy have yet to be achieved.

It is fair to say then that young people around the Mediterranean have shared experiences of social, economic and political exclusion, albeit differentially according to their unique intersectional identities and the specificities of geographic context. The last decade has witnessed the exacerbation of this exclusion as the global financial crisis has deepened the material vulnerability of young people and reduced the opportunities open to them. In the absence of trust in established political institutions and pathways for participation, young people have found their own ways to voice their demands for change.

Southern Europe

In southern Europe, youth movements have largely cohered around socio-economic agendas, at least to start with, and have become a vanguard for broader swathes of populations traumatized by prolonged neo-liberal measures and the scale of recent economic crises. Government reforms to education systems and labour laws have been particular triggers for protest since they symbolize the supremacy of markets over welfare. Consequently student and youth-based movements have worked in close coalitions with trade unions and leftist political groups.

In February 2006, French university students joined with workers to protest reforms to the labour market which would have made it easier for employers to fire young workers. This convergence was repeated in April 2016, although the agenda was by now widened as the Nuit debout (rise up at night) protests saw the Place de la Républic occupied by tents, sing-alongs and denunciations of everything from Google to tax evasion. The protests were led by young people but they were joined by pensioners, artists and others who shared their wider concerns.

The youth-worker alliance was also a feature of the 2008 protests in Greece. These were triggered by the killing of 15-year-old Alexis Grigoropoulos by a special police unit. Although this was not the first incidence of police brutality, the victim was the youngest, and school children and university students took to the streets in an outpouring of rage which simultaneously articulated their rejection of a proposed package of educational reforms. The reforms 'produced a widespread feeling of insecurity with respect to young people's prospects' (Sotiris, 2010: 205) and resonated with workers' unions concerned with high unemployment and under-employment rates, worsening pay and conditions, rising indebtedness, reforms to the pension system and privatizations. 'Police violence worked as a metonymy for all kinds of systemic pressure and violence facing Greek youth today' (Sotiris, 2010: 206). The protests articulated a new collective identity among Greek youth, the so-called 700 euro generation, a reference to the expectation that a graduate is lucky to find a job paying €700 a month (Kaimaki, 2009: 2).

The protests matured into a critique of the political institutions that had overseen the evolution of economic crisis, specifically the dominance of three political dynastic families, the rotation of power between just two political parties (New Democracy on the right and PASOK on the left) for over 30 years and the corruption within them.

Political parties previously at the margins of politics were now able to capitalize on the youth mobilization. The most successful was Golden Dawn, which constructed a xenophobic discourse blaming immigration for unemployment and rejecting the post-1974 political system entirely. Barely able to muster one town councillor in 2010, by 2012 it was enjoying electoral gains in national elections by presenting itself as a party of, and for, Greek youth. Exit polls suggested that the vote for Golden Dawn was higher among youth than the population as a whole. Only the new Syriza radical leftist coalition won more youth votes. Syriza, originally a small intellectualist party, grew through engagement of its horizontal networks with the anti-austerity agenda, expanding its electoral appeal well beyond the traditional hard-core left to become the second largest winner in 2012.

In Spain, according to Jover et al. (2014: 9), the mobilization of youth built on the circulation of two key texts; Stèphane Hessel's book, *Time for Outrage* (2011) and Rosa Maria Artal's edited collection of essays, *React* (2011). The books called for peaceful citizen insurrection to protest against the crises of modern society. They pulled diverse issues – the widening income gap, the diminished welfare state, corruption, the lack of a genuinely free press, a degraded environment, the treatment of illegal immigrants – into a narrative of institutional and capitalist failure, inspiring groups such as Democracia real ya, (real democracy now) to call for a day of protest on 15 May 2011 in advance of the Spanish elections. The first protest ended with the occupation of the Puerta del Sol, the main square in Madrid. Tent camps soon sprang up in public spaces in other cities, the movement – which became known as the 15-M or Indignados – bringing together many existing citizen groups and platforms as well as new activists, and being organized principally through social media. In the 2012 municipal and regional elections the proportion of young people exercising their vote was much as usual. However, a significant proportion (41.8 per cent) claimed the movement influenced *how* they voted (Jover et al., 2014: 9), the result being a decline in votes for the two main parties, especially the Spanish Socialist Workers' Party then in power. By 2014, youth activists had cohered around a new leftist party which they saw as largely their own, Podemos (We Can), around a 10-point critique of neo-liberal capitalism and aiming to reclaim what they see as 'constituent' or common power. The party recruited 100,000 members in 20 days, a figure which tripled in the next 15 months (*Público*, 17 August 2014) – by which time Podemos had 5 representatives in the European Parliament – but which still proved insufficient to bring the party to national power. As with Golden Dawn in Greece, not all Indignados saw the future in the reform of the existing political system. In late 2012 more radical elements set up the Plataforma ¡En Pie! ('Stand up!' Platform), which demanded the dissolution of parliament and a transition towards a different political model.

In Italy, a first wave of protests in February 2011 focused on the corrupt and illegal practices of the prime minister, Silvio Berlusconi, then caught up in three separate trials over allegations of vice and business misconduct. Protests in over 200 towns and cities saw youth joining with women's organizations to express outrage at the premier's involvement in a sex scandal. But the protest agenda widened when Berlusconi introduced an austerity plan, and raised taxes and healthcare costs even as the youth unemployment rate reached 28 per cent. In October 2011 a 'day of rage' saw over 200,000 people take to the streets. Berlusconi was forced to resign. His successors, Mario Monti, Enrico Letta and Matteo Renzi, have all sought to impose austerity budgets and public sector and labour reforms, none of which have revived the economy or created jobs for the growing legions of young unemployed. In 2013, youth and big business lined up against budget proposals which froze public sector wages but failed to cut oppressive corporate taxes, and in December 2014 students were marching with trade unions against the Jobs Act which cancelled protection against unfair dismissal.

Conventional political youth movements such as the Federation of Italian Communist Youth worked closely with trade unions in coordinated protests, while new groups such as the Centro Sociale Occupato Autogestitos (social centres) established communal squats in public spaces, bringing young people together with the wider population – including immigrants and the elderly – in collectivist efforts at local and social regeneration. The social centres were not always welcomed by local communities, which referred to their activists as communists, hippies or anarchists, and were made scapegoats for the frequent violence into which protests became mired (Amodeo-Vickery, 2011). With the main political parties understood to be corrupt and ineffective, young voters turned to new parties such as the Movimento Cinque Stelle (Five Star Movement), the name of which refers to key issues (public water, sustainable transport, sustainable development, right to internet access and environmentalism). The movement, which claims not to be a party as such, was established in 2009 by Beppe Grillo (a comedian and blogger) and Gianroberto Casaleggio (a web strategist), proposing a populist, anti-establishment, anti-globalist and Euro-sceptic agenda, endorsing direct democracy as an alternative to the dysfunctional national political system. In the 2013 national election the movement won the second largest number of votes for the Chamber of Deputies. Notably, in the 15–34 age group, 31 per cent of votes went to Five Star (Millennial Dialogue, 2016). A further 29 per cent voted for the Partito Democratico, the main Italian centre-left party, but the party's youth have not been captive to the agendas of their elders. After the elections in 2013, youth activists staged an occupation within the party headquarters in a number of districts under the name OccupyPD, demanding greater accountability of the leaders, more transparency within the party, the democratization of party structures and closer alignment with the anti-austerity agenda (Della Porta and Chironi, 2015: 60–1).

Podemos and OccupyPD demonstrate the potential for the overlap between social movements and political parties, suggesting that to argue that young people have rejected formal politics in southern Europe in favour of social movements is to over-simplify the complexities of efforts to formulate a new politics against a backdrop of mistrust of the old. However, it also remains the case in Italy, as in Spain and Greece, that younger cohorts are more likely to engage in unconventional forms of political participation such as demonstrations and social movements and less likely to be involved in political parties than older cohorts, creating an ever greater problem of representation (Quaranta, 2015: 806).

Eastern Mediterranean

If the activism of youth movements in southern Europe has been a response to declining faith in the capacity of democratic institutions to respond to economic crisis, in the eastern Mediterranean – where democratic models are tested by alternative religiously based political discourses, severe ethnic cleavages and the insecurity of the nation-state itself – youth activists have had to negotiate a more complex political terrain.

In Israel the quality of democracy for citizens is constrained by their ethnic or national status (Yiftachel, 2006). By July 2011, Israel too was experiencing a protest wave in which youth played a leading part. A 25-year-old woman, no longer able to afford her rent, set up a tent on the swanky Rothschild Street in Tel Aviv and announced the fact to her friends on Facebook. Within two days, there were 50 tents, within two weeks 400 in over 40 towns and cities. Youth and student organizations spread the word by Facebook, blocking roads and holding sit-ins in prominent locations. Young people were joined by other activist groups including parents, taxi-drivers, lifeguards, dairy farmers, lecturers and anarchists, and the protests included not just the working class oriental Jewish population, the backbone of previous protest movements, but middle class Ashkenazi Jews and some Israeli Arabs as well. At their height, and with the support of mainstream and social media, opinion polls found that 87 per cent of Israelis endorsed the protests. What had started as a protest against house purchase and rental prices expanded to include a wide range of demands that amounted to a radical reversal of economic policy, including reconstruction of the welfare state, a bill of rights for citizens, and a re-drawing of the tax system in favour of the working and middle classes rather than the cartels and monopolies run by the so-called '20 leading families' (Doha Institute, 2011).

A Protest Movement Committee and the National Tents Council emerged, working closely with the National Union of University Students and the Dror Israel Youth Movement (which had emerged out of the Labour Party), with decisions being taken by consensus and a clear commitment to remaining independent of political parties, both ideologically and financially. The decision to remain apolitical was vital to retain inclusivity: it was notable that they refrained from ever using the words occupy or occupation, preferring not to ignite sensitivities over the Israeli occupation of Palestinian lands, and rejecting notions of the movement as revolutionary since this might imply a rejection of Zionism itself and thereby fragment the coalition of left and right, or set Jews against Arabs. In sum, the fragility of the democratic claims of the political institutions inhibited a fundamental transference of socio-economic protest into the party political arena.

In Turkey, youth was a key component of the political culture which arose out of the nation and state-building process. A myth of youth had been built around the leaders who founded the republic in 1923, reproduced in the 1960s and 1970s through ideologically driven activism. The military coup in 1980 led to a de-politicization of society as well as the early neo-liberalization of the economy, during which time the apparent acquiescence of youth led to criticism that they were no longer living up to their assigned role. A new myth evolved of their supposed apathy and materially determined cultural identity, one which Lűkűslű fiercely contests (Lűkűslű, 2014).

She argues that, far from being uninterested, Turkish youth were highly critical of designated political spaces and distrustful of authoritarian and corrupt parties. But whilst they rejected conventional political spaces, they were politically active in choosing new spaces – in particular the Internet and social media.

In May 2013 their activism erupted as they took to the streets to protest against an urban management project in Istanbul which would have destroyed the Gezi public park and replaced it with a shopping mall. The project symbolized everything about the ruling AKP that was problematic for Istanbouli youth: its imposition (and the brutal police repression used against early protesters) signified the co-optation of corrupt, self-serving political elites into global capitalist networks. The protests were led by young people, not *against* the older generations (since they were themselves embedded in broader coalitions which included all age groups) but in part *on their behalf*. Turkish youth thus regained its vanguard status, coming together around the convergence of issue politics: environmentalism, anti-capitalism, civil rights and the defence of the individual. The movement was self-consciously democratic, in contrast to the personalization of power around the AKP's President Erdoğan.

The Gezi movement triggered a broader revival of grass-roots activism. With the traditional socialist left no longer a reference point, activists regrouped through new progressive forces located in horizontally structured organizations such as the workers' movement Başlangıç (The Beginning) or the 10danSonra (Past 10) movement. These were active in the run up to the parliamentary elections in 2015, urging leftists, liberals, LGBTQ and Kurdish oppositionists to unite in support of the People's Democratic Party (HDP) – long viewed as an essentially Kurdish party – in an effort to win at least 10 per cent of the seats and so stymie the president's efforts to change the constitution in favour of presidentialism (Goyette, 2015). Thus, youth movements in Turkey have mirrored their counterparts in Europe in creating coalitions of resistance to established structures and institutions which are inclusive of diverse identities and unencumbered by ideological divisions. The danger, of course, is that such coalitions can withstand the onslaught of established power but, once 'liberated', lack the glue to hold together through institutional rebuilding and policy decision-making.

Perhaps nowhere are the problems of this glue more pertinent than Lebanon which, despite having a tradition of student protest going back to the 1960s, has seen sectarian crisis consistently mitigating against nationwide youth solidarity. During the civil war youth was mobilized around, and divided by, sectarian community identities. In 2005 in the so-called Cedar Revolution, youth protesters were prominent in the large-scale protests against the Syrian occupation which had lasted for the best part of 30 years, demanding the removal of the pro-Syrian Karami government, an international commission to investigate the assassination of the former prime minister, Rafiq Hriri, the withdrawal of Syrian troops and free parliamentary elections. But no sooner had the Syrians retreated, than protesters divided once again along sectarian lines: the March 8 Movement led by Hezbollah's Hassan Nasrallah mobilizing Shia support for a pro-Syrian government and the March 14 Alliance, led by Hriri's son, demanding independence and recovered sovereignty. In 2011, inspired by events in Tunisia and Egypt and responding to Hezbollah's toppling of Saad Hriri's government, youth protesters returned to the street demanding an end to sectarianism. The initial agenda soon morphed into a range of demands including an end to rape and sexual violence against women, freedom of expression, the right to civil marriage and the lowering of the voting age.

But the reality of Lebanese politics meant their protests gained little real traction as regional power politics proved more salient determinants of domestic politics. In 2015 youth movements tried again by focusing on a shared everyday frustration, the piling up of uncollected trash on the streets. Their slogan – *You Stink* – referred as much to the corruption of political elites as to the garbage itself. The inability of political elites to negotiate through their sectarian disagreements, or to constrain their own avaricious self-enrichment, had led to gridlock in the provision of public utilities (Khoury, 2016: 3). The situation was compounded by disagreements on a new electoral law and an inability to comprise a stable government for any length of time. The new movement 'transcends all denominations, gathering young people from different religions and sects and calling for the removal of both literal and symbolic garbage' (Nader, 2015). But while it has had some successes in forcing the government to reopen files against corrupt politicians, to declare the establishment of a corruption observatory and even to put forward a comprehensive waste management plan, the movement has been weakened by the violence of some of its members and infiltrators from the sectarian parties. Maintaining the broad appeal attached to representing the everyday socio-economic frustrations of Lebanese youth requires a careful dance around other sensitivities which threaten at every turn to disrupt the solidarity needed to truly take back the streets for Lebanese citizens.

The Arab Spring

In Arab North Africa, where authoritarian rule over many decades has hollowed out formal institutions, the political participation of youth was until 2011 effectively contained within corporatist extensions of official parties, student, trade union and youth organizations. While youth played significant roles through these organizations at particular points in the narrative history of post-independence state-building, and despite common regime discourses which portrayed youth as 'being at the forefront of the forces of progress embracing noble universal values' (Morjane, 2010: 3) or 'pillars of the nation' (Ali and El-Sharnouby, 2014: 89), meaningful participation was stymied by securitized political structures and the absence of substantive rights. However, the younger generation was rapidly becoming the majority of the population and – as economic stagnation and staggering levels of youth unemployment took their toll on not just prospects for the future but the capacity to simply survive on a day-to-day basis – the tolerance of the young of their political exclusion was dramatically eroded.

Youth were visibly at the forefront of the protests in Tunisia in December 2010 which were initially an instinctive empathetic response to the self-immolation of a street vendor in the small town of Sidi Bouzid, described by Juan Cole as 'a typical Arab millennial' (Cole, 2014: 126). Bullied and harassed by police and officials, unable to continue even this meagre living, his life mirrored those of educated and uneducated, rural and urban youth alike, and his death unleashed a torrent of youth activism. The protesters soon connected with established civil society solidarities, and drew inspiration from the youth activism sweeping across southern and central Europe. Throughout the revolution and its transitional aftermath, Tunisian youth movements flourished, proliferating and formalizing around agendas designed to keep the momentum of political reform alive. Their street protests and online activism provided the backdrop to the efforts by the post-Ben Ali government to meet the demands of a Higher Committee for the Achievement of the Objectives of the Revolution, itself comprised largely of civil society and opposition political party representatives. But as the country moved towards elections in October 2011 young people had to decide how they would participate in the emerging political processes. As old and new political parties demonstrated a continued preference for paternalistic organization, youth organizations focused on holding politics to account rather than direct participation. Youth were active as election observers (Mourakiboun, Réseau Ofiya, Jeunesse sans Frontières and I-Watch Tunisia) (Honwana, 2013) and established effective information, monitoring and lobbying organizations promoting accountable, transparent politics (OpenGovTn, the Jeunes Indépendent Democrats and Sawt Chabeb Tounes). Just two weeks before the 2011 elections, it was estimated that only 17 per cent of eligible youth had registered to vote (McCurdy, 2011: 17), a pattern of non-participation that has been sustained through subsequent parliamentary and presidential elections (IRI, 2014). Today Tunisian youth activism is concentrated on social entrepreneurship, creative activities and educational opportunities. Their digital nativism, ably displayed in the 2011 Uprising, has continued to provide them with communicative space, but post-2014 government initiatives designed to counter Islamist violence have seen the contraction of conventional associational space. In a tragically disappointing denouement to the Uprising, the alternatives for youth have increasingly become recruitment into radical Islamist movements that promise not least some material reward, or emigration.

A wave of youth mobilization in Egypt had preceded the Tunisian uprising by several years. Youth were visible political activists in 2004, when the Kefaya (Enough) movement emerged out of pro-Palestinian and anti-Iraq war protests. A second wave of youth activism, including a branching out of Kefaya into the Youth for Change movement, was prompted by political reforms which groomed the president's son for succession and installed a cabinet comprised of his crony business allies. Youth activists allied themselves with the Muslim Brotherhood in opposing constitutional reforms and the emergency law, publicly demonstrating in the street and directly criticizing the president. They led political protests against rigged elections in 2005 and supported striking textile workers in Mahalla-al-Kubra in 2008, leading to the emergence of the April 6 Movement. The latter was notable for its Facebook presence which attracted tens of thousands of followers very quickly and showed how youth could occupy a new political space where they had the advantages of their digital skills. In 2010, when a young man was killed in police custody, Facebook was used again to establish the We are all Khaled Said (WAAKS) movement.

'The deteriorating economic conditions and closing political space kept the grievances high' (Lynch, 2012; Ali and El-Sharnouby, 2014: 91) so that, as the Tunisian uprising was sweeping away Ben Ali, Egyptian youth were already visible, competent and committed. As well as embedding their street politics in groups such as the Revolutionary Youth Coalition and the Revolution Continues, young Egyptians also turned to political parties. When old parties failed to internalize their demands, youth splinter parties were formed, such as Hezb Al-Tayyar Al-Masry (the Egyptian Current), which split from the Muslim Brotherhood in 2011, and youth were instrumental in the founding of parties like the Egyptian Social Democratic Party (Hellyer, 2016: 134). In 2013, many youth movements also aligned themselves with the Tamarod (Rebel) movement which demanded an end to Islamist Mohammed Morsi's rule and (ironically) cleared the path for a military coup d'état.

Ultimately Egyptian youth (and it is worth remembering that nearly 60 per cent of Egypt's population fall between the ages of 10 and 24) were unable to translate their formidable social mobilization into a consensus on the political path post-Mubarak. The multiple acts of protest did not amount to a strategy for political action which could resist the embedded power of the older generation of political elites or act as a unifying glue. Secker recounts how, when Muslim Brotherhood supporters took to occupying protest camps at Rabaa and al-Nahda, progressive young Islamists despaired at

> the unreconstructed sheikhs who insisted on preaching sectarian hatred about Christians and other supposed traitors to Morsi, rather than speaking about democracy and human rights. They shared a joke on Facebook: 'Please God, let these sheikhs have the honour of being martyred first.'
>
> *(Secker, 2016: 4)*

Under the presidency of Al-Sissi the space for youth activism has contracted, legal avenues for dissent have narrowed, and young people have found themselves again in prison. They have not engaged significantly with regime performances such as the constitutional referendum, are largely uninterested in regime-orchestrated dialogues, and are increasingly visible as either migrants or members of violent groups such as the pro-football Ultras (Hellyer, 2016: 137).

Youth movements elsewhere in North Africa have had even less long-term impact despite moments of high visibility. In Morocco protesters took to the streets in February 2011. Tens of thousands of young people in cities across the country held public 'general assemblies' to demand democratic reform, the rule of law, social justice and an end to corruption. The so-called February 20 Movement comprised diverse groups, including members of political parties such as the Baraka youth wing of the Islamist Justice and Development Party and the Omar Ben Jelloun group from the youth wing of the Socialist Union of Popular Forces (Desrues, 2012: 34) and of unaffiliated CSOs such as the anti-globalization ATTAC Maroc and the League of Young Unemployed Graduates. Websites and Facebook groups such as Mamfakinch (No Concession) claimed to be inclusive of a range of political affiliations united by a shared belief in democratic values and human rights. The king seemed quick to respond, promising consultation on speedy constitutional reform and releasing a number of political prisoners. The February 20 leaders refused to participate in the consultation and rejected the reforms ultimately proposed. However, the referendum showed widespread support for the monarch's proposals among the more conservative older generations and, whilst the implementation of the revised constitution has offered some small concessions to the balance of power between monarch and parliament, the reality has been a consolidation of power by the political establishment (*makhzen*) and an erosion of the February 20 Movement's traction among the wider body-politic.

In Algeria, where 70 per cent of the population falls under the age of 30, 2011 also witnessed a wave of youth protests and activism including the formation of the Mouvement de la Jeunesse Independente pour le Changement. However, the regime proved adept at confronting what was frequently violent opposition. Popular frustrations over the poor education system, unemployment, high food costs and inadequate housing infrastructure were met with a series of hand-outs funded by the country's hydrocarbon wealth, while calls for political change were met with a carrot-and-stick policy of constitutional reform and harsh political clamp-down. Ultimately only the student movement had the organizational structures and reach to sustain large-scale protests, so youth activism moved increasingly online. To some extent it cohered around a youth-based political party, the Jil Jadid (New Generation). The party has sustained relations with numerous other opposition movements around an agenda for democratic reform but its potential to translate into a significant force is limited. The public face is very much its leader, Djalali, repeating old traditions of personalized politics, and it lacks a clear and precise platform for policy innovation.

The outlook in Libya is bleakest of all. Libyan youth were at the forefront of the uprising against Muammar Gaddafi. Even diaspora youth played their part, through the online support forum of the Shebab Libya (Libyan Youth Movement). Initially youth were celebrated as the driving force for change, but as the uprising disintegrated into fractious division, youth became associated with armed groups, militia and Islamist militants. As Libyan political elites pursue a power struggle among themselves, youth have once again been marginalized and demonized, with effectively no public space other than social media open to them.

A regression into the 'youth as problem' paradigm has been the corollary of the regime securitization impelled by Islamist violence in North Africa. The brief moment in which youth movements were fêted as being the generation which would assume responsibility for national renovation, appears to have passed. Their ambivalence towards, or self-imposed absence from, the formal political arena does little to reassure older generations that they are ready or able to fill positions of leadership or develop credible policy options. At the same time, they continue to be excluded from those institutions which could offer meaningful routes to full participation and remain subject to the impositions of authoritarian modes of rule and failed economic strategies.

Conclusion

As the narratives above demonstrate, the new wave of youth activism around the Mediterranean has manifested itself in two discernible trends: through the evolution of horizontal social movements and mass protests, on the one hand, and through efforts to alter the terrain of formal politics by presenting new (or reviving old) political parties, on the other. Young people have become important components of what Castells (2012) terms the new 'networks of outrage and hope'. The trans-Mediterranean sharing of strategies and tactics, and the solidarities expressed for one another's struggles, have been indicative of the global structural challenges referred to at the start of this chapter (Murphy, 2012: 18–19) and were evidence not just of an Internet-fuelled learning process but of the fact that Mediterranean youth have identities which are shaped by neither national boundaries nor by the distinct life experiences of previous generations. They recognize the commonalities of their fates.

However, the narrative of youth activism set out here suggests that, so far, youthful political activisms have served largely as spheres of dissidence (Aouragh and Alexander, 2011) and resistance (Castells, 2012: 56). Whilst they have represented sites in which autonomous organization and deliberative artistic and political creativity could take place, they could not in themselves capture power from the formal political institutions. Youth-based movements have disruptive power; they can mobilize, resist and interject new discourses. But only when they have engaged in formal competitive politics have they relocated their voice into the spaces where decision-making takes place and – in doing so – they lose much of their energy, scale and plurality.

Nonetheless, political institutions and elites ignore them at their peril. Today's youth-based movements are simply the most visible and noisy elements of a much wider tide of popular resistance to the status quo, representing far more than a narrow youth agenda and indicating that the system itself needs fixing. The problems will only grow as today's youth mature and the next generation comes behind them demanding new and better ways of doing politics and enacting social justice.

Bibliography

Ali, A. and El-Sharnouby, D. (2014). 'Distorting Digital Citizenship: Khaled Said, Facebook and Egypt's Streets' in Linda Herrera and Rehab Sakr (eds), *Wired Citizenship: Youth Learning and Activism in the Middle East*, Routledge, Abingdon, 89–101.

Amodeo-Vickery, A. (2011). 'This Home Grown Youth Movement is Occupying Italy', *The Daily Good*, 24 December. Available from http://www.good.is/articlaes/this-homegrown-youth-movement-is-occupying-Italy-legally, accessed 6 September 2016.

Aouragh, M. and Alexander, A. (2011). 'The Egyptian Experience: Sense and Nonsense of the Internet Revolution', *International Journal of Communication*, 5, 1344–58. Available from http://ijoc.org/ojs/index.php/ijoc/article/view/1191/610.

Artal, R. (2011). *Reacciona*, Aguilar, Spain.

Bardak, U., Maseda, M. and Rosso, F. (2015). *Young People Not in Employment, Education or Training (NEET): An Overview in ETF Partner Countries*, European Training Foundation, Turin.

Bayat, A. (2010). 'Muslim Youth and the Claim of Youthfulness', in L. Herrera and A. Bayat (eds), *Being Young and Muslim: New Cultural Politics in the Global South and North*, Oxford University Press, Oxford and New York.

Benedicto, Jorge (2013) 'The Political Cultures of Young People: An Uncertain and Unstable Combinatorial Logic', *Journal of Youth Studies*, 16(6), 712–29. DOI: 10.1080/13676261.2012.744812.

Castel, R. (2006), 'Et maintenant, le precariat', *Le Monde*, 29 April. Available from http://multitudes.samizdat.net/Et-maintenant-le-precariat, accessed 2 April 2009.

Castells, M. (2012). *Networks of Outrage and Hope: Social Movements in the Internet Age*, Polity Press, Cambridge.

Catterall, B. (2013). 'Towards the Great Transformation: Locating Gezi Park', *City* 17, 419–22.

Cole, J. (2014). *The New Arabs: How the Millennial Generation is Changing the Middle East*, Simon & Schuster, New York.

Della Porta, D. and Diani, M. (1999). *Social Movements: An Introduction*, Blackwell, Oxford.

Della Porta, D. and Chironi, D. (2015). 'Movements in Parties: OccupyPD', *Partecipazione e Conflitto*, 8(1), 59–96.

Desrues, T. (2012). 'Moroccan Youth and the Forming of a New Generation: Social Change, Collective Action and Political Activism', *Mediterranean Politics*, 17(1), 23–40.

Doha Institute. (2011). *The Israeli Protest Movement: Motivations and Opportunities for Change*, Arab Center for Research and Policy Studies, UAE.

Eichhorst, W. and Neder, F. (2014). 'Youth Unemployment in Mediterranean Countries', Policy Paper No. 80, IZA Institute for the Study of Labour, Berlin.

Ermsone, D. (2015). *The Challenge of Youth Employability in Arab Mediterranean Countries: The Role of Active Labour Market Programmes*, European Training Foundation, Turin.

Fahmi, G. and Meddeb, H. (2015). *Market for Jihad: Radicalization in Tunisia*, Carnegie Middle East Center, Washington DC.

Göle, N. (2013). 'Gezi: Anatomy of a Public Square Movement', *Insight Turkey*, 15(3), 7–14.

Goyette, J. (2015). 'Meet the Young Activists who Upended Turkish Politics and Want a New Model for the Middle East', *Public Radio International*, available from www.pri.org/stories/2015-06-11/meet-the-young-activists-who-upended-Turkish-politics-and-want-a-new-model-for-the-Middle-East, accessed 21 June 2016.

Hellyer, H.A. (2016). 'Civil Society' in E. Hokayem and H. Taha (eds), *Egypt after the Spring: Revolt and Reaction*, IISS, London.

Hessel, S. (2011). *Time for Outrage/Indignez-vous*, Charles Glass Press, Imprint of Quartet Books, London.

Honwana, A. (2013). *Youth and Revolution in Tunisia*, Zed Books, London.

IRI. (2014). 'Tunisians Hold Credible Democratic Election, Lack of Youth Participation Cause for Concern as Country Moves Forward', International Republican Institute, Washington DC. Available from www.iri.org/resource/tunisians-hold-credible-domestic-election-lack-youth-participation-cause-concern-country-0, accessed 4 July 2016.

Jover, G., Belando-Montoro, M. and Guìo, Y. (2014). 'The Political Response of Spanish Youth to the Socio-Economic Crisis: Some Implications for Citizenship Education', *Journal of Social Science Education*, 13(3), 4–12.

Kaimaki, V. (2009). 'Mass Uprising of Greece's Youth', *Le Monde Diplomatique English Edition*. Available from http://mondediplo.com/2009/01/06greece, accessed 22 January 2016.

Khoury, N. (2016). 'Lebanon's Stalemate', *The Cairo Review of Global Affairs*. Available from http://www.thecairoreview.com/tahrir-forum/lebanons-stalemate/, accessed 24 May 2016.

Lamloun, O. (2015). *Experiences and Perceptions of Young People in Tunisia: The Case of Douar Hicher and Ettadhamen*, International Alert, London.

Lűkűslű, D. (2014). 'Cyberspace in Turkey: A Youthful Space for Expressing Powerful Discontent and Suffering', in L. Herrera and R. Sakr (eds), *Wired Citizenship: Youth Learning and Activism in the Middle East*, Routledge, Abingdon, pp. 76–88.

Lynch, M. (2012). *The Arab Uprising: The Unfinished Revolutions of the New Middle East*, Public Affairs, New York.

Matthjis, M. (2014). 'Mediterranean Blues: The Crisis in Southern Europe', *Journal of Democracy*, 25(1), 101–15.

McCurdy, D. (2011). *A Guide to the Tunisian Elections*, Project on Middle East Democracy (POMED), Washington, DC.

Millennial Dialogue. (2016). *The Millennial Dialogue: Key Findings*. Available from http://millennialdialogue.com/key-findings, accessed 12 April 2016.

Morjane, K. (2010). *Tunisia's Address to the 65th Session of the General Assembly of the United Nations*, UN, New York. Available from gadebate.un.org.

Murphy, E. (2012). 'Problematizing Arab Youth: Generational Narratives of State Failure', *Mediterranean Politics*, 17(1), 5–22.

Nader, S. (2015). 'Why Lebanon's "You Stink" Movement Lost Momentum', in *Al-Monitor*, Washington DC. Available from www.al-monitor.com/pulse/originals/2015/10/lebanon-civil-movement-protests-violence.html, accessed on 25 April 2017.

Quaranta, Mario (2015) 'An Apathetic Generation? Cohorts' Patterns of Political Participation in Italy', *Social Indicators Research*, 125, 793–812. DOI: 10.1007/s11205-015.0869.x.

Secker, H. (2016). 'Generation Revolution: How Egypt's Military State Betrayed its Youth', *The Guardian*, 2 June. Available from www.theguardian.com/news/2016/jun/02/generation-revolution-egypt-military-state-youth, accessed on 2 June 2016.

Silver, H. (2007). *Social Exclusion: Comparative Analysis of Europe and Middle East Youth*, Wolfensohn Center for Development, Dubai School of Government, UAE.

Sloam, J. (2013). 'The Outraged Young: How Young Europeans are Reshaping the Political Landscape', *Political Insight*, April.

Sotiris, Panagiotis (2010) 'Rebels without a Cause: The December 2008 Greek Youth Movement as the Condensation of Deeper Social and Political Contradictions', *International Journal of Urban and Regional Research*, 34(1), 703–9. DOI: 10.111/j.1468-2427.00949x.

Torreblanca, J. I. (2013), 'Europe has Lost its Citizens', *El País*, 11 March, available from http://voxeurope.eu, accessed on 17 April 2017.

Torreblanca, J. I. and Michou. H. (2013). 'Taking Stock: Political and Social Crisis in Mediterranean Europe. From Tahrir to Sol: The Unexpected Mediterranean Convergence', in *IEMed Mediterranean Yearbook 2013*, IEMed Barcelona, Spain, pp. 148–53.

Quaranta, M. (2016). 'An Apathetic Generation? Cohorts' Patterns of Political Participation in Italy', *Social Indicators Research*, 125(3), 793–812.

Yiftachel, O. (2006). *Ethnocracy: Land and Identity Politics in Israel/Palestine*, University of Pennsylvania Press, Philadelphia.

PART VI

Societal and cultural trends

30

NEW MEDIA, ACTIVISM, AND THE TRANSFORMATIVE ARAB POLITICAL LANDSCAPE

Sahar Khamis

This chapter addresses the evolving and transformative Arab media landscape, before and after the eruption of the so-called "Arab Spring" or "Arab Uprisings" of 2011. It highlights the most important and significant changes in the Arab media scene and their potential effects on and implications for civil society, civic engagement, political activism, and different forms of mediated communication and journalistic practices. Special attention is paid to the shift from the highly uniform mainstream media, which have been mostly controlled by the ruling regimes in the Arab world to consolidate their power, to the widely diverse new media, especially social media, which have been used by ordinary citizens, especially young activists, to inspire sociopolitical transformation and to enact change. The chapter investigates the various potentials and limitations of this new wave of citizen journalism before, during, and after the eruption of the "Arab Spring" movements, as well as the future prospects for this new wave of citizen journalism and its multiple implications moving forward.

The shifting Arab media landscape: from uniformity to diversity

For many years, the media ownership and media management pattern which prevailed in most Arab countries has been characterized by the hegemony and domination of the ruling minority over the majority. In other words, the consolidation of both political power, as well as the power of communication, in the hands of authoritarian regimes and their supporters. This resulted in a tightly controlled and highly uniform media landscape in the majority of Arab countries for many decades, with ruling regimes dictating the content and the agenda of mainstream media, which were for a long time the only available type of media, through ministries of information, which are officially appointed and directly manipulated by those in power.

The media landscape in the Arab world suffered from multiple challenges, which negatively affected its level of professionalism for a long time. These included technological barriers, lack of sufficient journalistic education and professional training for journalists and media people, censorship and tight governmental scrutiny and control, economic constraints, and high levels of illiteracy. Combined together, these factors posed serious barriers to the growth and development of the Arab media landscape. Needless to say, we have to avoid the danger of placing all Arab counties in one basket or lumping them all under one category, since there are, of course, significant political, economic, and social factors which distinguish them from each other.

However, we can say with a high degree of confidence that these were the general, prevailing characteristics of most Arab media systems until 1990.

An important defining moment in the history of Arab media came in 1990, with the so-called "CNN effect," when CNN started broadcasting to the Arab world free of charge. This exposed Arab audiences, for the very first time, to a different pattern of news coverage and news reporting, which moved away from the "talking head" traditional pattern to a much more instant, interactive, and field based pattern of television reporting. Other developments which also took place around that time included the introduction of cell phones, satellite television channels, and Internet access. Additionally, media privatization was introduced with the birth of a number of private satellite channels in many Arab countries for the first time.

Therefore, it could be said that prior to 1990 most media ownership in the Arab world fell with governments, and most media functioned under strict governmental supervision and control. During this era Arab media were mostly controlled by governments mainly to keep lay people uninformed and, thus, incapable of effectively participating in political controversies and rational debates. A new media revolution erupted in the Arab world after 1990, inspired by the introduction of both satellite television channels and the Internet (Abdulla, 2007; Khamis and Sisler, 2010). In the 1990s Internet penetration started to spread throughout the Arab world. Although the region generally suffered from being on the low end of the digital divide (Abdulla, 2007: 35) and faced many challenges, including the lack of human and economic information technology (IT) resources, illiteracy and computer illiteracy, the lack of funds for IT research and development, and the lack of solid telecommunication infrastructures (Abdulla, 2007: 35), this situation is rapidly changing, since many Arab countries are currently striving to increase Internet penetration rates.

Ironically, although many Internet websites and blogs were used to defy and resist autocratic governments and dictatorial regimes in the Arab world, a number of these governments took steps to encourage Internet proliferation and accessibility, mainly in order to boost economic development, as in the case of the Egyptian government, for example (Abdulla, 2006: 94). In other words, it could be said that these governments were unknowingly digging their own graves, since the very same tools they boosted and supported were the ones to be used later to defy them and end their rule. This provides clear evidence of the highly ambivalent and complex relationship between media and governments in the Arab world (Khamis and Sisler, 2010).

Overall, it could be said that the introduction of satellite television channels and the Internet represented an important shift from the monolithic, state-controlled, and government-owned media pattern to a much more pluralistic and diverse media scene, where many diverse and competing voices representing different political positions and orientations could be heard at the same time, adding to the richness of ongoing political debates and the formation of a wide array of public opinion trends (Khamis and Sisler, 2010; Khamis and Vaughn, 2011).

The Internet allowed for the dissemination of cultural content in the Arab world (Howard, 2011: 163). Much of the user-generated content is transmitted using social media, such as Facebook, the video-sharing portal YouTube, Twitter, and short message service (SMS) or text messaging. These media enable peer-to-peer communication between users and can be linked to each other, allowing users to transmit their ideas and images to large numbers of people. Therefore, it is safe to say that one of the most important avenues through which public opinion trends and public spheres are both shaped, as well as reflected, in modern Arab societies is the Internet (Zelaky et al., 2006: 5). The significance of the introduction of the Internet stems from the fact that it defies boundaries, challenges governmental media censorship, and provides an alternative voice to traditional media outlets, which echo official, governmental policies, and views.

Here it is important to bear in mind that although the world's attention mostly turned to the Arab world, and focused on the role of new media in instigating change in it, with the eruption of the "Arab Spring" movements in 2011, as will be discussed in the rest of this chapter, the fact remains that

> Even before the spread of populist revolts that have gripped the region, Arabs with digital access were taking part in a social media revolution that enabled unprecedented freedom of expression. Over the previous decade of Internet access, activists, writers, and lay citizens built capacities and networks.
>
> *(Ghannam, 2012: 7)*

The penetration and proliferation of the Internet, and its many related applications, in many parts of the Arab world allowed diversity of opinions and empowered journalists, political dissidents, and human rights activists, thus, promoting freedom of speech and democracy, in many unprecedented ways. For example, in his research on Egyptian opposition websites, Abdel-Latif (2004) argued that the Internet has emerged as a platform for voices denied a place in the mainstream, state-owned media, enabling the opposition to "break the monopoly of the state over the articulation of the political and social agenda" (Abdel-Latif, 2004: 1). Similarly, Zayani (2005) explained how new forms of media, especially the Internet, brought about a new era of diversity of opinions, vigorous public debates, as well as pluralism, which shifted away from the highly uniform and harshly controlled media arena, which characterized many Arab countries.

The presumed link between the spread of new information technologies and the process of democratization stems from the fact that, for a long time, the Internet was seen as an influential and subversive medium which inherently promotes democracy, encourages direct participation, and generally contests established and traditional authorities, especially in non-democratic environments (Khamis and Sisler, 2010).

New expectations of the democratization potential of the Internet have been associated with the phenomenon of blogging, which allows individuals holding different political, cultural, and religious opinions to debate and exchange views. As Anderson (2009) indicates "Blogging . . . has been hailed as a new opportunity for public communication, political activism, and a democratic public sphere from its very first appearances in the region – notably in Egypt, Syria, Saudi Arabia, [and] famously Iraq."

Indeed, blog users in the Arab world started to develop an increasing self-confidence and a growing belief in their own potential and their own individuality, because they became capable, for the first time, of developing and expressing their authentic views, which are separate from the traditional worldviews (Hofheinz, 2005: 92–5). Examples of the increasing influence of the political blogosphere and its expanding role as a news source allowing marginalized political voices to be heard, not just locally but also internationally, include the Israel–Hezbollah conflict in 2006 (Ward, 2007). Additionally, blogs have made their way into mainstream press in the Arab world, which is a large accomplishment enabling them to influence the agenda of traditional media coverage (Ward, 2007: 2–11). Such examples provide clear proof of the symbiotic relationship between "new" and "mainstream" media outlets, on both an international, as well as a regional, scale (Ward, 2007; Hofheinz, 2005).

The fact that the content of popular blogs started to influence mainstream media content deserves further attention, since there is a positive indication that the new "Arab blogosphere" effectively challenged the content of mainstream media through purposefully covering controversial events and topics, which may not be tackled in mainstream media, or at least covering them with more frankness and aggressiveness (Khamis and Sisler, 2010).

Through influencing the agenda of mainstream media, "blogs threaten to unravel the carefully managed, state-controlled narrative which frames government policy" (Al Malky, 2008). In other words, for the first time, and after many years of government hegemony, and even monopoly over the media, the average Arab citizen was being exposed to alternative venues for receiving both news and views, or coverage of ongoing current affairs, in addition to different viewpoints, varying analysis, and competing perspectives and viewpoints. Furthermore, blogs are relatively low-cost and easy to maintain and the changes in readership structure and composition can have very little influence over content. With greater privatization and increasing competition, mainstream media in many parts of the Muslim world sensed an increasing pressure to appeal to the tastes and interests of growing and diversified audiences in order to sustain themselves. Covering the war in Lebanon in 2006, the Iraq war in 2003, and even the sexual harassment of women on the streets of Cairo set bloggers apart from mainstream media, attracted larger and more diversified audiences, and increased public awareness. Thus, mainstream media's credibility could be seriously questioned and their popularity could be undermined, if they failed to keep up with the controversial and sensitive topics covered in blogs (Al Malky, 2008).

This spillover from the new emerging realm of citizen journalism, as in the case of blogs and other forms of social media, to the realm of mainstream media, had a number of important effects and implications. First, it allowed for a much more pluralistic and diverse media arena, where many different, or even conflicting, voices could be heard. This resulted in an increased level of mainstream media professionalism, as a result of increased media competition from both new private media, as well as from social media and new media. Second, this meant, in turn, that marginalized groups, which traditionally did not enjoy a lot of power or a lot of opportunities to express themselves were now given an opportunity for the first time to not only make their voices heard, but also to play a more active, interactive, and proactive role in shaping their own countries' future on all political, social, and cultural fronts. Third, in relation to the previous point, this shift from the more monolithic and uniform media arena to the more pluralistic and diverse media arena was certainly indicative of a new era of increased public awareness, thanks to the openness and transparency enabled via new media venues, which certainly paved the way for the tides of public protests, upheavals, and uprisings which erupted against a number of dictatorial regimes in the Arab region in 2011, in what came to be know as the "Arab Spring" or "Arab Uprisings."

One important point to bear in mind, however, is the fact that old media ownership and management patterns in the Arab region did not disappear or cease to exist, as a result of the new shifts and developments which were witnessed in the region. In fact, the most interesting observation about the Arab media landscape is the high level of parallelism which is manifested in it. This eclectic and paradoxical media landscape interestingly combines the binary opposites of authoritarianism and resistance, public ownership and privatization, official and popular spheres, mainstream media and new media, and secularization and (re)Islamization, reflecting a unique case of heterogeneity and divergence (Khamis, 2011). This highly eclectic, paradoxical, and complex media landscape could be said to have both caused and mirrored the equally unique, diverse journeys to democratization and transformation in different Arab countries, which have been far from straightforward, clear, or smooth.

The role of new media in socio-political transformation: the "Arab Spring" moment

The terms "Arab Spring" or "Arab Awakening" have been used interchangeably to refer to the massive wave of political upheavals and citizen revolts which swept many parts of the Arab region from 2011 (Khamis and Vaughn, 2011). This wave started in Tunisia, followed by Egypt, and then Libya, and, subsequently, Syria, Yemen, and Bahrain (Khamis and Vaughn, 2011). However, each of these countries witnessed different developments and, ultimately, had varying outcomes, based on a myriad of political, social, and economic factors.

This last point is of special importance since the Arab Spring movements have also been characterized by the significant role of new media, especially social media, which have been effectively utilized by the young protestors and activists to enact political change. This phenomenon is commonly known as "cyberactivism" (Howard, 2011), which refers to the use of online communication to advance a cause which is difficult to advance offline, such as paving the way for political transition, as witnessed in the Arab world since 2011.

The marriage between this growing phenomenon of cyberactivism, as defined by Philip Howard (2011), and the growing parallel phenomenon of citizen journalism, whereby ordinary citizens use modern communication technologies to document important events and to increase international attention and awareness around them (Bennett, 2008), was evident in many Arab Spring countries' uprisings. One example is the Syrian uprising, which witnessed a growing role for activists and opposition leaders in the diaspora, and whereby citizen journalism enabled the coverage and documentation of the horrors of the conflict inside Syria, which would not have been possible had it not been for these citizen journalists, due to the ban on foreign correspondents and journalists, who are not allowed to enter the country (Khamis, Gold, and Vaughn, 2012).

The Arab Spring movements granted Arab citizens, especially youth, unprecedented opportunities to increase their visibility, exercise their leadership, and execute their activism, mainly through the deployment of new forms of communication, such as social media, to spread their messages and to support their causes. The significance of youth stems from the fact that over 70 percent of the overall population in the Arab world today is under 30 years of age. Naturally, this is the age group which is most dynamic, passionate about change and reform, capable of organizing and mobilizing, and more technologically savvy.

The young activists relied on social media to achieve three main goals, namely: mobilization, documentation, and education. Mobilization refers to the use of social media to help people organize, coordinate and network, such as using Twitter to orchestrate minute by minute on the ground protests. Documentation refers to the use of social media to provide evidence of governmental corruption and violations of human rights, such as using cell-phone cameras to capture incidents of police brutality and harassment of protestors, a phenomenon commonly known as "citizen journalism" (Bennett, 2008). Education refers to increasing awareness about current social and political problems, in the hope of resolving them, as in the case of brainstorming and deliberating about key issues via political blogs (El Nawawy and Khamis, 2013).

Overall, it could be said that the "Arab Spring" uprisings were characterized by the instrumental use of social media, especially Facebook, Twitter, YouTube, and text messaging by protesters, to bring about political change and democratic transformation. These new types of media acted as effective tools for supporting the capabilities of the democratic activists by allowing forums for free speech and political networking opportunities; providing a virtual space for assembly; and supporting the capability of the protestors to plan, organize, and execute peaceful protests (Khamis and Vaughn, 2011).

These new media avenues also enabled an effective form of citizen journalism (Bennett, 2008), through providing forums for ordinary citizens to document the protests; to spread the word about ongoing activities; to provide evidence of governmental brutality; and to disseminate their own words and images to each other, and, most importantly, to the outside world through both regional and transnational media (Khamis and Vaughn, 2011).

Moreover, they have been effectively deployed as important weapons in the communication struggle which erupted between the Arab peoples and their governments, since the people engaged in both a political struggle to impose their own agendas and ensure the fulfillment of their demands, while at the same time engaging in a communication struggle to ensure that their authentic voices were heard and that their side of the story was told, thus asserting their will, exercising their agency, and empowering themselves in an unprecedented fashion. These aggregate efforts resulted in tilting the political and communication balance, at least initially, in favor of freedom fighters and political activists. However, the complex developments in the region moving forward were indicative of how these new media tools, or weapons, were very much a double-edged sword, since they had both strong potentials, but also numerous limitations simultaneously.

The potentials and limitations of new media in activism and transformation

The role that new media played at the heart of the so-called "Arab Spring" movements opens the door for tackling an important controversy and an ongoing debate regarding the potentials and limitations of new media in the realm of boosting democratization and paving the road for socio-political transformation. This controversy, which started well before the eruption of the "Arab Awakening" movements and is still very much going on until now, has two sides. On one hand, the optimists regarding the democratizing potential of these new media, such as Alterman (2005), and Lynch (2005), for example, herald them as potential agents of change and reform. They stress the power of new media in bringing about significant changes in the dynamics of Arab societies, as well as emphasizing their impact on shaping local, regional, and international public spheres and discourses.

Those who adopted this position expressed enthusiasm regarding the perceived role of new media in acting as motors of change, which have the capacity not just to shape and influence public opinion trends and attitudes, but also to inspire citizens to take collective action, such as protesting and demonstrating, rather than just passively venting their anger and frustration, and, thus, using their media usage experience as a "safety valve" (Seib, 2007). Those who adopt this position hailed the potential impact of satellite television channels and the Internet on encouraging public protests and opposition against autocratic regimes in the Arab world (Khamis and Sisler, 2010).

The adherents to this position predicted that the true winds of political change in many parts of the Arab world are most likely to result from the "information revolution," especially the proliferation of new information technologies, which have the capacity to break the barriers to effective communication, challenge authoritarian governments' hegemony, destroy traditional taboos, and bring people closer together, more than ever before (Khamis and Sisler, 2010).

There is no doubt that some evidence pointing to the power of the Internet and new mobile communication devices in helping actual political participation and organization was evidenced in the so-called Arab Spring or Arab Awakening movements, as in the case of the young political activists in Egypt who used websites and cell phones to organize strikes and mobilize effective political participation in demonstrations and other forms of political expression on the streets of Cairo (Khamis and Vaughn, 2011). A similar phenomenon was also detected in other Arab countries which witnessed political upheavals, such as Tunisia, Syria, Libya, Yemen, and Bahrain (Khamis, Gold, and Vaughn, 2012).

As Howard (2011) emphasized, the Internet is also a rapidly growing and expanding medium, especially among young people. Recent research studies indicate that Internet use is increasingly more prevalent among younger age groups within the Arab world, especially the 20- to

30-year-old age group, which uses the net more avidly compared to the rest of the population (Abdulla, 2007: 50). This can very well explain why and how new media were effectively deployed by young people in the Arab world to trigger political reform. In Egypt, for example, the segment of the population who are active Internet users are mostly youth, who were the driving force behind the Egyptian revolution.

What can be observed here is a phenomenon whereby the Internet, alongside other new means of communication, such as cell phones, were effectively deployed in not just sharing and exchanging political information, but also in expanding the possibilities of formulating an active civil society (Diamond, 1999) and vibrant public spheres that translate effective political discussions into organized political action, thus, expanding the horizons of democratic participation (Khamis and Sisler, 2010). Needless to say, however, the limitations of new media technologies in terms of contributing to a truly active and vibrant civil society were also evident.

On the other end of the spectrum, there were some scholars who voiced their concerns about the potential of the Internet and new media outlets to bring about democracy. Such concerns included the increasing possibilities of state control over the Internet, through such means as blocking websites, filtering content, or even the direct prosecution of posters (Kalathil and Boas, 2003; Zelaky et al., 2006; Abdulla, 2007: 77–90). Other scholars, such as Zayani (2005; 2008) and Seib (2007), were equally skeptical of the perceived trend of ascribing too much power to new media avenues in the process of mobilizing the public, or enforcing the required shift to democracy. Zayani (2008), for example, warns of the tendency to perceive the influence of new media on shaping public opinion in light of a simple "cause" and "effect" equation, by acknowledging the complexity and subtlety of the process of public opinion formation.

There is also some evidence that established political authorities, in other words autocratic regimes and their supporters, have started to reclaim the public sphere created by the Internet and new media by setting up their own media projects, blogs, and websites (Anderson, 2009). The "cyberwars" which erupted in the context of the Arab Spring uprisings between the regimes in power, on one hand, and their opponents, on the other hand, provide a clear illustration of this point.

For example, in countries such as Egypt and Syria, there were communication strategies and tactics deployed by activists and protestors to advance their political causes, such as setting up their own Facebook pages, Twitter accounts, and blogs to spread their messages, mobilize their supporters, and enact change (Khamis and Vaughn, 2011). However, there were also tactics and strategies deployed by the regimes in power to counter them and sabotage them, such as blocking the activists' websites, hacking their accounts, tracing their IP addresses, and launching counter campaigns in cyberspace, as in the case of the "electronic Syrian army," which was created by the Assad regime specifically for this purpose (Khamis, Gold, and Vaughn, 2012), or even shutting down the Internet completely for a whole week, through pushing down the kill switch, and suspending cell-phone services, as was witnessed during the Egyptian revolution of 2011 (Khamis and Vaughn, 2011).

Although such tactics and strategies were either proven to be ineffective, or they even backfired and proved to be counterproductive, as in the case of protestors flooding the streets of Cairo to express solidarity with fellow citizens and to ensure the safety of their families and friends after the Internet blackout and cell-phone disconnection, the fact remains that they are indicative of the "tug of war" between the regimes, on one hand, and their opponents, on the other hand, in cyberspace.

In other words, one important point to bear in mind is that, just like the activists and protesters build their own learning curves, so too do the regimes in power, who have been building their own learning curves since the eruption of the "Arab Spring" movements.

One of the most important features of the Arab Spring movements has been their so-called "leaderless nature." This refers to the fact that the Arab Spring revolutions have been mostly characterized as grassroots, across the board, bottom-up, horizontal, diffused tides of political transformation and social reform. The largely loose structure of these movements was subsequently viewed as a double-edged sword. On one hand, it increased the level of public participation, grassroots involvement, and civic engagement (El Nawawy and Khamis, 2013). On the other hand, it left a power vacuum, due to the absence of centralized, formal, hierarchical, and structured leadership. This was blamed for some of the setbacks witnessed in some of the Arab Spring countries, such as Egypt, which relapsed back to military dictatorship; Libya, which is suffering from chaos and tribal strife; Yemen, which is suffering from internal violence, which is worsened by external intervention; and Syria, which has an ongoing, violent fight, resulting in an exceptionally severe, unprecedented humanitarian crisis.

The lesson to be learned here is that the deployment of new media is not a substitute for civil society organizations and true civic engagement. While it is true that new media can act as amplifiers for the voices of protest and they can play the role of catalysts which can speed up the process of political mobilization, through numerous functions, such as increasing outreach, networking, and organization, they cannot, however, provide the needed mechanisms or the suitable environment for the transition to democratization and reform.

In fact, their role could be said to be more prevalent and more effective in paving the way for revolutionary change, through raising awareness about key issues which require change, as well as during the actual revolutionary phase, through networking, mobilization, and coordination. However, in the post-revolutionary phase, when the political scene becomes more complex and the challenges multiply and the tensions build up, proving the common saying that it is easy to oust a dictator from office, but it is difficult to figure out what to do next, the media alone cannot fill the power vacuum in society. The derailing of democratization in all the "Arab Spring" countries, with the exception of Tunisia, speaks volumes in support of this observation.

Moreover, one of these limitations is the digital divide, which points to the discrepancy between the haves and have nots in the realm of technological advancement, due to myriad factors including low literacy rates, especially in rural areas and among certain groups, such as the less economically fortunate and women, for example, as well as infrastructural barriers, and technical, technological and economic constraints which are widespread in many parts of the developing world, including the Arab region.

Another limitation is the danger of clicktivism and slacktivism—replacing doing with posting, sharing, and tweeting, a phenomenon through which individuals could cultivate a false sense of gratification and satisfaction by simply clicking the mouse and sharing a link or sending a tweet, without taking the necessary steps to change the realities on the ground and to improve the actual situation in the real world. Here, it is worth mentioning that we need to differentiate between a situation where someone has the capacity to take action, but chooses not to do so, and another situation where the only form of activism available for a person is, in fact, online posting, sharing, and tweeting, as in the case of Syrian opposition activists in the diaspora, for example (Khamis, Gold, and Vaughn, 2012).

Additionally, it is important to bear in mind the differing role of social media, depending on the surrounding political environment and the degree of unity and solidarity, or division and fragmentation, which is demonstrated in it. If there is a moment of unity and uniformity motivated by common goals, for example, during the Egyptian revolution of 2011 when all Egyptians across the board chanted the same slogans: "The people want to overthrow the regime" and "Mubarak must go," social media can be very successful in increasing this unity and amplifying the voices of protest, and they can help by acting as catalysts, mobilizers, and networking tools, which can aid the process of transformation and pave the way for change.

However, once this moment of solidarity is gone, and is replaced, instead, by deep divisions, severe polarization, and dangerous fragmentation, as witnessed in many "Arab Spring" countries today, including Egypt after June 2013, then social media can widen the gap between the different groups and increase the tensions and the divisions among them even more, since every group will use its social media venues as effective weapons to attack their opponents and defend themselves, while refusing to listen to their opponents' views. This is directly related to the finding that many people either use social media as echo chambers, which allow them to stay within their own comfort zones by adhering to similar people who share their worldviews, or they, to the contrary, use them as places to vent their anger, bash their opponents, and attack those who are different from them.

This ambivalent mixture of potentials and limitations pertaining to the role of new media in boosting transformation and aiding activism was best captured in Jeffrey Ghannam's (2012) analysis of the shifting Arab media landscape one year after the eruption of the "Arab Spring" uprisings. He noted that

> the year following the start of the Arab revolutions—in Tunisia, Egypt, Libya and violent uprisings in Syria, Yemen, and Bahrain—was followed by continued repression and threats to the exercise of free expression online and offline. But the year also saw great strides in the numbers of Arabs across the region turning to social media platforms and the ascendancy of online engagement.
>
> *(Ghannam, 2012: 6)*

Today, more than five years after the eruption of these sweeping waves of revolt and these popular uprisings, it could be said that the parallel tides of the simultaneous, yet conflicting, forces of authoritarianism and resistance are continuing, albeit in different forms, shapes, and strengths, based on the unique, individual conditions of each Arab county.

Concluding remarks

The shifting tides of change in the Arab media landscape before, during, and after the so-called "Arab Spring" or "Arab Uprisings" are indicative of a number of glaring findings which need to be highlighted. They indicate that the use of the Internet, and related new media technologies and applications, does not occur "in an information vacuum" (Kalathil and Boas, 2003: 143). In other words, such mediated usages and applications should be contextualized within the broader context of Arab media developments and their interrelated political, social, and cultural landscapes (Khamis and Sisler, 2010).

The high level of media hybridization, synchronization, interconnectedness, and interdependency, which we are witnessing now in the Arab media arena, which are closely intertwined with complex social, political, and economic factors, imply that any analysis of the impact of the Internet and new media technologies, and their multiple applications, on the shifting Arab media landscape has to transcend the "media-centric logic" (Allievi, 2003: 12) or the "technological determinism" approach.

Looking at the overall picture of the Arab media landscape in the five years following the eruption of the so-called "Arab Spring" movements, it becomes clear that some gains were made and some progress has been achieved in the realm of popular protest, as well as in the areas of popular participation, activism, and expression, despite some of the major hurdles and serious setbacks on the road to democratic transformation.

As previously discussed, the significant implications which the introduction of the Internet had in many parts of the Arab world in the various political, religious, social, and cultural arenas inspired the birth of new debates and discourses, the creation of new media effects, as well as growing waves of expectations of "liberalization" and "democratization" in the Arab world, while, ironically enough, providing platforms for many forces to resist these waves simultaneously.

In other words, it could be said that these new information technologies played the complex, dual, and, oftentimes, contradictory role of providing tools and platforms for both those in power, as well as their opponents; the mainstream voices, as well as the marginalized ones; the dominant discourses, as well as the alternative ones, to be heard and expressed simultaneously. Here, it is useful to remember that the Internet "connects on its own users' terms" (Seib, 2007).

This last point is in line with the "democratization debate." Some media analysts and observers predicted that new media developments, such as the increased level of Internet penetration, would intrinsically lead to a significant growth in democratization in the Arab world, while others say that these expectations do not seem to have materialized, so far (Khamis and Sisler, 2010).

This debate remains intact and highly relevant after the eruption of the "Arab Spring" movements in some Arab countries, such as Tunisia, Egypt, Syria, Libya, Yemen, and Bahrain, which manifested good examples of the presence of a "tug of war" or "cyberwars" between the regimes, on one hand, and their opponents, on the other hand, and which did not always yield the desired positive outcomes.

In line with this last point, it is especially important to transcend the "media-centric logic" when analyzing the impact of the Internet on any particular society (Khamis and Sisler, 2010). Philip Seib (2007), for example, reminds us that new media are only part of a complex and interrelated set of variables, and while, indeed, they may act as "catalysts" or "stimulators" of change and reform, one should be careful not to assign too much power to them in the transition toward democratization.

In other words, the media can only play the role of "facilitators" or "accelerators" of the transition to democracy. They can help in networking, spreading messages, widening outreach, and speeding up the impact, but they will always remain only catalysts for the process of change, whether in the political, social, or cultural domains. It will always be the members of society, in this case the Arab people, who can effectively bring about actual change and real transformation. In order for us to capture the complexity of this process of change and transformation, in all of these domains, we have to account for many interrelated and intersecting factors and variables, which move beyond the narrow focus on the used communication tools alone.

Moving forward, it is mandatory to adopt a much more comprehensive approach in assessing and analyzing the shifting roles of new media and their multiple effects in an equally shifting region, by taking into account a number of relevant factors and variables, such as the overall political environment in each country, the strength or weakness of civil society organizations and the related process of civic engagement, the barriers to full democratic engagement, and even the infrastructural barriers and other technical constraints.

This requires the emergence of a new form of media scholarship, which relies on more indigenous research from the Arab world, through adopting a culturally sensitive, locally informed, globally aware, and academically sound approach (Khamis, 2011). This, in turn, necessitates a high level of inclusiveness, comprehensiveness, and cultural sensitivity in mapping the developments in the region as a whole, as well as the consideration of specific dimensions, such as language, culture, historical background, and religion in studying each individual country's media system.

Analyzing the complexities and paradoxes of the transformative Arab media landscape to capture the cultural, historical, political, and social specificities of this region, as well as the specific conditions of each country in it, is especially important because of the political turmoil that is sweeping this region (Khamis, 2011). In other words, academics need to enhance their ability to localize, globalize, synthesize, and contextualize their approaches in studying the Arab media landscape, through adopting a deep, comprehensive, flexible, porous, and comparative media research approach, in an effort to capture the hybridity, complexity, fluidity, and dynamism of this ever changing region (Khamis, 2011).

It is only through such a comprehensive approach that the equally complex phenomenon of social media's role in boosting democratization, enhancing civic engagement, and paving the way for reform can be studied and analyzed. Looking ahead, it is safe to predict that many of these factors will continue to undergo constant change in a region which is itself in flux and undergoing a number of serious changes and transformations, and where the road to democratization and reform remains to be highly uncertain and uncharted.

References

Abdel-Latif, O. (2004) Cyber-struggle: Islamist websites versus the Egyptian state. *Arab Reform Bulletin*. Available at www.mafhoum.com/press7/220T44.htm (accessed 18 August 2016).

Abdulla, R. A. (2006) An overview of media developments in Egypt: Does the Internet make a difference? *Global Media Journal* (GMJ) (Mediterranean edition), 1, 88–100.

Abdulla, R. A. (2007) *The Internet in the Arab World: Egypt and Beyond* (New York: Peter Lang Publishing).

Allievi, S. (2003) Islam in the public space: Social networks, media and neocommunities, in: S. Allievi and J. Nielsen (Eds) *Muslim Networks and Transnational Communities in and across Europe* (Leiden: Brill), pp. 1–28.

Al Malky, R. (2008). Blogging for reform: the case of Egypt. *Arab Media and Society*. Available at http://www.arabmediasociety.com (accessed 20 August 2016).

Alterman, J. (2005) IT comes of age in the Middle East. *Foreign Service Journal*, 36, 42.

Anderson, J. W. (2009). Blogging, networked publics and the politics of communication: Another free-speech panacea for the Middle East? NMIT Working Papers, January 31. Available at: http://nmit.wordpress.com/2009/01/31/197/ (accessed 20 August 2016).

Bennett, W. L. (2008) Changing citizenship in the digital age, in: W. L. Bennett (Ed.) *Civic Life Online: Learning How Digital Media Can Engage Youth* (Cambridge: MIT Press), pp. 1–24.

Diamond, L. (1999) *Developing Democracy: Toward Consolidation* (Baltimore: Johns Hopkins University Press).

El Nawawy, M. and Khamis, S. (2013) *Egyptian Revolution 2.0: Political Blogging, Civic Engagement, and Citizen Journalism* (New York: Palgrave Macmillan).

Ghannam, J. (2012) Digital media in the Arab world: One year after the revolutions. A report to the Center for International Media Assistance (CIMA). The National Endowment for Democracy (NED).

Hofheinz, A. (2005) The Internet in the Arab world: Playground for political liberalization. *International Politics and Society*, 3, 78–96.

Howard, P. N. (2011) *The Digital Origins of Dictatorship and Democracy: Information Technology and Political Islam* (Oxford: Oxford University Press).

Kalathil, S. and Boas, T. C. (2003) *Open Networks, Closed Regimes: The Impact of the Internet on Authoritarian Rule* (Washington, DC: Carnegie Endowment for International Peace).

Khamis, S. (2011). The transformative Egyptian media landscape: Changes, challenges and comparative perspectives. *International Journal of Communication*, 5, 1159–77. Available at: http://ijoc.org/ojs/index.php/ijoc/article/view/813/592 (accessed 20 August 2016).

Khamis, S. and Sisler, V. (2010) The new Arab "cyberscape": Redefining boundaries and reconstructing public spheres. *Communication Yearbook*, 34, 277–316.

Khamis, S. and Vaughn, K. (2011) Cyberactivism in the Egyptian revolution: How civic engagement and citizen journalism tilted the balance. *Arab Media and Society*, summer, 13, Available at: www.arabmediasociety.com/?article=769 (accessed 19 August 2016).

Khamis, S., Gold, P. B. and Vaughn, K. (2012) Beyond Egypt's "Facebook revolution" and Syria's "YouTube uprising": Comparing political contexts, actors and communication strategies. *Arab Media and Society*, Spring, 15. Available at: www.arabmediasociety.com/index.php?article=791andp=0 (accessed 20 August 2016).

Lynch, M. (2005) Assessing the democratizing power of Arab satellite TV. *Transnational Broadcasting Studies Journal* (TBS), 1, 150–5. Available at www.tbsjournal.com (accessed 19 August 2016).

Seib, P. (2007) New media and prospects for democratization, in: P. Seib (Ed.) *New Media and the New Middle East* (New York: Palgrave Macmillan), pp. 1–17.

Ward, W. (2007) Uneasy bedfellows: Bloggers and mainstream media report the Lebanon conflict. *Arab Media and Society*. Available at: www.arabmediasociety.com/topics/index.php?tarticle=54 (accessed 19 August 2016).

Zayani, M. (2005) *The Al-Jazeera Phenomenon: Critical Perspectives on New Arab Media* (Boulder: Paradigm Publishers).

Zayani, M. (2008) The challenges and limits of universalist concepts: Problematizing public opinion and a mediated Arab public sphere. *Middle East Journal of Culture and Communication*, 1, 60–79.

Zelaky, E., Eid, G., Sami, S., and Ziada, D. (2006) *Implacable Adversaries: Arab Governments and the Internet* (Cairo: Arabic Network for Human Rights Information).

31

DIGITAL COMMUNICATIONS AND SOCIAL NETWORKS

Co-evolution of digital activism and repression during the Arab Uprisings

Ben Wagner

From Tahrir to Tunis to Tripolis, there are few topics in the past decade that have attracted greater global public interest than the 'Arab Spring'[1] (Pace and Cavatorta 2012). While there are many other events that feed into it from Teheran to Istanbul and London, the Arab Spring provides for a remarkably bright prism of potential imaginaries. The multitude of stories and narratives produced has obviously been influenced by global communications, but perhaps not exactly in the way such changes are commonly discussed. There are many popular narratives which drive the idea of the Internet, social media or simply modern technology as a liberating force, considering that 'online organizing has been a critical tool for advancing democracy' (Clinton 2010). This is reinforced by authors like Clay Shirky who suggests that many of the processes that led to democratization in former East Germany would have been impossible in a pre-Internet era (Shirky 2008: 161). However, as noted by more critical voices 'Shirky and others promote a decidedly one-sided view of empowerment that favours a social imaginary of a relatively conflict-free world enabled by progressive innovation in technology' (Mansell 2012: 108). Morever many of the

> analyses . . . led to attributing magical powers to Internet technology. By repeatedly putting the Internet corporations – Facebook, Twitter, and the like – at the center, it seemed as if particular Western characteristics were artificially being inserted into a genuine popular Arab revolution.
>
> *(Aouragh 2011: 1346)*

Together with the term 'Arab Spring', the ideas of Facebook or Twitter revolution have been increasingly critiqued as terms that were primarily of US origin and that do not adequately describe the conflict or associated struggles that actually took place in the Arab Uprising countries (Massad 2012). This chapter will be looking at Egypt, Syria, Libya and Tunisia and will not look specifically at Bahrain, Iraq, Morocco or Yemen which could also be considered within the context of the Arab Uprisings (Pace and Cavatorta 2012). In looking at these countries this chapter will trace some of the basic questions about digital communications and social networks during the Arab Uprisings and will attempt to provide a clearer perspective on what human beings actually do with technology. Particular attention will be paid to mobile networks and usage of communications as well as the state in communications flows to help or hinder certain information. It will also consider the global context within which digital communications and social networks interact with the Arab Uprisings. Finally the conclusion will provide a more coherent narrative for thinking about digital communications within the Arab Uprisings that allows for the existence and usage of technology without unnecessarily foregrounding technically mediated practices.

Many of the critiques discussed here previously will not be new to students of democratization theory and indeed many of the less critical perspectives on how states democratize flow naturally into narratives of technology-enabling masses rising up to claim democracy. While of course many of the critiques that apply to existing concepts of democratization (Hinnebusch 2006) also apply to such narratives, so too do critical perspectives on technology in international relations (van Eeten and Mueller 2012; Evgeny Morozov 2011; Mansell 2012).

While much of this 'utopian fantasy' (Aouragh 2011: 1345) is not lost on authors writing about Egypt or Tunisia (Ben Gharbia 2010), it is also not without effects. Intense global public interest in a string of protests and uprisings in Iran, Tunisia, Egypt, Libya, Syria from 2009 to 2012 has ensured that all of these events are discussed as part of one continuum. While there is certainly some inspiration and likely also different forms of learning involved between these individual events, many of their similarities are mystified and overstated (Anderson 2011). In order to then understand what took place during the Arab Uprisings and what role technology may or may not have played during them, it is first necessary to look more closely at what human beings actually used technologies for.

Basic questions about digital communications before and during the Arab Uprisings

Were digital technologies used during the Arab Uprising? Certainly, but this should not come as much of a surprise. In 2011 Libya had 163 mobile phone subscriptions per 100 inhabitants, Tunisia had 115, Egypt had 105 and Syria had 59.[2] This means the mobile phone connectivity was widely available to substantial parts of society, with at least half of the citizens in each country having access to a mobile telephony. Similarly, Internet users, while not as high a percentage of society as mobile phone users still represent approximately 39.1 per cent of the population in Tunisia, 25.6 per cent of the population in Egypt, 22.5 per cent in Syria and 14 per cent in Libya.[3] Thus it can be suggested that digital technologies were widely accessible in all countries in which the Arab Uprisings took place, with mobile telephony almost ubiquitous.

When looking more closely at the scholars that study actual uses of technology, they do not 'argue that activists only (or even mainly) relied on Internet tools and spaces to organize and engage in debate [but that rather] it is important to understand the dialectical relationship between online and offline political action' (Aouragh 2011: 1346). A similar point is made by Lotan et al. (2011) and Wagner (2011) who both argue for the importance of considering a dialetic relationship between traditional media sources like newspaper outlets or satellite television and bloggers, activists and other social media users. They suggest that the debate on social media platforms 'is being co-constructed by bloggers and activists alongside journalists' (Lotan et al. 2011: 1400) while also relying on 'television, a traditional medium, [to] disseminate information about the Tunisian protests, because those who could not access YouTube could still watch Al-Jazeera' (Wagner 2011: 1298).

The use of digital communications is not a new thing in the countries of the Arab Uprising. Quite the contrary, social movements using digital technologies were common for over a decade in Tunisia, Syria and Egypt. Howard and Hussain (2013) note that 'Even before their revolutions, Tunisia and Egypt had active blogospheres. Often the most critical coverage of government abuse was done not by newspaper reporters, but by average citizens using their access to the internet in creative ways' (Howard and Hussain 2013: 37). In particular Mohamed Zayani's (2015) historical analysis of Tunisian networked publics provides an excellent overview of the history of both offline and online social movements in Tunisia in the decades that led up to the Arab Uprisings, highlighting both the long and complex historical role of trade unions such as the UGTT which stretch back to the founding of the Tunisian republic as well as the history of Tunisian 'cyber activists' (Zayani 2015: 80) whose emergence he traces back to 1998 with sites such as 'Takriz, TUNeZINE, Reveil Tunisien, Tunisnews and Nawaat' (Zayani 2015: 83) playing a key role.

Similarly it is important to consider the

> decades-long history of social and political protest in Egypt, starting with the mobilizations in solidarity with the Second Intifada and the US (and British) invasion of Iraq, which led to huge protests expressing anger at leaders seen as the local lackeys of the US and Israel.
>
> *(Aouragh 2011: 1346)*

Egypt is perhaps different than other countries where the Arab Uprisings took place in the sense that its media landscape has historically been much bigger and more developed than in any other country in the region (Khamis 2011). The shifts in this landscape, however, affected not just Egyptians but citizens of the whole region with the mass introduction of satellite television providing a window on the world and critical discussions of politics that were previously not available (Sakr 2001). This has led some commentators to suggest satellite television has a 'democratizing power' (Lynch 2005), a theme that is not entirely uncommon in other literature on media and in particular the Internet in the Arab world (Abdulla 2007; Anderson 2007; Warf and Vincent 2007). This is particularly the case as significant parts of media framing and production and dissemination among elites take place in online spaces (Hofheinz 2007; Sakr 2012). This is particularly obvious on Twitter where much of the struggle for the initial framing of the debate and the narrative takes place, i.e. defining what the narrative will be about and what will be reported as opposed to Facebook whose primary function is increasingly becoming the dissemination of information rather than the creation of it.

One key aspect in regard to the role of digital communications that is always discussed is the role of diasporas in supporting the Arab Uprisings (Nagel and Staeheli 2010). While there is still far too little research on this topic, access to digital communications is crucial for networked diasporas to continue to play a role in political debates. This is the case both for traditional activists and in particular for digital activists with many of these individuals engaging these debates while based both in Tunisia, Egypt, Syria or Libya and from an international place of residence, typically in Europe but also potentially elsewhere in the world. Thus attempts to imprison individuals like Sami Ben Gharbia in Tunisia – one of the key actors of the political blog Nawaat (Zayani 2015: 99) – are far less effective if he can continue to engage in political activity and activism outside of Tunisia. This also extends to the location of much of the critical information about regimes: for 'Libyans and Syrians, this content was mostly hosted out of country, though the origin of contributors included both in-country citizens and members of widespread diasporas' (Howard and Hussain 2013: 37). Thus internationally connected networks have become the norm across all four countries being studied here.

Another important aspect is the shift in gatekeeping power around publicly available information from traditional and heavily regulated media elites to a wider audience. While this raises considerable challenges in regard to the verification of information in general (Chouliaraki 2009; Lynch and Galtung 2010), it also provides for an opportunity for previously unheard voices to insert themselves into a public debate. This in turn leads to particularly intense struggles about the appropriate framing of a debate (Chouliaraki 2009; Palmer 2012) in which deciding which message gets out is one of the most fundamental questions. Here the overwhelming 'Arab Spring' narrative of 2011 is – despite its many problematic aspects – useful in as much as it serves to counter state narratives which argue that terrorists, jihadis or criminals are at work and that demonstrators should be treated as such (Hussain and Howard 2013; Massad 2012). This legitimizing discourse is particularly important in places like Syria and Libya where protests were responded to with massive levels of violence, leading eventually to civil war in both countries. It is also important because protestors in both countries seem to have expected some kind of support or solidarity from a larger international community. Their protests were not just directed at their own societies but also at a wider international public which they hoped would be sympathetic to their concerns.

A further aspect of this phenomenon in regard to shifting boundaries of information is that of leaking platforms. In the years before the Arab Uprisings numerous platforms sprung up in the region, of which those operated by Al Jazeera, Nawaat and WikiLeaks are perhaps the most prominent. However, there were also examples such as Moroleaks or the work of newspapers such as the Lebanese *Al Akhbar* which were involved in publishing leaked documents (York 2013). Most of the leaks published were in relationship to the US State Department cables initially published by WikiLeaks which described in relatively unflattering terms what local American officials thought of their counterparts and the societies they were living in (Rusbridger 2010; WikiLeaks 2010). In particular, in relation to Tunileaks, which is run by Nawaat and WikiLeaks to disseminate the Tunisian parts of the cables, there has been some suggestion by Sami Ben Gharbia, one of the key Nawaat activists involved, that Tunileaks 'helped tip the balance' (York 2013: 229) during the Arab Uprisings in Tunisia.

As noted by Ibrahim Saleh

> The Arab Spring changed the political climate as it uncovered the previously hidden (or rather, suppressed) conflict between authoritarian rulers and those who promote political change. At its basis was the transformation of social spaces into political spaces where deliberation on the problems of society emerged and quickly started to spread to different social sectors and locations [. . .] WikiLeaks could play a significant role as a new window for unveiling the hidden ills of society, for naming and shaming individuals, and for establishing the issues that served as triggers for mobilization.
>
> *(Saleh 2013: 237)*

At the same time Jillian York notes that

> Egyptian activists stated WikiLeaks' influence on their uprising as minimal, yet the release of the cables – which exposed the brutality of the Egyptian government – created a shift in how US media covered the revolution, providing rich details on Mubarak's regime.
>
> *(York 2013: 230)*

There are clearly differences between countries, but what also seems evident is that a changing information environment supports different framings of conflict which in turn contribute to shifts in global and local narratives about the Arab Uprisings. These narratives are not only key anchors of protest movements, they also served to give context and meaning to many of the actions and interactions that took place during the Uprisings.

When linked to the previously suggested notion of international personal networks this does suggest that uprisings – whether Arab or otherwise – themselves have become a global mediatized phenomenon (Carafano 2009; Hussain and Howard 2013). The specifically mediatized form of protest is closely linked to uses of technology such as pervasive access to mobile phone video cameras (Padania et al. 2011; Wagner 2011), without being dependent on or driven by them. Instead these changes are indicative of the heavily technified and mediatized societies out of which protests emerge. Thus more heavily mediatized protests are a reflection on existing societies rather than a specific protest tool, precisely because – as will be discussed in the next section – tools of protest and the control of protest co-evolve with each other. Thus, deeply embedded social technologies such as mobile phones with cameras are both useful in protest and enable many forms of government surveillance. Thus, while the technologies are ambivalent to their many potential uses (Brey 2005), government actors are not and they strive to keep them under control. This will be discussed in greater detail in the next section.

An authoritarian Internet? The state and information flows

The Arab Uprisings also provide a fascinating stage on which government control of the Internet was re-negotiated in very short spaces of time. Opposition to censorship had already previously been an important part of anti-government mobilization in Tunisia (Zayani 2015: 146) and there is some indication that this was also the case in Egypt. This leads to the fascinating situation in which Tunisian dictator Ben Ali believed, just before he was forced out of office, that one of the key concessions he could make to his population (aside from lowering the prices for foodstuffs and instituting independent investigations of ongoing violence) was to restore access to the Internet and end censorship (Wagner 2011). This is not to overstate the efficacy of state censorship of the Internet in any way, but rather to emphasize its increasingly important role in Tunisia as a political bargaining chip during the course of the Arab Uprisings.

Notably invasive practices of censorship, surveillance and control were ratcheted up considerably during the course of the Tunisian Uprising, with individual users being 'hacked' by their own government in the final weeks before Ben Ali fled the country (Wagner 2012c). This practice, however, is more generally indicative of a long-term trend in which disciplinary practices in the Tunisian Internet were steadily increased (see Figure 31.1).

This steady increase in scale and technological sophistication of repressive Internet policies right up until the Arab Uprisings is typical of Egypt, Syria and Libya as well. In doing so they

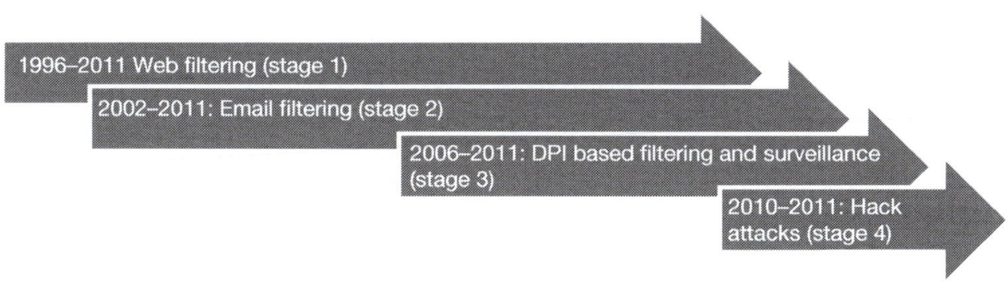

Figure 31.1 Stages of censorship and filtering on the Tunisian Internet

Source: Figure taken from Wagner (2012c).

primarily purchased control technologies from Europe and North America (Wagner 2012a). The gradual increase in control and surveillance was thus dependent on the willingness primarily of European and North American governments and companies to continue providing access to these technologies, something that became increasingly difficult to justify as the conflicts within the Arab Uprising became increasingly bloody (Elgin and Silver 2011).

Importantly Internet censorship was also not uniform across the countries being studied here. While Tunisia and Syria all had extensive Internet censorship regimes up until 2011, Egypt and Libya did not (Maher and York 2013; Noman and Zarwan 2007; Noman 2009; OpenNet Initiative 2005; OpenNet 2009).

In all four countries being studied here there was extensive government surveillance of the Internet, mobile phones and other digital communications; however, activists, academics and many other individuals living in these countries reported varying degrees of actually perceived surveillance (Filastò 2011; OpenNet Initiative 2009; OpenNet 2009; Silver 2011a; Wagner 2008, 2012a, 2012c; Warf 2010). While much of this surveillance was digitally mediated, at least as much was conducted through physical surveillance in all four countries being studied here. It was common for individuals working on sensitive political matters to assume their phones were being tapped and even conducting only slightly political academic research could lead an individual to be followed, their computers or phones stolen or their apartment searched. Another example of such government practices is Libya, where the 'Jamahiriya domestic surveillance committees involved between 10 and 20 percent of the population' (Howard and Hussain 2013: 27).

There have also been frequent reports of the reading – and at times even editing – of emails by government agencies in Tunisia and Syria (Silver 2011b). Perhaps most invasive of all techniques were the shutdowns of the Internet which took place in all of the Arab Uprising countries except Tunisia, i.e. in Egypt, Libya and Syria. While the shutting down of the Internet was most frequently reported in the case of Egypt in 2011, many other countries engaged in it previously and have engaged in it since (Purdon, Ashraf and Wagner 2015). However, the shutting down of the Internet and mobile phone networks in Cairo and to a degree in other parts of Egypt in 2011 is the first time that this issue received global public attention and was widely discussed (Aouragh 2011; Dainotti et al. 2011; Cowie 2011).

From 27 January 2011 until 2 February 2011 Internet connectivity was shut down by the government for five days across Egypt (Dainotti et al. 2011), mobile phone connectivity through phone calls and SMS was also blocked from 27 January until 2 February and in the case of some communications services like SMS until 6 February 2011 (Dunn 2011). In many cases these disconnection strategies were also closely linked to mass SMS campaigns by the government or military to influence and at times even threaten Egyptian citizens (Dunn 2011). Notably, the choices of the Egyptian government also had considerable effects and it was suggested that the shutdown cost 'Egypt's economy at least $90 million, and their reputation among technology firms as a stable place for investment' (Howard, Agarwal, and Hussain 2011: 231), which only refers to the direct costs of the shutdown to telecommunications providers and does not consider the indirect or secondary losses incurred in the course of the shutdown.[4]

Libya undertook repeated disconnections of Internet and telecommunications services between 17 February and 3 March, some of which lasted for several days (Dainotti et al. 2011). As in Egypt these disconnections lasted between six hours and four days and were closely linked.

There was also a separate set of disconnections that took place in Syria, however, with very different intentions. While disconnections in Egypt and Libya were primarily employed to disrupt information flows, they seem to have been employed in Syria as part of a military strategy to disrupt enemy communications as part of wider combat operations (Gohdes 2015). This is not the case for all forms of conflict; rather Gohdes suggests that the Syrian government 'implement large-scale disruptions selectively and purposely in conjunction with launching larger battles. Evidently, not all battles are accompanied by outages, but when they are, they tend to be preceded by a substantial increase in violence' (Gohdes 2015: 13).

This is particularly relevant as authors' work on the early stages of the Syrian protests suggests that social 'networks provided an important sense of solidarity and presented the background against which recruitment for mobilization took place' (Leenders and Heydemann 2012: 155). Thus network outages attack a key part of the infrastructure outside of the control of the Syrian government, infrastructure which provides 'key skills and resources for mobilization to be effective and to be sustained under prohibitive conditions of massive repression' (Leenders and Heydemann 2012: 155).

Notably, despite all of the attempts at shutdowns and other mechanisms to disrupt information flows, they do not seem to have hindered demonstrations in Egypt significantly. As noted by Tufekci and Wilson (2012: 364), the

> shutdown of Internet service between January 25 and February 2 slowed, but did not stop, the flow of information out of Tahrir Square, as a small but technologically savvy group of protestors continued to disseminate information and videos. Al-Jazeera, too, was focused on the events on Egypt, often replaying videos obtained through social media.

This is particularly important as the protests were themselves a key location for media co-production. Tufekci and Wilson's study of protests points to a 'high level of production and dissemination of multimedia content . . . Approximately half of our respondents were actively documenting and sharing images of the protests' (Tufekci and Wilson 2012: 376). Similarly to Tunisia where the strong inter-relation between different forms of media is key to understanding how the Arab Uprisings took place and were narrated (Wagner 2011), so too Egypt is characterized by a media landscape which shows the 'interrelated use of satellite television, the Internet . . . and the widespread use of Internet-enabled cellphones capable of transmitting photos and video' (Tufekci and Wilson 2012: 377). The information cascading between different mediums during the protests has been key to their successful dissemination, with videos spreading rapidly from social media to television to peoples home's and vice versa (Wagner 2011). Equally important is the close coupling between purely 'digital activism' which focuses on social media and 'offline' activism (Aouragh 2011).

Fear of the Spring

The Arab Spring is real. This statement may seem slightly surprising in the context of the ongoing scholarly debate on this issue, but it is important to look at the Arab Uprisings not just as an event in the region but also as a global event of global relevance. Only then does it make sense as a whole and only then is it possible to understand why the Arab Spring is a real thing that affects real people.

While scholars have now spent many years debunking the idea that the Arab Spring was caused by technology (Anderson 2011), or that the term Arab Spring should not even be used (Massad 2012), for much of the rest of the world the Arab Spring is a very real thing. This is because the term 'Arab Spring' or even just 'Spring' has become anchored as a global 'world-cultural script' (Meyer et al. 1997) that means many things to many people. Its most prevalent meaning seems to be around the potential for revolutionary movements in the twenty-first century, with evident resonance from Africa (Villa-Vicencio, Doxtader and Moosa 2015) to India (Gupta 2015). However, almost equally frequently it is cited as a key example of evidence of the transformative effects of technology/Internet/social media/Facebook/Twitter on politics and society across the world.

The Arab Uprisings have become a global symbol of what could be possible and thereby also more of an imaginary than an actual thing. Their inspiration is perceived as many things to many people which is perhaps why there is little agreement on even their name. Their particular emptiness as a signifier does not, however, mean that they do not exist, thus the Arab Spring and its Facebook and Twitter revolutions have taken on lives of their own as part of a global imaginary of technology enabled revolutions.

As the idea of an Arab Spring has solidified itself to a considerable degree as a global script there is also a need for substantive engagement with the idea itself, rather than simply dismissing it as false. Indeed, the shadow of Arab Spring weighs heavily on many domains, not least because it has created considerable fear among elites that their power is soon likely to be challenged. This 'Fear of the Spring' (Wagner 2012b) is typically linked to technology as it has led states around the world to increase repressive communications practices even further. Regardless of whether Facebook or Twitter revolutions actually took place, governments across the world are preparing for them anyway. It has been reported that China was the first country to censor the word 'Spring' in 2011,[5] and many other countries have taken similar measures to control and suppress information flows since then. Indeed it can be argued that, together with the Snowden revelations, fear of the 'Spring' creates a strong impetus for state actors to legitimize and justify repressive government practices affecting information flows.

This can also be observed in the countries where the Arab Uprisings took place, with communicative and physical repression closely linked in Syria (Al-Saqaf 2016; Gohdes 2015) and Internet censorship and surveillance rife in Egypt (Dixon, Ristenpart and Shrimpton 2016). At the same time the imaginary of Internet revolutions has been transposed into very concrete policy initiatives with associated funding and institutional support for 'Internet Freedom' (Clinton 2011; Ben Gharbia 2011). Whether we like it or not, the Arab Spring is here to stay.

Conclusion: The Arab Uprisings as globally embedded information landscapes

When looking at digital communications and the Arab Uprisings little takes place outside constant battles for framing and meaning. It is perhaps for this reason that so little is known about actual practices of individuals and so much is discussed in the context of popular 'world-cultural scripts' (Meyer et al. 1997) and opposition to those scripts. These scripts in turn are only loosely coupled to actual practices and it is true that technologies were certainly used before, during and after. When these are studied in greater detail, however, a far more messy and complex picture of technology usage emerges. For sure technologies were used in all of the Arab Uprising contexts, but this should hardly be surprising as all of the countries had considerable mobile phone and Internet penetration rates at the time. There is no credible evidence that social media or the Internet or any one factor 'caused' the Uprisings or that indeed such a causal relationship could be attributed to any individual factor. This is particularly the case when the co-determinate relationship of technological openness and repressive measures by states is considered. Rather human beings were the core drivers, shapers and agents in shaping the Arab Uprisings in ways that are as complex and indeterminate as much other human interaction. What is doubtless remarkable is the speed and scale with which the Arab Uprisings spread.

However, the speed and scale of the Arab Uprisings also came with the consequence of almost irreversibly creating an imaginary of the uprisings decidedly distant from many of the practices on the ground. This 'Arab Spring' imaginary has become a rallying call for those believing in peaceful protest and revolution, popular uprising and democratization just as much as for those who warn of the instability and unrest 'caused' by technology and globalization. That these scripts are now owned by the whole world does not mean they should not still be vigorously contested. Despite this point, it can also not be denied that the Arab Uprisings developed as they did in no small part due to massive global public interest. Thus, it is impossible to fully understand the Arab Uprisings without also understanding the hopes, dreams, fears and wishes that have been projected onto them.

Notes

1 For simplicity all future mentions of the Arab Spring will not include quotes.
2 This data on mobile phone subscriptions is provided by the World Bank and can be accessed here: http://data.worldbank.org/indicator/IT.CEL.SETS.P2?name_desc=false&start=2011
3 This data on Internet users per 100 people is provided by the World Bank and can be accessed here: http://data.worldbank.org/indicator/IT.NET.USER.P2?name_desc=false&start=2011
4 See www.oecd.org/countries/egypt/theeconomicimpactofshuttingdowninternetandmobilephoneservicesinegypt.htm for further details.
5 See www.businessinsider.com/words-china-banned-from-search-engines-after-tiananmen-square-2014-6?IR=T

References

Abdulla, Rasha A. 2007. *The Internet in the Arab World: Egypt and Beyond*. New York: Peter Lang.

Al-Saqaf, Walid. 2016. 'Internet Censorship Circumvention Tools: Escaping the Control of the Syrian Regime.' *Media and Communication*, 4(1), 39.

Anderson, Jon. 2007. 'Globalization, Democracy, the Internet and Arabia.' Georgetown University Center for Contemporary Arab Studies, 1–12.

Anderson, Lisa. 2011. 'Demystifying the Arab Spring.' *Foreign Affairs*, 90(3), 2–7.

Aouragh, Miriyam. 2011. 'The Egyptian Experience: Sense and Nonsense of the Internet Revolution.' *International Journal of Communication*, 5, 1344–58.

Ben Gharbia, Sami. 2010. 'The Internet Freedom Fallacy and the Arab Digital Activism.' Available at http://samibengharbia.com/2010/09/17/the-internet-freedom-fallacy-and-the-arab-digital-activism/ retrieved November 15, 2010.

Ben Gharbia, Sami. 2011. 'The Internet Freedom Fallacy and the Arab Digital Activism.' *OWNI*. Available at http://owni.fr/index.html.

Brey, P. 2005. 'Artifacts as Social Agents.' In Hans Harbers (Ed.), *Inside the Politics of Technology: Agency and Normativity in the Co-Production of Technology and Society*, Amsterdam University Press, pp. 61–84.

Carafano, J.J. 2009. 'All a Twitter: How Social Networking Shaped Iran's Election Protests.' *Heritage Foundation Backgrounder*. Available at www.heritage.org/global-politics/report/all-twitter-how-social-networking-shaped-irans-election-protests.

Chouliaraki, Lilie. 2009. 'Witnessing War: Economies of Regulation in Reporting War and Conflict.' *The Communication Review* (February 2013), 37–41.

Clinton, Hillary. 2010. 'Remarks on Internet Freedom.' Available at www.state.gov/secretary/rm/2010/01/135519.htm retreived June 21, 2011.

Clinton, Hillary. 2011. 'Secretary Clinton on Internet Freedom.' in *Freedom Online – Joint Action for Free Expression on the Internet*. The Hague, Netherlands: Bureau of Democracy, Human Rights and Labor, US Department of State.

Cowie, James. 2011. 'Egypt Leaves the Internet.' *Renesys Blog*. Available at www.renesys.com/blog/2011/01/egypt-leaves-the-internet.shtml retrieved April 2017.

Dainotti, Alberto, C. Squarcella, E. Aben et al. 2011. 'Analysis of Country-Wide Internet Outages Caused by Censorship.' Internet Measurement Conference (IMC). November 2–4, Berlin, Germany, 18 pp.

Dixon, Lucas, Thomas Ristenpart and Thomas Shrimpton. 2016. 'Network Traffic Obfuscation and Automated Internet Censorship.' ArXiv eprint available at https://arxiv.org/abs/1605.04044v2.

Dunn, Alexandra. 2011. 'Unplugging a Nation: State Media Strategy during Egypt's January 25 Uprising.' *The Fletcher Forum of World Affairs*, 35(2), 15–24.

Elgin, Ben, and Vernon Silver. 2011. 'Syria Crackdown Gets Italy Firm's Aid with US–Europe Spy Gear.' *Bloomberg*. Available at www.bloomberg.com/news/articles/2011-11-03/syria-crackdown-gets-italy-firm-s-aid-with-u-s-europe-spy-gear

Filastò, Arturo. 2011. 'Blue Coat Device Logs Indicate the Levels of Censorship in Syria.' Available at http://hellais.github.com/syria-censorship/ retrieved December 17, 2011

Gohdes, Anita R. 2015. 'Pulling the Plug: Network Disruptions and Violence in Civil Conflict.' *Journal of Peace Research*, 52(3), 352–67.

Gupta, Kanika. 2015. 'Trends in Democracy Promotion by Regional Organizations: The Arab Revolution of the 21st Century and the After Effects.' *IOSR Journal of Humanities and Social Science*, 20(6), 6–16.

Hinnebusch, Raymond. 2006. 'Authoritarian Persistence, Democratization Theory and the Middle East: An Overview and Critique.' *Democratization*, 13(3), 373–95.

Hofheinz, Albrecht. 2007. 'Arab Internet Use: Popular Trends and Public Impact.' In Sakr, N. (Ed.), *Arab Media and Political Renewal: Community, Legitimacy and Public Life*. London: I. B. Tauris.

Howard, Philip N., Sheetal D. Agarwal and Muzammil M. Hussain. 2011. 'When Do States Disconnect Their Digital Networks? Regime Responses to the Political Uses of Social Media.' *The Communication Review*, 14(3), 216–32.

Howard, Philip N., and Muzammil M. Hussain. 2013. *Democracy's Fourth Wave? Digital Media and the Arab Spring*. Oxford: Oxford University Press.

Hussain, Muzammil M., and Philip N. Howard. 2013. 'What Best Explains Successful Protest Cascades? ICTs and the Fuzzy Causes of the Arab Spring.' *International Studies Review*, 15(1), 48–66.

Khamis, Sahar. 2011. 'The Transformative Egyptian Media Landscape: Changes, Challenges and Comparative Perspectives.' *International Journal of Communication*, 5, 19.

Leenders, Reinoud, and Steven Heydemann. 2012. 'Popular Mobilization in Syria: Opportunity and Threat, and the Social Networks of the Early Risers.' *Mediterranean Politics*, 17 (January), 139–59.

Lotan, Gilad et al. 2011. 'The Revolutions were Tweeted: Information Flows during the 2011 Tunisian and Egyptian Revolutions.' *International Journal of Communication* 5, 31.

Lynch, M. 2005. 'Assessing the Democratizing Power of Arab Satellite TV.' *Transnational Broadcasting Studies Journal*, 14 Spring.

Lynch, Jake, and Johan Galtung. 2010. *Reporting Conflict: New Directions in Peace Journalism*. St Lucia, QLD: University of Queensland Press.

Maher, Katherine, and Jillian C. York. 2013. 'Origins of the Tunisian Internet.' In Muzammil M. Hussain and Philip N. Howard (Eds), *State Power 2.0*, Ashgate Publishing, p. 201.

Mansell, Robin. 2012. *Imagining the Internet: Communication, Innovation, and Governance*. Oxford University Press.

Massad, Joseph. 2012. 'The "Arab Spring" and Other American Seasons.' *Al Jazeera Online*. Available at www.aljazeera.com/indepth/opinion/2012/08/201282972539153865.html.

Meyer, John W., John Boli, George M. Thomas and Francisco O. Ramirez. 1997. 'World Society and the Nation-State.' *American Journal of Sociology*, 103(1), 144–81.

Morozov, Evgeny. 2011. 'America's Internet Freedom Agenda.' *New Perspectives Quarterly*, 28(2), 61–3.

Nagel, C., and L. Staeheli. 2010. 'ICT and Geographies of British Arab and Arab American Activism.' *Global Networks*, 10(2), 262–81.

Noman, Helmi. 2009. 'Middle East and North Africa.' *OpenNet Initiative*. Available at https://opennet.net/sites/opennet.net/files/ONI_MENA_2009.pdf

Noman, Helmi, and Elijah Zarwan. 2007. 'Internet Filtering in the Middle East and North Africa.' *OpenNet Initiative*. Available at https://opennet.net/research/regions/mena

OpenNet. 2009. 'Egypt.' *OpenNet Initiative*. Available at https://opennet.net/country/egypt

OpenNet Initiative. 2005. *Internet Filtering in Tunisia in 2005: A Country Study*. Available at https://opennet.net/studies/tunisia

OpenNet Initiative. 2009. 'Internet Filtering in Tunisia.' Available at https://opennet.net/research/profiles/tunisia

Pace, Michelle, and Francesco Cavatorta. 2012. 'The Arab Uprisings in Theoretical Perspective: An Introduction.' *Mediterranean Politics*, 17, 125–38.

Padania, Sameer, Sam Gregory, Yvette Alberdingk-Thijm and Bryan Nunez. 2011. *Cameras Everywhere Report 2011*, available at www.cmu.edu/chrs/documents/Final_WITNESSCamerasEverywhereReport.pdf

Palmer, Lindsay. 2012. 'iReporting an Uprising: CNN and Citizen Journalism in Network Culture.' *Television & New Media*, 14(5), 367–85.

Purdon, Lucy, Arsalan Ashraf and Ben Wagner. 2015. *Security v Access: The Impact of Mobile Network Shutdowns*. London.

Rusbridger, Alan. 2010. 'Editor's Note: Publishing the Cables.' *The Guardian*. November 28.

Sakr, Naomi. 2001. *Satellite Realms: Transnational Television, Globalization and the Middle East*. I. B. Tauris.

Sakr, N. 2012. 'Social Media, Television Talk Shows, and Political Change in Egypt.' *Television & New Media*, 14(4), 322–37.

Saleh, I. 2013. 'WikiLeaks and the Arab Spring: The Twists and Turns of Media, Culture, and Power.' In Brevini, B., McCurdy, P. (Eds), *Beyond WikiLeaks*. Palgrave Macmillan.

Shirky, Clay. 2008. *Here Comes Everybody: The Power of Organizing without Organizations*. New York: Penguin Press.

Silver, Vernon. 2011a. 'Italian Firm Said to Exit Syrian Monitoring Project.' *Bloomberg*. Available at www.bloomberg.com/news/2011-11-28/italian-firm-exits-syrian-monitoring-project-repubblica-says.html retrieved December 31, 2011.

Silver, Vernon. 2011b. 'Post-Revolt Tunisia can Alter E-Mail with `Big Brother' Software – Bloomberg.' *Bloomberg*. Available at www.bloomberg.com/news/2011-12-12/tunisia-after-revolt-can-alter-e-mails-with-big-brother-software.html retrieved December 14, 2011.

Tufekci, Z. and C. Wilson. 2012. 'Social Media and the Decision to Participate in Political Protest: Observations from Tahrir Square.' *Journal of Communication*, 62(2), 363–79.

van Eeten, M. J., and M. Mueller. 2012. 'Where Is the Governance in Internet Governance?' *New Media & Society*, 15(5), 720–36.

Villa-Vicencio, Charles, Erik Doxtader and Ebrahim Moosa, (Eds). 2015. *The African Renaissance and the Afro-Arab Spring: A Season of Rebirth?* Washington DC: Georgetown University Press.

Wagner, Ben. 2008. *Deep Packet Inspection and Internet Censorship: International Convergence on an 'Integrated Technology of Control'*. Tunis, Tunisia.

Wagner, Ben. 2011. '"I Have Understood You": The Co-Evolution of Expression and Control on the Internet, Television and Mobile Phones During the Jasmine Revolution in Tunisia.' *International Journal of Communication*, 5, 1295–302.

Wagner, Ben. 2012a. *After the Arab Spring: New Paths for Human Rights and the Internet in European Foreign Policy*. Brussels, Belgium.

Wagner, Ben. 2012b. 'Digital Diplomacy: The Fear of the Spring.' European Council on Foreign Relations (ECFR), 6 November.

Wagner, Ben. 2012c. 'Push-Button-Autocracy in Tunisia: Analysing the Role of Internet Infrastructure, Institutions and International Markets in Creating a Tunisian Censorship Regime.' *Telecommunications Policy*, 36(6).

Warf, Barney. 2010. 'Geographies of Global Internet Censorship.' *GeoJournal*, 76(1), 1–23.

Warf, Barney, and Peter Vincent. 2007. 'Multiple Geographies of the Arab Internet.' *Area*, 39(1), 83–96.

WikiLeaks. 2010. 'Secret US Embassy Cables.' *WikiLeaks*. Available at www.wikileaks.ch/cablegate.html retrieved January 5, 2011.

York, J. C. 2013. 'The Internet and Transparency beyond WikiLeaks. In Brevini, B., McCurdy, P. (Eds), *Beyond WikiLeaks*. Palgrave Macmillan.

Zayani, Mohamed. 2015. *Networked Publics and Digital Contention: The Politics of Everyday Life in Tunisia*. Oxford: Oxford University Press.

32

MEDITERRANEAN MIGRANTS AND REFUGEES

Historical and political continuities and discontinuities

Sarah Wolff and Leila Hadj-Abdou

Since 2015, the high volumes of arrivals of migrants and refugees to Europe have put the spotlight more than ever on the Mediterranean. Typically described in the public debate as the 'cradle of civilization' and a fertile space of mobility and exchange, the Mediterranean has lately become associated with scenarios of threat and tragedy: 'The Mediterranean is today the center of the world . . . [it] is the most problematic region in the world, and still the least integrated in the world' as Federica Mogherini (2015) the High Representative of the European Union for Foreign Affairs and Security Policy has put it. The Mediterranean Sea today stands for the 'deadliest stretch of water' (UNHCR, 2012) for people aiming to reach Europe. In 2014 and 2015 alone, 7,000 lives were lost in this sea (IOM, 2016a), mostly in the central Mediterranean route (ibid.).

The debate about refugees and the high death toll of migrants crossing the Mediterranean Sea has altered the common perspective on the region. It has also established a crisis narrative that suggests discontinuity, i.e. a breaking point in contrast to a previous linear pattern of normality (Lindley, 2014). This rupture narrative, however, conceals historical continuities, as well as the political process that has led to the contemporary situation. Migration and population movements are indeed common to the southern rim of the Mediterranean, but movement has never been so restricted and thus irregularized than in the past decades. Refugee protection in the Mediterranean region is also weak.

The EU's policies are also ill equipped and ignorant of these historically rooted dynamics of mobility. The EU's internal security interests have prevailed over the need for a common Mediterranean regional governance approach. Beyond its humanitarian narrative, the EU has had difficulties to use all possible aid, trade, economic, diplomatic and humanitarian tools to address the complex and interrelated root causes of migration such as poverty, conflict, socio-economic precariousness and climate change. This is nonetheless critical in building resilience in Arab Mediterranean societies, supporting their administrative and integration capacities, as well as relying on transnational non-state actors and increasing refugees, and migrants' protection in the Mediterranean. In the aftermath of the Arab uprisings, societal resilience amongst Syrian's neighbours, such as Jordan, Lebanon and Turkey, who are welcoming millions of refugees, is also at stake. But northern and southern EU member states have argued about 'burden-sharing' and 'solidarity' while new lines of cleavages have appeared between eastern and western EU member states as the western Balkan route became central to refugees' and migrants' journey to Europe. EU policies have proved to be driven by short-termism as they ignore the demographic challenge of an ageing EU and the consequent need for migrant workforces in European labour markets. This remains a major challenge given that Mediterranean countries are also undergoing a demographic transition with a declining fertility rate.

In order to unravel the underlying idea of discontinuity of the current crisis narrative, this chapter is divided into two parts. The first part focuses on highlighting the historical continuities in the Mediterranean migrations prior to the Arab uprisings. After analysing post-war migration patterns and refugee flows in the Mediterranean, explanatory factors for the ongoing crisis are found in the discussion of 1990s and 2000s policy developments. Irregularity, securitization and externalization of EU migratory policies are specifically scrutinized. The second part analyses the post-Arab uprisings developments. While Mediterranean migrants' vulnerabilities and precariousness are on the rise, it shows how EU policy remains risk averse and how migratory politics is used as an instrument of soft power by Mediterranean countries.

Migration as a historical defining marker of the Mediterranean

Migration has always been a central and defining feature of the Mediterranean. While the directions and patterns of movements have shifted over the years, the region was and continues to be a sending, receiving as well as transit region of immigration.

Mediterranean migration fuelled by post-war economic growth

Post-war economic growth has stimulated migration in the region since the 1950s. Initially migration movements were characterized by south to north flows within Europe, including a large degree of internal migration within European Mediterranean countries, as was the case with massive north–south movements within Italy. Growing sectors such as industry, mining, housing construction and agriculture (de Haas, 2007) in Europe's north were largely dependent on so called 'guest workers', which were recruited from Europe's south. Greece, Portugal, Italy and Spain were significant exporters of labour forces from the 1950s onwards, particularly to Germany, Austria, Belgium, France and the Netherlands. As labour supply from the northern Mediterranean started to slow down, immigration from the southern Mediterranean gained relevance. In the 1960s the new north African nation states, Algeria, Tunisia and Morocco, which had just gained independence from the colonial powers, but also Turkey, became important source countries of labour immigration to Europe.

Both waves of 'guest-workers' were initially regarded as temporary phenomena. Not only did most host societies expect post-war immigration to be temporary, but most migrants conceptualized their stay as limited. Many intended to return to their countries of origin after having saved sufficient means to acquire property back home (de Haas, 2007). However, many of these temporary 'guests' eventually turned into permanent residents. The transition from previous temporary, circular to permanent migration was paradoxically partly an – unintended – consequence of restrictive European immigration control policies. In the wake of the 1973 oil crisis, which set off a period of economic stagnation, European labour recruitment schemes were officially put to an end, and western European nation states closed their borders to reduce immigration. Many migrants chose to reunite with their families in their host countries, instead of returning back home and facing the risk of not being able to return. The active attempts of western European governments to prevent the settlement of immigrants at the time failed. Constitutional norms concerning the protection of the family, which were enforced by European national courts, were a major factor in preventing repatriation policies in the 1970s (Castles, 2004: 216).

Irregularity as an intrinsic feature of Mediterranean migration regimes

At the same time former northern Mediterranean emigration countries underwent an important transformation. In 1972 Italy had for the first time a positive migration balance, followed by Greece and Spain in 1975, and Portugal in 1981 (Montanari and Cortese, 1993: 221). Following political and economic integration into Europe, and steady economic growth, these former emigration countries started to attract significant numbers of immigrants from the south and eastern Mediterranean region especially throughout the 1990s and the 2000s. Spain witnessed the largest inflows in the region, becoming one of the largest recipients of absolute migration in the Organization for Economic Co-operation and Development (OECD), with migration rates multiplying by five from the 1990s to the 2000s (İçduygu, 2007: 154), including significant numbers from North Africa, particularly Morocco.

This type of migration, however, significantly differed from previous immigration flows in the region. Immigration in the northern Mediterranean was largely characterized by irregular entry, a mode of migration driven by the shadow economy, as well as the inappropriate regulation of labour migration in Europe's south, which was unable to address labour force shortages. Until the mid-1980s there were no legal avenues to enter Italy or Spain for work purposes (Barbulescu, 2012: 58). The introduction of visa requirements for Maghrebi immigrants in Spain and Italy in the early 1990s also contributed to foster irregular migration. The crossing of the Mediterranean Sea started in so-called *pateras*, small fishing boats often operated by smugglers (de Haas, 2008: 3). Migration up to the mid-2000s was largely managed through post-migration regularization schemes (Triandafyllidou, 2007). In spite of the late introduction of quota systems in Spain and Italy, large-scale irregular migration continued to match the real demand of the labour market (de Haas 2008: 12). To put it differently, irregularity became an intrinsic and permanent character of the migration regimes in the region (cf. İçduygu, 2007: 154). Southern European economies relied heavily on the supply of cheap foreign labour in order to keep their economies competitive and to sustain economic growth (cf. ibid.: 158).

During the 2000s, migration across the Mediterranean to Europe's shores continued. Migration patterns did not significantly alter until the economic recession in 2007. The economic downturn triggered a new emigration from southern Europe, the region that was most hit by the recession, to northern Europe (Castles et al., 2014: 118). However, while initially the recession was expected to lead to massive return migration this did not prove true. Return migration has been highest for EU migrants, who enjoy free movement rights, but was not significant for migrants from outside the EU, for whom returning would have often meant losing their residency rights (ibid.). Immigration, including labour migration, continued during the recession period, which suggests a persistent labour demand in certain sectors, such as the care industry (ibid.).

Eventually in the 2000s, north African states and Turkey became destination and transit countries of immigration (Düvell, 2014), partly due to developments in Libya under Gaddafi. Immigration flows into Libya had already started in the 1960s after the discovery of oil and hydrocarbon reserves (MPC, 2013: 1). Immigration was further fueled by the so-called 'open door' policy of the Libyan regime towards sub-Saharan African countries and used as an instrument of soft power in response to international isolation of the country following the 1992 UN embargo and the conflictual relationships of the regime with the neighbouring Arab countries (ibid.).

At the beginning of the 2000s a major anti-immigrant backlash in Libya eventually led to a tightening of immigration regulations in the country, and sub-Saharan migration started to shift towards Algeria, Morocco and Tunisia (de Haas, 2008: 3). Consequently sub-Saharan migrants started to settle in north Africa, but also increasingly joined north African migrants trying to come to Europe via the Mediterranean Sea route.

The construction of irregular mobility in the Mediterranean as a security problem

These developments were accompanied by a growing concern in Europe with irregular migration in the Mediterranean from the beginning of the 1990s onwards (Lutterbeck, 2006: 59). A securitized reading of migration became dominant and was sustained through a portrayal of immigrants as desperate and passive victims of ruthless traffickers and criminal smugglers (de Haas, 2008). The security imperative was further strengthened through an issue linkage of international migration to terrorism in the aftermath of 9/11, the 2003 Madrid and 2005 London attacks (Lutterbeck, 2006: 59; de Haas, 2008: 2).

This process of securitization of immigration is to be understood as a self-referential practice, and not a question of measuring de facto threat (Geddes, 2009:18). 'It is self-referential because it is in this practice [of securitization] that the issue becomes a security issue', as Geddes (2009:18) has aptly put it. One aspect of this securitization process was the increasing border militarization along the Mediterranean shores. Semi-military police forces, i.e. police forces with a military status, were increasingly employed by Italy and Spain to respond to irregular migration movements at sea (Lutterbeck, 2006: 64). Additionally European naval forces started to join forces to 'secure' Europe's southern borders (ibid.). In 2003, for instance, Operation Ulysses was pioneered in Spain. This joint mission of the navies of France, the UK, Spain, Portugal and Italy, was targeting irregular migration across the Straits of Gibraltar and the west Sahara towards the Canary Islands (Lutterbeck, 2006: 68). Bilateral patrolling with non-EU Mediterranean countries became common practice, the most successful examples being between the Moroccan Royal Gendarmerie and the Spanish Guardia Civil, or between the Italian Guardia di Finanza and the Libyan authorities under Gaddafi (Wolff, 2012). The EU started to train Arab Mediterranean law enforcement authorities and border guards.

A bundle of policy measures ranging from joint deportations, carrier sanctions, which co-opted private transport businesses into border control, and the adoption of various new surveillance technologies, as well as the establishment of a range of new agencies and institutions such as the border agency Frontex to implement these policies, complemented the militarization of European borders in the Mediterranean and beyond (Düvell and Vollmer, 2011: 8–11)

Fortress Europe? Externalization of migration control

These developments have been often characterized in popular discourse as the erection of a so-called 'Fortress Europe'. Such a depiction, however, is misleading for several reasons. For one, the idea of a 'Fortress Europe' implies to some extent that immigration inflows were actually stopped. However, there was no halt to immigration. Instead, immigration routes were reshaped and diversified across the Mediterranean (Triandafyllidou, 2014) which also made many of these journeys more deadly. The militarization of the Mediterranean border also led to a growing professionalization of smugglers (de Haas, 2008: 7).

The process of securitization was accompanied by the externalization of EU migratory policies, aiming at co-opting non-member states into European and EU migration and asylum policies through foreign policy tools (Geddes, 2009) The European Parliament and Commission did note the need for co-operation with non-EU states as early as 1987 (Triandafyllidou, 2014: 9). As a result of this foreign policy focus cooperation between north and south Mediterranean countries to control migration intensified. The Mediterranean became a 'laboratory' for the 'extra-territoralization' of European immigration control. Extra-territorialization in the realm of immigration can be understood as

> the way in which the EU and its Member States attempt not only to prevent non-Community nationals from leaving their countries of origin, but also to ensure that if they manage to do so, they remain as close to their country of origin as possible, or in any case outside EU territory. It furthermore covers measures that ensure that if individuals do manage to enter the EU, they will be repatriated or removed to 'safe third countries'.
>
> *(Rijpma and Cremona, 2007: 12)*

At regional level, the Euro-Mediterranean Partnership (EMP), launched in 1995 by EU ministers of foreign affairs and their Mediterranean counterparts to spread 'peace, prosperity and stability' was initially not concerned with migration, as Mediterranean partners considered discussions of migration of their citizens as 'taboo'. Yet the combined evolution of changing migratory fluxes in the region and the externalization of justice and home affairs (JHA) policy helped to 'depoliticize JHA' on the Euro-Mediterranean agenda. In 2002, a JHA regional programme was adopted within a wider package to re-launch the Barcelona Process, and was balanced by a strong commitment on the social, cultural and human partnership. Justice and home affairs and migration, with a strong emphasis on the readmission of irregular immigrants, became de facto the 'fourth basket' of the EMP (Wolff, 2012: 79–80). A milestone in curbing irregular migration was the 2002 Seville European Council (Geddes, 2009). Under the influence of the Spanish presidency of the EU, the Council for the first time introduced the provision that any future cooperation, association or any equivalent agreement with a non-EU country needed to include a joint management of migration flows and a compulsory readmission clause regarding irregular immigrants (ibid.). These targets were later integrated into the European Neighborhood Policy (ENP), which from the mid-2000s onwards became the main EU bilateral policy framework with Mediterranean countries.

EU migration cooperation with non-EU countries has often been described as strongly asymmetrical, the EU was exerting leverage to push for its own migration agenda and co-opt third countries in implementing control mechanisms outside the borders of the EU. This perspective, however, suppresses the fact that the EU fixation on migration control, at the same time also gave leaders in the region considerable power, using migrants and the willingness to implement control measures strategically as bargaining chips (Cassarino, 2012). Cooperation with northern neighbours provided authoritarian leaders such as Ben Ali in Tunisia or Gaddafi in Libya with the opportunity to 'boost their national prestige and international reputation in spite of their dubious domestic legitimacy' (Cassarino and Lavenex, 2012: 1). Under the prerogative of curbing migration, calls for democracy and human rights in the region became sidelined (Cassarino 2012). The EU and its member states reinforced cooperation with southern Mediterranean countries on border control and readmission of migrants, regardless of whether their governments respected basic human rights of those returned or not (Cassarino and Tocci, 2011: 8). In particular, the cooperation of Italy with Libya throughout the 2000s attracted repeated criticism from human rights associations and also from the UNHCR and the European Parliament (see Cuttita, 2010). Severe human rights abuses occurred to a large extent, leaving in particular sub-Saharan migrants in Libya in extremely vulnerable conditions (Bialasiewicz, 2012). Extra-territorialization of migration control created 'off-shore' black holes where European norms, standards and regulations' (ibid: 861) did not apply.

The major focus on control, readmission and return remained a continuous feature of the EU policy agenda towards its southern neighbours throughout the 2000s, and has de facto trumped other approaches also existent on the EU migration policy agenda, such as the facilitation of legal migration (Cassarino and Lavenex, 2012). More significantly it has shifted the attention away from refugee protection in the region. Displacement of people and the reception of refugees, however is equally defining the Mediterranean. Refugee flows are closely related to Mediterranean colonial history. For instance, the Algerian War of Independence (1954–62) alone displaced more than 200,000 people who fled to Tunisia and Morocco (UNHCR, 2000). The unsuccessful independence struggle of the West Sahrawi led to another 150,000–200,000 refugees in the 1970s (Farah, 2003). The largest numbers of displaced people in the region are Palestinians. The Palestine–Israel conflict has produced more than 5 million people in need of protection, of which a large number were received in Lebanon, Syria and Jordan (UNRWA, 2016). Turkey, moreover, has traditionally been another significant source country of asylum seekers.

The Mediterranean migratory space and politics post-Arab uprisings

Mass displacement is a major feature of post-World War II in the Mediterranean and has always been linked to socio-political and economic changes (Marfleet and Hanieh, 2014: 37). The recent Arab uprisings are no exception. Yet, following the Arab uprisings, migrants and refugees are increasingly facing vulnerabilities and precariousness, therefore highlighting the limits of protection regimes in the Mediterranean. EU policy has also been risk averse, continuing to privilege its own internal security over the widening of legal channels for migrants and increased protection for refugees – a situation complicated by the fact that increasingly EU's Mediterranean partners are using migratory politics as soft power to exert influence on the EU.

Mediterranean migrants' vulnerabilities and precariousness

The dismantlement of the Gaddafi regime and the Syrian conflict certainly explain the post-Arab uprisings influx of migrants and refugees ready to cross the Mediterranean Sea. Major regional geopolitical changes have led populations to flee conflict. Migratory patterns are also evolving rapidly due to the rise of socio-economic inequalities, poverty and climate change. New categories of displaced people have appeared, challenging conventional tools of international law. Next to the 'mixed migratory flows', the Arab uprisings have seen more 'stranded migrants'. These are migrants who are either in transit or at destination in north Africa, Yemen, Turkey and Greece but have no support from their governments (Chetail and Braeunlich, 2013). This was the case of workers from Vietnam, Thailand, Turkey and Ghana, and of Senegalese who were left behind by their companies with no way to get back home after the fall of the Gaddafi regime. State failure in Libya also meant that those who managed to return home, such as Egyptian migrants, returned to precarious conditions back in the Delta and Upper Nile, thus becoming potential candidates for crossing the Mediterranean (Marfleet and Hanieh, 2014).

Although initially it was mostly men crossing the Mediterranean, women are increasingly crossing it too. In 2016, the proportion of women reaching the Greek island of Kos was around 25 per cent (Freedman, 2016: 6). Women and children are more at risk of death in the Mediterranean as 'anecdotal reports indicate that during sea voyages women and children are more likely to be located in areas below deck where exposure to fumes, leaking water, and other hazards is likely' (Pickering and Cochrane, 2012: 33). Women are also increasingly fleeing precarious situations of living in refugee camps at the EU's borders, which involve not only conflict violence but also family violence (Freedman, 2016: 12). In spite of the emergence of a debate on the need for a gender-sensitive approach to EU migration and asylum policies, the diversity of implementation of EU asylum legislation by member states has created additional protection gaps for women and girls (Shreeves, 2016).

Refugees are confronted with growing precariousness in Arab Mediterranean countries of first refuge, which, in July 2016 were hosting almost 5 million refugees. This figure includes 2.1 million Syrians in Egypt, Iraq, Jordan and Lebanon, 2.7 million Syrians registered by the government of Turkey, as well as more than 29,000 Syrian refugees registered in north Africa (UNHCR, 2016a). In comparison, between April 2011 and April 2016 there have been 718,821 Syrian asylum applications in the EU (including Norway and Lichtenstein) (UNHCR, 2016b), putting in perspective the 'quantitative crisis' claimed by European media and policy-makers. Middle East and North African (MENA) countries host 39 per cent of them while Europe received only 6 per cent (UNHCR, 2016c). Refugees' hosting societies are under strain, with increased tensions between local communities and refugees. Getting access to basic needs such as jobs, healthcare, food or even psychological support is a daily struggle. In 2016, in Lebanon 70 per cent of refugee households lived below the poverty line and in Jordan 90 per cent of registered Syrian refugees in urban areas were living below the national poverty line (UNHCR, 2016d). Palestinian refugees continue to be in a precarious situation too with around 5 million registered by UNRWA (IOM, 2016b) and around 110,000 having fled from Syria (UNHCR, 2016b). This situation explains why after many years in MENA countries, refugees decide to cross the Mediterranean.

The continuities of an EU risk-averse policy

In the aftermath of the Arab uprising, the European Commission released a communication that proposed the establishment of 'a dialogue for migration, mobility and security with the Southern Mediterranean countries' (European Commission, 2011). The paper emphasized that the EU needed to provide 'clear support to the people in the Southern Mediterranean' through 'active management of migration flows, the strengthening of legal migration opportunities together with measures to address irregular migration'. Although the communication was based upon a 'root causes' narrative, which recognized the daunting 'challenge of creating jobs and improving living conditions throughout the region', little has been done so far (European Commission, 2011).

The focus on 'managing' and 'ordering' Mediterranean migratory flows was, as noted previously, a persisting EU concern. The Arab uprisings have accelerated the reliance on sophisticated biometrics, surveillance and smart border technologies to implement remote-control policies (Zaiotti, 2016: 6), presenting important internal, external and legal challenges (Wolff, 2008). Militarization is continuing with the EUNAVFORMED Operation Sophia launched to 'disrupt the business model of human smugglers and traffickers in the Southern Central Mediterranean'. As legal migration opportunities to come to Europe are seldom, refugees and migrants have opted out for riskier journeys, which are controlled by human smugglers. The absence of a competence for EU-wide search and rescue missions, which remains a member state competence, as well as the sanctioning of any commercial airlines and shipping companies for carrying persons without the proper visas or travel documents to enter the EU through Directive 2001/51 and lengthy visa procedures have contributed to the blossoming industry of human smuggling, putting migrants even more at risk (Wolff, 2015).

The decision to relocate 160,000 refugees under the influence of Germany revealed divisions amongst EU member states. Since 2015, walls and fences have been erected between Austria and Italy, Hungary and Austria, and on the Greek–Macedonian border, while Bulgaria announced the plan to construct a new wall with Turkey. These initiatives contributed to the rise of anti-immigrant and often anti-Islam movements such as Pegida in Germany or the Golden Dawn in Greece, which have spread all over Europe. Also the message of the president of the European Council, Donald Tusk, representing the European heads of states and governments, could not have been clearer when he declared 'Don't come to Europe. Don't believe traffickers. Don't risk your lives and your money' (Chadwick, 2016).

The evolution from an 'Arab Spring' to an 'Arab Winter' and the realization that EU's southern neighbourhood was becoming a 'ring of fire' rather than a 'ring of friends' has rapidly overshadowed EU's declarations for more mobility for Arab Mediterranean citizens. The 'crisis' narrative requiring exceptional measures was exploited by various EU member states as a trump card in EU negotiations. The traditional northern–southern dividing line on 'burden-sharing' and 'solidarity' resurfaced with southern EU member states pursuing specific strategies to gain financial and operational support to police EU's southern borders. Malta, Italy, Greece and Spain have been in the frontline of rescue at sea missions while coping with the lasting consequences of the 2007 financial crisis. Capacities to welcome and process asylum-seekers' applications have come under strain, to the extent that the European Court of Human Rights condemned 'northern' EU countries for transferring asylum-seekers back to the country of first entry such as Greece, unable to ensure their human rights and dignity.

Southern EU member states pursued strategies to resist 'policies that displace responsibility for migration and asylum away from the core of Europe towards its peripheries' (Mainwaring, 2012a: 38). This helped them to gain more influence and financial support from northern EU member states in order to control their borders (Wolff, 2008). Malta for instance retained up until January 2016 a detention policy of 18 months for any migrant arriving on Maltese soil, which was seen as a strategy of deterrence for migrants but also forced some EU member states to stop asylum-seeker transfers through the Dublin Convention to Malta (Mainwaring, 2012b). Faced with the immobility of its European peers, in October 2013 Italy launched a major military rescue operation called 'Mare Nostrum' following the death of 300 migrants close to Lampedusa Island, which shocked the Italian public. The operation, with a budget of €9 million per month and involving 900 personnel, saved 150,000 migrants (Carrera and den Hertog, 2015: 3–4). One year later, the operation was ended and succeeded by a much more modest Frontex operation, the Triton operation. The Mare Nostrum operation was accused of pulling more migrants as 'smugglers abused the proximity of this operation near to the Libyan coast to put more people in the sea with the assumption that they would be rescued very soon' (Frontex interim executive director Gil Arias, quoted in ibid.). Italy was also blamed by other EU member states for not systematically recording the fingerprints of asylum-seekers (Trauner, 2016: 315).

Mediterranean countries' migratory politics and soft power

The 2015 European Agenda for Migration, the European Agenda on Security but also the 2015 Valetta summit with African partners and the EU/Turkey 2015 and 2016 deals have shown the EU's continuous willingness to cooperate with third countries in organizing returns, and the fight against irregular migration in the Mediterranean. Thus, mobility partnerships concluded with Morocco and Tunisia, an EU external migration instrument that organizes mobility for 'short periods', is in fact used to 'combat illegal immigration, networks involved in the trafficking and smuggling of human beings, and to promote an effective return and readmission policy while respecting fundamental rights' (Council of the EU, 2013). The EU has also reactivated the negotiation of EU readmission agreements with third countries. Yet without clear mobility incentives in the form of visa facilitation, many non-EU southern Mediterranean countries have been resisting the EU's demands (Wolff, 2014). Morocco pursued an issue-linkage strategy by suspending EU readmission agreement negotiations following discontent with the negotiations on a Deep and Comprehensive Free Trade Agreement. In addition signing an EU readmission agreement would also not have been considered 'appropriate' by Moroccan officials who do not want to be regarded as the 'Gendarme of the European Union' by other Mediterranean and African partners. This issue of 'image' of Morocco in its own neighbourhood, including its own geostrategic interests, has been clearly overlooked by EU officials, thus reducing their leverage in the negotiations (Wolff, 2014).

While some argue that the EU has capitalized on the fragility and weakness of north African governments following the Arab uprisings to get them to sign mobility partnerships (Limam and Del Sarto, 2015), geopolitical concerns continue to prevail in the migratory politics choices made before and after the Arab uprisings (Natter, 2014). If in the 2000s the 'remote-control' demands of the EU matched Morocco's willingness to regain a regional power role in Africa after some years of isolation from its European and African neighbours (Natter, 2014: 19), the 2014 Moroccan immigration reform can similarly be explained by the geopolitical motives of the kingdom to gain new economic markets in west and sub-Saharan Africa. After 15 years of sub-Saharan migration, Morocco has become a destination country and cannot, geopolitically, afford to be seen as a violator of sub-Saharan migrants' rights in the region, as denounced by Médecins Sans Frontières in 2012.

Mediterranean countries can aptly use migrants and refugees as an instrument of soft power. Thus, Turkey became a key strategic partner in the EU's attempt to control the eastern Mediterranean route. After having welcomed millions of Syrian refugees, the country gained leverage and was able to capitalize on European internal divisions between Germany and other EU member states. The March 2016 EU–Turkey deal, complementing the October 2015 EU–Turkey Action Plan, and enacting the principle to return Syrian refugees back to Turkey in exchange for resettling other Syrian refugees from Turkey to Europe (the *one for one* approach), caused a general outcry for curbing refugees' rights. Human Rights Watch (2016) denounced deportations from the Greek islands of Lesbos and Chios. Refugees' and migrants' rights are at stake at two levels (Carrera and Guild, 2016). First, Turkey is indeed not yet considered a 'safe third country' by the UNHCR, where it would be considered safe to return refugees, following the *principle of non-refoulement*. Second, Turkey's geographical limitation to the 1951 Geneva Convention exempts the Turkish authorities from applying the Convention to non-European refugees, namely Syrian refugees. In exchange for this deal, Turkey has secured the opening of new chapter in its accession negotiations with the EU and an additional financial support of €3 billion. The refugee issue has thus enabled Turkey to return to the centre of attention of EU politics after years of being the pariah among EU's neighbours. Some have also maintained that the hosting of Syrian refugees is also providing the AKP government with 'loyal' supporters, and thus strengthening its position domestically (Parkes, 2015).

Conclusions

Controlling migrants and borders has become the main objective of states and international agencies at a global level, as a result of the growing geopolitical and socio-economic uncertainties deriving from globalization. Migrants and refugees are considered as 'transgressors' of the territorial borders of the nation state (Marfleet and Hanieh, 2014: 25), and the Mediterranean is no exception. The exceptionalism of the 2015 migrant and refugee crisis framed by European policy-makers and media as a security issue, has been oblivious of the social, economic and political reality of migration in the Mediterranean. Migration and mobility are a defining marker of the region, in spite of the many constraints that migrants and refugees face. Migration in the Mediterranean has been managed through a self-feeding dynamic: stricter migration controls and a lack of legal avenues, together with the persistence of economic needs, caused an increase in irregular migration, which in turn generated the need for more control.

In many ways the recent Mediterranean history of migration is a showcase of the core dilemma of migration governance, namely the conflict between economic interests and public resistance to migration, which Hollifield (1992) has pointedly framed as the paradox of open markets and closed political communities. The increase of border control, which is a consequence of this disjuncture of economic and political interests and the growing securitization of migration, however, drives migrants and refugees to undertake riskier journeys and to cooperate with human smugglers to make their way through Europe. The situation in the EU's southern neighbours, hosting millions of refugees, is clearly unsustainable for countries of first refuge whose societal resilience is at stake. Transregional governance is nonetheless absent in a region governed by state-driven migratory politics.

Bibliography

Barbulescu, R. (2012). The Politics of Immigrant Integration in Post-Enlargement Europe Migrants, Co-ethnics and European Citizens in Italy and Spain, PhD thesis, European University Institute.

Bialasiewicz, L. (2012). Off-shoring and Out-sourcing the Borders of Europe: Libya and EU Border Work in the Mediterranean, *Geopolitics*, 17(4), 843–86.

Carrera, S. and L. den Hertog (2015). Whose Mare? Rule of Law Challenges in the Field of European Border Surveillance in the Mediterranean. Brussels: CEPS Paper, No. 79, January.

Carrera, S. and E. Guild (2016). EU–Turkey Plan for Handling Refugees is Fraught with Legal and Procedural Challenges. Brussels: CEPS Commentary, 10 March.

Cassarino, J.-P. (2012). Reversing the Hierarchy of Priorities in EU–Mediterranean Relations, in: J. Peters (ed.), *The European Union and the Arab Spring: Promoting Democracy and Human Rights in the Middle East*, New York: Lexington Books, pp. 1–16.

Cassarino, J.-P. and N. Tocci (2011). Rethinking the EU's Mediterranean Policies Post-1/11. IAI Working Paper No. 11, June.

Cassarino, J.-P. and S. Lavenex (2012). EU Migration Governance in the Mediterranean Region: The Promise of (a Balanced) Partnership?, in *IEMed Mediterranean Yearbook*, Barcelona: IEMed, pp. 284–8.

Castles, Stephen (2004). Why Migration Policies Fail, *Ethnic and Racial Studies*, 27(2), 205–27.

Castles, S., H. de Haas Hein and M. Miller (2014). *The Age of Migration: International Population Movements in the Modern World*. New York: Palgrave Macmillan.

Chadwick, V. (2016). Donald Tusk Tells Economic Migrants: 'Don't Come to Europe'. *Politico*. Available online at www.politico.eu/article/donald-tusk-tells-economic-migrants-dont-come-to-europe/ [Accessed on 6 July].

Chetail, V. and M. A. Braeunlich (2013). Stranded Migrants: Giving Structure to a Multifaceted Notion, in Global Migration Research Papers, No. 5/2013 (December), pp. 4–5, available online at http://bit.ly/12Ksm3Q.

Council of the EU (2013). *Joint Declaration Establishing a Mobility Partnership between the Kingdom of Morocco and the European Union and its Member States*. Brussels, 3 June.

Cuttita, P. (2010). Readmission in the Relations between Italy and North African Mediterranean Countries, in: J.-P. Cassarino (ed.), *Unbalanced Reciprocities: Cooperation on Readmission in the Euro-Mediterranean Area*, Washington: Middle East Institute, pp. 30–53.

De Haas, H. (2007). Morocco's Migration Experience: A Transitional Perspective, *International Migration*, 45(4), 39–70. Preprint available online at https://heindehaas.org/articles/ [accessed 4 July].

De Haas, H. (2008). The Myth of Invasion: The Inconvenient Realities of Migration from Africa to the European Union, *Third World Quarterly*, 29(7), 1305–22, preprint available online at https://heindehaas.org/articles/ [accessed 3 July].

Düvell, F. (2014). Turkey's Transition to an Immigration Country: A Paradigm Shift. *Insight Turkey*, 16(4), 87–104.

Düvell, F. and B. Vollmer (2011). European Security Challenges. Working paper EU–US Immigration Systems No. 1. Robert Schuman Centre for Advanced Studies. European University Institute.

European Commission (2011). Communication on a dialogue for migration, mobility and security with the southern Mediterranean countries. Brussels, 24 May 2011.

Farah, R. (2003). Western Sahara and Palestine: Shared Refugee Experiences, *Forced Migration Review*, 16, 16–23.

Freedman, J. (2016). Engendering Security at the Borders of Europe: Women Migrants and the Mediterranean 'Crisis'. *Journal of Refugee Studies*, 29(4): 568–82.

Geddes, A. (2009). Migration as Foreign Policy? The External Dimension of EU Action on Migration and Asylum. Report by the Swedish Institute for European Policy Studies. No. 2.

Hollifield, J, (1992). *Immigrants, Markets and States: The Political Economy of Postwar Europe*, Cambridge: Cambridge University Press.

Human Rights Watch (2016). EU/Greece: First Turkey Deportations Riddled with Abuse. Available online at www.hrw.org/news/2016/04/19/eu/greece-first-turkey-deportations-riddled-abuse [accessed 7 July 2016].

İçduygu, A. (2007). The Politics of Irregular Migratory Flows in the Mediterranean Basin: Economy, Mobility and 'Illegality', *Mediterranean Politics*, 12(2), 141–61.

IOM (2016a). IOM Counts 3,771 Migrant Fatalities in Mediterranean in 2015. Available online at www.iom.int/news/iom-counts-3771-migrant-fatalities-mediterranean-2015 [accessed 4 July 2016].

IOM (2016b). Migration to, from and in the Middle East and North Africa, Data snapshot prepared by IOM Regional Office for the Middle East and North Africa, April. Available onlne at www.egypt.iom.int/Doc/Publications/Migration%20in%20MENA_Data%20snapshot_April2016.pdf [accessed 5 July 2016].

Liman, M. and R. Del Sarto (2015). *Periphery under Pressure: Morocco, Tunisia and the European Union's Mobility Partnership on Migration*, Florence: RSCAS 2015/75.

Lindley, A. (ed.) (2014). *Crisis and Migration: Critical Perspectives*, London: Routledge.

Lutterbeck, D. (2006). Policing Migration in the Mediterranean, *Mediterranean Politics*, 11(1), 59–82.

Mainwaring, C. (2012a). Resisting Distalization? Malta and Cyprus' Influence on EU Migration and Asylum Policies, *Refugee Survey Quarterly*, 31(4), 38–66.

Mainwaring, C. (2012b). Constructing a Crisis: the Role of Immigration Detention in Malta, *Population Space and Place*, 18(6), 687–700.

Marfleet, P. and A. Hanieh (2014). Migration and 'Crisis' in the Middle East and North Africa Region, in: Lindley, A. (ed.), *Crisis and Migration: Critical Perspectives*, London and New York: Routledge, pp. 24–45.

Mogherini, F. (2015). Keynote speech for the ISPI dinner at the conference 'Mediterranean Dialogue' in Rome. December 15. Available online at www.federicamogherini.net/keynote-speech-for-the-ispi-dinner-at-the-conference-mediterranean-dialogue-rome/ [accessed 6 July].

Montanari, A. and A. Cortese (1993). South to North Migration in a Mediterranean Perspective, in: R. King (ed.), *Mass Migration in Europe: The Legacy and the Future*, London: Belhaven Press, pp. 212–33.

MPC (Migration Policy Centre) (2013). *Libya Migration Profile*. Available online at www.migrationpolicycentre.eu/docs/migration_profiles/Libya.pdf [accessed 9 July].

Natter, K. (2014). Fifty Years of Maghreb Emigration. Oxford: IMI Working Papers Series, 95.

Parkes, R. (2015). *Turkey's Refugee Politics*. Paris: EUISS, Alert 44.

Patrillo, E. R. (2016). The Securitization of the EU External Borders and the Rise of Human Smuggling along the Eastern Mediterranean Route: The Case of Afghan Unaccompanied Minors, in: E. Ambrosetti, D. Strangio and C. Withol de Wenden (eds), *Migration in the Mediterranean: Socio-Economic Perspectives*, London and Abingdon: Routledge, pp. 276.

Pickering, S. and B. Cochrane (2012). Irregular Border-Crossing Deaths and Gender: Where, How and Why Women Die Crossing Borders, *Theoretical Criminology*, 17(1), 27–48.

Rijpma, J. and M. Cremona (2007). The Extra-Territorialisation of EU Migration Policies and the Rule of Law. EUI Working Papers Law No. 1.

Shreeves, R. (2016). *Gender Aspects of Migration and Asylum in the EU: An Overview*. Briefing, March 2016, PE 579.072, Brussels: European Parliamentary Research Service.

Trauner, F. (2016). Asylum Policy: The EU's 'Crises' and the Looming Policy Regime Failure, *Journal of European Integration*, 38(3), 311–25.

Triandafyllidou, A. (2007). Mediterranean Migrations: Problems and Prospects for Greece and Italy in the Twenty-first Century, *Mediterranean Politics*, 12(1), 77–84.

Triandafyllidou, A. (2014). Multi-levelling and Externalizing Migration and Asylum: Lessons from the Southern European Islands, *Island Studies Journal*, 9(1), 7–22. Available online at www.antigone.gr/files/en/library/selected-publications-on-migration-and-asylum/eu/ISJ-9-1-Triandafyllidou.pdf [accessed 4 July].

UNHCR (2000). *The State of The World's Refugees 2000: Fifty Years of Humanitarian Action*. Available online at www.unhcr.org/publications/sowr/4a4c754a9/state-worlds-refugees-2000-fifty-years-humanitarian-action.html [accessed 8 July 2016].

UNHCR (2012). *Mediterranean Takes Record as Most Deadly Stretch of Water for Refugees and Migrants in 2011*. Available online at http://www.unhcr.org/news/briefing/2012/1/4f27e01f9/mediterranean-takes-record-deadly-stretch-water-refugees-migrants-2011.html [accessed 4 July 2016].

UNHCR (2016a). *Syrian Refugee Regional Response*. Available online at http://data.unhcr.org/syrianrefugees/regional.php [accessed 5 July 2016].

UNHCR (2016b). *Syrian Refugee Regional Response*. Available online at http://data.unhcr.org/syrianrefugees/asylum.php [accessed 5 July 2016].

UNHCR (2016c). *Global Trends 2015*. Available online at www.unhcr.org/figures-at-a-glance.html [accessed 5 July 2016].

UNHCR (2016d). *3RP Regional Refugee and Resilience, Plan 2016–2017 in Response to the Syria Crisis, Mid-Year Report*, June 2016. Available online at www.3rpsyriacrisis.org/wp-content/uploads/2016/07/3RP-Mid-year-Report-June-2016.pdf

UNRWA (2016). *Palestinian Refugees*. Available online at www.unrwa.org/palestine-refugees, accessed 10 July 2016.

Wolff, S. (2008). Border management in the Mediterranean: Internal, External and Ethical Challenges, *Cambridge Review of International Affairs*, 21(2), 253–71.

Wolff, S. (2012). *The Mediterranean Dimension of EU's Internal Security*, London: Palgrave.

Wolff, S. (2014). The Politics of Negotiating EU Readmission Agreements: Insights from Morocco and Turkey, *European Journal of Migration and Law*, 16(1), 69–95.

Wolff, S. (2015). Migration and Refugee Governance in the Mediterranean: Europe and International Organisations at a Crossroads, Roma: IAI, October, 23 pp.

Zaiotti, R. (2016) Mapping Remote Control: The Externalization of Migration Management in the Twenty-first Century, in: R. Zaiotti (ed.), *Externalizing Migration Management: Europe, North America and the Spread of 'Remote Control' Practices*. New York: Routledge, pp. 3–30.

33

INTERCULTURAL DIALOGUE ACROSS THE MEDITERRANEAN TROUBLED WATERS

Challenges to the Anna Lindh Foundation

Stefania Panebianco

Introduction

The European Union (EU) regards intercultural dialogue and civil society activism as a strategic approach to advance cooperation with Mediterranean partners also in other policy areas. The EU fosters civil society activism, bottom-up strategies and thematic networking to provide a more receptive context to security cooperation (Malmvig, 2005). For several years the Partnership on Social, Cultural and Human Affairs has been regarded as one of the most promising fields to invest in within the Euro-Mediterranean Partnership (EMP) launched in Barcelona in 1995.

Ten years later, this framework has been institutionalized with the creation of the Anna Lindh Foundation (ALF). This is a 'network of national networks' bringing together civil society organizations and citizens across the Mediterranean. The ALF declared goal is to foster mutual understanding via specific cooperation projects. Since 2005 several initiatives have been conducted within the ALF network, but some action fields are more advanced than others and networking is *à la fois* active or highly hesitant.

The Foundation provides institutional support and funds to promote intercultural dialogue; thanks to the ALF network, NGOs and civil society associations are supposed to interact, exchange different views and experience cooperation in a neutral context, far from domestic control or political influence. Yet, cultural cooperation is not a linear process as this constructivist approach envisages, and cultural cooperation in the Mediterranean area is often jeopardized by domestic political conditions and regional systemic constrains, such as intolerance and extremisms mounting both in EU and Mediterranean countries. Moreover, the Foundation cannot involve society at large. Following the ALF procedures and internal rules, it is difficult to create truly new and wider Euro-Mediterranean networks. The analysis of ALF projects indicates that the ALF institutional mechanisms favour existing networks, including partners already socialized to the EU funding system, where EU associations play a pivotal role. By supporting existing networks, the Foundation can hardly produce the expected multiplier effect. Hence, if the Foundation involves actors with similar interests, scopes and values, the declared goal of appeasing cultural differences and experiencing a common language via cooperation is missed. This is inevitably the rationale of applying for a call: associations rarely come together if they have nothing in common.

This chapter challenges the ALF model of intercultural dialogue, because one thing is to foster regional cooperation and get people closer, another is the adoption of a shared cultural model based upon pluralism, portraying the added value of diversity and leading to the peaceful coexistence of different cultures. Today the Foundation is experiencing the same Euro-centrism of the global civil society discourse with a strong normative connotation laying at basis of the third chapter of the Barcelona Declaration. In the 1990s a social-constructivist approach based upon intercultural dialogue had emerged suggesting to invest in cooperation to appease differences and promote a common language. Over the years this naive assumption has been beset by various constraints rendering intercultural dialogue extremely difficult.

The Foundation seems entrapped in the myth of multiculturalism conducive to peaceful coexistence, as a result of the (short-sighted) view that cultural cooperation can automatically bring about transnational and cross-national initiatives devoid of any cultural specific traits, thus conducive to a common language and shared values. In a sense not much has changed since the 1990s, when the Mediterranean partners regarded the EMP – being an EU construction – as a distant entity. Institutional conditions and systemic constraints do not render civil society networking within the Foundation easier than in the past 20–25 years.

The constructivist framework at the basis of Euro-Mediterranean relations

In the 1990s, EU cooperation with Mediterranean partners was often explained via a constructivist interpretation: actors working together on a specific project are exposed to common values, ideas and stimuli that help the development of a common language that is eventually conducive to a more secure and cooperative environment.[1] Building confidence through confidence building measures (CBMs) was a new security approach that the EU was experiencing at the regional level.[2] As Claire Spencer explained

> [t]he utility of CBMs [was] perceived to derive from their gradual creation of an atmosphere of mutual trust, transparency and predictability – in slow and incremental steps, if need be – in order to provide alternatives to confrontation and conflict where differences between states recur or have been inflamed, or where new points of contention have arisen.
>
> *(Spencer, 1997: 23)*

The east–west context is clearly different from the Euro-Mediterranean area. Nevertheless, following the normalization of relations among European countries and the fading of the east–west cleavage, in 1995 the EU launched the EMP trying to experience CBMs also in the Mediterranean. The EMP was conceived as a region-building process based upon a multi-dimensional framework assuming the achievement of a security community as an eventual goal (Adler and Crawford, 2006) to be attained – among other instruments – through dialogue and the progressive development of shared understandings (Malmvig, 2005).

The EMP comprehensive approach was strengthened and made more explicit with the adoption of intercultural dialogue as one of the main cooperation areas of Euro-Mediterranean relations. The Barcelona Declaration, in fact, devoted its third chapter to the 'Social, Cultural and Human Partnership'. This was a firm political commitment of the 27 countries that adopted the Barcelona Declaration, in 1995,[3] to react against the rhetoric of the clash of civilizations and the debate that was sparked by the publication of Samuel Huntington's (1993) article in *Foreign Affairs*, followed by a book a few years later (Huntington, 1996). Dialogue among partners was then conceived as an alternative to the clash of civilizations discourses (Schäfer, 2007).

Despite its innovative approach, the third chapter encompassed very different cooperation areas under the same title, weakening de facto the outcomes of cooperation. Excluding the issues directly related to security and economics, different subjects were grouped within the third chapter of the Barcelona Declaration: human rights, health, sustainable development, environment protection, migration, youth, media and intercultural dialogue, rendering this basket an empty box without a specific identity (Schäfer, 2007: 334). As if all the issues of cooperation that 'could not be accommodated within the "political and security partnership" or within the realm of economics, were somewhat "thrown" into the third basket' (Del Sarto, 2005: 314).

Today, new challenges and threats have emerged in the Mediterranean area rendering the implementation of this framework rather difficult. Twenty years after the adoption of the Barcelona Declaration, the overstated optimism of that time seems more evident than ever.

Intercultural dialogue as a political goal of the Barcelona Declaration

Discourses on the role of dialogue and identity construction are not neglected in international relations research, and the Mediterranean, with its long-lasting Euro-Mediterranean relations, represents a prolific case study.[4] Intercultural dialogue across the Mediterranean has been one of the main pillars of the Euro-Mediterranean cooperation since the launching of the EMP in 1995. The third chapter of the Barcelona Declaration invited partners to 'cooperate with the aim of developing human resources, and promoting understanding between cultures and exchanges between civil societies' (Barcelona Declaration, 1995).[5]

The EMP cooperation framework assumed that EU and Mediterranean countries could develop mutual relations through dialogue (Pace, 2005a) in a wide range of issues. The Barcelona Declaration and its work programme acknowledged the importance of intercultural dialogue and dialogues between religions;[6] the role of media to favour the understanding of cultures; the respect of cultural identities fostered via cultural programmes; the participation of civil society in the EMP (including regional and local authorities), etc.

When the Political and Security Partnership was revealed as fragile – by the early 2000s – policy-makers re-launched the third chapter.[7] The Al Aqsa Intifada broke up in September 2000 and put security cooperation under stress; despite a long and sophisticated diplomatic effort, the adoption of the Charter for Peace and Stability in the Mediterranean was provisionally frozen and eventually discarded. The third chapter of the Barcelona Declaration was then considered as an indirect way to address security issues that for the time being could not be addressed within the first chapter. A popular argument was to invest in cross-cultural dialogue, involving greater contact and cooperation at the level of civil society, in order to facilitate cooperation in other fields. A new emphasis on the Social, Cultural and Human Partnership was seen as a means of regaining some momentum within the EMP at a time when the overall project was threatened by delays and blockages.

After an uneven development of the three chapters and a 'relative neglect of the third basket . . . [i]n the new millennium . . . the third basket of the EMP agenda [had] begun to acquire a more substantial script' (Gillespie, 2003: 22). Several EU initiatives and cooperation programmes were launched to develop mutual understanding via a better knowledge of 'the other' and eventually achieve peaceful coexistence.

Alongside the resurgence of the Israeli–Palestinian political violence, the 9/11 attacks initiated a new security threat series with various groups using and preaching terror as a diffuse strategy, from Al Qaeda to ISIS to – maybe – others to come. Without distinction between global, regional or domestic level, uncontrolled terrorist actions targeted both EU and Mediterranean countries. In the aftermath of the 9/11 terrorist attacks, the importance attached to intercultural dialogue within the EMP framework dramatically increased.

However, new or renovated systemic constraints soon affected the outcomes of the socio-cultural partnership. Some scholars denounced the 'lack of clear and specific plans regarding the cultural dimension of the [EMP] process' (Gillespie, 2002: 105). Others acknowledged the EMP idealistic goals: 'the Barcelona process [was] a laboratory where one of the most ambitious experiments in international relations may have started to take place' (Pace, 2005a: 293). Despite the goodwill inherent in the concept of 'cultural dialogue', its institutionalization was inevitably problematic, since 'cultural dialogue' is a paradoxical and conflictual operation (Stetter 2005: 332).[8] Moreover, cooperation within the third chapter remained subservient to European goals, ideals and values (Schäfer, 2007).

Following the naive assumption that culture is a force for good, conducive almost inevitably to peaceful coexistence and mutual respect, the EU had represented its EMP third basket policy aims in a highly idealized fashion (Schumacher, 2005). The third chapter of the Barcelona Declaration had envisaged the rapprochement between peoples through a social, cultural and human partnership in order to encourage understanding between cultures and exchanges between civil societies. This derives from the idea that cultural diversity in the Euro-Mediterranean area is a richness per se and provides an added value to be defended following the credo of pluralism, mutual respect and coexistence. Unfortunately, this is unattainable in turbulent times of fanaticism and extremism animated by alienation and destruction of otherness.

Challenges to intercultural dialogue in the Mediterranean

The Mediterranean is currently facing several crises and very few analysts would claim that a Euro-Mediterranean identity based upon a common language and shared practices (Panebianco, 2003; Pace, 2006) has eventually emerged. In the last two decades the optimism that had characterized the 1990s and the adoption of the Barcelona Declaration has vanished, overwhelmed by political instability, civil wars, terrorism, proliferation of weapons of mass destruction, religious extremism and mounting intolerance.

The social-constructivist paradigm emphasizing the role of culture, identity, norms and communication as fundamental vehicles for regional cooperation is being questioned by radicalization and socio-economic structural factors leading to widespread dissatisfaction. Security-related issues prevailing in the Euro-Mediterranean political realm endanger cultural cooperation. Systemic constraints such as poverty, unemployment, socio-economic dissatisfaction or violent ideologies supporting armed groups seriously challenge intercultural dialogue across the Mediterranean. In such a context, strategic interactions can hardly create shared meanings and mutual trust eventually leading to an identity-making process.

New analytical tools are required to understand the ongoing trends. The decreased political commitment in multi-dimensional regional cooperation frameworks marked by the adoption of the Union for the Mediterranean (UfM) has favoured a more pragmatic à la carte approach (Seeberg, 2010). Existing conflicts and wars, mounting intolerance, extremism and eventually terrorist attacks have threatened and almost frozen widespread regional cooperation projects. In the current Mediterranean troubled waters social actors alone cannot perform as successful actors of cooperation. A new *élan* in regional cooperation would require stronger institutional support and more political engagement both at domestic and regional level. In this context the ALF performance comprehensibly remains below expectations.

The Anna Lindh Foundation: size and features of a region-wide network[9]

The 'Anna Lindh Euro-Mediterranean Foundation for the Dialogue between Cultures' was created as an intergovernmental institution within the Barcelona Process.[10] The ALF international headquarters were inaugurated in 2005 in Alexandria, Egypt, with the first heads of national networks meeting.[11] In 2006 the first ALF call for proposals was issued, together with the launching of the Euro-Med award, the Journalist award, and the Euro-Med education programme. At the Paris summit that established the UfM, in 2008, the Foundation was mentioned as the main institution for intercultural dialogue in the region.

Fully in line with the goals of the Barcelona Declaration, the Foundation aims to contribute to the creation of a space of prosperity, coexistence and peace; works to restore trust in dialogue and bridge the gaps in mutual perceptions, as well as promoting diversity and coexistence. Its ambitious scope is to overcome the misunderstandings and stereotypes affecting relations between and within societies in the Mediterranean by setting up north–south networks.[12]

Since its foundation, it was conceived as a 'network of national networks'. Originally, it grouped national networks based in EMP countries; today the Foundation brings together national networks established in UfM countries.[13] Nevertheless, the original Mediterranean partners of the EMP (labelled here as MENA countries) still represent the core group of the ALF networks (see Figure 33.1).[14]

Not surprisingly, EU associations are extremely active within the ALF network. Out of the 4,062 associations belonging to the ALF network in 2014, almost 60 per cent of them are based in EU member states (2,382). With almost 300 associations, Italy and France are well represented within the ALF network and always act as project leaders in ALF projects.[15] Luxembourg and Latvia (respectively 11 and 15 associations) are the least active. Less than 10 per cent of the ALF associations belong to Balkan countries and Mauritania. More than 30 per cent (namely 1,315 associations) are registered in MENA countries, with the Palestinian Authority top of the list with 302 associations. When Syria was suspended in 2011, it had 59 associations.

Figures related to Tunisia are rather emblematic. In 2014 only 61 Tunisian associations were active within the ALF network, despite the fact that since the Jasmine Revolution of January 2011 that led to the collapse of Ben Ali's regime, the number of Tunisian associations has rapidly increased. There is a significant gap between the size of the Tunisian national network and the current figures of associations existing in the country. For small, newly established associations it is not an easy task to engage in regional networking generally dominated by EU

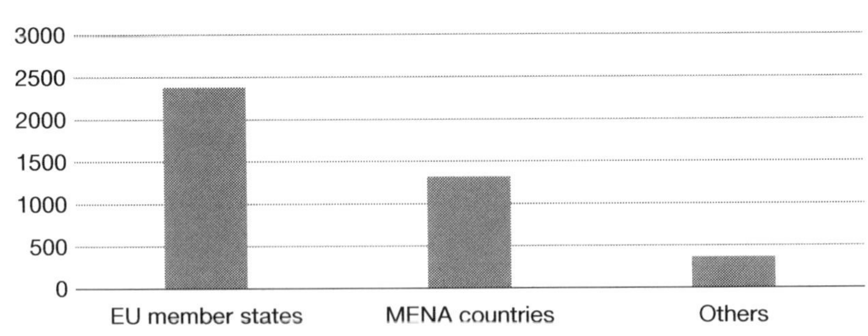

Figure 33.1 The ALF network by number of associations per groups of countries (2014)

Source: Author's elaboration from ALF Review (2005–15: 13)

associations that are familiar with EU complex forms and procedures.[16] To fill an ALF application, associations need an administrative staff mastering the EU bureaucratic language in order to provide clear need assessments, functional work-plans, detailed provisional budgets, etc. A successful application requires an ambitious project with a long-term impact because competition is hard: in 2015 less than 20 per cent of applications were funded. However, the goal at stake is usually a grant of €30,000–50,000, which might not be sufficient to implement a very ambitious project; extra funds can be a plus. EU associations often act as 'bureaucratic mediators' to socialize MENA partners.

Moreover, irrespectively of what happens on the ground, associations involved in ALF activities need a sort of official recognition from above.[17] Domestic conditions can favour or hinder the implementation of ALF projects. The Egyptian experience is a case in point. On the one hand, small associations denounce the undue political control exerted by the domestic political leadership,[18] on the other Egyptian associations are engaged in large cooperation networks.[19] Associations working in authoritarian MENA countries de facto require and benefit from a sort of political authorization.

The Foundation involves around 4,000 civil society organizations of very diverse nature. These are mainly NGOs (a bit less than 60 per cent), but also foundations (11 per cent), public institutions (8 per cent), individuals and private organizations (3 per cent), local and regional authorities (2 per cent) (ALF Review 2005–15: 12). About 40 per cent of the associations involved in ALF activities deal with youth and education, 37 per cent of associations act within the international cultural cooperation field (ALF Review 2005–15: 13).

The ALF main fields of action are: arts and culture; youth and education; cities and migration; peace and coexistence; values, religion and spirituality; media. Figure 33.2 shows the total amount of granted projects from 2006 to 2015 in each ALF action field. Arts and culture is by far and away the most relevant field of cooperation within the ALF. Religion and spirituality is the weakest field of ALF networking.

The ALF cooperation grants (€1,000,000 for the 2015 call) represent a 'window of opportunity' for regional cooperation. However, the goal of achieving 'peace and stability in the Mediterranean' seems unattainable via cooperation on thematic projects. Table 33.1 provides a general overview of the ALF grants from 2006 to 2015. The 2015 ALF call promoted projects falling within the fields of 'education for intercultural citizenship' and 'intercultural artistic co-productions'. The 2013 call promoted the so-called '4D Strategy' (i.e. intercultural dialogue,

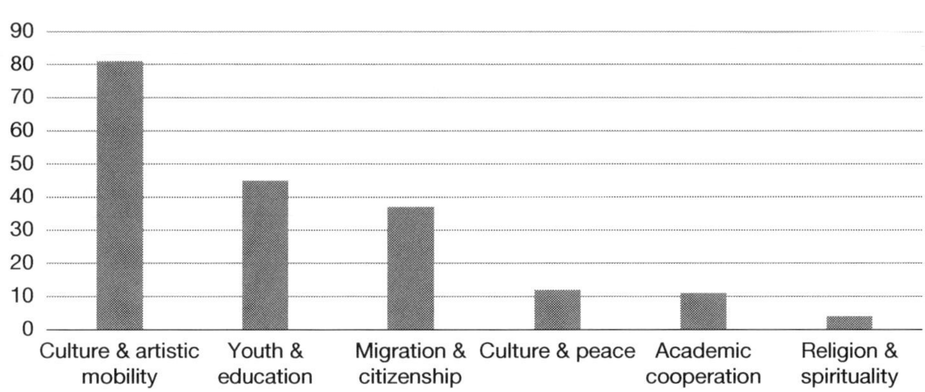

Figure 33.2 ALF projects in a nutshell (2006–15 grants)

Source: Author's elaboration from the ALF Review (2005–15) and the ALF Review (2005–11).

Table 33.1 The Anna Lindh Foundation grants (2006–15)

	Financial envelope	*Number of applications*	*Number of funded projects*	*Number of partners*	*Number of beneficiaries (estimated)*	*Number of involved countries (EU/MENA)*
Call 2015	€1,000,000	187	30 in process	–	–	25/5
Call 2013	€800,000	184	26	88+	105,626**	21/8
Call 2012	€1,350,000	264	40	142+	24,394	22/8
Call 2010	€500,000	231	27	86+	19,528	17/9
Call 2009	€2,300,000*	393	56	239+	21,476	27/9
Call 2007	€1,800,000	131	30	141+	30,934	21/8
Call 2006	€1,500,000	101	2,120	172+	30,046	18/9
Total	€9,250,000	1,304	218	868+	126,378	all EU/all MENA partners

Source: Author's elaboration from the ALF Review (2005–15) and the ALF Review (2005–11).

Notes: *In 2009, ALF launched two calls of proposals to support civil society's actions in the Mediterranean. One call financed 35 short-term projects with a financial envelope of €600,000. The other call financed 21 long-term projects with a financial envelope of €1,700,000. For 2009, therefore, the table shows the aggregated figure of the two annual calls.

** Direct beneficiary (mainly through social media, educative formats and large public events).

diversity, democracies and human development). What is put into question is the multiplier effect of ALF projects, since the cooperation effects remain limited to the actors involved and rarely have an impact outside the specific granted network.

The limited effects produced by these networks are mainly due to ALF internal rules. Following the 1+1 schema (one EU partner plus one Mediterranean partner), in many cases trans-cultural dialogue and mutual understanding are fostered within small thematic groups. The 1+1 networks represent the minimum requirement to apply. The number of partners usually varies between two and nine (i.e. four EU and five Mediterranean partners or vice versa). However, about 30 per cent of the 218 total ALF granted projects rely upon 1+1 networks. On the one hand, the small size of the ALF network can favour applications, but on the other ALF grants promote bilateral relations rather than true regional cooperation networks. The regional impact of the ALF network is thus weakened by this rule.

Furthermore, ALF granted projects address specific issues and can hardly produce dialogue between cultures in a broader sense. The voluntary basis upon which an application is set up necessarily implies an a priori sharing of values and interests among pre-existing networks (either formal or informal). On such narrow bases, the overall impact outside existing networks is limited, especially when and where this common understanding is lacking. ALF risks remaining a 'closed circle of friends'.

Also fostered domestically by national networks, the Foundation is becoming a well-known institution granting Euro-Mediterranean thematic networks. Figure 33.3 indicates that competition is hard and total funds allocated are insufficient to grant all applications. The caveat of 'national networks' risks limiting the effects on Euro-Mediterranean society at large, especially when national networks solicit applications.[20] Being an intergovernmental organization, national ministries influence the Foundation via national networks. Since national networks are organized along national lines, not around themes and issues, they risk building domestic barriers. The expectations on this model have been far too high, and 'it is [*still*] highly questionable

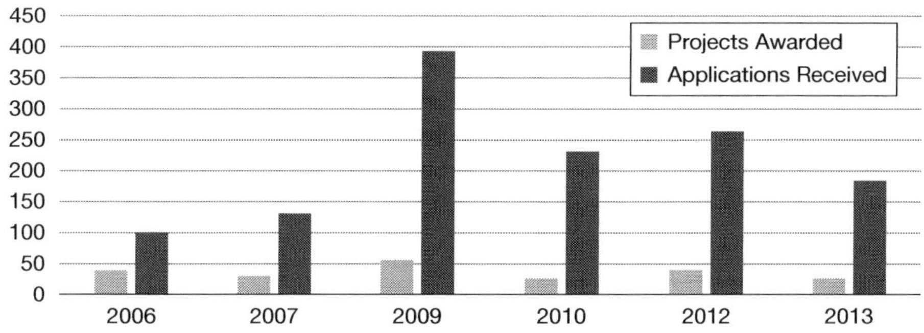

Figure 33.3 Ratio ALF grants/applications: calls 2006–13

Source: ALF Reviews (2005–11: 50) and (2005–15: 45).

whether nationally grouped civil society actors have the appropriate tools for effectively promoting education, sustainable development, and human rights'[21] (Del Sarto, 2005: 325).

Youth as a key actor of intercultural dialogue across the Mediterranean

Youth – one of the key target groups of the third chapter of the Barcelona Declaration – represents the most relevant ALF field of action following arts and culture (see Figure 33.2). The ALF reports consider 'youth and education' (Y&E) as one of the key areas of ALF activities, following the assumption that young people (and their teachers) engaged in regional networks learn 'to live together in diversity' and experience an 'intercultural citizenship by learning' (ALF Review 2005–11; ALF Review 2005–15). Four sets of initiatives address youth and education:

1 Actions to develop intercultural learning methodologies and new education resources (including education manuals).
2 Actions to create a network of teachers (e.g. regional training courses, workshops on cultural diversity and intercultural dialogue, workshops on teaching about interfaith issues).
3 Actions to coordinate different actors from the youth sector (e.g. Euro-Med Youth Workshops, Euro-Med Youth Parliament, the Euro-Arab Youth Forum).
4 Actions to grant activities coordinated by the partners from the two shores (e.g. projects based upon the use of video animation for youth leaders or for the promotion of citizenship among young people).

Table 33.2 provides a comparison of ALF networking divided by fields of action. While in terms of number of projects, Y&E represents the second area of activities after culture and artistic mobility (see Figure 33.3), in terms of network size Y&E is the largest area of cooperation. In fact, the highest number of associations is currently active in this sector. The number of ALF partners involved in Y&E has increased especially in recent years: until 2010, only 16 per cent of the ALF partners were active in this field, in 2014 the number of partners more than doubled with 40 per cent of partners.

However, in terms of net figures, data do not reflect the political will to invest more and foremost on young people. Out of the total projects funded for the period 2005–15, just 21 per cent were focused on Y&E, and more specifically just 15 per cent (23 projects) in the period (2005–10) and 35 per cent (22 projects) for the period (2011–15) (see Table 33.3).

Table 33.2 ALF network size by field of action

Fields of action	*2005–15 (%)*	*2005–10 (%)*
Youth and education	40	16
International/cultural cooperation	37	NA
Arts and cultural cooperation	28	27
Democracy and community development	27	10
Human rights	22	8
Environment/sustainable development	17	7
Media	14	6
Research	14	7
Gender	13	5.5
Heritage	11	6
Religion	6	2
Others	13	5

Source: Author's elaboration from the ALF Review (2005–15) and the ALF Review (2005–11).

Table 33.3 ALF grants to youth and education projects

Years	*Projects for youth and education (in numbers and percentages)*	*Total ALF granted projects*
2005–10	23 (15%)	152
2011–15	22 (33%)	66
Total	45 (21%)	218

Source: Author's elaboration from the ALF Review (2005–15) and the ALF Review (2005–11).

Over the years, the Foundation has tried to adapt to new challenges and threats in the Mediterranean and more specific issues have been identified as new priority areas. 'Moving beyond the extremist narrative' has become a relevant ALF political objective in order to search for 'alternatives to extremism'.[22] This implies a different labelling, but not necessarily a more effective strategy.

Considering that young people are the first victims of radicalization, the ALF assumption is that EuroMed policies need to address the majority of youth who are not attracted to violence to provide them with information on the context in which radicalization arises. The Foundation has launched large-scale public awareness campaigns aimed at positively framing youth in debates on participation in public life to ensure greater buy-in of young people.

The Foundation devotes specific attention to media, with the overt goal to leverage the positive benefit from the media's role in shaping public perceptions and attitudes in the Euro-Mediterranean region. Partnerships with media and civil society are envisaged to create a permanent observatory to monitor more effectively the role of journalists when it comes to reporting on cross-cultural issues. The Foundation also seeks to invest in a new generation of journalists with the skills to report on complex issues with an intercultural dimension. New media formats for intercultural dialogue are regarded as useful tools to reach a broad audience and provide examples of intercultural coexistence. Following the ALF approach, networks of journalism schools fostering new and innovative tools should inspire intercultural dialogue more broadly.

Limits to institutional networking: the need for new models

The Foundation reflects the constructivist approach that lays at the basis of the EMP, claiming that bringing together people from across the Mediterranean leads to the improvement of mutual respect between cultures and supporting civil society helps in the construction of the common future of the area. The EU has assumed that multi-dimensional cooperation within the EMP and intercultural dialogue fostered via the ALF network would be a successful model conducive to better understanding, mutual respect and peaceful coexistence. The EU has portrayed the richness of diversity and multiculturalism as the key towards a peaceful and prosperous Euro-Mediterranean area. Despite the best intentions that inspire it, this model is distant from the logic of cooperation fostered by the ALF network illustrated earlier.

Moreover, this model assumes that intercultural dialogue can move along a continuum, from a minimum of interaction to a maximum result, eventually leading to the adoption of a common language. Yet, several options can stand in between the two extremes of the continuum: intolerance, cultural closure, refusal of diversity, exchange of views, respect for different ideas, sharing values and principles (either a few or many). There is no linear process, because regional cooperation does not necessarily improve mutual perceptions or appease cultural differences.

Considering that some transnational actors have become globally influential by supporting terrorist strategies aimed at fighting any form of cultural dialogue and mutual respect, it is clear that intercultural dialogue cannot be assumed as a political panacea to overcome deep misunderstandings. Extremists and radicals have put into question the EU model based upon peaceful coexistence respecting diversity. Education, culture, media and civil society organization networks cannot foster mutual respect irrespectively of systemic constraints and challenges.

The regional scenario has become rather complex. The most relevant political issue is not any longer what we had experienced and researched in the last 20 years (namely the dichotomy between Islam and the West), but rather the spreading of radicalism and extremisms, with violence systematically applied against the others. The rising of extremisms is a global phenomenon of the current times, fuelled by political instability and socio-economic dissatisfaction. Radicalization has steadily progressed, more quickly and strongly than mutual understanding among different civilizations, religions and cultures. Alienation, lack of integration and societal exclusion are de facto impeding dialogue between cultures being fostered via education, mobility, youth or media.

The west, Islam, Europe or the Arab world involve variegated political entities with multiple actors, cultures and sub-cultures which are all menaced and threatened by terrorist groups who make use of logic of persuasion and proselytism. Faced with the recent terrorist attacks in Europe and the use of terror as a systemic act of aggression, many Muslims settled in European countries are declaring that these behaviours are 'not in my name'. Culture, traditionally associated with low politics, has become a very sensitive political issue. And dialogue among cultures cannot be left any longer to cooperation among civil society actors. States are brought back in world politics, not just because they have demonstrated great weakness to protect their citizens from generalized irrational violence and terrorist attacks, but also because they have to adopt new security strategies and engage in more effective cooperation at the intelligence level.

Although it is not an easy task to measure and evaluate the regional outcomes of the ALF networks, there is a clear expectations–capabilities gap in the performance of the Foundation. Without expecting to get information about the ALF intercultural effectiveness, the ALF Reports on Intercultural Trends and Social Change in the Euro-Mediterranean Region published in 2010 and 2014 provide useful indications on perceptions of respondents to Gallup polls conducted in 2009 and 2012. What strikes the most in terms of common definition of the Mediterranean is that respondents from EU, southern or eastern Mediterranean countries have a different perception of what the Mediterranean region is. Despite ALF investments in regional networking and cooperation projects, a common definition of Mediterranean is still missing, as if there were two different Mediterranean regions. When asked about the countries that spontaneously come to their mind when thinking about the Mediterranean region, Europeans tend to think about European countries bordering the Mediterranean Sea (mainly Italy), while respondents from southern and eastern Mediterranean countries rather think about their neighbours (ALF Report, 2010: 18).

Overall, the 2010 ALF Report reveals more optimism, with a consistent reference to shared values and a vision of the Mediterranean as a bridge. The 2014 ALF Report too refers to a common cultural heritage of the Mediterranean countries (ALF Report, 2014: 6), but reveals also that almost half of the respondents regard religious and cultural diversity as a threat to the stability of society (ibid.: 39). This argument is in contrast to the value of multiculturalism and the richness of diversity claimed by the Foundation.

Two different trends seem to coexist. On the one hand, there is the will to know more about the others (ibid.: 65), on the other there is a widespread feeling of fear, indifference and suspicion. The EuroMed survey adopts two meaningful indicators: 'Mediterranean as a source of conflict' and 'Mediterranean as a common and cultural heritage'. In 2010 only 32 per cent of the Europeans and 27 per cent of the MENA respondents considered the Mediterranean as a source of conflict (ALF Report, 2010: 19). In 2014, the percentage of respondents considering the Mediterranean as a conflictual area doubled, with 75 per cent of Europeans and 71 per cent of MENA interviewed (ALF Report, 2014: 16). Nevertheless, the Mediterranean is still appreciated for its common and cultural heritage. In 2010, 47 per cent of the Europeans and 36 per cent of the MENA respondents acknowledged the common and cultural heritage, while in 2014 this percentage has almost doubled.

The Mediterranean is currently faced with authoritarian resilience, civil wars and mounting radicalization; political regimes unable to provide political order and economic growth; socio-economic dissatisfaction and political disorder paralysing existing regional cooperation frameworks. In times of crisis all around the Mediterranean, the agreement on a definition of the Mediterranean area, acknowledging its relevant change dynamics, is the pre-condition of cooperation.

Conclusions

This chapter has challenged the constructivist assumption laying at the basis of intercultural dialogue in the Mediterranean, fostered by the EMP and more specifically by the Anna Lindh Foundation. The EU promotes civil society cooperation and regional networks as if networking could improve mutual perceptions in a sort of linear process, but this model is at risk both domestically and regionally.

Multiple Europes and multiple identities characterize the construction of Europe, currently put into question by Brexit, Grexit, Frexit or similar alternative political options. For decades the EU motto 'united in diversity' (or 'diversity in unity') has guided EU cooperation programmes. Current events such as domestic tensions on migration or severe terror strategies EU member states are experiencing on their soil, are putting Europe under stress.

The EU had adapted a similar approach to the Euro-Mediterranean area, regarded as a *laboratoire* to respect political, economic and cultural diversity. Yet the Mediterranean remains a troubled region. Similar popular protests and requests which emerged since 2010 have produced different political outcomes (or even none) (Panebianco and Rossi, 2012). Economic imbalances are triggering social dissatisfaction across the Mediterranean. Terrorism is mounting both within and outside the EU. Political instability, economic imbalances, social dissatisfaction and an increasing number of terrorist attacks in Europe and abroad provide a very bleak picture of the Mediterranean area. Such a variegated and complex scenario does not allow defending cultural diversity via networking and civil society activism. It is difficult to defend cultural diversity as an added value or a richness to protect in the Euro-Mediterranean area.

As scholars, we cannot be inclined to pessimism nor can we talk about a cultural war, but undeniably the Mediterranean is experiencing a very turbulent time. Pan-Mediterraneanism – as an inspiring ideology of the elites in the Mediterranean (Pace, 2005b: 435) – for the time being seems far unachievable.

What is currently missing is a regional collective identity, not only in the Mediterranean broadly conceived as a region, but also on each of the two shores. The self/other distinctions are framing intracultural debates along paradigms of radical extremist approaches rather than multiculturalist ones. A forceful rhetoric of intracultural inclusion/exclusion has become more appealing than the peaceful coexistence of diversity.

One thing is to set up institutions to foster dialogue and cooperation among civil society, another thing is to transform cooperation among peers into mutual understanding and peaceful coexistence on a regional level, ultimately conducive to a common and shared identity in the Mediterranean. The belief of the early 2000s that intercultural cooperation was the most promising EMP cooperation field has been challenged by systemic changes and threats. In just one decade or so a paradigmatic shift has reversed the causal nexus: cultural cooperation is useful, but cannot be a sufficient condition to favour coexistence; conversely, it can be easily paralysed by adverse systemic conditions.

The bottom-up approach which is at the basis of the ALF networking is currently put into question, as if there were a gap between civil society organizations and non-state actors, on the one hand, and political actors on the other. The distinction between high politics and low politics does not work and new platforms are needed to foster dialogue between politics and society.

The EMP elitist nature that many scholars denounced in the past (Gillespie, 2003: 32) seems reflected in the Anna Lindh Foundation, which is managed and controlled by national networks having good relations with (or at least not vetoed by) political institutions and rarely represent opposition groups. This is not the result of a spontaneous bottom-up process, but rather a bottom-up process favoured and supported from the top for political purposes. This kind of *dirigiste* model has not produced a multiplier effect, but has rather set up thematic cooperation networks separated from society at large.

Notes

1 On social constructivism, see Risse (2004).
2 The seminal article by Adler and Barnett (1998) is a departing point to understand the construction of security communities in Europe and beyond. On the failure of cooperative security systems, see Attinà (2013).
3 The 12 Mediterranean partners that signed the Barcelona Declaration together with the EU member states were: Algeria, Cyprus, Egypt, Israel, Jordan, Lebanon, Malta, Morocco, Syria, the Palestinian Authority, Tunisia and Turkey.
4 On the role of dialogue in the EMP, see Pace (2005a). For a discussion on the concept of cultural dialogue in the EMP context and the problematization of identity that relies upon communication, see Stetter (2005).
5 On the cultural dimension of the EMP, see Peresso (1998), Panebianco (2001), Pace and Schumacher (2004), Schäfer (2007). On civil society cooperation and the Euro-Med Civil Forum, see Jünemann (2003).
6 In the very first years of the EMP the interfaith dialogue had acquired a central role in intercultural practices within the Euro-Mediterranean context (Silvestri, 2005).
7 In 2002, at the Fifth Euro-Mediterranean Conference of Foreign Ministers in Valencia, the EMP partners agreed to establish a foundation specifically devoted to intercultural dialogue, the nascent ALF. On the political conditions that impeded any substantial advancement in the security partnership – mainly due to the recrudescence of the Arab–Israeli conflict – and the attempts to reinvigorate the Barcelona Process through the Valencia Action Plan, see Gillespie (2002).

8 On the political implications of institutionalizing a 'cultural dialogue', see Stetter (2005).
9 Many thanks go to Iole Fontana for data collection.
10 In October 2003 the high-level advisory group established at the initiative of the president of the European Commission had issued a report on intercultural dialogue recommending the creation of a Euro-Mediterranean Foundation. The ALF statute was approved on 30 November 2004 by the Sixth Euro-Mediterranean Conference of Foreign Ministers (called Barcelona VI).
11 The ALF governing structure includes a president, an executive director, a board of governors chosen by the UfM member states, an advisory council. For more information visit the ALF website: www.annalindhfoundation.org.
12 Article II of the ALF statute sets up its objectives and tasks.
13 In 2008, 43 countries adhered to the UfM: Albania, Algeria, Austria, Belgium, Bosnia and Herzegovina, Bulgaria, Croatia, Cyprus, Czech Republic, Denmark, Egypt, Estonia, Finland, France, Germany, Greece, Hungary, Ireland, Israel, Italy, Jordan, Latvia, Lebanon, Lithuania, Luxemburg, Malta, Mauritania, Monaco, Montenegro, Morocco, Palestine, Poland, Portugal, Romania, Slovakia, Slovenia, Spain, Syria, Sweden, the Netherlands, Tunisia, Turkey and the United Kingdom. Due to the civil war, Syria has been suspended from cooperation programmes since 2011.
14 The label 'MENA countries' used in Figure 33.1 refers to Algeria, Egypt, Israel, Jordan, Lebanon, Morocco, Palestinian Authority, Syria (until 2011) and Tunisia.
15 Yet some associations are inactive, therefore the Italian Network plans to conduct regular reviews.
16 Author's interview, Tunisian partner.
17 This is in line with what Del Sarto denounced ten years ago (Del Sarto, 2005).
18 Controls by the Egyptian authorities in 2011 have blocked ALF grants, allocated but never transferred. Author's interview, Egyptian association.
19 Almost half of the ALF projects with Egyptian project leaders have 5–6 partners. This strikes with the overall picture: Israelis are mostly *chef de fil* of networks with 2–3 partners, while Lebanese and Palestinians are mostly leaders of 1+1 projects. Author's analysis of the projects listed in the ALF Review (2005–15).
20 Author's interview, Italian association.
21 My comment in italics.
22 The Valletta Agenda adopted in view of the ALF Forum to be held in Malta on 24–25 October 2016 regards youth as 'the next generation of dialogue leaders'.

References

Adler, E. and Barnett, M. (1998). A framework for the study of security communities, in Adler, E. and Barnett, M. (eds), *Security Communities*, Cambridge: Cambridge University Press, pp. 29–65.

Adler, E. and Crawford, B. (2006). Normative power: the European practice of region-building and the case of the EuroMediterranean Partnership, in Adler, E., Crawford, B., Bicchi, F. and Del Sarto, R. (eds), *The Convergence of Civilizations: Constructing a Mediterranean Region*, Toronto: University of Toronto Press, pp. 3–50.

ALF Report (Anna Lindh Foundation) (2010). *Euro-Med Intercultural Trends*, online publication, available at www.alfpolska.org/public/editor/file/AnnaLindhReport2010.pdf

ALF Report (Anna Lindh Foundation) (2014). *Intercultural Trends and Social Change in the Euro-Mediterranean Region*, online publication available at www.slideshare.net/jamaity_tn/the-anna-lindh-report-2014-intercultural-trends-and-social-changes-in-the-euromediterranean-region

ALF Review (Anna Lindh Foundation) (2005–15). *The Anna Lindh Review*, online publication, available at www.annalindhfoundation.org/anna-lindh-review-2005-15

ALF Review (Anna Lindh Foundation) (2005–11). *The Anna Lindh Review*, online publication, available at http://communication.annalindh.org/key-figures-anna-lindh-review

Attinà, F. (2013). Mediterranean security revised, *Democracy and Security*, 9:1–2, 120–36.

Barcelona Declaration (1995), adopted at the Euro-Mediterranean Conference (27–28 November 1995), *Mediterranean Politics* 2/1 (Summer 1997): 177–87.

Del Sarto, R. (2005). Setting the (cultural) agenda: concepts, communities and representation in Euro-Mediterranean relations, *Mediterranean Politics*, 10:3, 313–30.

Gillespie, R. (2002). The Valencia Conference: reinvigorating the Barcelona Process?, *Mediterranean Politics*, 7:2, 105–14.

Gillespie, R. (2003). Reshaping the agenda? The internal politics of the Barcelona Process in the aftermath of September 11, *Mediterranean Politics*, 8:2–3, 22–36.
Huntington, S. P. (1993). The clash of civilizations?, *Foreign Affairs*, 72:3, 22–49.
Huntington, S. P. (1996). *The Clash of Civilizations and the Remaking of World Order*, New York: Simon & Schuster.
Jünemann, A. (2003). The EuroMed Civil Forum: critical watchdog and intercultural mediator, in Panebianco, S. (ed.), *A New Euro-Mediterranean Cultural Identity*, London: Frank Cass, pp. 84–107.
Malmvig, H. (2005). Security through intercultural dialogue? Implications of the securitization of Euro-Mediterranean dialogue between cultures, *Mediterranean Politics*, 10:3, 349–64.
Pace, M. (2005a). Imagining co-presence in Euro-Mediterranean relations: the role of 'dialogue', *Mediterranean Politics*, 10:3, 291–312.
Pace, M. (2005b). Conclusion: cultural democracy in Euro-Mediterranean relations?, *Mediterranean Politics*, 10:3, 427–37.
Pace, M. (2006). *The Politics of Regional Identity: Meddling with the Mediterranean*, London/New York: Routledge.
Pace, M. and Schumacher, T. (2004). Culture and community in the Euro-Mediterranean Partnership: a roundtable on the third basket, Alexandria 5–7 October 2003, *Mediterranean Politics*, 9:1, 122–6.
Panebianco, S. (2001). The EMP innovative dimension of a cultural dialogue: prospects and challenges, in Attinà, F. and Stavridis, S. (eds), *The Barcelona Process and Euro-Mediterranean Issues from Stuttgart to Marseille*, Milan: Giuffré, pp. 99–120.
Panebianco, S. (ed.) (2003). *A New Euro-Mediterranean Cultural Identity*, London: Frank Cass.
Panebianco, S. and Rossi, R. (eds) (2012). *Winds of Democratic Change in the Mediterranean? Processes, Actors and Possible Outcomes*, Soveria Mannelli: Rubbettino.
Peresso, E. M. (1998). Euro-Mediterranean cultural cooperation, *European Foreign Affairs Review*, 3, 135–56.
Risse, T. (2004). Social constructivism and European integration, in Wiener, A. and Diez T. (eds), *European Integration Theory*, Oxford: Oxford University Press.
Schäfer, I. (2007). The cultural dimension of the Euro-Mediterranean Partnership: a critical review of the first decade of intercultural cooperation, *History and Anthropology*, 18:3, 333–52.
Schumacher, T. (2005). Introduction: the study of Euro-Mediterranean cultural and social cooperation in perspective, *Mediterranean Politics*, 10:3, 281–90.
Seeberg, P. (2010). Union for the Mediterranean: pragmatic multilateralism and the depoliticization of EU–Middle Eastern relations, *Middle East Critique*, 19:3, 287–302.
Silvestri, S. (2005). EU relations with Islam in the context of the EMP's cultural dialogue, *Mediterranean Politics*, 10:3, 385–405.
Spencer, C. (1997). Building confidence in the Mediterranean, *Mediterranean Politics*, 2:2, 23–48.
Stetter, S. (2005). The politics of de-paradoxification in Euro-Mediterranean relations: semantics and structures of 'cultural dialogue', *Mediterranean Politics*, 10:3, 331–48.

INDEX

administration *see* public administration
Africa, sub-Saharan 1, 21, 66, 98, 110, 111, 113, 134, 166, 201, 233, 239, 249, 269, 280, 378, 384, 385, 387, 389, 390; *see also* North Africa
agriculture 18, 42, 62, 127, 222, 223, 260, 269, 270, 272, 311, 383
AKP (Justice and Development Party) 126, 132–6, 138, 161, 163, 164, 172, 175, 336, 349, 390
Al Albani, Nasir Al-Din 328
Al Assad, Bashar 78, 113, 116, 137, 163, 165, 228, 365
Al Assad, Hafiz 163, 228
Al Baghdadi, Abu Bakr 189
Al Bana, Hassan 321–5
Albania 17, 157, 158, 161–7, 271, 288, 312
Al Hudaybi, Hassan 322, 325
Al Jazeera 326, 372, 374, 377
Al Nusra 113, 328
Al Thinni, Abdullah 138
Al Qaeda 113, 114, 115, 116, 185, 186, 187, 189, 192, 397
Al Sisi, Abdel Fattah 80, 125, 137, 163, 213
Anna Lindh Foundation 8, 299, 312, 394, 398, 400, 404, 405
Arab Human Development Report 248
Arab–Israeli conflict 18, 29, 53, 54, 64, 100, 102–4, 111, 121, 124, 133, 171, 194, 324; *see also* Palestinian–Israeli conflict
Arab League 52, 56, 123, 124, 127, 137, 149, 312
Arab socialism 4, 5, 223, 321, 323, 324
'Arab Spring' *see* Arab uprisings/Arab Spring
Arab states, political views of/within 222
Arab unity initiatives *see* pan-Arabism
Arab uprisings/Arab Spring 1, 4, 5, 7, 8, 21, 24, 25, 31–4, 44, 56, 57, 61, 65, 68, 69, 72, 75, 76, 92, 93, 102, 105, 112, 120–4, 128, 132, 135–8, 151, 154, 157, 164, 165, 171, 172, 178, 194, 199, 201, 207–14, 232, 238, 250, 295, 296, 300–5, 310–16, 325–8, 331, 338, 350, 359, 361–8, 371–9, 382, 383, 387–90
'Arab World' *see* Arab states, political views of/within
armies *see* military
arms sales 61, 76, 80, 116, 126, 127
asylum seekers *see* refugees
authoritarianism 3, 24, 27, 32, 34, 76, 80, 97, 101, 112, 153, 157, 164, 166, 207, 213, 215, 222, 237, 298, 309, 362, 367; authoritarian actors/regimes(s) 1, 4, 5, 7, 24, 27, 30, 31, 32, 33, 55, 56, 63–7, 69, 98, 100, 105, 151, 157, 162, 176, 199, 202, 208, 213–15, 223, 228, 247, 249, 250, 251, 281–3, 285, 299, 300, 311, 322–5, 327, 328, 335, 336, 338, 339, 343, 349, 350, 353, 359, 364, 374, 375, 386, 399; authoritarian context 310, 316; authoritarian modernization 221; authoritarian resilience/persistence 4, 81, 207, 208, 212, 214, 215, 228, 404; authoritarian revival 154, 207, 229; post-authoritarian 160, 161; semi-authoritarian 325, 328

Ba'athist regime/party 223, 247, 321, 324
Baghdad Pact 18, 52, 61
Balkans 17, 113, 115, 117, 133, 134, 135, 136, 148, 157, 171, 174, 175, 176, 247, 279, 299, 383, 398
Barcelona Declaration (1995) 54, 62, 272, 273, 395, 396, 397, 398, 401
Barcelona Process *see* Euro-Mediterranean Partnership
Ben Ali, Zine El Abidine 63, 162, 165, 207–9, 214, 227, 228, 250, 326, 335, 336, 350, 351, 375, 386, 398
Berlin 56, 121, 287
Berlusconi, Silvio 347
Bin Laden, Osama 189, 328
blogs in political life 347, 360, 361, 362, 363, 365, 372, 373

borders 16, 145, 148, 150, 214, 280, 287, 390; Algeria 236; Egypt 66, 137; Europe 21, 41, 43, 60, 61, 67, 68, 77, 78, 80, 139, 154, 198, 201, 251, 269, 287, 383, 385, 386, 388, 389, 391, 404; Exclusive Economic Zones (EEC) 116; Greece 139, 150, 251; Islamic State (ISIS) 236; Israel 123, 124, 127, 128, 190, 191; Lebanon 191; Libya 137, 203, 236; Macedonia 77; 'Muslim' countries 138; Syria 67, 113, 133; Tunisia 66; Turkey 81, 113, 139, 150; Yugoslavia 20
Bosnia 17, 153, 157, 158, 162, 164, 165, 167, 176, 177, 200, 271
Bourguiba, Habib 162, 214, 223, 226, 227, 282, 335
Bouteflika, Abdelaziz 237
Brexit 404
Bulgaria 92, 297, 389
bureaucracy *see* public administration
Bush, George H. 28–30, 124
Bush, George W. 30, 112–15
business actors 74, 80, 147, 163, 165, 195, 209, 210, 212, 214, 222, 227, 228, 237, 261, 280, 284, 285, 337, 347, 351, 371, 385, 388

Cairo 80, 151, 282, 302, 320, 321, 322, 324, 333, 362, 364, 365, 376
capitalism 256, 282, 284, 288, 289; anti-capitalism 349; crony capitalism 5, 63, 69, 228; global capitalism 255, 283; liberal democratic capitalism 69, 245, 343; market-based capitalism 228; neo-liberal capitalism 347
censorship 359; challenges to/opposition to 360, 375; on the Internet 375, 376, 378
Ceuta 18, 88, 148
China (People's Republic of China) 33, 34, 66, 67, 99, 112, 116, 118, 136, 152, 250, 251, 378
CHP (Republican People's Party) 173
Christianity/Christians: Christians and Muslims 14, 16, 19, 24, 40, 51, 98, 106, 333, 351; presence in the Mediterranean 16, 17, 127, 148, 151, 288, 321
cities 79, 208, 209, 214, 223, 224, 275, 280, 282, 286, 288, 347, 349, 352
citizenship 302, 303, 305; Arab citizenship 304; citizenship laws 336, 338; citizenship rights 304; citizenship studies 305; conferences on citizenship 304, 399, 401; engagement for citizenship 300; equal citizenship 151, 304; meaningful citizenship 151, 155
civil society 6, 56, 65, 147, 154, 252, 309, 311, 314, 339; civil societal actors/organizations 55, 56, 76, 105, 297, 300, 312, 326, 352, 394, 396–400, 402, 403; civil society activism 32, 56, 74, 197, 261, 288, 296, 325, 339, 350, 404; European (EU and individual states) support (or lack of) for civil society 56, 76, 80, 105, 311, 314, 315, 317, 337, 340, 394, 404; global civil society 245, 249, 275, 395; Mediterranean civil societies 275, 314; non-governmental organizations (NGOs) 65, 74, 80, 105, 126, 146, 152, 154, 249, 261, 297–302, 309–16, 323, 335, 337, 394, 399; non-state actors 6, 7, 56, 57, 147, 153, 182–6, 189, 298, 309, 312, 331, 382, 405; perceptions/nature of civil society 7, 99, 104, 295–305, 315, 365, 366, 394, 401, 403, 405; relations between the state and civil society 335; Western/European civil societies 249
civil society organizations (CSOs) *see* civil society
civil wars 62, 69, 159, 171, 182, 397, 404; Algeria 29, 62, 73, 88, 188, 225, 236, 246, 326, 328, 336; Greece 161; Iraq 185; Lebanon 151, 186, 191, 283, 349, 374; Libya 66, 165, 167, 192, 213; Palestine 191; Spain 4, 161, 281; Syria 33, 113–14, 125–6, 129, 167, 182, 185, 192, 194, 199, 338, 374; Yemen 33
'Clash of Civilizations' 4, 73, 107, 395–6
clientelism *see* patron–client relations
climate change 197, 201, 232, 241; effects in the Mediterranean region 234, 268–70, 276; effects on migration 387; policy concerning 241, 268–71, 275–7, 382
Clinton, William Jefferson 28, 30, 115
Cold War 2, 4, 17, 19, 26, 27, 53, 55, 99, 111, 126, 147, 197, 199, 244, 260, 298; Cold War impact on Turkey 133, 134; colonialism 4, 18, 87, 104, 148, 182, 279; decolonization and the Cold War 18; historical analogies to the Cold War 16, 17; neo-colonialism 81, 87; post-Cold War 3, 19, 20, 25, 26, 27, 28, 31, 38, 56, 63, 89, 99, 111, 126, 196, 197; Soviet and US struggle for influence in the Mediterranean 24, 25, 26, 27, 33, 50, 56, 98, 110, 111, 147, 195
communism 3, 17, 27, 53, 111, 133, 161, 176, 177, 208, 282, 298, 321, 322, 347; post-communism 20, 176
Conference on Security and Cooperation in Europe (CSCE) 18, 54, 55, 89, 197
Conference on Security and Cooperation in the Mediterranean (CSCM) 89, 90
conflicts in Mediterranean area 21, 29, 43, 62, 68, 73, 93, 106, 107, 127, 145–55, 195–9, 277, 279, 299, 382, 397, 404; border conflicts 61; conflict prevention/resolution/management 77, 102, 111, 192, 299, 300; and energy resources 113–16, 126, 235–8, 275; EU/European states and conflicts 79, 81, 100, 388; hydro-conflicts 269–71; in the MENA region 44, 68, 76, 98, 102, 125, 160, 212, 250, 268; in the Sinai 115; stalled conflicts 26, 171–8, 194
consociationalism 172–8
constitutions and constitutionalism 164, 173, 177, 179, 207, 227, 304, 321–7, 339, 349–52, 384
corruption 32, 97, 151, 153, 188, 227, 300, 331, 332, 343, 346, 349, 350, 352, 363
Croatia 157, 158, 161–5, 167, 174, 281

Crusades 40, 41, 51, 104, 106, 328, 332, 333, 338
cyberactivism 363

decolonization 7, 18, 158, 160, 223
De Gaulle, Charles 4
democracy 21, 147, 148, 154, 248, 299; democracy promotion 56, 61, 64–9, 74, 93, 100–2, 107, 110–12, 154, 198, 199, 249, 250, 286, 312, 361; democratization 4, 7, 63–8, 80, 101, 102, 112, 164, 166, 188, 207–13, 244, 246, 249, 283, 296–300, 347, 361–9, 371–3, 379; perceptions of democracy 61, 104–6, 329, 351, 365, 368, 371, 372; status in Mediterranean 24–36, 148–52, 157, 161–7, 172, 207, 214, 249, 250, 283–6, 343–8, 386, 402
demography, as political factor 32, 44, 229, 270, 271, 277, 383
development strategies/sustainable development 221–30, 251, 260, 270, 271, 276, 303, 347, 396, 401, 402
DISY (Democratic Rally) 172, 174

eastern Mediterranean 18, 111–16, 122, 127–9, 132, 133, 136, 138, 148–51, 233, 235, 239, 240, 246, 247, 251, 268–77, 279, 282, 284, 287, 309, 310, 316, 343, 348, 384, 390, 403, 404; *see also* regionalism
EC–Maghreb Partnership 90
economy, of Mediterranean 7, 16, 27, 28, 32, 44, 63, 110, 126, 135, 136, 209, 212, 215, 221, 222, 225–30, 232, 233, 237, 238, 244, 250, 258, 261, 271, 273, 283–6, 289, 296, 337, 338, 344, 347, 348, 376, 384; GDP 44, 226, 227, 233, 235, 261; and global economy 28, 244, 245, 247, 250, 252, 282; *see also* agriculture; energy resources; globalization; industry; foreign direct investment; tourism; trade; unemployment
Egypt 13, 18, 21, 25–7, 30, 33, 44, 45, 50, 52, 53, 57, 61, 63, 64, 66, 67, 75, 76, 80, 87, 89, 98–101, 104, 105, 110–17, 120–8, 135–9, 148–54, 157–67, 172, 183, 186–8, 192, 199, 207–15, 222–9, 233–40, 247–51, 269–76, 279, 282, 283, 287, 298, 300–5, 315, 320–9, 332–9, 342, 344, 349, 351, 363–8, 371–78, 388, 398
Egyptian Current Party 351
Egyptian Social Democratic Party 351
elections 29, 64, 105, 127, 151, 159, 173, 175, 188, 189–92, 212, 225, 249, 301, 322, 325–8, 335, 336, 339, 343, 346–51
elites 3, 7, 15, 31, 33, 63, 67, 80, 99, 152, 161, 162, 164, 165, 166, 167, 173, 174, 175, 177, 201, 209, 210, 214, 222, 227, 228, 229, 237, 251, 273, 282, 284, 300, 313, 323, 327, 336, 343, 349, 350, 351, 352, 353, 373, 378, 405
employers' associations *see* business actors
energy resources 7, 61, 64, 102, 110–16, 125–7, 132–9, 148, 201, 224, 229, 232–41, 268–77, 283, 353; energy cooperation 273–7; hydrocarbons 232–8, 352, 384; natural gas 29, 113–16, 127, 139, 151, 211, 221, 224, 225, 230, 232–41, 261, 270, 274–7; oil 5, 18, 26, 29, 54, 61, 64, 66–8, 87, 111–16, 136, 211, 215, 221–30, 232–41, 247, 260, 261, 269, 274, 275, 283, 383, 384; pipelines 116, 235–41; renewable 232, 233, 241, 268–77; solar energy 241, 274, 275
Ennahda 80, 249, 305, 326
entrepreneurs *see* business actors
environment 39, 80, 147, 154, 200, 201, 241, 255, 258, 268–77, 288, 303, 346–9, 396, 402
Erdogan, Recep Tayyip 134, 137, 138, 167, 163
ethnicity 174, 178
Euro–Arab Dialogue 18, 41, 54, 61
Euro-Mediterranean Partnership (EMP) 2, 3, 20, 30, 42, 54–6, 60–6, 72, 73, 90, 100, 117, 123, 147, 197, 248, 260, 286, 310, 337, 386, 394; *see also* Barcelona Declaration
Euro-Mediterranean relations 19, 41–4, 72–81, 85, 90, 154, 259, 260, 265, 316, 395, 396; *see also* Euro-Mediterranean Partnership; Union for the Mediterranean
European Neighbourhood Policy (ENP) 43, 54, 55, 74, 77, 91, 123, 125, 260, 271, 273, 275, 277, 337, 339; 2015 review of 195
European Union (EU) 5, 13, 112, 117, 145, 174, 200, 248–51, 260, 274; Mediterranean policies of member states 56, 57, 68, 73, 77–9, 85, 88–94, 111, 133, 149–52, 197, 200, 271, 382, 383, 389, 390, 404; Mediterranean policy of EU 3, 5, 20, 21, 27–33, 50, 54, 56, 72, 80, 97–101, 115, 117, 194, 248, 260, 268, 269, 298, 300, 310–17, 334–6, 382, 390, 394; neighbourhood policy 30, 43, 54, 55, 74, 77, 91, 123, 125, 195, 260, 271, 273, 275, 277, 337, 339; position on the Cyprus stalemate 172, 176, 300

Facebook *see* information and communication technology
Fatah 186, 187, 191
federalism 172–8
feminism 215, 331–9; *see also* gender issues
financial crisis (2008) 21, 32, 227, 234, 250, 343–5, 389
FIS (Islamic Salvation Front) 188, 225, 249, 326, 334
Five Star Movement 347
FJP (Freedom and Justice Party) 327
food, as a political issue 103, 127, 183, 214, 226, 228, 248, 352, 375, 388; in relation to climate change 270, 272
foreign direct investment 63, 227, 240, 246, 247, 250; *see also* economy, of Mediterranean
France 4, 13–16, 25–7, 31, 33, 41, 61, 64–8, 78, 79, 85–92, 100, 103, 106, 110, 111, 115, 128, 133, 135, 136, 149–52, 157, 158, 161–3, 167, 195,

208, 213, 215, 247, 274, 281, 299, 310, 311, 324, 343, 383, 385, 398
free trade 31, 42, 62–4, 76, 91, 100, 110, 136, 239, 248, 251, 260, 261, 311, 390

gas *see* energy resources
geopolitics of the Mediterranean: energy resources 115, 225, 233, 236, 240, 241, 268, 273, 277; perspectives 20, 24, 72, 85, 98, 134, 240, 279, 286; policy/power 66, 73, 74, 77, 79, 81, 82, 85, 110, 111, 113, 114, 116, 132, 151, 236, 240, 251, 273, 276, 390; shifts in 225, 233, 240, 244, 274, 338, 387; stability 273, 287
gender issues 148, 154, 249, 255, 304, 314, 333–40, 345, 388, 402; women 106, 223, 297, 302, 303, 314, 349, 362, 366, 387, 388; women's movements 331–40, 347
generational dimension of Mediterranean politics 63, 222, 237, 280, 321, 324, 325, 342–53
Ghannouchi, Rached 326
Gibraltar 148, 199, 385
globalization: concept of/perspectives on 244–6, 252, 379; and democratization 3, 64, 249; economic aspects of 7, 245–8, 286, 390; politics of 248–51, 352; and states 65, 250, 251, 284; structure of 63, 146, 245
Global Mediterranean Policy, of European Economic Community 18, 41, 87, 123, 259, 260, 264
Golden Dawn 346
governance 30, 35, 38, 39, 43, 64, 74–81, 100, 103, 148, 150, 154, 155, 157, 255, 286, 299; energy/environmental governance 232, 237–41, 269, 270–6; EU/European states approach to governance 20, 65, 75, 77, 79, 80, 298, 343; global governance 37, 46, 245, 251, 252, 256; governance in the MENA region 29, 32, 63, 97, 106, 153, 196, 344; regional governance 309, 312, 382, 391
Grillo, Beppe 347
Gulf Cooperation Council (GCC) 213, 224–6
Gulf states 137, 148, 190, 213, 251
Gulf War (1990–1991) 28, 30, 62, 111, 226

HaAvoda (Israeli Labour Party) 348
Haftar, Khalifa 138
Hamas 105, 116, 126, 127, 138, 139, 151, 183, 184, 185, 186, 187, 189, 190, 191, 192, 249, 323
HDP (People's Democratic Party) 349
HDZ (Croatian Democratic Union) 174
historians, and the Mediterranean 14–16, 39, 46
Hizballah 114, 116, 124, 182–5, 190–2, 326, 349, 361
humanitarian missions 66, 68, 78–81, 117, 138, 288
human rights 146–51, 178, 249–52, 255, 279; human rights activism 32, 261, 299, 309–17, 352, 361; promotion of 4, 27–9, 55, 65, 74, 79, 100, 112, 154, 299, 396, 401; situation in Mediterranean 31, 56, 63, 73, 101–4, 154, 363, 386, 389
Hungary 91, 92, 287, 389
Hussein, Bin Talal 323
Hussein, Saddam 64, 173
hydrocarbons *see* energy resources

Iberia 16, 19, 247
identity, in Mediterranean politics 8, 50, 52, 55, 80, 123, 124, 136, 158, 173, 175, 183, 197, 199, 200, 213, 281, 289, 329, 335, 339, 346, 348, 396, 397, 405
immigration 55, 66, 89, 100, 101, 120, 127, 128, 311, 346, 383–99; *see also* migration
imperialism 13, 17, 34, 37, 60–9, 74, 147, 301, 338; anti-imperialism 25, 334; neo-imperialism 18
indignados, anti-austerity movement in Spain 250, 288, 346, 347
industrialization 62, 222–6, 230, 285
industry 223, 227, 233, 236, 238, 239, 255, 261, 272, 279, 284, 295, 383, 384, 388
information and communication technology (ICT) 65, 245, 251, 351, 360–8, 372, 375–9, 385, 388; Facebook 348, 351, 352, 360, 363, 365, 371, 373, 378; Internet 65, 245, 328, 347, 349, 353, 360, 361–9, 371–9; mobile phones 372, 375, 376, 378; social media 8, 301, 346, 348, 349, 352, 359–69, 371, 372, 377–9; Twitter 360, 363, 365, 366, 371, 373, 378
insurgency 182–92; counter-insurgency operations 151; *see also* Arab uprisings
intelligence services 67, 165, 209
intercultural dialogue 394–405; and youth 396, 401; *see also* Anna Lindh Foundation
interdependence 38, 97, 116, 196, 241, 244, 246, 250–2, 257, 262
international financial institutions 31, 32, 63, 153, 154, 224, 244, 299
International Monetary Fund (IMF) 117, 154, 226, 227, 233, 238, 248, 250, 299
international non-governmental organizations (INGOs) 146, 147, 153, 154
International Relations (IR), perspectives on Mediterranean 16, 24, 28, 37, 38, 145, 194, 208, 244, 372, 396, 397
Internet *see* information and communication technology (ICT)
Islamic Action Front 326
Islamic parties *see* Parties and party systems
Islamic State (ISIS) 33, 67, 76–81, 106, 113–16, 121, 135, 137, 165, 182–92, 199, 213, 235–6, 251, 280, 321, 324–9, 397
Islamism 27, 29, 33, 34, 99, 100, 105, 136, 320–9, 332, 336
Islam, presence in Mediterranean 24, 40, 136, 149, 154, 189, 299–304, 320, 321, 327, 329, 333, 335, 339, 340, 403
Istiqlal 321, 323, 336

Italy 5, 13, 15, 18, 25, 41, 66, 68, 78, 85, 87, 88, 89, 90, 91, 103, 110, 111, 112, 117, 135, 136, 149, 152, 153, 157, 158, 161, 173, 236, 239, 250, 274, 281, 285, 299, 343, 344, 347, 348, 383–6, 389, 398, 404

Jerusalem 51, 148, 190, 282, 288
Jewish communities 127, 288
Jil Jadid 352
Jordan 13, 20, 27–31, 44, 45, 76, 80, 99, 115, 117, 120–4, 127, 128, 139, 153, 207, 211–15, 225–8, 235, 238, 240, 247, 248, 270, 271, 274, 275, 282, 287, 314, 323, 326, 328, 334, 382, 387, 388
Justice and Construction Party 137
justice (system) 74, 78, 386; justice (social) 288, 303, 323, 337, 352, 353

Karami, Rashid 365
Kataeb 174
Kurdish communities 133, 137, 172–5, 178, 310

law 127, 183, 184, 189, 212, 221, 226, 245, 249, 261, 273, 323, 333, 335, 336, 338, 339, 345, 351, 352, 385, 387; electoral laws 188, 350; international law 27, 123, 139, 251, 272, 276, 147; Sharia/Islamic law 189, 327, 329; *see also* rule of law
left-wing movements 172, 174, 250, 310, 335, 339
legislatures *see* parliaments
Levant 13, 51, 67, 98, 111, 114, 148, 149, 151, 166, 186, 189
LGBT issues 215, 349
liberalism, economic 26, 100, 251, 281; political 26, 295, 320
Libya 1, 13, 20, 21, 25, 26, 33, 44, 56, 64–9, 76, 78, 81, 88, 98, 102–5, 111–16, 121, 127, 135–8, 149, 151, 157, 158, 163, 165, 167, 172, 186, 187, 190, 192, 199, 203, 207, 208, 213, 223–9, 232–40, 247–51, 271, 301, 304, 328, 334, 335, 336, 339, 352, 363–76, 384–9

Macedonia 77, 171, 174, 176–8, 287, 389
Maghreb 13, 52, 86–90, 97–9, 103, 111, 114, 149, 151, 154, 186, 235, 248, 275, 312, 323, 336
Mashrek 13, 51, 52, 99, 235, 275
media 102, 107, 137, 172, 175, 207, 250, 270, 287, 289, 300, 304, 359–69, 373, 374, 388, 391, 396, 399, 402, 403; and democratization/civil society 366, 377, 402, 403; media freedom 79, 367; new media 8, 359–69, 402; regime use of 359–62, 367, 373; social *see* information and communication technology; traditional media 361, 362, 372
Mediterranean Action Plan 268, 271, 272, 276, 277
Mediterranean, concept of 13–21, 37–46, 97–107; *see also* regionalism
Mediterranean Forum 89, 90
Mediterranean Sea 15, 39, 50, 74, 123, 127, 145, 166, 382, 384, 385, 387, 404; environmental issues 271–3, 274; and struggles for hegemony 16, 18, 28–30, 37, 43, 68, 81, 101, 102, 122, 150
Mediterranean Solar Plan 241, 274, 275
Melilla 18, 88, 148
Merkel, Angela 68
Middle East and North Africa (MENA) 5, 13, 10, 21, 25, 60–9, 73–82, 116, 132–5, 138, 145, 146, 160–2, 165, 223–9, 338, 388, 398–400, 404
Middle East, concept of 6, 38, 50–7, 73, 120, 123, 182
migration 45, 113, 351, 382–91, 396, 399; anti-migrant sentiment 68, 149, 287, 389, 404; attempts to manage 68, 79, 80, 88, 100–2, 385–90; and EU policy 20, 102, 118, 199, 201, 248, 251, 262, 287, 382, 385–91; flows 21, 45, 66, 68, 281, 383, 384, 386; and globalization 245, 251, 252, 390; routes 115; and security 61, 62, 66, 68, 69, 76, 103, 150, 262, 385, 389–91; and US policy 110, 116, 117, 118; vulnerability of migrants 45, 140, 277, 382, 383, 387–90; *see also* refugees
military, activity in Mediterranean 20, 26, 138, 149, 163, 185, 191, 208, 209; civil–military/relations 7, 80, 99, 152, 157–67, 172, 184, 190, 199, 208–10, 214, 215, 222, 228, 237, 249, 322, 332, 334, 385, 389; military and NATO *see* NATO; military occupations/repression 190, 213, 225, 226, 249, 322, 326, 339, 376; military bases (non-naval) 135, 148; military dictatorships/juntas 7, 18, 162, 366; military intervention/influence by external powers 26–8, 33, 34, 56, 60, 61, 64, 66, 78, 79, 104, 111, 112, 114, 116, 118, 133, 135–7, 146, 147, 149–54, 162, 212, 279, 281; military partnerships/cooperation/assistance 127, 133, 137, 138, 152, 153, 200, 212–15; military power/capacities 150, 160, 162, 196, 197, 200, 201, 209, 210, 212, 223; military spending 78, 223; role of military in politics 26, 29, 76, 151, 159, 162–4, 188, 199, 223, 225, 249, 251, 305, 326, 327, 328, 348, 351, 366; paramilitary forces 160, 162, 322
Mitterrand, François 88
monarchies 161, 211; Arab monarchies 208, 211, 212, 215; constitutional monarchies 321; Egyptian monarchy 322; Gulf monarchies 67, 207, 211, 213; Jordanian monarchy 211, 212, 247, 321, 322, 326; Libyan monarchy 163, 223; Moroccan monarchy 25, 211, 212, 223, 247, 327
Montenegro 157, 158, 162, 164, 167, 271
Morocco 4, 17, 18, 25–7, 31, 42, 44, 45, 63, 80, 86, 88, 98, 98, 102, 103, 110, 111, 117, 127, 128, 148, 149, 153, 154, 157, 158, 167, 177, 178, 194, 199–201, 207, 211–15, 223, 227, 228, 233, 235,

238, 240, 247, 248, 256, 261, 269–71, 274, 275, 301–4, 313, 314, 321, 324, 326–9, 336, 339, 342, 352, 371, 383–90
Morsi, Mohamed 121, 137, 138, 163, 213, 305, 327, 351
Mubarak, Gamal 63, 209, 228
Mubarak, Hosni 76, 80, 115, 117, 163, 165, 172, 207, 208, 209, 210, 214, 227, 228, 327, 335, 336, 338, 339, 366, 374
municipalities 74, 275, 326, 346
MUR (Movement for Unity and Reform) 326
Muslim Brotherhood 57, 76, 117, 121, 136, 137, 138, 151, 154, 172, 186, 187, 188, 190, 192, 249, 321, 322, 323, 324, 325, 326, 327, 328, 335, 339, 351

Nasrallah, Hassan 349
Nasser, Gamal Adbel 18, 52, 53, 61, 150, 163, 209, 223, 228, 282, 322–5, 335
National Democratic Party 336
nationalism 147, 171, 174, 177, 178, 190, 279–81, 321, 332, 334; Arab nationalism 61, 150, 171, 173; transnationalism 224, 252
nation-state *see* state
naval activity in the Mediterranean 17, 134; Chinese (PRC) naval activity 116; EU/NATO naval activity 140, 150, 154, 287, 385; naval bases 80, 113, 150; Russian naval activity 113, 150; Soviet naval activity 19; Turkish naval activity 135; US naval activity 110, 114, 117
neo-liberalism 61, 65, 227, 244, 250, 255–7, 263, 264
Netanyahu, Benjamin 121, 122, 124, 125, 126
New Democracy 346
non-governmental organizations (NGOs) *see* civil society
non-state actors *see* civil society
normative aspect of EU Mediterranean policy 25, 28, 31, 54, 62, 65, 74, 99, 102, 103, 120, 201, 202, 240, 263, 277
North Africa 13, 20, 24, 25, 31, 38, 45, 60, 63, 66, 73, 79, 85, 86, 88, 90, 100, 101, 106, 110, 111, 114–17, 120, 127, 128, 132, 134, 148, 160, 164, 182, 195, 199, 201, 223, 248, 282, 286, 302–4, 310, 313, 331, 350, 352, 384
North Atlantic Treaty Organization (NATO) 17–20, 25, 26, 33, 56, 64, 101, 113–17, 132, 133, 135–40, 149, 150, 154, 165, 196, 198, 200, 201; NATO's Mediterranean Dialogue 20, 98, 99, 117; non-NATO ally 99
northern Mediterranean 120, 128, 137, 150, 152, 194, 234, 269, 296, 383, 384; *see also* regionalism
north–south issues/relations 5, 6, 20, 255
Nour Party 327–8

Obama, Barack 33, 110, 112–18
oil *see* energy resources

Ottoman Empire 16, 17, 40, 41, 50, 51, 61, 132, 133, 134, 135, 138, 140, 147, 148, 149, 160, 171, 175, 177, 281, 332; neo-ottoman 134, 137; post-ottoman 176, 177

Palestinian–Israeli conflict 3, 87, 98, 100, 111, 124, 125, 126, 148, 150, 183, 190, 387, 396
Palestinian territories 13, 64, 104, 124, 125, 149, 190, 249, 279, 282, 302; Gaza 92, 106, 115, 116, 121, 124–7, 138, 148, 151, 184–6, 190, 191, 279; Palestinian Authority 124–6, 138, 139, 398
pan-Arabism 5, 122, 124, 150, 321, 324
parliaments 74, 312, 164, 174, 183, 188; Algerian parliament 225; Egyptian parliament 325, 327; Euro-Med Youth parliament 401; European Parliament 88, 286, 314, 347, 386; Greek parliament 161, 347; Jordanian parliament 326; Lebanese parliament 191, 192; Libyan parliament 339; Moroccan parliament 326, 352; Palestinian legislature 191; parliamentary democracy *see* democracy; parliamentary elections *see* elections; parliamentary system 321, 322, 324, 326; Tunisian parliament 351; Turkish parliament 175
Parties and party systems 164, 172, 174, 177–8, 250, 283, 301, 310, 323, 326, 342, 345, 349–50, 353; Arab/MENA parties 173, 303, 350; European parties 43, 68, 153, 283; Islamist parties 7, 29, 74, 80, 105, 188, 192, 334; nationalist parties 25, 187, 192; opposition parties 173, 192, 249, 350; populist parties 68, 247; secular parties 191, 249, 327, 334; single-party socialist/communist states 161, 162, 166, 176, 297, 321; social democratic parties 283, 284; *see also* individual party entries
PASOK (Panhellenic Socialist Movement) 346
patronage, patron–client relations 17, 32, 153, 211, 215, 222, 225, 237, 284, 286, 289
PD (Democratic Party) 347
peace processes (Middle East) 28, 30, 64, 73, 100, 120–7, 153, 178, 260, 298, 300
PJD (Justice and Development Party) 326, 327, 336, 353
PKK (Kurdistan Workers' Party) 137
Podemos 347
political economy 6, 110, 115, 215, 224, 229, 232–41, 244–7, 256, 277, 283, 285
political regimes 4, 157–67, 185–8, 207–15, 224, 249, 332, 334, 404; Algerian regime 225, 237, 324, 326, 336, 352; Al-Sisi/Egyptian regime 57, 76, 80, 207, 215, 352; Assad/Syrian regime 34, 66, 67, 78, 113, 116, 124, 137, 163, 165, 210, 211, 213, 228, 324, 326, 365; authoritarian/autocratic regimes 5, 27, 29, 31, 32, 55, 56, 63, 65, 98, 154, 157, 176, 199, 202, 208, 213, 223, 281, 283, 295, 299, 314, 325, 336, 338, 343, 359, 360, 364, 365; Ben Ali/Tunisian regime 80, 162,

165, 209, 210, 214, 228, 339, 398; communist regimes 161; Franco/Spanish regime 162, 164, 281–4; Gaddafi/Libyan regime 33, 66, 105, 115, 163, 165, 213, 225, 334, 335, 384, 387; Greek military regime 162, 164, 282; Gulf regimes 80, 211, 213; Hussein/Iraqi regime 173, 225; hybrid regimes 157; Jordanian regime 211, 215, 228; MENA regimes 20, 25, 31, 63, 64, 73, 74, 77, 99–107, 135, 138, 162, 176, 201, 208, 215, 223, 225, 228, 333, 336, 350, 359, 363, 365; monarchical regimes 211–13; Moroccan regime 80, 200, 211, 215, 228, 336; Morsi/Egyptian regime 339; Mubarak/Egyptian regime 101, 209, 210, 214, 228, 325, 335, 338, 366, 374; Nasser/Egyptian regime 163, 322, 324, 335; nationalist regimes 18, 336; opposition to/ protest against 57, 157, 159, 164, 166, 364, 365, 366, 368, 373; regime change/transition 6, 64, 65, 66, 105, 157–9, 164, 166, 207, 299, 300, 311, 343; Sadat/Egyptian regime 163, 212, 325; semi-authoritarian regimes 328; socialist regimes 166, 336; Tunisian/post-Arab awakening regime 80, 215

political violence 24, 182–92, 287, 396; *see also* civil wars; conflicts in Mediterranean; terrorism

population issues 31, 34, 62, 127, 165, 172, 191, 224, 225, 229, 281, 326, 350–2, 363, 365, 372, 376; population density 236; population growth 44, 225, 268, 272, 273, 280, 344; population movements 45, 268, 382, 387

populism 33, 63, 68, 222, 223, 224, 225, 287, 299, 325, 327, 347, 361

Portugal 3, 5, 13, 15, 19, 25, 26, 41, 42, 86–90, 103, 111, 134, 164, 246, 250, 274, 283, 285, 286, 343, 344, 383–5

private sector 32, 226–8, 245, 289; *see also* business actors

privatization 62, 63, 209, 221, 226–8, 260, 261, 283, 346, 360, 362

PSOE (Spanish Socialist Workers' Party) 347

public administration 237

public opinion: 'Arab street' 122, 126; European public opinion 105, 316; Israeli public opinion 121; in the Middle-East/Arab world 65, 104, 314, 360, 364, 365

public sector 63, 80, 223–6, 233, 284, 347

PYD (Syrian Kurdish Democratic Union Party) 113

Qutb, Sayyid 323–9

refugees 62, 66–8, 76–81, 93, 98, 113, 128, 135, 139, 140, 150, 153, 190, 251, 280, 287, 288, 382–91; refugee camps 154, 388; refugee crisis 1, 8, 139, 194, 199, 201, 250–2, 280, 281, 391; *see also* migration

regionalism, in Mediterranean 37–46, 123, 289; regional conflicts 150, 212; region-building initiatives 38, 39, 73, 196, 200, 395; *see also* Euro-Mediterranean Partnership; Renovated Mediterranean Policy (RMP); Union for the Mediterranean

regional security complexes *see* security

religion 51, 98, 134, 140, 154, 189, 192, 197, 302, 321, 329, 333, 345, 350, 368, 396, 399, 402, 403

Renovated Mediterranean Policy (RMP), of EU 19, 20, 88, 90, 260

rentier economies/states 215, 225, 226, 232, 236, 237, 285

Renzi, Matteo 347

repression 6, 8, 31, 65, 66, 76, 85, 105, 113, 162–5, 188, 189, 251, 300, 309, 322, 326–8, 349, 367, 377, 378

revolution 158, 183, 184, 211, 223, 315; 'Arab' revolutions 229, 230, 303, 339, 366, 367, 371, 378, 379; 'Cedar' revolution (2005) 349; counterrevolution 213; Egyptian (1952) 161, 163; Egyptian (2011) 183, 214, 339, 365, 366, 373, 374; European 166, 250; Iranian (1979) 50, 52, 53, 212, 301; Libyan (2011) 165, 186, 187, 339; revolutionary movements 314, 323, 348, 351, 378; revolutionary regimes 225, 237; revolutionary terrorism 188; Tunisian (2011) 209, 214, 339, 350, 351, 373, 398; 'velvet' revolutions 4

Rome 14, 39, 189, 272

rule of law 101–5, 221, 228, 352

Russia (Russian Federation) 33, 34, 43, 51, 66, 67, 91, 99, 113–18, 127, 135–40, 149–53, 190, 194, 213, 232, 233, 236, 239–41, 250, 251

Sadat, Muhammad Anwar 163, 209, 212, 226, 324, 325, 335

Sahel 1, 78, 101, 114, 116, 235

Salafism 189, 320, 323, 327–9

Sarajevo 17

Sarkozy, Nicolas 103

Second World War 17, 24, 25, 41, 51, 110, 111, 149, 150, 157, 160, 161, 166, 167, 175, 176, 197, 255, 279–82, 322, 323, 387

secularism and secularization 4, 105, 133, 172, 177, 210, 249, 300, 321, 322, 332, 334, 362

securitization 4, 68, 74, 101, 103, 146, 152, 153, 197–9, 287, 343, 352, 383, 385, 391

security, in Mediterranean 20, 50–7, 110–18, 134–9, 150, 152, 196–8, 255, 269, 277, 337, 391, 396; destabilization/problems 25, 28, 33, 45, 62, 77, 79, 81, 93, 97, 99, 121, 154, 162, 172, 229, 232–41, 385–9, 396, 397; energy security 61, 262, 273–5, 277; human security 269; impact of 9/11 64, 72, 74, 103; regional security complexes 28, 38–46, 100, 128; security communities 18,30, 50, 54, 56, 75, 76, 77, 101,

102, 124, 151, 152, 194–202, 395; security cooperation 31, 33, 34,50, 64, 65, 73, 78, 80, 87–90, 99, 100, 126, 139, 196, 199, 200, 213, 215, 286, 311, 315, 382, 394, 395; security organizations 18, 78, 93, 101, 103, 123, 197, 200, 286, 396; state/regime security 34, 78, 98, 101, 121, 124, 132, 157, 159, 162–5, 173, 184, 185, 190, 212, 215, 225, 249, 343, 403
Serbia 17, 173
Shia/Shiism 81, 121–5, 128, 135, 138, 152, 173, 207, 213, 303, 349
Sicily 19, 40
Slovenia 91, 157, 158, 161, 162, 164, 167
social class 20, 65, 106, 152, 191, 223, 226, 228, 245, 247, 255, 280, 284, 285, 288, 289, 295, 321, 324, 332, 334, 345, 348
social exclusion 188, 189, 228, 287, 302, 329, 343–50, 403, 405; *see also* unemployment
Socialist Union of Popular Forces 352
solar energy *see* energy resources
southern Mediterranean 4, 43, 45, 46, 62, 64, 69, 72–7, 80, 81, 85–94, 97–106, 120–8, 132, 136, 147–54, 194–9, 207, 208, 211–15, 232–8, 241, 269, 272, 273, 279, 280, 283, 284, 286, 296, 300, 331–8, 342–4, 383, 386, 388, 290; *see also* regionalism
Soviet Union 24, 25, 26, 27, 28, 31, 52, 56, 98, 110, 132, 133, 140, 149, 150, 157, 196; post-Soviet period 298; Soviet expansionism 53, 56, 110, 328; Soviet influence/interests 18, 19, 25, 26, 27, 52, 90, 111, 113, 132, 133, 195, 212, 298
Spain 3–5, 13, 18, 19, 25, 27, 31, 32, 40–2, 85–91, 103, 104, 110–12, 128, 134–6, 149, 152–4, 157, 158, 161, 162, 164, 166, 167, 172, 175, 178, 199–201, 239, 246, 247, 250, 274, 280–8, 299, 301, 310, 311, 315, 342–4, 346, 348, 383–5, 389
state, types of *see* authoritarianism; consociationalism; democracy; federalism; military; monarchies
students, activism among 162, 324, 325, 328, 346–53
Suez Crisis/War (1956) 18, 61, 111
Sufism 320, 321, 322, 327, 329
Sunni/Sunnism 135–8, 152, 165, 173, 189, 207, 210–13, 320, 323, 325, 326,
Switzerland 312
Syria 1, 13, 21, 27, 28, 33, 34, 44, 66–9, 76–80, 98, 102, 104, 112–16, 120–9, 135–40, 150, 153, 157–60, 163–7, 172–4, 177, 178, 182, 185–92, 194, 199, 208–15, 222–9, 235, 236, 247–51, 273, 282, 287, 297, 301, 321–8, 334, 338, 349, 361–8, 371–8, 387, 388, 398; as part of the United Arab Republic 87
Syriza 250, 346

telecommunications 227, 360, 376
television 360, 364, 372, 373, 377
terrorism 397, 404; anti-terrorism/counter-terrorism 56, 78, 80, 101, 112, 189, 192, 198, 200, 201; Islamist terrorism 105, 114, 189, 191, 192; North–South cooperation against terrorism 102; perceptions of terrorism 98, 101, 105, 115, 116, 182, 183–92; terrorism in Europe/EU 61–9, 78, 117, 118, 385, 404; terrorism in the MENA region 97, 111, 114, 116, 174, 183; 'War on terror'/international terrorism 57, 74, 88, 101, 112, 194, 197, 252, 287
Thatcherism 258
tourism 15, 135, 245, 276, 279–89; forms of 274, 280, 284–6, 288, 289; policy 280, 281, 282, 284, 285; protests against mass tourism 288; regional pattern of 128, 280, 281, 283; violence against 190, 287, 289; volume of tourism 138, 269, 280–5, 287
trade 15, 16, 19, 28–32, 44, 45, 54, 61–4, 86, 87, 91, 125–8, 132, 135, 136, 139, 195, 199, 221, 228, 240, 245–51, 259–61, 281, 284, 287, 288, 382; flow (of goods/commodities/tourists) 115, 128, 213, 215, 222–6, 248, 287, 305; *see also* free trade
trade unions 298–301, 310, 311, 324, 345–7, 350, 373
transnationalism across Mediterranean/transnational networks 7, 8, 34, 65, 146, 186, 187, 192, 195–7, 244–7, 251, 252, 256, 259, 268, 283–6, 297, 309–17, 328, 363, 382, 395, 403
Treaty of Rome (1957) 86, 259
tribal dimension, of political life 163, 221, 224, 228, 238, 366
Twitter *see* information and communication technology

UBP (National Unity Party) 174
unemployment 31, 32, 62, 106, 221, 227, 229, 250, 280, 285, 301, 343–7, 350, 352, 397
Union for the Mediterranean (UfM) 5, 20, 43, 44, 54, 74–6, 92, 93, 103, 117, 150, 260, 268, 271–7, 314, 316, 397, 398
United Nations 92, 111, 112, 124, 153, 154, 172, 268, 271, 317
United States 6, 17, 21, 24–34, 34, 50–5, 57, 60–8, 79, 89, 98–101, 110–18, 124, 125, 133, 135–9, 149–54, 174, 191, 194–6, 198, 200, 207, 208, 212–15, 224, 232–5, 238, 245, 248, 274, 280, 282, 283, 287, 288, 298, 328, 371–4
USSR *see* Soviet Union

Venice 134
VMRO–DPMNE (Internal Macedonian Revolutionary Organization – Democratic Party for Macedonian National Unity) 174

Wafd Party 321
Wasat Party 325

water scarcity 268, 269, 272
welfare 32, 65, 346; welfare state 154, 211, 247, 269, 346, 348
westernization 245, 246, 249
western Mediterranean 5, 88, 111, 199–201; *see also* regionalism
West, involvement in Mediterranean 6, 13, 16–20, 25–35, 61–9, 75, 81, 88, 104–7, 111, 137, 146, 148, 149, 152–4, 194, 212, 213, 226, 249, 295, 300, 301, 310, 332, 338
Wikileaks 374
women *see* gender issues
World Bank 154, 227, 248, 299
World Trade Organization (WTO) 248

xenophobia 287, 346

Young Egypt Party 321
youth 80, 104, 312, 322, 329, 396, 399; political activism among 7, 74, 211, 287, 301–4, 342–53, 363, 365; situation of 106, 363, 365, 401–3; unemployment among 62, 221, 227, 228, 301

Printed in Great Britain
by Amazon

54707254R00246